JURIDICAL STUDIES
IN
ANCIENT INDIAN LAW

PART II

L. STERNBACH LL. D.

MOTILAL BANARSIDASS
DELHI : VARANASI : PATNA

BUNGALOW ROAD, JAWAHAR NAGAR, DELHI-7
NEPALI KHAPRA, VARANASI-1 (U.P.)
ASHOK RAJ PATH, (OPP. PATNA COLLEGE), PATNA-4 (BIHAR)

First Edition 1967

PRINTED IN INDIA BY SHANTILAL JAIN AT SHRI JAINENDRA PRESS, BUNGALOW ROAD, JAWAHAR NAGAR, DELHI-7 AND PUBLISHED BY SUNDARLAL JAIN, MOTILAL BANARSIDASS, BUNGALOW ROAD, JAWAHAR NAGAR, DELHI-7.

PREFACE

Since the publication of Volume I of my *Juridical Studies in Ancient Indian Law* I have completed three more studies.

30. "Mahābhārata Verses in Cāṇakya's Compendia", which was published in the *Journal of the American Oriental Society*, Vol. 83. 1; pp. 30-67.
31. "Rāmāyaṇa Verses in Cāṇakya's Compendia", the the printing of which was completed; the study will appear in the *Paṇḍit Gopīnata Kaviraj. Commemoration Volume*; and
32. "Quotations from the Kauṭilya-arthaśāstra", which will appear in two or three installments in the *Journal of the American Oriental Society*, Vol. 87. 3.

I was able to include in this volume the additional study 30.

The original studies 29 and 30 have been expanded in the present volume, since new so-called Cāṇakya's Aphorisms came to my attention. I could add to study XXIV, 43 new Cāṇakya's Aphorisms which also occur in the Hitopadeśa; to study XXIV, 17 new Cāṇakya's Aphorisms which also occur in the Pañcatantra and to study XXVII, 9 new Cāṇakya's Aphorisms which also occur in the Mahābhārata. I also added to studay XXIV an extensive footnote 3 and in the *Post scriptum* my contributian to the XXIV International Congress of Orientalists in Munich, 1957 on "Various Versions of Cāṇakya's Compendia" published in the *Akten des XXIV Internationalen Orientalisten Kongresees*, München, 1957.

The present volume contains also the Subject Index for volumes I and II, for the preparation of which I wish to express to my sincerest thanks to Mrs. K. S.

The publication of any juridical text, particularly if it is intermingled with copious Sanskrit quotations in transliteration is a particularly difficult task. My sincere thanks are due to M/S. Motilal Banarsidass and in particular to Mr. Mulkh Raj Suri, Manager of Shri Jainendra Press for their untiring efforts, patience and skills in matters of detail.

Ludwik Sternbach LL.D.

TABLE OF CONTENTS
OF VOLUME II

PART II

INDIAN TALES AND THE DHARMA-AND ARTHA-SOURCES

XIX

THE PAÑCATANTRA AND THE SMṚTI-S*

INTRODUCTION

1. When we read a literary work we read it either from the point of view of its contents, or because of its literary form, or for thoughts contained in it. Very seldom, however, do we read it from the point of view of law. Yet, very often, imperceptibly, law enters into all our actions, into every step of our daily life. If we do shopping, if we go to a locksmith, if we go to a jeweller to order a ring, or step into a tram, or bus, or taxi in each of these cases we conclude one or more legal contracts, which from the legal point of view, very often are complicated. The same is the case when reading literary works. While reading the Mṛcchakaṭika, for instance, we had probably never noticed that in this beautiful drama we find the description of a juridical act, namely a contract of deposit. In this case the act was concluded between Carudatta and Vasantasenā and the whole drama is based on legal rules resulting from the conclusion of this contract of deposit. They relate to the responsibility of the depositor, the influence of *vis major* on the obligation of returning the thing deposited, etc. These juridical problems are the thread running through the whole of this drama. However no mention of this fact appears in any of the critical editions of the Mṛcchakaṭika.

2. In reading "The Arabian Nights" for the first time one reads it from the point of view of their contents, for the second time from the point of view of its contents as well as customs which were current. There it may be seem that some legal problems are raised in these tales. On reading "The Arabian Nights," for the third, fourth, and tenth time the conclusion is reached that this work reflects the daily life of the people, the life which really existed and not that which was contained in the books, on the basis of which legal contracts were concluded and legal actions were performed. The legal contracts, contained therein are clearer and more alive and are

* Previously appeared as JSAIL. 20. in the "Bhāratīya Vidyā", Vol. XI, Nos. 3-4, pp. 222-309.

a better illustration of the application of legal rules than the dull legal rules contained in the law-books.

3. When reading the Indian tales and, in particular, the Pañcatantra, perhaps for the twentieth time, I came to the same conclusion.

Many scholars have written much about the Pañcatantra and it is not easy to add anything to their works. However, it seems that the Pañcatantra, though it is a collection of fables, depicts quite faithfully the daily life in India and daily juridical problems.

4. The aim of this work is :

(1) to point out various juridical problems, raised in the Pañcatantra,

(2) to show first how the same problem was solved in the *Smṛtis* and in the Pañcatantra, and also

(3) whether, in the Pañcatantra, it was solved in conformity with the *Smṛti-s*.

On the basis of these considerations it can be shown how the legal rules contained in the *Smṛti-s* were applied in daily life. It is certain that the author or authors of the Pañcatantra were not jurists and did not know the legal rules in force. If some juridical problems were mentioned in the Pañcatantra and solved in accordance with the rules of the *Smṛti-s*, it shows that these rules were well-known to everybody, so that even laymen quoted them. In particular the Mānava-Dharmaśāstra was one of the authorities on which the Pañcatantra was based, as stated in the introduction to Pañc.[1]

Furthermore, if we interpret the Pañcatantra from the point of view of law, we often come to very interesting conclusions. We know that various versions of the Pañcatantra exist in which some of the tales, especially those which have something in common with law, were narrated in different ways. Some of them were in conformity with the rules contained in the *Smṛti-s*, and other were not. In particular, later texts, the longer versions (*textus ornatior*), tried to make the text conform to the legal rules in order to eliminate illogical passages which

1. *manave vācaspataye śukrāya parāśarāya sasutāya,*
cāṇakyāya ca viduṣe namo'stu nṛpaśāstrakartṛbhyaḥ. (Kathāmukham, śl. 1) and others.

might shock the reader, or listener. On the other hand, if some of the texts of Pañcatantra quoted some rules of the *Smṛtis*, we learn what wording was known in daily life at the time when the Pañcatantra was written, and what other legal rules, not contained in the *Smṛtis*, were in use.

5. This study seems to be the first experiment in the interpretation of Sanskrit literary works from the point of view of law. It seems therefore, that we cannot draw too broad conclusions from this interpretation. Only J. Dahlmann, in his "*Das Mahābhārata als Epos and Rechtsbuch*," interpreted MBh. also from the legal point of view, but books XII and XIII of MBh. are *par excellance* collections of legal rules. These books should be considered as a *Smṛti*; that is not the case as far as the Pañcatantra is concerned.

We should note, however, that the Pañcatantra, in the Introduction stated that, in order to increase intelligence, grammar, *Dharmaśāstra-s* should be taught through the works of Manu, *Arthaśāstra-s*—through the works of Cāṇakya, and *Kāmasūtra-s*—through the works of Vātsyāyana.[2]

6. This study is based in the first place, on the work of Prof. F. Edgerton "Pañcatantra Reconstructed" (P.) The Tantrākhyāyika ed. by J. Hertel (PTH.) which is the version nearest to P., the Viṣṇuśarman, *i.e.* the first text of the Pañcatantra edited in Europe. In particular the following text were used : the so-called *Pantchatantrum sive quinquepartitum de moribus exponens*, ed. by I.G.L. Kosegarten (PK), the critical editions by Kielhorn and Bühler in the BSS. (PKB.) and J. Hertel's recension of the Jaina monk Pūrṇabhadra (PHP.). From among many recently edited texts by Indian scholars the text edited by P.K. Parab and W. L. S. Panśikar (PPP) has been chosen.

I. THE TALE OF THE HONEST-MIND AND EVIL-MIND

7. *Contents of P.* (1-13) *and its Juridical Problems*

In P. Book I, *kathā* 13 (in PHT. Book I, *kathā* 15, in PK. Book I, *kathā* 19, in PHP. Book I, *kathā* 26, in PBK. Book I, *kathā* 19, in PPP. Book I, *kathā* 19) in the tale of Honest-

2. *deva dvādaśabhir varṣair vyākāraṇaṁ śrūyate; tato dharmaśāstrāṇi manvādīny arthaśāstrāṇi, cāṇakyādīni, kāmaśāstrāṇi vātsyāyanādini*. PKB. (Introduction p. 1, v. 24 to p. 2. v. 2 and PPP. (p. 2. v. 12 sqq.).

mind and Evil-mind we find a story of two men, Honest-mind and Evil-mind who found a thousand dinars, divided a part of this amount half-and half, between themselves and buried the rest in the ground. Afterward they again divided a part of this buried treasure.

Later Evil-mind took away all the remainder of the money and as, some time later, the rest of their common treasure could not be found, accused Honest-mind of having stolen the treasure. The matter was submitted to the court. The judge arrested both the litigants and, as Evil-mind declared that he had witnesses namely a tree, who should prove that Honest-mind did steal the money, the judge took sureties from them and let both of them go to their homes. Evil-mind went home and persuaded his father to enter the hollow trunk of a tree situated near the place where the money was buried to state that Honest-mind had stolen the money. During the nest day's hearing, after texts from the law-books had been read before the tree, a voice came forth from the tree stating that Honest-mind had stolen the money. The latter, supposing that it was a trick played by Evil-mind, climbed up the tree, collected a heap of dry wood and leaves, filled the hollow trunk of the tree and set fire to it. Then Evil-mind's father, half burnt, came out of the hollow tree trunk. The judges perceived the truth and commanded that the money be given to Honest-mind and ordered the impalement of Evil-mind.

From the juridical points of view, as described in the *Smṛtis*, three problems were solved in this tale :

(1) the fate of an object found,

(2) the surety in litigation,

(3) reading of texts of law-books in the court.

8. *Objects Found*

(A) *In the Smṛti-s*

The problem of the fate of an object found is closely connected with the problem of the finding of a treasure.

In the *Smṛti-s* it is stated that any object found must be given to the king or to a special office for lost property where it has to be kept for a period of time which varies in the sources of law; after the end of the term the property shall be taken by the king or by the finder, as well as by the king.

In particular G. (10.36-38) stated[3] : *pranaṣṭam asvāmīkam adhigamya rājñe prabruyūḥ. vikhyāpya rājñā saṁvatsaraṁ rakṣyam. ūrdhvam adhigantuś-caturthaṁ rājñaḥ śeṣaḥ.* (Similarly Vās. 16.19, 20[4]. See also Y. 2.33[5]).

According to Mn. 8.30)[6] the object found has to be kept for three years and after that term elapsed the king can take the whole object found.[7] Similarly Y. (2.173)[8] and K. (190.1-2).[9]

In K. (190. 4-5)[10] it was stated that every article lost should be first kept in the custom-office, which was a kind of office for lost property, and then if the owner did not appear during three fortnights, it should be given to the king. Similarly Y. (2.173)[11], although this term was extended up to one year.

The office for lost property was also mentioned in K. (146.16-17)[12] where it was stated that the *nāgaraka* should keep in safe custody all the things lost, forgotten, or left behind by others.[13]

3. "Those who find lost (property) the owner of which is not (known), shall announce it to the king. (36) The king shall cause it to be proclaimed (by the public crier), and (if the owner does not appear) hold it in his custody for a year. (37) Afterwards one fourth (of the value goes) to the finder (and) the remainder to the king. (38)".; according to G. Bühler's translation in SBE. II.

4. *prahīṇa-dravyāṇi rājagāmīni bhavanti* (19), *tato'nyathā rājā mantribhiḥ saha nāgaraiś ca kāryāṇi kuryāt* (20).

5. *pranaṣṭādhigataṁ deyaṁ nṛpeṇa dhanine dhanam,*
vibhāvayen na cel liṅgais tat samaṁ daṇḍam arhati.

6. Similarly also Agnipurāṇa, Rājadharma 222. 16, 1

7. *pranaṣṭa-svāmikaṁ rikthaṁ rājā tryabdaṁ nidhāpayet,*
arvāk tryabdād dharet svāmī pareṇa nṛpatir haret. Mn. (8.30) also stated that if the owner proved his ownership he had to pay to the king one-sixth, one-tenth, or one-twelfth of the value (Mn. 8.33). Similarly Y. 2.174, K. 190.6 ff.

8. *śaulkikaiḥ sthāna-pālair vā naṣṭāpahṛtaṁ ahṛtam,*
arvāk saṁvatsarāt svāmī hareta parato nṛpaḥ. (Y. 2.173. Also quoted in VyK. 118, SC. 133, VRK. 346, VCi. 148, SV. 490, VyPr. 297, VyM. 87, VT. 563, RDhK. 468, VV. 251, VyP. 84. VyS. 72, VVy. 43, AP. 257.24).

9. *nāṣṭikaṁ ca svakaraṇaṁ kṛtvā naṣṭapratyāhṛtaṁ labheta. svakaraṇābhāve pañcabandho daṇḍaḥ. tac ca dravyaṁ rājadharmyaṁ syāt.* (K. 190.1-2).

10. *śulkasthāne naṣṭāpahṛto'tpannas tiṣṭhet. tripakṣād ūrdhvam anābhisāraṁ rājā haret, svāmī vā.* (K. 190. 4-5).

11. See note 8.

12. *nityam udakasthānāmārgabhūmicchanna-pathavaprākārā-rakṣo-vekṣaṇaṁ naṣṭa-prasmṛtā-pasṛtānāṁ ca rakṣaṇam* (K. 146.16-7).

13. See also N. (7.8).

Even he who received an object lost from another person without informing the king had to be fined (Y. 2.172)[14], as this kind of acquisition of an object was considered as sale without ownership.[15]

As far as the treasure was concerned, the finder of it had to give notice of the fact of finding a treasure to the king[16], otherwise the treasure was not considered his lawful property[17], and the finder had to give up the entire treasure found[18] or even to pay a fine[19],[20] After the finding of the treasure has been announced, the finder was entitled to one sixth only (unless found by *bhṛtaka*)[21] of the value of the treasure found and the rest belonged to the king.[22]

The treasure-trove was the property of the king,[23] if found by members of the three highest castes, unless it was found by

14. *hṛtaṁ pranaṣṭaṁ yo dravyaṁ parahastād avāpnuyāt,*
anivedya nṛpe daṇḍyaḥ sa tu ṣaṇṇavatiṁ paṇān. (Y. 2.172. Also quoted in VyK. 138, SC. 213, VRK. 110, VCi. 44, VyN. 276, SCM. 17, DV. 329, NṛP. 171, SV. 495, VyPr. 292, VT. 574, RDhK. 468, VV. 140, VyS. 104, AP. 257.23).

See also K. 190.3, where we read : *naṣṭāpahṛtam anivedyo 'tkarṣataḥ svāminaḥ purvaḥ sāhasadaṇḍaḥ.*

15. See below.

16. See K. (203.7). Cf. note 21.

17. See N. (7.6) : (*pareṇa nihitaṁ labdhvā rājany upaharen nidhim*),- See also N. (7.8; NSM. 8.6. Also quoted in VrK. 643, DK. 345, DV. 289, NṛP. 174, VV. 292).

18. See Vi. : *aniveditavijñātasya sarvam apaharet.* (3.62) Also quoted in VRK. 642, DV. 286, VV. 291).

19. See Y. (2.35).

itareṇa nidhau labdhe rājā ṣaṣṭhāṁśam āharet,
anivedita-vijñāto dāpyas taṁ daṇḍam eva ca. (Also quoted in ViR. *ad Y.* 2.37, SC. 134, VRK. 644, VyN. 533, DV. 287, DT. 183, Rāgh. in MnM. *ad* 8.39, VyM. 88, VT. 564, VV. 292, VyP. 84, VyS. 73, VVCa. 97).

20. See Kāty. (949-50) and Bṛh. (29.13-4) :

niṣkṛtīnām akaraṇam ājñāsedha-vyatikramaḥ,
varṇā-śrama-vilopaś ca prarṇa-saṅkaralopanam.
nidhir niṣphalā-vittaṁ ca daridrasya dhanāgamaḥ,
etāṁś cāraiḥ suviditān svayaṁ rājā nivārayet.

(Also quoted in DV. 263, VyK. 164, VRK. 623).

21. Then it amounts to one-twelfth :
K. (203.8).

22. See note 21. See also K. (203. 8-9). The same is also stated in G. (10.45) where we read that some declare that the finder who is not a Brahmaṇ, is entitled to one-sixth part.

23. See G. 10.43: *nidhyadhigamo rājadhanam.* (Also quoted in VyK. 118, SC. 133, VRK. 347, DV. 274, VT. 564, VV. 252, VyP. 84, VyS. 72).

a Brahmaṇ.[24] Also every treasure worth more than 100,000 *paṇa-s*, had to be taken by the king (K.[25]).

Any Brahmaṇ who found a treasure could take everything[26] but had to give notice to the king at once.[27] According to Vi. if the finder was a *kṣatriya*, the king received one quarter, the Brahman one quarter and the finder one half; if he was a *vaiśya* one quarter went to the king, one half to the Brahmaṇs and one quarter to the finder; and if he was a *śūdra* five-twelfth went to the king, five-twelfth to the Brahmaṇs and one sixth to the finder.[28]

If the treasure was found by the king, he had to take a half of the treasure found for himself and give a half to the Brahmaṇs.[29]

However, of a treasure hidden in former times, members

24. *Pareṇa nihitaṁ labdhvā rājany upaharen nidhim,*
rājagāmi nidhiḥ sarvaḥ sarveṣāṁ brāhmaṇādṛte (N. 7.6; NMS. 8.6. Also quoted in VRK. 643, DK.34-53, DV. 289, NṛP. 174, VV. 292).

25. *śatasahasrāḍ ūrdhvam rājagāmī.* K. (203. 8).

26. *vidvāṁs tu brāhmaṇo dṛṣṭvā pūrvopanihitaṁ nidhim,*
aśeṣato 'py ādadīta sarvasyā 'dhipatir hi saḥ. (Mn. 8.37) Also quoted in SC. 134, DV. 289, VyP. 84, VyS. 73, Apar. *ad* Y. 2.34).
nidhiṁ brāhmaṇo' labhdhvā sarvam ādadyat. Vi. (3.58. Also quoted in VRK. 644, VyN. 533, DV. 288, VV. 293).
nidhy adhigamo rāja-dhanam. G. (10.43). Cf. fn. 23.
aprajñāyamānaṁ vittaṁ yo 'dhigacched rājā tad dhared adhigantre ṣaṣṭham aṁśaṁ pradāya. brāhmaṇaś ced adhigacchet ṣaṭsu karmasu varttamāno na rājā haret (Vās. 3.13-4. Also quoted in Mit. *ad* Y. 2. 35, Vīr. *ad* Y. 2.35, Apar. *ad* Y. 2.35, SC. 134, VRK. 643, DK. 35, DV. 287, VT. 564, VV. 292, VyP. 84, VyS. 73). Also one-sixth had to be paid to the finder. See also G. (10.43) (above note 23) and Y. (2.34).

27. *brāhmaṇo 'pi nidhiṁ labdhvā kṣipraṁ rājñe nive* dayet. (N. 7.7), NMS. 8.7. Also quoted in VRK. 643, DK. 35, DV. 292, NṛP. 174, VV. 292.

28. *kṣatriyaś caturthaṁ aṁśaṁ rājñe'paraṁ caturtham aṁśaṁ brāhmaṇebhyo 'rdham ādadyāt,*
vaiśyas tu caturtham aṁśaṁ rājñe dadyād brāhmaṇebhyo 'rdham aṁśam ādadyāt (Vi. 3, 59, 60). Also quoted in VRK. 644, VyN. 533, DV. 288, VV. 293).

29. *yaṁ tu paśyen nidhiṁ rājā purāṇaṁ nihitaṁ kṣitau,*
tasmād dvijebhyo dattvā 'rdham ardhaṁ praveśayet. (Mn. 8.38. Also quoted in SC. 134, VRK. 645, MPā. 226, VV. 293, VyS. 73, Apar. *ad* Y. 2.34).
nidhiṁ labdhvā tad ardhaṁ brāhmaṇebhyo dadyāt, dvitīyaṁ ardhaṁ kośe praveśayet (Vi. 3.56, 57) Cf. fn. 28. (for *nibandha-s*)
rājā labdhvā nidhiṁ dadyād dvijebhyo 'rdhaṁ dvijaḥ punaḥ,
vidvān aśeṣam ādadyāt sa sarvasya prabhur yataḥ (Y. 2.34. Also quoted in Vīr. *ad* Y. 2.36 MMu. 8.37, VRK. 643-4, VyN. 533, DV. 289, DT. 183, VyM. 88, VV. 292, VVCa. 97.

Y. used here the word *dvija* as the designation of a Brahmaṇ. Similarly Viṣṇudharmottara (Vīra-Rāja, 269 ff.), Agnipurāṇa 222. 14.

of all castes, with the exception of Brahmaṇs had to give one-sixth or one-twelfth to the king.[30]

Thus, we see that, according to the rules found in the *Smṛti-s*, objects found anywhere and treasure-trove did not belong automatically to the finder and that the finder did not acquire by the act of finding any property (unless the object found was a *res nullius*, or a *res derelicta*); we also see that the finder or finders could not freely dispose of every object found.

(B) *In the Pañcatantra*

In the tale of the Honest-mind and Evil-mind we read in P. the following passage :

(*atha*) *tatrā dharmabuddhir nāma yaḥ* (*sārthavāhasutas*) *tena* (*kasyacit sādhoḥ pūrvasthāpitaṁ*) *kalaśikāgataṁ* (*svabhāgyapracoditaṁ raupya*) *dīnārasahasraṁ prāptam.* (p. 1.13.501) *adhiṣṭhānasamīpe dharmabuddhinā 'bhihitam*: *dīnārā dharvibhāgena vibhajyantām.* (P. 1. 3. 503.)[31]

"(Now) on the way the one (merchant's son) who was named Honest-wit (because of the merit [acquired by past deeds],) found a thousand (silver) dinars in a purse (where a usurer had once hidden it)......When they were nearly home, Honest-wit said: 'Let us divided the dinars half and half......"[32]

It ought to be also emphasized that in P. (book 2 : *katha* 1, continuation, 141)[33], in the tale of the mouse and two monks, a treasure found by two men was divide between them in two halves.[34] (Identically PHT. 2.1, p. 66, v. 9-10).

We see here that the money found by Honest-mind and

30. *sva nihitad rājñe brāhmaṇa-varjaṁ dvādaśam aṁśaṁ dadyuḥ.* (Vi. 3.63. Also quoted in VRK. 642, MPā. 225, DV. 286., VV. 292).

mamā'yam iti yo brūyān nidhiṁ satyena mānavaḥ,
tasyā'dadita ṣaḍbhāgaṁ rājā dvādaśam eva vā. (Mn. 8.35. Also quoted in Mit. *ad* Y. 2.35, SC. 134, VRK. 642, MPā. 226. DV. 286, Vīr. *ad* Y. 2.35, VyM. 88, VT. 565, VV. 291, VyP 84, VyS. 73, Apar. *ad* Y. 2.35, Similarly Y. 2.35).

31. Almost identically PHT. (1-15, p. 46, v. 10-12 and v. 13-14. Similarly PHP. (1.26, p. 109, v. 13-14 and v. 17). According to PK., PBK. and PPP. the two friends did not divide the money found but gained it.

32. According to F. Edgerton's translation.

33. *ardhārdhaṁ ca vibhajya suhāsīnau sthitau.* (P. 2. 1, 141).

34. PK. PBK., and PPP. do not contain this sentence. However, compare PBK. (II.1, p. 19, v. 5 sqq.) and PBK. (v.3, p. 45). About treasure in PHP. see 2.1, *śl.* 67, 68, sqq.

Evil-mind was not given to any office for lost property, or to the king, but was only divided in half between the two finders.

We also see that a treasure found was not given either to the king or to the Brahmaṇs, but was divided between the two finders.

Therefore, we can state that these versions of Pañc. were not based on the *Smṛti-s*,as far as the problem of property found, or of treasure-trove is concerned.

However, it is to be noted that the same stories as found in PK., PBK. and PPP. in both tales (*i.e.* in the story of Honest-mind and Evil-mind, and in the story of the mouse and two monks) do not contain this problem at all. In the story of Honest-mind and Evil-mind the money buried by both friends was not *found*, but *gained*[35] and in the story of the mouse and and two monks we do not find any mention that the treasure found was divided into two equal parts.[36]

Therefore, it seems that these tales, in PK., PBK., and PPP., as far as the legal problems are concerned, solved this problem better, *i.e.* in accordance with the legal rules in force, the more so as, for the contents of this tale, it is irrelevant whether the money was found or gained, and in the second whether the treasure-trove was divided among the finders, or not.

It does not seem possible that by accident only, in both these tales, in P. and PHT., the property and treasure-trove was divided, and in the same tales, in PK., PBK., and PPP., we do not find this statement. It is likely that the latter versions *purposely* did not make mention of the division of property and treasure-trove, desiring to be in agreement with the legal rules then in force. These rules were probably older than the tales and it would therefore, be difficult to assume that this distinction was made between younger and older versions.

(C) *According to PHP.* (3.14)

In PHP. (3.14 p. 217) in the story of the bird whose dung was gold, the problem of what to do with the property

35. The same is also found in Kath. in the same tale (10.60, 212, 213).
36. The same can also be observed in Kath. (10.60, 212, 213 and 10.61, 87-96).

found was raised. According to this tale he who found a bird, whose dung was gold, reflected: "If anybody should ever discover his peculiarity it would be reported to the king......I will take the bird and report to the king myself."[37]

From this story it is evident that the object found should be reported to the king, which action was in conformity with the texts of the *Smṛti-s* quoted above.

9. *Surety in Litigation*

(A) *In the Smṛti-s*

Vāda was according to the *Smṛtis,* surety in litigation. Such a surety was introduced in order to safeguard the execution of justice. According to Mit. (*ad* Y. 2.10) the officer presiding over the court could ask both litigants to take surety who would be competent to satisfy the object of judgement *i.e.*, the payment of the amount decreed, or the fine.[38] This kind of surety may also be introduced in order to secure the appearance of the defendant in court (Śukr. 4 ch. 5, 125). Such a surety resembled a surety for appearance (*darśana, pradarśana,* or *upasthāna*).[39]

(B) *In the Pañcatantra*

In P 1. 13, 525-6 we read : (*atha*) *tair* (*dharmādhikṛtair*) *vismayād abhihitam : kathaṁ vanaspatir mantrayiṣyati. bhavatu, parasmin dine pratipādayiṣyatī'ti. kṛtapratibhuuvau* (*dvāv api sva*)-*gṛhaṁ visarjitau.*

(Then) the judges were astonished and said : "How shall a tree give evidence ? Very well, tomorrow he shall prove his statement.' And they let (both of) them go to their homes, taking surety from them."[40] (Almost identically PHT. 1.15, p. 47, v. 14-16; and similarly PHP 1.26, p. 111, v. 6-7).[41]

37. According to A.W. Ryder's translation.

38. *ubhayor arthipratyarthino sarveṣu vivādeṣu nirṇavasya kāryaṁ kārya nirṇayaḥ; āhitāgnyādiṣupā ṭhāt kāryaśabdasya pūrvanipātaḥ, nirṇayasya kāryaṁ, ca sādhitadhanadānaṁ daṇḍadāṇaṁ ca tasmin samarthaḥ pratibhūḥ pratibhavati tat kāryaṁ tadvad bhavatī'ti pratibhūr grāhyaḥ sasabhyena sabhāpatinā,* (Mit. *ad* Y. 2.10).

39. Cf. Above Sudy V. on 'Suretyship".

40. According to F. Edgerton's translation.

41. In PK., PBK. PPP. this sentence has not been found.

The various versions of Pañc. designated "suretyship" by the general word *pratibhū*, instead of *vāda*[42]; nevertheless, we see that the sense of the *Smṛti-s* was preserved here as the judge or judges sent both the litigants home, but before doing so took surety from both of them, *i.e.* surety in litigation.

This rule conformed with the *Smṛti-s* and shows that this kind of sureties, although mentioned only in Kāty. (530), and indirectly in Y. (2.10) and Śukr. (4, ch. 5, 125), was often ordered by the court and was frequently in use.

10. *Reading of Text-Books in the Court and Minor Juridical Problems*

(A) *In the Smṛti-s*

According to the ancient Indian civil procedure the judge had to collect evidence and then pronounce judgement. There are various kinds of evidence; however, the most important were documents, witnesses and ordeals.

In the tale of Honest-mind and Evil-mind the question arose which of this sort of evidence had to be applied in case when documents, witnesses and ordeals were offered.

In Kāty. (223) we read :

kriyā na daivikī proktā vidyamāneṣu sākṣiṣu,
lekhye ca sati vādeṣu na divyaṁ na ca sākṣiṇaḥ.

(Also quoted in VyMā. 306, 308, 315, Apar. *ad* Y 2.22, VyK. 39, DK. 33, VyCi. 27, 29, NṛP. 7, VyT. 216, DT. 575, VCa. 128, VySau. 37, VyPr. 83, VyM. 10, VT. 111, VV. 125, VyS. 25. VVy. 8).

Hence Kāty states that where documents exist witnesses could not be heard, and where witnesses existed ordeals were not admissible.

In Y. (2.22) it was stated :

pramāṇaṁ likhitaṁ bhuktiḥ sākṣiṇaś ce 'ti kīrtitam,
eṣām anyatamābhāve divyā 'nyatamam ucyate.

(Also quoted in ViR. *ad* Y. 2.22, VyK. 38, SC. 50, 95, SS. 95, VyCi. 28, SCM. 42, NṛP. 7, VT. 211, SV. 105, VySau. 37, Vīr. *ad* Y. 2.22, VyPr. 82, 156, 169, VyU. 42, VyM. 10, 60, VT. 110, RDhK. 393, VV. 110, VyP. 32, VyS. 25, AP. 253. 50-1).

42. Y. (2.10) also uses the word *pratibhū* instead of *vāda*.

According to J. R. Gharpure's translation "Evidence has been stated to consist of a writing, possession, and witnesses. In the absence of any of these, the ordeal is said to be another (means of evidence)."

Mit., Vīr, and Śūlapāṇi (*ad* 2.22) made it still clearer that the proof by ordeal could also be applied when other proofs were absent.

On the other hand Bṛh. (4.17)[43] stated that only when doubt arose with regard to a document or oral evidence, and when ratiocination also failed, purgation through ordeal was the proper test.[44]

The difference between these two *Smṛti-s* was small, but the sense was the same—the proof by ordeal could only be introduced when all other proofs have given no positive results.

The same was also the opinion of N. (1.247)[45], Kāty. (218)[46], and others.[47]

(B) *In the Pañcatantra*

In the tale of Honest-mind and Evil-mind in P. (1.13, 546), after the judges came to the field in order to examine the tree as witness we read :

(*atha*) *prabhāt* (*asamay*)*e dharmādhikaraṇa-prakṛtipratyakṣaṁ dharma* (*śāstra*) *vacanābhiśrāvitād vanaspater niḥsṛtā vāk.* (Similarly PHT. 1.15, p. 48, v. 16 sqq.).

According to F. Edgerton's translation : "(Then) in the morning, after texts from law books (*dharmaśāstra*) had been

43. *likhite sākṣi-vāde ca saṇdigdhir jāyate yadi,*
anumāne ca saṁbhrānte tatra divyaṁ viśodhanam. (Bṛh. 4.17). Also quoted in VyMā. 314, 333, Apar. *ad* Y. 2.22, VyK. 39, SC. 53, 91, SV. 108, VCa. 128, VySay. 38, VyM. 11, VT. 133-4, VyP. 32, VyS. 26-7).

44. According to Jolly's translation in SBE 33.

45. *yadā sākṣi na vidyeta vivāde vadataṁ nṛṇām,*
tadā divyaiḥ parikṣeta śapathaiś ca pṛthag vidhaiḥ. (N. 1.247). Also quoted in Apar. *ad* Y. 2.95, VyK. 39, SC. 51, SV. 106, VCa. 129, VySau. 38, VyPr. 84, VyP. 32, VyS. 25, VVy. 10).

46. *yady eko mānuṣīṁ brūyād anyo brūyāt tu daivikīm,*
mānuṣīṁ tatra gṛhṇīyān na tu daivīṁ kriyāṁ nṛpaḥ. (Kāty. 218). Also quoted in Śukr. 4.757-8, Mit. *ad* Y. 2.22, VyMā. 315. Apar. *ad*.Y. 2.22, VyK. 38, SC.51, VyC. 27, SC. 41, NṛP. 7, SV. 107, VySau. 37, VyPr. 82, VyM. 10, VT. 110, RDhK. 393, VyP. 33, VyS. 25).

47. See also N. 1.76, Bṛh. 7.34 and 4.15, Kāty. 242, 243, where the list of evidence is enumerated in the order in which it was to be applied.

read before the tree in the presence of the court officials, a voice came forth from the tree saying......"

From the legal point of view it is difficult to understand what this sentence meant, what texts of law-books were read, since this action was not in conformity with the *Smṛti-s*. Therefore, it seems, that from the legal point of view, the tale as quoted in PK., PHP., and PPP. was better. We read there:

Evaṁ dvav api tau vivādamānau dharmādhikaraṇaṁ gatau, procatuś ca parasparaṁ dūṣayantau, atha dharmādhikaraṇādhiṣṭhita-puruṣair divyārthe yāvan niyojitāu tāvat pāpabuddhir āha, aho na samyag dṛṣṭo'yām nyāyaḥ, uktaṁ ca :

vivāde 'nviṣyate patraṁ tad abhāve 'pi sākṣiṇaḥ,
sākṣyabhāvāt tato divyāṁ pravadanti manīsiṇaḥ. (451)

Tad atra viṣaye mama vṛkṣa-devatā sākṣibhūtā tiṣṭhati, sā 'py āvayor ekataraṁ cauraṁ vā sādhuṁ kariṣyati, atha taiḥ sarvair abhihitaṁ : bho yuktam uktaṁ bhavatā, uktaṁ ca yataḥ :

antyajo 'pi yudā sākṣī vivāde saṁprajāyate,
na tatra yujyate divyaṁ kiṁ punar yatra devatā. (452)

(PK 1.19, p. 96, v. 25-p. 97.9, PM 1.174).

"So quarreling they carried their dispute to court, pleaded and accused each other. And when the judges decreed an ordeal for each the Evil-mind said: "This judgment is not proper. For it is said : "Best evidence is a document, if this is lacking witnesses have to be examined and when these are lacking, ordeals have to be decreed' " (*śl.* 451).

"In the present case, I have a witness, the Goddess of the tree. She will state which one of us is a thief or an honest man. And they replied: 'You are quite right as it is also stated: 'Even if a man of the lowest class could be examined as witness, proof by ordeals is not to be taken, of course, much less if a deposition of a God is available' " (*śl.* 452).

(Similarly PHP. 1.26, p. 110, v. 18 to 111, v. 4, PBK. 1.19, p. 86, v. 16-25, and PPP. 1.19, p. 87, v. 24 to p. 88, v. 5).

The first sentence (*śl.* 451) expressed very well the teachings of Kāty. (223), Y. (2.22), Bṛh. (4.17) and others, and stated in general words that in the court, firstly, evidence by documents was decisive; if documents were not available then evidence of witnesses should be decreed; and if witnesses were not available then ordeals had to be decreed. This sentence conformed entirely with the *Smṛti-s* and the second *śloka* (452) repeated the same general *śloka* relating it more to the specific case, narrated in the tale of Honest-mind and Evil-mind.

Therefore, it is to be assumed that, from the legal point of view, the latter texts were more accurate (than P. and PHT.), as they were based on the *Smṛtis*.

(C) *Minor Juridical Problems*

The tale of Honest-mind and Evil-mind mentioned also some minor juridical problems, such as the choice of the judge, or judges; examination of witnesses in the field; sentences and punishments. However, these references were too vague to be discussed at this point.

11. *Conclusions*

In interpreting this tale from the legal point of view, we come to the conclusion that the Viṣṇuśarman's Pañc., as far as it referred to the division of the object found, was, perhaps, the proper version rather than PHT 1.15, p. 46, v. 10 ff. and 2. 1, p. 66, v. 9-10 (P. 1. 13, 501 ff.), which was completely strange to the Indian listener's sense of legal order, even though it was narrated in a fictitious tale.

Similarly, the question of the reading of law-books in the court was not too clear in PHT 1. 15, p. 48, v. 16 ff. (P. 1. 13, 546) although explicitly it was stated there that it referred to the *Smṛti-s*; the other versions (PBK 1 10, p. 86, v. 16 ff., PK 1. 19, p. 96, v. 25 ff. PPP. 1. 19, p. 87, v. 24 ff. and even PHP 1. 26. p. 110, v. 18 ff. however, express the thoughts of the *Smṛti-s*.

On the other hand, it is evident that rules on sureties in litigation, not mentioned in a detailed way in the *Smṛti-s*, were often ordered by the court and were frequently in use.

II. THE TALE OF THE CAT AS JUDGE BETWEEN THE PARTRIDGE AND THE HARE

A. *According to P.*

12. *Contents of P. (III-4) and its Juridical Problems*

In P., book III, *kathā* 4 (in PK. Book III, *kathā* 2, p. 163;

in PHP. Book *kathā* 3; in PPP. Book III *kathā* 2; in PBK. Book III, *kathā* 2; in PHT. Book III, *kathā* 4 we find the tale of the cat acting as a judge between the partridge and the hare. The story tells of a partridge who had possession of a hole. One day he vacated the hole and did not return to it for some time. When he did, he found that the hare occupied his old dwelling. The partridge asked the hare to vacate it, but the hare refused to do so, saying that a dwelling could be enjoyed by whomever was at hand. The partridge then proposed to refer the question to a judge and to summon witnesses to give testimony. They chose the cat as judge. The cat won their confidence by reciting some sacred texts. The cat, pretending to be hard of hearing, asked the partridge and the hare to come quite close to him, and then, with one stroke, caught and killed them. The tale ended with a maxim that by applying to a mean judge both of the litigants will be doomed to destruction.

From the juridical point of view as described in the *Smṛti-s*, two problems were solved in this tale:

(1) the dwelling could be enjoyed by whomever was at hand,

(2) in the case of a dispute regarding a dwelling the testimony of neighbours was decisive.

This tale also contains some interesting quotations from the *Smṛti-s* by means of which the cat won the confidence of the partridge and the hare.

Further the tale demonstrated that the king had to decide in the case of a dispute between his subjects. However, the maxims and the conclusion in this case were not interesting from the legal point of view.

13. *Res Derelicta-Occupatio*

As far as it was possible to ascertain, we do not find in the *Smṛti-s* any rule that a dwelling could be enjoyed by whomever was at hand.

In the tale quoted above the partridge possessed the hole, or possessed its use. The hole, before being taken possession of by the partridge was a *res nullius.* Here the use along with the *animus utendi* was the *titulus acquirendi* and no special act was necessary. From the legal point of view, the hare was wrong in stating that he could take possession of the hole.[48] This could be taken possession of only if it were abondoned by the partridge and had thus become a *res derelicta*: then as a *res nullius* it could be taken possession of by the hare (*occupatio*). However, as is evident from the tale quoted above the partridge had the *animus utendi* the hole, and did not abandon the hole completely, and intended to return there. The judge therefore passed the judgement in favour of the partridge.

14. *Witnesses*

In order to pass judgment the judge had to proceed with the trial. For that purpose he had to examine witnesses as to whether the partridge has used the hole before leaving, whether he had the *animus utendi* the hole, etc. Therefore, the partridge proposed to examine witnesses[49] and quoted the following *śloka*:

vāpīkūpataḍāgānāṁ gṛhasyā'vasathasya ca,
sāmantapratyayā siddhir ity evaṁ manur abravīt (P. 3.4, *śl.* 47).

This *śloka* is quoted almost identically in PHP. (3.3, 83)[50] and PK. (3.2, 91)[51] however, differently in PHK. (3.2, 93)[52] and PPP. (3.2,91). It is undoubtedly based on the *Smṛti-s*.

Mn. (8.262) stated :

kṣetra-kūpa-taḍāganām ārāmasya gṛahasya ca
sāmantapratyayo jñeyaḥ sīmā-setu-vinirṇayaḥ.

(Also quoted in VyK 97, VRK 218, VCi 97, SCM 23, VV 190, VyS 115.)

Kāty. (734) stated:

kṣetravāstutaḍāgeṣu kūpopavanasetuṣu,
dvayor vivāde sāmantaḥ pratyayaḥ sarvavastuṣu.

(Also quoted in VyK 171, VRK 207, MR 114, Vyr Pr. 358, VT 692).

Y. (2.154) stated:

48. As it could be enjoyed by whomever was at hand, i. e. took a *res nullius* into possession. P. (3.4, 93) stated : *mūrkha, (kiṁ na te viditam, upasthānabhogya āvāso (bhuktiś ca).*

49. In P. (3.4, 94) we read : *kapiñjala āha: santy atra prāśnikāḥ, pṛcchāmo (deśarūpam iti. uktaṁ ca dharma śāstre).*

50. Instead of *gṛhasyā'vasathasya* there is *gṛhasyopavanasya.*

51. Same text as of PHP. However, PK. wrongly stated *sāmantapratayāt* instead of *sāmantapratyayā*. See also PS. 3.35, PN. 3.28.

52. *vāpī-kūpa-taḍāgānāṁ devālaya-kujanmanām,*
utsargāt parataḥ svāmyam api kartuṁ na śakyate.

ārāmāyatanagrāmanipānodyānaveśmasu,
eṣa eva vidhir jñeyo varṣāmbupravahādiṣu.

Also quoted in ViR 2.158, VyK 98, VRK 218, MR 114, VCi 97, NṛP 32, VyPr 358, VyU 107, VT 692, VV 190, VyS 115, VVy 47, AP 257.5).

Vās. (16,13) stated :

gṛha-kṣetra-virodhe sāmanta-pratyayaḥ.

Thus, according to these *Smṛti-s,* in the cases enumerated above, covering wells (*kūpa*), tanks (*taḍāgana*), houses (*gṛha*), gardens (*ārāma, upavana*), etc. the neighbours' evidence was decisive.

P., PK., PHP. (and PBK., as well as PPP., as far as the first part of the first verse in concerned) were based on Mn. (8.262).[53] However, they unfortunately quoted this *śloka* wrongly. Instead of *kṣetra* they quoted *vāpī* which is almost identical with *taḍāga* and was unnecessarily introduced. Completely distorted is the second part of the second verse in which P., PK., and PHP quoted the authority (Mn.: *ity evaṁ manur abravīt*) and omitted the very important sentence—*sīmāsetuvinirṇayaḥ,* which explained the use of the *genetivus* of *ārāma,* and *taḍāga.*[54]

Although from the point of view of Mn., it was very important to state that there were boundary marks, Kāty., Y., and Vās. did not emphasize this fact so clearly.

Nearer to the text of Mn. was the text of PK. and PHP. Instead of *āvasathasya* both these texts used the word *upavanasya* as the latter word also meant garden, similar to *ārāma.* For this reason the text of this *śloka,* used in PK. and PHP. seems to be nearer the original version.[55]

Thus, we see that from the legal point of view, the partridge was right when asking the testimony of witnesses, *i.e.* of neighbours, as this testimony, according to the *Smṛti-s,* in the case of the dwellings (*gṛha*), was decisive.

53. That was stated *expressis verbis* in these texts.

54. In this connexion it should be stated that G. N. Jhā's translation of Mn. (8.262) in Vol. IV, p. 2 (p. 303) seems not to be correct. (G. Bühler's translation in SBE. XXV is much better.

55. Numerous editions and MSs of Mn. have been checked but no text of this *śloka,* as quoted in P., PK., or PHP.. could be found.

15. *Sentences Recited in P. by the Cat in order to win Confidence*

A. *According to P.*

P. (3.4, *śl.* 49-51), when quoting the *śloka-s* recited by the cat in order to obtain the confidence of both of the litigants, based them partly on the *Smṛti-s*.

We read there :

dharma eva hato hanti dharmo rakṣati rakṣitaḥ,
tasmād dharmo na hantavyo mā no dharmo hato vadhīt (49).
eka eva suhṛd dharmo nidhane 'py anuyāti yaḥ,
śarīreṇa samaṁ nāśaṁ sarvam anyad dhi gacchati (50).
andhe tamasi majjāmaḥ paśubhir ye yajāmahe,
ahiṁsāyāḥ paro dharmo na bhūto na bhaviṣyati (51).
mātṛvat paradārāṁs tu paradravyāṇi loṣṭavat,
ātmavat sarvabhūtāni yaḥ paśyati sapaśyati (52).[56]

P. (3.4, *śl.* 49) stated : "when righteousness is destroyed, it destroys in turn; when righteousness is preserved, it preserves. Therefore, we must not destroy righteousness lest it, being destroyed, destroy us." This is the well-known verse from Mn. (8.15) and of MBh. (3.313, 28; cf. Jātaka 422.9,1).).

P. (3.4, *śl.* 50) stated : "Righteousness is our only friend that follows us even in death; for all else goes to destruction together with the body." This is the well-known verse from Mn. (8.17).[57]

P. (3.4, *śl.* 51) stated : "In blind darkness are we sunk who offer sacrifices with beasts. A higher religious duty than harmlessness has never been nor shall be." This *śloka* cannot be identified by the present writer. As far as known, it is not a quotation from the classical *Smṛti-s*, since animal sacrifices were allowed in the *Smṛti-s* and are well described in the *Gṛhyasūtra-s*.[58]

P. (3.4, *śl.* 52) stated : "Whoever regards other men's wives like a mother, other men's possessions like clods of earth, and all creatures like himself—he has true vision". This *śloka* could not be identified as a quotation from the *Smṛti-s*. It seems

56. These *ślokas* were also quoted in PHT. (3.4, 60-63).

57. See also MBh. (12.173, 14, 15) (ed. in Jagadiśvara Press), MBh. (13.90, 17) and some so-called Cāṇakya maxims (CNŚ A. 17, etc.).

58. See *Āśv.-Gṛh.* (1.11), *Pāraskara-Gṛh.* (3.11), *Khādira-Gṛh.* (3.4), *Gobhila-Gṛh.* (3.10, 18; 4-1), *Hiraṇyakeśi-Gṛh.* (2.15), Bṛhadāraṇyakopaniṣad (4.4,10), Iśopaniṣad (9.12) and others.

to be a sentence of a general character and is quoted very often by various authors. It is found with small variations in various *Cāṇakya's* collections,[59] in the *Saṁskṛtapāṭhopakāraka* (53), in H. (1.14) and in PK. (1.450), PHP. (1.26, 390), PBK (1.9, 402), PPP. (1.19, 435), etc. It was a well-known maxim.

B. *According to Other Versions*

The tale of the cat as judge between the partridge and the hare as quoted in P. was almost identical with that quoted in PHT.

From the juridical point of view the same story was told in another manner in PK. and PHP., as well as in PBK. and PP. The differences between PK. and PHP. were insignificant; similarly between PBK. and PPP. There were however, some slight differences between PK. and PHP. on the one hand, and PBK. and PPP. on the other.

16. *Animus Utendi. Bona Fides*

A. The substance of the story of the cat as judge between the partridge and the hare was the same. According to the *Viṣṇuśarman's* Pañcatantra the partridge or sparrow Kapiñjala, in order to gain his livelihood (*prāṇayātrārtham anyaiś caṭakaiḥ*), went to another place but was expected to return (PK. 3.2, p. 163, 223; PBK. 3.2, p. 56-6; PPP. 3.2, p. 148-7.

This clearly shows that Kapiñjala intended to return to his hole; the hole, therefore, was not a *res derelicta* and the previous possessor of the hole still had the *animus utendi.* Therefore, it is clear that, from the legal point of view, *occupatio* did not take place.

B. However, a new problem arose in these versions because it was stated in these texts that the hare was not warned that the hole was in possession of anybody else and, therefore, occupied it, and then possessed it, *in bona fide.*

This is evident from the texts in which it was stated that nobody had forbidden (*nivāritaḥ*) him to occupy the hole (PK.

59. CVND. 12.14, CVM. 12.6, CRCa. 2.18, CNJV. 5, CNS. 73, CNF. 27, CNN. 28, CNPh. 72, CNP. 2.145, CNI I 1.25, CNG. 218, CNŚC. 3, CNŚI. 3, CNŚ. 3, CNŚL. 10, CNNM. 3, CNŚT. 3, CNŚK. 4, CnT. II. 19.6, CnT. III.52.1, Garuḍa-purāṇa 1.111,12.

3.2, p. 164.5 ; PHP. 3.2, p. 56.12; PPP. 3.2, p. 148.14).

C. Therefore, Kapiñjala said to the hare: "It is not right that you occupied my dwelling. Vacate it as soon as possible." And the hare replied : "It is not your dwelling place. It is mine...." "If you think so" Kapiñjala replied "then let us ask the neighbours" because :

vāpī-kūpa-tadāgānāṁ gṛhasyopavanasya ca,
sāmantapratpayāt siddhir ity evaṁ manur abravīt (PK. 3.2, *śl.* 91, PHP. 3.3, *śl.* 83), or because:

vāpī-kūpa-ṭaḍāgānāṁ devālaya-kujanmanām,
utsargāt parataḥ svāmyam api kartuṁ na śakyate. (PBK. 3.2, *śl.* 93, PPP. 3.2, *śl.* 91).

These *śloka-s,* as cited in PK. and PHP. were almost identical with those of P. (3.4, *śl.* 47) quoted above and identified with the *Smṛti-s* (Mn. 8.262, Kāty. 734, etc.).

In PK. and PHP. the same maxim was repeated in other words in the subsequent *śloka.* It was stated there :

gṛha-kṣetra-vivādeṣu kūpo-pavanabhūmiṣu,
samutpanne vivāde tu sāmantāt pratyayo bhavet. (PK. 3.2 *śl.* 92, PHP. 3.3, *śl.* 84).[60]

From the legal point of view the *śloka,* as cited in PBK. and PPP. presented the legal cases, as described in the tale in question, much better because it was stated there that if a person left any land, wells, etc.[61] he was no longer entitled to lay claim on them.

This was a general rule, taken from the *Smṛti-s,* but based on the principle that a *res derelicta* and then a *res nullius* could be taken possession of (*occupatio*) by anybody and that the person who abandoned an object had no more claim to it. This had to be, however, a *res derelicta* towards which the previous possessor had no more *animus possedendi* or *animous utendi.*

17. *Res Nullius, Possessio, Detention, Usucapio. Praescriptio*

(A) *In the Smṛti-s*

A. In solving some legal institutions the ancient Indian

60. In this wording it could not be found in any of the Smṛti-s. See PHP 3.84.

61. This *śloka* added temples and trees.

law is excellent and stands at the highest level, of development. To these legal institutions belonged the problems of possession and ownership, their acquisition, and the juridical problems *usucapio* and *praescriptio* connected with them.

B. To exhaust this problem, a special monograph should be written. Here, it needs only to be pointed out that the ancient Indian law knew the principle of a *res nullius*, or a *res derelicta*, *i. e.* an object which belonged to nobody or which the owner no longer wanted either to possess or use (had no *animus possedendi vel utendi*) and which could be subjected to *occvpatio*.[62]

C. The ancient Indian law also knew the distinction between *possessio* and *detentio*[63] and the legal consequences of this distinction (viz. it was stated in the *Smṛti-s* that objects which were given only into detention could not be acquired by *usucapio*[64]). The *Smṛti-s* distinguished also between acquisition of some objects by *usucapio*[65] and *praescriptio*[66]. They also stated that it might happen that the owner had no right to claim the return of his property, even though the possessor of this object did not acquire it (by *usucapio*)[67]. In order to acquire a certain object by *usucapio*, the *Smṛti-s* prescribed an uninterrupted[68] possession *in bona fide*,[69] without any hindrance[70] for many years.[71] *Mala fides* excluded the possibility of acquisition of an object by *usucapio*. *Usucapio* created the *titulus acquirendi* of ownership which excluded the possibility of proving ownership of an object by the previous owner by means of witnesses, documents, etc.[72] The period of time necessary for *usucapio* depended on the objects to be acquired by *usucapio*;

62. Cf. Mn. (9.44) and J. Jolly's *Recht and Sitte*, § 26.
63. Cf. above study II on *Law of Deposits*, § 4.,
64. Cf. above study IV on *Pledge*, § 40.
65. Mn. (8.148), N. (1.78, 80), G. (12.37), Vi. (5.187), Bṛh. (7.28, 41), Kāty. (327).
66. Mn. (8.147), Y. (2.24), Vās. (16-16, 17), N. (1.79), Bṛh. (7.43), Śukr. (4.5, 221-223).
67. Śukr. (4.5, 223-224).
68. Bṛh. (7.28).
69. N. (1.84-88), Śukr. (4.5, 223).
70. Mn. (8.147), Y. (2.24), N. (1.78), Bṛh. (7.28, 41), Śukr. (4.5, 221).
71. N. (1.90), Bṛh. (7.28), Kāty. (329), Vi. (5.187), also in Smṛ. C. 3 p. 166.).
72. Bṛh. (7.41). Compare Kāty. (299).

it extended to ten years or more.[73] In different *Smṛti-s* ownership could be created after the lapse of different periods of time[74] and originally some objects could not even be acquired. After some time, however, with the development of legal rules they could be acquired in varying periods of time.[75]

D. If we compare these rules with Roman law we can see that Roman law, at its highest level of delopment, contained similar rules which were already known to the oldest Indian *Smṛti-s*.

E. These *Smṛtis* also stated clearly that, in spite of possession of some objects during a period necessary for *usucapio*, these objects were not to be acquired by *usucapio*. This problem was solved in Mn.,[76] Y.[77] Vās.[78] N.,[79]

73. According to Mn. (7.147) every object was acquired by *usucapio* after the lapse of ten years (see also G. 12.37). Similarly N. (1.79). According to Y. (2.24) land could be acquired by way of *usucapio* after a lapse of twenty years of time, and money after ten years of time. According to Vās. (16.16-17) a property inherited from a father, an object bought etc. could be acquired by *usucapio* after the lapse of ten years. According to Śukr. (4.5, 437-440) small properties could be acquired by *usucapio* after the lapse of ten years and land after twenty years. According to Bṛh. (7.28, 43) uninterrupted possession for thirty years, or by three generations created ownership. Compare also Kāty. (299, 300, 301), N. (Quot. 2.21).

74. For instance according to Mn. (8.147) land could be acquired after ten years, and according to Y. (2.24) after twenty years. Compare Vyāsa in Śūlpāṇi (*ad* Y. 2.24), G. (12.39), and others.

75. According to G. (12.39) animals, land and females were not lost by adverse possession, Immemorial possession was mentioned in Bṛh. (Saṁs. (327-9). According to Bṛh. (Saṁs. 327). Vi. (5.187) land could be acquired by *usucapio* after possession by three generations.

76. *ādhiḥ sīmā bāladhanaṁ nikṣepo'panidhi striyaḥ,*
rājasvaṁ śrotriyasvaṁ ca na bhogena praṇaśyati (Mn. 8.149. Also quoted in VyMā. 351, VyK. 74).

77. *ādhisīmopanikṣepajaḍabāladhanairvinā,*
tathopanidhirājastrīśrotriyāṇāṁ dhanair api (Y. 2.25. Also quoted in ViR. *ad* Y. 2.25, Subodhinī 2.24, VyT. 224, SV. 126, VyPr. 165, VT. 150, VV. 89, VyP. 44, VyS. 47, VCi. 138, AP. 253.53-4.)

78. *athāpy udāharanti,*
paitṛkaṁ krītam ādheyam anvādheyaṁ pratigraham,
yajñād upagamo veṇis tathā dhūmaśikhāṣṭamīti (Vās. 16.16).
tatrā bhuktānubhuktadaśavarṣam (Vās. 16.17).
anyathāpyudāharanti,
ādhiḥ sīmā bāladhano nikṣepo'panidhi-striyaḥ,
rājasvaṁ śrotriyadravyaṁ na saṁbhogena hīyate (Vās. 16.18).

79. *ādhiḥ sīmā bāladhanaṁ nikṣepo'panidhī striyaḥ,*
rājasvaṁ śrotriyadravyaṁ na bhogena praṇaśyati (N. 1.81, NMS. 2.73. Also quoted in VyMā. 351, VyK. 74, SC. 107, VyC. 75, SCM. 50, VySau. 69, VyPr. 166, VVy. 20).

K.,[80] Bṛh.[81] Śukr.,[82] G.,[83] N. Quot.[84] Some of these objects could not be acquired by *usucapio* because of the nature of the contract (lack of *bona fides*), or of the object to be acquired by *usucapio* (real exceptions), or because of the person who was the owner (personal exceptions).

To the first group (because of lack of *bona fides*) belonged *ādhi*[85], *nikṣepa* or *upanidhi*[86], *nidhi*[87]; and because of the nature of the object to be acquired by *usucapio*: *bhūmi*,[88] *sīmā*,[89] *paiśu*,[90] female slaves and boats.[91]

Personal exceptions were more numerous. The aim of their introduction was either protection of the said person, or *praesumptio* of lack of *bona fides*. To the first group belonged the estates of the king (*rājan*)[92], ministers (*amātya*)[93], children (*bala*)[94], mentally backward people (*jaḍa*)[95], women (*strī*)[96], ascetics (*śrotriya*)[97], and heretics (*pāṣaṇḍa*)[98]; to the second

80. *jñātayaś śrotriyāḥ pāṣaṇḍā vā rājñam asannidhau paravāstuṣu bivāsanto na bhogena hareyuḥ; upanidhim ādhiṁ nidhiṁ niksepam striyaṁ sīmānaṁ rājaśrotriyadravyāṇi ca* (K. 191-1.3).

81. *asvāminā tu yad bhuktaṁ gṛhakṣetrāpaṇādikam,*
suhṛdbandhusakulyasya na tad bhogena hīyate (Bṛh. 7.44. Also quoted in Apar. *ad* Y. 2. 28, VyK. 73, SS. 107, VyC. 70, SCM. 49, VyT. 227, DT. 180, VCa. 155, VySau. 69, VyPr. 166, VV. 93, VyP. 45, VyS. 47, VVC. 93).

vaivanya srotriyairbhuktam rājnāmātyais tathaiva ca,
sudīrgheṇāpi kālena teṣāṁ sidhyati tanna tu (Bṛh. 7.46. Also quoted in VyMā. 351, DK. 33-4, SS. 107, VyC. 71, Vīr. *ad* Y. 2.25, VT. 151, VVy. 19. See above *ad* Bṛh. 7.44).

82. *ādhiḥ sīmā bāladhanaṁ nikṣepo'panidhis tathā,*
rājasvaṁ śrotriyasvaṁ ca na bhogena praṇaśyati. (Śukr. 4. 5, 225).

83. *aja dāpogaṇḍadhanaṁ daśavarṣabhuktaṁ paraiḥ san nidhau bhoktuḥ. na śrotriyapravrjtarājanyapuruṣaiḥ. paśubhūmistrīṇāmanatibhogaḥ* (G. 12.37, 38, 39).

84. N. (Quot 7.12).

85. Mn, N., Vās. Śukr., N. Quot. Cf., above Study IV on "Pledge".

86. Mn., Y., Vās., N., K., Śukr., N. Quot.

87. K.

88. G.

89. Mn., Y., Vās., N., K., Śukr.

90. G. Compare also N. Quot. (7.12).

91. N. Quot. (7.12); Compare also for females G.

92. Mm., Y., N., K., Bṛh., Śukr.

93. Bṛh.

94. Mn., Y., N., Vās., K., Śukr.

95. Y.

96. Mn., Y., N., Vās., K., Śukr.

97. Mn., Y., N., Vās., Bṛh., Śukr.

98. K.

group belonged the estates of the son-in-law,[99] or of kinsmen.[100]

F. As far as the tale of the cat as judge between the partridge and the hare was concerned, the most interesting problem was that of *usucapio*, or rather of objects which could be acquired by *usucapio*. Land (*bhūmi*) was only enumerated in G., *i. e.* probably, in the oldest *Smṛti*, which seems to indicate that only in the ancient times land could not be acquired by *usucapio*, although in more recent times *usucapio* of the land *in bona fide* gave the *titulus acquirendi* and, consequently, ownership. However, Mn. Y., N., Vās., K., and Śukr. enumerated *sīmā* as an object which could not be acquired by *usucapio*. Medh. (*ad* Mn. 8.149) added the following commentary on *sīmā*:

> '*sīmā maryādā grāmādīnām, bahusādhāraṇyād-dhi tatro'pekṣā saṁbhavati, gṛhādīnāṁ tu prākāraparikhādirūpā dvitrihastaparimāṇarūpā dvayoḥ sādhāraṇī yā'nyatare kathaṁcid upajīryamāṇā svalpatvād bhogaś ca kaścit kiyantaṁ kālam upekṣyetāpi, tatrāpi dānādisvatvāpagamahetuṁ saṁbhāvayataḥ, atas tat putrāḥ paitrā vā gūacihnādinā prajñāpitasīmatvād ācchindanty eva.*[101]

Hence *sīmā* were only boundaries or objects which were in the boundary line.

(B) *In the Pañcatantra*

Now let us interpret the story of the partridge and the hare as described in PK., PBK., and others with the legal rules quoted above.

A. In PK., after having quoted the maxims relating to

99. Bṛh.
100. K.
101. '*Boundary*'—the boundary-line between villages, etc. It is quite possible that it being a public concern, men are likely to ignore encroachments upon it. In the case of houses, the boundary line, marked by ditches or walls, two, three or four cubits in size, is common to both; and if either side of it happens to crumble down in time, as the matter would be a slight one, even encroachment might be ignored for some time by a certain person. But since in such matters also the owner fearing the loss of ownership through gift, etc., his sons or grandsons do discover some hidden marks of the original boundary and assert their claims to the recovery of the boundary encroached upon. (Medh. According to G. N. Jhā's translation in *Manu Smṛti*, Vol. 4. part 1, p. 183).

the evidence of neighbours in cases of disputes regarding land, field, tanks, pools, etc.[102] the hare replied.

pratyakṣaṁ yasya yad bhuktaṁ kṣetrādyaṁ daśa vatsarān,

tatra bhuktiḥ pramāṇaṁ syān na sākṣī nākṣarāṇi vā. (PK. 3.2, 93, and identically PPP. 3.2, 92; cf. PM. 3.30).

PBK. (3.2, 94) quoting the same rule used however, instead of *kṣetrādyaṁ* the word *gṛhādyaṁ*.

PHP. (3.3, 85) quoted the first part of this *śloka*, as in PK. The second part runs: *pramāṇaṁ nākṣarāṇy atra sākṣī vā tasya tad bhavet.*

On the basis of the *Smṛti-s* we can accept that the text of PK. and PPP. was the nearest to the original. This text was based on the *Smṛti-s*, in particular, on Mn. (8.147), according to which land could be acquired by *usucapio* after ten years. In PK. (and others) it was stated that in the case of a public (*i. e.* not interrupted[103]) possession of land during a period of ten years the evidence of witnesses and documents was not admissible. It was admitted *eo ipso* (Mn.) that its possessor acquired ownership of the land or houses (PHP)[104] by *usucapio*.

The hare, in order to support his statement, quoted according to PK. and PHP. the following sentence ascribed to N ā r a d a. With a few variations the same *śloka*, without mentioning the authority of N ā r a d a, was also quoted in PBK., where we read:

mānuṣāṇām ayaṁ nyāyo munibhiḥ parikīrtitaḥ,

tiraścāṁ ca vihaṁgānāṁ yāvac chiśusamāśrayaḥ (PBK. 3. 2, 95).

In PPP. (3.2, 96) it was stated :

mānuṣāṇām ayaṁ nyāyo munibhiḥ parikīrtitaḥ,

tiraścāṁ ca vihaṁgānāṁ yāvad eva samāśrayaḥ.

This sentence of N ā r a d a could not be found in N., or other *Smṛti-s* and, probably, was invented *ad hoc* by the hare in order to prove his right to the hole. It must also be noted that the period of time quoted in the tale would be too short to prove the acquisition of the property by *usucapio*, and

102. Similarly in P.
103. Cf. Bṛh. (7.28).
104. Some of the texts, used instead of *kṣetra* (land) the word *gṛha* (house).

that no special rules were promulgated for animals.

It should be noted that, from the legal point of view, *usucapio*, was inadmissible because of lack of time necessary for *usucapio*, even if we admit that the hare was *in bona fide*. Therefore, the following statement of the hare was not correct: *tan mamaitad gṛhaṁ dharmato na taveti* (PK. 3.2, p. 165.1).

B. In PK. (and similarly in PHP. and PPP.) the litigants asked the cat for judgment. The cat won their confidence by quoting some well-known sentences and maxims. Those quoted in PK. (3.2, 95 to 107 and 111), in PHP. (3.3, 88 to 93 and 96), in PBK. (3.2, 96 to 106 and 110), in PPP. (3.2, 94 to 105) are of no interest from the legal point of view.[105] However, some others were based on the *Smṛti-s*.

In particular, in PK. (3.2, 109) the following sentence was quoted :

pañca paśvan ṛte hanti daśa hanti gavān ṛte,
śataṁ kanyān ṛte hanti sahasraṁ puruṣān ṛte

This sentence was identically quoted in PHP. (3.3, 98), PPP. (3.2, 107) and, as far as the first part of this *śloka* is concerned probably, wrongly, in PBK. (3.2, 108).[106]

It was stated in PK. and other texts that by false testimony regarding cattle[107] one killed five, regarding a cow—one killed ten, regarding a girl—one killed a hundred, and regarding men—one killed a thousand.

This sentence was undoubtedly based on the *Smṛti-s*, or on the epics. We find the same idea in Mn. (8.98) where we read :

pañca paśvan ṛte hanti daśa hanti gavān ṛte,
śatam aśvān ṛte hanti sahasraṁ puruṣān ṛte (identically B. 1.10, 19, 12 *bc* and MBh., Bhāṇḍarkar edition 5.35, 26).

105. PK. (3.2, 105-106) and identically PHP. (3.3, 94-95) and PBK. (3.2, 104-105), PPP. (3.2, 103-104) stated :

ahiṁsā pūrvako dharmo yasmāt sadbhir udāhṛtaḥ,
yūkamatkuṇadaṁśādīṁs tasmāt tān api rakṣayet.
hiṁsakāny api bhūtāni yo hiṁsati sa nirghṛṇaḥ,
sa yāti narakaṁ ghoraṁ kiṁ punar yaḥ śubhāni ca.

These *śloka-s* were also based on legal rules or, rather religious literature.

106. Instead of *pañca paśvanṛte* PBK. had *ekam aśvān ṛte.*

107. PBK. had "regarding horses one kills one."

Vās. (16.34) quoted this sentence in the following way:
pañca kanyān ṛte hanti daśa hantigavān ṛte,
śatam aśvānṛte hanti sahasraṁ puruṣān ṛte.

G. (13.14, 15; GMH 13.15.6) quoted this sentences in the following way :

kṣudrapaśvanṛte sākṣī daśa hanti, go'śvapurusabhūmiṣu daśaguṇottarān.

Similarly it was also quoted in the *Rāmāyaṇa* (Bombay edition, 4.34, 9) where we read :
satam aśvān ṛte hanti sahasraṁ tu gavān ṛte,
ātmānaṁ svajanaṁ hanti puruṣaḥ purusān ṛte.

We see that this sentence was quoted in various versions. MBh. (in $G._1$ $G._4$ G_5 MSs)[108] and identically Vās. (16.34) introduced *kanyā* instead of *paśv°*. However, PK., PHP., PPP., and others introduced *kanyā* instead of *aśva*. *Aśva* was however, quoted in Mn. and others, as well as in PBK.[109] The original text was probably that of Mn., MBh. and B. and it is probably this text which was quoted in PK., PHP., and PPP. The texts in P., PK., PHP., PBK., and PPP. were only corruptions of these texts.

C. PK. introduced two more *śloka-s*; :
mānād vā yadi vā lobhāt krodhād vā yadi vā bhayāt,
yo nyāyam anyathā brūte sa yāti narakaṁ naraḥ (PK. 3.2, 108, identically PBK. 3.2, 109, PPP. 3.2, 108), and:
upaviṣṭaḥ sabhāmadhye yo na vakti sphuṭaṁ vacaḥ,
tasmād dūreṇa sa tyājyo nyāyo vā kīrtayed ṛtram (PK. 3.2, 110; identically PBK. 3.2, 109, PPP. 3.2, 108).

In the first *śloka* it was stated that he who judged falsely because of pride, hostility, timidity, or fear, would be punished with hell. In the second *śloka* it was stated that he who did not describe the history of the case clearly in the court would have his case dismissed.

The existence of these *śloka-s* could not be traced to the *Smṛti-s*. However, it seems to be certain that they were based

108. We read there :
pañca kanyān ṛte hanti daśa hanti gavān ṛte,
śatam aśvān ṛte hanti sahasraṁ puruṣān ṛte
(MBh. in G_1, G_4, and G_5, Mss in the Bhandarkar Oriental Research Institute in Poona.

109. In the place of *paśv°*.

on general rules contained in the *Smṛti-s* and in repeating them the cat could easily win confidence.

18. *Other Passages in the Pañcatantra relating to Occupation*

The tale of the cat as judge between the partridge and the hare was not the only one in which the problem of the acquisition of a *res nullius* (the hole), occupation of a hole, etc. was raised. This problem seemed to be very popular in the various versions of the *Pañcatantra.*

A. In the tale of the jackal and the war-drum a hungry jackal, hearing a war-drum, crept near it thinking that he would get food; "having come to this conclusion he picked a pot, gnaved a hole and crept in." (PHP. 1.2, p. 13, v. 20).[110]

B. In addition, in the tale of the lion and the wary jackal, a hungry lion came to a great mountain and thought that some animal would come into the cave during the night. Then a jackal, the owner of the cave, came and began to sing (PHP. 3.15, p. 218; 11.12).[111]

In this tale it was stated that he who quitted even, for some time, the object that was taken into his possession (the hole), having still *animus utendi*, was always considered as owner of this object (*svāmin*). This fact proves, once more, that the hare, in the tale of the cat as judge between the partridge and the hare, in the later versions, had the right to the hole.

C. On the other hand, in the tale of the frog's revenge, when the frog-king after having given his relative to the black snake to be eaten by him said that he should return home, the black snake replied that certainly in the meantime his hole had been occupied by a stranger (PHP. 4.1, p. 234.3; see also PBK. 4. p. 7.22).[112]

D. The fact of the occupation of the hole by strangers during the absence of its owner can also be observed in the frame-story to Book 4., where the crocodile was informed that during

110. *evam avadhārya kasmiṁścit pradeśe vidāryā'ntaḥ praviṣṭaḥ* (PHP. 1.2, p. 13.20).

111. *atha guhāsvāmī dadhimukho nāma śṛgālo dvāri phūtkartum ārebhe* (PHP. 3.15, p. 218.11).

112. *madīyabiladurgam anyai ruddhaṁ bhaviṣyati* (PHP. 4.1, p. 234.3 Cf. also PBK. 4, p. 7.22).

his absence his house had been occupied by another crocodile (PHP. 4. p. 250.20; see also PBK. 4. p. 29.12)[113] Having returned, the crocodile killed the intruder and recovered his home (PHP. 4. p. 256).[114]

E. In these tales it was not stated that somebody warned the intruders, saying that the hole was in the possession of another. That was clearly stated in PK., PHP., PPK., and PPP. versions of the tale of the cat. These passages, written only in order to maintain the action of the tales, throw no additional light on this problem.

19. *Conclusions*

From the various versions of the tale of the cat as judge between the partridge and the hare it is evident that all these versions were based upon legal rules which we can find in the *Smṛti-s*; that the juridical problems contained in the tale were presented by both litigants (the hare and the partridge) from the legal point of view and in conformity with the rules contained in the *Smṛti-s*; that, although the hare very wisely quoted juridical arguments, his case ought to be dismissed; and that the longer versions (PK., PHP., PBK., and PPP.) are clearer and better insofar as the legal problems are concerned.

According to the short version (P.), the legal problem was not clearly defined and it is difficult to understand the hare's arguments. It is not clear whether the hare abandoned the hole; on the other hand, the very interesting problem of the possible acquisition of the hole by *usucapio* was lacking.

The longer versions, in particular, PK., PBK., and PPP. contained the explanation that the partridge did not abandon the hole, since he went away only to find some food (and *eo ipso* still had the *animus utendi* the hole). This version also raised a new problem, viz. whether the hare, who was *in bona fide* (nobody has forbidden him the use of the hole), could acquire it by *usucapio*. The hare based his claim upon the following rule :

mānuṣāṇāṁ pramāṇaṁ syād bhuktir vai daśavārṣikī,

113. *yad aho tvadīyagṛham apy apareṇa mahāmakareṇa saṁgṛhītam* PHP IV, frame story, p. 250.20. Cf. also PBK. 4, p. 29.12.

114. PHP. (4 frame story, p. 256).

vihaṅgānāṁ tiraścāṁ ca yāvad eva samāśrayaḥ.[115] i. e. that in case of animals the period of ten years was not necessary in order to acquire ownership by *usucapio*, but only the fact of taking possession of the object. It seems to be clear that this rule was invented *ad hoc* and was not based on the *Smṛti-s*. A special legal rule for animals could not be promulgated. However the hare could plead in the court that, being *in bona fide*, he took possession of a *res nullius*, and in this way proved his *titulus acquirendi*. The judge, however hearing the case and basing his judgment on the deposition of witnesses-neighbours (Mn. 8.262)[116] ought to pronounce his judgement in favour of the partridge, because the witnesses-neighbours could only state that the hole was a *res nullius* or a *res derelicta*, that, in spite of *bona fides* of the hare, it could not be acquired by him by *usucapio*, as the period of time necessary for *usucapio* had not elapsed; that the rule contained in G. that *bhūmi* could not be acquired by *usucapio*, should not be applied in this case, because *bhūmi* was mentioned only in G. and, according to all the other younger *Smṛti-s* (even in Mn.) might be acquired by *usucapio*.

In connexion with the legal interpretation of the tale of the cat as judge between the partridge and the hare, it is possible to come to the conclusion that the longer versions were clearer and more logical and, although the text, as quoted by F. Edgerton, may be the original one (as it is almost identical with PHT.), the value of the tale and of the logical solution of the problems raised there, increased in the longer versions, in particular in the *Viṣṇuśarman's Pañcatantra*, (PK., PBK., PPP.), thus becoming easier to read and to understand by the Indian reader.

III THE TALE OF THE MOUSE-MAIDEN WHO WAS TO WED A MOUSE[117]

20. *Contents of P. (3.9) and its Juridical Problems*

In P. Book 3. *kathā* 9 (in PHT Book 3, *kathā* 9, in PK. Book 3, *kathā* 12 in PHP. Book 3, *kathā* 9, in PBK. 4, *kathā* 9,

115. PK. 3.2,94, PHP. 3.3,86, PBK. 3.2,95, PPP. 3.2,93. See. § 9.
116. And others. See above.
117. See Supplement to Bhāratiya Vidyā, Vol. VII, Nos. 3-4.

PPP. Book 3, *kathā* 12) in the tale of the mouse-maiden who was to wed a mouse, we find the story of a sage who changed the mouse (which was dropped by a falcon into his hands) into a maiden. He gave her to his wife and brought her up as his daughter. When she reached the age of twelve he began to think about her marriage, because it would be considered a sin on his part if the daughter were to attain puberty in her father's house. For this reason the sage wanted to give her away in marriage to a worthy husband. Neither the sun, nor the cloud, nor the wind, nor the mountain found themselves strong enough to take the girl. Finally the mountain said that stronger than she was the mouse, because mice made countless holes, Since the maiden was of the same kind as the mouse, she wanted to be turned back into a mouse.

In some of the versions it was stated that the sun, cloud, wind, etc. did not find themselves strong enough to take the girl, but that the girl did not like them, and that only when she saw a mouse and found that she was of the same kind as the mouse, she wanted to be turned back into a mouse.[118]

From the juridical point of view, as described in the *Smṛti-s*, three problems were solved in this story :

(1) at what age the father should give his daughter away in marriage,

(2) what happened if the father did not give away his daughter in marriage at the prescribed time,

(3) whom the father should choose as husband for his daughter.

21. *General Problems relating to Marriage*

(A) *In the Smṛti-s*

(i) *Two Problems*

P. (227) stated that when a girl reached her twelfth year of age she should be given in marriage by her father or guardian and in any case she should not attain puberty in the father's house, as this fact would constitute a sin on the part of the father.

118. For similarities between this story and other stories of antiquity, see *Benfey's* Pañcatantra, Vol. I. p. 373 sqq.

This sentence was undoubtedly based on the rules contained in the *Smṛti-s*; it regulated two different questions:

(a) the age at which a maiden became marriageable, and

(b) consequences of the fact of attainment of puberty in the father's house.

It is clear that this question, as it was worded, contained the statement that the father of the girl was obliged to give her away in marriage. Only in the case of his failure other persons were obliged to perform his duty. According to Y.[119] (1.63) the father (*pitar*), the paternal grandfather (*pitāmaha*) the brother (*bhratar*), the kinsmen (*sakulya*) and the mother (*jananī*) were obliged to give the maiden away in marriage *i.e.*, in cases of failure of one the next in order was obliged to do it. Vi. (24.38, 39)[120] put between the kinsmen and the mother (*matār*), the maternal grandfather [121] (*mātamana*) N. (12.20-1)[122] gave the following list : *pitar*, *bhrātar*, *pitāmaha*, *mātula* (maternal uncle), *sakulya*, *bāndhava* (cognates) and *mātar* and Kāty. quoted in Vīr. (*ad.* Y. 1.63) p. 127 25, 26; *pitar*, *bāndhava*, *mātāmaha*, and *mātar*[123],[124].

It is evident that according to these *Smṛti-s* [125] the father, in the first place, was responsible for giving away his daughter in marriage and only if he failed some other persons, enumerated in a similar, but not identical order, were obliged to perform the duty of the father. In all these *Smṛti-s* the mother was the

119. *pitā pitāmaho bhrātā sakulyo jananī tathā,*
kanyā-pradaḥ pūrvanāśe prakṛtisthaḥ paraḥ paraḥ. (Also quoted in ViR. *ad* Y. 1. 63, GMH. 18.22, VyPr. 457-8, VBh. 92).

120. *pitā pitāmaho bhrātā sakulyo mātāmaho mātā, ce'ti kanyā-pradāḥ.*
pūrvabhāve prakṛtistheḥ paraḥ paraḥ iti.

121. See also Vīr. *ad* Y. 2.63, p. 127, v. 17 sqq. wrongly attributed by *J. R. Gharpure* in "Yājñavalkya Smṛti" (in "The Collection of Hindu Law Texts." Vol. II, p. I. 182) to Viṣṇu Purāṇa.

122. *pitā dadyāt svayaṁ kanyāṁ bhrātā vānumate pituḥ,*
pitāmaho mātulaś ca sakulyā bāndhavas tathā.
mātā tv abhāve sarveṣām prakṛtau yadi vartate,
tasyām aprakṛtisṭhāyāṁ dadyuḥ kanyāṁ sanāmayaḥ.

123. *svayamevaurasīṁ dadyāt pitā'bhāve svabāndhavāḥ,*
mātā-mahas tato'nyāṁ tu mātā vā dharmajām sutām.
(Not found in Kane's edition).

124. Other *Smṛti-s* were not quoted here.

125. Mn. (5.151) quoted also the father and the brother as those who could give the maiden away in marriage with the father's permission.

last upon whom the obligation fell[126] and never were both the parents even allowed jointly to give away their daughter in marriage; this duty rested solely and exclusively on the father and only in the event of his failure, on other persons, *inter alia* on the mother.

In PBK. we find the following sentence:

mātā caiva pitā caiva jyeṣṭha-bhāratā tathaiva ca,
trays te narakaṁ yanti dṛṣṭvā kanyāṁ rajasvalāṁ.

(PBK. 4, 9, *śl* 70). That is the only sentence not completely conformed with the *Smṛti-s*; according to it in the first place the father, and if he failed, the mother and then the oldest brother were responsible for giving away the girl in marriage.

(ii) *Suitable Age*

The first question, *i.e.*, at what age the girl became marriageable, was regulated in different ways in many sources of law. These sources of law gave rather an advice then stated what really was the suitable age of a girl and a boy.

Aśv.-Gṛh. (in Vīr. Saṁs. p. 767.8 sqq.)[127] stated that the girl of seven should marry a boy of eighteen, and Bṛh. (Saṁs. 329)[128] and Āp. (in Vīr. Saṁs. p. 767.1-3)[129] a boy of twenty-one. Raghunandana quoting an anonymous *Smṛti* stated that the suitable age for a girl was seven[130] years.

According to Mn. (9.94)[131] a girl of eight years had to

126. According to N. (2.22). (If none of the persons mentioned above exist the king could give the maiden his permission for self-choice).

127. *yadā tu naiva kaścit syāt kanyā rājānam āśrayet,*
anujñayā tasya varaṁ pratītya varayat vayam.
saptābdā kanyakānāmnī śaiśavī syāc chubhānvitā,
tām aṣṭā-daśa-varṣīyo vivahed vidhivat pumān.
aṣṭa-varṣā bhaved gaurī putra-pautra-pravardhinī.
pañca-viṁśati-varṣīyas tāṁ kānyām udvahevijaḥ.
rohiṇī nava-varṣā syād dhana-dhānya-vivardhinī,
tām udvaheta matimān sarva-kāmā'rtha-siddhaye,
ūrdhvaṁ daśābdād yā kanyā prāg rajodarśanāt tu sā,
gāndhārī syāt samudvāhyā ciraṁ jīvituṁ icchunā. Cf. NMS. 13.22.

128. *triṁśad-varṣo deśābdāṁ tu bhāryā vindeta nagnikām,*
eka-viṁśati-varṣo va sapta-varṣām avāpnuyāt. See note 139.

129. The text is found in note 128.

130. *saptasaṁvatsarād ūrdhvaṁ vivāḥaḥ sarva-varmikaḥ.*

131. *triṁśad-varṣo vahet kanyāṁ hṛdyāṁ dvādaśaṁvarṣikīm,*
tryaṣṭa-varṣo'ṣṭa-varṣāṁ vā dharme sīdati sat varaḥ.

marry, and Ya. (in Vīr. Saṁs. p. 766.13, 14)[132] a man of twenty-four, and according to Āśv.-Gṛh. (in Vīr. Saṁs. p. 767.5 sqq.)[133] a man of twenty-five. Dak.[134] and Saṁv. (68)[135] were of the opinion that the suitable age of a girl was eight.

According to Āśv.-Gṛh.[136] a girl of nine, called *rohiṇī* had to be wed by a wise man.

A girl of ten had to be taken as wife by a man of thirty, Bṛh.,[137] Āp.[138] and MBh.[139] stated. According to Aṅg.[140] the marriageable age of the girl was ten. A girl of over ten, called *gāndhārī*, had to be taken by a man desirous of living long, Āśv.-Gṛh.[141] stated.

According to Mn. (9.94)[142], a girl of twelve had to marry a man of thirty. This age was a suitable marriageable age for girls, according to Ya. (22)[143] Par. (7.7)[144] and Rājamārtaṇḍa.[145]

A girl of sixteen had to be married by a man of thirty or twenty-one in MBh.[146] stated.

We even find some texts according to which the marriageable age for girls was six, five and even four years of age.[147]

The *Viṣṇu Purāṇa* stated, generally, that a man should

132. Identically as Mn. (Vīr. p. 766.12 sqq.).
133. See note 127.
134. *vivāhayed aṣṭa-varṣā evaṁ dharmo na hīyate,*
135. *vivāho'ṣṭama-varṣāyāḥ kanyāyastu praśasyate*
136. See note 127.
137. See note 128.
138. See note 129.
139. *triṁśad-varṣo daśa-varṣāṁ bhāryāṁ vindeta nagnikām, eka-viṁśati-varṣo vā sapta-varṣām avāpnuyāt.* See notes 128 and 129.
140. *tasmāt saṁvatsare prāpte daśame kanyakā budhaiḥ pradātavyā prayatnena.*
141. See note 127.
142. See note 131.
143. *prāpte dvā-daśame-varṣe yaḥ kanyāṁ na prayacchati, māsimāsi rājas tasyāḥ pitā pivati śoṇitam.* See note 174.
144. The text is identical with that given in note 143.
145. See J. Jolly's Zur Geschichte der Kinderehen, ZDMG. vol. 46, pp. 413 sqq.
146. *triṁśad-varṣaḥ ṣoḍaśa-varṣāṁ bhāryāṁ vindeta nagnikām eka-viṁśati-varṣo vā sa purveṣām avāpnuyāt.* (Vīr. Saṁs. 766. 16.7). This text is probably a corrupted text of MBh. (13.14, 14) and cannot be taken into consideration. See note 139.
147. Three anonymous authors stated : *ṣaḍabda madhyeno'dvāyā kanyā varṣadvayaṁ tataḥ aṣṭama-varṣa-paryantī garbha-pañcama-prabṛti kanyā-vivāhaḥ ucitaḥ kālaḥ und janmato garbhādhānād vā pañcamā'bdāt paraṁ śubham; kumariṇāṁ tathā dānam.*

select a wife whose age was one third of his own[148] and Kām. stated that the wife should be younger than her husband by three years.[149]

From these few (out of many) quotations we see that the suitable age for the girl could be according to the *Smṛti-s* from four to twelve years of age.[150]

(iii) *Different Kinds of Maidens*

A great many sources of law stated that the maiden should be given away in marriage by her father before attaining puberty. Such a maiden was called in the *Suṛti-s nagnikā* or the like.

The *Smṛti-s* differentiated between a *śauśavī*, *gaurī*, *nagnikā*, *gāndhārī*, *kanyā* (*kanyakā*), *śyāmā*, *rohiṇī* (or *rohinī*), *rajasvalā* and *kumārī*.

We find the respective rules in Par., Ya,[151] Saṁv.,[152] Kaś.,[153] Aṅg.,[154] Bhav. P.,[155] and Āśv.-Gṛh.[156]

According to these sources :

(a) a *śauśavī* was a girl of seven (Āśv.-Gṛh.).

(b) a *gaurī* was a girl of seven years of age (according to Kaś., Āśv.-Gṛh. and Bhav. P.), or a girl of eight years of age (according to Par., Ya., Saṁv., and Āśv.-Gṛh.). Aṅg. and Bhav. P. described her as a girl before attaining puberty (before she has commenced her monthly course in her father's house).

148. *varṣair eka-guṇāṁ bhāryām udvahet tri-guṇaḥ svayam* (3.10,1).

149. *tasmāt kānyām abhijano'petāṁ mātā-pitṛ-matīṁ tri-varṣāt prabhṛti* (190.19)

150. The question of the real marriage, the taking of the girl into the husband's house, or the question of child-marriages discussed here.

151. *aṣṭa-varṣā bhaved gaurī nava-varṣā tu rohiṇī,*
daśa-varṣā bhavet kanyā ata ūrdhvaṁ rajasvalā (Vīr Saṁs. 768.19-20).

152. *aṣṭa-varṣā bhaved gaurī navame nagnikā bhavet,*
daśame kanyakā proktā dvā-daśe vṛṣalī matā. (in Vīr. p. 768. 5-6).

153. *sapta-varṣā bhaved gaurī daśa-varṣā tu kanyakā,*
prāpte tu dvā-daśe varṣe kumarī'ty abhidhīyate. (in Vīr. 769. 3-4).

154. *anavāptarajā gaurī prāpte rajasi rohiṇī,*
avyañjana-kucā śyāmā kucahīna tu nagnikā.
vyañjaneṣv atha jāteṣu somo bhuṅkte tu kanyakām,
payodhareṣu gandharvo vahnir bhuṅkte rajasvalām. (in Vīr. p. 769.6-9).

155. *aprāpta-rajasā gaurī prāpte rajasi rohiṇī,*
avyañjana-kucā kanyā kucahīnā tu nagnikā.
sapta-varṣā bhaved gaurī dasa-varśā tu nagnikā.
dvā-daśe tu bhavet kanyā ata ūrdhvaṁ rajasvalā. (in Vīr. p. 768.23 sqq.. Similarly PK. (3.213) and PHP. (3.13, 183).

156. The text can be found in note 127

(c) a *nagnikā* was a girl who had not attained puberty. She was a naked girl, without breast (*kucahīnā*) (Aṅg., Bhav. P.); she was a girl of ten years of age (Bhav. P.).[157]

(d) a *gandhārī* was a girl who was more than ten years old and had not yet attained puberty. (Āśv. Gṛh.).

(e) a *kanyā* was a girl of ten years of age (Par., Ya., Aṅg., Saṁv.) or a girl of twelve years of age (Bhav. P.). Her breasts were not yet developed (*avyañjanakuca*) (Bhav. P.).[160]

(f) *śyāmā* was a synonym for *kanyā*. A *śyāmā* was also described in Aṅg. as a girl whose breasts were not yet developed.

(g) a *rohiṇī* was a girl of nine years of age (Par., Ya., Saṁv., Āśv.-Gṛh.), who had already commenced her monthly course, *i.e.* a maiden after atainment of puberty (Aṅg., Bhav. P.).[161]

(h) a *rajasvalā* was a maiden who had already commenced her monthly courses and attained puberty. She was more than ten years old (Par., Ya., Saṁv.), or more than twelve years old (Bhav. P.)[162]

(i) a *kumārī* was also a maiden after attainment of puberty of more than twelve year of age (Kaś.).[163]

Many sources of law stated either :

(1) that the father had to give his daughter away in marriage before she had started her monthly courses in her father's house, or

(2) that a man had to take as wife a maiden who had not yet commenced her monthly courses in her father's house.

This was, certainly, the same rule, but for the father it was a duty to give away his daughter in marriage before she started her monthly courses, and for the suitor it was an advice to marry such a maiden, since she was considered as suitable for him.

157. Hem. (510) stated that the girls before menstruating were called *gaurī*, *rajā* and *nagnikā*. Amar. (2.6, i, 8) stated that they were called *gaurī*, *nagnikā* and *anāgatārtavā*.

160. For more details see Aṅg. (in Vīr. p. 769-8).

161. Amar. quoted *rohiṇī* in the meaning of a cow.

162. For more details see Aṅg. (in Vīr., p., 769.9).

163. Hem. (510) stated that a girl who had attained puberty was called *kanyā kanī* or *kumarī*; Amar. (2.6, 1, 8) stated that such a girl was called *kanyā* or *kumārī*.

(iv) *Consequences*

A. Mn. (9.4) declared only generally : *kāle'dātā pitā-vācyo*. Medh. (*ad* Mn. 9.4) explained what was meant: *i. e.* that the father who did not give his daughter away in marriage "in proper time was reprehensible." Supported by Mn. Medh. stated :

kaḥ punaḥ kanyāyā dānakālaḥ; "*aṣṭamād varṣāt pribhṛti prāgṛtor iti*" *smaryate*; *ihā'pi liṅgam asti......tiḥ*.

Hence Medh was here of the opinion that the proper age for the maiden to be married by her father was eight *i. e.* as long as she was a *nagnikā*[164] although Mn. (9.94)[165] stated that a maiden of twelve years of age was also marriageable.[166]

On another place we read:

sa ca svāmyād atikrāmed ṛtūnāṁ pratirodhanāt (Mn. 9.93).

Interpreting this rule in connexion with the preceding *śloka*, we see that according to Mn. the father who did not take precautions against the first appearance of the daughter's monthly courses at home, lost his authority over his daughter.[167]

Hence, according to Mn.: (a) the father had to give his daughter away in marriage before her attainment of puberty, (b) otherwise he was reproachable, and (c) lost his authority over her. More definite rules were to be found in other *Smṛti-s*. And so Vās. (17.70) declared:

prayacchen nagnikāṁ kanyām ṛtu-kālabhayāt pitā,
ṛtu-matyāṁ hi tiṣṭhantyāṁ doṣaḥ pitaram ṛcchati.

Vās. stated here: (a) that the father had to give his daughter in marriage as long as she was a *nagnikā*; (b) otherwise he committed a sin; (c) the reason for this rule was that

164. See *J. Jolly's* "*Beiträge zur indischen Rechtsgeachichte*"; ZDMG Vol. 46, p. 416.

165. For text see note 131.

166. It should be added that Mn. (9.88) stated in another place that the father should give his daughter to the bridegroom in the proper form, though she had not attained the proper age.

utkṛṣṭāyābhirūpāya varāya sadṛśāye ca,
aprāptām api tām tasmai kanyāṁ dadyād yathāvidhi (Mn. 9.88. Also quoted in VyS. 118). Medh. rightly stated that this should be a *nagnikā* i.e., an eight-year-old girl. This rule was connected closely with the problem of child-marriages.

167. Medh. stated that according to some authors this *śloka* did not belong to Mn. This opinion does not seem to be right.

a maiden could not see her monthly course in her father's house (out of fear of the appearance of the menses).[168]

This was also the opinion of B (4.1, 11) where we read:

dadyād guṇavate kanyāṁ nagnikāṁ brahmacāriṇe,
api vā guṇahīnāya no'parundhyād rajasvalām.

and Ya. quoted in Smṛ. C. (Saṁs. pp. 216, 19-20) where we read:[169]

dadyād guṇavate kanyāṁ nagnikām eva śaktitaḥ,
na tv eva guṇahīnāya no'parudhyād rajasvalām.

Here it was declared that: (a) the father should give his daughter away in marriage as long as she was a *nagnikā*, (b) that the father could not keep her in the house after her attainment of puberty.[170] B. (4.1, 13), basing his opinion on Mn., in addition stated that by such an act the father committed a sin at each appearance of the menses.[171]

A similar opinion was also held by G. (18.21-3) where we read:

pradānaṁ prāgṛtoḥ; aprayacchandoṣī, prāgvāsaḥ pratipatterity eke.

Here it was stated that : (a) the father had to give his daughter away in marriage before her attainment of puberty, (b) as long as she was a *nagnikā i. e.* before she wore clothes, (c) otherwise he committed a sin.

Also N. (12.25, 27, NMS 13.26, 28) stated the same. We read there :

kanyā nartum upekṣeta bandhavebhyo nivedayet,
te cen na dadyustāṁ bhartre te syur bhrūṇāhabhiḥ samāḥ.
ataḥ pravṛtte rajasi kanyāṁ dadyāt pitā sakṛt,
mahad enaḥ spṛśed enan anyathaivaṁ vidhiḥ satām.

Hence N. declared that : (a) the maiden could not reach the period of maturity without giving notice of it to her relations,

168. Vās. (17.69) declared :
pituḥ pramādāt tu yadī'ha kanyā vayaḥpramāṇaṁ samatītya dīyate
sā hanti dātāram udīkṣamāṇā kālā-tiriktā guru-dakṣiṇeva.

This rule was almost identical with Vās. (17.70). Here it was only stated that such an act "destroyed" the father.

169. The same sentence was also quoted in Smṛ. C. (Saṁs. 216.16, 17). The second verse runs : *apivāguṇahīnaya no 'paroddhyā rajasvalā.* This seems to be a wrong rendering. See also Ya. which was identical with Hultzsch's edition.

170. Ya. quoted in the commentary on Par. (7.5, 7) stated also *tasmād udvāyeta kanyāṁ yāvan nartumatī bhavet.*

171. *ekaikasmin nṛtau doṣaṁ pātakaṁ manur abravīt.*

(b) that the father had to give his daughter away in marriage before her attainment of puberty, (c) otherwise he committed a great crime.[172]

B. We have seen that, according to some *Smṛti-s*, the father committed a sin if he did not give his daughter away in marriage before her attainment of puberty *i.e.*, if she had seen her monthly courses in his house. B. 4.1, 13),[173] and others declared that at each appearance of the menses the father incurred the guilt of a mortal sin. Par. (7.7, 8) and identically Ya. (22, 23)[174] and Saṁv. (7)[175] stated:

prāpte tu dvādaśe-varṣe yaḥ kanyāṁ na prayacchati,
māsi māsi rājas tasyāḥ pivanti pitaraḥ svayam.
mātā caiva pitā caiva jyeṣṭho bhrātā tatthaiva ca,
trayaste narakaṁ yānti dṛṣṭvā kanyāṁ rajasvalām.

According to these *Smṛti-s* at each appearance of the menses the father, or other persons responsible for arranging the girl's mariage "drunk her menstrual fluid", or "went to hell by seeing her in this condition." MBh. (13.24, 9) even stated that he who did not give a grown-up daughter in marriage was equal to a Brahmaṇa-murderer.[176]

Other *Smṛtis* gave a more detailed definition of the kind of sin committed by the father. B. (4.1, 12) stated:

trīṇi varṣāny ṛtumatīṁ yaḥ kanyāṁ na prayacchati,
sa tulyaṁ bhrūṇa-hatyāyai doṣam ṛcchaty asaṁśayam.[177]

Hence, according to B. (4.1,12), interpreted together with the preceding *śloka*, if the father did not give his daughter away in marriage three years after her attainment of puberty, he committed a sin similar to that of destroying an embryo. Similar was the opinion of Y. (I.64) where we read:[178]

172. Equal to that of killing an embyo.

173. For text see note 171.

174. Ya.'s reading was as follows:
prāpte dvā-daśame varṣe yaḥ kanyāṁ na prayacchati,
māsi māsī rajastasyāḥ pitā pivati śoṇitam. (Dutt's edition has wrongly *kanyāṁ*.

175. Only identical with Par. (7.8) and Ya. (23).

176. *ātmajāṁ rūpa-sampannāṁ mahatīṁ sadṛśe vare,*
na prayacchati yaḥ kanyāṁ taṁ vidyād brahmaghātinam.

177. See also N. (12.25). The text has been quoted above (§21 (a).

178. Cf. above Study XV. Infanticide and Exposure of New-born Children and Y. (1-27) Mn. (5.89), Vṛddha Manu in Apār. (p. 876).

aprayacchan samāpno'ti bhrūṇa-hatyām ṛtāvṛtau. (Also quoted in ViR. *ad* Y. 1.64, GMH. 18.22, VyPr. 458, VBh. 4) and of Vās. (17.71) where we read:

yāvantaḥ kanyām ṛtavaḥ spṛśanti tulyaiḥ sakāmām abhiyācyamānām,
bhruṇani tavanti hatānı tābhyāṁ māta-pitṛbhyam iti dharmavādaḥ
(Also quoted in DBh. 176, VBh. 4).

In N. (12.26) it was also stated:

yāvan taścartavas tasyāḥ samatīyuḥ patiṁ vinā,
tāvat yo bhrūṇa-hatyāḥ syus tasya yo na dadāti tām.

Hence, according to these three *Smṛti-s* each time the daughter had her monthly courses in the father's house, he was guilty of a crime equal to that of killing an embryo.

C. Also Vy. (2.7) declared that the father, if he did not give his daughter away in marriage before her attainment of puberty, was guilty of a crime equal to procuring abortion and, in addition, became degraded.[179]

Bṛh. (in *Saṁs.* 373) also stated that such a father was guilty of a crime equal to that of killing an embryo, but did not state that he became degraded, but, on the contrary, was of the opinion that such a maiden became degraded *vṛṣalī*[180] and unmarriageable. This latter statement was completely contradictory to that found in MBh. (12.44, 17) where it was declared that the union with such a maiden was not disgraceful, that her children did not lose respectability, and even that such a maiden personally should look for a husband.[181]

The statement found in Bṛh, was probably more recent and, possibly, have been introduced with the development of child-marriages which though not entirely unknown, were infrequent in older times.[182]

It must be noted that Vi.'s opinion (24.41) was almost

179. *yadi sā dātṛ-vaikalyād rajaḥ paśyet kumārikā,*
bhrūṇa-hatyāś ca yāvat yaḥ patitaḥ syāt tadapradaḥ.

180. *pitu-gṛhe tu yā kanyā rajaḥ paśyaty asaṁskṛtā,*
bhrūṇa-hatyā pitus tasyāḥ sā kanyā vṛṣalī smṛtā.

181. *prajā na hīyate tasyā ratiś ca bharatarṣabha,*
ato'nyathā vartamānā bhaved vācyā prajāpateḥ.

182. See J. Jolly's "*Zur Geschichte der Kinderehen*; ZDMG., Vol. 46, p. 413 and ZDMG., Vol. 47, p. 610. Bibliography on this subject was quotted by J. Jolly.

identical with that of Bṛh. In Vi., however, we did not find the rules regarding the obligation of the father to give away his daughter in marriage before attainment of her puberty; however this rule is evident from the fact that the right of self-choice was given to maidens after their attainment of puberty. The following sentence was almost identical with that of Bṛh., quoted above :

pitṛ-veśmani yā kanyā rajaḥ paśyatyasaṁskṛtā,
sā karyā vṛṣalī jñeyā haraṁstāṁ na viduṣyati (Vi. 24.41)

Hence a maiden who was not given in marriage by her father before attainment of puberty also became degraded—*vṛṣalī* and *eo ipso* unmarriageable. Also Par. (7.9) was of the opinion that the maiden became unmarriageable. Par. declared that even he who performed the marriage of such a girl (a Brahmaṇa) became degraded.[183] Almost identical with the wording of Par. was that of Ya. (24. 25).[184]

(v) *Counsels for the Suitor*

As far as the same question, from the point of view of the suitor is concerned, it was stated in various *Smṛti-s* that the suitor should take as wife[185] a *nagnikā* or a maiden before she has seen her monthly courses in her fathers house;[186] even if the proper age of the marriageable maiden was fixed, it was declared that in any case the suitor should marry her before she attained puberty.[187]

It is clear that these rules were only counsels for the suitor : to take as wife a maiden before her attainment of puberty.

183. *yas tāṁ samudvavet kanyāṁ brāhmaṇo 'jñānamohitaḥ,*
asambhaṣyo hy apāṅkteyaḥ sa vipro vṛṣalīpatiḥ.

184. *yas tāṁ vivāhayet kanyāṁ brāhmaṇo madamohitaḥ,*
asambhāṣyo hy apāṅkte yaḥ sā vipro vṛṣalīpatiḥ.

bandhyā tu vṛṣalī jñeyā vṛṣalī tu mṛta-prajāḥ,
śūdrī tu vṛṣalī jñeyā kumārī tu rajasvalā.

185. Gobh. Gṛh. (3.4, 6) stated that the best was a *nagnika*, Mn.-Gṛh. (1.7, 8) and Vaikhanāsa-Gṛhyasūtra (3.2, 1) stated that a suitor should take a *nagnikā* as wife.

186. *tasmād vivāhayet kanyāṁ yāvan narttumatī bhavet.* (Saṁv. 68).

187. Āp. (in Vīr. 767-2, 3), stated that a man of thirty years of age should take a wife ten years old before she attained puberty. (For text see note 129).

(iv) *Conclusions*

From these few quotations it is evident that although the marriageable age of the maiden was fixed in some *Smṛtis*, the maiden had to be given away in marriage by her father before she attained puberty. If the father did not give his daughter in marriage, he committed a sin equal to that of slaying an embryo and became degraded and even the future husband of such a maiden became degraded. In other words the maiden became unmarriageable.

Probably these rules were subject to evolution. In the most ancient times the *Smṛti-s* regulated the marriageable age of the maiden only by way of advice; the father was then responsible for giving his daughter away in marriage before she attained the age (Mn.) and, if possible, before she attained puberty, because otherwise the father's action would be considered reproachable and he would lose authority over his daughter. In the course of time such an act of the father was considered to be a sin on his part equal to that of killing an embryo. In later times, the father who did not give his daughter away in marriage before her attainment of puberty became degraded and the girl unmarriageable.

(B) *In The Pañcatantra*

In P. (3.9, 227a) it is stated:

atha kālena dvā-daśa-varṣe prāpte vivāhakārye tasyāś cintām ṛṣir āpede

Hence, at the age of twelve the girl should be given in marriage by her father.

According to Bhav. P. a girl of twelve was a *kanyā*.[188] A *kanyā* or a *śyāmā* (Aṅg.) was a girl whose breasts were not yet developed (Bhav. P., Aṅg.) and was not expected to have

188. It should be noted that in PK. (3.213) and PHP. (3.13, 183) we find the following sentence :

asamprāptarājā gaurī prāpte rajasi rohiṇī,
avyāñjanā bhavet kanyā kucahīna ca nagnikā.

This sentence, defining what was to be understood by the words *gaurī*, *rohiṇī*, *kanyā* and *nagnikā* was identical with that of Aṅg. and Bhag. P. (in Vīr. p. 768-23, 24). Similarly also Gṛhyasaṁgraha (2.28) sqq. This sentence was probably interpolated later along with PK. (3.214-215) PHP. (3.13, 184, 185).

attained puberty. That was also the intention of the Pañc.; as we shall see below, according to the Pañc., and in accordance with other *Smṛti-s*, the girl should be given in marriage by her father before she attained puberty.

Mn. (9.94) mentioned a girl of twelve years of age as suitable to be married; also Par. (7.7) and Ya. (22) were of the opinion that the girl should be married before reaching her twelfth year.

P. (3.9, 227a) based his statement—that the age of twelve was suitable for the girl—on these *Smṛti-s*, or rather on the general rules. This statement was generally accepted. In this connexion it can be noted that PK. (3.215) and PHP. (3.13, 185)[189] in the same story (Mouse maiden will wed a mouse) declared :

vivāhaś cā'ṣṭa-varṣāyāḥ kanyāyās tu praśasyate[190]

This shows that the marriage of a girl of eight years of age was also recommended. This *śloka* seems to be interpolated along with the preceding ones (PK. 3.213, 214 and PHP. 3.13, 183, 184) later *i. e.* with the introduction of child marriages. In PBK. we read the following sentence :

anūḍha mandire yasya rajaḥ prāpnoti kanyakā,
patanṭi pitaras tasya svargasthā api tair guṇaiḥ.

(PBK. 4.9 *śl.* 67). This sentence is also similar, as far as its contents are concerned to P., but is rather similar to the contents of Par. (7.7, 8), Ya. (1.22, 23) and Saṁv. (67), quoted above.

Interpreting this sentence on the basis of the *Smṛti-s*, we come to the conclusion that P. (3.9, 227a) was based on the older *Smṛti-s* which did not introduce child-marriages. As, moreover, in the whole P. we do not find any mention of child-marriages, we can state that P. (3.9, 227a) was based on Mn. and the like, and did not introduce any rule regarding child-marriages, and even, on the contrary, recommended

189. As far as the story "Mouse-maiden will wed a Mouse" was concerned PPP. (3.12, 199 to 209) was completely identical with PHP. (3.13 181 to 191), except in 202 where PPP. had *payodhārābhyaṁ* instead of *payodhareṣu*.

190. PHT. did not contain this *śloka*.

marriages of grown-up maidens *i.e.* of maidens twelve years old, and before their attainment of puberty.[191]

22. *Non-fulfilment of the Duty of the Father to give his Daughter away in Marriage*

(A) *In the Smṛti-s*

A. Before this last stage of evolution occurred the maiden had the right, or even the obligation, according to the *Smṛti-s*, to choose a husband for herself. Here we come to the second question *i.e.*, what happened if the father did not give his daughter away in marriage at the prescribed time. The answer is as follows : the maiden had the right of self-choice—*svayaṁvara*, as the father lost authority over her.[192] However, the maiden could exercise her right of self-choice only in case the *Smṛti-s* did not state that she became unmarriageable and her wooer degraded if he married her; these rules *eo ipso* excluded the possibility of self-choice.[193]

The *svayaṁvara* which could be considered, from the point of view of theory of law, as a separate form of marriage,[194] took place in three different cases.[195] The first was "the festive *svayaṁvara* found in the epics (Kuntī, Savitrī, Damayantī, Sitā, Draupadī, Rukmiṇī, etc.) which took place with the consent of the father and could be divided into three sub-groups;[196] the second is the *svayaṁvara* which took place when there was no legal guardian of the girl; then the girl could select a hus-

191. Compare PBK. (4.9, 69) we read:
yāvan na lajjate kanyā yāvat krīḍati pāṁsunā,
yāvat tiṣṭhati gomārge tāvat kanyāṁ vivāhayet.

192. Compare also the tale of the blind man, the hunchback and the three-breasted princess in PHP. (5.10), PK. (5.12), PBK. (5.12), PPP. (5.11). From this tale it seems to be clear that these texts were of the opinion that the girl should be given in marriage before attainment of puberty. See Chapter IX.

193. When Vi. stated in one place that the maiden became degraded, and in the other that she was given the right of self-choice, he quoted—as he often did—two different schools or two different authorities.

194. In this form of marriage the father lost authority over his daughter; the Brahmaṇic school of law did not consider the *svayaṁvara* as a separate form of marriage.

195. Cf. above study of on Forms of Marriage in Ancient India and their Development.

196. See J. Jolly's "Hindu Law and Custom," Calcutta, 1928; p. 111, note 2.

band for herself (Y. 1.64, N. 12.22, 23, Ya. 2.6); the third *svayaṁvara* took place if the father (or other legal guardians) had not given the maiden away in marriage before attainment of puberty. This latter *svayaṁvara* was described in almost all the *Smṛti-s* in a similar manner. In particular, it was similarly described in Mn. (9.90),[197] B. (4.1, 14),[198] Vās. 17.67, 68),[199] G. (18.20)[200], Vi. (24.40),[201] and MBh. (13.44, 15).[202]

B. It is clear from the text quoted in the notes, that the maiden should wait in her father's house for three years after she attained puberty (after the appearance of the first menses), then choose a husband for herself, who should be of equal caste and rank or blameless (Mn. Vās. B., G.) or even a destitude of good qualities (B.) as she then had full power to dispose of herself freely (Vi.).

kanyā dvā-daśa-varṣāṇi sā'pradattā gṛhe vaset,
bhrūṇahatyā pitus tasyāḥ sā kanyā varayet svayam.

Hence, according to this *Smṛti-s*, the maiden had the right to self-choice twelve years after her attainment of puberty. Also Kām. (222.8-10) stated :

mandāpadeśā guṇavaty api kanyā dhanahīnā kulīnā'pi samānairāyācyamānā mātā-pitṛ-viyuktā vā jñāti-kulavatinī vā prāpta-yauvanā pāṇigrahaṇaṁ svayam abhīpseta.

Jayamaṅgalā added the following commentary:

prāpta-yauvane'ti praty ekaṁ yojyam; svayam īpseta; tadānīṁ svayaṁ varasyā-bhyanujñānāt; yathoktam" trīṇi varṣany upāsīta kumaryanumatā satī; ūrdvaṁ tu kālāde tasmād vindeta sadṛśaṁ patim."

Hence Kām. and Jayamaṅgalā, basing their opinion on

197. *trīṇi varṣaṇy upāsīta kumāry ṛtumatī satī,*
ūrdhvaṁ tu kālāde tasmād vindeta sadṛṣaṁ patiṁ. (Also quoted in MV. and VyS. 116).

198. *trīṇi varṣaṇy ṛtumatī kāṅkṣeta pitṛ-śāsanam,*
tataś caturthe varṣe tu vindeta sadṛśaṁ patiṁ,
avidyamāne sadṛśe guṇahīnam api śrayet.

199. *kumāry ṛtumatī trīṇi varṣāny upāsīta.* (67).
tribhyo varṣebhyaḥ patiṁ vindet tulyam. (68).

200. *trīn-kumāry ṛtūnatītya svayaṁ yuñjītāninditeno'tsṛjya pitryānlaṅkārān.*

201. *ṛtu-trayam umāsyaiva kanyā kuryāt svayaṁ varam,*
ṛtu-traye vyatīte tu prabhavaty ātmanaḥ sadā.

Vi. (24. 40-1) gave two different views of two different schools. See note 187.

202. *trīṇi varṣāṇy udīkṣeta kanyā ṛtumatī satī,*
caturthe tv atha samprāpte svayaṁ bhartār amarjayet.

Mn. (9.90), also stated that the girl had the right of self-choice three years after her attainment of puberty.

The same was also evident from K. (231.6-10) where we read :

saptārta-prajātāṁ parāṇāṁ ūrdhvam alabhamānāṁ prakṛtya prakāmīsyāt na ca pitur apahīnaṁ dadyāt; ṛtu-pratiro'dhibhiḥ svāmyād apakrāmati.

trivarṣa-prajātārta-vāyas-tulyo gantuma-doṣaḥ; tataḥ parama-tulyo'py analaṅkṛtāyāḥ; pitṛ-dravyādāne steyaṁ bhajeta.

K. stated, that it was not an offence to have intercourse with an unmarried maiden, who has spent more than three years after attainment of puberty in her father's house, and it was not an offence to have such intercourse with a married woman (*prāptaphalāṁ prakurvato madhyama - pradeśinīvadho dviśato vā daṇḍaḥ*), (K. 231.1). We can assume, in connexion with the preceding sentence, in which it was stated that the father lost authority over the girl, that such a girl according to K., was also entitled to self-choice.

The maiden was not only entitled to self-choice, but, according to MBh. (13.44, 16), was even compelled to a *svayaṁvara.*[203]

C. Some of the *Smṛti-s*, quoted above, as G. (18.20) and Vi. (24.40), used the word *ṛtu* (monthly period) instead of *varṣa* (year).[204] Therefore, according to these *Smṛtis*, the maiden had the right to choose a husband for herself, if she saw that three monthly courses (and not three years) have passed in her father's house. We cannot, however, base our statement on verbal interpretation and we must accept that G. and Vi. used the word *ṛtu* in the meaning of *varṣa.*

D. As the maiden was legally allowed to choose a husband for herself,[205] neither she nor the chosen husband incurred any guilt by marrying each other. This statement of Mn.

203. *ato'nyathā vartamānā bhaved vācyā prajāpateḥ.*

204. See J. Jolly's "The institutes of Vishnu", SBE 7. p. 109 note 40 *Ṛtu* was also used in the sense of menses in K. (231.7) and others.

205. Although she could not hope to get a husband. This statement is not convincing.

pradāna-kāṅkṣiṇīnāṁ ca kanyānāṁ vayasi sthite,
śrutvā kathās tathā yuktāh mā'śā kṛśatarī mayā. (MBh. 12.128, 18).

(9.91)[206] was so clear, in this *Dharmaśāstra*, that it was not necessary to add it. It is, therefore probable that this rule was a later interpolation, in order to show that according to Mn., the maiden, after attainment of puberty in the father's house, was marriageable and that neither she nor her future husband became degraded, as opposed to the statements found in later *Smṛti-s*, such as in Vi. (24.41), Par. (7.9) and Ya. (24).[207]

In the case of such a self-choice the husband of the maiden was not obliged to pay his father-in-law any *śulka* as the latter has lost authority over her[208] and the maiden was allowed to take her *strīdhana*.

As to the non-obligation of the son-in-law to pay the *śulka* we read in Mn. (9.93) as follows :

pitre na dedyāc chulkaṁ tu kanyām ṛtumatīṁ haran,
sa ca svāmyād atikramed ṛtūnāṁ pratirodhanāt.

As to the losing of the *strīdhana* by the girl in such a case it was stated in Mn. (9.92); also quoted in GMH 18.20 and VyS 119) that she had no right to take with her any ornaments given by her father, or her mother, or her brother. We read there :

alaṅkāraṁ nādadita pitryaṁ kanyā svayaṁvarā,
mātṛkāṁ bhrātṛ-dattaṁ vā steyaṁ syād yadi taṁ haret.

(similarly G. 18.20)[209] and K. (231.10).[210] Although Mn. and G. used only the word *alaṅkāra* it is to be assumed that the inherited family jewels and all other goods given by her parents or brothers etc., or even what was obtained from them, etc. *i.e.* generally speaking, the *strīdhana*, could not be taken away by the maiden when she chose a husband for herself.

(B) *In the Pañcatantra*

A. In continuation of the question cited above, the sage after having stated the age suitable for the marriage of his daughter, declared :

ayukto 'syāḥ kālātikramo yat kāraṇaṁ mamai'vā'yam adharmaḥ (*uktaṁ ca*). (P. 3.9, 227 b).

206. *adīyamānā bhartāram adhigacched yadi svayam,*
nainaḥ kiṁcid avāpnoti na ca yaṁ sā'dhigacchati.
207. See notes 182 and 183.
208. Mn. (9.93), K. (231.7), and others.
209. For text see note 200.
210. For text see above.

Here P. stated that in any case the father gives his daughter away in marriage before she attained puberty, because otherwise he would be committing a sin. In order to confirm this statement P. quoted the following *śloka* :

pitur gṛhe tu yā kanyā rajaḥ paśyaty asaṁskṛtā,
avivāhyā tu sā kanyā dempatī vṛṣalau smṛtau. (74). (Cf. PHT. 3. 86, PTem, 3.75, PS. 3.53, PN. 342, PHP. 3.188, PBK, 4.67, PK. 3.218).

Edgerton translated it in the following way : "But if a maiden beholds her flux in her father's house, unmarried, that maiden is unmarriageable; her parents are considered to be *Śūdras.*"

PBK. in a beautiful stanza stated similarly as follows:

yāvan na lajjate kanyā yāvat krīḍati pāṁsunā,
yāvat taṣṭhati gomārge tāvat kanyāṁ vivāhayet.

(PBK. 4.9, *śl.* 69). The girl must be a *kanyā* before her attainment of puberty.

B. Both PK. and PHP. in the prose text, referred in different ways to the subsequent *śloka-s* in which it was explained why women were guiltless and clean, and why they were divided into several classes depending on their sexual capacity :

vyañjanais tu sam utpannaiḥ somo bhuṅkte hi kanyakām,
payodharābhyāṁ gandharvā rajasy agniḥ pratiṣṭhitaḥ.
tasmād vivāhayet kanyāṁ yāvad ṛtumatī bhavet,
vivāhaś cā'ṣṭa-varṣayāḥ kanyā yās tu praśasyate,
vyañjanaṁ hanti vai pūrvaṁ param caiva payodharau,
rati-riṣṭāṁs tathā lokān hanyāc ca pitaraṁ rajaḥ.
ṛtumatyāṁ tu tiṣṭhantyāṁ svecchādānaṁ tu dīyate,
tasmād udvāhayen nagnāṁ manuḥ svāyaṁbhuyo'bravīt,
pitṛ-veśmani yā kanyā rajaḥ paśyatyasaṁskṛtā,
avivāhyā tu sā kanyā jaghanyā vṛṣalī smṛtā.

(PK. 3.214 to 218 and almost identically PHP. 3.13, 184 to 188).

Hence PK. and PHP. advised that the maiden should be married by her father before attainment of puberty because "the menses destroyed the father and if the daughter was not given in marriage by her father at the proper time, she had the right, of self-choice." Then PK. (3.218) and PHP. (3.13, 188) declared in a similar *śloka* to that of P. (3.9, *śl.* 74) that if the maiden beheld her flux in her father's house unmarried, she became unmarriageable and she was considered as the lowest Śūdra. [PHT. (3.9 p. 112.6, 7) omitted the second part of P. (3.9, 227b) being probably of the opinion that PHT. (3.9, 86) was the repetition of P. (3.9, 227b).][211]

In continuation of the preceding *śloka-s* PHT. (3.9 p. 112.8, 9) quoted also the same *śloka* as PK. (3.13, 218), PHP. (3.13, 188; also PTem. 3.75, PS. 3.52, PN. 3.42, PM.4.97) and P. (3.74) of which the first part was almost identical with thepreceding texts, and the second part was slightly different.

PHT. (3.9, p. 112.8, 9, *śl.* 86) declared:

pitṛ-gṛhe tu yā kanyā rajaḥ paśyati cakṣusā,
vṛṣalī sā tu vijñeyā na śūdrī vṛṣalī smṛtā.

C. The statement of P. (3.9, 227b) was based on the *Smṛti-s.* P. stated here that if the father did not give his daughter away in marriage before her attainment of puberty, he committed a sin. This statement was vague and did not contain any answer to the question as to what kind of sin was committed by the father. We have seen above, that according to some sources of law, this sin was not specified, however, according to most of them it was considered to be equal to that of killing an embryo. Undoubtedly that was also the meaning of P. (3.9, 227b).

In continuation of the preceding statement (P. 3.9, *śl.* 74) declared, that if an unmarried girl beheld her flux in her father's house, she became unmarriageable (*avivāhyā*). The *Smṛti-s* did not use the same expression (*avivāhyā*), but stated that the girl became a *vṛsalī* which also meant that she was unmarriageable as everybody could take her and nobody marry her. If we compare Bṛh. (Saṁs. 373) and Vi (24.41) we see that these *śloka-s* were almost identical with P. (3.9, *śl.* 74), at least with P. (3.9, *śl.* 74a). Therefore, we can admit that P. (3.9, *śl.* 74a) was based on these two *Smṛti-s*, which, probably, favoured child-marriages. These *Smṛti-s* declaring that the maiden who attained puberty in her father's house was unmarriageable, *eo ipso* did not admit the possibility of her self-choice. We have seen in Par. (7.9) and Ya. (24) that a Brāhmaṇa who gave such a maiden away in marriage also became degraded, consequently, that author

211. PBK. (4.9, 67) stated similarly as the *Smṛti* :
anūḍhā mandire yasya rajaḥ prāpnoti kanyakā;
patanti pitaras tasya svargasthā api tairguṇaiḥ.

who admitted that the maiden became unmarriageable, could not contain any sentence permitting the self-choice of the maiden who attained puberty in her father's house. Therefore, we may assume that, from the legal point of view, the placing together of PK. (3.217) as well as 218, and PHP. 3.13, 187 and 188, was wrong. PK. (3.218) excluded PK. (3.217) and PHP. (3.13, 187) excluded PHP. (3.13, 188) and vice-versa.[212] Which *śloka* was original and which was interpolated is difficult to state. PHP. contained a similar *śloka* to that of PK. (3.218) and PHP. (3.13, 188). F. Edgerton in P. has also chosen these last *śloka-s*. However, it seems to be more likely that the right of self-choice had to be selected, as it was based on Mn. (3.90), MBh. (13.44, 16), B. (4.1, 14), etc. In addition, it should be emphasized that, as we have seen before, P. liked to base his statements on Mn., quoted Mn. as an authority (Intr. v. 1) and did not support the idea of child-marriages. (It must be noted that P.'s opinion that the maiden who attained puberty in her father's house became degraded, was caused by the introduction, or favourable inclination to the introduction of child-marriages).

This assumption is, however, doubtful; nevertheless, it seems to be certain that P. (3.9, *śl.* 74b) should be considered as the correct text.

In PK. (3.218b) and identically in PHP. (3.13, 188b) we read:

avivāhyā tu sā kanyā jaghanyā vṛṣalī smṛtā.

In PHT (3.9, *śl.* 86b) we read:

vṛṣalī sā tu vijñeyā na śūdrī vṛṣalī smṛtā.

On the contrary P. (3.9, *śl.* 74b) had:

avivāhyā tu sā kanyā dampatī vṛṣalau smṛtau.

No reason can be seen for the use in this context of *dualis*. Both the parents could never become degraded. The father was solely and exclusively obliged to give his daughter away in marriage. The mother had no obligation and even had no right during the life of her husband to look for a husband for her daughter. That was the right and obligation of the father

212. That was however, the legal point of view. Pañc. is a collection of maxims, often illogically quoted and even contradictory, therefore it is possible that the original text of PK. and PHP. contained these two rules. Even Vi. (24.40 and 51) quoted these two points of view; it undoubtedly, quoted two different schools.

only. If he did not fulfil his duty, for which he was responsible, he could be degraded, but never his wife.[213] Therefore, on the basis of the *Smṛti-s* and general notions of ancient Indian law, the verse concerned could be reconstructed only on the basis of the Viṣṇuśarman's Pañcatantra.

It should be noted that the contents of this *śloka* were based on Bṛh. (Saṁs. 373), Vi. (24.41) and others.

23. *Eligible Suitor*

(A) *In the Smṛti-s*

The question as to whom the father chose as husband for his daughter was not dealt with in a uniform way in the Sanskrit literature. This problem was not as well settled in the *Smṛti-s* as it was in the *Gṛhyasūtra-s* and *Kāmasūtra-s*. Again, the attributes of a suitable husband were not legal rules but counsels for the father which did not entail any legal consequences.

The rules dealing with this subject are to be found in Mn. (9.88),[214] Y. (1.55),[215] G. (in Vīr. Saṁs. p. 754.22-24),[216] Āp. (in Vīr. Saṁs. p. 755.1-2),[217] and B. (4.1, 11).[218]

This problem was treated much better in the younger *Smṛti-s*, *i. e.* in Ya. (in Vīr. Saṁs. p. 754.15-17),[219] La. in

213. However, it should be noted that in PBK. (4.9, 70) we find the following statement, which was not based on the *Smṛti-s* :

mātā caiva pitā caiva jyeṣṭha-bhrātā tathaiva ca,
trayaste narakaṁ yānti dṛṣṭvā kanyāṁ rajasvalām.

214. *utkṛṣṭāyabhi-rūpāya varāya sadṛśāya ca,*
aprāptam api tāṁ tasmai kanyāṁ dadyād yathā vidhi. (Also quoted in VyS. 118).

215. *etair eva guṇair yuktaḥ savarṇaḥ śrotriyo varaḥ,*
yatnāt parīkṣitaḥ puṁstve yuvā dhīmān janapriyaḥ.

216. *vidyā-caritra-bandhu-śila-sampannāya dadyād iti.*

217. *bandhu-śila-lakṣaṇa-sampannaḥ śratavān aroga iti varasampad iti.*

218. *dadyād guṇavate kanyāṁ nagnikāṁ brahmacāriṇe,*
api vā guṇahīnāya no'parundhyād rajasvalām. (For small changes in this text see Smṛ. C. 216.19-20).

219. *kulaṁ ca śilaṁ ca vapur vayaś ca vidyāṁ ca viṭtaṁ ca sanāthatāṁ ca;*
etān guṇān sapta parīkṣya deyā kanyā budhaiḥ śoṣam acintanīyam.

Vīr. Saṁs. p. 754.19-21)[220] and Śāt. (in Vīr. Saṁs. p. 755.3-5).[221]

Among the Gṛhs. this problem was best treated in Āśv.-Gṛh. (1.5, 2)[222] and Āp. Gṛh. (1.9, 19).[223]

Among the Kāmasūtras this problem was also very well dealt with in An. (8.7)[224] and Pa. (35.7).[225]

These sources often used different words for the designation of the same attribute of the future husband. Classifying these attributes we come to the conclusion that, according to these sources, the suitable husband whom the father should choose for his daughter should have the following attributes :

(a) He should be descended from a good family (*kula*—Ya., *sukula* An.; *bandhu* Āp. Gṛh. , Āśv.-Gṛh.) and his caste and other qualifications should be remarkable (*utkṛṣṭaya*—Mn.)[226] That means also that the future husband should be equal to the wife (*sadṛśa*—Mn.) *i.e.*, both should be descended from a respectable family *prakhyato'malavaṁśajo*—Pa. or caste (*jāti*—La).[227] In particular Y. stated that the husband should be *savarṇa*, i.e. as Mit. (*ad* Y. 1.55) explained: *sava utkṛṣṭo vā na hīna-varṇa.*

This rule introduced the rule of hypergamy which prohibited a woman from marrying a man belonging to a caste lower than her own.

(b) be wealthy (*dhana*—Pa, An.; *vitta*—Ya.) or gainfully employed (*artha*—La.);

(c) having guards (*sanāthatā*—Ya.);

(d) be honourable, respectable, distinguished (*śila*—

220. *jāti-vidyā-vayaḥ śīlam arogyaṁ bahu-pakṣatā,*
arthitvaṁ vipra-sampattir aṣṭav ete vare guṇaḥ.

221. *varo varayitavyo'rthī kula-śīla-samanvitaḥ,*
rūpavan paṇḍitaḥ prājño yudha doṣa-vivarjitaḥ.

222. *buddhīm ete kanyāṁ prayacchet.*

223. *bandhu-śīla-lakṣaṇa-sampannaḥ śṛiavān aroga i.i varasaṁmet.*

224. *vidyā-śaurya-dhanā-śrayo guṇanidhiḥ khyāto yuvā sundaraḥ,*
sācāraḥ sukulodbhdaro madhura-vāg-dātā dayā-sāgaraḥ.
bhogī bhūri-kuṭumbavān sthiramatiḥ pāpārti-hīno balī,
jāmātā parivarṇitaḥ kavivaraiḥ evaṁ vidhaḥ sattamaḥ.

225. *prakhyāto'malavaṁśajo navavayāḥ śūraś ca śīlā'śrayaḥ,*
sācāraḥ sthira-sauhṛdo guṇanidhir-nānā-kuṭumbī valī.
ārthā-bhogarato viśiṣṭa-vacano dākṣiṇyadhairyā-śriyaḥ,
jāmātā jagatītale kavivarair evaṁ vidho varṇitaḥ.

226. This is the explanation of Medh. (*ad* Mn. 9.88).

227. This was also the meaning of Mn.'s *sadṛśāya*. Medh. stated : *jātyātibhiḥ.*

Ya, Āp., G., La., Śāt., Āśv.-Gṛh., Pa.; *utkṛṣṭa*—Mn.), virtuous (*guṇa*—B., An., Pa.; *guṇair-yukta*—Y.[228]), brave (*śaurya*—An., *śūra*—Pa.), firm (*sthiramati*—An.), of good character (*caritra*—G.; *viprasampattir*—La);

(e) be wise, intelligent, learned, erudite, scholarly (*vidyā*—Ya., G., La., An., *śrotriya*—Y.)[229], *śrutavata*—Āp., Āśv.-Gṛh.; *paṇḍita*—Śāt.; *dhairya*—Pa.; *dhīmata*—Y.[230]; *prajñin*—Śāt.; *buddhimat*—Āp.-Gṛh.; *brahmacārin*—B.), celebrated (*khyāta*—An. as well as capable and fit ((*sampanna*—Āp.; G., Āśv. Gṛh.);

(f) be good-looking, handsome, have a good figure, be of distinguished appearance (*vapusa*—Ya.; *abhirūpa*—Mn.[231]; *rūpavat*—Śāt.; *sundara*—An.), have a nice voice (*madhuravac*—An.; *vasiṣṭhavacana*—Pa.), young (*yuvana*—Y.[232], Śāt., La.; *vayas* or *vayasvat*—Ya.; *navayavas*—Pa.), healthy (*aroga*—Āp., La., Śāt.) and strong (*balina*—Pa., An.);

(g) have a big family (*bhūrikūmbavān*—An.; *nānākuṭumbī*—La.);

(h) of good conduct and behavious (*sacāra*—An., Pa.), courteous, polite (*dakṣinya*—Pa.), strong in friendship (*sthira-sauhṛda*—Pa.),

(i) fond of pleasure, pleasure-seeking (*bhogin*—An.; *bhogatara*—Pa.);

(j) generaous (*dātṛ*—An.), merciful (*dayāsāgara*—An.) and generally speaking faultless (*doṣavivarjita*—Śāt.), free of sins (*pāpārti-hīna*—An.) and beloved by all men (*janapriya*—Y.).[233]

Y. also added that the virile power of the future husband should be carefully examined (*yatnāt-parīkṣitaḥ puṁstve*—Y. 1.55) and Mit. (*ad* Y. 1.55, p. 16. 8-9) added : *yatnāt-prayatnena puṁstve parīkṣitaḥ*. The method of testing the virile power of the future husband was described in N. 12. 8-10; (NMS. 13.8-10); it was based on the external appearances of the suitor (bones, shoulders, hair, neck, etc.) and on the experiment with

228. *doṣaiś ca varjito* (Mit. *ad* Y. 1. 55, p. 16-7).

229. *svayaṁ ca śrutā' dhyayana-sampannaḥ* (Mit. *ad* Y. 1. 55, p. 16).

230. *laukika-vaidika-vyavahāreṣu nipuṇa-matiḥ* (Mit. *ad* Y. 1.55, p. 16.13).

231. Medh. *ad* Mn. (9.88) stated : "*abhirūpaḥ*"—*svabhava-vacano vā; susvabhāvo vidhān-apy abhirūpā ucyate.*

232. *na vṛddhaḥ* (Mit. *ad* Y. 1. 55, p. 16.13).

233. *smita-pūrva-mṛdvabhi-bhāṣaṇādibhir anurakta-janaḥ.* Mit. *ad* Y. 1.55, p. 16.14).

his semen and urine.[234] Similarly also Apar. (on Y.) and K. (193.17).

These counsels should guide the father of the girl in choosing a husband for her. Certainly they were not binding on him. These rules were *leges imperfectae.*[235]

(B) *In the Pañcatantra*

A. P. after having quoted śloka 74 continued in prose : *ato'ham enāṁ sadṛśāya* (*balavate*) *prayacchāmi*; (*uktaṁ ca*) (228) and concluded in verse :

yayor eva samaṁ vittaṁ yayor eva samaṁ kulam,
tayor vivāhaḥ sakhyaṁ ca na tu puṣṭavipuṣṭayoḥ. (*śl.* 75).

PTem. (3.76) PS, (3.53), PN (3.43), PK. (3. p. 189, v. 16 and *śl.* 220) PHP. (3.13, p. 214, v. 13 and *śl.* 190 and 1.288), PBK. (3.220; cf. 1.313 and 2.28), as well as PHT. (3.9, p. 112, v. 10 and *śl.* 87) contained the same text.[236]

PK. (3.221) and PHP. (3.13, 191), PBK. (4.9, 71), added however the following *śloka* :

kulaṁ ca śīlaṁ ca sanāthatā ca vidyā ca vittaṁ ca vapur vayaś ca
etān guṇān sapta vicintya deyā kanyā budhaiḥ śeṣam acintanīyam.

F. Edgerton translated the text of P. (3.9, 228 and *śl.* 75) in the following way: "therefore, I will give her to a hus-

234. *parīkṣyaḥ puruṣaḥ puṁstve nijair evā'ṅga-lakṣaṇaiḥ,*
pumāṁś ced avikalpena sa kanyāṁ labdhum arhati.
subaddhajatrujānvasthiḥ subaddhāṁ śaśiroruhaḥ,
sthūlaghātastanūrutvag avilagna-gati-svaraḥ.
reto'syo'tplavate nāpsu hlādi mūtraṁ ca phenilam,
pumāt syāl lakṣaṇair etair viparītais tu ṣaṇḍhakaḥ.

235. As far as *kula* is concerned, compare CVND 3.3, CVM 3.13, CvP IV 7.6, CvH 7.7, CRC 3.9, CRB 3.9, CRP 3.9, CRBh I 3.9, CRBh II 3.10, CRCa 3.9, CSBD 31, CSB. I 31, CSJ 31, CSC I I 31, CSC II 31, CSB II 31, CSLd 31, CNP I 16, CNG 53, CNT IV 14. CNM-15, CNMN 15, CnT II 9.8, CnT III 7.4, CnT V 16, CnT VII 17, CnT I 4. As far as *kula, śīla* and *vitta* are concerned compare Kath. (30.29) and Subhāṣitārṇava (117) where we read :

vapuḥ śīlaṁ kulaṁ vittaṁ vayo vidyā sanāthatā,
etāni yasya vidyante tasmai deyā nijā sutā.
Compare also Subhāsitārṇava (186):
nātidūre na cā'sanne dhanāḍhye nātidurbale,
vyādhite cā'ṅga-hīne na ṣaḍbhyaḥ kanyā nā dīyate.

and similarly Subhāṣitārṇava (300), as well as PBK. (4.9, 72-73) and similarly Subhāsitārṇava (362).

dūrāsthānām avidyānāṁ mokṣa-margānukāriṇām,
śūrāṇāṁ nirdhanānāṁ ca na deyā kanyakā buddhaiḥ.

236. In PK. and PBK. with small variations.

band worthy of herself. (And it is said); Only between two persons who are well matched in means (*vitta*) and in blood (*kula*) should there be marriage or friendship, but not between the high and the low."

P. did not repeat the latter *śloka* in other places, but PHP. (1., p. 74, v. 15, 16) repeated it and gave the same wording. PK. (1.313 and 11.28), PBK. (1.281 and 2 *śl.* 27, 2 p. 7, 22 S 22.) and PPP. (1.304 and 2.30), referring this *śloka* not to marriage but to friendship, repeated it, slightly changing the wording of the second verse.[237] In the latter wording this verse was also quoted in the anthology Śārṅgadhara-apaddhati (1475).[238]

B. PBK. (4.9, *śl.* 72) in addition to *śl.* 71 gave some details about the eligible suitor for the girl, stating:

durasthānam avidyānāṁ mokṣa-dharmānuvartinām,
śūrāṇāṁ nirdhanānāṁ ca na deyā kanyakā budhaiḥ.

PBK. did not state here the positive attributes of the suitor, but gave only the negative ones which excluded the suitor from eligibility for the girl. Though having the attributes enumerated in *śl.* 71, or not having those enumerated in *śl.* 72 PBK. stated that, in any case, the girl should marry only a man whom she loved :

aniṣṭaḥ kanyakāyā yo varo rūpānvito'pi yaḥ,
yadi syāt tasya na deyā kanyā śreyobhivañcchatā.

(PBK. 4.9, *śl.* 73). This statement did not conform with the *Smṛti-s*.

C. P. undoubtedly based his statement on the *Smṛti-s* and not on the Gṛhyasūtra-s and Kāmasūtra-s, as those gave more far-reaching counsels.

Mn. (9.88) declared that the future husband whom the father should find for his daughter should be *sadṛśāya*, he should belong to a respected family (*kula*) Ya., Āp., G., La., Āśv.,Gṛh., An., Pa.), equal to that of the girl (Y.) and wealth (*vitta*) (Ya., La., An., Pa.) like her.

Therefore, it is evident that the Pañc., as far as the ques-

237. *tathor maitrī vivāhaś ca.*

238. Edited by P. Peterson, BSS., No. 37, Bombay, 1888. Compare also Bhāgavata Purāṇa (4-60, 15) where we read:

yayor ātmasamaṁ vittaṁ janmaiśvaryākṛtir bhavaḥ,
tayor vivāho maitrī ca no'tta-mādhamayoḥ kvacit.

tion "whom the father should choose as husband for his daughter' was concerned, confirmed the rules contained in the *Smṛti-s*. This statement can be better seen from the fact that PK. (3.220) and PHP. (3.13, 191) contained the same text as that found in Ya. (quoted in Vīr. P. 754.16, 17).[239]

Most probably this *śloka* contained in PK. and PHP. was a later interpolation. It is not found in P. and PHT.[240]

24. *Conclusions*

Returning now to the question put at the beginning of this chapter, we can conclude that the three problems solved in the story of the Mouse-maiden, as reconstructed by F. Edgerton, were based on the *Smṛti-s*, which, however, were not valid during the same period of time.

The first question about the age at which the father should give away his daughter in marriage, was solved on the basis of Mn. and other *Smṛti-s* which did not support the idea of child-marriage. The answer was in her twelfth year but before attainment of puberty. It is clear that this question, as it was worded, contained the statement, based on the *Smṛti-s*, that the father of the girl was obliged to give his daughter away in marriage. This statement resulted also from the story of the Mouse-maiden.

The second question, as to "what happened if the father did not give his daughter away in marriage at the prescribed time" was solved in various texts in different ways. The uniform answer, based on the *Smṛti-s*, was that then the father com-

239. *kulaṁ ca śīlaṁ ca sanāthatā ca vidyā ca vittaṁ ca vapur vayaś ca* PHP. 3.13, 191).
kulaṁ ca śīlaṁ ca vapur vayaś ca vidyāṁ ca vittaṁ ca sanāthatāṁ ca (Vīr. in Saṁs. 754.16).
etān guṇān sapta vicintya deyā kanyā budhaiḥ śeṣam acintanīyam (PHP. 3.13, 191).
etān guṇān sapta parīkṣya deyā kanyā budhaiḥ śeṣaṁ acintanīyam (Ya. in Vīr. Saṁs. 754.17).

240. PK. (3.219), PHP. (3.13, 189) and PPP. (3.12, 207) added the following sentence :
śreṣṭhabhyaḥ sadṛśebhyaś ca jaghyanyebhyo rajasvalā,
pitrā deyā viniścitya yato doṣo na vidyate.

This verse, which was contradictory to the preceding *śloka* was also contradictory to the Smṛti-s. It was only a counsel for the father and shows that, if he could not find a suitable husband for his daughter before she attained puberty, he should try to give her away, as soon as possible, even to a non-suitable husband in order to be free from any sin.

mitted a sin. P. gave the answer that the girl became unmarriageable and her parents degraded. The unmarriageability of the girl was probably caused by the introduction of child-marriage and was not in conformity with the answer to the first question. Therefore, the answer contained in PK. and PHP., that the girl had the right to self-choice, was more likely. The degradation of both the parents, as contained in P., seems to be wrong. It could only be stated that the result was the degradation of the father who did not give his daughter away in marriage at the proper time. This would conform with some of the *Smṛti-s* in which child-marriages also prevailed and could be the result of the principle that the maiden became unmarriageable.

There was no difficulty about the third question as to "whom the father should choose as husband for his daughter." This question was solved in conformity with the *Smṛti-s* and was based on them. The answer was that the husband chosen by the father of the girl should be wealthy and equal to the girl, particularly as far as his family and fortune were concerned.

From the statement that the best husband was he who was of the same kind, it could be assumed that according to this tale the girl should be given away in marriage to a member of the same caste as her father.

It should be noted that similarly as in tale it was stated in Kath. 10.61, 204-213) :

tad ālokya uttamaṁ matvā śunaś caṇḍāla-putrakam,
sva-jāti-tuṣṭā vavre sā tam eva patim antyajā. (10.61, 213).

From this sentence it is obvious that the husband should belonging to the same caste as his wife. Kath. stated it *expressis verbis.*

IV. THE TALE OF THE MICE THAT ATE IRON

25. *Contents of P.* (1.15) *and its Juridical Problems*

In P. 1, *kathā* 15 (in PHT. Book 1, *kathā* 17, in PK. Book 1, *kathā* 21, in PHP. Book 1, *kathā* 28, in PBK. Book 1, *kathā* 21, in PPP. Book 1, *kathā* 21) in the tale of the mice that ate iron, we find the story of a merchant's son who decided to travel abroad to seek his lost fortune. He had in his house a balance made of iron which he deposited with another merchant's son before he departed for foreign countries. After his return he asked the merchant's son to return him the balance. 'However, the latter replied that mice had eaten the balance'. The depositor then went to take a bath and asked the depositary to send his things with him. After having taken his bath, he hid the boy who had carried his things and returned. When asked where the boy was, he replied that he had been carried away by a falcon. The depositary dragged the depositor into court. There the depositor, when examined by the court, declared that where mice could eat a heavy balance made of iron there a falcon could carry off an elephant and also a boy. Then the judges ordered the restoration of the balance of iron and the boy to their respective owners.

From the juridical point of view, as described in the *Smṛti-s*, four problems were solved in this tale that :

(1) *nikṣepa* was an open deposit,

(2) the object deposited should be returned to the depositor in the same condition in which it was deposited, immediately when the depositor asked for it,

(3) the depositary was not responsible for the loss of the object deposited in the case of *vis major*,

(4) the keeping of a minor in confinement was a crime,[241]

26. *Nikṣepa—an Open Deposit*

The various texts of Pañc. used here, for the designation of the deposit, the word *nikṣepa* which is used in the *Smṛtis* very often, as the principal word for the designation of deposits.[242]r We ead in P. (1.15, 565) that the merchant's son deposited the balance of iron with another merchant's son :

sa cā'nyasmin vaṇik-putrake tāṁ nikṣipya deśāntaram arthopārjanāya prāyāt (similarly in PHT. 1. p. 50.20-21).[243]

In PK. (1.21; p. 99.25-100.1) we also read that the

241. The problem as to the submitting of controversial cases to the judge was also solved in this tale.

242. Mn. (8.4, 179-181, 185, 186, 188, 190-192, 194, 149), N. (2.1, 5 7-10, 13, 14; 3.230), Bṛh. (heading of chapter 11 and 11.1, 15, etc.), Vi. (5.169-171; 36.3; 52, (p. 493, 496), etc.

243. PHT. (50.20-1) has :

so'nyasmin-vaṇik-putrake tāṁ nikṣipya deśāntaram artho'pārjanāya prāyāt

balance of iron was deposited with another person : *tāṁ ca śreṣṭinandukasya gṛhe nikṣepe-bhūtaṁ kṛtvā deśāntaraṁ prasthitaḥ*; and that the depositor asked for the return of the deposited balance of iron: *bho śreṣṭin dīyatāṁ me sā nikṣepa tulā* (PK. 1.21; p. 100.3). Similarly PHP. (1.28-114,20 and 1.28-114-22-23,[244] PBK. (1-21, 89.10-11 and 1.21, 89.13)[245] and PPP. (1.21, 90.16-17[246] and 1.21-90.19).[247]

Mit. (*ad* Y. 2.65 p. 162.25-26) and VyM. (p. 190.10-11) quoted an unpublished text of N.[248] according to which *nikṣepa* was an unsealed deposit, while *upanidhi*, was a sealed deposit. In spite of this definition some translators[249] of Sanskrit texts did not accept this interpretation and translated the word *nikṣepa* as sealed deposits.[250]

From this tale it is, however, obvious that *nikṣepa* was not a sealed, but an open deposit, the more so as not money but a special object, named in the tale, was deposited openly.

27. *Return of the Objects Deposited*

(A) *In the Smṛti-s*

The *Smṛti-s* stated that the object deposited should be returned to the depositor in the same condition in which it was

244. *tāṁ ca śreṣṭhilakmaṇasya nikṣepa-bhūtāṁ kṛtvā deśāntaraṁ prasthitaḥ ....bho lakṣmaṇa samarpaya me nikṣepa-tulām,*

245. *tāṁ ca kasyacid vaṇijo gṛhe nikṣepa-bhūtāṁ kṛtvā deśāntaraṁ prasthitaḥ ... bhoḥ śreṣṭhindīyatāṁ me sā nikṣepa-tulā.*

246. Identically as PBK. has only *kasyacic cheṣṭhino* instead of *kasyacid vaṇijo.*

247. Identically with PK.

248. *asaṁkhyatam avijñātaṁ samudraṁ yan nidhīyate,*
taj jānīyād upanidhiṁ nikṣepaṁ gaṇitaṁ viduḥ. (Also quoted in SC. 2, MMu. 8.149, DK. 33, SCM. 14, VyPr. 280, VyU. 79, VT. 554-5, VV. 89, VyS. 87, VCi. 138, Rāmacandra in MnM., Apar. *ad* Y. 2.65); see also N.2.1:
svaṁ dravyaṁ yatra viśrambhān nikṣipatya-viśaṅkitaḥ,
nikṣepo nāma tat proktaṁ vyavahāra-padaṁ budhaiḥ. (Also quoted in Mit. *ad* Y. 2.25, Apar. *ad* Y. 2.25, VyK. 130, SC. 2, VRK. 83, DK. 38, VCi. 36, SCM. 14, Vīr. *ad* Y. 2.67, VyPr. 279, VyM. 84, VT. 554, VV. 129, VyS. 87, VVy. 31, AP. 253.14).

249. Shama Shastry in K. (180.6 sqq.).

250. Cf. above Study I on the "Different Types of Deposits".

deposited, immediately after the depositor asked for it. In particular, Mn. (8.180) and, identically, N. (2.3)[251] stated that the object deposited had to be returned in the same condition in which it had been delivered.[252]

As to the return of the object deposited by the depositary to the depositor, immediately when the depositary was asked for it, we read in Bṛh. (11.9):

nyāsa-dravyaṁ na gṛhṇiyāt tan nāśayatv aśaskaraḥ
gṛhītaṁ pālayed yatnat sakṛdyayācitam arpayet.[253]

(B) *In the Pañcatantra*

Legal rules were mirrored in the tale of the mice that ate iron; this could be deduced from the fact that : (1) the depositor went to the depositary and requested him to return the object deposited *i.e.* in the same condition in which it was delivered, and (2) the depositary, who did not intend to return the object deposited, did not object at the time of the return but felt obliged to return it immediately when asked for it.

28. *Loss of the Objects Deposited. Vis Major*

(A) *In the Smṛti-s*

The depositary (the merchant's son) when asked to return the object deposited, objected only that he could not return it as the object deposited had been eaten by mice. He stated: *tulā mūṣakair bhakṣite'ti* (P. 1.15, 567).[254] That was his only objection, *i.e.* that because of *vis major* he was unable to return the object deposited.

251. *yo yathā nikṣiped dhaste yam arthaṁ yaṣya mānavaḥ,*
sa tathaiva grahītavyo yathā dāyas tathā grahaḥ. (Mn. 8.180 and N. 2.3. Also quoted in VyK. 131, SC. 181, VRK. 86, NṛP. 23-4, SV. 269, VyPr. 285, VT. 556, VyS. 88).

252. See also Mn. (8.194, 195) quoted above in Study II on the "Law of Deposits" para. 12A.

253. See also Kāty. (606) and above Study II on the "Law of Deposits" para. 12B.

254. Similarly PHT. (2.17; p. 50.22-3 :
sā mūṣakair bhakṣite'ti; and PK. (1.21; p. 100.4) : *tvadīyā tulā mūṣakair bhakṣitā*. See also identically PHP. (1.28; p. 114.23-4), PBK. (1.21, 89.14) and PPP. (1.21; p. 90.20) :

(B) *In the Pañcatantra*

In this tale, the rule contained in the *Smṛti-s* that in case of *vis major*, the depositary was not obliged to return the object deposited, was not quoted. However, the argument quoted by the depositary showed that the depositary based his objection on the rules of non-responsibility for the return of the object deposited in case of *vis major*.

The most casuistic rule relating to this was quoted in K. (177.13-17) where we read: "Whenever forts, or country parts are destroyed by enemies, or wild tribes; whenever villagers, merchants, or herds of cattle are subjected to the inroads of invaders; whenever the kingdom itself is destroyed; whenever extensive fires or floods bring about entire destruction of villages, or partly destroy immovable properties, movable properties having been rescued before; whenever the spread of fire, or rush of floods is so sudden that even movable properties could not be removed; or whenever a ship laden with commodities is either sunk or plundered (by pirates), deposits lost in any of the above ways shall not be reclaimed."[255]

N. (2.12) stated :

caurair hṛtaṁ jale magnam agninā dagdham eva ca
na dadyād yadi tasmāt sa na saṁharati kiṁcana.[256]

Here we see clearly that destruction of an object deposited by water or by fire, or any other destruction of the object which was caused by a fate, independently of the will of the depositary, was considered a *vis major* which excluded the responsibility of the depositary for the loss of the object deposited. This casuistic enumeration was only an interpretation of the general rule, namely, that *vis major* was caused by an act of the king or by fate.[257]

255. According to Shama Shastri's translation. *paracakrāṭavikābhyāṁ durgarāṣṭra-vilope vā, pratiro 'dhakair vā grāmasā'rtha-vrajā-vilope cakra-yukte pāśe vā grāmamadhyā' gnyudākābādhe vā kiṁcid amokṣayamāṇe kupya manir hāryavariam eka-deśam uktadravye vā, jvālāvegopavṛddhe vā, nāvi nimagrāyāṁ muṣitāyāṁ svayam uparūḍho no'penidhim abhyābhavet.* (p. 177, 13-7).

256. "What has been stolen by thieves, carried away by water, or burnt by fire need not to be restored (by the depositary), unless he should have appropriated something out of it:." According to J. Jolly's translation, in SBE. 33. Similarly Mn. 8. 189; also quoted in VyK. 131, SC. 179, VRK. 88, VCi. 37, VCa. 31-2, Vīr. *ad* Y. 2.67, VyPr. 282, VV. 131, VyS. 87-8, VVy. 32, Apar. *ad* Y. 2.66.

257. Y. (2.66), Mn. (8.189), Kāty. (593.4), Bṛh. (12.10), N. (2.9), etc.

The merchant's son objected that the balance of iron had been eaten by mice, *i.e.* was lost by an act of God (*vis major*). If this objection could be proved, then the depositary would be free from responsibility and would not be obliged to return the balance of iron. However, his objection, although based on the *Smṛti-s*, was baseless and illogical and could not be proved, as mice could not eat iron.

29. *Keeping of a Minor in Confinement*

(A) *In the Smṛti-s*

K. (199.12-13) stated : *puruṣam abandhanīyaṁ badhnato bandhayato bandhaṁ vā mokṣayato bālamaprāpta-vyavahāraṁ badhnato bandhayato vā sahasra-daṇḍaḥ.*[258]

Also Y. (2.243) stated:

abadhyaṁ yaś ca badhnāti baddhaṁ yaś ca pramuñcati,
aprāpta-vyavahāraṁ ca sa dāpyo damam uttamam.[259]

(Also quoted in ViR. *ad* Y. 2.249, VyK. 122, VRK. 368, VCi. 160.1, DV. 335, Vīr. *ad* Y. 2.243, VT. 768, VV. 257, VyS. 158, AP. 258.37).

We see here that keeping a person (in K.—minor) in confinement without any reason was considered a crime, for which even the highest punishment had to be inflicted (fine).

(B) *In the Pañcatantra*

In the tale of the mice that ate iron, the depositary, when aware that his son had been kidnapped (hidden in a friend's house or thrust into a mountain-cave, etc.) seized the depositor and dragged him into court, in other words considered this act as a crime which should be examined by judges.

30. *Conclusions*

Interpreting the tale of the mice that ate iron on the basis of the *Smṛti-s*, we come to the conclusion that the author (or

258. "When a person keeps or causes to keep another person in illegal confinement, releases a prisoner from prison, keeps or causes another to keep a minor in confinement, he shall be punished with a fine of 1,000 *paṇas*."

259. "He, moreover, who restrains one who ought not to be restrained or releases one who is restrained before the decision (in his case) is arrived at, such a one shall be fined in the highest amercement."

authors) of the tale were well acquainted with the legal rules contained in the *Smṛti-s* and relating to deposits as well as to kidnapping of men.

In this tale the legal rules were not quoted *expressis verbis*, as the author was probably of the opinion that these rules were too well-known to everybody, so that quotation of them would be superfluous. All the *Smṛti-s* considered the depositary's objection as definitely just as they were logical and very often in use.

Though these rules, as to the place and time for returning of deposits and of the depositary's objection of *vis major* and others (kidnapping), were not quoted in the tale of the mice that ate iron, we can assume that this tale was based on the respective legal rules and that the juridical problems raised in this tale were solved in conformity with the legal rules contained in the *Smṛti-s*.

V. THE TALE OF THE WEAVERS WIFE

31. *Contents of P.* (1.3 *c.*) *and its Juridical Problems*

In P. (Book 1, *kathā* 3c), in PHT. (1-3), in PK. (1. p. 35 sqq.), in PHP. (1.4c), in PBK. (1.4), in PPP. (1.4) in the tale of the weaver's wife, we find the story of a weaver who, though drunken, when seeing his wife nicely adorned, suspected her of being unfaithful to him. The weaver tied his wife firmly to a post and fell asleep. Then a barber's wife came and induced the weaver's wife to go to her lover. In the meantime she was tied to the post to which the weaver's wife had been previously tied. The weaver awoke from sleep and began to scold his wife in the same way as before. The barber's wife afraid of being recognized, did not dare to answer. The weaver, in anger, cut off her nose and went to sleep again. Then the weaver's wife returned and the barbar's wife, after having told the full story, tied the weaver's wife to the post and went away. As the weaver awoke and scolded his wife again, she invoked the gods and asked them to return her nose to her if she was unfaithful to her husband. After this the weaver lighted a lamp and saw that her face was not disfigured, though he found blood on the floor. Hence he set his wife free and asked her for forgiveness. In the meantime the barber's wife, with her nose in her hands, went home and when her husband arrived home and asked her to bring him his razor-case, she threw him only the razor. The barber, filled with wrath, threw the razor back and his wife pretended that at this moment her husband had cut her nose off without any reason. The barber was brought before the judge who sentenced him to death. However, the monk, who had observed the whole course of events went to the court, told the true story and the judge spared the barber.

From the juridical point of view, three problems were solved in this tale:

1. The legal penalty for assaulting a woman,
2. The penalty for the unfaithfulness of the wife.
3. Quotations from the *Śāstra-s.*

32. *Assaulting a Woman*

K. (229.3-5) stated : *prasabha-strī-puruṣa-ghātakā...hiṁsakān stenān vā śūlānāroha yeyuḥ.* Hence those who killed men, women etc. should be impaled (*śūla*).

Mn. (9.232) stated :

kuṭa-śāsana-kartṛś ca pṛakṛtīnāṁ ca dūṣakān,
strī-bāla-brāhmaṇa-ghnāṁś ca hanyād dviṭ-sevinas tatha.

(Also quoted in VyK. 122, SC. 324, VRK. 370, VCi. 162, VyN. 504, DV. 266, 317, SV. 475, VV. 307, VyS. 157, Apar. *ad* Y. 2.294).

According to G. Buhler's translation[260] "Forgers of royal edicts, those who corrupt his ministers, those who slay women, infants, or Brahmaṇas, and those who serve his enemies, the king shall put to death (*han*).

Similarly Vi. (5.9, 10, 11) where it was stated:

kūṭa-śāsana-kartṛṁś ca rājā hanyāt. kūṭa-lekhyakārāṁś ca. garadāgnidaprasahyataskarān-strī-bāla-purūṣa-ghātinaś ca.[261]

(Also quoted in VyK. 22, Apar. *ad* Y. 2.294, SC. 324, VyS. 187).

The ancient Indian law developed independently spiritual and worldly punishments. The quotations cited above belonged to the last named; however, it

260. In SBE. 25.
261. See also N. Quot. (1.11).

should be noted that spiritual punishments for killing a woman were to be also found in the *Smṛtis* (Mn. 11.88, 89, G. 22.12., 13, B. 2.1, 1, 12 sqq., Āp. 1.9, 24, 5, Vās. 20.34-40, Vi. 50.8-10, etc.).

From these quatations it is evident that a killer of a woman had to be put to death (*han*), or impaled (*śūla*).

(B) *In the Pañcatantra*

PHP. (1.4, p. 33, v. 4-5) stated :

strī-dharṣanād vadhya iti śūlāyām āropyatām.[262]

Hence, the assaulter (violator) of a woman had to be impaled (*śūla*).

P. (1.3c, 169) stated only :

tadā dharmādhikṛtāḥ śūle'vataṁsyatām ity ājñāpitavantaḥ.

Though PHP. (PK., PBK., and PPP.) used the word (*strī*)*dharṣa* and not *hiṁsa* (K.), or others we may assume that both the quotations related to almost the same case and that PHP.'s (and others) quotations were based on the *Smṛti-s* and were in accordance with them.

33. *Adultery*

(A) *In the Smṛti-s*

For adultery worldly as well as spiritual punishments were prescribed in the *Smṛti-s*. According to Mn. (8.371), G. (23.14), Hār. (in Viv. p. 396), Ya. (in Viv. p. 398), MBh., (12.165, 64), and others, if a woman committed adultery the king had to cause her to be devoured by dogs in a public place.[263] According to others (Vi. 5.18[264] and others) she had to be put to death.[265]

262. Similarly PBK. (1.4, p. 36, v, 6-7) : *strī-dharṣaṇād-vadhya iti; tac chūlāyām āropyatām iti.* (See also similarly PPP. (1.4, p. 37, v. 17-8), PK. (1. p. 41, v. 14-5).

263. *bhartāraṁ laṅghayedyā tu strī jñāti guṇa-darpitā,*
tāṁ śvabhiḥ khādayed rājā saṁsthāne bahusaṁsthite. (Mn. 8.371. Also quoted in VyK. 127, SC. 323, VRK. 399, VCi. 178, DV. 174, VV. 273, VyS. 155, VVy. 54).

264. *striyam aśakta-bhartṛkāṁ tad atikramaṇīṁ ca.* (Also quoted in VyK. 127, VRK. 399, VCi. 186, DV. 175, VV. 273).

265. The following spiritual punishments were described in N. (12.91): the woman's head to be shaved; her lieying on the ground, her receiving bad

These were the punishments prescribed in the *Smṛtis*. Y. (2.286) stated :

sajātāv uttamo daṇḍa ānulomye tu madhyamaḥ,
prātilomye vadhaḥ puṁso nāryāḥ karṇādikartanam.

(Also quoted in ViR. 2.228, VyK. 525-6, SC. 321, VRK. 390, MR. 130, VCi. 183, VyN. 400, DV. 166, NṛP. 207, SV. 469, VyPr. 399, VyU. 136, VyM. 106, VT. 801, RDhK. 484, VV. 267-8, VVy. 65, AP. 258.68-9).

In K. (236. 7-8) we read :

śūdraśvapākasya bhāryā-gamane vadhaḥ striyāḥ karṇa-nāsācchedanam.

A better reading of the latter text was given by J. J. Meyer in his "Das alt-indische Buch vom Welt-und Staatsleben" (p. 364.19). His reading was as follows:

svapākasya bhāryā-gamane vadhaḥ striyāḥ karṇa-nāsacchedanam.

Hence according to these texts, if in a case of adultery the woman belonged to a higher caste than the man, the man had to be put to death and the woman's ears and nose had to be cut off. It was stated there that the ears, etc. *ādi* had to be cut off, but Mit., as well as Śūlapāṇi (both *ad* Y. 2.286) explained that by the word *ādi*, cutting off of the woman's ears as well as nose had to be understood.[266]

(B) *In the Pañcatanta*

A. The punishment of the cutting off by the husband of the nose of his unfaithful wife, was very common in ancient Indian literature. Particularly, in the Pañcatantra we come very often across this punishment; in the tale of the weaver's wife her screaming "I was always a faithful wife. Look ! he, cut off my nose.[267]" showed that she accepted as punishment for adultery the cutting off of her nose by her husband.

In PHP. (1.4, p. 33, v.16 sqq.) it is also stated that as soon

food and bad clothing, removal of sweepings to be assigned to her as her occupation:

vyabhicāre striyā mauṇḍya-madhaḥ śayanam eva ca,
kadannaṁ vā kuvāsaś ca karma cā'vaskarojhanam. (N. 12.91, NMS 13.93. Also quoted in SC. 242, VRK.426, MR. 134, VyPr. 410, VyU. 141, VT. 814, VBh. 16, VyS. 121).

266. *nāryāḥ punar-hīnavarṇaṁ vrajantyāḥ karṇayorādigrahaṇānnāsādeś ca kartanam.* (Mit. *ad* Y. 2.286).

267. PHP. 1.4., p. 32, v. 11 sqq.).

as it was proved that the barber's wife has cheated, besides the cutting off of her nose (by her own act), the additional punishment of cutting off of her ears has been ordered.[268]

In addition to the tale of the weaver's wife we also find mentions of cutting off by the husband of the nose of his unfaithful wife in PHP. (3.17, p. 224 v. 20 sqq.) in the tale of the cuck-old's revenge. However, according to this tale, the husband was also allowed to cast off, *i.e.*, to repudiate his wife. We find in this tale[269] the institution of *repudiatio uxoris*, well-known to the *Smṛtis*.[270]

(C) *Conclusions*

Comparing the text of P. (PHP. and others) of the tale of the weaver's wife with the texts of the *Smṛti-s*, as far as the penalty for the unfaithfulness of the wife was concerned, we must come to the conclusion that in some *Smṛti-s* and in some special cases the *pratilobha*, the penalty of cutting off the woman's nose, was prescribed, though the principal penalty was putting the woman to death.[271] In this tale, however, only the punishment of cutting off of the nose was ordered, which penalty was not against the legal rules but not in conformity with them. This penalty was, probably, often used, and was executed by the husband himself without the participation of the court. It was rather a custom than a legal rule.

34. *Quotations from the Śāstra-s*

In PHP. (I.4c, p. 32, v. 16 sqq.), when the barber was caught by the police for the alleged unjustified cutting off of his wife's nose, he was asked by the judge why he did it; he was so astonished that he could not give any answer, and then the jurymen quoted the following *śloka-s* (*śāstra*).[272]

268. *tad asyāḥ svakarma-vaśād eva nāsikāchedaḥ saṁvṛttaḥ; tato rājanigrahaḥ karṇac-chedaḥ kāryaḥ.* PHP. (1.4, p. 33, v. 16 sqq.)

269. *tām api duṣta-patnīṁ chinna-nāsikāṁ kṛtvā visasarja.* PHP. (3.17, p. 224, v. 20-1).

270. Cf. above Study 13 on the "Subjects of Law and Law of Family according to Yājñavalkya Dharmaśāstra, para. 21.

271. Compare the story of "The Gullible Carpenter" (PHP. 3.12).

272. In the sense of *Smṛti*. For the first *śloka* see also PHT. (1.86), PTem. (1.153), PS. (1.140), PN. (2.113), PBK. (1.197), PK. (1.212), P. (1.157).

bhinnasvaramukhavarṇaḥ śaṅkita-dṛṣṭiḥ samutpatitatejāḥ,
bhavati hi pāpaṁ kṛtvā svakarmasaṁtrāsitaḥ puruṣaḥ. (151)

tathā ca :

āyāti skhalitaiḥ pādair mukhavaivarṇyasaṁyutaḥ,
lalāṭasvedabhāg bhūrigadgadaṁ bhāṣate vacaḥ. (152)
kampamānam adho'vekṣī pāpaṁ prāptaḥ sadā naraḥ,
tasmād yatnāt parijñeyaś cihnair etair vicakṣanaiḥ. (153)

anu ca,

prasannavadano hṛṣṭaḥ spaṣṭo vācā saroṣadṛk,
sabhāyām vakti sāmarṣaḥ sāvaṣṭambho naraḥ śuciḥ. (154)
(PHP. 1.4c, p. 32, v. 19—p. 33, v. 3).

A. W. Ryder translated these *ślokas* in the following way:

"The guilty man is terrified
By reason of his crime. His pride
Is gone, his powers of speaking fail,
His glances rove, his face is pale.

And again:

The sweat appears upon his brow,
He stumbles on, he knows not how,
His face is pale, and all he utters
Is much distorted; for he stutters.
The culprit always may be found,
To shake, and gaze upon the ground :
Observe the signs as best you can
And shrewdly pick the guilty man.

While on the other hand :

The innocent is self-reliant;
His speech is clear, his glance defiant;
His countenance is calm and free;
His indignation makes his plea."

These *ślokas* could not be traced in any of the *Smṛti-s*; but similar thoughts aapear often in the *smṛti-s.*

PK. (1.p. 41, *śl.* 212-215), PBK. (I.4 p. 35, v. 22), PPP. (1.4, p. 37, v. 6) also quoted the same *śloka-s,* but did not mention that they belonged to the *śāstra-s.*

VI. THE TALE OF THE WEAVER AS VIṢNU

35. *Contents of PHP* (1.8) *and its Juridical Problems*

In PHP. (1.8) we find the story of the weaver as Viṣṇu, which was completely omitted in P.

According to this story a weaver who was a Vaiśya and who fell in love with a princess, could not take a Kṣatriya girl as wife. Therefore, the weaver's friend constructed a mechanical bird, like Garuḍa. The weaver went to the princess on this mechanical bird. She thought that Viṣṇu had come to her and "married him according to the Gāndharva form of marriage." The king, when informed about the visits of a strange man cursed his daughter but she explained that her lover was Viṣṇu himself. The king, proud of his relationship with Viṣṇu, did not want to pay his yearly tribute to the king Valour of the South. The latter, furious, began hostilities. Garuḍa, afraid that if the mechanical bird were to be defeated, the whole population might cease to worship Viṣṇu induced Viṣṇu to help the princess's father. He did it and defeated king Valour.

From the juridical point of view three problems were solved in this tale :

1. how many wives were allowed to members of different castes,
2. whether the girl could belong to a higher caste than the husband, and
3. what did the Gāndharva form of marriage mean.

The problems *ad* 1 and 2 were too well known and consequently so well settled in the *Smṛti-s* that it is sufficient to mention only the most important rules.

36. *Number of Wives and their Castes as Allowed to Members of Different Castes*

(A) *In the Smṛti-s*

In the *Smṛtis* it was stated that a man could always have wives of his own caste and of lower castes than his own[273], but

273. Some of the *Smṛti-s* permited that Śūdra-women were taken as wives; others did not.

the girl could never belong to a higher caste than her husband.

Mn. (3.13) stated:

śūdraiva bhāryā śūdrasya sā ca svā ca viśaḥ smṛtā,
te ca svā caiva rājñaś ca tāś ca svā cāgrajanmanaḥ.

Hence a Brahmaṇ could have as wife a Brahmaṇa-girl and girls of the Kṣatriya, Vaiśya and Śūdra castes; a Kṣatriya girl and girls of the Vaiśya and Śūdra castes; a Vaiśya, a girl of his own caste and a Śūdra-girl; and a Śūdra a girl of his own caste only. The same was the opinion of B. (1.1; 8, 16, 2-5)[274], Vi. (24.1-4)[275], Ya. (in Vīr. Saṁs. p. 748),[276] etc.

N. (in Vīr. 748. 19-22) stated:

brāhmaṇasyā'nulomyeṇa striyo'nyās-tisra eva tu,
śūdrāyāḥ pratilomyena tathā'nye patayas trayaḥ.
dve bhārye kṣatriyasyānye vaiśyasvaikā prakīrttitā,
vaiśyāyā dvau patī jñeyāveko'nya kṣatriyā patiḥ.

Hence according to N. a Brahmaṇa could have as wife a Brahmaṇa-girl and girls of the Kṣatriya, Vaiśya and Śūdra castes; a Kṣatriya, girls of the Kṣatriya, Vaiśya and Śūdra castes; and the Vaiśya—a Vaiśya girl only.

The opinion of other *Smṛti-s* on this subject was similar. And so Y. (1.57) stated :

tisro varṇānu-pūrvyeṇa dve tathaikā yathākramam,
brāhmaṇa-kṣatriya-viśāṁ bhāryā svā śūdrajanamanaḥ.

Y. (1.57) was identical with Mn. (3.13), with one exception only *i.e.* that Śūdra-women were not mentioned at all.

Vās. (1.24-5) stated: *tisro brāhmaṇasya bhāryā varṇānupūrveṇa dve rājanyasya ekaikā vaiśya-śūdrayoḥ. śūdrām apy eke mantravarjaṁ tadvat.*

This rule was almost identical with the preceding with the exception that a Vaiśya and a Śūdra could have one wife only.[277]

274. *teṣāṁ varṇānu-pūrvyeṇa catasro bhāryā brāhmaṇasya. tisro rājanyasya. dve vaiśyasya. ekā śūdrasya.*

275. *atha brāmaṇasyā varṇānukrameṇa catasro bhāryā bhavanti. tisraḥ kṣatriyasya. dve vaiśyasye. ekā śūdrasya.*

276. *ānupūrveṇa bhārvāḥ syuś catasro brāhmaṇasya tu,*
kṣatriyasyā'nupūrvyeṇa jñeyāstrisro'dharāḥ striyaḥ.
vaiśyasya cāvare dharme dve bharyety abravīn manuḥ,
śūdraḥ svajārti vindeta tāsvapatyaṁ samaṁ bhavet.

Cf. Paiṭhīnasi (in Vīr. Saṁs. p. 748).

277. Similarly Pāraskara-Gṛhyasūtra (1—4, 8-11) and many others.

J. Jolly in his *Recht und Sitte* rightly stated:[278] "The necessity of equality in birth is pronounced already in the marriage rules of the Gṛhyasūtra-s and Kāmasūtra-s and it is particularly emphasised in all the *Smṛti-s* as well as in the MBh. Of course, in this respect too, the gradual process into harder rules cannot be mistaken. Thus it was an ancient topic of dispute whether the marriage between a man of a higher caste and a Śūdra woman may be allowed or not and, not infrequently, both the views are found one immediately after the other, as, *e.g.* B. (1.16, 2), Mn. (3.13), N. (12.5 sqq.) and Vi. (24.1) allow the Brahmaṇa to marry women out of the four classes in the order, but on the other hand B. (2.27 nnd 4.1, 5), Mn. (3.14 sqq.), N. (12.108), Vi. (26.4 sqq.) etc. decisively condemn connections with Śūdra women. Also Āp. (1.26, 7), Vās. (1.25 sqq.), Y. (1.56), Pārask. (1.4, 11) etc. unequivocally declare themselves against the permissibility of such marriages even if they are performed without the usual marriage-*mantra-s*, and other ancient authors such as Uśanas, Hār., G. etc. fell out only over the question whether in such cases the excommunication of the culprit should take place immediately or later.

They were more tolerant towards the marriage of a Kṣatriya-woman and a Brahmaṇa and generally towards mixed marriages where the female is only one step lower than the male. Thus according to B. (1.17, 3 sqq.) (similarly 1.16, 6 and G. 4.16) sons of equal status are said to be born of such marriages, and also according to the unpublished Dharmasūtra of Uśanas (4) the son of a Brahmaṇa by a Kṣatriya wife will be a Brahmaṇa, the son of a Kṣatriya by a Vaśya wifea Kṣatriya and that of a Vaiśya by a Śūdra wife a Vaiśya. The MBh. too knows of marriages between Brahmaṇas and daughters of kings."

As to whether the girl could belong to a higher caste than the husband, the answer was in the negative. J. Jolly in his work, quoted above, stated.[279]

"Marriages between men of lower castes and women of higher castes are universally disapproved and the sons born of those unions are identified with the most hated castes as contrary to the natural order (*pratiloma*). Only the wife of

278. According to B. Ghosh's translation, p. 135.

279. According to B. Ghosh's translation, p. 136.

equal position is regarded as the *dharmapatnī* and the mixing of castes is generally a grave sin and the king must take care to prevent it. In later texts the marriage of Aryans (*dvija*) with women of unequal position is mentioned among the usages no longer permissible in this age of sins (*kalivarjya*)."

And so e.g. Vi. (16.3) stated : *pratiloma-svārya-vigarhitāḥ* (on women of higher caste than their husbands sons are begotten who are despised by the twice-born.[280]

Interpreting these two problems from the point of view of the Pañc., the most important seemed to be the rule quoted in Ya. (in Vīr. Saṁs. 747) where we read : *bhāryā sajāt yāḥ sarveṣāṁ dharmaḥ prāthakalpikaḥ.*

This rule was conform with other quotations mentioned above.

(B) *In the Pañcatantra*

In PHP. (1.18, p. 49, v. 12-3) we read : *kṣatriyasya tisro bhāryā dharmato bhavanty eva*; *tad eṣā kadācid vaiśyāsutā bhaviṣyati.*

Hence according to the *dharma* a Kṣatriya could have three wives and the girl could be the daughter of a woman of the same caste as the wooer.

In this connexion the following sentence was quoted, though it was not very closely connectedwith the text :

asaṁśayaṁ kṣatraparigrahakṣamā yad āryam asyām abhalāṣi me manaḥ,
satāṁ hi saṁdehapadeṣu vastuṣu pramāṇam antaḥkaraṇapravṛttayaḥ

(PHP. 1-7, *śl.* 211). The *śloka* was translated by A.W. Ryder as follows :

"Surely, she may become a warrior's bride,
Else, why these longings in an honest mind ?
The motions of a blameless heart decide
Of right and wrong, when reason leaves us blind."

We also find this sentence in Śāk.[281] and Sāhityadarpaṇa.[282]

In addition to these sentences, we find in PHP. the following rule :

kṣatriyo'sau rājā, tvaṁ ca vaiśyaḥ sann adharmād api na bibheṣi. (PHP. 1.7, p. 49, v. 10-1).

280. According to J. Jolly's translation in SBE. 7.
281. Ed. by Böhtlingk, 1. 21
282. 71. Sar. 585.37 and Kuv. *ad* 212.

We see in PHP. that the carpenter after some reflection said, "The king is a Kṣatriya and you are a Vaiśya. Have you no reverence for the *dharma* ?" Hence, PHP. expressed the opinion that a marriage with a girl of a higher caste than her future husband could not to be performed.

Comparing these two juridical problems (as described in PHP.) with the *Smṛti-s* we come to the conclusion that they were in conformity with the rules contained in the *Smṛti-s*.

37. *The Gāndharva-Vivāha*

(A) *In the Smṛti-s*

From the juridical point of view the Gāndharva form of marriage can be either combined with the Rākṣasa-vivāha, or be a separate Gāndharva-vivāha.[283]

The Gāndharva-vivāha could be defined as a voluntary (spontaneous) (Mn. 3.32, K. 3.151, 14, Kām. p. 207.213, G. 4.10, MBh. 1.73, 27) union (*saṁyoga*) (Mn. 3.32, Āp. 2.5, 11, 20, G. 4.10, B. 1.11-20, 7, Śaṅkh., 4.5, Vi. 24.23, N. 12.42, K. 151.74, Kām. p. 207.213, MBh. 1.73, 27, Dev. in Vīr. p. 855) of a loving (willing) (G. 4.10, Vās. 1.33, B. 1.11, 20, 7, N. 12.42) maiden (bride, girl, damsel, woman) Mn. 3.32, Āp. 2.5, 11, 20, Vās. 1.33, B. 1.11, 20, 6, Śaṅkh. 4.5, Āśv.-Gṛh. 1.6, 5, N. 12.42, K. 151.14, Dev. in Vīr. p. 855, Hār. in Vīr. p. 856) and her lover (bridgroom) (Mn. 3.32, Āp. 2.5, 11, 20, G. 4.10, Vās. 1.33, B. 1.11, 20, 7, Śaṅkh. 4.5, Āśv.-Gṛh. 1.6, 5, N. 12.42, K. 151.4, Dev. in Vīr. p. 855, Hār. in Vīr. p. 856).

Basing the definition on Kām. (228.18-21 and 229.1-4)[284] we should assume that the Gāndharva-vivāha was a concubinage only.

283. See above study 11 on the "Forms of Marriage in Ancient India and their Development" para. 52 sqq.

284. *pratipannam abhipretāvakāśa-vartinīṁ nāyakaḥ śrotriyāgārād agnimānāya kuśanāstīrya yathā smṛti hutvā ca triḥ parikramet; tato mātari pitari ca prakāśayet; agni-sākṣikā hi vivāhā na nivartanta ity ācārya-samayaḥ.*

duṣayitvā caināṁ śanaiḥ svajane prakāśayet; tad bāndhavāś ca yathā kulasyāghaṁ pariharanto daṇḍa-bhayāc ca tasmā evaināṁ dadyus tathā yojayet; anantaraṁ ca prītyupagraheṇa rāgeṇa tad bāndhavān prīṇayed iti; gāndharveṇa vivāhena vāceṣṭeta. Kām (228.18—229.4).

(B) *In the Pañcatantra*

In PHP. (1.7, p. 50, v. 20-p. 51, v. 3) it was stated: *evaṁ vādinyāṁ rājaduhitari kauliko gambhīraś-lakṣaṇayā girā śanair idam uvāca; bhadre, tvad artham eve'daṁ ihā'gamanam; sā'bravit; mānuṣī kanyā vā'ham; tenā'bhihitam; śāpabhraṣṭā tvaṁ mamaiva pūrvapatnī; mayā caitāvantaṁ kālaṁ mānuṣasaṁparkād rakṣita; tasmāt tvām ahaṁ gāndharveṇa vivāhena vivāhayāmi; tatam tayā, manorathānām apy agamyam, iti matvā, tathā, iti pratipannam; tenā'sau gāndharveṇa vivāhena pariṇītā;*

and again (PHP. 1.8, p. 52, v. 13-6) : *tac chrutvā sā prahasitavadanā, pulakitasarvāṅgī satvaraṁ gatva rājānam uce; deva, diṣṭyā vardhase; niśīthe nityam eva bhagavān nārāyaṇaḥ kanyakāpārśve svayaṁ samabhyeti; tena gāndharva-vivāhena pariṇītā sa.*[285]

In both these quotations the Gāndharva-vivāha was only a concubinage and not a real form of marriage. Therefore, these PHP. sentences were rather based on the Kāmasūtra-s than on the *Smṛti-s*.

In PBK. (1.5, p. 38, v. 20-24) it was even stated that as Garuḍa married the girl according to the Gāndharva-vivāha and carried her away, they spent the rest of the night in the way in which Vātsyāyana taught.[286]

It should be noted that always in ancient Indian literature any intercourse between unmarried people was discreetly called *gāndharva-vivāha.*[287]

285. According to A. W. Ryder's translation : "To the princess' words the weaver, indignified and sweetly modulated accents, made stately answer: 'Yourself, dear maiden, are the occasion of this visit to earth'. 'But I am merely a mortal girl', said she. And he continued : 'Nay, you have been my bride, now fallen to earth by reason of a curse. It is I who have so long protected you from contact with man. I will now wed you by the ceremony used in heaven". And she assented, for she thought: 'It is a thing beyond my fondest aspirations.' And he married her by the ceremony used in heaven." And again: "Thereupon the queen, with laughing countenance and thrilling in every limb, hastened to the king and said: 'O King, you are indeed fortunate. It is blessed Viṣṇu who comes each night in person to our daughter's side. This very night you and I are to hide in the window niche and have sight of him. But with mortals he does not exchange words."

286. *tvaṁ gāndharveṇa vivāhenā'tmānaṁ prayaccha; no cec chāpaṁ dattvā sānvayaṁ te pitaraṁ bhasmasāt kariṣyāmī'ti;evam abhidhāya garūḍā-davatīrya satye pāṇau kṛtvā tāṁ sabhayāṁ salajjāṁ vepamānāṁ śayyāyāmanayattataś ca rātri-śeṣaṁ yāvad vātsyāyano'ktavidhinā niṣevya pratyūṣe' lakṣito jagāma.* PBK. (1.5, p. 38, v. 20-4).

287. In Pañc. in PHP. (2.5, p. 149, v. 22); in Śāk.—the story of Śakuntalā and Duṣyanta, and many others.

38. *Minor Juridical Problems and Conclusions*

In the tale of the weaver as Viṣṇu we find some other minor problems connected with law and politics, in particular, the problem of collecting yearly tribute from a tributary king (PHP. 1.7, p. 58).

As far as the juridical problems were concerned the problems raised in this tale were solved in conformity with the common, well-known rules.

39. *Others Forms of Marriage. Dowry*

It should be noted that in addition to the Gāndharva-vivāha we find in the Pañc. the mention of the Āsura-vivāha. In PHP. (3.9, p. 205, v. 12-14) in the tale of the old man, young wife and thief, we find some mention of buying a girl from her father.[288]

On the other hand we also find in another place, *i.e.* in PHP. (3.11, p. 208), in the tale of the prince with a serpent in the belly, that the girl received the dowry from his father; this custom was common in connexion with the so-called orthodox forms of marriage.[289] The same statement regarding the dowry was also included in PHP. (5.7, p. 276, v. 12-15)[290] and PBK. (2.4, p. 25) as well as in PBK. (5. p. 56, v. 26, sqq.).

It was also stated in the Pañc. that the father used to arrange the wedding of his daughter at his own expense. (PHP. 1.4, p. 23, v. 9 sqq.).

VII. THE TALE OF THE GIRL WHO MARRIED A SNAKE

40. *Juridical Problems in PHP.* (1.23)

In the tale of the girl who married a snake (PHP. 1.23, *śl.* 379, and others) we find a very interesting *śloka* which runs as follows :

288. *tena ca kāmo'pahatacetasā mṛta-bhāryeṇa kācit nirdhanavaṇiksutā prabhūtadhanaṁ dattvo'dvāhitā* PHP. (3.9, p. 205, v. 12-4). See also PBK. (4., p. 25, v. 13 sqq.).

289. Cf. above study 11 on the "Forms of Marriage in Ancient India and their Development.

290. *tataś ca kaścin mama gṛham abhyetya prāptavarāṁ rūpāḍhyaṁ kanyāṁ pradāsyati.* PHP. (5.7, p. 276, v. 12-3).

sakṛj jalpanti rājānaḥ sakṛj jalpanti sādhavaḥ,
sakṛt kanyāḥ pradīyante trīṇy etāni sakṛt sakṛt.

A. W. Ryder translated it in the following way :

"Do once, once only, these three things :
Once spoken, stands the word of kings;
The speech of saints has no miscarriage;
A maid is given once in marriage."

The same *śloka* was to be also found in Vetālapañcaviṁśatikā (4. *śl.* 29).[291]

We see that in this *śloka* the opinion was expressed that a girl was given only once in marriage. This sentence was well-known; much has been written about it. It is certain that, as far as the problem of giving a girl to one bridegroom only was concerned, it was based on the *Smṛtis.*

In Mn. (9.47) we find a similar *śloka.* This *śloka* runs as follows:

sakṛd aṁśo nipatati sakṛt kanyā pradīyate,
sakṛd āha dadāmīti trīṇy etāni satāṁ sakṛt.

(Also quoted in SC. 311, DT. 182, VCa. 20, DN. 6, VyPr. 534, VT. 331, 475, BBh. *ad* Y. 2.149, VV. 83, VyS. 146, VVCa. 95).

The same was also the wording of N. (12.281)and almost the same of MBh. (Āraṇyaka-Parvan, Adh. 278.25),[292] and Bṛh. (Saṁsk. 266).[293] Y. (1.65) stated also that the girl could be given away once only.[294]

We find here another example of quoting, in the text of the Pañc. legal rules from the *Smṛti-s.*

291. Ed. by H. Uhle in *Abhandlungen für die Kunde des Morgenlandes,* Leipzig 1881; in the Jambhaladatta's version this *śloka* does not appear. (See M.B. Emeneaux's Vetālapañcaviṁśati in 'American Oriental Series, Vol. 4). It also appears in CV. 4.11, several MSs of the CN, version, in the Vikramacarita, Metric recension (2. 70-1) and the Bhaviṣya-purāṇa (4. 102, 29)

292. In the edition of the Bhandarkar Oriental Research Institute, Poona : same as above, but in has *gīṇy* instead of *trīṇy* (?)

293. The texts of MBh. and Bṛh. are identical.
It should be noted that in some versions of Mn. we find instead of *dadāmīti—dadanīti* and instead of *satāṁ sakṛt* we find *sakṛt sakṛt.* (See in Jhā's Manu Smṛti, Notes, part I, p. 396). On the other hand in MBh. K4 and D1 we find *dadāmīti* instead of *dadānīti* and in K1-3, D 5 *satāṁ sakṛt* instead of *sakṛt sakṛt.* It should be also noted that in K3 we find *sakṛj jalpanti bhūmiśāḥ.* (See PHP and Vet.).

294. See also Kāty. (in Vīr. *ad* Y. 1.65)

41. *The Same Problem in PHP.* (2.5)

The same problem was also raised, though not so clearly, in the tale of "Mr. What-fate-ordains" (PHP. 2.5, and others)[295] In this tale Varakīrti, when seeings that his bride has been given to another man, exclaimed with indignation: "Father-in-law: This is hardly respectable ! You promised your daughter to me, and then gave her to another man."[296] Though this act was contradictory to the general rules that the girl could be given to one man only in marriage, in this particular case the father could base his act on Y. (1.65)[297] according to which, if he found for her daughter a better bridegroom, he could take her back.

VIII. THE TALE OF MR. WHAT-FATE-ORDAINS

42. *Juridical Problems in PHP.* (2.5)

In PHP. (2.5, *śl.* 94-95 and almost identically in PK. 2, *śl.* 115 in PBK 2.4, *śl.* 107 sqq. in PPP. 2.4, *śl.* 114 sqq.) in the tale of Mr. What-fate-ordains the following *śloka-s* were quoted :

guroḥ sutāṁ mitrabhāryāṁ svāmisevakagehinīm,
yo gacchati punāṁl loke tam āhur brahmaghātakam,
aparaṁ ca,
ayaśaḥ prāpyate yena yena cā'dhogatir bhavet,
svārthāc ca bhraśyate yena tat karma na samācaret.

These *śloka-s* were translated by A.W. Ryder as follows :

"A Brahman-slayer, so they say,
Is he who tries to house
With teacher's child, or wife, of friend,
Or royal servant's spouse.

And again :

A deed that brings dishonour,
Whereby a man must fall,

295. See Chapter 8.

296. *bhoḥ śvaśura viruddham idaṁ tvayā'nuṣṭhitaṁ, yan mahyaṁ pradāya kanyā'nyasmai pradattā, iti.* (PHP 2.5, p. 150, v. 18. sqq.) See also PBK. (2.4, p. 25, v. 5 sqq.) and others.

297. *sakṛt pradīyate kanyā haraṁstāṁ caura-daṇḍa-bhāk,*
dattām api haret purvāc chreyāṁś ced vara āvrajet. (Also quoted in ViR. 1.65, Medh. in MnM. *ad* 8.227, Mit. *ad* Y. 1.65, VRK. 521, DV. 186, RDhK. 459, VyS. 119).

That causes disadvantage,
Don't do it—that is all".

These *śloka-s*, loosely connected with the tale itself, were based on the *Smṛti-s* and were in conformity with them.

In Mn. (9.235) we read :

brahmahā ca surāpaś ca taskaro gurutalpagaḥ,
ete sarve pṛthag jñeyā nahāpatakino narāḥ.

Hence, he who slew a Brahmaṇ, as well as he who violated a *guru's* bed committed a mortal sin (*mahāpātaka*).

Similar was also the opinion of Mn. (11.54 or 55 where we read :

anṛtaṁ ca samutkarṣe rājagāmi ca paiśunam,
guroś-cālika-nirbandhaḥ samāni brahma-hatyayā

We also find a similar opinion in B. (1.10, 18, 19), N. (in Vīr. p. 634) and others. All these *śloka-s* expressed the opinion that a Brahmaṇ-slayer, and he who violated a *guru's* bed, committed the same sin.

In the same tale the problems of the Gāndharva-vivāha, of giving the girl in marriage only once[298] and of *repudiatio filii*[299] were also mentioned. The Gāndharva-vivāha of this tale was rather settled in accordance with the Kāmasūtra-s than with the Dharmaśāstra-s.[300]

IX. THE TALE OF THE BLIND MAN, THE HUNCHBACK AND THE THREE-BREASTED PRINCESS

43. *Contents of PHP.* (5.10) *and its Juridical Problems*

In PHP. book 5, *kathā* 10 (in PK. Book 5, *kathā* 12, in PBK. Book 5, *kathā* 12, in PPP. Book 5, *kathā* 11) in the tale of the blind man, the hunchback and the three-breasted princess, we find the story of a king who wanted to expose his new-born daughter with three breasts, as it was believed that she would bring misfortune to her father. However, he decided to give her away in marriage and ordered a proclamation that anyone who would marry the three-breasted princess would receive hundred thousand gold-pieces, but would be exiled. Nobody wanted to marry the three-breasted princess and she grew to

298. See Chapter 7.
299. PBK. (2.4, p. 23, v. 2 sqq.).
300. See §. 37.

young womanhood. Then a blind man, who had a hunchback as his companion, decided to marry her. They went into exile and there the hunchback fell in love with the three-breasted princess. They decided to poison the blind man. Therefore, the princess cooked for him a black poisonous snake. The poisonous steam of the cooked snake reached the blind man's eyes and the film began to peel off. He saw that a poison was prepared for him, but behaved as a blind man. When he saw that the hunchback was beginning to kiss his wife, and so on, he seized him, whirled him about his head and dashed him against the chest of the three-breasted woman. This blow forced the third breast in, while the hunchback when his hump crashed against her boom, became straight.

From the juridical point of view, as described in the *Smṛti-s*, two problems were raised in this tale :

(1) exposure of new-born girls,

(2) duty to declare the defects of the girl before giving her in marriage.

44. *Exposure of New-born Girls*

(A) *In the Smṛti-s*

In spite of some passages which could show that exposure of new-born children, and particularly of new-born girls, was admissible in ancient India (Ṛg. 2.29, 1, Kāthaka 27.9, Maitrāyaṇī Saṁhitā 4.6, 11, Taittiriya Saṁhitā 6.5, 10, 3, etc.), on the basis of legal rules contained in the *Smṛti-s* we must exclude the possibility of the existence of such a custom.

Foeticide (*garbhavadha* or *bhrūṇahattya*) was considered as one of the greatest sins,[301] the woman who committed foeticide could be repudiated by her husband (*repudiatio uxoris*)[302] and libations of water could not be offered to those who had committed foeticide.[303] The Gṛhyasūtra-s did not mention

301. Vṛsiṁha Tapanīya Upaniṣad (1.5, 4, 1), Kāth. (31. 7), Taittirīya Brāhmaṇa (4. 2, 8, 12), Taittir. Ār. (10, 38, 40, 2, 7, 3), Ṛg. (10, 115, 2), etc. See *A. Weber'a* "Indische Studien", Vol. 9., p. 117, sqq.

302. *vyabhicāradṛtau śuddhir garbhe tyāgo vidhīyate,*
garbha-bhartṛ-vadhādau ca tathā mahati pātake. (Y. 1.72).

303. *pāṣaṇḍam āśritānāṁ ca carantīnāṁ ca kāmataḥ,*
garbha-bhartṛ-druhāṁ caiva surāpīnāṁ ca yoṣitām. (Mn. 5.89) and similarly Apar. (p. 876): *balībādyā modakaṁ kuryuḥ stenā vrātyā vikarmiṇaḥ garbha-bhartṛ-druhaś caiva surāpyaś caiva yoṣitaḥ.*

any case of exposure of new born children.[304] Infanticide was legally prohibited.[305]

These rules show that exposure of new born children, even girls, whose birth was not greated with the same joy as that of boys, was legally prohibited in ancient India.

(B) *In the Pañcatantra*

In PHP. (5.10, p. 285, v. 5-8) we read: *astyuttarā-pathe sadhupuraṁ nāma nagaram. tatra madhuseno nāma rājā; tasya kadācit tristanī kanyā jajñe; atha tāṁ tristanīṁ jātāṁ śrutvā, rājā kañcukinam āhūya provāca; bhoḥ, tyajyatām iyam araṇye, yathā na kaścid eva jānāti.*

(Similarly PK. 5.12, p. 257, v. 22 to p. 258, v. 1, PBK. 5.12, p. 64, v. 1-5, PPP. 5.11, p. 234, v. 5-8).

This passage was translated in A. W. Ryder's "Pañcatantra" in the following way : "In the north country was a city called Honey-Town, where the king was named Honey-Host. And once there was born to him a daughter with three breasts. As soon as he learned of the birth of the three-breasted girl, he summoned the chamberlain and said : 'Sir let this girl be exposed in the forest, so that not a single soul may learn the fact."

It is clear that, according to this tale, this exposure, or rather intention to expose the girl, was caused by the belief that abnormal children (a three-breasted girl) bought misfortune.[306]

304. See Āśv.-Gṛh. (1.15, 7 and 10), Gobh.-Gṛh. (2.8, 25), Āp. -Gṛh. (6.15, 11 and 13), etc.

305. *kūṭa-śāsana-kartṛṁś ca prakṛtīnāṁ ca dūṣakān,*
strī-bāla-brāhmaṇa-ghnāṁś ca hanyād dviṭsevinas tathā. (Mn. 9. 232.

Also quoted in Apar. *ad* Y. 2.294, VyK. 122, SC. 324, VRK. 370, VCi. 162, VyN. 504, 508, DV. 266, 317, SV. 475, VV. 307, VyS. 157). See also Vi. (5.9-11) reading : *kūṭa-śāsana-kartṛṁś ca rājā hanyāt. kūṭa-lekhya-kārāṁś ca. garadā'gni-dapra-sahya-taskarān strī-bāla-puruṣa-ghātinaś ca.* (Also quoted in VyK. 122, SC. 324, VyS. 157, Apar. *ad* Y. 2.294).

Cf. above study XV on "Infanticide and Exposure of New-born Children in Ancient India.

306. *hināṅgī vā'dhikāṅgī vā bhaved yā kanyakā'tra sā,*
bhartuś ca syād vināśāya svaśīlanidhanāya ca, (71),
yā punas tristanī kanyā yāti locanag ocaram,
pitaraṁ nāśayanty eva sā drutaṁ nātra saṁśayaḥ. (72).

PHP. (5.10, *śl.* 71-72). Similarly PK. (5.12, *śl.* 81, 82), PBK. (5.12, *śl.* 95, 96, PPP. (5.11, *śl.* 89, 90), PM. (5.545)

"A daughter fitted out with limbs
Too numerous or few,
Will lose her character, and will
Destroy her husband, too.

Though the king first intended to expose his daughter, he decided not to do so, probably, because he was afraid of the legal consequences of such an act.

Therefore, we could assume that this king's action was based on the legal rules contained in the *Smṛti-s* and that his action was in conformity with the legal rules.

45. *Declaration of Defects of the Girl Before Giving her in Marriage*

(A) *In the Smṛti-s*

The duty of the father or the guardian of the girl to declare all her defects before giving her in marriage was a legal rule contained in almost all the *Smṛti-s*.

If the father or guardian of the girl declared openly all the defects of the girl given in marriage, he was not liable to punishment,[307] but if he did not do so, then he was punished by the king[308] (the punishment varied between the first and the highest amercement), [309] and the suitor could annul the contract with this man[310] and abandon, or repudiate the girl who had some defects.[311]

But if the father sees a girl
With triple breast about,
She dooms him to a speedy death
Without a shade of doubt."
(According to A. W. Ryder's translation).

307. *no''nmattāyā na kuṣṭhinyā na ca yā spṛṣṭa-maithunā,*
pūrvaṁ doṣān abhikhyāpya pradātā daṇḍam arhati. (Mn. 8. 205. Cf. Rāmacandra in MnM.)
anākhyāya dadad doṣaṁ daṇḍya uttama-sāhasam,
aduṣṭāṁ ca tyajan daṇḍyo dūṣayaṁs tu mṛṣā śatam. (Y. 1.66).
yas tu doṣavatīṁ kanyām anākhyāya prayacchati,
tasya kuryān nṛpo daṇḍaṁ pūrva-sāhasa-co'ditam. (N. 12.33, NMS. 13.33. Also quoted in Apar. *ad* Y. 1.66).

308. *yas tu doṣavatīm kanyām anākhyāya prayacchati,*
tasya kuryān nṛpo daṇḍaṁ svayaṁ saṇ-ṇavatiṁ paṇān. (Mn. 8. 224. Also quoted in BBh. *ad* Y. 2. 289, VyS. 119, 157).
kanyā-doṣam aupaśāyikām anakyāya prayacchataḥ kanyāṁ ṣaṇ-ṇavatir daṇḍaḥ śulka-strīdhana-pratidānaṁ ca. K. (188.7-8). For other texts see note 307.

309. Y. and N. See also K. and J. J. Meyer's *Das altindische Buch vom Welt-und Statsleben* (p. 797 sqq.) and others.

310. *yas tu doṣavatīṁ kanyām anākhyaya prayacchati,*
tasya tad vitathaṁ kuryāt kanyā datur durāt manaḥ.
Mn. (9.73). *A contrario* Vi. (5.162), N. (12.35) and others. According to some *Smṛti-s* the father or guardian ought not only pay an amercement but also return the *śulka* and the *strīdhana*.

311. *vidhivat pratigṛhyā'pi tyajet kanyāṁ vigarhitām,*
vyadhitāṁ vipradraṣṭāṁ vā chadmanā co'papāditām. (Mn. 9.72).

We see that these rules were very strict and common,

(B) *In the Pañcatantra*

In PHP. (5.10, p. 286, v. 16-22) we read : *tasmād etad-darśanaṁ pariharatu devaḥ; yadi kaścid enām udvāhayati, tat tasmai dattvā deśa-tyāgena niyojayitavyaḥ, iti; evaṁ kṛte lokadvayāviruddhatā kṛtā bhavati, iti; teṣām tad vacanam ākarṇya rājā sarvatra paṭaha-ghoṣaṇām ājñāpayām āsa, yathā; aho, tristanīṁ rājakanyāṁ yaḥ pariṇayati, tasya rājā suvarṇa-lakṣaṁ dattvā deśatyāgaṁ kārayati; evam āghoṣaṇāyāṁ kriyamāṇāyāṁ prabhutakālo vyatītaḥ.*

(Similarly PK. 3.12, p. 261, v. 5 sqq. PBK. 5.12 p. 65, v. 12 sqq., PPP. 5.11, p. 235, v. 8 sqq.).

This passage was translated by A. W. Ryder as follows:

Therefore, O King, shun the sight of her. Give her to anyone who will marry her, but banish him from the country. If this is done, there is no offense to laws human of divine.'

When the king had listened to this opinion, he ordered a proclamation to be made everywhere with beat of drum, as follows : 'Hear ye : There is a three-breasted princess. To anyone who marries her the king will give a hundred thousand gold-pieces, but will exile him.' "

Hence we see that the king decided to order a proclamation in which he has stated that his daughter had some defects, *i.e.* that she was three-breasted. In this way he was free of responsibility and could give her in marriage before she attained puberty.[312]

This act of the king and father of the deformed girl was in conformity with the *Smṛti-s* and was based on them. In this way the king-father was not obliged to expose his daughter and in this connection commit a sin (he ordered the proclamation immediately after his decision was taken not to expose her) and was free from any responsibility towards the future husband of his daughter.

X. THE FRAME-STORY TO BOOK I

46. *Juridical Problems in PHP.* (5.22)

In PHP. (in the first part of the frame story to Book 5, *śl.* 22), in PK. (in the first part of the frame story to Book 1, *śl.* 16) we find the following *ślokas* :

312. See Chapter 3.

nikṣepe gṛhapatite śreṣṭhī saṁstauti devatāṁ nityam,
nikṣepeśo mriyatāṁ dāsyāmy upayācitaṁ tubhyam (PHP. 5.22)

and

nikṣepe patite harmye śreṣṭhī stauti svadevatāṁ,
tadīśo bhriyatām āśu tubhyāṁ dāsyāmi yācitam (PK. 1. 16).

According to both these texts if a trader had in his possession a deposited object, he asked God to kill the owner of the object deposited.

It is not clear from where this *śloka* came, as the rules contained in it were contradictory to the rules contained in the *Smṛti-s*.

According to the *Smṛtis* the object deposited had to be returned to the depositor himself; if not, the depositary had to be punished (K.180.7). In particular, the object deposited could not be returned to the next-of-kin (son, brother, wife—Medh. *ad* Mn. 8.185). Especially in joint families e.g., the brother of the depositor could come to the depositary and ask for return, saying that it belonged to him. If this person committed a dishonest act, the depositary had no proof and lost the object deposited which then had to be restored by him; but the object deposited did not become lost if no accident occurred (Mn. 8.185, similarly Bṛh. 11.10). However, the depositary could restore the object deposited to the depositor's next-of-kin, if the depositor has died (Mn. 8.186 and identically N. 2.10).[313]

Mn. (8.186) and identically N (2.10) stated :

svayam eva tu yo dadyān mṛtasya pratyanantare,
na sa rājñābhiyoktavyo na nikṣeptuś ca bandhubhiḥ.

Therefore, it is evident that the object deposited might be returned to the next-of-kin. Also the general rules regarding succession have to be applied in this case. According to these rules the heir entered into the rights and obligations of the deceased.

Hence no reason is seen why the object deposited should not be returned to the heir of the deceased depositor.

These *ślokas*, as not based on the *Smṛtis*, and even contradictory to them, were probably wrongly interpreted in PHP. and PK. In P., PHT., PBK., and PPP. these *śloka-s* were not included. It is very likely that the last versions purposely omitted these *ślokas*.

313. Cf. above Study II on the "Law of Deposits"

XI. QUOTATIONS FROM THE MĀNAVA-DHARMA-ŚĀSTRA

47. *Mn.* (8.26)

We also find in the Pañc. some sentences from Mn. which were quoted without the real understanding of the text. The best example is in citing Mn. (8.26) without quoting Mn. (8.25) with which it is closely connected. It is not possible to understand Mn. (8.26) without the preceding *śloka.* They both refer to the commencement of a trial and the way in which the judge should examine witnesses.

It was stated in Mn. (8.25, 26).[314]

bāhyair, vibhāvayel liṅgair bhāvam antargataṁ nṛṇām.
svaravarṇeṅgitā-kāraiś cakṣuṣā ceṣṭitena ca. (25)
ākārair iṅgitair gatyā ceṣṭayā bhāṣitena ca,
netra-vaktra-vikāraiś gṛhyate'ntargataṁ manaḥ. (26).

Jhā translated these two *ślokas* in the following way : "He shall discover the internal disposition of men by external signs: by variations in their voice, colour and aspect, as also by means of the eye and by gestures. (25). The inner mind is indicated by such variations as those of aspect, gait, gesture, speech, and by changes in the eye and the face (26)."

If we read both the *ślokas* the text is intelligible : "the inner mind is indicated by such variations as those of aspect, gait, gesture, speech, and by changes in the eye and the face" does not make any sense.

PHP. (1. frame story, *śl.* 21), PK. (1. p. 13, *śl.* 50), PBK. (1. *śl.* 44), PPP. (1, *śl.* 45), PM (1.22) quoted only Mn. 8.26 with some small variations. We read there :

ākārair iṅgitair gatyā ceṣṭayā bhāṣaṇena ca,
netra-vaktra-vikāreṇa gṛhyate'ntargataṁ manaḥ[315].

This text did not add any sense to the frame story of Book

314. See also similarly Y. (2.14-5):
pariśuṣyat skhalad vākyo viruddhaṁ bahu bhāṣate,
vāk cakṣuḥ pūjayati no tathoṣṭau nirbhujaty api.
svabhāvad vikṛtiṁ gacchen mano-vāk-kāya-karmabhiḥ.
abhiyoge ca sākṣye vā duṣṭah sa parikīrtitaḥ.

315. Cf. CRC 2.55, CRB 2.62, CRB. 2.59, CRBh. I 2.59, CRBh. II 2.49, CRCa 2.49 CNG 265, HJ 2.47, MKS 148, Vet 1. 8.

I. This proves once more, that some well-known sentences were very often put into the text of the Pañc. though they were not related to the text at all. This also happens often in anthologies. On the other hand, this proves that the sentences of Mn. 8.25, 26 were well-known all over India.[316]

48. *Attribution of Different Śloka-s to Mn.*

It should also be noted that in the Pañc. we find sentences, sometimes well-known which could not be found in the Mn., but, in the Pañc. were attributed to Mn. This shows once more the high authority of Mn. but also a lack of accuracy on the part of the author, or authors, or rather later compilors, of the Pañc.

A. And so we find in PBK. (3.1, p. 53, v. 26 and *śl.* 84) the following passage :

uktaṁ ca manunā vyāsena ca:
tyajed ekaṁ kulasyā'rtha grāmasyā'rthe kulaṁ tyajet,
grāmaṁ janapadasyā'rtha ātmā'rthe pṛthivīṁ tyajet.[317].

(Similarly PPP. 3.1, p. 146, v. 2 and *śl.* 82, PS. 1.105, PN. 2.83). The same *śloka* was also quoted in P. (1.8, *śl.* 117), PHT. (1.9, *śl.* 118; PTem 1.107), PK. (3.81), but without quoting the authority of Manu and Vyāsa.

This *śloka* could not be traced in Mn. and it is not likely that it could be found there, as it was a typical *śloka* from Nītiśāstras-s. It is to be found in MBh. (Ādiparvan, crit. ed. *Adhy.* 107, *śl.* 32[318] in Sabhāparva 32, *Adhy.* 55, *śl.* 10[319] in Udyogaparvan, *Adhy.* 37, 16 and 126, 48[320] in various Cāṇakya's MSS. and editions, 117. CVND. 3.10, CVM 3. 3, CvA. 1.7, CvS. 1.7, CvW 1.8, CvP IV 1.7, CvP V 1.7, CvGt 1.7, CvTb 1.8, CvH 1.8, CvI 1.7, CvL I 1.7, CvL II 1.7, CvLd 1.7, CRB 2.2, CRP 1.7, CBBh. 2.7, CRBh II 2.3, CRC 10, CNJV 36, CNS 41, CNF 14, CNP I 58, CNPh 6, CNP II 94 8316, CNG 20, CNT

316. It should be noted that in PBK. and PPP. the authority of Manu was quoted *expressis verbis*. Compare below.

317. F. Edgerton translated it as follows: "For the sake of a family an individual may be sacrificed; for the sake of a village a family may be sacrificed; for the sake of a nation a village may be sacrificed for the sake of one's self the world may be sacrificed" (P. 1.8, *śl.* 117).

318. Many MSS. read for the first quarter of this *śloka*:
tyajet kulaye puruṣam

319. First quarter of this *śloka* as in note 318.

320. See note 312.

IV 58, CNM 58, CNS-A 10, CNNM 26, CNST 27, CNI1124, CnT II 1.12, CnT III 1.12, CnT VI 13.31,in the Vṛddhacāṇakya MS. (No. 834 of 1886-92, dated Saṁ. 1864, in the Bhandarkar O. R. Institute, fol. 7b. *Adhy.* 1, v. 8) in the Caṇakyarājanīti-samuccaya MS. (No. 833 of 1886-92, dated Saṁ 1828, in the same Institute, fol. 1 b, v. 6) with some insignificant changes in Cāṇakyanīti (MS. No. 74 of 1883-84, dated Saṁ. 1845, Govt MSS. Library at the same institute, fol. 4a, adhy. 2, v. 3,[321] and MS. No. 400 of 1887-91, at the same Institute, fol. 1 b, v. 4),[322] in Saṁskṛtapath. (54), in Sama-P. Kāśika (13.90), in Benfey's edition, in Hit. (ed. Schlegel and Lassen 1.14), in Vikramacarita (VCsr. 28.3), in Śukasaptati (Śts. 21.4-5) Kathārṇava (in ZDMG. 16.544) and in Paddhati of Śārṅgadhara and some others.

However, it must be emphasized that only the later versions attributed these *śloka-s* Mn. and MBh. while the younger ones did not. This is another proof that the later and longer versions tried to avoid all the inaccuracies and illogicalities which could be perceived in the Pañc.

B. Also PBK. (1.13, *śl.* 317), PPP. (1.13, *śl.* 346) attributed to Mn. one *śloka* though it could not be traced in Mn.[323]

Pañc. quoted the authority of Mn. *in majorem gloriam* In the first case it was completely unnecessary, as this *śloka* was a well-known one and was quoted in MBh. and in the *Nīti-śāstras*.[324]

Other examples of the quoting of the Mānava-Dharma-śāstra as an authority (for the reason of importance) are some passages in PBK. (3.1, p. 53, v. 26 and *śl.* 84,) PPP. (3.1, p. 146, v. 2 and *śl.* 82), etc.

C. Also the God of justice—Dharma was quoted in the Pañc. We find in PBK. (5, p. 48, v. 26) the following quotation : *dharmasya tvaritā gatiḥ*; *eṣa dharmas tāvat.* (Quick is the march of Dharma. This is the God of Justice).

It should be noted here that the first part of this quota-

321. *tyajed daśaṁ kulasyā'rthe grāmasyā'rthe kulaṁ tyajet,*
grāmaṁ janapadasyā'rthe svātmā'rthe pṛthivīṁ tyajet.
322. *tyajed ekaṁ kulasyā'rthe grāmasyā'rthe kulaṁ tyajet,*
sāmaṁ janapadasyā'rthe ātmā'rthe pṛthivīṁ tyajet.
323. See Chapter 12.
324. Though it was not possible to trace it in K. either.

tion was probably a not-well-understood and only partially quoted *śloka*, the whole of which runs:

kṣaṇaṁ cittaṁ kṣaṇaṁ cittaṁ kṣaṇaṁ jīvati mānavaḥ,
yamasya karuṇā nāsti dharmasya tvaritā gatiḥ.

We also find in PBK. (1.16, p. 78, v. 13-18) and in PPP. (1.16, p. 80, v. 9-14) some mentions of the God of Justice as surety.

Following is the text of PBK. *paramatra dharmaḥ pratibhūr iti te vicintya sarve siṁha-sakāśam ājagmuḥ.........tad yadi svāmī dvi-guṇaṁ śarīraṁ prayacchati tataḥ śaṅkukarṇo'yaṁ dvi-guṇa-vṛddhyā svaśarīraṁ prayacchati dharma-pratibhūvā; ......vyavahārasyā'sya dharmaḥ pratibhūḥ kriyatām iti.*[325]

XII MINOR JURIDICAL PROBLEMS FOUND IN THE PAÑCATANTRA

49. We find in P. and other versions many other references to juridical problems, but they were of no great interest. There are in the Pañc. some references to: possession and ownership,[326] guarantee,[327] safety,[328] suretyship,[329] secured loans,[330] service,[331] contracts of work (workmen who were employed,[332]) appointing of guards,[333] unworthy employment,[334] marriage of the husband

325. Quoted in PBK. (p. 81 *ad* p. 48).
326. PBK. (2.6, p. 34).
327. See PBK. (1.11, *śl.* 290, sqq.) and many others.
328. *na gopradānaṁ na mahīpradānaṁ na nānpradānaṁ hi tathā pradhānam,*
yathā vadantīha budhāh pradhānaṁ sarvapradāneṣv abhayapradānam.
PHP. (1.13, *śl.* 298).
329. *param atra dharmaḥ pratibhūr iti te vicintya sarve simha-sakāśamājag-muḥ......tad yadi svāmī dvi-guṇaṁ śarīraṁ prayacchati tataḥ śaṅku-karṇo'yaṁ dvi-guṇa-vṛddhyā sva-śarīraṁ prayacchati dharma-pratibhhuvā;...vyavahārasyā'sya dharmaḥ pratibhūḥ kriyatām iti,* PBK. (1.16, p. 78, v. 13-8). Similarly PPP. (1.16, p. 89, v. 9-14).
330. See PBK. (4.14, p. 33 sqq.).
331. It is very interesting to note that PHP (*śl.* 266) in the first *pāda* used the third *pāda* of Mn. (4.6) *seva śvavṛttir ākhyātā*. Hence, both Mn. and Pañc. considered the service as *śvavṛtti*, i.e. impure (a dog's life). Similarly PBK. (1.268) and others.
332. *tatra ye karmakarāḥ sthapatyādyas te madhyāhnāvelāyām āhārārthaṁ nagaramadhye praviśanti.* P. 1.1.28).
tatra ye ca karmakarāḥ sthapatyā dayaste madhyāhnavelāyām āhārā'rthaṁ nagara-madhye vrajanti. PBK. (1.1, p. 6, v. 15-6).
dravya-prakṛti-hīno'pi sevyaḥ sevyaguṇānvitaḥ,
bhavaty ājīvanaṁ tasmāt phalaṁ kālāntarād api. PHP. (1. frame story, *śl.* 33. Similarly PBK. (1. *śl.* 48) and PPP. (1. *śl.* 49).
333. *tadā tasya rakṣipuruṣān niyojya śeṣasārtha saṁrakṣanārthaṁ bahvapāyaṁ vanam iti matvā yathābhilāṣitaṁ digantaraṁ prāyāt. anyedyus tv ātmabyāt tat-parai rakṣipuruṣair apy āgatya tasya mṛto'ktam.* P. (1. frame story 13-4).
334. *asamaiḥ samīyamānaḥ samaiś ca parihīyamāṇasatkāraḥ,*

after the death of his first wife,[335] power of the husband over his wife,[336] (beating and mutilating of the wife by the husband if she is not guilty[337]), polygamy and relations between husband and wife[338] (the true wife should obedient),[339] property rights of women,[340] *repudiatio filii*,[341] succession,[342] *praesumptio* in case of death,[343] trading,[344]

adhuri viniyujyamānas tribhir arthapatim tyajati bhṛtyaḥ. P. (1. frame story. *śl*. 38). See also PHP. (1. frame story, *śl*. 115 and others.)

api sammānasaṁyuktaḥ kulīnā bhaktitatparāḥ
vṛttibhaṅgān mahīpālaṁ tyajanty eva hi sevakāḥ. PHP. (1. *śl*. 115; also PBK. 1. 153, PK. 1.169).

335. PBK. (4. p. 25, v. 13) and others.

336. *so'pi bhūyas tām tad evā'ha. atha sā yāvat pratyuttaraṁ na prayacchati; tāvat sa kupito darpān mama vacasy uttaramātram api na dadāsī'ty uktvo'tthāya tīkṣṇaśastreṇa tasyā nāsikām achinat, āha ca: tiṣṭhai'vaṁlakṣaṇā, kas tvām adhunā vārttām pṛcchati*. P. (1.3c. 147 sqq.) cutting off her nose.

337. PBK. (1. p. 31, v. 20 sqq.), P. (1, 3c, 147) quoted above, P. (1. 3c, 171) (guilt).

338. See PBK. (3.86).

339. *sa snigdho'kuśalān nivārayati yas tat karma yan nirmalaṁ*
sā strī yā'nuvidhāyinī sa matimān yaḥ sadbhir abhyarcyate
sā śrīr yā na madaṁ karoti sa sukhī yas tṛṣṇayā no'hyate
tan mitraṁ yad ayantraṇaṁ sa puruṣo yaḥ khidyate ne'ndriyaiḥ.

P. (1. frame story, *śl*. 82). (Also PHT. 1.81, PTem. 1.74, PS. 1.73, PN. 2.54, PHP. 1.251). See also PBK. (1. *śl*. 85).

340. See PBK. (4. p. 25, v. 10 sqq.).

341. PBK. (2.4, p. 23, v. 2. sqq.).

342. PHP. (2.8, p. 166, v. 9-10).

343. PBK. (1.10, *śl*. 274) quoted even the authority of Manu:
viśrambhād yasya yo mṛtyum avāpnoti kathaṁcana,
tasya hatyā taduttha sā prāhedaṁ vacanaṁ manuḥ. (Cf. PK. 1.306).

The authority of Manu was also quoted in PBK. (1.13, *śl*. 317):
mitrā'rthe bandhavā'rthe ca buddhimān yatate sadā
jātāsv āpatsu yatnena jagād edaṁ vaco manuḥ. (Cf. PK. 1.359).

344. *parivartamāne vyavahāre gṛhapatiḥ samāyātah; tenā'bhihitam: kathaṁ tilāḥ parivartyante sā tam āha: samārghās tilā mayā labdhāḥ, śuktāḥ. kṛṣṇaiḥ. tato'sau vihasyā'bravīt; kāraṇenā'tra bhavitavyam. ato'haṁ bravīmi, nā'kasmāc chāṇḍvlī mālā, iti*. P. (2.134).

tatra dharmopārjitavṛttir vardhamānako nāma sārthavāhah prativasati sma; tasya kadācic cittaṁ utpannaṁ yat; prabhūte'pi vitte'rthavṛddhiḥ karaṇīye'ti P. (1. frame story, v. 4-5). Also PBK. (1.22, p. 91, v. 25 sqq.) and many others.
In PHP. (5.2, p. 262, v. 16-19) the profitable trade was divided into seven branches: (1) false weights and balances, (2) price-boosting, (3) keeping of deposit-shops. (4) getting regular customers, (5) a stock company, (6). articles of luxury such as perfumes. (7). foreign trade. We read there :

tac ca vāṇijyaṁ saptadhā vittāgamāya syāt, tad yathā; kūṭa-tulā-mānaṁ mithyākrayakathanaṁ, nikṣepapraveśah, paricitagrāhakāgamah, goṣṭhikakarma, gāndhikavyahāro deśāntarabhāṇḍanayanaṁ ca, iti.

Very similar was the opinion of PK. (1. frame story p. 7, v, 15-7) where we read : *tac ca vāṇijyaṁ saptaviddham vittāgamāya syāt; tad yathā kūtā-tulā-mānaṁ mithyākrayathanaṁ nikṣepa-praveśaḥ paricitagrāhakāgamo goṣṭhikakarma ca gāndhika-vyavahāro deśāntara-bhāṇḍānayanaṁ ceti*.

robbery,[345] bribery,[346] procedure,[347] punishments.[348]

All these references did not exhaust any of these problems and, therefore, are not dealt with in this study.

XIII. CONCLUSIONS

50. It is clear that we do not find in the Pañc. any system of Indian law but only separate juridical problems which are related to various sections of civil or penal law, as well as civil procedure and did not exhaustively solve any of the problems raised.

As far as the law of things was concerned, we find in the Pañc. general references to *res nullius*, *res derelicta*, treasure-trove, acquisition of ownership, possession, detention, occupation usucaption, praescription, boundary disputes, etc.

As far as the law of obligations was concerned we find references to deposits, (their return, *vis maior*, etc.,) suretyship, relationship between copartners employees and employers, commercial-contracts, trade, etc.

We find most frequently in the Pañc. references to the family law and, in particular to the law of marriage. The following juridical problems were found in the Pañc. : different kinds of maidens, the obligation and right of the father or other guardian of a girl to give her away in marriage, choosing of a suitable husband for a girl, suitable age for marriage, obligation of the father to declare the defects of the girl before giving her in marriage, inter-caste marriages, giving of a girl in marriage once only, the *Gāndharva-vivāha*, *Āsura-vivāha*, *Ārṣa-vivāha* and dowry, self-choice, relations between husband and wife, assaulting of women, adultery, and violation of a *guru's* bed, and, even, exposure of new-born children, or keeping a minor in confinement.

We also find in the Pañc. some references to the law of in-

See also PBK. (1. frame story, p. 4, v. 10-3) where we read: *tac ca vāṇijyaṁ saptavidham arthāgamāya syāt tad yathā gāndhika-vyavāhāro nikṣepa-praveśo goṣṭhika-karma paricitagrāhakāgamo mithyākrayakathanaṁ kūṭa-tulāmānaṁ deśāntarād bhāṇḍānayanaṁ ceti.* Almost identical with the latter was the text of PPP. (1. frame story, p. 5, v. 10-3).

345. P. (1. frame story, v. 104, PhP. (3. frame story, p. 206, v. 9-15).

346. P. (1. frame story 134)

347. PHP. (5. frame story p. 259).

348. Impalment—P. (5.2, 54) and many others. See also above.

heritance, legal procedure, in particular, general remarks relating to proofs, particularly, of witnesses, documents and ordeals, sentences, punishments, sureties in litigation, etc.

In addition to these juridical problems which were contained in the *Smṛti-s,* we find in the Pañc. customs, as they were applied in daily life, which could not to be traced to the *Smṛti-s,* such as, for instance, the custom of cutting off the unfaithful wife's nose.

51. If we compare the juridical rules contained in the *Smṛti-s* with those contained in various versions of the Pañc., we must come to the conclusion that all these juridical problems,—though the respective rules were not quoted *in extenso,*[349] with the exception of a few only and the most complicated ones,—were pictured in the Pañc. in accordance with the legal rules contained in the *Smṛti-s.* This proves (1) that these rules were really applied in daily life, and (2) generally known so well that they were even reproduced by lay-men. It is clear that in the first place the Mānava-Dharmaśāstra was quoted. On the other hand, it seems that the author or authors of the Pañc. tried to compose the tales in conformity with the legal rules generally known and contained in the *Smṛti-s.* It seems that, in particular, this was the aim of the author or authors of the later and longer versions. The oldest recensions did not show this tendency. However, this tendeney could be noticed in the later versions, as well as in the Kath., which was based on the Pañc. This tendency caused even a complete change of the text of some tales in these parts which, from the point of view of their contents, were insignificant, but were not in accordance with the *Smṛtis.*

The best example is to be found in the tales of Honest-mind and Evil-minded and in the story of the mouse and the two monks. In the older texts we find the statement, contradictory to the *Smṛti-s* that the finders divided between themselves some money they had found or that the treasure-trove was divided among the finders. In order to avoid any contradiction to the legal rules, the later versions changed the tale in these parts which were insignificant for the contents of the tale, and declared in the first tale that the money divided between two persons was not found by them but gained by them, since it was in accordance with the legal rules that money acquired in such a way should be divided. It should be noted that for the contents of this tale the statement that some two persons were co-partners in some amount of money, was necessary. In the second tale the later versions completely omitted the passage stating that the treasure-trove was undivided among the finders, as this fact was entirely insignificant for the contents of the tale.

Another good example may be found in the tale of the cat as judge between the partridge and the hare. The older versions were unclear and illogical as to the legal rules contained in this tale, but the later versions tried to remove all the inconsequences and doubts by interpolating some additional explanations.

On the basis of the legal interpretation of the Pañc. we can also show in some cases,—if not in what manner the Pañc. might be reconstructed, then in any case negatively,—in which way the Pañc. should not be reconstructed.[349] We find the best example for this statement in the tale of the mouse-maiden who was to wed a mouse, with reference to the reconstruction of the words *vṛsalī* or *vṛṣalau*.

52. It was mentioned before, in the introductory notes, that we could read the Pañc. from various points of view. In this study the tales were interpreted from the point of view of the *Smṛti-s*[350] and it seems that the juridical problems raised in the Pañc. offered a splendied picture of the real application of legal rules from the *Smṛti-s* in daily life. It is clear that only the most popular and most common cases were mentioned, but these were most easily and most frequently subjected to changes, as life was stronger than legal rules. The Pañc. interpreted from the point of view of *Smṛti-s* shows that the legal problems raised and solved there did not change the legal rules as they were worded in the *Smṛti-s* and that they were applied in daily life. Therefore, it can be stated that the Pañc. mirrored legal rules contained in the *Smṛti-s* and proved that these rules were not dead letters, but were applied in daily life also.

349. It must be noted that sometimes some versions of Pañc. referred to the *Smṛti-s* though the rules quoted there could not be found there. See Chapter 12.

350. It would be perhaps, constructive and interesting to read the Pañc. from the point of view of the *Arthaśāstra-s* and *Kāmasūtra-s*. The Pañc. contained many quotations from K. and some from Kām.

XX
THE TALE OF THE GULLIBLE HUSBAND AND HIS CUNNING WIFE*

I THE TALE OF THE GULLIBLE HUSBAND AND HIS CUNNING WIFE IN DIFFERENT SANSKRIT AND OTHER SOURCES

1. The story of the gullible husband and his cunning wife was well-known in the classical Sanskrit literature. We find it in Pañc.[1] in H.,[2] in KB.,[3] in SK.,[4] in S.,[5] and in TN.[6] It spread westward and can be found in KD.,[7] in AiS.,[8] in SVez.[9] in Tṭ.[10] and even in modern tales in Romanian Transylvania and in the Slovak part of northern Hungary.[11]

The story has two main versions which may be called the *textus simplicior* and the *textus ornatior*.

2. *Textus Simplicior Version*

A. According to the *textus simplicior* a husband, usually a carpenter, had an unchaste wife. Not being sure whether she was faithful to him he has told her that he was going away to

* Previously appeared at JSAIL 23 in the "Annals of the Bhandarkar Oriental Research Institute" Vol. XXXIV, pp. 128-65.

1. In various versions (Pts. 4.7, PtsK. 3.11, Ptsh. 4.6, PT. 3.8, PP. 3.12 PRE. 3.8, PN. 3.8, PM. 4.9, PSo. 3.8, PX. 3.16).
2. In various versions (HJ. 3.7, HK. 3.6, HM.3.6, HP. p. 96, HS. 3.6)
3. 16.491 sqq.
4. 10.62, 104 sqq.
5. In various versions (Śto. 38 and 41, Śts. 24, ŚtsA. 26, ŚtsM. 24).
6. 41.
7. 3.7. For various versions (Syrian, Hebrew, Greek, Spanish and others) cf. PB. 1.371. Also see I. Guidi, Studii sul testo arabo del libro di Calila e Dimna, Roma 1872, 54 sqq.
8. 4.10.
9. CB. 8.174, No. 197.
10. 26. (3.7). For various version (Persian, Turkish, Malaian) cf. JHP. p. 14; W. Pertsch, Über Nachschabī's Papageinbuch (ZDMG. 21.533 sqq.; twenty ninth night) and Ṭūṭīnāmah, Das Papageienbuch (Eine Sammlung orientalischer Erzählungen nach dur türkishchen Bearbeitung zum ersten Male übersetzt von. G. ROSEN Leipzing 1858; twenty eighth night. 2.202).
11. Heinrich V. Wlislocki, Beiträge zu Benfey's Pantschatantra in ZDMG. 42. 113 sqq. The Slovak version was recorded in Henzlova, Gömörer Comitat.

another village. He really went away but returned, stole into his own house and hid under bed. In the meantime his wife has sent for her paramour. When she went to bed with her paramour, she lightly touched the body of her husband hidden under the bed and immediately guessed that her husband was testing her. Then her paramour asked her whom she loved more—him or her husband. She replied with indignation that though women were light-minded they loved their husbands best; for the sake of her husband she would surrender her life. When the husband heard this statement he came out from under the bed convinced of his wife's devotion to him and lifted both, i.e., his wife and her paramour and carried them about joyfully while all the people laughed at him.

We find this *textus simplicior* in PRE. (3.8) PT. (3.8), PSo. (3.8), HJ. (3.7), HK. (3.6), HL. (78.10), HS. (3.6), HP. (96.12), HM. (3.6), SK. (10.62, 104 sqq.), KB. (28; XVI. 489), Śts. (24), ŚtsM. (24), Śto. (38), KD. (3.7, p. 240), AiS. (4.10), SVez. (in CB. 8.174, No. 197).

B. The different sources were not completely identical. Some texts added either that the husband before leaving home asked his wife to make ready provision for a few days, and to lock the door; or that the wife summoned her paramour through a go-between; or that she touched her husband's knee or foot; H. quoted several aphorisms very loosely connected with the story itself, which show the fondness for wives to their husbands. All these additions were of no importance for the tale itself. However, some texts made important changes. Thus according to some (e. g. PP.), the husband when returning home, came with his apprentice and hid with him under the bed in order to have a witness of his wife's disloyalty.

C. When the wife discovered by chance that her husband was under the bed, then (*tato*) according to most Sanskrit sources, her lover asked her whom she loved more—him or her husband. This part of the story does not make sense, since it is difficult to understand why the lover should suddenly wish to know from the woman beside him whether she loved him better than her husband. The non-purely Indian versions, based on the *textus simplicior*, removed this illogicality by adding that the wife, became disconcerted and sought a way out of the almost impossible situation by asking the lover in a low voice to ask her whom she liked most-him or her husband. Only then her lover asked this unexpected question.

Ś. solved this question somewhat differently, in a less sophisticated way. The cuckold husband did not wait until his wife and her lover went to bed but seized her by her hair as soon as she entered the bedroom. The wife, seeking a way out of this awkward situation, said to her lover that she had told him before that her husband was not at home but that when he returned, he would return the money which he owed him; therefore he should rest assured that he would receive the money back. This version is found in Śts. and ŚtsM. In Śto. (38), which was nearer to the original story, the wife, when she noticed that her husband was under the bed, rose (on the bed) and then was seized by the hair, not by her husband but by her lover.

Ś. combined the two elements in the story of the gullible husband and his cunning wife, i.e. the trickish reply of the wife with her lifting by her husband. In Śts. and in Śts.M. the sly reply of the wife was much less convincing than in other versions, since the husband, irrespective of how gullible he was, would have to be utterly stupid to believe the cunning words of his wife caught *in flagranti*. According to Śts. and ŚtsM. the husband caught his wife before she gave her cunning reply, so it was evident that she knew already her husband's whereabouts, while in the other versions he might have been convinced that she did not know that he was around and therefore could easier believe her sly words. In Śto. this difficulty was removed because the wife could not have known that her husband was under the bed and therefore her reply was more credible. Therefore, from that point of view the story, as found in Śto., was nearer to the original, but on the other hand the second element, i.e. the lifting of the wife by her husband, has been twisted, since she was lifted, or caught by her hair, not by her husband but by her lover.

The latter element which, probably, could not be understood among non-Sanskrit speaking people was changed in KD., AiS. and SVez., based on Ś. In KD. and AiS. the husband, hearing the cunning words of his wife did not come out from under the bed but remained there until the next morning when he said that being restrained by a regard for her reputation, he had not called her visitor to account. In SVez. the cuckold husband even begged his wife's pardon and in AiS. he said he had to close his eyes to her failings and to fix his eyes on her merits.

3. *Textus Ornatior Version*

A. The *textus simplicior*, even in the most plausible versions, was not plausible at all, and the husband had to be very gullible, indeed, in order to believe the story of his cunning wife. On the other hand the *textus ornatior* seems to be much more plausible and more refined. It is found in Pts. (4.6), PtsK. (3.11), PP. (3.12), PM. (4.9), TN. (41), Śto. (41), Ṭṭ. (26), RT. and SH.

B. The story of the gullible husband and his cunning wife in the *textus ornatior* follows the *textus simplicior* until the moment when the wife has noted that her husband is hidden under the bed. Then the cunning wife thinks that she will give her husband "a taste of women's tricks." When her paramour became insistent she forbade him to touch her. Replying to his question as to her purpose in inviting him, she told him that she had gone to a goddess temple; there the goddess warned her that in six months her husband would die. When she asked the goddess for a remedy to make her husband live one hundred years, the goddess told her that if she would go to bed with another man and if she would embrace him, the death destined for her husband would pass on to him and her husband would live another hundred years. When the husband heard this story he came out from under the bed full of joy being convinced of the faithfulness of his wife. He embraced her and lifted her to his shoulder and in token of his gratitude to his wife's paramour who had "saved his life", forced him to mount his shoulder and then went dancing.

C. The different sources were not completely identical. In TN. the wife asked her paramour what he would do if her husband would come back, to which he replied : *sādhu-pūjayāmi*. This was probably the remains of a longer and more conciliatory speech.[12]

In Śto. (41) the wife did not go to the goddess's temple but had a dream; in that dream the goddess told her that she should invite a stranger and embrace him on the bed, but if he wished to have sexual intercourse with her, she should not allow him to

12. The Tantrākhyāna, a Collection of Indian Folklore from a unique Manuscript discovered in Nepal by C. Bendall in JRAS. NS, 20, 1888. 465 sqq.

touch her. By such an action, the life of her husband would be saved. But if the stranger should violate her then he would lose half of his life. Therefore, the cunning wife asked the stranger not to use force, the more so as she sacrificed herself for her husband and the more so as he would lose half of his life. She then asked the stranger to go away and threatened that otherwise she would shout loudly. When the gullible husband heard this he came out from under the bed and began to dance joyfully.

PM. introduced an additional element which added piquancy to the whole story. According to PM. the wife profited by her husband's stupidity and enjoyed her paramour after the husband turned her over to her paramour.[13]

The non-Indian version of the story of the gullible husband and his cunning wife followed the story of Śto. (41) and intelligently adapted it to the specific conditions existing in the place in which they were told. And so, for instance, according to Ṭṭ the wife saw in the dream an old man with a long beard; according to RT. the Virgin Mary and according to SH. St. Petrus.[14]

Ṭṭ. followed the story of Śto. (41) very closely[15], however RT. combined the elements found in Śto. (41) with those of PM.; there, the cunning wife having made sure that her husband could hear her, asked her paramour not to touch her, yet enjoyed his love; in addition the husband gave her to her paramour and asked him to have sexual intercourse with his wife, for which he paid him ten ducats; the paramour became afterwards a frequent guest of the cunning wife.

13. Cf. J. Hertel, Eine vierte Jaina-Recension des Pañcatantra in ZDMG., 57, 639 sqq.

14. In RT. the husband was hidden under the bed with his mother and the wife noted her frock under the bed. (Mothers-in-law are in Romanian folk-tales objects of derision).

The story in SH. had only few common elements with the tale of the gullible husband and his cunning wife, namely the dream, the hiding under the bed and the cunning explanation of the woman found on the bed with a stranger. The story ended differently; the woman was killed by the man whom she invited but with whom she had no sexual intercourse; this man was killed by her wooer who came out from under the bed. He in turn was executed; thus, her dream and St. Petrus's warning came true. Cf. H. V. Wlislocki, Beiträge zu Benfey's Pantschatantra in ZDMG. 42.113 sqq.

15. In Ṭṭ., similarly as in KD. and AiS, the husband remained under the bed until his wife fell asleep; then he sat at her bed and kissed her, being convinced that she was a very faithful wife.

4. *Relation between the Textus Simplicior and the Textus Ornatior*

A. The *textus ornatior* was much superior to the *textus simplicior*, since the story was more plausible there. In none of the versions of the *textus ornatior* was there any mention of the husband being aware that his wife's explanation given to the lover was caused by the fact that she had found out his presence under the bed. The goddess's warning seems to be more plausible than the sudden question of the wife's paramour as to whom she loved more. Particularly the wife's explanation seemed to be plausible, if she had no sexual intercourse with the man whom she invited, as told in Śto. (41). Therefore, the version, as we find it in Śto. seems to be the best one, though Hertel thought that the PM. version was preferable, since there the husband was saved, according to the goddess's warning, only through sexual intercourse; in PM. and in some versions of PP.[16] sexual intercourse really took place while in others it did not.[17] This understanding would be valid if the goddess's warning would necessarily contain the requirement to have sexual intercourse with a stranger, but Śto. (41) did not contain this requirement; on the contrary the goddess, according to Śto. (41), warned the wife not to allow herself to be touched by the stranger and added that if the stranger should violate her then he would loss half of his life. Therefore the wife asked the stranger to go away and warned him that if he did not go, she would shout loudly. Firstly, this explanation seems to be more plausible and, secondly, it seems that the husband would have to be very stupid to believe that, despite the warning of the goddess that the death destined for the husband would pass on to the stranger, the latter would have accepted such an explanation calmly and as stated in some versions (PP., PM.), would remain in the arms of the cunning wife. Certainly the story, as described there, was more spicy, but less plausible. RT., as stated above, contained also the additional element of adultery under the

16. Cf. J. Hertel, The Pañcatantra—text of Pūrṇabhadra, Critical introduction and list of variants, Cambridge, Mass. 1912. HOS. 12. 54-5; Das Pañcatantram (*textus ornatior*), eine alt-indische Sammlung zum ersten Male übersetzt von R. Schmidt, Leipzig 232. J. Hertel, Eine vierte Jaina Recension des Pañcatantra in ZDMG. 57. 639 sqq.

17. J. Hertel, Eine vierte Jaina Recension des Pañcattantra in ZDMG, 57.639 sqq.

eyes of the cuckold husband, but did not contain the warning to the stranger that death destined for her husband would pass on to him. Therefore the *textus ornatior* of the story of the gullible husband and his cunning wife, as narrated in RT., seems to be both logical and full of piquancy.

B. The two versions have many common points but in the main theme, viz. the explanation given by the cunning wife to her gullible husband, they differed greatly. It may be therefore argued that two different stories of a gullible husband and his cunning wife existed, the more so as we know other stories also in which the wife used cunning words in order to deceive her husband. This argument might be supported by the fact that in Śto. we find both versions i. e. the *textus simplicior* in the thirty-eighth and the *textus ornatior* in the forty-first tale.

II. THE TALE OF THE GULLIBLE HUSBAND AND HIS CUNNING WIFE IN THE HITOPADEŚA

5. H. contained the story of the gullible husband and his cunning wife in the shorter version (*textus simplicior*). H. added several aphorisms in the body of the tale which, as was usual for H., were often loosely connected with the story itself. In H. the cunning wife, replying to the question put by her paramour as to why she did not want to spend the night with him, said that her heart was breaking at thinking about what might happen in the village, a strange place to her husband, if he came there; of what he has had to eat; or how he would be lodged. When her paramour wondered about her sudden affection towards her husband, the cunning wife cited the following three aphorisms—

puruṣeṇā'pi[18] *co'ktā yā*[19] *dṛṣṭā vā*[20] [21]*kruddha-cakṣuṣā,*
[22]*suprasanna-mukhī*[23]*bhartuḥ sā nārī dharma-bhāginī*[24]. (HJ 3.27)

[Virtuous (is) that woman, who, when roughly spoken to, or viewed with a scowling eye, maintains a very placid countenance toward (her) husband].[25]

18. *puruṣaṇy api* HS., HP. HN. HK.
19. *co*° (*pro*°) *yā* tr. HM.; *yā proktā* HSer.
20. *yā* HM, HK.
21. *krodha*° HS., HM., *kuddha*° HK.
22. *yāpra*° HL.
23. °*mukhī* HPet.
24. °*bhājan* HPet., HP., HK., (or better °*bhāgiṇī*).
25. According to F. Johnson's translation.

nagarastho vanastho vā pāpo vā yadi vā śuciḥ,[26]
yāsāṁ strīṇāṁ priyo bhartā tāsāṁ lokā[27] *mahodayāḥ.*[28] (HJ.3.28)

[Realms of exalted bliss (are the portion) of those women whose husband (is) beloved, be he citizen or forester, sinner or saint].[29]

We find the same aphorism in VRK., R. 2, 117, 23 and in its v. l. in RG. where we read:

samastho viṣamastho vā pāpo vā yadi vā śuciḥ,
yāsāṁ strīṇāṁ priyo bhartā tāsāṁ lokā mahodayāḥ (RG. 3.2,22)

The third aphorism quoted by the cunning wife was:

bhartā hi paramaṁ nāryā[30] *bhūṣaṇaṁ bhūṣaṇair-vinā,*
eṣā[31] *virahitā tena śobhanā'pi*[32] *na śobhate*[33]. (HJ. 3.29)

[For, a husband (is) a wife's chiefest ornament, without (other) ornaments. Deprived of him, she shineth not, although adorned].[34]

6. We find the same aphorism in MBh. (3.38, 18b19a-) After having quoted the three above cited aphorisms, the wife said that she occasionally made use of a paramour in the same way, as if she would make use of a betel-leaf, flower or perfumes, but that her legal husband was her master. As such, he was free to sell her or to give her away to the gods or the Brāhmaṇas. She was living in him and followed him in death[35]. This statement allowed the author of H. to add, in the body of the story of the gullible husband and his cunning wife, three aphorisms losely connected with the story itself, glorifying the *sati*.

The first of these aphorisms reads :

26. *śubhaḥ* VRK. 2.117,23.
27. *loke* HL., A in HP., B in HP.
28. *sukhodayaḥ* HL; *mahodayaḥ* A in HP., *mahotsavaḥ* B in HP.
29. According to F. Johnson's translation.
30. *strīṇāṁ* HS; *nāryaḥ* edd. in HS.
31. *hi rahitā* HPet., HP; *sahita* N in HP.
32. *sobhitā'pi* HS.
33. *śobhanā* edd. in HS., N. in HP., HM., HK.
34. According to J. Johnson's translation. This *śloka* meant that the husband was the most precious ornament of the wife, even if she would be deprived of other ornaments; because the wife without a husband, even if she would be decorated with ornaments would be without grace.
35. In HS. and in HL. this idea was expressed in the following aphorism.

tasmin jīvati jīvāmi mṛte tasmin mriye punaḥ,
tan maraṇe'numaraṇam eṣa me dṛḍha-niścayaḥ. (HS. 3.28; HL. 79.5-6).

[36]*tisraḥ* [37]*koṭyo'rdha-koṭi ca*[38], *yāni*[39] *lomāni*[40] *mānave.*[41]
tāvad varṣaṁ[42] *vaset*[43] *svarge*[44], *bhartāraṁ yā'nugacchati.*[45]

[There grow upon a man alive
some thirty million hairs and five;
So many years in heaven spend
wives following husbands to the end[46]].

This aphorism is also found in PP. (3.164). PtsK (3.186), VCsr (30.5) and PŚ (608)[47] as well as in Aṅg. and Śaṅkha in Mit. (Śaṅkha-Likhita in Mit. Vij.) *ad* Y. I. 86, Vivā, 287 and VJT. 24.

The second of these aphorisms reads :

vyālagrāhī yathā vyālaṁ[48] *vilād uddharate balāt*[49],
[50]*tadvadbhartāram ādāya* [51]*tenaiva saha modate.* (HJ. 3.32).

[As a snake-catcher by force draws up a serpent from (its) hole, in the same manner shall she, taking (her) husband enjoy felicity with him].[52]

This aphorism is also found in VCsr (30.6), in Vyāsa quoted in Apar. (110. 23-3), in Mit. (Vij.) *ad* Y. 1.87 and in VR. (442); its first two *pāda-s* are found in Brahmavaivarta-purāṇa

36. *narāṇāṁ sordhako'tiś ca* Q in VCsr.

37. or wrongly *tisraḥ*.

38. *ko'ṭyarddha koṭī ca* HL., Q. in VCsr.; ⁰*koṭiś* Nd. in VCsr; *koṭyaś* M. in VCsr. *kodyordhakoṭiś* ca HP; *koṭyordhakāṭiś* ca PŚ; *koṭyadurdakoṭī ca* HScr.

39. *yāvana* Pr. in PP. PŚ.

40. *romāṇi* HP., PP., PtsK., VCsr.

41. *mānuṣe* Pr in PP., PŚ.; *mānadhe* V. in VCsr. Mit.

42. *tavat kāle* ŚL in Viv.; *tāvat kālaṁ* Mit., HS., HP., HM., HK., PP., PtsK., VCsr., PS; *tāvan kālam* (or *tāvān*) PL. in PP.

43. *tāvanty abdāni sā* VR.

44. *svargaṁ* HP., Nd., Q. in VCsr.

45. ⁰*gacchati* HS.; ⁰*nuyāsyati* M., Nd. Q. in VCsr.

46. According to A. Ryder's translation in "The Pancatantra", University of Chicago Press, 340.

47. Also quoted in "Andjira", according to M. Abel-Remusat in Mélanges Asiatiques, on choix de morceaux de critique et de mémoires—Paris 1825, I, 393.

48. ⁰*bilād*⁰ HP., PŚ.; ⁰*bilāt* T in VCsr; *balād*⁰ N. in HP., *bilād* HM, VCsr; *balāt* tr. N., Q in VCsr; *bilād gṛhṇātyaśaṅkitaḥ* Vy. in Apar. and VR.

49. *bilāt* HS., N.in HP., HM.; *bilāt* HK., VCsr.

50. *tathā strī patim uddhṛtya* VCsr.

51. *svargaloke mahīyate* HS., HM., *te*⁰ *sa*⁰ tr. VCsr.; *divaṁ yāti tapobalāt* Vy. in Apar. and VR.

52. According to F. Johnson's translation.

3.28.6),[53] in Skanda-purāṇa, Kāśikhaṇḍa (57) and in PŚ; (609) its first *pāda* is also found in Skanda-purāṇa, Kāśikhaṇḍa (45.7).[54]

The third of these aphorisms, which is not found in HP., reads :

citau pariṣvajya vicetanaṁ[55] *patiṁ*
priyā hi yā muñcati[56] *deham ātmanaḥ,*
hatvā'pi[57] *pāpaṁ* [58]*śatalakṣam apy asau*
patiṁ gṛhītvā suralokam āpnuyāt. (HJ. 3.32)

[The loving one who, embracing (her) lifeless husband, resigns her own body on the pyre: she having effaced a hundred thousand sins, a hundred times told (and) taking (her) husband shall obtain a mansion among the gods].[59]

Aphorisms which glorified the *sati* were very common in Sanskrit classical literature and the first two quoted above were very well-known. Even the legal Sanskrit literature contained many aphorisms relating to *satī*; out of the three aphorisms quoted in the story of the gullible husband and his cunning wife, two were quoted by the commentators on the Smṛti-s, and the commentaries of Mit. and Vīr. on Y. (1.86) contained a long list of rules praising and criticising the custom of *satī.* VCsr (30), in the story of the clever mountebank, first quoted seven aphorisms dealing with the custom of *satī* (among them also the two quoted in H.) and dealing with the sad plight of a widow. In the tale of the clever mountebank these aphorisms followed logically the story itself, since it was based on the wish of a young woman who lost her husband on the battlefield to enter the fire. But there was no reason for the author of H. to include in the story of the gullible husband and his cunning wife the three aphorisms quoted above, save that his aim in writing the Hitopadeśa was to include as many aphorisms as possible. It was even less logical to include in the story the last aphorism.

53. In Ān. S.S. 102, Vol. I (b) *bilā*; *balātū* probably mistakenly for *balāt*.

54. °*grāhiṇyabhūt kacit*. Cf. Halāyuddha's Abhidhānaratnamālā ed. Th. Aufrecht. 1861; 351.

55. *vicetanaṁ* HS., HM., HK.

56. *muṁciti* HM.

57. *kṛtāti* HS. ; *kṛtvā'pi* HM., HK.

58. *śatasaṁkhyaṁ* HM., HK.,

59. According to F. Johnson's translation.

7. This last aphorism quoted in H.'s version of the tale of the gullible and his cunning wife reads :

yasmai dadyāt pitā tvenāṁ[60] *bhrātā cānumate:*[61] *pituḥ,*
[62]*taṁ* [63]*śuśrūṣeta jivantaṁ*[64] *saṁsthitaṁ ca na*[65] *laṅghayet*[66]. (HJ. 3.33)

[Him, to whom her father may give her, or her brother with the paternal consent, she should be obedient to while he lives and after his death shall never disregard him].

This verse is found only in two main editions of H. viz. in HJ., and HL. and was taken from the Smṛti-s viz. from Mn. (5.149).[67] Mn. (5.149) was also quoted in SC., VK., MR. in VyS.[68]

8. *Duty of giving the Girl in Marriage*

A. The main thought of Mn. (5.149) was the description of the duties of the wife towards her husband, but Mn. added in this *śloka*, as if in parenthesis, another thought, viz. who was responsible for giving a girl away in marriage. The reply to this latter question was : it was the father or her brother with paternal consent. The same thought was also expressed in N. Even the same words were used there.[69] However N. dealt only with the question of who was responsible for giving a girl away in marriage. This question was solved not only in N. but also in Y. and Vi., but was conspicuously missing in Mn. with the only exception mentioned above in Mn. (5.149). The of order persons who were responsible for giving away marriageable girls was as follows :

60. *vaināṁ* VK.; *pyenāṁ* SCŚ; *pi*⁰ *tve*⁰ tr. MnM.
61. *yā'numate* Mn., VK. v. l. ⁰*numataḥ* Mn.; *calumatum* SCŚ.
62. *śuśrūj jīvitaṁ hi taṁ vṛttaṁ cā'nuśayed iti* HL.
63. *tūṁ* SCGh.
64. *duṣthitaṁ* SCGh.
65. *ca na* tr. Gov., Kash.
66. *laṁghayet* MnH., MnL.
67, MnJh. 5.149, MnJ. 5.151, MnK. 5.151, MnH. 5.151, MnL. 5.151, MnM. 5.151. Cf. MnJh. 9.153. (Kāty. 835, Dev. in VR. 1245) and Y. 1. 63-4, 77 and 83, No. 12. 20-2, Vi. 24. 38-40, 25.15.
68. VK. 579, SCGh. 251, SCŚ. 7.223.
69. N. 12.20 second *pāda* (*bhratā yā'numate pituḥ*). *Cf.* NMS. 13.20.

Mn.[70]	N.[71]	Y.[72]	Vi.[73]
Father	Father	Father	Father
		Paternal grand-father (*pitāmaha*)	Paternal grand-father (*pitāmaha*)
Brother (with the father's consent *anumate pituḥ*)	Brother (with the father's consent *anumate pituḥ*)	Brother	Brother
	Maternal grand-father[74] (*mātāmaha*)		
	Maternal uncle (*mātula*)		
Further details not available	*Sakulya*	*Sakulya*	*Sakulya*
			Maternal grand-father (*mātāmaha*)
	Bāndhava		
	Mother (if she was competent	Mother	Mother
	King		
	Svayaṁvara[75]	*Svayaṁvara*[75]	*Svayaṁvara*[75]

B. It seems that in Mn., as well as in N., the brother of the girl could have given her in marriage when the father was alive, since it was stated in both these Smṛti-s that this choice

70. Mn. 5.149.
71. N. 12. 20-2.
72. Y. 1.63-4.
73. Vi. 24. 38-40.
74. According to NMS. in N. Jolly also mentioned that the Nepalese MS. had in the text the paternal grandfather (*pitāmaha*). This does not seem to be correct. The commentator of NMS. stated : *tad abhāve mātāmahaḥ, tato mātulaḥ.*
75. Cf. above Study XI on Forms of Marriage in Ancient India and their Development, par. 56 sqq. and P.V. Kane, History of Dharmaśāstra, Vol. II. p. 1, p. 501.

could have been made with the father's consent and this consent should be given during his lifetime. Medh.[76] and Sarvajñanārāyaṇa[77] commented on this part of Mn.'s *śloka*, but were not convincing, since no reason is seen for introducing the mother as co-responsible with the father for marrying their daughter, especially in view of the fact that in Y., N. and Vi. she was at the bottom of the list of those who were responsible for giving away marriageable girls. This part of the *śloka* could, however, mean that the father wanted to pass by the paternal grandfather as long as he was alive and consented that after his death his son, who was in any case his successor, should replace his paternal grandfather, as provided for in Y. and Vi. This interpretation elucidates the difficult understanding of the words *anumate pituḥ*; no reason for permission seems to be needed for the brother to give his sister in marriage unless a special reason existed for the father to give such permission during his lifetime, as for instance when, due to some kind of intervention, he was unable to give his daughter in marriage and then asked his son to act on his behalf.

9. *Description of the Duties of the Wife towards her Husband*

A. The description of the duties of the wife towards her husband is found in the second part of the *śloka* which contained two different rules. The first referred to the duty of the wife to obey her husband during his lifetime and the second to her duty not to disregard the husband after his death.

Rules relating to duties of a wife were found in almost all Smṛti-s and *nibandha-s* and also in epics, Puraṇa-s and other sources in classical Sanskrit.[78] The first of these duties mentioned in the *śloka* in question was very often repeated while the second was rather rare.

76. *bhrātā vā'numate pituḥ: yathaiva pitrā'nujñātasya bhrātur dātṛtvam evaṁ pitur nirapekṣasyā'pi datṛtva śrutau bhāryāyā anumate sati dānaṁ boddhavyam; sarvatra sahādhikārād ubhayoś ca duhitari svāmyāt; asati pitari mātrā'pi deyeti navame darśitam; mātrā-pitror-apatyaṁ tan nimittaṁ ca svāmyām iti yuktā itaretarāpekṣā* (*ad* MnJh. 5.149).

77. *bhrātā-veti-dānādhikāry-anraro'palakṣaṇam* (*ad* MnM 5.151)

78. Cf. P.V. Kane, History of Dharmaśāstra, Vol. II, p. 1, p. 561 sqq.

10. *Duty of the Wife to Obey her Husband*

A. The duty of a wife to obey her husband during his lifetime was expressed in Mn. (5.149) as follows : *taṁ śuśrūtṣeta jīvantaṁ*. Medh. explained that the duty to obey (*śuśrūṣeta*) was equal to the duty to serve (*ārādhayet*). Mn. in 5.153b repeated this rule in other words, saying *patiṁ śuśrūṣate yena*[79] *tena svarge mahīyate*[80] [it is by obeying her husband that she (the wife) will be exalted in heaven]. Medh. also explained that to obey was equal to serving[81]. Vi. (25.15b) used the same language as Mn. (9.153 b).[82]

(Also Y.[83] stated : *strībhir bhartṛ-vacaḥ kāryam eṣa dharmaḥ paraḥ striyāḥ*...observe the husband's word; this is the highest duty of women).[84] In other words, according to Y., to obey the husband was the highest duty of wives. Y. used in 1.77. the words *bhārtṛ-vacaḥ kāryam* and again in 183 stated that the wife should show to her husband her obedience (*bhartṛ-tat-parā*). Mit. explained (*bhartṛ-tat-parā*) as meaning acting on demand of her husband[85] and Vir. explained that *bhartṛ-tat-parā* meant obeying or serving the husband.[86]

Also Kāty. (835)[87] and Devala in VR. (1245)[88] mentioned as the duty of the wife her *obligation* to obey her husband. Both Kāty. and Dev. used the word *śuśrūṣā* for denoting obedience towards the husband.

B. The Sanskrit classical literature contained many instances where the duty of wives to obey their husbands was men-

79. *yat tu* Vi. SCGh.

80. Also quoted in Vi. 25.15, SCGh. 252.10, VyK. 135, VyS. 124, VBh. 21.

81. Or worship; *śuśrūṣate, paricarati*.

82. Vi. has *yat tu* instead of *yena*.

83. Y. 1.77 (a).

84. Also quoted to SCGh 251, VyM. 108, MR. 135, ViR. 1.76, VyS 124, VivT. 823.

85. *bhartṛ-tat-parā bhartṛ-vaśavartinī satī pūrvoktaṁ kuryāt.* (Mit. *ad* Y.1.83).

86. *bhatṛ-tat-parā bhartṛ-śuśrūṣaṇādi-śīlā.* (Vīr. *ad* Y.1.83).

87. *patyā cā'py aviyoginyā śuśrūṣyo'gnir-vinītayā,*
saubhāgyavad-avaidhavya-kāmyayā bhartṛ-bhaktayā. (Kāty. 835).

88. *asvātantryaṁ, pati śuśrūṣā, sahadharma-caryā, tat pūjya-pūjanam, para-veśmā-gamanaṁ, tad dveṣyamāṇa-dveṣaṇaṁ, aduṣṭā bhāvanā, nityā'nukālyaṁ, tat kārya-paratvam iti strī-dharmaḥ.* (VR. 1245).

tioned. Thus, in R.[89], Rāma addressed his mother Kausalyā saying that wives must obey their husbands and that by obeying their husbands they would win heaven. This part of Rāma's address was almost identical with the statement found in Mn. (9.153b). In the next *śloka* Rāma referred to Mn. since he stated that obedience of the husband was an eternal law for wives, already established in the Vedas and the Smṛti-s.

We also find in two place in MBh. a statement that by obeying their husbands wives could win heaven.[90] Similar were some *śloka-s* found in MP.[91] and in SRBh.[92] MP. added that women by obedience to their husbands obtained half of the entire merit painfully earned by their husbands and that the wives, minds should always be turned towards obedience to their husbands.[93] Similar were also the statements found in the Brāhmadharma, according to which those women were real wives who, in their

89. *vrato pavāsa niratā yā nārī paramo'ttama,*
bhartāraṁ nānuvarteta sā ca pāpagatir bhavet.
bhartuḥ śuśrūṣayā nārī labhate svargam uttamam,
api yā nirnamaskārā nivṛttā devā-pūjanāt.
śuśrūṣam eva kurvīta bhartuḥ priyahite ratā,
eṣa dharmaḥ striyā nityo vede loke śrutaḥ smṛtaḥ. (R. 2.24, 25b-28a).

90. *naiva yajñakriyāḥ kāścin na śraddhaṁ no'pavāsakam,*
yā tu bharttari śuśrūṣā tayā svargaṁ jayaty uta. (MBh. 3.204, 22b-23a).
nā'sti yajñakriyā kācin na śrāddhaṁ no'pavāsakam,
dharmaḥ sva-bhartṛ-śuśrūṣā tayā svargaṁ jayanty uta. (MBh. 13.46, 13).
Also found with variations in ŚP. 606. SRBh. 156.142 and other *subhāṣita-saṁgraha-s.*

91. *nā'sti strīṇāṁ pṛthag yajño na śrāddaṁ nā'py upoṣitam,*
bhartṛ-śuśrūṣa-yaivaitān lokāniṣṭān vrajanti hi. (MP. 16.61)

92. *yasya putro vaśībhūto bhāryā chāndānugāminī,*
vibhave yaś ca saṁtuṣṭastasya svarga ihaiva hi. (Pras. 14. Also found in CVND. 2.3, CVM. 2.2, CvA. 2.3, CvṢ. 2.3' CvW. 2.3, CvP. IV. 2.3, CvP V. 2.3, CvGt. 2.3., CvTb. 2.3, CvH. 2.3, Cvī. 2.3, CvL. I 2.3, CvL II. 2.3, CvLd. 2.3, CSBD. 191, CSB. I.2.92, CSJ. 2.97, CSC. I.2.91, CSC II.191, CSB II. 191, CSLd. 2.90, CNPN. 23, CNI I.62, CnT. II. 2.10, CnT. III. 2.2, CnT. VII. 23, Ŝto. 325.28-9, SRBh. 498, 489, SRHt. 191. 47, Subhāṣitārṇava in IS.

93. *striyas tv evaṁ samas tasya narair duḥkhārjitasya vai,*
puṇyasyā'rdhāpahāriṇyaḥ pati-śuśrūṣayaiva hi. (MP. 16.60)
tasmāt sādhvi mahābhāge pati-śuśrūṣaṇaṁ prati,
tvayā matiḥ sadā kāryā yato bhartā parā gatiḥ (MP. 16.62).
yad devebhyo yac ca pitrā-gatebhyaḥ kuryād bharttā'bhyarccanaṁ sat kriyātaḥ,
tasyā'py arddhaṁ kevalān anyacittā nārī bhuṅkte bhartṛ-śuśrūṣa-yaiva.
(MP.16. 63).

words and actions were pure and who obeyed their husbands,[94] or in MBh. according to which the strength of women laid in obedience.[95] Other aphorisms stated, for instance that obedient wives were a real treasure[96] or that in a country without a king there was no order and peace and even students did not obey their *guru* nor sons their fathers, nor wives their husbands.[97]

11. *Duty of the Wife not to Disregard her Husband after his Death*

A. The second duty of the wife towards her husband contained in Mn. (5.149), was not to disregard her husband after his death. This duty cannot be often found in this form in the Smṛti-s or in the classical Sanskrit literature. This duty of the wife was expressed in Mn. (5.149) as follows: *saṁsthitaṁ ca na laṅghayet.* Kull. explained this expression as *vyabhicāreṇa tadīya-śrāddha-tarpaṇādi-virahitaya pāra-laukika-kṛtya khaṇḍanena ca.* Other commentators gave similar explanations.[98] On the other hand Medh. stated : *laṅghanam atikramaṇam; na svātantryeṇā-sītety arthaḥ; yathā jīvati bhartari tat paravatī evaṁ mṛte'pi tadaiva tat paratantrayā bhavitavyaṁ; yata āha—"pradānaṁ svāmya kārakam." tadaiva pitrā dattā tadaiva pituḥ svāmyaṁ nivartate yasmai dīyate tasyo'tpadyate; ataś ca na vivāha-kāla eva dānaṁ prāg api vivāhād-varaṛakāle, asti dānam.*

Both commentators seem to be right when they said that not disregarding the husband after his death meant not acting in

94. *sā bhāryā yā patiprāṇā sā bhāryā yā prājāvatī,*
manovāk karmabhiḥ śuddhā pati-deśā 'nuvartinī (better *patyādeśa*)
(BrDh. 2.2, 7).

95. *hiṁsā balam asādhūnāṁ rājñāṁ daṇḍa-viddhir balam,*
śuśrūṣā tu balaṁ strīṇāṁ kṣamā guṇavatāṁ balam. (MBh. 5.33, 74).

96. *yā tu bhāryā surūpaiva bhartāram anugāminī,*
nityaṁ madhurabhāṣitrī sā śrīyo na śriyaḥ śriyaḥ (CvP. IV. 7.3. Also CvP. V. 7.3, CvTb. 7.4, CvL. I. 7.7, CSBD. 183, CSB I. 2.84, CSJ. 2.82, CSC I. 2.83, CSC II. 183, CSB II. 182, CSLd. 2.82, CNG. 16, CnT. V.55 and many similar aphorisms in C.)

97. *nārājake janapade bījamuṣṭiḥ prakīryate,*
nārajake pituḥ putro bhāryā vā vartate vaśe. (R.2.67, 10).
nārājake patim bhāryā yathāvad anutiṣṭhati,
nārājake guroḥ śiṣyaḥ śṛṇoti nivataṁ hitam (RG. 2.69,10).

98. Rāmacandra : *saṁsthitaṁ mṛtaṁ tat karma na laṅghayet na vyabhicaret.*
Nandana : *saṁsthitaṁ ca na laṅghayet : mṛte patyau puruṣā'nṭaraṁ na bhuñjed ity arthaḥ.* Cf. also Sarvajñanārāyaṇa : *taṁ saṁsthitaṁ mṛtaṁ ca na laṅghayan na vyabhicaret.*

an imprudent way and not to neglect to prepare the necessary oblations as well as not to behave as if the wife were her own mistress. Medh. was right in saying that disregarding meant not minding; however his further explanation that the wife should remain subservient to her deceased husband (since she, by the fact of being given away by her father, came under his ownership and remained so after his death) are not convincing. This explanation is not contradicted by stipulations contained in Mn. (9.3 and 5.146)[99] according to which woman were subject to their fathers in childhood, to their husbands in youth, but to their sons after their husbands' death, since they could never be independent. They, therefore, after the death of their husbands came under ownership of their sons.

B. The same explanation, as found in the interpretations given by the commentators of Mn., relating to the wife's behaviour after the death of her husband can be found in Mn. as well as in other Smṛti-s Mn. stated that wives, even after the death of their husbands, should never do anything that might displease their husbands,[100] that is, that widows should be strict in their conduct ; freedom of life was thus forhidden to them.[101] Mn. also stated that widows should be abstinent and emaciate their bodies by living on pure flowers, roots and fruit and under no circumstances mention the name of another man i.e. live with another man.[102] In particular widows should be patient (that, is control

99. *pitā rakṣati kaumāre bhartā rakṣati yauvane,*
rakṣanti sthavire putrā na strī svātantryam arhati. (Mn. 9.3).
bālye pitur vaśe tiṣṭhet pāṇigrāhasya yauvane,
putrāṇaṁ bhartari prete na bhajet strī svatantratām. (Mn. 5.146. In other editions 5.148).

Mn. 9.3 was also quoted in SCGh. 240, VR. 119, BBh. 2.135, 2.295, SCi. 27, VyP. 406, VyK. 128, VBh. 2.53, VyS. 120, Vivā. 281, U. 2.14, 2, GMit. 28. Similarly MBh. 13.20, 21, Vās. 5.3, VRK. 2.29, 18- N. 13.31, NMS. 14.31, B. 2.2, 3, 45, Apar. *ad* Y. 2.124, DBh. 209, Viv. 2.136, VyP. 529, VivT. 334.

Mn. 5.146 was also quoted in Maskari Bhāṣya on G. 18.1, GMit. 18. 1. SC. 249, VR. 1239, VyK. 133, VivT. 17, VyṢ. 123.

100. *pāṇigrāhasya sādhvī strī jīvato vā mṛtasya vā*
pāṇigrāhasya sādhvī strī jīvato vā mṛtasya va,
patilokam abhipsantī nācaret kiṁcid apriyam. (Mn. 5.154). Also quoted in MR. 135, VyK. 136, VivT. 21.

101. *na hi mṛtasya kiṁ priyam apriyaṁ vā śakyam avasāṭum; na ca jīvato yat priyaṁ tad eva mṛtaṣya: bhavāntaro'papannānaṁ tu prītibhedāt; tasmād yat pratiṣiddhaṁ svātantryaṁ tad evāpriyam; tan nācaret.* (Medh. *ad* Mn. 5.154).

102. *kāmaṁ tu kṣauayed dehaṁ puṣpa-mūla phalaiḥ śubhaiḥ,*
na tu nāmā'pi gṛhṇīyāt patyau prete parasya tu. (Mn.5.155).

their passions, or not be disturbed by hardships),[103] self-controlled and chaste;[104] if they remained constantly chaste they were sure to go to heaven, even if they had no sons.[105] Thus Mn. stated that widows should remain chaste, not disturbed by passion, self-controlled, abstinent, not live freely and never do anything which, could displease their husbands if they were alive. Widows could emaciate their bodies but nowhere in Mn. was it stated that self-immolation was ordered or even recommended.

C. Constant chastity of widows was ordered in all the Smṛti-s which dealt with that subject. Y. stated that women should never have sexual intercourse with other men, irrespective of whether their husbands were alive or dead.[106] Vi. (26-17) used the same words as were used in Mn. (5.158) and also[107] prescribed chastity of widows. Bṛh.[108] and Śuk.[109] prescribed virtuous life for widows.[110] Hār., speaking about the duties of wives, stated that widows should remain chaste; their chastity cancelled all their sins and made it possible for them to join their husbands in heaven.[111] Also Yama prescribed chastity to widows and pious

Also quoted in Mit. *ad* Y. 2.127 and 2.290, VR. 1282, VyK. 138, VyK. 238, VyP. 472, Vivā. 288, VBh. 28, SV. 388.

103. *kṣāntā; tat kṛtaṁ duḥkham avadhīrayanti; na brahamacāryaṁ kṣudut kṛtyaṁ yena cittaṁ kallolena khaṇḍayet* (Medh. *ad.* Mn. 5.156).

104. *āsitā-maraṇāt kṣāntā ṇiyaṭa brahmacāriṇi,*
yo dharma eka-patnīnāṁ kāmkṣanti tam anuttaman. Mn. 5.156.

Also quoted in Mit. *ad* Y. 2. 127. VR. 1282, VyS. 138, VyK, 238, VyP. 472, Vivā. 288, VBh. 38.

105. *mṛte bhartari sādhvī strī brahmacarye vyavasthitā,*
svargaṁ gacchaty aputrā'pi yathā te brahmacāriṇaḥ. (Mn. 5.158. Also quoted in Mit. *ad* Y. 2.127, VR. 1282, SCGh. 254, VyK. 238, VyP. 472, VyS. 125, VBh. 28. V. 1. of the first two *pāda-s* is found in VivT. 393.)

106. *mṛte jīvati vā patyau yā nā'nyam upagacchati,*
sena kīrtim avāpnoti modate comayā saha (Y. 1.75. Also quoted in Mit. Apar, ViR. *ad* Y. 1.75, VyK. 136).

107. *mṛte bhartari brahmacaryāṁ tad anvārdhaṇam vā.* (Vi. 25.14).

108. *anvārūḍhā jīvatī* (*°ntī*) *ca sādhvī bhartur-hitāya sā.* (Bṛh. 25.14, *cd.* Also quoted in Apar. *ad* Y. 1.87, VyK. 137, VBh. 27).

109. *mṛte bhartari saṅgacched bhartur vā pālayed vratam,*
paraveśma-rucir na syād brahmacarye sthitā satī,
maṇḍanaṁ varjayen nityaṁ tathā proṣita-bhartṛkā. (Śuk. 4.4, 28-9).

110. Vi. and Bṛh are those few which mentioned self-immolation. Śuk. also mentioned self-immolation. Medh. *ad* Mn. 5.155 (strongly) objected to the practice of self-immolation.

111. *pativratā tu yā nārī niṣṭhaṁ yāti patau mṛte,*
sā hitvā sarva-pāpāni pati lokam avāpnayāt. (Hār. 3.9. Also quoted in VR. 1280, SCGh. 254, VyK. 137, VyS. 125, VBh. 28).

austerity;[112] similarly Kāty.[113] where chastity of widows and their celibacy was recommended.[114]

Similarly, as in Mn. the provision that widows should control their passions was also contained in Śuk.[115]

What "not neglecting to prepare the necessary oblations" meant (as the commentators of Mn. explained *ad* 5.140 by saying *saṁsthitaṁ ca na laṅghayet*) was explained in Hār.[116], Śuk.[117] and in an unidentified Smṛti quoted in the digest Vivādabhaṅgārṇava compiled by Jagannātha Tarkapañcānana of Triveṇi.[118] It meant burning of sacred fire (Hār.), making of offerings for the deceased husband daily with *kuśa*-grass, *tila* and water (VJT.), performing oblations, making gifts travelling to places of pilgrimage and repeatedly uttering the name of Viṣṇu (VJT.) controlling of the tongue, hands, feet, senses (Hār.), giving up daily ornamentation of the body (Śuk.), and perfuming (VJT.), fasting (Hār., VJT.), or preparing only one repast daily (VJT.), and not going to houses of others (Śuk).

12. *Interpretation of HJ.* 3.33

From the interpretation of the last *śloka* contained in the Hitopadeśa's story of the gullible husband and his cunning wife (HJ. 3.33), or rather from the interpretation of Mn. (5.149), which was the source for the *śloka* found in H., it is

112. *yāvajjīvaṁ sadāsīta niyatā brahmacāriṇī,*
yo dharma eka-patnīnāṁ taṁ dharmam anukāṅkṣatī...
aputrā jāta-putrā vā kanyā patim anuvratā,
prāpnuyāt svargaṁ eve'ti manuḥ svayambhuvo'bravīt. (Yama quoted in VR. 1283. Also quoted in VyK. 138, VBh. 28).

113. *mṛte bhartarī yā sādhvī brahmacarye vyavasthitā,*
sā'rundhatīsamācārā brahmaloke mahīyate. (Kāty. 837. Also quoted in SCGh. 254, VR. 1284, Vyā. 138, VyS. 125).

114. K., though preached celibacy of widows, gave detailed rules on disposition of property in case a widow remarried or did not remarry (K. 152. 12 sqq.).

115. Cf. fn. 3 above.

116. *āhitāgniś cet pramīyeta aupasanā'vakṣāṇagniṁ parigṛhya sarirājñībhir anusavanam iṣṭvā vaset anāhitāgniś ced anyam ādadhy ājjanāgniṁ vā parigṛhya bhartuḥ pituḥ svajana-gṛha-vasjaṁ ji ta-jihvā-hasta-pāde 'ndriyā svācāravatī divārātraṁ svabhartāram anuśocantī vratopayāsaih kṣāntā'yuṣo'nte patilokaṁ jayati sā bhūyaḥ patilokamāpnotī'ty evaṁ hy āha.* (Hār. 3.9).

117. Cf. fn. 3 109.

118. Book IV., ch. III., par. 135. Also quoted in VR. 1280, SCGh. 253-4, VyK. 137, VBh. 28, VyS. 125.

evident that : after the death of the father his son was responsible for giving the girl in marriage, and that after her marriage she came under the protection of her husband and had to obey him as long as he was alive and remain faithful to him after his death, as well as to prepare the necessary oblations for her deceased husband; since doing so she would not disregard her deceased husband.

This is a strange *śloka* ; it contained three completely different thoughts squeezed into one stanza. Almost all *Smṛti-s* contain the same thoughts but there they were more logically amplified; each of these thoughts was there described separately, while in Mn. they were scrambled together and the very important rule, viz., who was responsible for giving a girl in marriage, not found elsewhere in Mn., was mentioned in this *śloka* of Mn. as if in parenthesis. It is likely that this *śloka*, because of lack of clarity, was almost forgotten; it was even very rarely quoted in the *nibandha-s*,[119] As far as it could be ascertained, it was only quoted in H. and could not be found in other sources of classical Sanskrit literature, including the main Subhāṣita-saṅgraha-s. Why the author of H. had chosen this *śloka* of Mn. and included it in the story of the gullible husband and his cunning wife, is completely incomprehensible. The only explanation for including this *śloka* in H. was the wish of its author, or may be a scribe, to include as many aphorisms from well-known authors in the body of his work, though they were sometimes loosely connected with the story itself. In this case, in particular, no reason is seen for any use of including this *śloka* in the story.

When the cunning wife discovered that her husband was hidden under the bed, she, according to H., quoted several aphorisms which had to convey the principle that for wives the husband was the chief ornament and therefore they had to be faithful to him. Already the conception of self-immolation, mentioned in the story, was at least unnecessary, but the conceptions of who was responsible for giving the girl in marriage or of the duty of the wife to obey her husband during his lifetime and to remain faithful to him a f t e r (!) his death and to prepare oblations a f t e r (!) his death were completely out of

119. SCGh. 251, SCŚ.1, 123.

place. Moreover, the author of H. combined this *śloka*, taken from Mn., with three *śloka-s* on self-immolation, while Mn., did not mention self-immolation at all and according to some commentators on Mn. was not in favour of self-immolation. That is one more reason for considering that the inclusion of Mn. (5.149) was not only out of place but obviously the author's mistake. If the author of H. found it necessary to quote any *śloka* from Mn. in the tale of the gullible husband and his cunning wife, he could have chosen for instance Mn. 5.156[120] or 5.162[121] and 5.164[122], or 5.154[123] which were better connected with the main thought contained in the tale; but he should not have chosen Mn. 5.149 which was not only one of the poorest rules contained in Mn. and was not connected with the tale, but was ill-chosen, particularly since Mn. was opposed to self-immolation.

Such a thoughtless and ill-judged inclusion of unsuitable aphorisms into the body of H. was not unexpected and was not uncommon for the author (or authors) of H., but as far as the story of the gullible husband and his cunning wife was concerned, might not have been made by the author himself ; possibly this *śloka* was interpolated later by a scribe or "revisor" of H., since it was found only in HL., and HJ., and is not quoted in HP., HS., HM., HK., HPet. and HSer.

III. THE TALE OF THE GULLIBLE HUSBAND AND HIS CUNNING WIFE IN THE ŚUKASAPTATI (41)

13. Śto. (41) contained the story of the gullible husband and his cunning wife in the longer version (*textus ornatior*).[124] Śto. (41) added in the body of the tale one aphorism which could not be found in other sources containing this tale. This aphorism, though not taken verbally from the Smṛti-s, was based on them.

In Śto. (41) when the cunning wife had seen that her

120. Cf. fn. 102.

121. *vyabhicāre tu bhartuḥ strī loke prāpnoti nindyatām,*
sṛgāla-yonim prāpnoti pāparogaiś ca pīḍyate. (Mn. 5.162 and 9.30. Also quoted in VR. 1262, SCGh. 242, SCi. 28, VyK. 136, VyS. 121, VBh. 21).

122. *anena nārī vṛttena mano-vāg-deha-saṁyatā,*
ihāgṛhyāṁ kīrtim āpnoti patilokaṁ paratra ca. (Mn. 5.164. Also quoted in VR. 1258, SCGh. 252, VyK. 136, VyS. 124, VBh. 21).

123. Cf. fn. 100.

124. Cf. par. 3B-4A.

husband was hidden under the bed, she narrated to him her dream in which the goddess (Tripurasundarī) told her that she might save the life of her husband if she would embrace a stranger on the bed; but if he would endeavour to have sexual intercourse with her. she ought to turn away from him; if the stranger should use force, then he would lose half of his life. Therefore she asked the stranger not to use force because :

apāṁsulāṁ puṣpiṇīṁ ca balād bhuṅke naro hi yaḥ[125],
[126]*kṣiṇam āyur bhavet tasya mūḍhasy āviditātmanaḥ.*[127] (Śto. 41 365, 30-1)

[A man—a fool who does not know himself—who violates a chaste and menstruous woman is threatened with the loss of his life.]

14. As far as could be ascertained, this *śloka* is not found in Śts. nor in any other source of Sanskrit classical literature.

This *śloka* stated that he who, using force, cohabited against the will of a virgin who had already reached puberty, might be convicted to death.

The Smṛti-s contained two categories of rules : one referring to sexual intercourse in general, the other to adultery.

The story of the gullible husband and his cunning wife indicated that the *śloka* quoted above ought to be understood as referring to adultery. On the other hand this *śloka* was couched in general terms and therefore could be interpreted as if it would refer to sexual intercourse in general and in particular to the rape of a virgin who had already reached puberty.

15. According to Bṛh., which dealt with adultery (*saṅgrahaṇa*) there were three kinds of adultery, *viz.* connected with violence, with deception and with springing from sensual desire.[128] The same categories referred to sexual intercourse in general. Those connected with violence and deception were considered as rape, though the penalty was not the same.'[129]

125. V. 1. *yādahuḥ* HKB.
126. V. 1. *kṣiṇam ayurma tasya* B
127. *viditātmanaṁ iti* HB; °*tmanaḥ iti* K
128. *pāpamūlaṁ saṅgrahaṇaṁ triprakāraṁ nibodhata;*
balopādhi-kṛte dve tu tṛtīyam anurāgajam (Bṛh. 24. 1 γδ -2 α β. Also quoted in DhSP. 462, DV. 154, SCGh. 8, VR. 1101, MR. 129, VyK. 124, VyP. 397, VyS. 153-4, VyU. 135).
129. Cf. Bṛh. 24. 13-4.

According to different *Smṛti-s* the penalties prescribed were different.

A. Kāty. (830) gave a general rule in which it was stated that when a man using force has had sexual intercourse with a woman, the king should inflict capital punishment since it was a violation of a good conduct.[130]

B. According to Bṛh. (24.13) when a man violated an unwilling woman, the king had to order the cutting off of his penis and scrotum, as well as the confiscation of his entire wealth and his being paraded on an ass;[131] and when he enjoyed a woman by fraud the king had to order the confiscation of his entire wealth, brand him with the mark of a female part and banish him from the town.[132]

C. Mn. (8.364) stated that he who violated an unwilling girl deserved death on the spot; when she was willing he did not deserve death, if he was of the same caste as she.[133] Medh. explained that violating an unwilling girl meant depriving her of virginity through sexual intercourse; for that act the offender should be killed[134] without delay on the same day, or on the spot.[135] Mn. stated however that in case of only defiling an unwilling girl not through sexual intercourse but through sheer audacity the offender's two fingers should be instantly cut

130. *strīṣu vṛttopabhogaḥ syāt prasahya puruṣo yadā,*
vadhe tatra pravarteta kāryā'tikramaṇaṁ hi tat. (Kāty. 830. Also quoted in SCGh. 320.16, VR. 1131, VyK. 125, VyP. 397, VyMGh. 105).

131. *sahamāyaḥ kāmayate dhanaṁ tasyākhilaṁ haret,*
utkṛtya liṅga-vṛṣaṇau bhrāmayed gardabhena tu. (Bṛh. 24.13. Also quoted in Viv. 117.15, Apar. *ad* Y. 2.286, SCGh. 320.8-9, VR. 1129, PS. 166, DV 164 SV. 467, VyP. 396, VyM. 244).

132. *chadmanā kāmaved yas tu tasya sarvaharo damaḥ,*
aṅkayitvā bhagāṅkena puran nivāsayet tataḥ. (Bṛh. 24.14. Also quoted in PS. 472, Apar *ad* Y. 2.286, VR. 1129, SCGh. 320, MR. 130, VyM. 105, VyK. 125, VyP. 398, VyS. 154, VyU. 136, VivS. 266-7, DV. 165)

133. *yo'kāmaṁ dūṣayat kanyāṁ sa sadyo vadham arhati,*
sakāmāṁ dūṣayaṁs tulyo na vadhaṁ prāpnuyān naraḥ. (Mn. 8.364). Also quoted in Mit. *ad* Y. 2.288, Apar. *ad* Y. 2.288, DhSP. 471, VR. 1161, DV. 183, VC. 175, SCi. 27, VivT. 817, VivS. 274, VV. 54, VyK. 127, VyP. 403, VyU. 403, VyS. 153. Cf. SCGh. 27).

134. According to some translators not "killed" but "suffered corporal punishment". It was beginning and ending with actual killing; *anye tu yo'kāmāṁ dūṣayed ity asyaiva vadhy arthasyopasaṁhāro'yam, tāḍanāt prabhṛti-māraṇaṁ yāvad vadyarthaḥ. tatre'māṁ nikṛṣṭa-jātīyāṁ ca dūṣayan na māryate'pi tv aṅguli yasya cchidyeta.* (Medh. *ad* Mn. 8.367).

135. *so'nicchantīṁ kumārīṁ dūṣayet kaumāryād apacyāvayet strī-puruṣasaṁbhogena—sadyas tasmin nevāhanyavilaṁbaṁ hantavyaḥ.* (Medh. *ad* Mn. 8.364).

off or he should pay a fine of six hundred *paṇa-s.*[136] A very similar rule was found in Y. where it was stated that for defiling a girl the offender's hand should be cut off, if the girl was of the same caste as the offender and in case of a girl of a higher caste the offender should be punished with death.[137] What defiling meant was explained in Mit. where we read : *yadyakāmāṁ kanyāṁ balātkāreṇa nakha-kṣatā-dinā dūṣayati tadā taṣya karaśchet tavyaḥ*; *yadā punas tām evā'ṅguli-prakṣepeṇa yonikṣataṁ kurvan dūṣayati tadā manūkta ṣaṭ śatasahito'ṅguli-cchedaḥ.* (Mit. *ad* Y. 2.288)[138].

The punishment of cutting off the hand or finger was probably the consequence of the general principle which we find in Śaṅkha.[139] According to this source by whatever limb a man misbehaved that limb should be cut off or a fine of eight thousand should be imposed (*lex talionis*), except in the case of Brāhmaṇas who were immune from such punishment.[140]

Mn. (8.378) contained also a rule that a Brāhmaṇa who violated an unwilling, protected (*gupta*) Brāhmaṇa girl should be fined one thousand and in the case of a willing one he should be fined five hundred.[141]

D. K. in three different places stated that a man should never have sexual intercourse with a woman against her will.[142] K. differentiated between violation of a girl who had not reach-

136. *abhiṣahya tu yaḥ kanyāṁ kuryād darpeṇa mānavaḥ,*
tasyāśu kartyā aṅgulyo daṇḍaṁ cā'rhati ṣaṭ-śatam. (Mn. 8.367. Also quoted in Mit. *ad* Y. 2.288, Apar. *ad* Y. 2.288, Vīr. *ad* Y. 228, DhSP 470, VR. 1167, DV. 182, VC. 176, VivT. 816, VivS. 275, VyK. 127, VyP. 403, VyU. 137. VyS. 156)

137. *dūṣaṇe tu karaccheda uttamāyāṁ vadhas tathā* (Y. 2.288. Also quoted in VR. 1170, DhSP. 469, VR. 2.292, VC. 177.

138. Cf. DV. 185, SV. 472, VivT. 816, VivS. 276, VyK. 127, VyP. 403, VyU. 137, VyS. 156.

139. *yena yenā'ṅgenā parādhaṁ kuryāt tat tasya chettavyam aṣṭa-sahasraṁ vā daṇḍo'nyatra brāhmaṇāt, adaṇḍyo hi brāhmaṇaḥ.* (ŚL. quoted in Viv. 111. 20-2). Also quoted in VR. 1127, VC. 174, DV. 159, VivT. 806, VivS. 263, VV. 54, VyM. 107, VyK. 125, VyS. 162.

140. A Brāhmaṇa could not be punished with death according to some Smṛti-s (Bṛh. 9.27, Mn. 8.830. Cf. B. 1.10, 18, 17; 3.2, 4, 1, Vi. 5.2, N. 14, 9, Pariśistam 41, ŚL. in VR. 634.)

141. *sahasraṁ brāhmaṇo daṇḍyo guptāṁ viprāṁ balād vrajan,*
śatāni pañca daṇḍyaḥ syād icchantyā saha saṅgataḥ. (Mn. 8.378). Also quoted in Mit. *ad* Y.2.81, BBh. 2.86, Vīr.2.286, DhSP 464, SCGh. 320, VR. 1139, DV. 167, VC. 180, SV. 151, VivT. 187, VivS. 170, VV. 55, VyP. 396, VvU. 134, VvMā. 105, VyS. 154.

142. *na ca prākāmyam akāmāyāṁ labheta.* (K. 231.3; 231.12; 232.1).

ed her maturity and a menstruous girl. In the first case the offender's hand had to be cut off,[143] or he had to pay a fine of 400 *paṇa-s* and if the girl died in consequence of his act,the offender had to be put to deaṭh; in the second case the offender's middle finger had to be cut off, or he had to pay a fine of 200 *paṇa-s* as well as to give an adequate compensation.[144]

E. N. did not differentiate between girls who did not reach their maturity and menstruous girls, but prescribed a similar punishment for violating unwilling girls. If the girl belonged to the Brahmaṇa caste the offender had to be punished with death and confiscation of his entire property and in other cases with cutting off of his two fingers.[145]

F. From this short examination of the different rules found in different Dharma- and Artha-śāstras we see that the penalties imposed on the offender who violated an unwilling girl were different. Generally, the more ancient the sources were, the more severe punishments were prescribed. Punishment depended on the form in which the violation took place and also on the caste of the offender and the girl. If the girl was of a higher caste than the offender then capital punishment was prescribed,in other cases the punishment was lighter.[146] The punishment also depended on whether the woman was guarded (*gupta*) or not, and was more severe in the first instance. The same general rules are found in the Sanskrit legal sources and *nibandha-s* as to adultery brought about by force, deceit, or sensual passion. Each case was very well described in these sources and many details concerning different penalties were given depending on the caste of the man and woman who committed adultery.[147] In case of adultery both men and women were liable to punishment, while in case of rape only the man,

143. If the girl was of the equal caste.

144. *savarṇam aprāpta-phalam kanyāṁ prakurvato hastavadhaś catuś-śato vā daṇḍaḥ; mṛtāyām vadhaḥ. prāptā-phalāṁ prakurvato madhyama-pradeśinīvadho dviśato vā daṇḍaḥ; pituś cā'pahīnaṁ dadyāt.* (K. 230. 16-231.2).

145. *kanyāyām asakāmāyāṁ dvy aṅgulasyā'vakartanam,*
uttamāyāṁ vadhas tv eva sarva-saṁgrahanaṁ tathā. (N. 12.71. Also quoted in VR. 1165, DV. 171, VivS. 275, VyK. 127).

146. Regarding violation of prostitutes, see above Study VI on the Legal Position of Prostitutes according to Kauṭilya's Arthaśāstra, par. 18.

147. Cf. P. V. KANE, History of Dharmaśāstra III, p. 531-7 and G. Bühler's translation of Mn. in SBE. 25 *ad* Mn. 8.359.

who was the only offender, was liable to punishment; women were liable to different punishment.[148]

16. The *śloka* quoted in Śto. (41), though not taken literally from any Dharma- or Artha-śāstra, was based on legal scriptures, particularly the older ones which stipulated a more servere punishment than the younger legal scriptures. Therefore it may be stated that this *śloka* reflected existing legal rules.

IV. OTHER APHORISMS QUOTED IN THE TALE OF THE GULLIBLE HUSBAND AND HIS CUNNING WIFE

17. Śto. (38) contained the story of the gullible husband and his cunning wife in the shorter version (*textus simplicior*),[149] Śto. (38) added in the body of the tale one aphorism reading : *durdivase*[150] *ghanatimire*[151] *gatasaṁcārāsu*[152] *nagara-vīthīṣu*[153], [154]*patyur-videśa-gamane*[155] *paramaṁ*[156] *sukhaṁ jaghana-capalāyāḥ*[157] (Śto. 38.363.14-5).

[When the weather is bad, when the night is falling, when the streets of the town are full of life, and when the husband left for abroad, the libidinous woman is filled with highest delight.]

This *śloka* is also found in PP. (3.177 and 1.33), Pts. (4.53 and 1.173), PtsK. (3.203 and 1.189) and in several Subhāṣita-saṁgraha-s, such as SRBh. (352.4) and SRK. (119.19). This

148. However, if the man was of a lower caste than the woman, she was also liable to capital punishment. Cf. Bṛh. 24. 18-9;

anicchantī tu yā bhuktā guptāṁ tāṁ vāsayed gṛhe,
malināṅgīm adhaḥ śayyāṁ piṇḍa-mātro'pajīvinim.
kārayen niṣkṛtiṁ kṛcchraṁ parākaṁ vā same gatām,
hīna-varṇo'pābhuktā yā tyājyā vadhyā'thavā bhavet.

149. Cf. par. 3A.

150. *durdiṇa* v. l. in SRBh.

151. *asitapakṣe* PP. 1.133, Pts. 1.173.

152. *duḥsaṁcāreṣu* PP.3.177; *duḥsamcārāsu* PP. 1.133, Pts, PtsK.1.189, SRBh., SRK.; *varṣāti jalade* PtsK. 3.206; *niḥsaṁcārasu* Bh. in PP. *ad* 3.177.

153. °*mārgeṣu* PP. 3.177; °*vithīṣu* RB., *Śto.* ; *mahāṭavīpramṛtau* PtsK. 3.206.

154. *pratyu*° B. in Śto.; *patyau* Bh. in PP. *ad* 3.177, Pts.

155. °*gamanaṁ* KRB. in Śto; *virdeśe gamane* Pr. in PP. *ad* 3.177; *videśayāto* Bh. in *ad* 3.177, Pts.

156. *parama* H. in Śto., PP., Pts., PtsK., SRBh., SRK., *paraṁ* K. in Śto., Bh. in PP. *ad* 3.177.

157. *jana capalāyāḥ* M in PP. *ad* 3.177. Bh. in PP. *ad* 3.177 has only *durdivase ghanatimiretyādi* and omits the rest. In A. in PP. *ad.* 3.177 the second, third and fourth *pāda-s* run as follows :

varṣabhi (better *varṣati*) *jalade mahā'tavī-prabhṭau,*
viṣamasthāne bharttaś tvayā na gaṁttavaṁ tu sabhaye'pi.

aphorism found in PP. (3.177), Pts. (4.53) and PtsK. (3.203) was quoted in the story of the gullible husband and his cunning wife.

18. In Pañc. in the *textus ornatior* and in the *textus simplicior* of the story of the gullible husband and his cunning wife, we find three additional aphorisms.

The first of them reads :

yadi syāt pāvakaḥ śītaḥ proṣṇo vā śaśalā'ñchanaḥ,

strīṇāṁ [158]*ca tat satītvaṁ* [159]*syād yadi syād*[160] *durjano hitaḥ.*

(PP. 3.175).

[If fire were cold, if the moon were burning hot, or a bad man became good, only then faithfulness would be found in woman].

This *śloka* is also found in Pts. (4.51), PtsK. (3.204) and in some Subhāṣitasaṁgraha-s, as for instance in SRBh. (348.23). Similar aphorisms were often found in Sanskrit classical literature.[161]

The second *śloka* reads :

yac ca[162] *vedeṣu śāstreṣu na dṛṣṭam*[163] *na ca saṁśrutam,*

[164]*tat sarvaṁ vetti loko'yaṁ yat syād brahmāṇḍamadhyagam.*

(PP. 3.176).

[All what happens in the world is known among the people, also that what is not included in the Veda-s and the Śāstra-s, and even that what was never heard].

This *śloka* is also found in Pts. (4.52) and PtsK. (3.205).

The story of the gullible husband and his cunning wife started and ended in both the shorter and longer versions with a third aphorism which was also the starting *śloka* in H. This *śloka* reads :

158. *tadā* Pts., SRBh.

159. *ca syād* Pr. in PP.; om. in P. in PP.

160. *vā* PtsK.

161. Cf. L. Sternbach, Gaṇikā-vṛtta-saṁgraha, Hoshiarpur, 1933; 359-416.

162. *yan na* Pts.

163. *tad dṛṣṭaṁ* bh. in PP. *tad daṣṭaṁ* N. in PP.

164. *t* Pr. in PP.

pratyakṣepi [165]*kṛte pāpe*[166] *mūrkhaḥ* [167]*sāmnā praśāmyati*[168],
rathakāraḥ[169] *svakāṁ*[170] *bhāryā sajārāṁ śirasāvahat.*[171] Pts. 4.48, 64)

[Although an offence is committed before his eyes, the fool is appeased by nice words ; the wheelwright carried on his head his own wife with (her) lover.]

This *śloka* which was the quintessence of the whole story of the gullible husband and his cunning wife was also quoted in PtsK. (3.203 and 207), PRE. (3.68), PT. (3.81),PP. (3.174),HJ. (3.26), HP. (3.23), HS. (3.24), HK. (3.24) and HM. (3.24). [172]

19. Two more aphorisms were contained in some versions of the *textus simplicior* of Pañc. only. The first of those *śloka-s* reads:

nadīnāṁ ca kulānāṁ ca munīṇāṁ ca mahātmanām,
parīkṣā na prakartavyā strīṇāṁ duścaritasya ca (Pts. 4.49).

[Inquiry should not be carried through about rivers, families, magnanimous ascetics and about the bad conduct of women].

This *śloka* was also found in SRBh. (165.540) with a remark that its source is Cāṇakya.[173] This aphorism is a v.l. of an aphorism found in MBh. (3.34,72)b-73a).[174]

The second of these aphorisms reads :

vasor-vīryo'tpannām-abhajata munir matsyata-nayāṁ,
taṭha jāto vyāsaḥ śata-guṇāni-vāsaḥ kim aparam,
svayaṁ vedān-vyāsañchamita-kuruvaṁśa-prasavitā
sa evā'bhū-cchrīmānahaha viṣamāḥ karmagatayaḥ. (Pts. 4.50).

[A sage loved the daughter of a fish who came from the semen of Vasu; so the virtuous Vyāsa was born. However that is not all : he alone set asunder the Vedas, was the progenitor of the extinct family of Kauravas and lived happily. Oh, the road of destiny can be understood only with difficulty].

165. v. l. *pratyakṣeṇa* HS,.
166. *doṣe* PRE., PT., HP., HS. HK., HM.
167. *sāntvena tuṣyati* PRE., PT., HJ., HP., HM., v. l. *śantvena* HS., or *śāntvena* HS., B. in HP., HM., or *śāntena* HP., HPet., HSer.
168. *pratuṣyati* PP
169. *sthakāro* HJ. , HP., HS., HM., HK.
170. *nijāṁ* HJ., HP., HS., HM., HK.
171. ⁰*karot* HJ. HP., HS., HM., HK.
172. An introductory stanza to Śts. (89.10-90.1) reads :
yāhi devi vijānāsi yadi jārasamanvitā,
sajjanīva purā vaktuṁ bharturagre kacagrahe.
173. This is probably an error. In none of the 127 editions and 44 MSS which the author studied and analysed in detail could this aphorism be found. (It is not identical with CVND 1.15 and those based on this aphorism).
174. The first *pādas* read : *ṛṣīṇāṁ ca nadīnāṁ ca kulānāṁ ca*⁰; the third *pāda* reads : *prabhavo nādhigantavyaḥ.*

20. All these seven aphorisms,[175] though not important for the understanding of the story of the gullible husband and his cunning wife, were well suited and appropriate to the story itself. The *śloka* Pts. (3.48) was an introductory *śloka*[176] as well as a closing *śloka* and the quintessence of the story in question. The *śloka* PP. (1.76) was also an introductory *śloka*; it stated that gossips were wide-spread; it was related to the fact that everyone, with the exception of the husband himself, knew that the wife of the gullible husband was not faithful to him. The *śloka-s* of Śto. (38.363). 14-5)and PP. (1.175) stated that women were fickle, libidinous and not faithful, while *śloka-s* of Pts. (4.49 and 4.50)[177] emphasized the bad conduct of women and the difficulty in understanding destiny; they accentuated the characteristics of the main figure in the tale of the gullible husband and his cunning wife and therefore were closely connected with the story itself. That is the most important difference between the Pañcatantra and the Śukasaptati on the one hand and the Hitopadeśa on the other, since the author (or authors) of H. had included into his work, in order to make of it a Subhāṣitasaṅgraha, unsuited and inappropriate aphorisms.

V. CONCLUSIONS

The tale of the gullible husband and his cunning wife in two different versions was well-known in India. It was included in most of the important collections of Indian tales. Through translations, revisions and elaborations the tale became known in Persia and the Near East and then, probably through gypsies, who travelled either directly from India, or more probably from Persia and the Near East,[178] became known in Europe. The tale was adapted to the specific circumstances existing in each country in which it has been told; therefore a development of the tale can be noticed. Some inconsistencies,or naivetés disappeared; some lacunae have been filled and the tale became more congruous, more logical and more plausible,at least,with respect the cuckold

175. Including the introductory *śloka* to Śts.

176. Similarly as Śts. 89.10-90. 1.

177. These *śloka-s* were the least connected with the story itself.

178. The *textus ornatior* was adapted to the special circumstances in Slovakia and Romania. The dream in RT. and SH. resembled closely the dream in Ṭṭ.

husband. This evolution can be clearly observed if we compare the crude original with the highly elaborated tale found in RT.; however, it can also be observed in India in each group; for instance the story as found in the longer version of Śto. (41), seems to be more developed, than that found in Pts. As far as the shorter version is concerned, the text found in H. became more amplified but it is difficult to admit that it became more developed. Rather a retrogression from the original could be noticed in the story as found in H., because the author (or authors) of H., as was usual for him, wanted to include in the story as many aphorisms as possible, even if they were very losely, or not at all, connected with the story itself. In order to show the foundness of the wife towards her husband, we find in H. inappropriate and unsuited aphorisms to the story itself, as for instance HJ. 3.28 or HJ. 3.33, or very loosely connected ones, as for instance HJ. 3. 30-32.

Fortunately the interpretation of Indian tales in conjunction with the Smṛti-s leads very often to some interesting conclusions.[179] This interpretation leads, for instance to the conclusion that in H. one of the unsuited and inappropriate *ślokas*, viz. HJ. 3.33 was a later interpolation.

The interpretation of the tales from the point of view of the Smṛti-s leads also to other conclusions. For instance, in the case of the tale of the gullible husband and his cunning wife it leads to the conclusion that the legal rules concerning rape, as stipulated in the Smṛti-s, were well-known in daily life. They were so well-known and so congenial to the Sanskrit speaking people that they were even included by non-legally minded authors in collections of common tales. That also means that they were still in force at the time when the Pañcatantra and the Śukasaptati were reduced to writing.

179. Cf. above Study XVIII on the Pañcatantra and the Smṛti-s, para 50.

XXI

THE TALE OF THE YOUNG WIFE AND THE OLD HUSBAND (HJ. 1.6)*

1. *Contents of the Tale of the Young Wife and the Old Husband in H. and Other Sources.*

A. In H.[1] we find in the first book a short inserted story of an old and wealthy merchant, Candanadāsa, who wedded a young merchant's daughter, Līlāvatī. Līlāvatī, through excitement caused by youth, fell in love with a certain son of a merchant. One day, when she was engaged in confidential talk with her paramour, her old husband arrived unexpectedly. At that moment she rose quickly, pulled him by his hair, closely embraced him and kissed him. In the meantime, her paramour escaped.

B. In a similar story, though not the same found in Pañc.[2] SK.[3] and KB.[4], the young wife of an old husband, every night when they were lying abed turned her body away. One night, a thief got in the house of the old husband. When the wife saw the thief, she was afraid and embraced her husband. The old husband not accustomed to such a sign of fondness on the part of his young wife, looked around for the explanation for her affection towards him. Then, he saw the thief in a corner. Since the thief had done him a benefit he spared his life and allowed him to escape.

C. The story of the young wife and the old husband, as included in the H., was more refined than the similar story found in Pañc., SK. or KB.; it contained additional elements, so often mentioned in classical Sanskrit literature, viz. the fickleness of women and their art to outwit their husbands.

D. The story of the young wife and the old husband, in the version found in H., was brought to Europe not directly, but probably via Arabia or Persia. We find it in P. Alfons

*Previously appeared as JSAIL. 22 in "Professor P.K. Gode Commemoration Volume", Wesley Press, Mysore. Submitted to the 163rd meeting of the American Oriental Society Washington 1953.

1. HJ. 1.6; HK. 1.5; HP., 25 sqq.; HS. 1.6.
2. PRE 3.6; PP. 3.9; Pts. 4.10; PtsK. 4.10; PT. Appendix II (138-9).
3. SK. 10.62; SKD. 10.62, 83-7.
4. KB. 16, 27.

Disciplina Clericalis and *Ex gestis Romanorum historiae notabiles de vitiis virtutibusque tractantes, cum applicationibus moralizatis et misticis* (Ch. 122, fol. 127, ed. 1517).[5]

2. *General Analysis of the Tale of the Young Wife and the Old Husband*

A. As usual for H., this simple story of the young wife and the old husband contained as many as 14 didactic stanzas taken from various sources or composed by the author (or authors) of H. They were mostly aphorisms connected only loosely with the main story of the tale.

B. The story of the young wife and the old husband, as found in H., could be divided into two groups.

The first group dealt with the feelings of the young wife toward her old husband and vice versa, and the second group dealt with fickleness of women and the need to protect them. This second group was more important for the analysis of this story from the point of view of the Smṛti-s, though it was loosely connected with the story itself. There were three stanzas in this second group, which were based on the Smṛti-s.

3. *Need to Protect Women*

A. We find in H. the following stanza dealing with the question of the need to protect women:

pitā rakṣati kaumāre bhartā rakṣati yauvane,
putrāś ca sthavire bhāve na strī svātantryam arhati

[The father protects[6] (a woman) in childhood, the husband in youth, and the sons in old age; a woman is never fit for independence.]

This stanza is found in HJ. 1.128, HK, 1.122, HL.24. 26-7, HC. 33. 17-8, HM. 1.119, HN. 1.92, HP. 1.91 and HS. 1.113.[7]

B. The stanza was introduced in this story in order

5. Schmidt on Peter Alfons, Disciplina Clericalis, c. XI. Cf. Benfey, Pantshatantra Leipzig 1859, 1 Theil, par. 153; Hitopadeśa *ou* l' *l'instruction utile,* trad. par E. Lancereau, Paris 1855.

6. Guards.

7. The text is almost identical in various versions. HK. has in (*c*) *rakṣanti sthāvire putrā na*⁰. The Nepalese MS has in (*c*) *putrāstu sthāvire.* The Bhaṇḍarkar's Collection MS. No. 326 has in (*c*) *putrāś ca vārdhake*; the Paris MS (in HS.) has in (*c*) *putrastu* (*putrāstu* ?) and the Petersburg MS (in HS.) has in (*c*) *sthavire kāle.*

to convey the idea included in its last part, that is, to show that women were never fit for independence, since they were fickle and always willing to be disloyal to their husbands; therefore they should always be protected by someone, that is, by their fathers until they were married, during marriage by their husbands and during their widowhood by their sons.

C. This principle was well known in the Smṛti-s. The same stanza as in H. was quoted in the following main Smṛti-s: Mn. (9.3), B. (2.3.45), Vās. (5.3), GM. (3.10,1), N. (13.31) and NMS. (13.31), MBh. (13.20, 21 and 13.46, 14) as well in *nibandha-s* which quote the texts of the main Smṛtis, such as VR. (410-1), SCM (27), DhSP (2.1.; 38.2 and 2.1; 355.6). NṛP. (Saṁsk. 666), Saṁskāra ratnamālā (674), VyK (128. 133), U. (2.14,2), SC. (240), VyS. (120), VyP. (406), VyB. (608), VyU. (140), MR. (133), VT. (821), VRV. (281)[8] and R. 2.39, 32. The same idea was also found in Mn. (5.146)[9], Y. (1.85-6),[10] Vi. (25.13).[11] G. (18.1)[12] as well as in Mahānirvāṇatantra (8.106)[13] and C. compendia (CRB 8.68, CRP 8.65, CRBh I 8.66, CRBh II 8.55, CNF 58, CNPh 92, CNI I 155, CNG 180, CNL 46.[14]

D. Though we find this aphorism in various versions of H. and in many Smṛti-s, we do not find, with the exception of the HK., text any version of H. which would be completely identical with any text of the Smṛti-s. The first two *pādas* of H. are identical in all the sources but the third *pāda* is very often different. The classical text of Mn. runs: *rakṣanti sthāvira* (or *sthavire*) *putrā*......The nearest to H. is the text of Vās, which

8. Dh. 1031, 1045, 1076, 1099, 1555, 1388, 1977, 1059, 1106.

9. *bālye pitur vaśe tiṣṭhet pāṇigrāhasya yauvane,*
putrāṇām bhartari prete na bhajet strī svatantratām. (Mn. 5.146)
(According to other versions 5.148. Also quoted in VR. 427, VyK. 133, MaBh. 18, 1, SCM 249, VRV. 281, VyS. 120, VV. 56).

10. *rakṣet kanyāṁ pitā vinnāṁ patiḥ putrās tu vārdhake,*
abhāve jñātayas teṣāṁ na svātantryaṁ kvacit striyāḥ (Y.1.85).
Also quoted in DhSP. 2.1; 355, 6, VK. 128, VR. 410, VC. 189, VyP. 406, VyU, 140, VyM. 50, VRV. 281, VyS. 120, VV. 56.

11. *bālya yauvanavārdhakyeṣv api pitṛbhartṛputrādhinatā* (Vi. 5.13).
Also quoted in VR. 428, VRV. 286.

12. *asvatantrā dharme strī* (G. 18.1). Also quoted in GM. 18.1.

13. *tiṣṭhet pitror vaśe bālye bhartus saṁprāpta yauvane,*
vārdhakye patibandhūnam na svatantrā bhavet kvacit (8.106)

14. See also below Study XXI on the "Mānava-dharmaśāstra Stanzas in the Hitopadeśa" paras 17-9.

has *putraś ca* (instead of *putrāś ca*; *putrāś ca* is in FH. in Va) *sthavire* (instead of *sthāvire*) *bhāve*, but in the fourth *pāda* has *marhatīti*.

Putrāś ca is also found in MBh. (13.20, 21 and 13.46, 24). *Putrās tu* is also found in R. in Mn., B. (*putras tu*) DhSP. (2.1; 355.7) when quoting Mn., N., GM., and VR. *Putraḥ* is found in DhSP (2.1; 38.3) when quoting Mn. *Rakṣanti*, as in Mn. is found in NMS. and some MSs of H.[15] *Vārdhake* (or *vārdhake*) in the Bhaṇḍarkar MS of H. instead of *sthāvire* (or *sthavire*) is also found in NMS. GM. and B. combine *sthāvire* (or *sthavire*) with *bhāve* and have °*virībhave*, while DhSP (2.1.; 38.3) when quoting Mn. has *sthavirabhāve*. *Putrā* instead of *bhāve* is found in Mn. and NMS. and *kāle* instead of *bhāve* in MBh. and in the Petersburg MS of H.

As to the fourth *pāda* the only changes[16] can be found in MBh. (13.20, 21)[17] and in SR.[18]

It is interesting to note that Mn. mentions the same idea in two different places, that is in the ninth and in the fifth book. According to the ninth book the dependence of women was caused by the fear of their fickleness; they had to be kept in dependence day and night[19] and they had to be restrained from their vicious attachment[20], because they attached themselves easily to sensual enjoyments. In the ninth book Mn. used the word *rakṣā* i.e., protection against ruin[21] and in the fifth book declared that women could not act independently even in their own houses.[22]

In addition to the general rule that women could not be

15. See above.
16. In addition to that quoted above (Vās).
17. *nāsti strīṇām svatantratā* (no change in MBh. 13.46.24).
18. *Ad* Mn. *na svātantryaṁ kvacit striyāḥ*.
19. *asvatantrāḥ striyaḥ kāryāḥ puruṣaiḥ svair divā niśam*
viṣayeṣu ca sajjantyāḥ saṁsthāpyā ātmano vaśe. Mn. 9.2.
See also Hār., Paith, and Āp. quoted by H. T. Colebrooke: A digest of Hindu Law, II, 381-4.
20. *ātmano vaśe sthāpyā yathā na sajyante* (Nār. *ad* Mn.)
21. N. 13.30 stated that through independence women went to ruin even if they were born in a noble family and that therefore that dependency was assigned to them.
svātantryād vipraṇaśyanti kule jātā api striyaḥ,
asvātantryam atas tāsāṁ prajāpatir akalpayat.
22. *bālayā vā yuvatyā vā vṛddhayā vāpi yoṣitā,*
na svātantryeṇa kartavyaṁ kiṁcit kāryaṁ gṛheṣv api. Mn. 5.147.
Also quoted in GM. 28.1, VR. 427, SC. 249, VyK. 133, MaBh. 28.1, Vivā. 285, VyS. 123.

independent and had to be protected by their fathers before mariage (in childhood), by their husbands during married life (in their youth) and by their sons in widowhood (in their old age), N. added that in widowhood, if women had no sons, the relatives of their fathers had to guard and maintain them[23] and if the deceased husbands had no family[24]—*sapiṇḍa* had to guard women, and in case *sapiṇḍa* were also not available their fathers[25] or his relations[26] had to protect them.

According to N.,[27] if any of these persons could not protect women the king had to be their protector and maintain them.[28]

E. In H. the better known and more important of the two rules included in Mn. (9.3 and 5.148) had been chosen, that is, Mn. 9.3, since the author of H. wanted to heighten the idea of fickleness and disloyalty of women. That idea was elevated in Mn. 9.2-3, while in Mn. 5.147 the idea of non-dependency of women in their own houses was heightened.

It is also clear that the author of H. has chosen to include in the story of the young wife and the old husband the simple and so often repeated rule found in Mn., B., Vās. GM., N., and MBh. and not the more elaborate rule found in N. and Y.; the latter introduced relatives of the deceased husband, *sapiṇḍa*, and finally the king as a person responsible for protecting women, if any of them was not available. These rules were too legalistic, too elaborate and too casuistic and, what was probably the most important reason for not introducing them

23. *mṛte bhartary aputrāyāḥ patipakṣaḥ prabhuḥ striyāḥ,*
viniyogātmarakṣāsu bharaṇe ca sa īśvaraḥ. N. 13.28.
Similarly Y. 1.85 (*jñātis*).

24. No male members of the family was extinct or too poor.

25. N. 13.29 mentioned only the father's relations, but it is clear that the father had greater rights and obligations than his relations.

26. *pariksīṇe patikule nirmaṇuṣye nirāśraye,*
tatsapiṇḍeṣu vāsatsu pitṛ pakṣaḥ prabhuḥ striyāḥ. N. 13.29

27. Not found in the text published by J. Jolly or NMS. quoted by Mit. and Vij. *ad* Y. 1.85.

28. *tatsapiṇḍeṣv arakṣatsu pitṛpakṣaḥ prabhuḥ striyaḥ.* (Same as N. 13.29 b).
pakṣadvayāvasāne tu rājā bhartā prabhuḥ striyāḥ,
sa tatsyā bharaṇaṁ kuryām nigṛhṇiyāt pathaś cyutām. (Vij. *ad* Y. 1.85, p. 150.

Quoted with some variants in NMS. 13.29 and in the Nepalese MS. of N. Also quoted in Mit. and Ś. (SBE 33.29), Ang. (*ad* Y. 1.185 transl. in SBH), VR. 412, SC. 240, MR. 130, VRV. 281, VTV 821, VyK. 129, VyP. 406, VyU. 140, VyS. 120.

into H., they were not so universally known as the similar rule found in Mn. (9.3). That can be deduced from the fact that the latter rule was so often quoted not only in other Smṛtis but also by its commentators, in the *nibandha-s*[29] and in the classical Sanskrit literature.[30]

4. *Need to Avoid Contact with Women*

A. The second legal rule in the story of the young and the old husband, dealing with the need for men to shun contact with women, immediately followed the first one and reads as follows:

mātrā svasrā duhitrā vā na viviktāsano bhavet,
balavān indriyagrāmo vidvāṁsam api karṣati.

[One should not sit in a lonely place near to mother, or sister, or daughter; for powerful is the assemblage of sense organs which overcomes even a learned man].

This stanza is found in HJ. 1.129 and HL. p. 25. HK., HP., and HS. omit it, but HS. mentions it in the notes.

B. This stanza was borrowed from Mn. 2.215 and can also be found in BhP. (9.19, 17), Garuḍa Purāṇa (1.114, 16) Bhaviṣya Purāna, Brāhma Parvan (4.184), CRC. (7.9), PS (654),[31] VS. (2780) and SB. (IS. 4809). The first *pāda* of this stanza is also quoted in ŚŚ. (3.18a).[32]

29. Compare paragraphs B. and C. above.

30. In the classical Sanskrit literature we often find statements to the effect that women (maidens or wives) should be guarded or held fast as the head of a venomous snake should be held, though that might be most difficult. They should be guarded because otherwise they would either run into destruction or abandon their protectors (husbands).

kṛṣir vidyā vaṇig bhāryā svadhanaṁ rājyasaṁpadaḥ,
sudṛhaṁ caiva kartavyaṁ kṛṣṇasarpamukhaṁ yathā. (VCsr. 14.2 Similarly VCmr. 14.27, VCbr. 14.1)

śāstraṁ sucintitam api praticintanīyaṁ,
svārādhito'pi nṛpatiḥ pariśaṅkanīyaḥ,
aṅke sthitāpi yuvatiḥ parirakṣaṇīyā
śāstre nṛpe ca yuvatau ca kuto vaśitvam. (Vān. in HKS. 2, in KSG. 2; ṢR. in HKS. 1; in KSG. 1; CNW. 65; CnT. VII 9; HS. *ad* 110. 18; SB. 101, 136 (6443).

ṣaḍ imāni vinaśyanti muhūrtam anavekṣaṇāt,
gāvaḥ sevā kṛṣir bhāryā vidyā vṛṣalasaṁgatiḥ. MBh. 5.32, 86.

svadāradhanaratnāni nijavaśyāni kārayet,
anyathā tāni gacchanti tyaktvā kāpuruṣādhamam. BD. 75 (7611.)

31. 37, 57

32. See also below Study XXI on the "Mānava-dharmaśāstra Stanzas in the Hitopadeśa" paras 20-4.

The text is identical in HJ. and Mn. Only SB. has in (α) *ca* instead of *vā*; HL. in (β) *na* instead of *no* (similarly SB). In ŚŚ. (β) reads *nātyantaikāntikaṁ bhavet* and in SB. *viśat* instead of *bhavet* and in (γ) °*indriyaḥ*: *grāmam* instead of °*indriyagrāmo*; BhP. in (δ) has *vidhvāṁsaṁ*° instead of *vidvāṁsam.*°

C. The stanza quoted in paragraph 12 above, taken from Mn., was included in the second part of book 2 of Mn. which deals with studentship and should not be read separately from the two preceding stanzas, that is, Mn. 2.213 and 214.[33] These stanzas declared that it was the very nature of women to seduce men, and therefore wise men should never be unguarded in the company of women (*pramadā*), since they were capable to lead astray every man, a fool and a learned man, and to make him a slave of desire and passion. Then Mn. continued with the stanza in question (Mn. 2.215). Medh. commenting on these three stanzas made it clear that they referred to a student.

MBh. in the Anuśāsanaparvan (48.37-8)[34] also mentioned the same but repeated only the first two stanzas and omitted Mn. 2.215. As to Mn. 2.213, MBh. changed the last two *pādas* and concluded that wise men should never become too much attached to women.

BhP. did not quote Mn. 2.215 without an introduction. It was first stated there that a man was a slave of desire[35] and then Mn. 2.94[36] was quoted where it was declared that desire was never extinguished by the enjoyment of desired objects; it only grew stronger. Therefore, BhP. continued that one should not sit in a lonely place near to mother, or sister or daughter because of fear that desire towards one of them, that is a woman, might overcome a man.

HJ. in 1.129 took Mn. 2.215 out of context and included it in the story of the young wife and the old husband with-

33. *svabhāva eṣa nārīṇāṁ narāṇāṁ iha dūṣaṇam,*
ato'rthān na pramādyanti pramadāsu vipaścitaḥ. Mn. 2.213.
avidvāṁsam alaṁ loke vidvāṁsam api vā punaḥ,
pramadā hy utpathaṁ netuṁ kāmakrodhavaśānugam. Mn. 2.214.

34. *avidvāṁsam alaṁ loke vidvāṁsam api vā punaḥ,*
nayanti hy apathaṁ nāryaḥ kāmakrodhavaśānugam. MBh. 13.48, 37 (MBh. 13, 48, 38 is almost identical with Mn. 2.213).

35. *yat pṛthivyāṁ vrīhiyavaṁ hiraṇyaṁ paśavaḥ striyaḥ,*
nālam ekasya tat sarvam iti paśyan na muhyati. BhP. 9.19, 19.

36. *na jātu kāmaḥ kāmānām upabhogena śāmyati,*
haviṣā kṛṣṇavartmeva bhūya evābhivardhate. Mn. 2.94.

out any introduction; that made this aphorism partly not clear the more so as stanza 2.215 of Mn. in the context of its second book had a specific meaning. Mn. referred it clearly to students and their duty to remain chaste during apprenticeship. These rules were found in several Dharma-śāstra-s. Thus, G. stated that a student should not gaze and touch women, if there was danger of a breach of chastity (G. 2.16)[37] and Āp. stated that a student should not touch a woman with his face, so as to inhale the fragrance of her body (Āp. 1.2.7, 8)[38], nor touch her at all without a particular reason (Āp. 1.2, 7-11).[39] B. (1.2, 3, 23)[40] and Āp. (1.1, 3, 16)[41] stated that a student should talk with women only as much as was necessary and should not salute (or stand too close)[42] to young wives of brothers and the young wives of the teacher (B. 1.2, 3, 33)[43], nor look at a naked woman (Āp. 1.2, 7, 3).[44]

D. The rule of Mn., as included in HJ. and HL., has lost its specific meaning. It was considered by the author of H. as an aphorism relating to women in general. The same could also be seen from MBh., BhP. and ŚŚ.[45] That meant, what was so clearly stated in some places in MBh., that women were the root of all faults and that they had a sinful disposition; they were never faithful and they always excited men and led them astray[46]; they were false, thoughtless, trickish, foolish, greedy, impure and cruel[47]; their passion was eightfold that of men.[48] Therefore, every man had to avoid them, because even sitting near them—his own mother, sister or daughter—might evoke men's passion and lead astray even the most learned men. The root for that did not

37. *strīprekṣaṇālambhane maithinaśaṅkāyām*. G. 2.16.
38. *nopajighret striyaṁ mukhena*. Āp. 1.2, 7.8.
39. *nākāraṇād upaspṛśet*. Āp. 1.2, 7,10.
40. *yāvadarthasambhāṣi strībhiḥ*. B. 1, 2, 3, 23.
41. *strībhir yāvadarthasaṁbhāṣī*. Āp. 1.1.3, 16.
42. Govinda.
43. *na samavāye 'bhivādayed atyantaśaḥ*. B. 1.2, 2, 32.
bhātṛpathīnām yuvatīnāṁ ca gurupatnīnāṁ jātavīryaḥ. B. 1.23, 33.
44. *na prekṣeta nagnām striyam*. Āp. 1, 2, 7, 3, Cf. Mn. 4.37, MBh. 13.104, 17b-18a, Y. 1.135, G.9.32, Vi. 71, 26, Hār. in Apar. 180, Ś. Gṛh. 4.11.1.
45. ŚŚ. incorporates the rule in the chapter on general principles on morality.
46. MBh. 13.38 sqq.
47. *bṛhat pārāśara* p. 121.
48. *anṛtaṁ sāhasaṁ māyā mūrkhatvam atilobhitā,*
aśaucatvaṁ nirdayatvaṁ strīnāṁ doṣaḥ svabhāvajāḥ.

necessarily lie in the character of women but also in the nature of men and their sexuality which might easily evoke passion towards any woman and overcome any man. That was the meaning of Mn. 2.215, as incorporated in HJ. and HL. However, this meaning was loosely connected with the preceding aphorism dealing with the principle of unfitness of women for independence. That was probably the reason why the greater number of texts of H. did not contain the quotation from Mn. (2. 215). Yet, it should not be forgotten that the preceding stanza (unfitness of women for independence) was introduced in order to heighten the principle of fickleness of women, the problem dealt with in the story of the young wife and the old husband.

5. *Factors Causing Corruption of Women*

A. The third legal rule in the story of the young wife and the old husband quoted in H., and dealing with factors causing corruption of women, cannot be interpreted without the preceding one which, though not taken verbatim from any of the Dharmaśāstra-s or Smṛti-s, contained some elements included in the Dharmaśāstra-s and dealt with the same subjects. The two stanzas read as follows:

svātantryaṁ pitṛmandire ca vasatir yātrotsave saṅgatir,
goṣṭhī-pūruṣa-sannidhāv aniyamo vāso videśe tathā;
saṁsargaḥ saha puṁścalībhir asakṛd vṛtter nijāyāḥ kṣatiḥ,
patyur vārdhakam īrṣitaṁ pravasanam nāśasya hetuḥ striyāḥ.
pānaṁ durjanasaṁsargaḥ patyā ca viraho'ṭanam,
svapnaś cānyagṛhe vāso nārīṇām dūṣaṇāni ṣaṭ.

[Liberty, dwelling in (her) father's house, attendance at festive processions, careless way of acting in the presence of distant male relatives, living in a foreign country, frequent entertainment with wantom women, loss of (her) livelihood, old age of (her) husband, (his) jealousy, (or his) setting out on journeys are the causes which ruin women.

Drinking, associating with bad people, separation from (her) husband, roving about, sleeping (at unsuitable hours), residing at other (men's) houses are the six causes which corrupt women].

These stanzas are found in HJ. (1.121-2), HK. (1.114-5), HP. (1.85-6), HS. (1.107-8), HL. 24.12-5, HC. 33.5-8), HM. 114-5 and HN. 1.87-8.

B. The second stanza (HJ. 1.122, HK. 1.115, HP. 1.86, HM. 1.114, HN. 1.88, HL. 24.12-3, HC. 33.5-6, HS. 1.108) which was most closely connected with legal texts was taken from Mn. (9.13)[49]. It was also quoted in VR. (431), VRV. (287), VyS. (120.1), SCM (27). VR. (431), after quoting Mn., added that what was mentioned in that stanza was only presented by way of a few examples of what led to the ruin of women's character.[50] We see that this comment was very just since we find in other Dharmaśāstra-s other examples of the reasons which led women to ruin. They were enumerated in Vi. (25.3, 9, 10-12)[51], Bṛh. (25.9-11).[52] Śaṅkha (quoted in Apar. 108)[53]. Vy. (quoted in Apar. 108)[54]. Hār. (3.37)[55], and ŚŚ. (3.19-20)[56].

The first stanza could not be traced in any of the Dharmaśāstra-s but was better known and was more often quoted in classical Sanskrit literature. It was quoted with some variants

49. See also below Study XXI on the "Mānava-dharmaśāstra Stanzas in the Hitopadeśa" paras 5.

50. *sarvāṇy etāni cāritradūṣaṇaupayikāni vivakṣitāni*. VR. 431.

51. *svaśrūśvaśuragurudevatātithipūjanam*, Vi. 25.3.
bhartari pravasite'pratikarmamriyā, paragṛheṣv anabhigamanam, dvāradeśagavākṣeṣv anavasthānaṁ, sarvakarmasv asvatantratā. Vi. 25, 9-12.

52. *bhartā pitrā sutair na strī viyuktānyagṛhe vaset,*
asatsaṅge viseṣeṇa garhyatam eti sa dhruvam. Bṛh. 25.9.
pūrvotthānaṁ guruṣv arvāk bhojanavyañjanakriyā,
jaghanyāsanaśāyitvaṁ karma strīṇām udāhṛtam. Bṛh. 25.10.
pānātanad ivāsvapnakriyā dūṣaṇaṁ striyāḥ. Bṛh. 25.11.

53. *nanūktā gṛhān nirgacchet, nāruttarīyā na tvaritam vrajet na parapuruṣam abhibhāṣetānyatra vaṇikpravrajitavṛddhavaidyebhyaḥ. na nābhiṁ darśayet āgulphād vāsaḥ paridadhyāt, na stanau vivṛtau kuryāt, na hased anapāvṛtaṁ, na bhartāraṁ na tad bandhūn vā vidviṣet, na ganikā-dhūrtā--vyabhicāriṇī--pravrajiteksaṇikā--māyāmūlakuhakakārikāduśśilādibhiḥ sahaikatra tiṣṭhet. saṁsargeṇa hi cāritraṁ duṣyatīty ādiśanti*. Śaṅkha in Apar. 108.

54. *dvāropaveśanaṁ nityaṁ gavākṣāvekṣaṇām tathā,*
asatpralāpo hāsyaṁ ca dūṣaṇaṁ kulayoṣitām. Vy. in Apar. 108.

55. *anyapuruṣeṇa sahekṣaṇābhibhāṣaṇaṁ duṣṭapravajitasaṁsargaṁ ca varjayet;*
paragṛharathyācatvaravīthipravrajitālayāṁś ca nābhigacchet;
kūpapathasthānaṁ sandhivelāsaṁcaraṇaṁ ca varjayet;
paraśayanāsane vastrābharaṇāni manasāpi nādhyavaṣyed āpunaḥ saṁskārāt;
tathaikapātryāṁ madyamāṁsani; ucchiṣṭanirmālyaṁ cā'nyatra
gurubhartṛsutebhyaḥ, ananyapuruṣalolupā' narthān varjayet. (Hār. 3.3).

56. *sahavāso 'nyapuruṣaiḥ prakāśam api bhāṣaṇam.*
svātantryaṁ na kṣaṇam api hy āvāso 'nyagṛhe tathā. ŚŚ. 3.19.
bhartrā pitrāthavā rājñā putraśvaśurabāndhavaiḥ;
strīṇāṁ naiva tu deyaḥ syād gṛhakṛtyair vinā kṣaṇaḥ. ŚŚ. 3.20.

in Śto. and SRK[57].

The two stanzas did not exclude themselves but rather completed each other, as far as the classical Sanskrit literature was concerned. However, they would exclude themselves in the Dharmaśāstra texts because the same ideas were expressed in both stanzas in other words. Thus in both stanzas we find the idea of separation of the wife from her husband (HJ. 1.122) and setting out of the husband for journeys (HJ. 1.121); association with bad people (HJ. 1.122) and association with wanton women (HJ. 1.121); or residing of a women in other men's homes (HJ. 1.122) and living of women in a foreign country (HJ. 1.121).

C. The six causes which corrupted women (Mn. 9.13 and HJ. 1.121) although, properly speaking, were not real legal reasons for women to lose their good reputation, were more closely based on legal rules than the other causes mentioned in HJ. 1.121.

Pāna—drinking, meant drinking spirituous liquors and was also mentioned in Bṛh. (25.11). According to Mn. (9.80) and Y. (1.73) women who drank spirituous liquors (*madyapā* in Mn. and *surāpī* in Y.) could be abandoned by their husbands.[58] Drinking of spirituous liquors was one of the legal reasons for the *repudiatio uxoris*.

Anyagehavāsa—residing in other men's houses and *durjana-saṁsarga*—association with wicked people, were also mentioned in other words in Bṛh. (25.9), Vi. (25.10), Hār. (3.3), Śaṅkha (in Apar. 108), Vy. (in Apar. 108), Śukr. (3.39-43)[59] and Mn. (9.5) where it was clearly stated that women must be particularly guarded against even small attachments, that is, as Medh. explained, association with women of unknown character such as those whose habit was to stand at the doorway, looking at gaily dressed young men passing by and so forth.[60] Such association with women of unknown character was better defined

57. *svātantryaṁ pitṛmandireṣu vasatir yātro'tsave saṁgatiḥ,*
goṣṭhīpūruṣasannibhāv aniyamo vāso videśe tathā,
saṁsargaḥ saha puṁścalībhir asakṛd vṛtter nijāyāḥ kṣatiḥ,
patyur vārdhakam īrsyit-apravasanaṁ nāśasya hetuḥ striyāḥ.
(Śto. 328.10-3, and similarly SRK. 114.5)

58. Cf. DhSP. 10.26 quoted *ad* Y. 1.73, Vās. 21.11, 15, Y. 3.256.

59. Includes speaking with other men.

60. Medh. *ad* Mn. 9.5. The same was also the opinion of Vi. 25.11 and Vy. in Apar. 108.

in HJ. 1.121 : *puṁścalī* and Śaṅkha : *gaṇikā* (in Apar. 108). It was also mentioned in PP. (1.141)[61] and C. (CVND) 5.6, CVM 5.18, CNP. I 29, CNT IV 28, CNM 28, CNMN 28.

Atanam—roving around, was also found in Bṛh. (25.11), Hār. (3.3)[62] and Śaṅkha (in Apar 108)[63] and *svapna*—sleeping, was also found in Bṛh. (25.11) and meant sleeping too much or at unsuitable hours as for instance by day-time.

The same idea as conveyed in the expression *viraha*—separation from her husband, was also found in HJ. in the expression conveying the meaning of setting out of the husband for journeys. This idea was not mentioned in other Dharmaśāstra-s, however Vi (25.9) stated that a woman should not decorate herself with ornaments while her husband was absent from home.[64]

From this enumeration of the six causes which corrupted women (HJ. 1.129) we see that all were either directly or indirectly enumerated in the Dharmaśāstra-s and the Smṛti-s and, generally, had legal implications[65] while others enumerated in HJ. 1.121 had no such implications at all and were only counsels for women or their guardians that certain actions of women might be considered by some people as injurious to their good reputation (e.g., too great liberty granted to them,[66] dwelling in her father's home,[67] careless way of acting in the presence of male relatives) or could give them better opportunity of not being chaste (old husband, jealous husband,[68] wife's loneliness in case the husband set out for journeys). Therefore it seems

61. And Pts. 1.416, PtsK. 1.467.

62. Roaming around in the evening (standing on the road to the wells).

63. Go out of the house.

64. In HJ. 1.121 we also find a rule prohibiting women to attend celebrations.

65. Other reasons which could corrupt women and had legal implications were those enumerated in Bṛh. 25.11 (neglect of daily duties), in ŚS. 3.39-43 (living with other men), in Śaṅkha (going around without upper garment or exposing navels or breasts, laughing without covering faces, bearing ill-will towards the husband or his relations) and in Hār. 3.3 (using the bed-seat, clothes and ornaments belonging to others), and so forth. Cf. fns. 52-56 on the preceding page).

66. Also mentioned in ŚS. 3.39-43.

67. That means she had a bad reputation and nobody wanted to marry her.

68. His jealously could also be caused by her bad beh'viour.

to be clear why in the Dharmaśāstra-s we could find a stanza containing causes which corrupted women enumerated in Mn. (9.13) and HJ. (1.122) and not those enumerated in HJ. (1.121), Śto. (328.10-3) and SRK. (114.5).

6. *Fickleness and Unchastity of Women*

(a) *Reasons Causing Chastity of Women*

A. After having quoted two similar stanzas on the causes which ruined women, we find in H. other stanzas of a general character. These stanzas conveyed the very often repeated idea in classical Sanskrit literature that women were fickle and unchaste. According to these stanzas only in one case a woman was chaste and that was in the case of lack of a paramour. In H. this idea was repeated twice. The two stanzas read as follows :

sthānaṁ nāsti kṣano nāsti prārthayitā naraḥ,
tena nārada nārīṇāṁ satītvam upajāyate.
na lajjā na vinītatvaṁ na dākṣinyaṁ na bhīrutā,
prārthakābhāva eveti satītve kāraṇaṁ striyāḥ.

[Only for lack of (appropriate) place, (favourable) moment or of a paramour, oh Nārada, women are chaste.

Neither shame, nor decency, nor piety, nor fearfulness, but lack of a paramour is the cause that a woman is chaste].

The first stanza is quoted in HJ. 1.123, HK. 1.117, HP. 1.88, HL. 24.14-5, HC. 33.7-8, HM I.115, HN. 1.89 and HS. 1.109[69] and the second in HJ. 1.126, HK. 1.121, HP. in MS B (No. 56 of Bühler's collection of 1873-4) after 1.87 and HL. (quoted in HS. *ad* 1.111).[70]

B. The first stanza is also found in PP. 1.107; Pts. 1.138; PtsK. 1.154; Vet. 24.2; VCsr. 6.11; NP. 1.14, 76 and ŚP.

69. Instead of *sthānam* PP., Pts., PtsK, VC. has *rāho,* VN in VC. *aho,* Q in VCsr. *ahar* M in VCsr. *dhakṣo,* Nd in VCsr. *pakṣo*; instead of *kṣaṇo* NHP. has *kṣaṇaṁ,* Q in VCsr. has *kṣaṇo,* IS. *kṣaṇe*; instead of *prārthayitā* Pr in PP. has *prārthayatā* (similarly IS.,), IS. *prārthavito*; instead of *naraḥ* VCsr. has *janaḥ*; instead of *tena* VC sr. and NP have *itthaṁ*; instead of *satītvaṁ*⁰ VCsr. has *pātivratyaṁ,* Q in VCsr. *satitvaṁ*; instead of *upajāyate* M in PP. has *upajñāyate,* VCsr. *prakalpyate,* VJ. in VCsr. *hi kalpate*; Nd in VCsr. *kalpayat,* MNVJ in VCsr. *kalpate.*

70. Instead of *vinītatvaṁ* HL. has *vinitātvaṁ*; instead of *prārthakābhāva* HL. has *prārthanāl‘āva,* instead of *eveti* HL. has *evaikaṁ* and HP. *evaikaḥ.*

80; the second, being a repetition of the first one, is not found in other classical Sanskrit sources.

A similar idea was expressed in MBh. (13.38, 23) where we read that women remained chaste only because of lack of a paramour, or because of fear of relatives, or fear of a death sentence (corporal punishment), or of imprisonment.[71] The same idea was also often repeated in other sources.[72]

As to the two stanzas found in HJ. it may be remarked that the second one seems not to be either necessary at all or, as was the case in HP. or HL., should precede or immediately follows the first stanza. It seems wrong to divide the two stanzas by other stanzas, since the main idea, that is lack of a paramour as cause for chastity of women, was the same in both stanzas. HJ. 1.123 added however to that idea the lack of appropriate place and favourable moment and HJ. 1.126 shame, decency, piety and fearfulness.

(*b*) *Inborn Unchastity of Women*

A. Other stanzas in the second part of the story of the young wife and the old husband dealt also with the subject of unchastity of women. HJ. 1.124 declared, in the same spirit as the two stanzas described above, that for women every man was good because it was the nature of women that they were like a jar of ghee, while men were like glowing coal; consequently no one should place ghee near glowing coal. In this connection HP. and HK. added that women became very excited when they saw a person of an opposite sex. HJ. 1.125 also declared that women were fickle and that it was most difficult to keep them chaste.

B. We read in H. :

na strīṇām apriyaḥ kaścit priyo vāpi na vidyate,
gāvas tṛṇam ivāraṇye prārthayanti navaṁ navam.

[To women no one is disagreeable or agreeable; (they), similarly as cattle in forest which continually seek fresh grass, seek for a new man].

71. *alābhāt puruṣāṇām hi bhayāt parijanasya hi,*
badhabandhabhayāc cāpi svayaṁ guptā bhavanti tāḥ. MBh. 13.38.23

72. Cf. *pañca me patayas santi mahyaṁ ṣaṣṭho 'pi rocate,*
puruṣāṇām abhāvena sarvā nāryaḥ pativratāḥ. NŚ. 9 See par. A.

This stanza is found in HJ. 1.124 and 4.7, HK. 1.119 and 4.7, HP. 1.155 and 4.7, HS. 1.189, HL. 24.16-7, HC. 33.9-10 and 133.10-1, HM. 1.116, HN. 1.156 and 4.7 as well as in CNF. 40.

A very similar stanza is found in MBh. (13.39, 5)[73] and RV. (414.15-6)[74] and is in accordance with Mn. (9.14) and MBh. (13.38, 17) where it was stated that women did not care for beauty or for youth in their paramours; it was enough for them that it was a man; then they gave themselves up irrespective whether he was handsome or ugly.[75]

The conception of inborn unchastity of women was described in H. in accordance with many classical Sanskrit sources in which we read *inter alia* that women like plants wrapped around any man[76] and like rivers strove after vulgar ones.[77] Women forsook men endowed with good qualities, renowned, handsome, adepts in the art of love, rich and young and betook themselves to men destitute of amiability, merit and the like.[78]

73. *na cāsāṁ mucyate kaścit puruṣo hastam āgataḥ,*
gāvo navaṭṛṇānīva gṛhṇanty etā navaṁ navam. MBh. 13.39,5.

74. *naivāṅganānāṁ dayito nāpi dveṣyo 'sti kaścana,*
sarvam evāvalambante latā gahanajā iva. RV. 414.15-6.

75. *naitā rūpaṁ parīkṣante nāsāṁ vayasi saṁsthitiḥ,*
surūpam vā virūpaṁ vā pumān ity eva bhunjate. Mn. 9.14.
nāsāṁ kaścid agamyo 'sti nāsāṁ vayasi niścayaḥ,
virūpam rūpavantaṁ vā pumān ity eva bhuñjate. MBh. 13.38, 17.
Cf. *na kāmabhogān vipulān nālaṁkārān na saṁśrayān,*
tathaiva bahu manyante yathā ratyām anugraham. MBh. 13.38- 28.

76. *latā pārśve sthitaṁ vṛkṣaṁ bhṛtyāḥ parśve sthitam nṛpam,*
pārsvasthaṁ puruṣaṁ yoṣid veṣṭayanti na saṁśayaḥ. CSBD. 178.
Also in CSB I 2.79, CSJ. 2.77, CSC I 2.78, SCSC II. 178, CSB II. 177, CSLd. 2.77.
āsannam eva nṛpatir bhajate manuṣyaṁ
vidyāvihīnam akulīnam asaṁstutaṁ vā,
prāyeṇa bhūmipatayaḥ pramadā latāś ca
yat pārśvato bhavati tat pariveṣṭayanti. PP. 1.28.
(Also in PRE. 1.20, Pts. 1.35, PtsK. 1.41, HJ. 2.55, KP. 2.51, HS. 2.55, Śts. 21.11-4).

77. *mahābhijanajātānām api hā dhiṅ nisargataḥ,*
saritām iva nārīnāṁ vṛttir nimnānusāriṇī. KR. 6.316
hā dhig nimnābhiyāyinyo lolā dūrād manoramāḥ,
sukṣobhyā na striyaḥ śakyāḥ pātuṁ śvabhrāpaga iva. SK. 10.64. 149b-150a.

78. *guṇāśtrayaṁ kīrtiyutaṁ ca kāntaṁ patiṁ ratijñaṁ sadhanaṁ yuvānam.*
vihāva śīghraṁ vanitā vrajanti narāntikaṁ śīlaguṇādihīnam. HJ. 2.116.

That was very common among them,[79] since through their passion to men, through their mutable temper, through their natural heartlessness, they became disloyal towards their husbands, however carefully they may have been guarded in this world.[80] Among thousands of women, or perhaps among hundreds of thousands, sometimes only one, devoted to her husband, could be found.[81] Women had never shown sufficient regard for those husbands who accomplished all their wishes, as they always did what was agreeable to them and protected them from want and danger.[82] Women used to show liking for any man who courted them, who approached them, or was gallant towards them even to the slightest extent.[83] Even those women who were loved and respected by their husbands admitted to their favours men that were hump-backed, that were blind, that were idiots, that were dwarfs or that were lame.[84] They were always looking for new paramours and could not be kept in obedience; their diposition was such that they were incapable of being restrained; they were unseizable and unintelligible as words.[85] They were exceedingly fond of sexual intercourse; even Agni, Varuṇa and other celestials were not so agreeable to them as the deity of desire.[86] When they were under the influence of desire they did not care for their family,

Asad dharmas tv ayaṁ strīṇām asmākaṁ bhavati prabho,
pāpīyaso narān yad vai lajjāṁ tyaktva bhajāmahe. MBh. 13.38, 14
nīcam āśrayate lakṣmīr akulena sarasvatī,
apātraṁ bhajate nārī girau varṣati vāsavaḥ. HJ. 2. 156.
kulajātiparibhraṣṭaṁ nikṛṣṭaṁ duṣṭaceṣṭitam,
aspṛśyam adhamaṁ prāyo manye strīṇām priyaṁ varam. VCsr. II.15.

79. *durjanagamyā nāryaḥ prāyeṇāpātrabhṛd bhavati rājā,*
kṛpaṇānusāri ca dhanaṁ devo girijālādhivarṣī. HJ. 2.155.

80. *paumścalyāc calacittavān naissnehyāc ca svabhāvataḥ,*
rakṣitā yatnato 'piha bhartṛṣvetā vikurvate. Mn. 9.15.

81. *sahasre kila nārīṇām prāpyetaikā kadācana,*
tathā śatasahasreṣu yadi kācit pativratā. MBh. 13.19, 92.

82. *kāmānām api dātārāṁ kartāraṁ manasāṁ priyam,*
rakṣitāraṁ na mṛṣyanti svabhartāram alaṁ striyaḥ. MBh. 13.38, 27.

83. *striyaṁ hi yah prārthayate sannikarṣaṁ ca gacchati,*
īṣac ca kurute sevāṁ tam evecchanti yoṣitaḥ. Mbh. 38,15.

84. *yāś ca śaśvad bahumatā rakṣyante dayitāḥ striyaḥ,*
api tās samprasajjante kubjāndhajaḍavāmanaiḥ. MBh. 13.38,. 20
paṅgāṣv api ca devarṣe ye cānye kutsitā narāḥ,
strīṇām agamyo loke 'smin nāsti kaścin mahāmune MBh. 13.38, 21.

85. *calasvabhāvā duhsevyā durgrāhyā bhāvatas tathā,*
prājñasya puruṣasyeha yathā vācas tathā striyaḥ. MBh. 13.38, 24.

86. *nānilo 'gnir na varuṇo na cānye tridaśā dvija,*
priyāḥ strīṇām yathā kāmo ratiśīlā hi yoṣitaḥ. MBh. 13.19, 91.

or father, or mother, or brother, or husband, or sons, or husband's brothers; in pursuit of what they considered happiness they destroyed their families; they also became then most capricious and did not feel any pain even if they walked over a desert of burning sand.[87] There was no pleasure more agreeable to them than sexual intercourse with persons belonging to the opposite sex, since such intercourse was considered as the most delicious and ripe fruit of joy.[88] As fire was never satiated with fuel, as ocean could never be filled with waters of rivers, as the god of death was never satiated with slaying all living creatures, similarly women were never satiated with men.[89] Women suffered from fever arising from their passionate feelings; for their lovers' sake they left their sons, husbands, houses, wealth and everything else.[90] If they found a young man they were ready to leave the country, but when they found a better one they were ready to leave the first one.[91] When they found a young man exceptionally strong in sexual intercourse they left their families, fear, shame, *dharma*, friends, fame, wealth and so forth. They could leave everything and could even poison their well qualified husbands.[92]

C. The comparison between a woman and a pot of ghee and between a man and glowing coal was given in H. where it was stated :

ghṛta-kumbha-samā nārī taptāṅgāra-samaḥ pumān,
tasmād ghṛtaṁ ca vahniṁ ca naikatra sthāpayed budhaḥ.

[A woman is like a pot of ghee (and) a man like a glowing coal; therefore a prudent man should not bring ghee and fire together].

87. *naitā jānanti pitaraṁ na kulaṁ na ca mātaram,*
na bhrātṝn na ca bhartāraṁ na ca putrān na devarān. MBh. 13.19, 93.
līlāyantyaḥ kulaṁ ghnanti kūlānīva saridvarāḥ,
doṣān sarvāṁś ca matvāśu prajāpatir abhāṣata. MBh. 13.19, 94.
ātmacchandena vartante nāryo manmathacoditāḥ,
na ca dahyanti gacchantyaḥ sutaptair api pāṁśubhiḥ. MBh. 13.19, 87.

88. *nātaḥ paraṁ hi nārīṇām vidyate ca ksdācana,*
yathā purusasaṁsargaḥ param etad dhi naḥ phalam. MBh. 13.19, 86.

89. *nāgnis tṛpyati kāṣṭhānāṁ nāpagānāṁ mahodadhiḥ,*
nāntakaḥ sarvabhūtānāṁ na puṁsāṁ vāmalocanāḥ. HJ. 2. 114.

90. *vicetanā bhavet sā ca kāmajvaraprapīḍitā,*
sarvaṁ tyajati taddhetoḥ putraṁ kāntaṁ gṛhaṁ dhanaṁ. NP. 1.14, 78

91. *labdhvā yuvānaṁ puruṣaṁ deśatyāgaṁ karoti sā,*
taduttamaṁ punar labdhvā taṁ tyajet sā kṣaṇena ca. NP. 1.14, 79.

92. *tyajet kulaṁ bhayaṁ lajjāṁ dharmaṁ bandhuṁ yaśaḥ śriyam,*
samprāpya ratiśūraṁ ca yuvānaṁ suratonmukham. NP. 1.14, 81.
viṣaṁ dātuṁ samarthā sā svāminaṁ guṇināṁ varam,
mlecchaṁ yuvānaṁ samprāpya sarvasvaṁ dātum utsukā. NP. 1.14.80.

This stanza is found in HJ. 1.127, HK. 1.120, HP. 1.90[93], HL. 24.24-5, HC. 33.13-4, HM. 1.117, HN. 1.91, HS. 1.112, as well as in C (CNJV 77, CNŚ. 34, CNF. 101, CNPh. 112, CNPN. 52, CNI II 18) and was quoted with variants in ŚV. Intr. 1 and 3.10, PdP., Sṛṣṭhi-khaṇḍa 54.21 and SRBh 162. 408; in the latter, the last two *pādas* were different.[94] A similar idea was also conveyed in SB. 228[95] and in BhP. 7.12, 9[96] and many other Sources.

D. Some editions of H. added between the two stanzas another one, which described the nature of women as full of passion towards men. This stanza reads :

surūpam puruṣaṁ dṛṣṭvā bhrātaraṁ yadi vā sutam,[97]
yoniḥ klidyati nārīṇāṁ satyaṁ satyaṁ hi nārada.

(*Feminae virum pulchrnm, sive fratrem, sive filium intuitae pudendum madescit ; vero, Nārada, vero*).

This stanza found in HK. 1.116, HP. 1.87[98], HS. 1.110, HC. 33.10-1 and HL. 24.18-9; HJ. does not quote this stanza. It is also found with some variants in some Cāṇakya's compendia (CRP. 2.45, CRBh. I. 2.45, CRCa I. 2.39, CNI I. 159, CnT II.23.9, CnT III. 57.3), the Garuḍa-purāṇa (1.109, 37), and in SB. 273 (IS. 7134)[99]; the same idea was also repeated in SB (IS. 7128)[100], MBh. 13.38, 26[101], ŚV. 3.9[102], VCsr. II 13, NŚ. 8[103] and NP. 1.14, 17.[104] These stanzas which

93. In HP. the last *pāda* reads : *pṛthak sthānena dhāvayet.* B MS is the same as HJ. and HK.

94. *ghṛtakumbhasamā nārī taptāṅgārasamaḥ pumān,*
saṁśleṣād dravate kumbhaḥ tadvat strīpuṁsabhāvitā, ŚV. 1.1.

ŚV. 3.10 reads : when they are both brought together the ghee melts; such is the nature of women.

95. *agnikuṇḍasamā nārī ghṛtakumbhasamo naraḥ,*
saṁgamena parastrīṇāṁ kasya no calate manaḥ. SB. 228 (IS. 62).

96. *nanv agniḥ pramadā nāma ghṛtakumbhasamaḥ pumān,*
sutām api raho jahyād anyadā yāvadarthakṛt. BhP. 7.12, 9.

97. Or *nārīṇām āmapātrām ivāṁbhasā*

98. B MS No. 56 of Bühler's Collection of 1873-4.

99. *suveṣaṁ puruṣaṁ dṛṣṭvā bhārataraṁ yadi vā sutam,*
yonih klidyati nārīṇāṁ satyaṁsatyaṁ hi nārada. SB. 273 (IS 7134).

100. *surūpaṁ puruṣaṁ dṛṣṭvā pitaraṁ bhārataram sutam,*
dehaṁ klidyati nārīnam paśya kāmasya ceṣṭitam. SB. (IS. 7128)

101. *idam anyac ca devarṣe rahasyaṁ sarvayoṣitām,*
dṛṣṭvaiva puruṣaṁ hṛdyaṁ yoniḥ praklidyate striyāḥ. MBh. 13.38,26.

102. *susnātaṁ puruṣaṁ dṛṣṭvā sugandham malavarjitam,*
klidyante yonayaḥ strīṇām āmapātram ivāṁbhasa. ŚV. 3.9.

103. *sundaraṁ puruṣaṁ dṛṣṭvā bhrātaraṁ pitaraṁ sutam,*
yonir dravati nārīṇāṁ satyaṁ satyaṁ janārdana. NŚ. 8 (IS. 7107).

104. *suveṣaṁ kāmukaṁ dṛṣṭvā kāminī madanatūrā,*
tadgrātaṁ ca pulakitaṁ yonau kaṇḍūyanaṁ param. NP. 1.14- 77.

in different words expressed the same idea showed that it was considered that even the nearness of a man caused passion in women for which they were not responsible.[105]

(c) *General knowledge about Unchastity of Women*

A. The last from this group of stanzas (HJ. 1.121 to 129) is the following:

striyo hi capalā nityaṁ devānām api viśrutam,
tās cāpi rakṣitā yeṣām te narāḥ sukhabhāginaḥ.

[It is well-known that women, even those of celestials, are fickle. Happy, indeed are those men who can guard them].[106]

This stanza is quoted in HJ. 1.125, HK. 1.118, HP. 1.89[107], HL. 24.20-1 and HS. 1.111.

B. The idea contained in the first part of this stanza was well-known and was in accordance with many classical Sanskrit literary works. In the first place the text of the Bārhaspatya Artha śāstra should be quoted where we also find the thought that it was well-known that women were fickle.[108] The same thought was also found in C (CNW. 54, CNPh. 58 v.l., CSBD. 209, CSB I. 3.9, CSJ. 2.17, CSC I. 2.9, CSC II. 209, CSB II 209, CSLd. 3.9)[109]. PP.[110] (Pts. 4.115, PtsK. 4.81), MBh.[111] and R.[112] However the second part of this stanza could not be traced, though it is also in conformity with some classical Sanskrit sources.[113] This stanza might be considered as a bridge connecting this group of stanzas which dealt with

105. Cf. also : *naitā jānanti pitaraṁ na kulaṁ na ca mātaram,*
na bhrātṝn na ca bhartāraṁ na ca putrān na devarān.
MBh. 13.19, 93.

106. Protect them.

107. A, B, C, an N MSs used by Peterson omitted this stanza.

108. *strīsu cāpalaṁ dūratvaṁ jñātiṣu sauhṛdaṁ patrajalabinduvat.* BS. 5.14.

109. *vidyate śiśucāpalyaṁ vidyate brāhmaṇe tapaḥ,*
pāruṣyaṁ vidyate nīce dayā sādhuṣu vidyate. CNW. 54.

110. *saṁbhāvyaṁ goṣu saṁpannaṁ saṁbhāvyaṁ brāhmaṇe tapaḥ,*
saṁbhāvyaṁ strīṣu cāpalyaṁ saṁbhāvyaṁ jñātito bhayam. PP. 4.64.

111. *saṁpannaṁ goṣu saṁbhāvyaṁ saṁbhāvyaṁ brāhmaṇe tapaḥ,*
saṁbhāuyaṁ cāpalaṁ strīṣu saṁbhāvyaṁ jñātito bhayam. MBh. 5.35, 58.

112. *vidyate goṣu saṁpannaṁ vidyate jñātito bhayam,*
vidyate strīṣu cāpalyaṁ vidyate brāhmaṇe tapaḥ. RB. 6.16, 9.

113. Cf. *dhātāpi na prabhuḥ prāyaś cāpalānāṁ tu raksaṇe,*
mattā nadī ca nārī ca niyantuṁ kena pāryate. KS. 7.36, 8.
na tāsāṁ rakṣaṇaṁ kartuṁ śakyaṁ puṁsā kathañcana,
api viśvakṛtā tāta kutas tu puruṣair iha. MBh. 13.40, 12b-13a.

fickleness of women with the idea expressed in HJ. 1.128 and taken from Mn. and other Dharmaśāstra-s which dealt with the necessity of protecting women in their childhood, youth and widowhood. H. explained the reason for this principle in the same manner as Mn. and other Dharmaśāstras did. The reason for protection of women was not caused by women's helplessness or their weakness but by their fickleness, evil inclinations[114] and particularly passion for men.[115] Their protection was mandatory in order to protect the family of their fathers and their husbands[116] and in order to preserve their husbands and the purity of their offspring.[117]

C. It seems that HJ. 1.125 which formed a bridge between the stanzas dealing with fickleness of women and stanza HJ. 1.128 should have been put immediately before HJ. 1.128 in order to convey in a more logical way the idea of the Dharma-, artha-śāstra-s and many classical Sanskrit literary works,[118] the more so as the author of H. wanted to convey to the readers of his work the same idea. Yet unfortunately the author[119] of H., as it was so usual to him, put together several aphorisms dealing with the same or similar subjects without thinking about the order in which they should be logically put together and without thinking, as was also the case in the story of the young wife and the old husband, whether the story itself necessitated the quotation of the stanzas included. The theme of fickleness of women and particularly the need for their protection does not seem to add very much to the story.

The situation was different, however, as far as the four stanzas in the story of the young wife and the old husband were concerned. These stanzas dealt with the feelings of an old man towards his young wife and vice versa, the problem dealt with in the story.

114. Cf. Mn. 9.5.
115. Cf. Mn. 9.15.
116. Cf. Mn. 9.5.
117. Cf. Mn. 9.7.
118. Cf. MBh. 13. and chapters 39 and 19.
119. Or authors.

7. *Feelings of the Young Wife towards Her Old Husband and Feelings of the Old Husband towards His Young Wife*

The first four stanzas in the story of the old husband and the young wife could be divided into two groups. The first referred to the feeling of the young wife to her old husband and the second to the feelings of the old man to his young wife.

A. The first group dealing with the feelings of the young wife towards her old husband consists of two stanzas. The first reads :

śaśinīva himārtānāṁ gharmārtānāṁ ravāvi'va,
mano na ramate strīṇām jarājīrṇendriye patau.

[As the heart of those tortured with cold is not satisfied with the moon, nor of those tortured with heat with the sun, (so the heart) of women (is not satisfied) with the husband whose organs of sense become dulled by old age.)

paliteṣv api dṛṣṭeṣu puṁsaḥ kā nāma kāmitā,
bhaiṣajyam iva manyante yad anyamanasaḥ striyaḥ.

[When a man becomes grey-haired how, indeed, can be a paramour, since women regard him like a drug and direct be their desire towards others.]

The first stanza is found in HJ. 1.117, HK. 1.110, HP. 1.81, HL. 23.24-5, HC. 32.9-10, HM. 1.109, HN. 1.83 and HS. 1.103.[120] (Also quoted in SRBh. 95.3 and SRK. 97.3).

The second stanza is found in HJ. 1.118, HK. 1.111, HP. 1.82, HL 23.26-7, HC 32.11-2, HM 1.110, HN. 1.84 and HS. 1.104.[121] (Also quoted in Subhāṣitaratnakoṣa 1524)

B. In both the stanzas the author expressed the opinion that every young wife who had an old husband disliked him and directed her desire toward other men.

Both these stanzas could not be traced to any classical Sanskrit literary works, but were certainly in accordance with them. We find the same thoughts in many of those sources. It was considered that since young and beautiful women could never find satisfaction with old husbands[122] they shunned them

120. The readings were not always the same. In (*d*) HP. (A. and C. MSS) has *jarāgrastendriye* while N. MS. has *jarāpitandriye*. HS. has *jārākṣīṇendriye*. HS. quoted also HL. as having *jarayā pīḍite patau*. It seems that the best reading is *jarāpitendriye*.

121. The readings are all identical. Only HS. mentions that the P. MS. has in (*c*) *paliteṣu* and that the S. edition has in (*b*) *kāmāmakāmitā*; the latter seems to be wrong.

122. *prāgalbhyahīnasaya narasya vidyā śastraṁ yathā kāpuruṣasya haste*
na tṛptim utpādayate śarīre vṛddhasya dārā iva darśanīyāh.
Jyotiṣṭattva in Śabdakalpadruma (IS. 4297).

like poison[123], or ran away from them[124], because old age of husbands caused ruin to them,[125] while husbands' youth was considered as their main and most important attribute.[126] Since young women shunned old men, if they visited them they did it always for a special purpose.[127]

C. The second group of stanzas dealing with the feelings of an old husband towards his young wife consists also of two stanzas. The first reads :

dhanāśā jīvitāśā ca gurvī prāṇabhṛtāṁ sadā,
vṛddhasya taruṇī bhāryā prāṇebhyo'pi garīyasī.

[The desire for wealth, (the desire) for keeping his life is at all times strong among human beings; however, to an old man a young wife is dearer than life itself].

The second reads :

nopabhoktuṁ na ca tyaktuṁ śaknoti viṣayān jarī,
asthi nirdaśanaḥ śveva jihvayā leḍhi kevalam.

[A decrepit old man cannot enjoy sensual pleasure nor can he renounce it; he is like a toothless dog which (is) only (able) to lick a bone with (his) tongue.]

The first stanza is found in HJ. 1.119, HK. 1.112, HP. 1.83, HL. 24.2-3, HC. 32.14-5, HM. 111, HN. 1.85 and HS. 1.105. (Also quoted in SBRh 166.584).

The second stanza is found in HJ. 1.120, HK. 1.113, HP. 1.84, HL. 24.4-5, HC. 32. 16-7, HM. 112, HN. 1.86 and HS. 1.106.[128] Also appears in BhS 583)

123. *ratiśūraṁ priyaṁ dṛṣṭvā kṣīraṁ ghṛtam ivācaret,*
gate vayasi jīrṇaṁ taṁ viṣaṁ dṛṣṭvā tyajet kṣaṇāt. NP. 1.14, 88.

124. *varnaṁ sitaṁ jhaṭiti vīkṣya śirohāṇaṁ*
sthānaṁ paraṁ paribhavasya tad eva puṁsām,
āropitāsthiśakalaṁ parihṛtya yānti
caṇḍālakūpam iva dūrataraṁ taruṇyaḥ. BhŚ. 323.

Also in Pts. 4.77, PtsK. 3.193, SB. 316 (IS. 6599), ŚP. 4146, SRBh. 95.14, SRK. 97.6. Śatakāvalī 106.

125. HJ. 1.121 *op. cit.*

126. *vayo rūpaṁ kulaṁ śīlaṁ vittaṁ ceti varasya yat,*
mṛgyate sakhi tatrādyaṁ vayo vaṁśādikaṁ tataḥ. SK. 6. 30, 29.

127. *akasmād yuvatī vṛddhaṁ keśeṣv ākṛṣya cuṁbati,*
patiṁ nirdayam āliṅgya hetur atra bhaviṣyati. HJ. 1.116

This is the introductory stanza to the story of the young wife and the old husband.

128. The readings are not always the same. HK. has in (*b*) *viṣayābjarī* and HP. *viṣayāñjarī*. In (*c*) HP. in the B. MS has *nirdaśanasyeva* and in the A. MS *nirdaśanaśveva* (similarly the S. editeon in HS.); HL. (quoted in HS.) has *nirdaśanaś caiva*.

D. In both these stanzas the author expressed the opinion that old husbands desired young women though could not enjoy them.

Both these stanzas could not be traced to any classical Sanskrit literary works, but were certainly in accordance with them. We find the same thoughts in many sources. And so we read that despite old age, men desired young women[129] though they were considered as an object of mockery.[130] For an old husband a young wife was like a poison.[131]

E. If we compare these two groups of stanzas with those analysed before, we see that they form an entirety and give somewhat of an explanation for the reasons of the author of H. why he quoted the stanzas on fickleness of women. Stanza HJ. 1.117 explained why the young wife did not love her old husband and became unchaste. This stanza may be considered as forming a bridge between the four first stanzas in the story of the young wife and the old husband and the other stanzas which conveyed the idea of fickleness of women and the need of protecting them

129. *vapuḥ kubjībhūtaṁ gatir api tathā yaṣṭiśaraṇā*
viśīrṇā dantāliḥ śravaṇavikalaṁ śrotrayugalam,
śiraḥ śuklam cakṣus timirapaṭalair āvṛtam aho
mano me nirlajjaṁ tad api viṣayebhyaḥ spṛhayati.
Kavitāmṛtakūpa 64; Calcutta.
jarāgrastaṁ rūpaṁ hasitalalitosāharahitam
śirah śuklībhūtaṁ timirapaṭalair akṣi pihitam,
śanair yaṣṭyutthānaṁ gatir api ca mandākulapadā
samīpastho mṛtyur vilasati na ccchā viramati. SB. 72 (IS. 2349)
valibhir mukham ākrāntaṁ palitair aṅkitaṁ śiraḥ,
gātrāṇi śithilāyante tṛṣṇaikā taruṇayate. BLŚ. 156. Also quoted in ŚP. 419, SRBh. 76.4, VS. 3242. SRK. 67.6.

130. *vṛddhakāle mṛtā bhāryā bandhuhastagataṁ dhanam,*
bhojanaṁ ca parādhīnaṁ tisraḥ puṁsāṁ viḍambanāḥ. CVND 8,9.
mūrkhasya kāvyakaraṇaṁ gītam akaṇṭhasya lalitam adhanasya,
vṛddhasya viṣayavāñchā parahāsyakarāṇi catvāri. SB. 33 (IS. 4913).
mūrkho 'śāntas tapasvī kṣitipatir alaso matsaro dharmaśīlo
duḥstho mānī gṛhasthaḥ prabhur atikṛpaṇaḥ śāstravid dharmahīnaḥ,
ājñāhīno narandraḥ śucir api satataṁ yaḥ parānnopabhogī
vṛddho rogī dardhaḥ sa ca yuvatipatir dhig viḍambaprakārān.
Navaratna 5 in HKS.

131, *dur adhītā visaṁ vidyā ajīrṇe bhojanaṁ viṣam*
viṣaṁ goṣṭhī daridrasya vṛddhasya taruṇī viṣam.

CVND. 4.15, (CVM 4.10, CvTb 8.14; CvL. I. 8.23, CvL II. 8.17, CSBD. 15, CSB. I. 1.15, CSJ. 1.15, CSC. I. 1.15, CSC. II. 15, CSB. II. 15, CSL1. 1.15, CNJV. 98, CNS. 42, CNW. 78, CNF. 11, CNP. I. 26, CNPn. 56, CNPN. 21, CNP. II.69, CNI. I.229, CNG. 144, CNT. IV. 25, CNM. 25, CNMN. 25, CNMN. 97, CNL. 21, CNI II. 13, CnT. V. 44, CnT. VII. 58) SB. 11.123 (IS 2896)

during their lifetime. These four stanzas which were not based on the Smṛti-s and which could not be found in the Smṛti-s were necessary in the story of the young wife and the old husband and were most closely connected with the story itself.

8. *Closing Stanza of the Story*

A. The story of the young wife and the old husband ends with the following stanza :

uśanā veda yac chāstraṁ yac ca veda vṣhaspatiḥ,
svabhāvenaiva tat sarvaṁ strībuddhau supratiṣṭhitham.

[Whatever Śāstras, Uśanas as well as Bṛhaspati knows, all that is, by nature, firmly implanted in women's intelligence.]

This stanza is found in HJ. 1.130, HK. 1.123, HL. 25. 7-8, HC. 34.4-5, HM. 1.120 and HS. 1.114 (HP. and J. in HS. do not quote this stanza).[132] (Also quoted in SRBh 348.20).

Though this stanza mentions Uśanas, an author of a Dharmaśāstra, and an Arthaśāstra,[133] and Bṛhaspati (Vṛaspati) also an author of a Dharmaśāstra and an Arthaśāstra[134] it cannot be interpreted from the legal point of view. It shows only that these two authorities enjoyed great popularity and esteem in this part of India where H. was written.

B. Almost the same stanza, as that quoted in paragraph 7E above, is found in PP. 1.142[135] (Pts. 1.185, PtsK. 1.199), Skanda-puraṇa, Nāgarakhaṇḍa 193.6 and MBh. (13.39,8[136]). P. C. Roy translated this stanzas as follows[137] : That science of polity which the preceptor of the Asura-s knew canot be regarded to be deeper or more distinguished for subtlety than what woman's intelligence naturally brings forth. Verily, how can women, therefore, be restrained by men ?[138]

132. HK. has in (*b*) *Bṛhaspati* and in (*c*), similarly as the S. edition in HS. *tacchāstraṁ*.

133. Cf. P.V. Kane, History of Dharmaśāstra, I.110 sqq.

134. op. cit. I.123 sqq. 207 sqq.

135. *uśanā veda yac chāstram yac ca veda bṛhaspatiḥ,*
strībuddhyā na viśiṣyeta tasmād rakṣyāḥ kathaṁ hi tāḥ. PP. 1.142.

136. *uśanā veda yac chāstraṁ yac ca veda bṛhaspatiḥ,*
strībuddhyā na viśsiyete tās tu rakṣyāḥ kathaṁ naraiḥ. MBh. 13.39.8

137. Vol. 10.4.

138. A. W. Ryder translated this stanza from PP. as follows :
Learn science with the gods above
or imps in nether space,
Yet women's wit will rival it;
How keep them in their place !

This stanza, as quoted in H., could not be traced to any other classical Sanskrit source. It seems that H. either used the text as it was known in that part of India where its author lived or changed it to fit better the story of the young wife and the old husband. However, the reason for the change is not clear, because the text, as quoted in MBh. (or P.) was more suited to the contents of the story, since it gave a final touch to the story and formed a perfect frame to it. This stanza conveyed the idea that because of women's inborn intelligence they could never be kept chaste by men, despite the fact that they had to be always protected, *viz.*, by their father in their childhood, by their husband during their marriage and by their sons during their widowhood. Their fickleness and unchastity was stronger than any bonds which could be imposed on them.

In the story of the young woman and the old husband all these principles were described and, therefore, it seems that this stanza would form an excellent closing of the story, while the ending, as quoted in H., though not bad, seems to be unfinished; it conveyed the same idea as that contained in Pañc. and MBh., *viz.*, that women were clever and had the knowledge of the Śāstra-s, that this knowledge was inborn to them, but did not contain the conclusion that because of the intelligence of women they could not be guarded and remained fickle and unchaste. Even stanza HJ. 1.125 would seem to form a better ending than HJ. 1.130[139].

9. *Conclusions.*

A. An analysis of H. from the point of view of the Smṛti-s is quite difficult because of the nature of the work. The author (authors) of H. introduced in his work different tales more or less already known to the Indian people only to be able to incorporate in them as many aphorisms as possible which were either very well-known, or known in some parts of India or composed by him/them, irrespective of the fact whether they were closely connected, somewhat connected or very losely connected with the thread of the story in which they had been incor-

139. Cf. paragraph 6 (c) B.

porated. These various aphorisms took more place in H. than the stories themselves. Therefore H. impresses one as being rather a Subhāṣita-saṅgraha than a collection of tales. The stories which form a frame for various aphorisms were very short and contained very little material which could serve as the basis for its analysis from the point of view of the Smṛti-s.

As far as the various aphorisms were concerned, they were sometimes quoted from the Dharmaśāstra-s, particularly Mn. Sometimes they were quoted *verbatim* but sometimes some changes have been introduced.

It is well-known that Manu enjoyed in India the highest esteem and was always considered as the highest authority. The story of the young woman and the old husband also mentioned Uśanas and Bṛhaspati, both authors of a Dharmaśāstra and a Arthaśāstra as other authorities.[140] However H. quoted these authors citing the texts of MBh and Pañc.

B. In the story of the young wife and the old husband the author of H. quoted three aphorisms from the Dharmaśāstra-s. He has chosen the best known quotations from the highest authority, *i.e.*, from Mn., though the same subject was also touched upon and solved in the same manner but in different words in various Dharmaśāstra-s. The author of H. tried to choose and incorporated into his work the least legalistic, the least elaborate and the least casuistic rule not only because it was the most popular one, but also because it was the easiest to digest for an average reader.[141]

C. One of the greatest drawbacks of the author of H. in selecting aphorisms to his story, is the fact that he had selected them sometimes indiscriminately and took them out of the context in which they had some specific meaning which was lost in the text incorporated in the story of the young wife and the old husband. That was, for instance, the case when the author of H. quoted Mn. 2.215. This stanza in Mn. referred not to all men in general but to students only and cannot be interpreted as a general rule. However, to give the author

140. Cf. paragraph 8 A-B.
141. Cf. paragraph 3 C.

of H. his due, it must be pointed out that he probably did not take this rule directly from Mn., but may be from BhP. in which it was also quoted out of context[142] and as in H. had the same general meaning as referring to men in general[143] and not to students and their special duty to remain chaste during apprenticeship. On the other hand, it is felt that a conscientious author ought to refer to the original and not quote a stanza which had a specific meaning not expressed in the text of H. The only explanation for that would be the fact that the stanza in question, in popular use, has lost its real meaning in the time when it was taken by the author of H. and was generally accepted as referring to men in general and not to students only.[144] It may be added that HK., HP. and HS., did not quote Mn. 2.215 at all and that this stanza was quoted only in HJ. and HL. That, probably, did not happen by accident; it could be considered that the omission of this stanza in some MS was a sign that some felt that it had a different meaning or no bearing on the subject and found it unnecessary in the text of the story of the young wife and the old husband.

D. The other drawback of the author of H., was his lack of legal background. Wanting to make of his work a Subhāṣita-saṁgraha containing as many stanzas as possible dealing with similar subjects, he did not think that some stanzas excluded others. That was for instance the case when the author of H. quoted side by side Mn. 9.13 and the text also found in Śto. (328.10-3)[145]. These two texts[146] dealing with the same subject, *viz.*, factors causing corruption of women, repeated the same factors in different words, a wrong conception for a legal minded author, but not necessarily wrong for a work which may be considered as a Subhāṣita-saṁgraha.[147]

E. The most important feature in the legal interpretation of the story of the young wife and the old husband is the fact that the spirit of the Dharmaśāstra-s was preserved in it. H.

142. Though with an introduction and explanation.

143. MBh. which contains in Anuśāsanaparvan Mn. 2.213 and 214 omits Mn. 2.215; MBh. also did not mention that these two stanzas referred to students and apprenticeship.

144. Cf. paragraph 4 C-D.

145. Also quoted in SRK. 114.5.

146. HJ. 1.121 and HJ. 1.122.

147. Cf. paragraph 5 B.

expressed the same philosophy as Mn. did regarding the reason for which women should be protected. The reason for protecting them was not, as some authors tried to show, that women were weak and helpless, but the reason was that they were fickle, unchaste and had inborn evil inclinations and therefore had to be protected in order to preserve their husbands and the purity of their offspring.[148] This philosophy, so well expressed in Mn. and MBh. was repeated in H., and gave probably to its author the incentive for inclusion in the story of the young wife and the old husband several aphorisms relating to fickleness of women.

F. Some of the aphorisms dealing with fickleness of women were not original ones but were taken from different sources. They were, as usual for the author of H., indiscriminately chosen and as if thrown together in one kettle without carefully considering whether the particular aphorism, which came to his mind, was really necessary in the story, whether it added anything to its content and, if included, in what order it should appear. Being more an author of a Subhāṣita-saṁgraha than an author of tales, the author of H. collected only aphorisms which he thought dealt more or less with the subject and incorporated them in the story of the young woman and the old husband. That gave rather an unfortunate result.

The aphorism dealing with passion of men towards women[149] seems to be completely out of place and not necessary in the story; the same refers to two aphorisms dealing with factors causing corruption of women.[150] These three aphorisms could be very well omitted from the story of the young woman and the old husband without any loss to its content; if the first of these stanzas had to be necessarily included it might have been preferably included immediately after HJ. 1.127 with which it has some connexion; the two other stanzas, if included, might better fit at the end of the story following the main stanza dealing with the need for protection of women (HJ. 1.128).

The other stanzas also seem to be very often included in wrong places. Only the first four stanzas dealing with feelings of the young wife towards her old husband and vice versa were

148. Cf. paragraph 6 (c) B.
149. HJ. 1.129.
150. HJ. 1.121 and HJ. 1.122.

really necessary for the proper understanding of the story of the young wife and the old husband and had to be put at its beginning; then logically the stanza dealing with relations between man and woman could follow (HJ. 1.127)[151] and then the two stanzas HJ. 1.123 and HJ. 1.126 dealing both with the same subject, that is, reasons causing chastity of women. Following these stanzas the two stanzas dealing with fickleness of women could have been inserted (HJ. 1.124 and HJ. 1.125). In particular the second of them explaining the philosophy of H., and Mn. about the need of guarding women should immediately precede the main stanza taken from Mn. 9.3 (HJ. 1.128). That could preferably be the last stanza in the story of the young wife and the old husband (if any stanza in addition to the first four and the last stanza were at all necessary[152]) followed only by the frame stanza dealing with inborn intelligence of women.

G. Many of the stanzas, in addition to those taken from the Dharmaśāstra-s, were taken from well-known sources in classical Sanskrit, but even then, it may be added that the author of H. having the possibility of choosing similar stanzas from different sources did not always choose that one which most suited to the story. This remark refers, for instance, to the closing stanza which was partly taken from Pañc. and MBh. Instead of inserting in full the stanza from Pañc. or MBh. which would form a perfect closing to the story of the young wife and the old husband, the author of H. has chosen to change the two last *pādas* making the whole stanza less clear and with an unfinished thought.[153]

H. Nevertheless, despite these few short comings, familiar also to its main source—the Pañcatantra—H.'s story of the young woman and the old husband, though extremely short, was very witty, interesting and more refined than its original.[154]

151. If included, HJ. 1.129 might follow HJ. 1.127.

152. If necessary HJ. 1.121 and 122 might have been added after HJ. 1.128 and before HJ. 1.130.

153. Cf. paragraph 8 B.

154. Cf. paragraph 1 C.

XXII

THE MĀNAVA-DHARMAŚĀSTRA STANZAS IN THE HITOPADEŚA*

I. INTRODUCTION

1. A. An analysis of the *Hitopadeśa* leads to the conclusion that this work was primarily an anthology of maxims and aphorisms, in which aphorisms were interpolated. The *Hitopadeśa* is only to a lesser degree a compendium of stories based on the *Pañcatantra.*

Nārāyaṇa who is believed to be the author of the *Hitopadeśa*, often tried with success to interweave the tales, mostly borrowed from the *Pañcatantra*, with such maxims and aphorisms known to him as in his view have had some connexion with the respective stories themselves.

In this way Nārāyaṇa tried to compose a *subhāṣita-saṁgraha* containing mostly good counsels for the teaching of the sons of Sudraśana, the king of Pāṭaliputra.[1]

B. The main editions of the *Hitopadeśa* contain 786 stanzas from amongst which the origin of 557 stanzas has been traced in HAIS.[2]

The main sources for Nārāyaṇa were the *Pañcatantra*, various Cāṇakya compendia,[3] the *Kāmandakīya Nītisāra* and other *nīti* works, the *Mahābhārata*, the *Rāmāyaṇa*, some Purāṇa-s (particularly the *Garuḍa Purāṇa*), some other *kathā* works and finally the Dharmaśāstra-s, and in particular the *Mānava-Dharmaśāstra.*

C. There are 18 and one half stanza in the *Hitopadeśa* which, either directly or indirectly, have been borrowed by Nārāyaṇa from the *Mānava-Dharmaśāstra.* Some other stanzas contain similar thoughts expressed in different words and were probably inspired by the *Mānava-Dharmaśāstra.* A few other

* Previous appeared as JSAIL. 25 in "St. Schayer Commemoration Volume", Rocznik Orientalistyczny, Vol. XX, ps 427-54.

1. Cf. HAIS par. 48-9.
2. Cf. HAIS par. 48 and table VI.
3. Cf. Below Study XXIV on Cāṇakya's Aphorisms in the Hitopadeśa.

stanzas have been borrowed from *Dharmaśāstra-s* other than the *Mānava-Dharmaśāstra*, but only the 18 stanzas directly borrowed from the *Mānava-Dharmaśāstra* comprise the subject matter of this study.

2. A. Nārāyaṇa knew the *Pañcatantra* very well. As he stated himself, he extracted from it the material for the four books of his *Hitopadeśa*.[4] He also knew well some of the *nīti* literature, the *kathā* literature; unfortunately however he was poorly acquainted with the *dharma* literature, including even such a well-known work as the *Mānava-Dharmaśāstra*. He had little training and probably never went through the *Mānava-Dharmaśāstra* itself. As most authors of his times, he knew by heart some of the *dharma* stanzas by Manu, possibly without knowing their origin; without referring to the original he included them in the stories, where he assumed they belonged. His ignorance of their origin and context led him often to serious mistakes.

He quoted sometimes stanzas out of context, depriving them thus of their real meaning.[5] On other occasions, the memory of Nārāyaṇa failed him when he quoted some of the stanzas from the *Mānava-Dharmaśāstra*, without referring to the original. This occurred for instance in the case of tales 3.7b and 3.8[6], where he first quoted the second part of stanzas Mn. 7.198, then stanza Mn. 7.199, and finally the whole of stanza 7.198.[7] In another passage, Nārāyaṇa first quoted first the part of stanza Mn. 7.195. then stanza Mn 7.192 and finally returned to the second part of the stanza Mn 7.195. Inserting stanza Mn 7.192 between the two parts of stanza Mn 7.195, Nārāyaṇa destroyed the logic and sequence of the latter stanzas.[8] Not knowing the original from which he borrowed, i.e. the *Mānava-Dharmaśāstra*, Nārāyaṇa quoted sometimes two stanzas leaving out one or more preceding or following stanzas by which he changed the sense of the original[9] or, without any apparent reason, the order of the stanzas.[10] Sometimes by selecting only

4. HJ. Intr. 9.
5. Cf. below, § 3 BC F,5 6 c.
6. Cf. HAIS table II.
7. Cf. par. 10 C below.
8. Cf. par. 11 B. below.
9. Cf. par. 4 E, 7 B, 8 B, 11 B below.
10. Cf. par. 8 B, 10 C below.

one stanza from a group dealing with the same subject, Nārāyaṇa missed his own objective which was to include in his *Hitopadeśa* as many aphorisms as possible dealing with the same subject, and to create a perfect *subhāṣitasaṁgraha.*[11]

Nārāyaṇa showed also poor judgment in choosing certain stanzas from the *Mānava-Dharmaśāstra.* He sometimes included in his work poorly worded[12], or little known[13] stanzas from the *Mānava-Dharmaśāstra,* or exceptional rules.[14] or rules not well fitted to his text[15], although he had a choice of stanzas from the *Mānava-Dharmaśāstra* better suited to his story.[16]

Because of his inexperience in the *Dharmaśāstra-s* (which was obviously a handicap to a *subhāṣita-saṁgraha* author), Nārāyaṇa included in one and the same story two or more stanzas which from the legal point of view were imcompatible.[17]

B. The list of mistakes committed by Nārāyaṇa in selecting stanzas from the *Mānava-Dharmaśāstra* is certainly impressive. However, Nārāyaṇa cannot always be blamed for them. In a number of cases in the selection of a stanza from the *Mānava-Dharmaśāstra* he followed blindly his master-work, the *Pañcatantra,* where the stanza had already been quoted mistakenly.[18] Sometimes a stanza originating from the *Mānava-Dharmaśāstra* lost its specific meaning at the time when it was used by Nārāyaṇa.[19] It has to be added that we do not know the original text (the ur-text) of the *Hitopadeśa* nor do we know whether all the dubious stanzas were in fact included in the *Hitopadeśa* by Nārāyaṇa himself. It is possible, particularly in cases when a stanza was quoted only in certain editions, that it was added later by a scribe or a "reviser" of the *Hitopadeśa.*[20]

C. The analysis of each stanza quoted below shows that Nārāyaṇa was not always as careless as all that. On the contrary, at times, he appeared to know the meaning of the original

11. Cf. par. 4 F, 10 C, D, G, 11 C below.
12. Cf. par. 9 C below.
13. Cf. par. 3 C below.
14. Cf. par. 4 C below.
15. Cf. par. 3 C, 9 D below.
16. Cf. par. 4 C, 9 E below.
17. Cf. par. 5 J below.
18. Cf. par. 3 D, 4 E, 6 C below.
19. Cf. par. 3 C, 6 C below.
20. Cf. par. 5 G, 9 F below. Very few such cases were noted, as far as the stanzas borrowed from the *Mānava-Dharmaśāstra* are concerned.

stanza well, changed some of its words merely to apply the stanza more meaningfully to the text treated. And so for instance in the case of stanza HJ 2.8 he made some fortunate verbal changes so as to adjust the text to the requirements of the story.[21]

On occasions, he omitted, probably deliberately, a stanza similar to that already quoted, because it did not suit the line of his story.[22] In other cases he chose the less legalistic, less casuistic and most palatable rules.[22]

II. ANALYSIS OF TEXTS

3. *Tale* 1.2 *b of the Old Tiger and the Traveller*

A. In the story 1.2 (b) we find the following stanza:
āpad arthe[23] *dhanaṁ rakṣed*[24] *dārān*[25] *rakṣed*[26] *dhanair api*
[27]*ātmānaṁ satataṁ*[28] *rakṣed*[29] *dārair api*[30] *dhanair api*[31].

[Let him preserve (his) wealth against misfortune ; let him preserve (his) wife even (at the expense) of (his) wealth; (but) let him always preserve himself even (at the expense) (his) wife and (his) wealth].

This stanza is found in the *Hitopadeśa* (HJ. 1.43, HS. 1.36, HM. 1.41, HP. 1.31, HN. 1.31, HK. 1.42, HH. 12.15-6, HC. 17.1-2) and Mn. (7.213; also quoted in VRR. 413.2-3, RRK. 31.6-7, Kṛtyakalpataru, Rājadharma 142.2 and Dh. 3.1978). It is also found in MBh. (1.160. 27; 5.36, 18; *cf.* MBh. Bhandarkar ed 12.136, 173 Bṛ), in Cāṇakya's compendia (CVND. 1.6, CVM. 1.6, CvA. 1.6, CvṢ. 1.6, CvW. 1.7, CvP. IV 1.6, CvP. V 1.6, CvGt. 1.6,CvTb 1.6, CvH. 1.6, CvL. I 1.6, CvL. II

21. Cf. par. 6 D below.
22. Cf. par. 5 C below.
23. *āpadarthaṁ* HP., HN, HK, P in HS. VCsr (VJENd in VCsr as above), GŚ in VCjr, Śto, BhB., DhV, most of the C. compendia, Mn (all editions), VRR; *āpadārthaṁ* A in HP, Pp in HS; *āpadārthe* B in HP.
24. *rakṣyaṁ* Ś in VCjr; *rakṣet* HP 3.122, HK 3.126, BhB, most of the C. compendia.
25. *dārām* HH. (corrupt); *dārā* Ś in VCjr, MBh (Bhandarkar edition 5.37, 17), VRR.
26. *rakṣyā* Ś in VCjr, VRR; *rakṣet* DhV, CRC, MnJh (notes) wrongly.
27. *ātmā tu sarvato rakṣyā* (*rakṣyo* CRC) Ś in VCjr, CRC; *ātma tu sarvathā* MBh. (Bhandarkar edition 5.37, 17).
28. *sarvato* M_9K in MnJ, VRV; *sarvadā* G in MnJ (also quoted in MnJh); *tu tathā* Nd in MnJ (also quoted in MnJh).
29. *rakṣet* CNW wrongly.
30. *dānair api* KRB in Śto; *rakṣet putradāra* HN; *paśva dārai* IS 958.
31. *apīti* RRK (*contra metrum*).

1.6, CvI 1.6, CvLd. 1.6; CRC 2.1, CRB. 2.1, CRP. 2.1, CRBh. I. 2.1, CRBh. II 2.1; CNJV 29, CNS 12, CNW 8, CNF. 45, CNPh. 4, CNPN 7, CNI I 95, CNG. 19, CNT. IV 195, CNŚ. A 11, CNNM 68, CNŚT 25, CNI. II 21) and GP. 1.109,1.

Moreover we find this aphorisms in the *kathā* and *kāvya* literature (Pts. 1.356; 3.86; VCsr, 12.1; VCjr 20.1, Śto. 321. 12-3, Vet. 19:16 and DhV. 14, the Mādhavānalakathā 106).

HJ. 1.43 *a* is also found in HP. 3.122 *a* and HK. 3.126*v*; it forms there a part of another aphorism also found in the same form in HP. 3.122 (HK. 3.126), BhP. 198 and in C. (CVND. 1.7, CVM. 1.10, CRC. 2.2, CRB. 2.3, CRP. 2.2, CRBh. I 2.2, CRBh. II. 2.2, CVGt. 1.5, CvW. 1.6, CnT. V. 131.)[32]

The main editions of the *Hitopadeśa* contain minor variants. The main editions of Mn. are identical. Some MS. of Mn. and quotations of Mn. found in digests contain minor variants.[33]

The HP., HN. and HK. editions and the P MS. of HS. are identical with Mn.[34]

B. In the *Hitopadeśa* this stanza formed part of story I.2(b)[35], while in Mn. it was contained in the chapter dealing with *nīti*, viz. the king. Although the king was not mentioned *expressis verbis*, it is evident from the foregoing and following stanzas that Mn. meant that the king should preserve money, and not necessarily all men, against misfortune, since *kośa* was the basis of the elements of State.[36] However Medhātithi, commenting on Mn. 7.213, stated that although this rule was laid down in the *Rāja-dharma-prakaraṇa*, it should be applicable to all persons since it served a useful purpose.

In the *Hitopadeśa* this stanza clearly did not apply to kings, but was quoted by Nārāyaṇa in order to illustrate the saying of Hiraṇyaka that the protection of dependents[37] (wife

32. HJ. 1.43 is quoted in IS. 958, while HP. 3.122 is quoted in IS.959.

33. MBh. is identical with H. The Pañc. VCsr, VCjr, Śto, Vet., most of the C. compendia and other sources are identical with some editions of H. Some changes are noted in MS.

34. M in MnJ. is identical with HJ.

35. Cf. HAIS. table *ad* I.2.

36. Cf. P. V. Kane, *History of Dharmaśāstra* 3.184 sqq.

37. Wife was taken in this stanza as a *pars pro toto* (for dependents). Cf. Medhātithi on wives *ad* Mn. 7.213.

was here taken as a *pars pro tato* for dependants) was not approved at the cost of one's life.

C. Nārāyaṇa was fully justified for quoting stanza Mn. 7.213 out of context and for attributing to it universal application since, as Medhātithi had already pointed out, this stanza applied to all men; but Nārāyaṇa chose a stanza which had no direct bearing on the maxim under consideration; no corresponding stanza is found in other Dharma-or Arthaśāstra-s.

D. This stanza is also found in the *kathā* literature, in particular in Pañc. and therefore it is possible that Nārāyaṇa may have made his choice not directly from Mn.

4. *Tale 1.4a of The Blind Vulture, The Cat and The Birds*

A. In the story 1.4(a) we find the following stanza :

tṛṇāni bhūmir udakaṁ [38]*vāk caturthī ca sūnṛtā*[39],
[40]*etāny api satāṁ gehe no'cchidyante*[41] *kadācana*[42].

[Grass, place (to sit on), water and, fourthly, a kind word; these (things) are never missing in the house of good men].

This stanza is found in H. (HJ. 1.61, HS. 1.53, HM. 1.59, HP. 1.45, HN. 1.47, HK. 1.60, HH. 15.23-4, HC. 21.14-5) and Mn. (Mn. Jh. 3.91; other editions, viz. MnJ. Mn.N. MnH., MnK., MnL., MnM. 3.101, also quoted in Mit *ad* Y. 1.107, VRA. 441.7-8)[43]. It is also found in MBh. 3.2, 53; 5.35, 34; PP. 1.131, Pts. 1.171, PtsK 1.187 and NV. 32.13.[44] (Also quoted in ŚP 642 aud SRHt. 23.7).

The main editions of H. are identical.[45] Also the main editions of Mn. are identical. The texts of H. and Mn. are identical. MBh., PP., Pts. differ from H. and Mn. in γ. (The Pañc. text is probably a variant of MBh.).[46]

38. *vācā caiva tu* NV.
39. ⁰*thī su*⁰ (*ca* om.) IS 2589; *sūnatā* IS 2589.
40. *satām etāni harmyeṣu* PP. Pts, Śp; *satām etāni geheṣu* MBh; *daridrair api dātavyaṁ samāsannasya cārthinaḥ* NV.
41. *'cchidyanti* N. in HP; *'chidyanta* IS. 2589.
42. *kadādana* MBh. 5.35, 34, MBh. 3.2,51 (printing error).
43. Cf. Hār. in VRĀ 449; Pr in VRĀ 440; DhŚP. in VRĀ 442-3; Yama in VRĀ 443.
44. This stanza was ascribed to a *guru*; it contains variants in β, while γδ are different. It is probably a different stanza.
45. Only one minor variant was noted in N in HP, but HN is identical with HJ.
46. ŚP. 642 quoted also this stanza, γ reads there *satam etāni harmyyeṣu*. Th. Aufrecht (ZDMG 27.209) ascribed this stanza to Mn. and H. wrongly,

B. In H. this stanza formed part of story 1.4 (a). (A corresponding story is found in Pañc. 3.4[47]). it was there one of the first six stanzas recited by a cat wishing to win confidence. These stanzas were introduced there as deriving from *dharmaśāstra* works. In the corresponding story in Pañc. other stanzas were quoted.[48] The stanzas quoted in H. were congruous and dealt with hospitality to be given to a guest. Chapters on hospitality were also found in the main Smṛti-s.[49]

In Mn. one of the stanzas dealing with guests is identical with HJ. 1.61. This stanza was not quoted in other Smṛti-s but its contents were identical with Āp. (2.2, 4, 14); Y. (1.107), partly G. (5.35-6) and *Baudhāyana Gṛhyasūtra* (2.9, 21-3).[50]

It was an important stanza relating to hospitality. As Mit. (*ad* Y. 1.107) explained, it meant that if the host was so poor that he could not find food in his house, he should honour the guest with grass (bedding[51]), place (space for sitting, sleeping and moving about[51]), water and kind words (in the form of conversation[51]).

C. This was an exceptional rule to be found in the Smṛti-s. A more general rule was found in Mn. 3.89[52] which stated that the main responsibility of the host was to give the guest food, a seat and water. Only if the host was so poor as not to be able to afford food to the guest, he should give him only a seat (grass, room), water and a kind word.

If Nārāyaṇa had been better acquainted with the Dharmaśāstra-s, he would have included before HJ. 1.61, the better known and general rule of the Smṛti-s[53] viz. Mn. 3.89; and had he wanted to combine both concepts, i.e. the general concept (each host) with the specific concept (host too poor to afford food) he would have been chosen Y. 1.107.

since this text was variant of the Pañc. On the other hand SRBh 163, 444 which has in J the text identical to that found in Mn. and H, ascribes it to Pañc.

47. In PP. and Pts. Cf. RO 17.220-39.

48. Cf. RO 17.226.

49. Mn. 3.94-118; Y. 1.104-13; Vi 67.28-46; Āp. 2.4, II, 13-20; 6.5-9; G 5.25-45; Vās. 8. 4-15; Dakṣa 3.5-8, B 2.5, 11-8; 6.36-7 and others.

50. Cf. MBh quoted in VRĀ 441, 448, Vās, Śaṅkha-Likhita, Parāśara, Hārita, Yama, Praccheta and Viṣṇudharmottara, all quoted in VRĀ 412-3, 419, 440-3, 448.

51. Medhātithi.

52. MnJ., MnN, MnH, MnK, MnL, MnM 3.99. Cf. 1.107, Vās 4.12, Vi 67.45, G 5.32-4, Āp 2.2, 4, 13-6.

53. Cf. P. V. Kane, *History of the Dharmaśāstra* 2.2, 752 sqq.

D. In the same story 1.4(a) we find another stanza recited by a cat in wishing to win confidence, which is also found in Mn. This stanza reads in H:

eka eva suhṛd[54] *dharmo nidhane'py anuyāti yaḥ,*
śarīreṇa samaṁ nāśaṁ sarvam[55] [56]*anyat tu*[57] *gacchati.*

[*Dharma* is the only friend that follows (men) after death; everything else perishes together with the body].

This stanza is found in H. (HJ. 1.67, HS. 1.59, HM. 1.64, HP. 1.49, HN. 1.50, HK. 1.66, HH. 16, 16-7, HC. 22.12-3) and Mn. 8.17 (also quoted in VyK. 15[58], VyP[58], VyS 8[58], VySau 11[58], Hemādri, Vrata 14, *Nṛsiṁhaprasāda Saṁskāra* 17a, *Kṛtyakalpataru* 11a and VyN. 17; the latter wrongly ascribed this stanza to Kāty. where it could not be found). It is also found in Pañc. (PN. 3.30, PS. 3.37, PT. 3.,61 PTem. 3.47, PRE 3.50), among Cāṇakya's aphorisms (CNŚ. A 17, CNŚL 47, CNMN 80), and in BrDh. 2.14, 10.

The main editions of H. are almost identical, only one minor variant is found in the HN. and the HK. editions respectively; some minor variants are also found in some MS. of H.; one of them which contains a minor variant in δ *viz.*, the P. MS., in HS., is identical with PN., PT., PTem, PRE. and NA. MS. in PS. This MS. is identical with all the Mn. editions and with all digests which quote the Mn. stanza.

E. Stanza HJ. 1.67 was one of those recited by the cat to gain confidence, similarly as in Pañc. in the tale of the cat acting as judge between the partridge and the hare; it was the only one quoted in both Pañc. and H[59]. It seems most likely that Nārāyaṇa, who plagiarized quite excessively Pañc., borrowed this stanza not directly from Mn. but through Pañc. It is not clear why when quoting Mn. 8.17, he did

54. *śatāṁ* PN.

55. *sarvan* HK.

56. *atra* PS.

57. *anyatra* Pp in HS. HP. (Edd. in HP. as above) HN.NA. in PS; *hi* PS (HO in PS as above); *anyad dhi* P. in HS. PN, PT. PTem. PRE, Mn. (and all editions and most digests quoting Mn. with the excepion of VyK which reads as in the text quoted above).

58. According to Dh. 1.36.

59. HJ. 1.61 is also quoted in PP. 1.131 and Pts. 1.171 (see above); HJ. 1.64 is also quoted in PD. 305.85; and HJ. 1.70 is also quoted in PN. 1.45 and PS. 2.49.

not quote the preceeding stanza in Pañc.[60] also found in Mn. 8.15.[61]

F. Nārāyaṇa revealed once more that he was not well acquainted with the Smṛti-s. Had he known the Smṛti-s better, he would have certainly included another stanza from Mn. very closely connected with the stanza quoted above, viz. Mn. 4.241.[62]

5. *Tale* 1.6*a of The Old Man and His Young Wife*

A. The story 1.6(a) of the old man and his young wife (described in a more detailed manner in Study XX above) contains three stanzas also found in Mn. The most important of them is HJ. 1.128 which reads :

pitā rakṣati kaumāre bhartā rakṣati yauvane[63]
[64]*putrāś ca sthavire*[65] *bhāve*[66] *na* [67]*strī svātantryam arhati*[68]

[The father protects (her) in maidenhood; the husband protects (her) in youth; (her) sons in old age. A woman is never fit to be free.][69]

This stanza is found in H. (HJ. 1.128, HS. 1.113, HM. 1.119, HP. 1.91, HN. 1.92, HK. 1.122, HH. 24.26-7, HC. 33.17-8) and Mn. (9.3; also quoted in DhSP. 2.1; 38.2; 355.6, SC. 2.240,16, U. 2.14, 2, VRV 406, DhNP. 2.50, BBh.

60. PN. 3.30, PS. 3.37, PT. 3.61, PTem. 3.47, PRE. 3.50.

61. *dharma eva hato hanti dharmo rakṣati rakṣitaḥ,*
tasmād dharmo na hantavyo mā no dharmo hato vadhīt. (also found in MBh. 3.313, 28 and Brāhmadharma 2.14, 9).

62. Leaving the dead body on the ground like a log of wood, or a clod of earth, the relatives depart with averted faces; but *dharma* follows (the soul).

63. *yāvane* IS.

64. *putrās* (*putras*) *tu* N. in HP., HN., P. in HS., GP., MBh. in Dh., CNF., B., N., RNd. in MnJ., GMH., U., VRV., VyP., VyS., DhSP. 2.1.355, DhNP., VRK., SRBh.; *putraś ca* Vās. (FH. in Vās. as above); *putraḥ sthavira bhāve tu na*⁰ DhSP. 2.1, 38; *putra rakṣanti vārdhake* R in D ; *rakṣanti vārdhake putrā* NMS.; *rakṣanti sthā*⁰ HS., HK., Mn. (all editions), SC., SCM., MBh., VBh., VyS.,

65. *sthāvire* HM., HC., U., CNF., MBh. 13.10, 21; SRBh.; *sthavirī* GMH., B. (ed in B. as above; *sthāvire co in* B, B. in KSS. 2.3, 46; B. in ĀnSS. 2.2, 52).

66. *kāle* Pp in HS., GP., MBh., 13.20, 21, CNF.; *putrā* HK., Mn. (all editions and most digests quoting Mn; differently GMH, DhNP., U., VRV., VRK., VyP., VyS).

67. *svātantryaṁ kvacit striyāḥ* Saṁskāraratnamālā; *nāsti strīṇāṁ svātantratā* MBh. 13.20, 21.

68. ⁰*arhatīti* B. (BS. in B. as above) G. Vās.

69. Cf. above Study XX on the Tale of the Young Wife and the Old Husband para 4.

Vyavahāra Prakāśa 195.33 αβη. BBh. *Vivāha Prakāśa* 342.24-5, 211.17, VRK. 1191, VyK. 128, VyP. 406, SCM. 27, VV. 281, VBh. 2.53, VyS. 120, VT. 821, *Nṛsiṁhaprasāda Saṁskāra* 66 b, *Saṁskāraratnamālā* 674)[70]. It is also found in other Smṛtis, such as B 2.2,3,45, GMH. 28.1, Vās. 5. 3. N. 13.31, NMS. 13.31 and in MBh. 13.20, 21 (also quoted in Dh. 2.1031), 13.46, 14, R. 2.39, 33 (2.29, 18), GP. 1.115, 63, *Padma Purāṇa*, *Sṛṣṭikhaṇḍa* 54.23[71] and in some C. compendia (CRB. 8.68, CRP. 8.65, CRBh. I 8.66, CRBh. II 8.55, CNF. 58, CNPh. 92, CNI I 155, CNG. 180, CNL. 46.)

The main edition of H. and its various MS. contain minor variants. The main editions of Mn. and the digests quoting Mn. contain two variants in *j* but some MS. of Mn. are sometimes almost identical with the texts of H. Of all the Smṛti-s, only the text of Vās. is identical with the text of H. Also MBh. (13.46, 14) and the C group[72] are identical with the texts of H. Other sources contain minor variants.

B. This stanza was introduced by Nārāyaṇa to illustrate the idea conveyed in the story of the young wife and the old husband that women were never fit to be independent since they were always fickle and disloyal to their husbands; therefore, they should always be protected by someone i.e. by their fathers until thay are married, by their husbands during marriage and by their sons during widowhood. This idea was also conveyed in Mn. 5.146 (in other editions 5.148). While in Mn. 9.3 the fickleness and disloyalty of women was highlighted, in Mn. 5.146 the idea of independence of women in their own houses was highlighted. The first idea was more pertinent to the story of the young wife and the old husband.

C. Independently of how far Nārāyaṇa was unacquainted with the Smṛti-s, it is difficult to assume that he did not know both the stanzas i.e. Mn. 9.3 and Mn. 5.146, since the latter was also very well-known. He, must have failed to include the latter rule deliberately, since the idea behind that rule did not suit his purpose. Similar rules of N. 13.31 and

70. Cf. fn. 69, para 3.

71. See also SRBh. 166.575 ascribed to GP. and compare Vi 25.13, Smṛtyantara in Apar. 109, N. in Vivādaratnākara 411 and Mahānirvāṇatantra 8. 106.

72. Cf. below Study XXIV on "Cāṇakya's Aphorisms in the Hitopadeśa".

Y. 1.85-6 which was too legalistic, too elaborate and too casuistic were equally not included, although Nārāyaṇa, the compiler, should have included them.

It is also conceivable that Nārāyaṇa knew only rule Mn. 9.3 and the omission of other similar rules from Mn. and other sources was due to his ignorance.

D. The second legal rule in the story I.6 (a) reads :

mātrā svasrā duhitrā vā[73] [74]*na*[75] *viviktāsano bhavet*[76]
[77]*balavān indriya-grāmo* [78]*vidvāṁsam aui karṣati*

[One should not sit in a sequestered place with (his) mother, sister, or daughter; the assemblage of sense-organs (is) powerful and overpowers even a wise man].[79]

This stanza is found only in two main editions of H. viz. HJ. 1.129 and HH. 25.1-2 (it is also quoted *ad* HS. 1.113) and in Mn. (2.215). It is also found in GP. 1.114,6 Bhaviṣya Purāṇa, Brahmaparvan 4.184, CRC. 7.9, BhP. 9.19, 17 and ŚŚ. 3.18 αβ [30] and is also quoted in ŚP. (654), VS. 2780 and SRBh. 154. 45. (IS. 4809).

All the main editions of H. are identical with the exception of one minor variant in HH.; all editions of Mn. are also identical. The text of H. is identical with the text of Mn., with the exception of MnN. which contains the same minor variant that is found in HH. The *Bhaviṣya Purāṇa* is identical with H. GP. and BhP. contain only one minor variant each. ŚŚ. differs in γδ and contains some variants in β[81].

E. This stanza (Mn. 2.215) was borrowed by Nārāyaṇa from the second book of Mn. which dealt with studentship and cannot be read separately from the two preceding stanzas. These stanzas said that the very nature of women was to seduce men and therefore wise men should never be unguarded in the company of women, since the latter were capable of leading astray every man, be it a fool, or a sage and of making him a

73. *ca* ŚP.
74. *nātyantaikāntikaṁ vaset* ŚŚ; *naikaśayyāsano* SRBh.
75. *no* HH., MnN. (var.).
76. *vaset* GP. (*cf.* fn. 73); *viśat* IS. 4809.
77. *balavān indriyaḥ grāmaṁ* IS 4809; *yathā sambandham āhūyād ābhāṣyāśvāsya vai striyam* ŚŚ.
78. *vsdhvāṁsam api* BhP.; *paṇḍito'py atra muhyati* VS.
79. Cf. fn. 69.
80. Cf. Āp. 1.2, 7, 3; 7.11; 1,3; 16; B. 1.2, 3, 23; 33; MBh. 13.48, 37-8.
81. ŚP, VS. and SRBh. contain minor variants.

slave of desires and passion. Then Mn. continued with the stanza in question (Mn. 2.215). Medhātithi commenting on these three stanzas made it clear that they were referring to students.

MBh. (13.48, 37-8) also mentioned the same idea but repeated only the first two stanzas and omitted Mn. 2.215. BhP. did not quote Mn. 2.215 without an introduction. It first stated that men were slaves of desires and then quoted Mn. 2.94 according to which desire was never extinguished by the enjoyment of desired objects, but was growing stronger. In this connexion BhP. continued with the idea contained in Mn. 2.215.

F. Nārāyaṇa probably not understanding Mn. 2.215 well, borrowed this stanza out of the context and without introduction included it in the story of the young wife and the old husband ; this made the aphorisms partly ununderstandable, the more so as the stanza in its proper framework had a special meaning, viz. it referred clearly to students and their duty to remain chaste during the period of apprenticeship.[82]

G. It is however possible that Nārāyaṇa himself did not make this mistake and that stanza Mn. 2.215 was added later by a scribe. This may be deduced from the fact that neither HN., nor HP., nor even most of the H. editions contained this stanza. It was only found in the HJ. and HH. editions which were known to have the greatest number of stanzas, possibly added at a later date.[83]

H. The third legal rule in the story 1.6(a) reads :

pānaṁ durjana-saṁsargaḥ patyā ca viraho 'ṭanam[84],
[85]*svapnaś cā'nya-gṛhe vāso* [86]*nārīṇāṁ dūṣanāni ṣaṭ.*

82. Similar rules are found in the various Smṛti-s. Cf. G. 2.16, Āp. 1.2, 7, 3; 8-11; 16; B. 1.2, 3, 23.

83. It may be also argued that this stanza lost its specific meaning and could be applied to women in general. That may be deduced from ŚŚ. which incorporates the rule in the chapter dealing with morality, as well as from MBh. and BhP. Cf. fn. 69.

84. *virahe'ṭanam* MnJh. (notes); k, kh, gh in Apar.

85. *svapanam-anya*⁰ HP., P. in HS., HC., SRBh; *svapno'nya gṛhe vāsaś ca strīṇāṁ saṁdūṣaṇāni ṣaṭ* HN., N. in HP., *svapno'nya geha* (*gehe* MnJh. notes, SC., SCM., Apar. BBh; *gṛha* VRK) *vāsaś ca nārī sāṁdū*⁰ (*nārīṇāṁ* G in MnJ, MnJh notes, VRK., SCM., VV) Mn (all editions), Apar, BBh., SC., SCM., VRK, VyN, VyK., VyS., VV., VBh.

86. *strīṇāṁ vai* B. in HP., K. in MnJ (also quoted in MnJh.); *strīṇāṁ saṅdū*⁰ Pp in HS, VV; *strīṇāṁ dṛ*⁰ SCM.

[Drinking, close contact with wicked people,[87] separation from husband, gadding about, (too much) sleeping and dwelling in another (man's) house are the six causes of ruin to women].[88]

This stanza is found in (HJ. 1.122, HS. 1.108, HM. 1.114, HP. 1.86, HN. 1.88, HK. 1.115, HH. 24.12-3, HC. 33.5-6) and in Mn. (9.13; also quoted in Apar 108.9-10, BBh. 3.211, 29, SC. 2.241, 33, VRK. 1253, VyN. 389.19-20, VyK. 134, VyS. 120, 121, VV. 287, VBh. 18, SCM. 27[89]).

The main editions of H. and its various MSS. contain same minor variants, particularly in γ. The editions of Mn. and the digests quoting Mn. contain some changes in γ and some minor variants.

I. This stanza cannot be interpreted without the preceding stanza in H. which, although not taken verbatim from the Smṛti-s, contained elements included in the Smṛti-s and dealt with the same subjects. This stanza was well-known and was often quoted in the classical Sanskrit literature. For instance, it was quoted in the *Śukasaptati* (*texts ornatior* 328.10-3) and in Kokkoka's *Ratirahasya* (4.22).

VRK. after quoting the first stanza borrowed by Nārāyaṇa from Mn. added that what was mentioned in that stanza was only presented by way of a few examples of what lead to the ruin of women's character. This comment was partinent, as we find in other Smṛti-s examples of women being led to ruin; such examples were particularly enumerated in Vi., Bṛh., ŚŚ., Śa., Vy. and Hār.[90]

J. The two stanzas found in H. did not exclude but rather completed each other. Thus, in both stanzas we find the idea of separation of a wife from her husband (HJ. 1.122) and the husband setting out for journeys (HJ. 1.121); association with bad people (HJ. 1.122) and association with wanton women (HJ. 1.121); a woman residing in orther man's house (HJ. 1. 122) and a woman living in foreign countries (HJ. 1.121). (Causes of corrupting of women listed in HJ. 1.121, complet-

87. viz. other unfaithful wives (Nārāyaṇa *ad* Mn.); adulteres (Rāghāvānanda *ad* Mn).

88. Cf. JSAIL. above Study XX on the Tale of the Young Wife and the Old Husband.

89. Cf. Vi. 25.3; 9.10-2; Bṛh 25.9-11; ŚŚ. 3.19-20, Śa and Vy in Apar 108; Hār. in VRK. 1256; Dh. 2.1048; SRBh. 166.576.

90. Cf. fns. 87-8.

ing the list of causes given in HJ. 1.122 and Mn. 9.13, had no legal implications, but were only suggestions for women or their guardians that their actions might hurt their reputation, or may offer opportunities to unchastity). In a work like the *Hitopadeśa*, where stanzas were but losely assembled and where the question of homogeneity did not arise, mutual exclusion of stanzas did not arise either. However in those portions of a Dharmaśāstra which formed a kind of a legal code, such incongruity would be inadmissible. A more careful writer and one better acquainted with the Dharmaśāstra-s would have refrained probably from selecting these particular stanzas.

6. *Tale* 2.1 *of The Bull, The Two Jackals and The Lion*

A. In the first frame-story of the second book of H. (story 2.1) we find the following stanza :

alabdhaṁ [91]*caiva lipseta* [92]*labdham* [93]*rakṣed avekṣayā*[94],
[95]*rakṣitaṁ vardhayet samyag*[96] *vṛddhaṁ*[97] *tīrthesu*[98] *nikṣipet*[99].

[Let him strive to gain (what he has not yet) gained; let him preserve with care what he has gained; let him increase what he has preserved; let him spend on *tīrtha-s* what he has increased].

This stanza is found in H. (HJ. 2.8, HS. 2.7, HM. 2.8, HP. 2.8, HN. 2.8, HK. 2.8, HH. 41.1-2, HC. 54.11-2) and Mn. (7.99; also quoted in DhSP. 1.1; 472.11, VRR. 131.20-1, RRK. 7.15-6). It is also found in Pañc. (PS. 1.2, v. l. PT. 1. 2, PM. 1.6, PRE. 1.2) and in SRBh. 163.468.

91. *arthaṁ* PTem., PRE; *īhed dharmeṇa* PS.

92. *labdho'pi parirakṣituṁ* A in HP. (cf. fn. 94).

93. *rakṣet prayanataḥ* PRE., Mn. (all editions), PRK., *rakṣeta yatnataḥ* G. in Mn. (also quoted in MnJh.); *rakṣec ca yatnataḥ* MR. in MnJ. DhSP., VRR.; *yatnena pālayet* PS. (cf. fn. 94).

94. *apekṣayā* HS. (Pp. in HS. as above) N. in HP., HN., HH., Nd. in MnJ. (also quoted in MnJh.); *avkeṣayā* IS. 630; *apakṣayāt* IS. 630; *avakṣayāt* HM., HN.; *ca paripālayet* C. in HP.; *labdho'pi parirakṣitum* A in HP. (cf. fn. 92).

95. *pālitaṁ vardhayen nityaṁ* PS.

96. *samyag* HS., HM., HN., HK., SRBh. (better); [0]*yen nityaṁ* HP. (PN., Edd. in HP. as above) [0]*yec caiva* Mn. (all editions), DhSP., VRR., RRK.; [0]*yec cainaṁ* PT.

97. *vṛddhim* B. in PS.

98. *pātreṣu* PS., PT, PRE., Mn (all editions), DhSP., VRR., RRK., (cf. fn. 99).

99. *niḥkṣipet* edd., Pp in HS., HH., MnK., Calcutta edition of Mn., as quoted in MnL.; *nirúṣipet* MnH. (notes), DhSP., RRK.. *vinyaset* BC. in PS.; *tīrthe vinikṣipet* P. in HS.

The main editions of H. contain several minor variants, while the main edition of Mn. are identical but some MSS. of Mn. and digests quoting the Mn. stanza contain some minor variants.

The various *Pañcatantra* versions contain some unimportant variants. A comparison of the H., Pañc. and Mn. texts shows that there were some differences between the H. text on the one side and the P. and Mn. texts on the other, though some differences were noted betwteen the Mn. and Pañc. texts (particularly PTem. and PRE. texts). In any case the texts of Mn. and P. were closer to each other than the texts of Mn. and H.

B. This stanza was a well-known *nīti* stanza which in all Dharma- and Nītiśāstra-s referred to the king and particularly to his duties.[100] The same idea as in Mn. 7.99 was also conveyed in Y. 1.317, KN. 1.18, 11.55, 13.57, K. 9.2-3 and partly Vās 16.6. However the maxim could very well apply to all men, perhaps with the exception of the fourth *pāda* which in Mn. applied to the kings rather than to ordinary men, since it said that one should strive for more and more money and preserve what was gained. Further one should not spend all that he got and finally what was increased he should bestow upon visits to *tīrthas* (H.), or upon worthy persons (Pañc. and Mn.).

C. This stanza again was included in H. out of context. Nārāyaṇa probably borrowed it not from Mn., but from Pañc. where it applied to men in general and not to kings. This stanza at the time of the composition of Pañc. and H. had certainly a general meaning;[101] that seems particularly evident from δ, according to which the king ought to bestow money upon worthy persons (*pātra*).

D. In applying this stanzas to story 2.1, containing several stanzas on the subject of increased riches, Nārāyaṇa showed a good deal of initiative by changing in δ the word *pātreṣu* (found not only in Mn. but also in Pañc. to *tīrtheṣu*. In this way, he made it clear that this stanza applied to men in general. This meant that while spending money on worthy persons (*pātra*) was the king's obligation, there was no such obligation binding ordinary men. The word *pātra* did not mean a holy person

100. Cf. in Mn. the prceding and following stanzas.

101. Cf. also KN. 13.57 which may also apply to men in general.

(on whom an ordinary person should spend money), but rather a capable or competent person[102] who, according to the Smṛti-s ought to be supported and patronized by kings.

7. *Tale 2.3 b of The Dear, The Jackal and The Crow*

A. In the story 2.3(b) we find the following stanza :

[103]*ākārair iṅgitair*[104] *gatyā ceṣṭayā bhāṣaṇena*[105] *ca,*[106]
netra-vaktra-vikāreṇa[107] *lakṣyate*[108] *'ntargataṁ manaḥ*[109].

[By external appearances by motions, by gait, by gestures and by speech; by changes in the eye or the face, the inward thought is discovered].

This stanza is found in H. (HJ. 2.47, HS. *ad* 2.46, HM. 2.50, HK. 2.50, HH. 47.15-6, HC. 63.5-6, and 106.3-4[110]) and Mn. (8.26; also quoted in DhSP. 3.1; 55.12, SC. 49.17, GMBh. 186. 12-3, GMH. 11.23, Apar 620.21-2, SV. 104, 8-9, VRV 71.13-4, VyMā. 313, VyN. 70.2-4 (wrongly ascribed to N.) VyS. 24, VyP. 21.31, VyK. 32, VySau 31, VVy 10, GR. in Dh., SCM 41, 42, NV. 10.27, 117.10-1 (wrongly ascribed to Vallabhadeva), VS 2803, SRHt. 146.29, SRBh. 147.226). It is also found in Pañc. (PP. 1.21, Pts. 1.44, PtsK. 1.50, PM 1.22), Mādhavānalakathā 148, Vet. (1.8), C. compendia (CRC. 2-55, CRB. 2-62, CRP. 2.59, CRBh. I 2.59, CRBh. II 2.49, CRCa. I.249, CNCr. 259, CnT. II 27.8, CnT. VII 57). and GP. (1.109, 52).

The main editions of H. are identical. The main editions of Mn. are also identical but some variants are noted in different MS. of Mn. and in the *nibandha-s* quoting Mn. Some of these digests, e.g. SV., contain a text identical with that of H. That proves that both versions were well-known.

102. An adept in, e.g. an actor, a king's counsellor, or a minister.

103. *ākareṇe' ṅgitair* Apar., SV., VyK.

104. *aṅgitair* N *ψ* PL.$_1$ PrMBh. in PP.

105. *bhāṣitena ψ* PL.$_1$ Pr. in PP., Mn. (all editions), SC., DhSP., GMBh., Apar. k, ch in VyN. (VyN. as above), VyMā, VyK., SCM., VySau., VRV. 71, VVy., VyS., VyP., GR., SV., GP.; *harṣitaja* GMBh.

106. *tu* GP.

107. *cak(t)ra-vikārais ca* A in PP., ⁰*vikārais ca* Pts, Vet., Mn. (all editions) VvMā GMBh., SCM., VySau., VVy, VyS., VyP., GR., Apar., VyN., GMBh., SC., DhSP., VyK., VRV; *vikāreṇa* BDce in Vet; *vikārais tu* a in Vet; *vikārābhyāṁ* A in Vet, GP., SV., CRC.

108. *gṛhyate* PP., A in Vet (d in Vet as above), Mn. (all editions), VyMā, SCM., VySau., VVy., VyS., DhSP., Apar, SC. SV., VyN., VyP., GMBh., NV., *jñāyate* A in PP. Vet. G in MnJ. (also quoted in (MnJh.), VRV., SV., CRC., *śaya*⁰ GR.

109. *nṛṇāṁ* CRC.

110. Not found in HP. and HN.

The text of H. contains three distinct minor variants as compared with Mn; the sme variants partly occur in Pañc.

B. This stanza referred to false witnesses and contained a thought expressed in various Smṛti-s not in same words as in Mn. We find it in Y. 2.13-5, N. 1.193-6, N. *Pariśiṣṭa* 10-1, Bṛh. 5.43a, Kāty. 386, Śaṅkha-Likhita in VRV 124.13 and R in Vyavahāradatta 51.

In these Smṛti-s as well as in the various digests, Mn. 8.26 was not quoted without the preceding stanza 8.25, since both these stanzas formed a unit. Mn. 8.25 stated that the king should discover the internal disposition of men by external marks, such as voices, colour, motions, eyes and gestures; in the following stanza Mn. stated that by external appearances, by hints, gait etc. their inward thought was revealed.

Medhātithi stated in his commentary to Mn. 8.26 that this stanza was a supporting stanza of the preceding one and was therefore not repeated in it.

Here again Nārāyaṇa has proved that he was not well acquainted with Mn. He should not have quoted Mn. 8.26 without the preceding stanza, particularly since Mn. 8.26 was only an explicatory and supporting stanza of Mn. 8.25.

C. It is possible that Nārāyaṇa borrowed this stanza not from the original text but through Pañc., where it was also quoted without the preceding stanza from Mn.[111]. This explanation, however, does not justify his choice.

8. *Tale* 2.3 c *of The Deer, The Jackal and The Crow* (Continuation)

A. In the story 2.3 (c) we find the following two stanzas:

yasya prasāde prajñā'ste[112] *vijayaś ca parākrame*
mṛtyuś ca vasati[113] *krodhe sarva-tejomayo hi saḥ.*[114]

[In whose favour prosperity resides, in whose valour victory rests in whose anger death resides, he unites, indeed, in himself the essence of majesty].

111. PP., Pts. PtsK. and PM. quote also the preceding stanza of HJ., while other editions of Pañc. mention only HJ. 2.46. Cf. above Study XVIII on the Pañcatantra and the Smṛti-s, par. 47.

112. *padmā'ste* HJ., HK., HN., HP., HC., Pp. in HS., DhSP., SRBh., SRK; *padmāsti* H; H. *padmā śrīr* HS. Mn. (all editions), VRR.

113. °*yuḥ saṁvasati* R. in MnJ. (also quoted in MnJh).

114. °*yoḥ nṛpaḥ* HH.

bālo'pi nā'vamantavyo manusya iti bhūmipaḥ,[115]
mahatī devatā hy esā[116] *nara-rūpeṇa*[117] *tiṣṭhati*

[The king, even a child must not be despised (because of the idea) that he is an (ordinary) mortal; for he is a great divinity which (appears) in human form].

The first stanza is found in H. (HJ. 2.80, HS. 2.79, HM. 2.81, HP. 2.73, HN. 2.72, HK. 2.81, HH. 52.6-7, HC. 68.13-4) and Mn. (7.11; also quoted in DhSP. 1.1; 448.13-4, VRR. 18.20-1, Dh. 1.574); it is also found in SRBh. 142.9 and SRK. 122.7 (attributed to Sabhātaraṅga).

The second stanza is found in H. (HJ. 2.81, HS. 2.80, HM. 2.82, HP. 2.74, HN. 2.73, HK. 2.82, HH. 52.8-9, HC. 68.15-6) and Mn. (7.8; also quoted in DhSP. 1.1; 448.7-8, 3.1; 4.1-2, VRR 17.21-2, RRK. 68.16-7); it is also found in MBh. (Bhandarkar ed. 12.68.40; *a* is different), NPr. (8.5), Cāṇakya's compendia (Vṛddha-Cāṇakya-nīti-samuccaya, Ahmedabad 1916, 16.21), SRHt. 62.23 and SRBh. 142.8.

Regarding the first of these stanzas most of the main editions contain one variant in *a*; otherwise, with the exception of the HH. edition, the other main editions are identical . The main editions of Mn. are identical[118]; they and the *nibandha-s* quoting Mn. are also identical with the HS. edition which contain one variant in *a*.

Regarding the second of these stanzas, the main editions of H. are identical, but some MS. contain minor variants. The main editions of Mn. are identical, as well as the digests quoting Mn. (with one exception of one MS. of a digest). H. is identical with the main editions of Mn. Other sources are also identical with H. and Mn.

B. The two consecutive stanzas of H. were borrowed by Nārāyaṇa from the seventh book of Mn. i.e. stanzas 11 and 8. Both these stanzas dealt with one subject, viz. the important position of the king (Mn. 7.1-13). It is starnge that Nārāyaṇa chose from this sub-chapter stanzas 8 and 11 only, that he changed their order and did not quote stanzas Mn. 7.9-10, nor those preceding and following dealing with a similar

115. *bhūpatiḥ* A in HP., *na hi jātu avamantavyo manuṣyair iti bhūmipaḥ* MBh.

116. *hy'etā* gh in RRK; *pūjyā* P. in HS.

117. *'nanta-rū*⁰ B in DhSP. 3.1.

118. One variant is only found in a MS. of Mn.

subject. It is likely that Nārāyaṇa knew stanzas Mn. 8 and 11 from hearsay only but did not know the other stanzas from Mn. dealing with the same subject.

9. *Tale* 3.7 a *of The Huntsman, The Deer, The Boar, The Serpent and The Jackal*

A. In the story 3.7 (a) we find the folowing stanza :
yasmai dadyāt pitā tvenāṁ[119] *bhrātā* [120]*cā'numate*[121] *pituḥ,*
[122]*taṁ* [123]*śuśrūṣeta jīvantaṁ saṁsthitaṁ*[124] *ca na*[125] *laṅghayet.*

[Him, to whom (her) father, or (her) brother with the paternal consent may give, let her dutifully obey (as long as he) lives, and when he is dead, let her never disregard him after death].

This stanza is found in H. (HJ. 3.33, HS. *ad* 3.31, HH. 79.15-6) and Mn. (5.149; in other editions Mn. 5.151; also quoted in SC. 251.25[126], VKK. 579.3, BBh. 3.213, 16, MRP. 319.19-20, DhNP. 2.50, VyS. 124).[127]

The main editions of H. are identical. The main editions of Mn. are also identical but various MSs. and the *nibandha-s* which quoted Mn., contain minor variants. The text of H. with the exception of one minor variant in β, is identical with that of Mn.

B. The main topic of Mn. 5.149 was the description of the duties of the wife towards her husband, but Mn. added in this stanza parenthetically another topic, namely the question as to who was responsible for giving a girl away in marriage. The reply to this question was her father, or her brother with the paternal consent. The same thought was also expressed in N. (12.20; cf. NMS. 13.20). However, N. dealt only with the question as to who was responsible for giving a girl away in marriage. This question was also treated in Y. (1.63-4 and

119. *vaināṁ* VKK; *pyenāṁ* SC. 223; *kanyāṁ* MRP.
120. *vā*⁰ Mn. (all editions), SC., VKK., DhNP., BBh., VyS., MRP.
121. *numataḥ* VKK. (also quoted in MnJh.); *numatau* SC. 223 (also quoted in MnJh).
122. *śūṁ* SC.; ⁰*śuśruṣej jīvitaṁ hi taṁ vṛttaṁ cānuśayed iti* HS (cf. fn. 123).
123. *śuśrūṣayec ca* MRP. (cf. fn. 122).
124. *duḥsthitaṁ* SC., VyS., MRP., (in Bikaner Skt. MSS. Library); *svaryāta* SC. 223 (var.).
125. *ca na* tr. GK. in MnJ.
126. In the Govt. Oriental Library Series 43, 223, 14-5.
127. of HJ. 3.33 is also found in Agni Purāṇa 222.20.

Vi 24.38-40) but is conspicuously missing in Mn., with the only exception of Mn. 5.149. (As stated above, Mn. 5.149 dealt also in this stanza with the duties of the wife towards her husband[128] and with the obligation of the wife not to disregard her husband after death[129]).

C. This is a strange stanza; it contained three almost entirely different topics squeezed into one stanza. Almost all the Smṛti-s contained the same topics but there they were more logically developed; each of these topics was described there separately, while in Mn. they were scrambled together. The important question, viz., who was responsible for giving away a girl in marriage, not found in Mn. elsewhere, was casually mentioned in this stanza. It is possible that this stanza, not so clear anyway, was almost forgotten. As far as could be ascertained, it was quoted in H. only and in no other source of classical Sanskrit literature, including the main *Subhāṣita-saṁgraha-s.*

D. Nārāyaṇa quoted this stanza immediately after stanzas dealing with self-immolation of widows. With this stanza Nārāyaṇa introduced amongst others, two conceptions which grossly contradict each other. On the one hand, he quoted a stanza recommending obedience of the wife to her husband during his lifetime, and faithfulness and oblations after his death, while on the other hand, he had no hesitation in introducing the conception of self-immolation of widows in the immediately preceding stanza. It may be noted that Mn. did not mention self-immolation and, according to some commentators on Mn., was not in favour of this practice.[130]

E. The inclusion of stanza Mn. 5.49 in the story 2.7(a) was not necessary. If Nārāyaṇa found it convenient to quote in the body of his story any stanza from Mn. dealing with the subjects mentioned above, he should have chosen better

128. Also found in Mn. 9.153, Vi. 25.15, Y. 1.77, 83, Kāty. 835, Devala in VRK. 1245, Cf. also R. 2.24, 25b—28a; 2.67,10 (RG. 2.69,10), MBh. 3.204, 22b-23a; 5.33, 74; 13.46, 13; MP. 16.60-3, Brāhmadharma 2.2,7, Prasaṅgābharaṇa 14.

129. Cf. Rāghavānanda, Rāmacandra and other commentators of Mn. on Mn. 9.149; Mn. 9.3; 5.146; 5.154-8; Y. 1.75; Vi. 25.14, Bṛh. 25.14b; ŚS. 4.4,28-9; Hār. 3.9, Yama in VRK 1283, Kāty. 837.

130. Cf. above Study XIX on the "Tale of the Gullible Husband and his Cunning Wife", para 14.

suited and ones better connected with the story, e.g. Mn. 5.156 or 5.162, and 5.164 or 5.154.

F. This stanza is found only in the HJ. and HH. editions; therefore, it is possible that Nārāyaṇa himself did not include it in the *Hitopadeśa*, but that an unknown scribe or "reviser" has interpolated it at a later date.

10. *Tale* 3.7 b *of The Huntsman, The Deer, The Boar, The Serpent and The Jackal*
(Continuation)

A. In the story 3.7 (b) we find the following two stanzas:

[131]*vijetuṁ prayat etārin*[132] *na yuddhena*[133] *kadācana,*
anityo vijayo yāsmād[134] *dṛśyate* [135]*yudhyamānayoḥ.*

[He should strive to conquer (his) foes (but) never by war, because between two combatants victor is seen (to be) uncertaīn].

sāmnā [136]*dānena bhedena samastair athavā*[137] *pṛthak,*
sādhituṁ[138] *prayat etārin*[139] [140]*na yuddhena*[141] *kadācana.*

[By conciliation, (well applied) gifts (and) by creating diversions, using either all or some of them, he should strive to destroy (his) foes, (but) never by war].

The first of these stanzas is found in H. (HJ. 3.42, HM. 3.39, HP. 3.38, HN. 3.38, HK. 3.39, HH 81.4-5, HC. 107.15-6) and Mn. (7.198b-199 a); the second is found in H. (HJ. 3.43, HS. 3.40, HM. 3.40, HK. 3.40, HH. 81.6-7, HC. 107.17-8) and Mn. (7.198), Both these stanzas of Mn. are also quoted in DhSP. 1.1; 459.13-460.2,VRR 404. 16-8, Smṛtitattva 742, RRK. 58.12-4, SRHt. 151.7, and SRBh. 148.230-1.

With regard to the first stanza, the main editions of H. are

131. *vijetuṁ prayatete yorīn na yuddhet kadācana* A. in HP. (cf. fns. 137-8).
132. *'rim* MnJh. MnN. (var.); *yateta cārīn* HH. (*cf.* fn. 138).
133. *yuddheta* B. in HP.; *yuddhyeta* BCDEFGH in DhSP. (cf. fn. 141).
134. *yasya* A. in HP.
135. *yuddha*° ṅ in RRK.
136. *bhedena daṇḍena* M_8G. in MnJ. (also quoted in MnJh), VRR.
137. *uta vā* VRR.
138. *vijetuṁ* P. in HS., Mn. (all editions); *viyuktaṁ* M_8. in Mn. (also quoted in MnJh.), VRR. DhSP., RRK. (cf. fn. 131).
139. *'riṁ* MnJh., MnN. (var.); *prayate cārin* edd. in HS. (cf. fn. 132).
140. *vijetuṁ sahasā na tam* M_8. in MnJ. (also quoted in MnJh).
141. *yuddhyeta* BCDEFGH in DhSP. (cf. fn. 133).

identical, with the exception of the HH. edition which contains one minor variant. (Some MSS. of H. contain minor variants).[142] The main editions of Mn. are identical, with the exception of one variant in MnJh[143]. The text of H. is identical with the text of Mn. As for the second stanza, the main editions of H. are identical but some MSs. contain minor variants. The main editions of Mn. are identical, but some MSs. contain also minor variants[144]. The texts of Mn. and H. are not identical, i.e. H. has *sādhitum̐*, while Mn. has *vijetum̐*.

B. Mn. 7.198 contained an advice to kings as to how to win peace, viz. not by war, but by conciliation, well applied gifts and by creating dissension. Mn. 7.199 contained an explanation of the advice, viz. victory was uncertain between two fighting parties.

This advice and its explanation were also repeated in Mn. 7.200 and in other sources, e.g. in KN. (there they were repeated on several different occasions: KN. 9.59[145], 60.74; 10.32; 19.15) and partly in Matsya-purāṇa 224.1-8[146] (On the contrary K[147] stated that peace should be chosen only when the advantage derivable from peace and war were of equal character).

C. The three Mn. stanzas, viz. 7.198 to 200 comprise a unit. They contain one single thought, but Nārāyaṇa chose to quote only two of the stanzas and this in reversed order. He quoted first the second part of stanza Mn. 7.198 and the first part of stanza Mn. 7.199 and then quoted the entire Mn. 7.198. In this way γδ of Mn. 7.198 were repeated twice and in HJ. 3.42 were quoted in a corrupt form (*vijetum̐* instead of *sādhitum̐*). Nārāyaṇa probably did not know the origin of stanzas HJ. 3.42-3 and included them in the story 3 (b) without the realization that αβ of HJ. 3.42 were identical with γδ of HJ. 3.42 and that in Mn. another similar stanza could be found.

D. A similar thought to that expressed in HJ. 3.42-3 is also found in KN. 9.59. Instead of quoting this stanza also

142. In addition *αB* in the A MS. in HP. contain some variants.
143. Also in one MS. of the MnN. edition. The digests quoting Mn. are identical with the text of Mn. with the exception of one variant in a MS. of RRK.
144. The *nibandha-s* and their various MSS. quoting Mn. contain minor variants.
145. KN. 9.59 is also quoted in H. in another place (HJ. 4.22).
146. Well-applied gifts.
147. Book 7, chapter 2.

in the story 3.7 (b) together with the similar stanzas Mn. (7.198-9), he included KN. 9.59 in the tale 4.8 (HJ. 4.22). He could have also included in the tale 3.7 (b) other stanzas of KN. dealing with the same subject, viz. KN. 9.60, 9.74, 10.37 and 19.15; but he most likely did not know about their existance, although he quoted many other stanzas from KN., in particularly in the fourth book.

E. In the story 3.7 (b) we also find the following stanza :

ekaḥ[148] *śataṁ*[149] *yodhayati*[150] [151]*prākārastho dhanur-dharaḥ,*
śataṁ [152]*daśa-sahasrāṇi tasmād durgaṁ vidhīyate*[153].

[A single bow-man placed on a rampart can fight against a hundred; one hundred (against) ten thousand; therefore a fortress is recommended].

This stanza is found in H. (HJ. 3.53, HS. 3.50, HM. 3.50, HP. 3.48, HN. 3.48, HK. 3.50, HH. 82.2-3; HC. 108.20-109.1) and Mn. (7.74; also quoted in RRK. 24.3-4, RDhK. 113.6-7, NM. 52.2, VRR. 202.24-5, VRL. 238.12-3). It is also found in ŚŚ. 4.6, 11 and in SRBh. 144.67. Similar stanzas, conveying the same idea, but using different words in γδ, are also found in Pts. (1.229, 2.14) PtsK (1.260) and PP. (1.88).

The main editions of H. are almost identical with the exception of HJ. which in δ has *vidhīyate* instead of *viśisyate.* In addition, HN. and NB. in HP. contain one small variant in *a*. The HH. edition contains a printing error in γ.

The main editions of Mn. are almost identical with the exception of some editions and several MSS. which contain a variant similar to that in HJ. Therefore, it may be assumed that both versions were known and used. Generally, the main editions of H. (with the exception of the HJ. edition) are identical with the main editions of Mn. Some *nibandha-s* which quote Mn. contain minor variants.

148. *ekaś* RRK.
149. *śatāni* NB. in HP., HN. (*contra metrum*).
150. *yodhayate* SRBh.
151. *durgasto' stradharo yadi* ŚŚ.
152. *śata-sa*⁰ HH. (printing error); *daśa-hasrāṇi* MnJh. (printing error ?); *sahasrāṇi tathā sahasraṁ lakṣam eva* SRBh.
153. *viśiṣyate* HS., HM., HP., HN.- HK, (var.), HH., MnL. (Calcutta and London editions as above), RKNdW in MnJ., Rāghavānanda in MnJh., Bombay copy in Mr. Wilkin's MS. (as quoted in MnH); *viśeṣyate* IS. 1377; *durgāṇi kārayet* Nos. V, VI., VII in MnH., MnL., M. in MnJ. (also quoted in MnJh.); *ca kārayet* MnJh. (notes); *samāśrayet* NM. quoted in MnJh. ŚŚ.

F. This Mn. stanza was well-known[154]; it stated that a single archer under the shelter of the fort-wall could fight a hundred enemy while a hundred archers could fight ten thousand.

G. H., though quoting several different aphorisms relating to forts, did not go into detail as to the capital and the fort[155], or the use of the fort[156], or different kinds of forts[157], nor even did he quote the preceding stanzas in Mn. (i.e. Mn. 7.70-3), nor the following one (i.e. Mn. 7.75).

11. *Tale* 3.8 *of The Blue Jackal*

A. In the story 3.8 we find the following three stanzas:
padātīmś[158] *ca mahipālaḥ*[159] *puro'nīkasya yojayet,*
[160]*uparudhyārim āsīta*[161] *rāṣṭraṁ ca'syo'papīḍayet.*

[The king should assign foot soldiers to the front of the army ; after having besieged the foe, let him sit encamped and proceed to harrass his kingdom" (viz. territories outside the fortress occupied by the enemy].[162]

[163]*syandanā'śvaiḥ*[164] *same yudhyed*[165] [166]*anūpe naudvipais tathā,*
vṛkṣa-gulmāvṛte cāpair asi-carmāyudhais[167] *sthale.*[168]

[On a plain let him fight with chariots and horses; on marshy grounds with boats and elephants; on grounds covered with trees and shrubs with bows ; on dry grounds with swords, shields and (other) weapons.]

154. The use of forts as described in this stanza was well-known (Medh *ad* Mn. 7.74).
155. Cf. Mn. 9.294.
156. Y. 1.321.
157. Cf. P.V. Kane, *History of Dharmaśāstra* 3.178 sq.
158. *padātiś* edd. in HS., HH.
159. *mahīpāla* HH.
160. *uparuṁdhyārim* B. in HS.; *upavadhyā-ratin(m) āsid* Pd in HS.; *uparudhyārātim ārāt* Pp. in HS. (var.).
161. *āsīt* HH. (*contra metrum*); *āsīd* IS. 3905 (*contra metrum*); *āsīc* ca HC., *āsināṁ* A. in HP., *āsāṁta* B. in HP.
162. Medhātithi.
163. *yudhyeta syandanāśvena* (⁰*ta*) *same'nūpo'nnate dvipan* (⁰*paiḥ*) VRR. (also quoted in MnJh); *yuddhyeran syan danā'śvaiś ca* (*ścaiva* DG. in DhSP.) *same'nūpe ca nau* (*no* DG. in DhSP)-*dvipaiḥ* BCDEFG in DhSP.
164. *'śvais* MnH., RRK.
165. *yojayet* RRK. (var.).
166. *anupe* HH.; *anape ity aśuddhaḥ pāṭhaḥ* ṅ in RRK.
167. *'yudhaiḥ* HS., HM., HP., HN., HK., HH., Mn. (all editions) VRV., DhSP., RRK.
168. *tathā* K. in MnJ. (also quoted in MnJh).

dūṣayec cāsya satataṁ [169]*yavasānnodakendhanam,*
[170]*bhindyāc caiva taḍāgāni*[171] *prākārān*[172] *parikhās*[173] *tathā*[174].

[Let him continually destroy fodder, provisions, water and fuel; likewise let him destroy tanks, ramparts and ditches].

The first of these stanzas is found in H. (HJ. 3.83, HS. 3.80, HM. 3.80, HP. 3.78, HN. 3.78, HK. 3.80, HH. 87.19-20, HC. 115.5-6) and Mn. (7.195 αβ; this part of the stanza is also quoted in DhSP. 1.1; 459.7, VRR 403.23 and BRK. 37.15[175]).

The main editions of H. are identical with some exceptions in HH. in α and γ, and in HC. in γ. The various MSs. contain several minor variants, αβ of Mn as well as the digests which quote this stanza are identical. γδ of the H text is identical with the Mn. text (αβ).

The second of these stanzas is found in H. (HJ. 3.81, HM. 3.81, HP. 3.79, HN. 3.79, HK. 3.81, HH. 86.21-2, HC 115.7-8) and Mn. (7.192; also quoted in DhSP 1.1; 459.1-2, VRR. 405-1-2 and RRK 36.14-5) (*Cf.* KN. 18,46 and RR. 40.7-8).

The main editions of H. are identical with the exception of two minor variants, or rather spellings. The main editions of Mn. are identical with one difference in spelling. Some MS. and the *nibandha-s* which quote this stanza contain minor variants. The text of H. is identical with the Mn. text.

The third of these stanzas is found in H(HJ. 3.85, HS.3.82, HM. 3.82, HP. 3.80, HN. 3.80, HK. 3.82, HH. 86.23-4, HC. 115.9-10) and Mn. (7.195b-196a; these parts of the two stanzas are also quoted in DhSP. 1.1; 459.8-91[176], VRR. 403. 24-5 and RRK. 37.16-7).

The main editions of H. are identical with the exception of HH. which contains one minor varient. The various MS. of H. contain three minor variants. The main editions of Mn. are

169. *yavasā 'nnaidane' ndha*° Pp. in HS; *yavaśāly-udake'ṁdha*° A in HP.

170. *bhindec* codd. in HS.

171. *taṭakāni* I in DhSP.

172. *prākāra* Mn. (all editions), VRV., DhSP.; *prākāraṁ* RRK. (gh in RRK. as in Mn.); cf. fn. 173).

173. *parikhāṁs* edd. in HS., HH.

174. *balam* MnJh. (var.); *api* MnJh. (var.).

175. According to MnJh. (noteṣ); also in Mit. *ad* Y. 1.342.

176. Omitted in BCDEFG in DhSP.

identical, but some *nibandha-s* which quote Mn. contain minor variants. The text of H. is identical with Mn. with one exception in δ. (Mn. has *prākāra*, while H. has *prākārān*).

B. These three stanzas were included by Nārāyaṇa among many others dealing with the conduct of war. But Nārāyaṇa chose these stanzas from Mn. in a very strange manner. Mn. had stanzas 7.190-200 or rather stanzas 7.190-6, which dealt with the conduct of war. Nārāyaṇa first quoted the first part (*xB*) of Mn. 7.195, then Mn. 7.192 and then the second part (αβ) of Mn. 7.195 and the first part αβ) of Mn. 7.196. Particularly, the insertion of Mn. 7.192 between Mn. 7.195 αβ and γδ destroyed the continuity and logic of the latter stanza which dealt in its entirety with the question on what the king should do after having besieged the foe.

Nārāyaṇa overlooked here the very closely connected stanzas Mn.7.190-1, 7.194[177] and 7.196 γδ and did not include them among the similar stanzas which he quoted.

C. Nārāyaṇa included the three stanzas quoted above without reference to the original. His memory failed and he quoted some of them wrongly.

12. *Other Stanzas Found in, or Inspired by, the Mānava-Dharama-śāstra*

In addition to the eighteen stanzas[178] analyzed above, the origin of which can be clearly traced to Mn. one half stanza is identical with Mn. (viz. HH. 99.20 γδ[179] which is identical with Mn. 9.14[180]); also several stanzas of H. contain thoughts similar to those included in Mn. but apply different wording, viz. HJ. Intr 27 (Mn. 2.136), HJ. 1.62 (Mn. 3.107, 99, 4.29), HJ 1.127 (Mn. 2.94), HJ. 1.218 (Mn. 7.22), HJ. 2.41 (Mn. 7.21), HJ. 2.109 (Mn. 7.80, 142-4, 9.253), HJ. 2.111 (Mn.

177. Mn. 7.193 as a particular stanza (though closely connected in Mn. with the preceding and following stanzas) has no place in H.

178. Stanza HP. 3.122 (HN. 3.122, HK. 3.126) was added to HJ. 1.43.

179. Not found in other main editions of H.

180. HH. 99.19-20. Also quoted in SC. 2.240, 3, SCM. 27, VRK. 1200, BBh. 3.211, 30, Dakṣa in VRK. 413, R. in VRK. 414, VyN. 389.21, VyK. 129, VyP. 407, VyS. 120, VyU. 140, VVy. 56, VCi. 190, VBh. 5. Cf. MBh. 13.38, 17; 13.28, 20-3, Pts. 1.143, JSAIL 22.20-6, L. Strenbach *Gaṇikā-vṛtta-saṁgraha*, Hoshiarpur 1954, 315-416.

8.86), HJ. 2.142-3 (Mn. 8.126), HJ. 3.20 (Mn. 7.64), HJ 3.55 (Mn. 7.70-1), HJ. 3.56 (Mn. 7.75), HH. 82.10-3 and HC. 108.8-11[181] (Mn 9.294), HJ. 3.72 (Mn. 7.188). HJ. 3.149 (Mn. 9.294) and HJ. 4.88 (Mn. 6.66). These stanzas were not borrowed by Nārāyaṇa from Mn., nor, with one exception, from other Dharmaśāstras (HJ. 2.47 was probably borrowed from Bṛh 5.43), but were probably inspired by Mn and other Dharmaśāstra-s, or borrowed rom other sources[182], as was the case of HJ. Intr 27 (Pañc., C, GP., Vet), HJ. 1.127 (C, *Padma-Purāṇa*, *Vet*), HJ. 1.218 (KN), HJ 2.41 (Pañc., GP., VCsr), HJ. 2.111 (Pañc., MBh, *Agni Purāṇa*), HJ. 2.142 (MBh.), HJ. 3.20 (GP.), HJ. 72 (KN., ŚŚ) and HJ. 3.149 (KN)[183]

181. Cf. HJ. 3.149.
182. Cf. HAIS table V.
183. Cf. HAIS. table VI.

XXIII

SOME DHARMAŚĀSTRA STANZAS IN THE HITOPADEŚA*

INTRODUCTION

1. In JSAIL 25[1], where the Mānava-Dharmaśāstra texts in the Hitopadeśa were analyzed, it was contended that the Hitopadeśa was primarily an anthology of maxims and aphorisms, and only to a lesser degree a collection of stories based on the Pañcatantra in which such aphorisms were interpolated. Nārāyaṇa, the presumed author of the Hitopadeśa, often tried with success to interweave tales with maxims and aphorisms which in his view were in a way connected with these tales. In this way, he tried to compose a *subhāṣita-saṁgraha* containing mostly good counsels for the teaching of the sons of Sudarśana, the king of Pāṭaliputra, for whom the Hitopadeśa was composed as a text-book of *nīti*.[2]

2. Eighteen and a half stanzas of the Hitopadeśa which, directly or indirectly, were drawn upon by Nārāyaṇa from the Mānava-Dharmaśāstra, have been analyzed in JSAIL 25[1]. The present study will now analyze twelve additional stanzas borrowed by Nārāyaṇa from the Dharmaśāstra sources other than the Mānava-Dharmaśāstra. These sources are the Yājñavalkya-Dharmaśāstra, the Viṣṇu-Smṛti, the Nārada-Smṛti and the Bṛhaspati-Smṛti. However, in some cases the stanzas found in the Hitopadeśa were not found in the Dharmaśāstra-s themselves, but were quoted only in some *nibandha-s*; they were explained to have originated in some well-known Smṛti-s, but they could not be found in the printed texts of the Dharmaśāstra. They usually contained elements of *dharma* or *nīti* and formed either a part of some genuine but unknown MSs of the respective Dharmaśāstra-s or Smṛti-s mentioned in the *nibandha-s*, or were

* Previously appeared as JSAIL. 26 in "Dr. S. K. Belvalkar Felicitation Volume", Banaras 1957, pp. 127-48.

1. Cf. above Study XXII. on the "Mānava-Dharmaśāstra Stanzas in the Hitopadeśa", para. 1.C.

2. Cf. above Study XXII, as quoted above.

more or less known stanzas whose origin, for reason of prestige, has been attributed by the authors of the digests to some celebrated Dharmaśāstra-s or Smṛti-s.[3]

3. Nārāyaṇa's main source for the Hitopadeśa was notably the Pañcatantra.[4] As was shown in JSAIL 26[5], Nārāyaṇa was poorly versed in Sanskrit *dharma* literature and his legal training was meagre. His knowledge of the Dharmaśāstra-s was limited. For his quotations in the Hitopadeśa drawn from this source, he often had to rely merely on his memory, as was the case with many of his contemporaries. He may even not have been fully aware that when he did so he was quoting from the Dharmaśāstra sources.[6] It is difficult to resist the suspicion that he never got thoroughly acquainted with such well known Dharmaśāstra sources as the Mānava-Dharmaśāstra, the Yājñavalkya-Dharmaśāstra, the Viṣṇu Smṛti, and the Nārada Smṛti which he quoted.

4. In his work, Nārāyaṇa followed the traditional postulate by which each of the tales told in the Hitopadeśa, was to be accompanied by an adage or a legal precept of a general or specific nature tending to convey a moral principle. Yet, Nārāyaṇa's imperfect knowledge of the Dharmaśāstra necessarily affected his ability to select from it the proper stanzas containing pertinent precepts and, to no less a degree, influenced his method to apply the selected precepts appropriately.[7] Where more general legal precepts would have been suitable, he cited stanzas that contained specific or exceptional rules but less pertinent. Since relevant precepts of general nature were available and plentiful, their omission must be obviously attributed to Nārāyaṇa's ignorance of the Dharmaśāstra texts.

In other instances Nārāyaṇa quoted in the Hitopadeśa stanzas which were obviously singled out from among a group of legal regulations related to the same subject. Had he consulted the original text rather than his memory, he would have included the remaining stanzas or at least a part thereof.[8] This is parti-

3. Cf. below paras 11 A and 11 F.
4. Cf. HAIS, part II and Tables I-II.
5. Cf. Study XXII above.
6. Cf. below paras 6 B, 7 B, 8 C.
7. Cf. below para 7 B.
8. Cf. below para 6 D and 10 B.

cularly true for thequotation of stanza Y 3.9 and the simultaneous omission of stanza Y 3.8 which is almost a variant of HJ 4.74.[9]

This weakness of Nārāyaṇa is also reflected in the usage of sources other than the Dharmaśāstra-s and the Smṛti-s which he undoubtedly knew[10] and which in specific cases were closely related to the subject matter of his particular tales.[11] Such somewhat casual treatment of sources militated against the objective which Nārāyaṇa had set for himself, i.e. to turn the Hitopadeśa into a perfect *subhāṣita-saṁgraha.* The failure to achieve this object in respect of all but one chapter is demonstrated below.[12]

Yet there is still another feature characteristic of Nārāyaṇa's treatment of his Hitopadeśa resulting from his zeal to achieve as complete a *subhāṣita-saṁgraha* as possible. He sometimes overburdened his work with citations from the Dharmaśāstra-s, which fitted only loosely or not at all with Hitopadeśa's specific tales. The reason for the occasional zeal manifested by these unduly lavish quotations could be also explained by the great authority enjoyed by the Dharmaśāstra literature, and equally by the significance of the quoted precepts to those who were to learn from them.[13]

5. Notwithstanding these inadequacies in the application of quotations, passages were frequently found from the Dharmaśāstra-s and the Smṛti-s which were both well-suited and well considered.[14] It was therefore not a rare occurrencethat a tale was accompanied by a quotation properly selected and based on good judgment; such quotations produced an excellently worded and homogeneous precept.[15]

II. ANALYSIS OF TEXTS

6. *Introduction to the Hitopadeśa*

A. In the Introduction to the Hitopadeśa we find the following stanza :—

9. Cf. below para 9 F.
10. E.g. in the case of Pañc. or MBh, See below para. 11.
11. Cf. below paras 6 B, D, 7 B, 9 C, 9 F, 10 B.
12. In connexion with tale 3.8.
13. Cf. below paras 8 B and D.
14. Cf. below paras 9 F and 10 B.
15. Cf. below para 10 A.

[16]*ko'rthaḥ putreṇa jātena*[17] *yo na vidvān na dhārmikaḥ*[18],
[19]*kāṇena cakṣuṣā kiṁ vā cakṣuḥ pīḍaiva kevalam.*[20]

"What is the benefit from a son born, who has neither knowledge nor virtue; or what is the benefit from a sightless eye; [such an] eye is simply an annoyance."

This stanza is found in the Hitopadeśa (HJ) Intr. 12; HS Intr. 12 ; HM Intr. 12 ; HP Intr. 12 ; HN Intr. 11 ; HK Intr. 12 ; HH 2.14-5; HC 4.14-5) and Bṛh (26.36[21] also quoted in DBh. 101; VRV 561.3; VyN 419; SC 271.12; VR 1383; MRP 357 1-2; VyK 144; VT 433; VyS 131 ; Vyavahāramādhava 305). It is further found in Cāṇakya's compendia (CNŚC 7, CNŚl 7, CNŚ 7; αβ are also found as γδ in CVND 4.9 ; CVM 4.5; CRC 7.68, CRB 7.63, CRP 7.62, CRBhI 7.61); in the *kathā* literature (PS Intr. 4; PN Intr. 3; PP Intr. 3, Pts. Intr. 4; PRE Intr. 3; VCsr 21.2) and in NV (27.16, ascribed wrongly to Vallabhadeva).[22]

Only αβ were identical in H and in other sources, while γδ were different,[23] but the main thought of all these stanzas was identical. Technically the stanza found in H formed an aphorism different from that quoted in the other sources.[24]

The main editions of the Hitopadeśa were identical with the exception of HN which contains one small variant of δ; γδ of H were different in other sources; they contained some variants.

B. In the Hitopadeśa this stanza formed a part of the "Introduction". The Introduction explained the reason for the composition of the Hitopadeśa; the purpose was to teach the

16. In Bṛh. DBh, MRP, SC, VR, VRV, VT, VyK, VyN, VyS, C, PP. Pts, VS αβ are γδ Cf. fn. 19 below.

17. *tena tu putreṇa* VR, VyN, DBh; *vā tena* VS.

18. *vidvān adhārmikaḥ* B. in PS.; *bhaktimān* PP, Pts, *CVND*; *śaktimān* M in PP.

19. *tayā gavā kiṁ kriyate* (*śriyate* E in PS) *yā na doghdrī* (*dhetur* DBh, MRP, VR, VRV, VT, VyN, VyS) *na* (*ca* VyN) *garbhiṇī* Bṛh, DBh, MRP, VR, VT, VyN. VyS, PS, PRE, CRC, VS; *kiṁ tayā kriyate dhenvā yā na sūte na dugdhadā* (*na dogdhrī na garbhiṇī CVND*) PP, Pts, *CVND*, NV.

20. *yat phalam* HN, N in HP.

21. Cf. Bṛh. 26.37.

22. This stanza was also quoted in IS (Nos. 1940 and 1748); see fn. 24 below and VS 2727.

23. In these sources (quoted above) αβ formed the second part of the stanza, while the rest was different.

24. In IS the H stanza was quoted as No. 1940, while the other sources as No. 1748.

king's sons about the books of *Artha-* the *Niti-śāstra*[25] and other learned writings. Consequently, it was necessary for Nārāyaṇa to preface this thought by stanzas saying that an unlearned and unwise son brought only unhappiness to his father, while one who was learned and wise brought true happiness to the family. HJ contained seven stanzas on this subject.[26] The first of these stanzas was that quoted above and was borrowed by Nārāyaṇa from the Pañcatantra. Nārāyaṇa probably did not even know that the stanza quoted from Pañc. was the same as that found in Bṛh or C. Had he known Bṛh, he would have certainly quoted the next stanza (Bṛh. 26-37) which also dealt with the same subject and was closely connected with the preceding stanza.

Nārāyaṇa did not show in this case his great acquaintance with the Sanskrit literature, as he did not quote the numerous stanzas dealing with the same subject; e.g. PP[27] Intr. 2, Intr. 3, 3.23; Pts.[27] Intr. 3, Intr. 6, 4.6-9; CVND 6.11[27]; VCsr[27] 21.3, 21.4; these and several other stanzas, if quoted would have certainly enlarged Nārāyaṇa's *subhāṣita-saṁgraha* on the subject. However, Nārāyaṇa adhered again to his master-work, the Pañcatantra and did not try to collect similar aphorisms on the subject, though he collected seven stanzas, some unknown to Pañc.[28]

C. In the Introduction we find also a second stanza borrowed by Nārāyaṇa from the Dharmaśāstra reading :

yathā hy ekena cakreṇa na rathasya[29] *gatir bhavet,*
evaṁ[30] [31]*puruṣa-kāreṇa vinā daivaṁ na sidhyati.*

"As indeed there cannot be any motion of a chariot by one wheel, so without human effort, destiny cannot be fulfilled.

This stanza is found in the Hitopadeśa (HJ Intr. 32; HS Intr. 31; HM Intr. 32; HP Intr. 20; HN Intr. 19; HK Intr.

25. HJ Intr.
26. HJ Intr 12.8.
27. And other editions.
28. HJ Intr. 3 identical with VCsr (21,3); Intr. 14 identical with *CRC* (8.35), *CṚB* (8.35) and BhŚ (74); Intr. 16 identical with MBh (5.132, 23b-24a) and *CRC* (8.36); Intr. 17 identical with *CVND* (4.5) and other editions of *C*. For more details see L. Strenbach, Various Versions of Cāṇakya's Aphorisms. An Attempt at Revised Analysis.
29. *na ra*° tr. Y (ChSS ed. as above with a note that in some MSs. *na* and *rathasya* are transposed).
30. *tathā* B in HP.
31. *purusa* HN (printing error).

32; HH 4.8-9; HC 6.8-9) and Y. (1.350 in Stanzler's edition; 1.351 in ChSS and in the Nirṇaya Sāgar editions; 1.349 in the ĀnSS edition; 1.347 in the TSS edition).[32]

The main editions of H were identical with the exception of the HN edition, which contained one small error. The main editions of Y were identical. The text of H was identical with that of Y with the exception of one small variant.[33]

D. The H stanza was one of the eight stanzas[34] quoted by Nārāyaṇa in the Introduction in order to explain that to gain knowledge and to achieve anything a person had to make an effort, because effort was superior to fate and adverse fate could be overcome by effort.

Most of the stanzas dealing with this subject were borrowed by Nārāyaṇa from Pañc.[35], some from C[36], and some from the MBh, etc.[37] These stanzas, however, were borrowed by Nārāyaṇa from Pañc., but they were not borrowed consistently. This seems to be evident from the fact that Pañc. dealt with the same subject not in the Introduction but in book 2 (Pts. tale 5)[38] and contained several stanzas on the subject. Nārāyaṇa picked out only some of these stanzas. He did not include in his Hitopadeśa the Y stanzas on the subject, in spite of the fact that the preceding two stanzas (Y 1.348-9) dealt also with human effort. Furthermore, he did not take into consideration the most classical stanzas on the subject found in Mn. (7.205 identical with Y. 1.348); MBh (3.32, 14.5; 5.192, 15; 10.2, 3; 10.2, 10; 12.24, 22; 12.139, 81; 13.6, 7, 8, 23, 43-47 etc.), RG (5.33. 30b-31a; 6.37, 12 and VRR 314), MP (23.26), Agni Purāṇa (in Śabdakalpadruma *sub pauruṣa*), KN (6.41[39]; 9. 36[40]; 11.29;

32. This stanza was also quoted in SRBh (82.7), where it was ascribed to Y, and in IS (5161).

33. However the ChSS edition was identical with that of H.

34. HJ Intr. 30—8.

35. HJ Intr. 30 from PT (2.83), PP (2.145) and Pts (2.140); HJ Intr. 31 from Pts (2.130 and 1.361) also found in Vct (Intr. 6), GhN (13) and NV (29.6); HJ Intr. 36 from Pts (2.131) and PP (2.139); also found in ŚŚ (4.7, 293) and NV (29.9).

36. HJ Intr. 38. See fn. 28.

37. HJ Intr. 34 from MBh (13.1,74) and Padma Purāṇa, Bhūmikhaṇḍa (81.42; first *pāda-s* only).

38. See also Pts (5.29 and other editions; also quoted in VC), Pts (1.360; 2.126 and other editions).

39. Also quoted in P (PP 1.190, Pts (1.223, 348) and others.

40. Also quoted in HJ 4.47.

13.10-1; 13.21), Viṣṇudharmottara (in VRR 31.3), Vyāsa (in VRR 315), Yogayātrā (1.3[41]) and many others which would have certainly suited well in this part of the Introduction.

It seems to be clear that Nārāyaṇa used, as before, his memory and inserted only such stanzas on the subject as came to his mind. He did not take the trouble to consult the original source; had he done so, he would have quoted at least the two preceding stanzas of Y.[42] He also probably forgot about the existence of the stanzas from MBh and other sources quoted above.

7. *Tale 1, 4a of the Blind Vulture, the Cat and the Birds*

A. In the story I.4 (a) we find the following stanza :

atithir yasya[43] *bhagnāśo gṛhāt*[44] *pratinivartate,*[45]
[46]*sa tasmai*[47] *duṣkṛtaṁ*[48] *dattvā puṇyam ādāya* [49]*gacchati.*

"A guest who departs from a house, disappointed in his expectations, leaves [the householder] with [his own] sins, [while] taking away from him [the latter's] virtues."

This stanza was found in H (HJ 1.64; HS 1.56; HM 1.61; HK 1.63; HH 16.5-6; HC 22.1-2)[50] and Vi (67.33αβ). It is also found in MBh (Bh) 12.184, 12; MP 29.31b--32 a; NPR 1.6,43 αβ, PD 305.85. It is further quoted in Gṛhastha Ratnakara (302.4 αβ), where it is ascribed to Parāśara, as well as in Smṛtimuktāphala 416.4 (*ab*) and in Śabdakalpadruma *āhnikatattva sub bhagnāśa*[51].

The main editions of H were identical. α and β in H were also identical with Vi and other *nibandha-s*, as well as with

41. In A. Weber's *Indische Streifen* (10.164).
42. Y (1.348-9) Stenzler' edition.
43. °*yāsya* K4 in MBh (Bh).
44. *gṛhaṁ* M1 in MBh (Bh).
45. *pratinivavartate* HK (printing error); *nivirtate* K1 in MBh (Bh).
46. *sā* K1 in MBh (Bh); *tasmāt sukṛtam ādāya duṣkṛtaṁ tu prayacchati.* Vi;...*na tasya pitaro'śnanti* (*pitaras tasya nā'śnanti* Smṛtimuktāphala; *pitara tasya devāś ca puṇyaṁ dharma-vratāśanāḥ* NPR) *daśavarṣāṇi pañca ca* NPR, Smṛtimuktāphala, Gṛhastha-ratnākara.
47. *datta*° *tas*° tr. MBh (Bh), T2 in MBh (Bh) as above, MP, PD; *dattvā sa* K1, $D_{5, 6, 9}$ in MBh (Bh); *sa tasya* D7 $TG_{1-3, 6}$, 6M5 in MBh (Bh); *tasya* B3 in MBh (Bh), PD; *tasyai* M_1 in MBh (Bh).
48. *kilviṣaṁ* P in HS.
49. *ādāti* G2 in MBh (Bh).
50. This stanza is not found in HP and HN.
51. This stanza was also quoted in IS (134).

NPR; γ and δ were different. Both parts of this stanza were however identical with H on one side, and MBh, MP and PD on the other.[52] Technically, therefore this stanzas as found in H, MBh. MP and PD was different from that found in Vi, the *nibandha-s* quoted above, and NPR. However, the thought in both groups of stanzas was the same. The same thought is also found in MBh 13, 2, 93; RG 3. 18, 35 and PP 3.137 (PtsK 3.159). Although the thought was the same in Vi and NPR on one side and MBh, MP and PD on the other, it must be assumed that Nārāyaṇa borrowed stanza HJ 1.64 from MBh (or PD, or MP) and not from Vi, since the text in Vi $\gamma\delta$ was different from that found in H.

B. In H this stanza was quoted among six others dealing with hospitality and guests (H 1.60 to 65). One of the preceding stanzas, viz.HJ 1.61, was borrowed by Nārāyaṇa from Mn[53], others from MBh. (HJ 1.60), Cāṇakya's compendia (HJ 1.63, 1.65) or Viṣṇu-Purāṇa (HJ 1.62). As was explained in JSAIL 25[54] Nārāyaṇa's choice of stanzas concerning hospitality was not too happy, for he selected rather exceptional Dharmaśāstra rules, but did not quote the more general ones, such as Mn 3.89 or Y 1.107.[55]

When analyzing stanza HJ 1.64 one comes to the same conclusion. It is rather incomprehensible why Nārāyaṇa did not quote next to HJ 1.64 the very similar stanzas PP. 3.137 (PtsK 3.159), MBh 13.2, 93 and RG 3.18, 35 which he must have known. He did not quote there the other stanzas dealing with hospitality found in Vi (67.34 and following), Mn (3.102 and following), Pañc. (PP 1.130; 2.49; 8.147; 4.5[56]) or Cāṇakya's compendia (CVND 15.11[56]) etc.

8. *Tale 3.8 of the Blue Jackal*

A. The story of "The Blue Jackal" 3.8 contained the following well-known stanza :

52. With few minor variants.
53. MnJh. 3.91. Cf. above Study XXII quoted above; para. 4.
54. Cf. above Study XXII quoted above; para 4B, C.
55. Cf. P.V. Kane's History of Dharmaśāstra, 2.2, 752.
56. Also found in *CVM* 15.10,*CNP* II.154, *CNT* IV.134, *CNM* 120.

na[57] *sā*[58] *sabhā yatra na santi vṛddhā*[59]
vṛddhā[60] *na te ye na vadanti*[61] *dharmam*[62],
dharmaḥ[63] *sa no yatra na*[64] [65]*satyam asti*[66]
satyaṁ[67] *na tad*[68] [69]*yad bhayam abhyupaiti.*[70]

"That is not a council where there are no elders; those are not elders who do not apply *dharma* justly; that is not *dharma* where there is no truth; that is not truth when it is associated with fear."

This stanza is quoted in H (HJ 3.64; HS 3.61; HM 3.61; HP 3.59; HN 3.59; HK 3.61; HH 84.16-7[71]) and in N (3.18; also quoted in NMS 1.80; MBh 220.1-2, ascribed to N; DhSP 3.1; 35.13, ascribed to MBh; SC 23.24-5, ascribed to N; Apar *ad* 2.4, ascribed to Vyāsa; SV 70; VyP 13; VyS 9; VyK 15; VyN 20; VySau 11; AsBh 31). It is also found in MBh 5.34, 59 (MBh (Bh) 5.35,49); R 7.59 (3) 33; GP (1.115. 52); Cāṇakya's compendia (CRC 8.54; CRB 8.57, CRP 8.54, CRT 8.29, CRBh II 8.49, CNG 330); BhŚ 568; PrC 2.129 and VA 385. 6-7, (cf. KSS 14.106, 168).[72]

57. *sa CRC* (wrongly).

58. *nāsau* Apar.

59. *vṛddhāḥ* HL, GP, DhSP, SC,SV, VyK, VyN, VyP, VyS, VySau, AsBh.

60. *na te vṛ*⁰ (tr.) MBh (Bh)(K4, D_5, D3, 4 in MBh (Bh) as above), NMS, SC, SV.

61. *vidanti* B4, D7 in MBh (Bh); *ye pravadantya* Pp in HS.

62. *dharmān* Pp in HS, K_2 in MBh (Bh).

63. *dharmo na vai yatra ca nāsti* SRBh; *nāsau dharmo yaṁ* MBh (Bh),R, N, NMS, GMBh, DhSP, Apar.; SC, SV, VyN, VyP VyS, VySau, AsBh, ŚP; *nāste sa dharmo na hi yatra satyaṁ sa*⁰ VA.

64. *no* N, GMBh, Apar. (var.), SC, VyN, VySau, AsBh.

65. *cā'sti satyaṁ sa*⁰ BhŚ, PrC (BP in PrC. as above).

66. *naivā'sti satyaṁ* IS; *na cā'sti satyaṁ* BhŚ, ŚP.

67. *na tat* (*naita* Apar (var.); *naitat* GP) *satyaṁ* (*sa*⁰ *na tat* D_5 in MBh (Bh); *yac chalenā'nuviddham*) R. NMS, GMBh, SC, DhSP, SRBh; *chalenā bhyupetam* IS; *kapaṭenā*, B in DhSP) MBh (Bh), R, GP, N, NMS. GMBh, DhSP, Apar, SC, SV, VyN, VyP, VyS, VySau, AsBh, ŚP; *no satyaṁ yac chalenā'nuviddham* IS (cf· 69).

68. *naitat* G4 in MBh (Bh).

69. *yac chalam* HS (L in HS as above) HM, HK (IP in HK as above), AB in HP, VyK; *yac chamam* HP, HN; *yac chale-doṣa-yuktaṁ* CRC; *yac chalenā 'nuviddham* R, NMS, GMBh, DhSP, SC, SRBh; *yac chalenā'bhyupetam* MBh; *yat kapatānu* (*kṛtakānu* PrC) *viddham* BhŚ; *yat kapaleṇa viddham* B in DhSP, VA (cf. fn. 67 above).

70. *anuviddham* IS; *abhyupetaṁ* N in MBh (Bh).

71. This stanza is not found in HC.

72. This stanza is also quoted in ŚP (1344), SRBh(174. 884) where it is ascribed to GP and in IS (3483).

Pāda δ in the HJ edition was different from all other editions; otherwise only one variant was noted in HH. There were some variants between H and other sources. The HS, HM, HP, HN, HK and HH editions were nearest to MBh[73] and GP.

B. Nārāyaṇa included this stanza immediately after the story of the blue jackal, which "met the fate of one who leaves his proper party." Then in H the king called his Court and invited the Crow, the Parrot and others. During the ensuing session numerous stanzas were uttered; we do not find them, however, in Pañc. as the continuation of the blue jackal story.[74] Very few of these stanzas were borrowed by Nārāyaṇa from Pañc.[75] Most of them, which deal with *nīti*, were borrowed from KN[76] (3.68 to 70; 72 to 77; 79; 80; 82; 86; 964 to 97) and other *nīti* sources.[77] Nārāyaṇa, having constantly in mind his objective of turning the Hitopadeśa into as complete a *subhāṣita-saṁgraha* as possible, inserted the stanza in question, which was a well-known *nīti* aphorism. This, however, was unneccessary as the thought in this stanza was very remote from the tale itself, the latter dealing mostly with war. Nārāyaṇa must himself have noticed the unsuitability of the stanza and included it at the beginning of the tale before the other stanzas.

C. Nārāyaṇa borrowed this stanza probably from MBh or GP and not from N. though it is also found in this Smṛti. This is evidenced by the wording of MBh [but not MBh (Bh)], which was the nearest to the text of all the editions of H, with the exception of the HJ edition; the editor of HJ chose a wrong wording not found in any other primary sources. The differences between MBh, GP and H.,[78] and all the other sources are not significant, but since MBh and MBh (Bh) respectively contained both versions, it is evident that both versions were current and Nārāyaṇa chose one of them subjecting it to slight changes.

D. Despite the fact that this stanza was not connected with the story itself, it mattered little, since it was a well known stanza

73. But not MBh (Bh).
74. Some of these stanzas were found in the last part of book 2 of HJ.
75. We find only HJ 3.67 and 3.69 in PKS and PP (Pts)respectively.
76. Nārāyaṇa changed often the wording of KN.
77. C, ŚŚ, MŚ, Cf. HAIS, Table VI.
78. With the exception of HJ.

and of pedagogical value to young princes for whom, after all, the Hitopadeśa was written.

9. *Tale* 4.12 *of the Old Serpent and the Frogs*

A. According to the story of the "Old Serpent and the Frogs" an old serpent no longer able to obtain his own food was interrogated by a certain frog as to why he had given up caring for food. He replied that some twenty years ago he bit a son of a holy Brāhmaṇa, of which the youngster died. The Brāhmaṇa cursed the serpent with the curse that he should be a carrier of frogs and have nothing to eat. The frog-king who was told about the story and was sorry for the old serpent asked him to eat a few of his subject-frogs. The old serpent waited only for that, began to eat the frogs until the pond became clear and finished with the frog-king himself.

B. Nārāyaṇa interpolated in this story nearly 30 stanzas spoken by the Brāhmaṇa, which related to life and mortality. Among these stanzas some texts of H. contained three stanzas taken from Dharmaśāstra sources, viz. Vi and Y. The first two of these stanzas were not quoted in any of the printed editions of H. They were found in a Hitopadeśa MS described by Theodor Zachariae in his article in ZDMG entitled *Bericht über eine Handschrift des Hitopadeśa.*[79]

The date of this MS was not given, but Th. Zachariae did not consider it old. He felt that it was the nearest to the HH edition, but that it contained a number of interpolated *śloka-s*, some of which were not found in any printed editions and were not even mentioned in any of them. To this kind of *śloka-s* belonged three which were quoted between HJ 4.77 and 4.78, two of which viz. the first and third, are also found in the Smṛti-s.

C. The first of these *śloka-s* reads,

dehino'smin yathā dehe kaumāraṁ yauvanaṁ jarā.
tathā dehāntara-prāptir dhīras tatra[80] *na muhyati* :

"As an embodied person (soul) undergoes childhood, youth and old age, so also he will obtain another body : the wise man is not worried about it."

79. ZDMG 61, 342-55.
80. *vīram* K., Dar. D_3 in MBh (Bh).

This stanza is found in Vi 20.49 and MBh (Bh) 6.24.13 (Bhagavadgītā 2.13).

The second of the *śloka-s* is connected with HJ 1.77 and the third of them reads :

ākramya sarvaḥ kālena paralokaṁ ca nīyate,
karma-pāśa-vaśo jantus tatra kā paridevanā.

"Every living being is seized upon by Kāla death and brought into another world; a living being is the slave of its actions. Why then should you wait (on its death)?"

D. This stanza is found in Vi 20.28. Vi in its twentieth chapter contained numerous stanzas[81] dealing with life and mortality and many of the stanzas quoted there could have been profitably included in the story of the old serpent and the frogs; nevertheless the two stanzas included in the MS described by Th. Zachariae were in the right place and well-chosen.

E. The third stanza borrowed from the Dharmaśāstra and included in the story of the old serpent and the frogs is found in only one edition of H, viz. in HS (4.71).[82] It reads:

saṁsāre[83] *kadalī-stambhe niḥsāre*[84] *sāramārgaṇam,*
yaḥ karoti[85] *sa saṁmūḍho*[86] *jalavudbuda-saṁnibhe.*

"Who in [this] human world, which is unsubstantial and sapless like a plantain tree and resembles a water bubble, attempts to seek the supreme reality is a foolish person."

This stanza is also found in Y (3.8); and is quoted in Smṛtimuktāphala 604.12 and in the Śabdakalpadruma *sub niḥsāra, mānuṣya* and *saṁmūḍha*.[87]

The text of H was not completely identical with that of Y. H has *saṁsāre* while Y has *mānuṣye* ; however, this one major variant and the two or three[88] minor ones do not change the thought of the aphorism.

F. The Y 3.8 stanza well chosen by Nārāyaṇa from Y,

81. Vi 20, 22 to 53.

82. In HJ it would have been inserted between 4.76 and 4.77.

83. *mānuṣye* Y.,Smṛtimuktāphala; *stamba* and *stambhe* Śabdakalpadruma; *manuṣī*⁰ Y (ĀnSS ed.) var.

84. *kadalīstambe* Y (k, kh, pu in ChSS ed.as above); ⁰*stamba*⁰ k, ṅ in TSS ed.

85. *yaḥ ka*⁰ tr. Y (Nirṇaya Sāgara Press ed., Ān. SS ed.) Smṛtimuktāphala; *korāti* IS (printing error).

86. *sa mūḍho vai* Smṛtimuktāphala; *saṁpūrṇo* (ĀnSS ed.) (var.)

87. This stanza is also quoted in IS. (4823)

88. In some editions of Y there were three variants.

and inserted in the right place, was followed in Y by Y 3.9 which claimed a very similar thought to that expressed in stanza HJ 4.74.[89]

In order to create a better *Subhāṣita-saṁgraha* the Y (3.9) stanza should have been inserted by Nārāyaṇa among those quoted between HJ 4.74 and 4.84. It is even possible that he did so, since in HS the Y stanza (Y 3.9) was quoted[90] after HS 4.71 (found only in the HS edition and quoted as *codd.*), but could have been preferably quoted after HS 4.68 (HJ 4.74).

It is, however, more likely that a scribe and not Nārāyaṇa added this stanza in *codd*, since only in this one MS this stanza was quoted. The scribe probably inserted the stanza, which followed in Y the stanza quoted before, as he knew the text of Y which Nārāyaṇa apparently did not.

10. *Last Frame-Story in H*

A. Nārāyaṇa, coming to a close of his Hitopadeśa, quoted the following stanza :

aśvamedha-sahasraṁ[91] *ca*[92] *satyaṁ ca tulayā dhṛtam*[93],
[94]*aśvamedha-sahasrād-dhi*[95] [96]*satyam evā 'tiricyate.*[97]

"If truth and a thousand horse-sacrifices [were] weighed in a balance against each other, truth would certainly outweigh a thousand horse-sacrifices."

This stanza is quoted in H (HJ 4.135; HS 4.129; HM 4.131; HP 4.136; HN 4.136; HK 4.138; HH 118.26-7 ; HC 160.3-4) and in Vi (8.36) and N (4.211; NMS 1.189); it is also quoted in SC 47; SS 121; VCa 147; VV 122; VyCi

89. *pañcabhir nirmite dehe pañcatvaṁ ca punargate,*
svāṁ svāṁ yonim anuprāpte tatra kā paridevanā. (HJ 4.74)
pañcadhā saṁbhṛtaḥ kāyo yadi pañcatvam āgataḥ,
karmabhiḥ svaśerīrothais tatra kā paridevanā. (Y 3.9)

90. Codd. quoted in HS.

91. *sahasrāṇi* (*ca* om.) HL, HK, HM, HP, HN; *sahasrāṇī ca sahasraṁ ca* IS.

92. *tu* Vi. (in Dh.), VyK, VyM, VyT, AsBh.

93. *ghṛtaṁ* HL (printing error); *kṛtaṁ* HM.

94. *tulayitvā tu paśyāmi sa*⁰R; *nā'bhijānāmi yad yasya satyasyārdham avā'pnuyāt* MBh (13.22, 14) ; *atyaricyate satyaṁ ca iti vedavido viduḥ* Urdh.

95. ⁰*srāṇi* VV; ⁰*srāttu* N, NMS, VCa, VyK, VySau, AsBh; ⁰*srādi* SRBh; *srasya* HP, HN.

96. *matyaṁ* S in HS.

97. *eva viśiṣyate* MBh (Bh) (1.69,22) (Ñ in MBh) (Bh) as above), MBh (12.162, 26; 13.75, 31), Vi, SS, VyK, VyMā; *eva viśeṣyate* NMS (var.); *evāviśiṣyate* VyCi.

48, 56; VyK 52; VyMā 331; VyT 215; VySau 50; AsBh 71). It is also found in MBh (MBh (Bh) 1.69, 22; MBh 12.162, 26; 13.75, 31 and similarly MBh 13.22, 14), R (2.61, 10 αβ), MP (8.42) and in Pañc. (PT Annex 4.20).[98]

Most of the editions of H contained one minor variant in α. HM contained also one variant in β and HP and HN in γ. In addition, HH contained one printing error in β. HJ, HS and HC seem to be nearest to the original.

The texts of Vi, N, the *nibandha-s*, MBh, MP and PTem contained minor variants only. R, MBh (13.22, 14) and Ūrdhvāmnāyas are identical with the other sources in αβ, while γδ are different in each case.

The Hitopadeśa on the one side, and other sources on the other, were respectively identical with the exception of one important variant in δ (minor variants were noted in δ and γ), but some texts, as for instance N in MBh (Bh) (1.69, 22) as well as VyT and SCM (quoting Vi or N), had the same wording as H. The wording used in H was somewhat better than that used in other sources, since *atiricyate* conveys a better meaning in this aphorism than *viśiṣyate*.

B. Nārāyaṇa had included at the end of his Hitopadeśa a very well-suited stanza concerning truth. Stanzas on this subject were included in the Smṛti-s in the chapters on witnesses. In Vi the stanza in question was the only one which conveyed a general meaning, but in N the stanza was among several others dealing with truth (N 4.210 to 216[99]), which should have been preferably included in the Hitopadeśa.

It would be improper to conclude from this that Nārāyaṇa borrowed this stanza from Vi and not from N. for if he had known N he would have also quoted the preceding and following stanzas dealing with the same subject. It is more likely that he did not know the source of this stanza but knew it by heart only, and included it at the end of his work. If he had known the Sanskrit literature better, he would have certainly included such stanzas as MBh. (1.74, 101; 1.74, 104; 5.32, 51; 12.162, 24; 12.276, 24; 12.329, 12), R (2.109, 11 to 14; 2.118, 12; RG 2.61, 13 to 17),

98. Also similarly Ūrdhāmnāyas. (1. 19 in IS 730); it is also quoted in SRBh (83.2), wrongly ascribed to Mn. and in IS (731).

99. The stanza quoted here is found in N (4.211).

KN (4.24), CVND (5.19, 18), Brāhmadharma (2.6, 9)[100], etc. which reflected the same thought as that intended by Nārāyaṇa; they all praised truth.

11. *Stanzas found in the nibandha-s*

A. In the Hitopadeśa we find also five stanzas which according to some *nibandha-s* were originated in the Smṛti-s, but could not be traced in these sources.

B. The first of these stanzas was found in the story I.1 (a) of "The Crow, the Tortoise, the Deer and the Mouse"; it reads :

utthāyot thāya boddhavyaṁ[101] *mahad bhayam upasthitam,*
maraṇa-vyādhi-śokānāṁ[102] *kim adya nipatiṣyati.*

"Having arisen one should consider (each day that) a great danger (may be) approaching : death, illness, pain may befall today."

This stanza is quoted in H (HJ 1.3; HS 1.3; HM 1.3; HN 1.3; HK 1.4; HH 7.2-3; HC 9.11-2) and according to Smṛtimuktāphala (210.17) and DhSP (1.1; 220.16-7) is attributed to Vi.[103]

This stanza is identical in all H editions; it was also identical with that quoted in Smṛtimuktāphala and DhSP. It was not typical for the Smṛtis.

C. The second and the third stanzas were found in the story II.3 (b) of "The Jackal and the Crow" : it reads :

[104]*alpecchur dhṛtimān prājñaś chāye-vā'nugataḥ sadā,*
[105]*ādiṣṭo na vikalpeta*[106] *sa rāja-vasatiṁ*[107] *vaset.*

"(He) who (is) moderate in his wishes, steady, wise, at all times following like a shadow and not hesitating when ordered (to do what he was ordered), may reside in the king's palace."

This stanza is quoted in H (HJ 2.53, HS 2.53, HM 2.56, HP 2.49, HN 2.48, HK 2.46, HH 48.5-6, HC 63.20-1) and

100. And N (4.210, 212 to 216). See above.

101. *yad bhayaṁ samupa°* DhSP.

102. *śokāni* Pp. in HS.

103. The stanza is also quoted in SRBh (162.432); it is there wrongly ascribed to ŚP) and in IS (1205).

104. *alpeṣu* HL (wrongly); *alpeccho* BN in HP, RR; *alpecchaḥ* RR (notes); *alpekṣaḥ* RR (notes).

105. *ādiṣṭosmi na vikalpet* HN; *āditosmi na vikalpet* N in HP.

106. *vikalpedyaḥ* RR.

107. *rājavastau* S in HS, HM, HK.

according to RR (12.9-10) is attributed to N and Hār.[108] αβ are also found with variants in MBh (Bh) 4.4, 37; αβ and γδ in MBh (Bh) 4.4, 39 γδ.

The various texts of H contained some minor variants in αγδ, one of which was also found in RR. The text found in RR. was almost identical with that of H with the exception of one minor variant in γ. This stanza was a typical *nīti* stanza which defined the attributes of a good king's attendant.[109]

The other stanza in the same story reads :

dūrād avekṣaṇaṁ hāsaḥ smapraśne sādaro[110] *bhṛśam,*
parokṣe'pi guṇa-ślāghā smaraṇaṁ priyavastuṣu.

"A look from a distance, asking questions with an amiable, smile, deep respect, praising even in absence, recollection of pleasant things (are signs showing that a master is well disposed towards his servant)."

This stanza was quoted in H (HJ 2.56, HS 2.56, HM 2.59, HP 2.52, HN 2.51, HK 2.59, HH 48. 18-9, HC 64.12-3) and according to RR (12.11-2) is ascribed to N and Nār.

The various texts of H contained one minor variant in β. The same variant was also found in RR.

It is difficult to read HJ 2.56 without the following stanza i. e. 2.57; by mistake RR did not quote HJ 2.57, both stanzas referred to servants and masters.

D. The fourth stanza was found in the story of "The Lion, the Mouse and the Cat", 2.4; it reads :

nā'nivedya[111] *prakurvīta*[112] *bhartuḥ kiṁcid api svayam*[113],
kāryam āpat pratīkārād anyatrā[114] *jagatīpate.*[115]

"O Lord of the world, (a servant) should not do anything spontaneously without having informed (his) master, unless he does it in order to overcome a threatening calamity (which could befall the master)."

This stanza is quoted in H (HJ 2.90, HS 2.86, HM 2.90,

108. The stanza is also quoted in SRBh (145.138) and IS (650).

109. Cf. MBh (4.4,89) and many others.

110. *saṁpraśneṣv ādaro* HM, HP, HN, HK, RR.

111. *atividyaṁ* IS.

112. *bhṛtyaḥ* IS; *bhartum* SRBh.

113. *priyam* RR.

114. *kārātnānyatra* HL.

115. *jagatīpateḥ* HS, HP, HN, HK, RR, SRBh (better).

HP 2.80, HN. 2.79, HK 2.89, HH 55.23, HC 72.13-4) and according to RR (12.15-6) is attributed to N and Hār.[116]

The various texts of H were identical with the exception of two minor variants in δ. One of these variants was also found in RR. This stanza dealt with the obligation of servants; many similar stanzas were found in the Smṛti-s and Nītiśāstra-s[117] several similar stanzas were also found in H in other places.[118]

E. The fifth and last of these stanzas was found in the story of "The Cow-keeper, the Barber and their Wives", 2.6 (b); it reads :

atathyāny api[119] *tathyāni darśayanti hi*[120] *peśalāḥ,*[121]
same[122] *nimnonnatānī'va citra-karma-vido janāḥ.*[123]

"Skilful men can make even false things to appear as true ones, just as persons skilled in the art of painting [can make appear] hill and dale[on their painting] whose surface is plain."

This stanza was quoted in HJ 2.112, HS 2.109, HM 2.113, HP 2.101, HN 2.100, HK 2.111, HH 59.23-4, HC 79.-3) according to RR (12.13-4) is attributed to N and Hār. It is also quoted in Dh (1.1, 69) and ascribed to VyK 7, SCM 7 and VySau.[124]

The various editions of H are identical with the exception of one minor variant in β which is also found in RR. Otherwise, RR is identical with H. The *nibandha-s* contain minor variants in αβ, but some MSS of RR contain major variants in γδ. This stanza is a typical *dharma* stanza and seems to be well-known, since such digests as SCM, VyK., VySau had quoted it.

F. The four stanzas quoted above contained elements of *dharma* or *nīti* and probably belonged to some unknown texts of Smṛti-s, although their origin could not be traced to any of the published Smṛti-s, and in particular to Vi, N or Hār (including the Laghu-Hārīta-Smṛti and Vṛdha-Hārīta-Smṛti-).

116. The stanza was also quoted in SRBh (1.6142) and IS (3580).
117. Cf. P. V. Kane's History of Dharmaśāstra 3. 159-60.
118. Cf. tale 2.3 (a) of "The Thief, the Ass and the Dog."
119. °*ni ca* SCM, RR (notes).
120. °*yantyati* HH, HS, HM, VySau, RR.
121. °*vicakṣaṇāḥ* SCM, VyK.
122. *sama* Pp in HS.
123. *citrakarmāvido janā ityaśuddhaḥ pāṭhaḥ* RR (notes).
124. The stanza is also quoted in IS. (125).

These seems even more likely, since some *nibandha-s* ascribe their origin to Vi, N or Hār. However, the latter argument does not seem to be irrefutable, since it has been often proved that some authors ascribed the origin of stanzas to well-known authorties in order to add some prestige to their sayings.

12. *Other Stanzas*

In addition to the thirteen stanzas analyzed above, the origin of some stanzas could be traced to some Dharmaśāstra sources[125] other than Mn, viz. HJ Intr. 27 (Vāsiṣṭhadharmaśāstra 13.56-7, Vi 32.16[126]); HJ 1.15 (DhSP 1.11; 183. 16-7 (Bh); HJ 1.62 (Gautamasmṛti 5.25, Āpastambīyadharmasūtra 2.2, 4, 11-2[127]); HJ 1.110-2 (Vi 71.66); HJ 1.121-2 (Vi 25.3; 9.10-2, Bṛh 25.9-11); HJ 2.30 (N 6.2, Bṛh. 16.11); HJ 2.111, (N 1.277-9, Vyāsa in Apar, Pitāmaha in Mit[128]); HJ 2.142-3, (Y 1.367, N Pariśiṣṭa 38[129]); HJ 3.30 (Vyāsa and Hār in DhSP, Āṅgiraḥ Smṛti in Śaṅkha-Likhita-dharmasūtra and Śaṅkha in Mit); HJ 3.31 (Āṅgiraḥ Smṛti in Mit and in Apar); HJ 3.32 (Mit. Vīramitrodaya *ad* Y 1.86); HJ 3.55 (Vi[130] 3.6), HJ 3.56 (Bṛh in VRR[131] 204); HH 82.10-3 and HJ 3.149 (Y 1.353, Vi 3.33[132]); HJ 4.88 (Vāsiṣṭhadharmaśāstra[133] 10.18); and HJ 4.100 (Vyāsa in RR 12.3-4). Some of these stanzas e.g. HJ 1.15, HJ 3.30, HJ 3.31, HJ 3.32 and HJ 4.100 were probably borrowed by Nārāyaṇa directly from these sources.

125. For the purpose of this paper the MBh stanzas of books 12 and 13 were not considered as Dharmaśāstra stanzas.
126. Also Mn 2.136.
127. Also Mn 3.107, 99; 4.29.
128. Also Mn 8.86.
129. Borrowed from MBh 12, 85, 25, Cf. Mn 8.126.
130. Also Mn 7.70-1.
131. Cf. MBh 3.56 in VRR 199.
132. Also Mn 9.294.
133. Also Mn 6.66.

XXIV

CĀṆAKYA'S APHORISMS IN THE HITOPADEŚA*

I. INTRODUCTION[1]

1. Nārāyaṇa, who is generally believed to be the author of the Hitopadeśa, prepared his work as a text-book for teaching the sons of Sudarśana, the king of Pāṭaliputra.

As the basis for his work, Nārāyaṇa chose the Pañcatantra, from which he omitted completely the fourth section (*Labdhanāśam*). Out of 71 motives of the Pañcatantra tales, he selected 56 and included them in the Hitopadeśa.[2] Two hundred forty-one or near one-third of Hitopadeśa's didactic stanzas could be traced to the various versions of the Pañcatantra. This was the highest number of stanzas borrowed by Nārāyaṇa from one source.

The other source from which Nārāyaṇa borrowed lavishly were Cāṇakya's sayings, or compendia of aphorisms which are known today under numerous titles.[3] Of 557 stanzas quoted in

* Previously appeared as JSAIL. 24 in the "American Oriental Society Offprint Series, No. 28" (JAOS 76.2,pp. 115-30; 77.1, pp. 26-31; 77.2, pp. 107-15; 77.3, pp. 166-83).

1. Due to further studies made by the author on the subject of Cāṇakya's aphorisms and due to the fact that he was able to collect many more Cāṇakya's editions and MSs., the references to Cāṇakya's editions and MSs. in the original study (JSAIL. 24) seemed to him insufficient. Therefore in this reprint of JSAIL. 24, in the third paragraph of each particular aphorism references to the various editions and MSs. of Cāṇakya's collections have been enlarged. However in the footnotes to the various aphorisms containing different readings, the original text with the original abbreviations has been retained.

2. *Cf.* HAIS § 48.

3. See below, § 10.1 and footnote 2 to the Post-Scriphen.

Prof. Daniel H. H. Ingalls in his recent study "The Cāṇakya Collection and Nārāyaṇa's Hitopadeśa" (JAOS 86.1; pp. 1-19) disputes this contention and expresses the opinion that Cāṇakya's collections of sayings, of which he considers the Cv version as the oldest, borrowed from the Hitopadeśa and not vice versa. This author does not see any validity in the arguments adduced by Prof. D. H. H. Ingalls for considering the Cv version as the oldest of the C versions. It is sheer speculation not based on any facts to consider one or another version older than the other. This author does not

all the main editions of the Hitopadeśa no fewer than 165 stanzas or parts of them i.e. nearly one-fifth are found in the Hitopadeśa and at least one of Cāṇakya's compendia.

2. Nārāyaṇa was a compiler in the first place and tried to render his Hitopadeśa into a subhāṣita-saṁgraha as complete as possible, by interweaving the contents of the tales with aphorisms that in his opinion were pertinent to the subject matter of single stories. Since his Hitopadeśa was intended to become a textbook for princes, he had to serve the purpose better than Cāṇakya's aphorisms.

3. It is possible that Nārāyaṇa had knowledge of all the

know whether the Cv version grew out or is a reduction of the CV version, but he considers the CV version as the most popular of all C versions and it seems to him that it is more likely that Cv borrowed from CV rather than vice versa. It seems to him that Cv and CL were composed at the same time (and not that the CL version is younger than the Cv version), since these two texts were usually contained in the same MSs and CL complimented Cv; as Prof. D.H.H. Ingalls himself suggests (p. 13), a selection "was made from most parts of the longer version" i. e. from CV (see the table on pp. XLV-XLVII of Vol. I.1 of his Cāṇakya-nīti Text Tradition) and as may be seen from table IV of his "The Hitopadeśa and its Sources" the number of stanzas identical in the Hitopadeśa and in any other version of Cāṇakya's sayings is the largest in the CR version, and in any case larger in the CV version than in the Cv version. If any C version could be considered as the oldest, this would be the CR version, and in particularly its Tibetan translation. This translation was known as in the second half of the tenth or in the beginning of the eleventh century A. D.

It seems to this author that the question of the dating of the versions is of secondary importance. The collections of Cāṇakya's sayings as such may be of much later date than the sayings themselves. Prof. D.H.H. Ingalls overlooks the fact that, though the author of the Hitopadeśa (as be rightly points out) admits that he has extracted from the Pañcatantra and another book (not books) i.e. the Kāmandakīya-nītisāra, the author of the Pañcatantra pays homage *inter alia* to Cāṇakya (PT Km 2, PS Km 1, PN Km 1, PRE Km 1), thus admitting that he, and *eo ipso* also the author of the Hitopadeśa, borrowed from the teachings of Cāṇakya. At that time probably these teachings, in the form of aphorisms, sayings and adages, did neither appear in written form nor were they composed in strict versions, but were the common knowledge of the Hindus. This common knowledge was based on the oral tradition on which the authors of the Pañcatantra and of the Hitopadeśa were often drawing sometimes even unaware that the sayings were the sayings of Cāṇakya or that they were usually attributed to Cāṇakya.

compendia known to us today[4] or of another compendium, or an ur-text of Cāṇakya's compendia, not yet discovered by scholars; it is however most likely that he knew, as so many Indians did then and do even today, Cāṇakya's sayings by heart but paid little attention to their origin and inserted them in his work wherever they seemed to fit.[5]

There is little difficulty in accepting in principle the thesis that Cāṇakya's aphorisms were composed prior to the composition of the Hitopadeśa. M. Winternitz[6] believed that the Hitopadeśa was composed after the ninth and before the fourteenth century A. D. Neither he nor anybody else has tried to fix the date of the composition of Cāṇakya's aphorisms. M. Winternitz, as other historians of Indian literature, emphatically rejected the possibility that the so-called Cāṇakya's aphorisms were written by Cāṇakya, the minister of Candragupta.[7] He concluded rightly that *es ist...nicht richtig in (der Cāṇakya-Sprüchsammlung) Volkspoesie zu sehen und sie mit Sprichwörtern gleich zusetzen, die von Mund zu Mund gehen, ohne dass an einen einzelnen Autor zu denken ist. Diese Sprüche sind vielmehr in litterarischen Kreisen entstanden, sie stammen teils aus Werken der Litteratur, teils rühren sie von Verfassern her, deren Namen vergessen worden sind. Es versteht sich, dass wir eine derartige Sammlung keiner bestimmten Zeit zuweisen können.*[8]

Though the date of the composition of Cāṇakya's aphorisms is a matter of speculation, it is safe to assume that they were known as early as the seventh century A. D.,[9] since the

4. This can be assumed from the fact that the Hitopadeśa, quoted verses which were peculiar to each of the Cāṇakya's versions now known to us. Thus, the following stanzas are only quoted in the *CN* version: 2, 3, 9, 21, 31, 35, 38, 50, 53, 54, 56, 59, 65, 66, 76, 79, 87, 88, 108, 123, 128, 136, 138, 141, 143, 144, 153, 154, 156; in the *CR* version: 6, 8, 17, 22, 39, 49, 57, 62,63, 73, 85, 98, 99, 106, 118, 125, 132, 138, 147, 150, 151, 152, 154, 155; in the *CV* version : 1, 15, 137, in the *CL* version: 28; and in the *CS*. version 14.

5. *Cf.* HAIS § 32.

6. *Geschichte der Indischen Litteratur* 3.291.

7. *Dass der Minister Cāṇakya...der Verfasser dieser Sprüche ist, daran ist nicht zu denken* (M. Winternitz, *Gesch. d. Ind. Litteratur* 3.135-6).

8. *Op. cit.* 3.136. Similarly *CKr* 7, H. v. Glasenapp, *Die Literaturen Indiens* 176, S. N. Dasgupta and S. K. De, *History of Sanskrit Literature*, 196.

9. Daṇḍin's *Daśakumāracarita* was probably written in the seventh century (*cf.* W. Ruben, *Die Erlebnisse der zehn Prinzen* (Berlin, 1952), p. 5).

Daśakumāracarita mentioned that Ācārya Viṣṇugupta compiled for the king six thousand *śloka-s* on political science.[10] Viṣṇugupta and Cāṇakya were one and the same person and the work mentioned by Daṇḍin probably referred to the compendia of Cāṇakya, though it could equally well refer to Kauṭilya's Arthaśāstra.[11] The latter is however less probable, as Kauṭilya's Arthaśāstra was written in prose and Daṇḍin referred to it as a work written in about 6,000 *śloka-s*,[12] the type of verse mostly used in Cāṇakya's compendia.[13]

Even if the seventh century should be accepted as the date *a quo* for the composition of some of the Cāṇakya compendia, M. Winternitz's suggestion that some of the aphorisms were composed in literary circles and originated from various works still is valid.

4. We find among Cāṇakya's aphorisms some that probably originated in the Pañcatantra or the Hitopadeśa; such for instance is the case with aphorisms Nos. 7, 104, 129, 143-4[14] which originally formed the prefatory or concluding stanzas of of Pañcatantra or Hitopadeśa framework stories. The maxims contained in these stanzas were reflected in the body of the story that follows, similarly as the animals around which the subsequent story was built were also the principals of the stanzas.

For instance, in Nos. 143-144 the maxim in $\alpha\beta$ reads : "that which could not be accomplished by prowess may be effected by stratagem." $\gamma\delta$ referred to the next tale dealing with a hen crow and a black serpent and reads : "a hen crow by [means of] a gold chain caused a black serpent to be put to death."[15]

Since all the above-mentioned stanzas originated from the Pañcatantra, the main source for the Hitopadeśa, it could be also assumed that a compiler of Cāṇakya's aphorisms or a scribe

10. *adhiṣva tāvad daṇḍanītim; iyam idānīm ācārya-viṣṇuguptena mauryā'rthe ṣaḍbhiḥ śloka-sahasraiḥ saṁkṣiptā* (BSS 10, 42 p. 131.10-2).

11. See BSS 10, 42, p. 344 *ad* p. 131 1.11; D. D. Kosambi; the text of the Arthaśāstra, JAOS 78.3 p. 169 sqq.

12. Verses. Cf. *CKr* 16.7.

13. Cf. *CKr* 13. Kressler did not know yet about the existence of Kauṭilya's Arthaśāstra.

14. See the second part entitled "Texts".

15. HJ 2.119 (No. 143).

included these stanzas at a later date from the Pañcatantra or the Hitopadeśa in a later Cāṇakya's compendium. In these cases it was not the Hitopadeśa that borrowed from Cāṇakya, but as it were, the opposite happened.

5. Moreover, if a stanza found in the Hitopadeśa was also extant in Cāṇakya's compendia as well as in the Mahābhārata, the Rāmāyaṇa or the Mānava-Dharmaśāstra[16] it would be fairly obvious to assume that the stanza incorporated in the Hitopadeśa would originate from sources other than Cāṇakya's compendia; as is well known these sources were older than the Cāṇakya's aphorisms and of greater authority. The text from which Nārāyaṇa may have borrowed was either the Mahābhārata, the Rāmāyaṇa or the Mānava-Dharmaśāstra directly or through a compendium of Cāṇakya's aphorisms.

6. The situation however was rendered less clear when the aphorism occurring in the Hitopadeśa occurred also in Chapters 108 to 115 of the Garuḍa Purāṇa or in other books of the *kathā* literature, e. g. the Vikramacarita and in one of Cāṇakya's compendia. Considering that little is known of the time of the composition of these texts, it is difficult to ascertain which stanza served as the source for the other stanza. However, if the text of a Cāṇakya aphorism is closer to the text of the Hitopadeśa than, say, to the text of the Vikramacarita, Śukasaptati or Vetālapañcaviṁśatikā, it may be assumed that the Cāṇakya text was that used by Nārāyaṇa.

Any identity of stanzas does not always imply direct borrowing one from the other, in view of the fact that earlier works or the floating mass of oral traditions may serve as common depositories for the borrowing.[17]

7. Despite the conclusions cited at the beginning of paragraph 5, a similar analysis of Cāṇakya's sayings leads to the conclusion that for some of his aphorisms Nārāyaṇa made no use of the Pañcatantra directly, but availed himself of other sources in which aphorisms similar to those in the Pañcatantra occurred.

So, for instance, this seems to be true for HJ 1.13[18] where

16. Or some other sources of an earlier date.

17. Cf. N. N. Law, in *Foreword* to the first edition of the Cāṇakya-rāja-nīti-śāstram.

18. Cf. No. 43 below.

the text of the Garuḍa Purāṇa was closer to the text of the Hitopadeśa than any text of the Pañcatantra, or for HJ Intr. 12, 1.165, 1.185 or 1.225[19] where the text of Cāṇakya was closer to the text of the Hitopadeśa than any text of the Pañcatantra. A similar inference may be made in the case of the Mahābhārata and the Pañcatantra. Thus, HJ Intr 16, being closer to Cāṇakya's aphorisms, was probably borrowed by Nārāyaṇa from one of Cāṇakya's compendia, while HJ 1.159, being closer to the Pañcatantra, was probably borrowed by Nārāyaṇa from the Pañcatantra and not from the Mahābhārata.[20]

8. The analysis of the texts included in the body of this study may be therefore of some use to those who wish to analyze Cāṇakya's aphorisms in the light of their origin, a task not undertaken by this author. Such an analysis is still wanting, though many scholars have dealt with Cāṇakya's aphorisms; they did not tackle, however, this particular difficult problem.[21] It may be also of some interest to those who study critically the poetical portions of the Hitopadeśa.

9. A. Weber[22] in 1864, O. Kressler[23] in 1904, J. Klatt[24] in 1873, E. Monseur[25] in 1887,[26] E. Teza[27] in 1878 and 1887, B. C. Dutt[28] in 1890, E. Bartoli[29] in 1911, 1920, Narendra

19. Cf. Nos. 92, 148, 20, 97 in the second part of this article entitled "Texts."

20. Nos. 90 and 119 respectively. See second part entitled "Texts."

21. It seems that this type of work could be done, even if not without mistakes, despite Kressler's statement that *die Rekonstruktion des Original-Cāṇakya wird sich durch blosses Ausscheiden überlieferter Sentenzen niemals bewerkstelligen lassen* (*CKr* 8.)

22. *Über hundert Sprüche des Cāṇakya,* Monatsberichte der kön. Akad. d. Wiss. 1864, pp. 400-30 and *Indische Streifen* 1.253-73.

23. *Stimmen indischer Lebensklugheit,* Indica, 4.

24. *De treeentis Cāṇakyae poetae indici sententiis* (Halis Saxonum, 1873).

25. *Cāṇakya Recension de cinq recueils de stances morales* (Paris, 1887).

26. See also in 1887 : J. Gray, *Ancient proverbs and maxims from Burmese sources: or the nīti literature of Burma* (London, 1887).

27. *Laghu-cāṇakyam. Sentenze di Viṣṇugutto figlio di Cianaco il furbo pubblicate...* (tomo XVI-o degli Annali delle Università Toscane, Pisa, 1878) ; and *Un nuovo codice del Cianakyo minore Giornale della Societá Asiatica Italiana* I, 41 sqq.

28. *Foreword* to Bodhi Cāṇakya (Calcutta, 1890).

29. *Cāṇakyam Codice indiano* 1911; *Un secondo codice fiorentino inedito di Cāṇakya, RIGI* III, pp. 151-66 (1920); *Il codice napoletano di Cāṇakya, RIGI* IV (1921), 129-33; v (1922), 115-9.

Nath Law, Johan van Manen[30] in 1921 and O. Botto[31] in 1950—to mention only some of the important scholars writing about Cāṇakya—were less interested in the origin of each of his maxims than in various editions of the various compendia of Cāṇakya's sayings. None of the scholars[32] dealt in particular with the sources of sayings of Cāṇakya although in some editions one-third of Cāṇakya's aphorisms was also found in the Hitopadeśa.[33] Scholars writing about the Hitopadeśa did not tackle this problem either.[34]

10. Cāṇakya's aphorisms exist in a very large number of recensions of which Kressler (in *CKr*) distinguished 17. A number of scholars have accepted the division into 17[35] recensions rather undiscerningly even though its accuracy merits little confidence. Since 1904 many new recensions have been discovered and, what is more important, the so-called "recensions" mentioned by Klatt were often different editions or MS. of one and the same recension. And so, for instance, the VB, VAg, G and Wk "recensions" mentioned by Kressler were different editions or MS, of the same Cāṇakya compendium, while Wb and EH are two different versions of anothers Cāṇakya Compendium. E. Monseur reduced the number of recensions of Cāṇakya's aphorisms to five: the Vṛddha-Cāṇakya, Cāṇakya-śloka, Laghu-Cāṇakya, Cāṇakya-nīti-śataka and Cāṇakya-nīti-śāstra, but did not take into account the Cāṇakya rāja-nīti-śāstra, not published at that time, but already known to Kressler as Bhj.

11. After having studied one hundred and twenty-seven editions and forty-four MS. of compendia of aphorisms attributed to Cāṇakya, it can be assumed that these com-

30. *Foreword* to Cāṇakya-rāja-niti-śāstram (Calc. Or. Ser. 2., 2nd ed., Calcutta, 1926).

31. "*Un testo politico indiano. Dal trattato di scienza politica di Cāṇakya.*" In Rivista di Filosofia XLI, D Ser. 3.5.

32. Cf. J. van Manen in the *Foreword* to the second edition of *Cāṇakya-rāja-nīti-śāstraṁ* stressed the point that scholarly work on Cāṇakya's aphorisms has only rarely been undertaken in India (vii).

33. For instance 37 aphorisms of the *CNW* compendium (which contains 109 aphorisms) were found in the Hitopadeśa.

34. O. Böhtlingk in IS gave sometimes the Hitopadeśa and Cāṇakya's aphorisms as sources of the aphorism quoted, but these data are far from complete.

35. M. Winternitz, *Geschichte der indischen Litteratur* 3.135; S. N. Dasgupta and S. K. De, *A History of Sanskrit Literature*, 1.196; L. Renou *Littérature sanskrite*, 32.

pendia should be divided into six versions which could be termed: (1) the Vṛddha-Cāṇakya, *textus ornatior* (or Cāṇakya-nīti-darpaṇa) divided into 17 *adhyāyas*[36]; (2)the Vṛddha-Cāṇakya, *textus simplicior* divided into eight *adhyāyas*[37]; the (3) the Laghu-Cāṇakya, divided into eight short *adhyāyas* (this version is often copied together with that under 2)[38]; (4) the Cāṇakya-rāja-nīti-śāstra, divided into eight but long *adhyāyas*, of which *adhyāyas* from sixth to eighth are particularly long; this version is almost identical with the Bṛhaspati Saṁhitā of the Garuḍa-Purāṇa;[39] (5) the Cāṇakya-sāra-saṁgraha, divided into three *satakas* [40] and (6) the Cāṇakya-nīti-śāstra not divided into *adhyāyas* or *śatakas*; the number of maxims in this version varies from 78 to 343.[41] The nomenclature of these varsions is rather arbitrary.[42], [43]

12. From the analysis of the body of this study it would appear that the greatest number of Cāṇakya's aphorisms were borrowed by Nārāyaṇa from the CV version but that the CN version was his main source, since the latter group contained the smallest number of differences between the Hitopadeśa and Cāṇakya's aphorisms and had the smallest number of variants. It may be added that the variants noted in these two works were of rather minor significance.

It would be unwise however to draw any far-reaching conclusions from this type of choice by Nārāyaṇa. No doubt, oral tradition, as it was current in its variations according to particular geographical areas, must have been a major factor in the selection of aphorisms; it may be assumed that the CN

36. Cf. Abbreviations beginning with *CV*.
37. Cf. Abbreviations beginning with *Cv*.
38. Cf. Abbreviations beginning with *CL*.
39. Cf. Abbreviations beginning with *CR*.
40. Cf. Abbreviations beginning with *CS*.
41. Cf. Abbreviations beginning with *CN* or *Cn*.
42. Cf. L. Sternbach, *Cāṇakya's Various Versions of Aphorisms, with a pratika Index of Aphorisms Attributed to Cāṇakya* (*An Attempt at a Revised Analysis*).
43. Cf. fn. 1 and 42. In the footnotes the old division of Cāṇakya's aphorisms in *CŚ* (Cāṇakya-śloka), *CV.* (Vṛddha Cāṇakya) *CR* (Cāṇakya-rāja-nīti-śāstra), *CL* (Laghu Cāṇakya), *CN* (Cāṇakya-nītiś-ataka) was used. In the division given above the *CŚ* and *CN* groups were merged into the *CN* group but some of the *CŚ* and *CN* editions or MSs were incorporated into the new *CS* version and the *CV* group was divided into the *CV* and *Cv* versions. See also footnote 2 to the Post Scriptare.

and the CS versions were best known in Beṅgāl between the ninth and fifteenth centuries.[44]

II. TEXTS

13. In the light of the somewhat complex position of the Hitopadeśa vis à vis its sources in general, and in particular vis à vis the compendia of Cāṇakya, the author has set himself primarily the task of answering the question as to which aphorisms cast by Nārāyaṇa into the medley of stories entitled Hitopadeśa, were borrowed by Nārāyaṇa from the various compendia of Cāṇakya's aphorisms, or were also found in the various compendia of Cāṇakya's aphorisms.

14. An attempt has been made to present this study in a manner which would allow as much detailed study as the subject requires, and preserve as much clarity as the variety of sources and the number of problems involved permits.

Accordingly the study will treat : (a) stanzas of the Hitopadeśa found in at least one compendium and (b) parts of stanzas of the Hitopadeśa which have at least two *pāda-s* identical with any part of the stanza found in any one of the compendia of Cāṇakya's aphorisms.

Each stanza was subjected to an analysis which was executed in the following four stages :

(i) the first paragraph reproduces the stanza as it is found in HJ edition;

(ii) the second paragraph presents the stanza in F. Johnson's translation;[45]

(iii) the third paragraph contains the enumeration of sources in which the quoted stanza occurs. First are indicated the main editions of the Hitopadeśa[46] followed by various

44. According to J. Hertel, *Das Pañcatantra, seine Geschichte und seine Verbreitung* (Leipzig-Berlin, 1914) 39 sqq, and Kressler (*CKr* 7), the Hitopadeśa was composed between the eighth century and 1373 in Bengal. M. Winternitz narrowed this period to the ninth and fourteenth centuries. *Op. cit.* 3.291.

45. Where F. Johnson's translation was found not completely satisfactory or when a stanza was not translated by F. Johnson, the author's translation was supplied.

46. HJ, HS, HM, HP, HN, HK, HH, HC and IS. In the final stage of this work i. e. in the preparation of various readings, the author could not consult the HC edition, because the book was mislaid in the Library of Congress. HC had to be quoted from HS.

Although HJ has been chosen as the main edition, it is not the best. On compendia of Cāṇakya in the six versions mentioned above, and finally follow other sources which can be divided into the *kathā* literature (particularly the various versions of the Pañcatantra), the Nīti literature, the Dharma-literature, Epics, the Purāṇas and others;[47]

(iv) the fourth paragraph contains a brief analysis of the pertinent stanza of the HJ edition as juxtaposed against other editions of the Hitopadeśa, against most[48] of Cāṇakya's aphorisms[49] as well as against other sources.

The abundant raw material found in the footnotes may, if examined further, be of use for the reconstruction of some of the original stanzas of Cāṇakya. On the other hand, it may be of some value to those interested in the reconstruction of some Hitopadeśa's stanzas.[50]

the contrary, the comparison of the Hitopadeśa with Cāṇakya's aphorisms shows that this edition is fairly poor, since many changes were introduced by the editor. These changes were unnecessary, particularly as the original of the stanza, as for instance one deriving from Cāṇakya's sayings, was different. (Cf. fn. 50). However, this edition, in comparison particularly with the HP and HN editions, is an *editio ornatior*. For the purpose of this paper,—for which aphorisms form the basis,—it has been deemed better to choose the HJ edition as the basis.

47. Most of these stanzas are also found in various *subhāṣita-saṅgrahas*, such as Śārṅgadhara's Paddhati (BSS 37), Vallabhadeva's Subhāṣitāvalī (BSS 31), Subhāṣita-ratna-bhāṇḍāgāra (Nirṇaya Sāgara Press, 1952), Subhāṣitaratnākara (Bombay, 1872), Sūktimuktāvalī (GOS 82), Bṛhacchārṁgadhara-paddhati (Banaras, 1875), Śatakāvalī (Calcutta, 1850), Kavīndravacanasamuccaya (Bibl. Ind.)., Kavitāmṛtakūpa (Calcutta, 1828), Bahudarśana (Bahoodursn, Serampore, 1826) and many others. They are in principle not quoted in this paper, since they could not serve as original source; they are collections of sayings assembled from original sources compiled much later.

48. Cf. footnote 1.

49. First the inter-connection between the various editions of the Hitopadeśa is described, then follows the analysis of inter-relation between various groups of the compendia of Cāṇakya's aphorisms and the Hitopadeśa texts. Finally, the inter-relation between other sources and the Hitopadeśa texts is looked into.

50. The comparison of sources used by Nārāyaṇa with the various MS. used for the HJ, HS, HM, HP, HN, HK or other editions shows for instance that : in No. 11 the MS. or MS. used in the HH edition is the closest to the original; in No. 67 the MS. or MS. used in the HK edition is the closest to the original; in No. 73 the MS, used in the HS, HM, HP, HK and HH editions are the closest to the original; in No. 78 the MS, used in the HM, HP, HN, and HK editions are the closest to the original; in No. 108 the MS, or MS. used in the HS edition is the closest to the original; in No. 132 the MS. used in the HS, HP, HN and HK editions are the closest to the original; in No. 148 the MS. used in the HP and HN editions are the closest to the original, and others (cf. fn. 46).

The Hitopadeśa stanzas are not quoted in numerical or alphabetical order but are grouped in ten different categories viz. ; (1) The king and his officials; state policy; (2) wealth and poverty; (3) knowledge and ignorance; (4) virtue and vice; (5) women in general and as wives; (6) sons; (7) friends, foes, and various types of association; (8) guests and hosts; (9) servants; service; (10) miscellaneous.

This grouping has been decided upon since not only in the Hitopadeśa but also in the various compendia of Cāṇakya it is possible to select and separate groups of stanzas dealing with similar topics. The grouping of the stanzas according to topics makes it possible to analyze together similar stanzas, sometimes coming from one and the same prototype stanza, as for instance in the case of Nos. 5 and 6 or Nos. 143 and 144, or Nos. 11 and 12, Nos. 23 and 24.

15. *The King and His Officials; State Policy*

No. 1

bālo'pi nā'vamantavyo manuṣya iti bhūmipaḥ[1],
mahatī devatā hy eṣā[2] *nara-rūpeṇa*[3] *tiṣṭhati.*

The king even as a child must not be despised [because of the idea] that he is an [ordinary] mortal; for he is a great divinity which appears in human form.

HJ 2.81, HS 2.80, HM 2.82, HP 2.74, HN 2.73, HK 2.82, HH 52.8-9, HC 68.15-6, IS 4446; *CV* (Vṛddha-Cāṇakya nīti-Samuccaya, Ahmedabad 1913) 16.21, Mn. 7.8 (also quoted in (DhPS 1.1—448.7.8; 3.1—4.1-2 Rājanīti-ratnākara 68. 16-7); VRN 17.21-2, NPr 8.5.

The main editions of H are identical; some MSs contain minor variants. Other sources are identical with H.

Footnotes to No. 1 : [1]*bhūpati* A in HP [2]*pūjyā* P in HS; *by etā* Gh in Rājanīti-ratnākara [3]*'nanta-rū*⁰ B in DhPS 3.1.

No. 2

[1]*śāstraṁ sucintitam api*[2] *praticintanīyam.*[3]
ārādhito[4] *narapatiḥ*[5] *pratiśaṅkanīyaḥ*[6],
[7]*aṅke sthitā'pi yuvatiḥ*[8] *pariśaṅkanīyā*[9]
śāstre nṛpe ca[10] *yuvatau ca kuto vaśitvam*[11]

A statute of law, though it has been ever so well considered, is still to be reconsidered. A king, who has been propitiated, is still to be apprehended. A young woman, although seated in the lap, is altogether to be suspected. How can one ever secure complete mastery of a text-book, a king, or a young woman ?

HH 99.21-4, *ad* HS 110. 18, IS 6443; *CNW* 65, CnT II 30.10, CnT VII 97; ṢR 1; Vānary 2.

The main editions of H are identical. *CNW* contains several minor variants; it is nearer to Vānary and ṢR than to H. Other sources contain several minor variants.

Footnotes to No. 2 : [1]*śās*⁰ *aṅke* tr. IS [2]*atho* ṢR [3]*paricin*⁰ IS; *suniścitadhiyā paricin*⁰ IS; *suniścitadhiyā'pi hi cuntanīyaṁ* IS [4]*svārā*⁰ Vānary; *saṁsevito* IS [5]*'pi nṛpatiḥ* ṢR, Vānary, *CNW* [6]*pariśaṅkanīyaḥ* ṢR, Vānary, *CNW*; *parirakṣaṇīyaḥ* IS [7]*ātmā'kṣatā'pi* IS; (cf. fn.1) [8]*yuvatī* *CNW* [9]*parirakṣaṇīyā* ṢR, Vānary, *CNW* [10]*nṛpeṣu* IS [11]*vaśatvam* IS; *vaśatāvasannā* *CNW*; *sthiratvam* IS

No. 3

ājñā-bhaṅgo narendrāṇāṁ [1]*brāhmaṇānām anādaraḥ,*[2]
[3]*pṛthak-śayyā ca nārīṇām* [4]*aśastra-vihito vadhaḥ*[5].

Breaking the commands of kings, disrespect to Brāhmaṇs, and a separate bed for women [is] death though not inflicted by a weapon.

HJ 2.84, HS 2.52, HM 2.85, HH 48.3-4, HC 70.7-8, IS 878; *CNP II* 211, *CnT II* 12.4, *CnT III* 7.38, *CnT V* 65; VCsr 5.4, VCmr 5.62-3, VCbr 5.2, VCjr 5.6; PrC 1.22; cf. KN 13.66.

The main editions of H are identical with the exception of one minor variant; *CNP II* is identical with H with the exception of β. Other sources contain some important variants.

Footnotes to No. 3 : [1]*viprāṇāṃ* (*viduṣāṁ* VCmr; *mahatāṁ* VCjr) *māna-khaṇḍaṇā* (⁰*khaṇḍanam* VCsr VCmr, VCjr) VCsr, VCbr, VCmr, VCjr, *CNP II*; *avajñāviduṣāṁ tathā* N in VCsr; *vṛttic chedo'nujīvinām* (*dvijannanām* P in PrC)PrC [2]*anādaraṁ* HK, HH [3]*pṛthak chayyā CNP* II; *marmavākyaṁ ca lokānām* VCjr [4]*aśastra* (*aśāstra* IS; *aśastro* Dn in VCmr, H in VCjr, PrC; *saśastra* N in Vcsr) *vadha ucyate* VCsr, VCmr, VCbr, VCjr, PrC [5](*vadhaḥ*) *vadham* Nd in VCsr, GOKF in VCjr.

No. 4

[1]*asantuṣṭā dvijā naṣṭāḥ*[2] [3]*santuṣṭāḥ pārthivāḥ sadā,*[4]
salajjā gaṇikā naṣṭā [5]*nirlajjā ca*[6] *kulāṅganā.*[7]

Discontented Brāhmaṇs [and] contented monarchs [are] always ruined. A modest courtezan and an immodest woman of family [are alike] undone.

HJ 3.67, HS 3.64, HM 3.64, HP 3.62, HN 3.62, HK 3.64, HH 85.5-6, HC 113.5-6, IS 755; *CVND* 8.18, *CVM* 8.15;

CLṢ 4.2, *CLB* 4.3, *CLT* 4.3, *CLI* 4.3, *CLP V* 4.3, *CLP IV* 4.3, *CLP II* 4.3, *CLTb* 4.3, *CLH* 4.3, *CLL I* 4.3, *CLLd* 4.3, *CRB* 8.139, *CRP* 8.137, *CRBh I* 8.148, *CRBh II* 8.92, *CSLd* 80; *CNJV* 80, *CNS* 9, *CNW* 36, *CNF* 93, *CNN* 37, *CNPh* 79, *CNPN* 90, *CNP II* 289, *CNG* 299, *CNŚT* 63, *CNL* 40, *CnT II* 10.9, *CnT III* 7.18, *CnT V* 34, *CnT* I, 17. PKS 10 (ZDMG 64, 62); cf. Samayamātṛkā 4.68 and 4.70.

The main editions and various MSs. of H contain several minor variants. All the *C* groups contain minor variants. Other sources also contain minor variants.

Footnotes to No. 4 : [1]*asantuṣṭāḥ dvija naṣṭā santoṣeṇa mahīpati* *CLT* (variant); *asantuṣṭo dvijo* PKS, *CLB* 1.37; *asantoṣā* *CLC* [2]*naṣṭā* HH, *CLT*, *CLM*; *naṣṭaḥ* *CLB* 1.37 [3]*santuṣṭā iva pārthivāḥ* HS, HM, A in HP, HH, *CŚH*; *santuṣṭa pārthiva* P in HS; *santuṣṭāḥ pārthivās tathā* HP; *santuṣṭaś ca* (°*tuṣṭā* *CVND* var.) *mahībhujaḥ* (*mahībkṛtaḥ* IS)HK, *CVND*; *santuṣṭaś ca pāthivoḥ* PKS; *santuṣṭā* (°*tāś* *CLB*, *CLT*, *CLE*, *CLI*, *CŚP*, *CŚlB*) *ca mahīpatiḥ* B in HP, *CLB* 4.3, *CLT*, *CLE*, *CLI*, *CŚP*, *CŚlB*; °*tāś ca saṁtoṣeṇa mahīpatiḥ* *CLC*, *CLD*, *CLM*; °*tāś cai'va pārthivāḥ* *CŚF*, *CŚW* [4]*vās tathā* HN, *CŚN*; *pṛthivīpatiḥ* *CLB* 1.37 (cf. fn. 3) [5]*nirlajjāś* HS, HM, HP, HN, HK, HH, *CVND*, *CŚF*, *CŚH*, *CŚN*, *CŚP*,*CLB*; 4.3, *CLT*, *CLC*, *CLD*, *CLE*, *CLI*, *CLM*, *CŚlB*, *nirlajjāḥ sukulastryaḥ* *CŚW*; *nirlajje'va* IS (cf. fn. 8) [6]*va* *CŚF* [7]*kulāṅganāḥ* B in HP; *kulastriyaḥ* HS, HM, HP, HN, HK, HH, *CŚF*, *CŚH*, *CŚN*, *CŚP*, *CLB* 4.3, *CLT* (*CLT* variant as above), *CLC*, *CLD*, *CLE*, *CLI*, *CLM*, *CŚlB*

No. 5

rājā kulavadhūr[1] *viprā*[2] [3]*mantriṇaś ca payodharāḥ,*
sthāna-bhraṣṭā[4] *na śobhante dantāḥ*[5] *keśā narā nakhāḥ.*[6]

A king, a respectable woman, Brahmiṇs, councillors, and women's breasts, if they fall, are not beautiful; similarly teeth, hair, men and claws.

ad HS 1.162, HM 1.168, HK 1.170, (cf. HJ 1.104), IS 5750; *CRC* 8.68, *CRB* 8.75, *CRP* 8.72, *CRBh I* 8.73, *CRBh II* 8.61, cf. *CNP II* 203, cf. *CNI I* 204; cf. PS 2.52 (αβ), cf. PN 1.49, PT 2.92 (γδ) PTem 2.81 (γδ), cf. PP 2.118 (αβ), cf. PRE 2.57 (αβ); cf. GP 1.115, 73, (αβ); (cf. No. 6).

γδ are identical with No. 6 αβ. The main editions of H are almost identical. *CNP II* contains some minor variants. Cf. fns. to No. 6 αβ.

Footnotes to No. 5 : [1] °*vadhū* *CNP II* [2] °*vidyā* IS [3]*niyogī yogino* IS; *narīṇāṁ ca* IS; *niyogi mantriṇas tathā* [4] *CNP* 11 °*bhraṣṭaḥ* IS [5]*śophante* N in PS; *sa*° *ke*° tr. *PT*, GP, *dantā t* HH, PT, GP, *pūjyante dantāḥ* PS (A in PS as above) *CRC*; *pūjyante keśā* PT, GP [6]*na*° *na*° tr. HP; *nakhās tathā* IS; *keśaḥ nakhā* (*nakhāḥ* IS) *narāḥ* HK, PS, *CRC*; *keśa nakhās narāḥ* *CNP* II; da° *nakha*° *nar*° tr. PT. GP

No. 6

[1]*sthāna-bhraṣṭā na śobhante*[2] *dantāḥ*[3] *keśā*[4] *nakhā narāḥ*[5],
[6]*iti vijñāya matimān svasthānaṁ*[7] *na*[8] *parityajet.*[9]

Knowing this, that teeth, hair, claws [and] men, removed from their place, appear not to advantage, a prudent man should not quit his own station.

HJ 1.104, HS 1.94, HM 1.168, HP 1.130, HN 1.131, HK 1.170, HH 21.21-2, HC 41.19-20, IS 7223, cf. IS 5750; cf. *CRC* 8.68, *CRB* 8.75, *CRP* 8.72, *CRBh I* 8.73, *CRBh* II 8.61, PS 2.52, PN 1.49, PT 2.92, PTem 2.81, PP 2.118, PRE 2.57, GP 1.115, 73 (cf. No. 5).

αβ are identical with No. 5. The main editions of H are not identical, in particular as far as γδ are concerned. The *CR* group is different in γδ. γδ are also different in Pañc and GP which contain minor variants in αβ. Cf. fns. to No. 5.

Footnotes to No. 6 : [1]*sthā°* *iti* tr. HM, HK, GP [2]*pūjyante* PS (A in *PS* as above), *PT*, GP *CRC*; *śophante* A in PS [3]*dantā* HH, PT, GP [4]*da°* *°ke* tr. PT, GP [5]*narā nakhāḥ* HP [6]*sthānasthitāś ca śobhante pavitratvaṁ bhajatiu te CRC*; *sthānasthitāni pūjyante pūjyante ca pade sthitāḥ* GP; *etaj jñātvā tu ma°* PT, PRE; γ in PP missing [7]*nāśu sthānaṁ* PS; *aśu sthā°* NEF in PS; *svaṁ sthā°* PP; *saṁsthānaṁ* M in PP [8]*na sva* tr. PT, PRE [9]*parityajyet* bhN in PP.

No. 7

[1]*buddhir yasya balaṁ tasya*[2] [3]*nirbuddhes tu kuto balam*
paśya[4] [5]*siṁho*[6] *madnmattaḥ*[7] *śaśakena*[8] *nipātitaḥ.*[9]

He who has sense, has power; but whence has a fool power? See (how) a lion, intoxicated with pride, was hurled to destruction by a hare.

HJ 2.121, HS 2.116, HM 2.122, HP 2.108, HN 2.107, HK 2.120, HH 61.12-3, HC 81.4-5, IS 5386; *CVND* 10.16, *CVM* 10.4; cf. *CNW* 64, cf. *CNPN* 58, cf. *CNI I* 207, *CnT II* 18.12, *CnT III* 8.6, PS 1.54, PN 2.39, PT 1.62, PTem 1.55, PP 1.172, Pts 1.214, PRE 1.63; Śto 365. 4-5, cf. Śts 101.6-7; cf. KSS 10.60, 91 and 107; cf. KṣB 16.292; Śiva Purāṇa, Rudra saṁhitā 4.219, 52.

The main editions of H are almost identical . All the *C* groups are almost identical with H, but *CNW*, *CNPN* and *CVND* contain some minor variants. Other sources contain minor variants.

Footnotes to No. 7 : [1]*bu° ya°* tr. PT, PP, Pts, PRE, *CŚP*; *yasya buddha sukuto balaṁ* M in PP [2]om. bh in PP (*contra metrum*) [3]*nirbuddhis tat* IS; *nirbodhasya* HH; *nirbuddheś ca* *CVND*; *durbuddhes* Śto; *abuddhis* IS;

abuddhasya Boltz 46.22, PT; *abodhasya CŚW* [4]*vane* PP, Pts, *CNPN*, *CVND*; *kūpe* Śiva P [5]*jātibalas* (°*laḥ* PTem) *siṁhaś* (°*haḥ* PTem) *śa*°, PT [6]*siṁhaṁ* PS, Śto; *siṁhe* Śiva P; *siṁha* PS [7]*madonmattaṁ* (°*taś* Śiva P) PS, Śto; *madod mattaḥ* Boltz 46. 22; *balon mattaḥ CNW*, *CNPN*; *madon matto CVND* [8]*śaśikena* Pr. in PP; *maśakena* N in PS; *sasakena* IS; *jambukena CVND* (other editions as above) [9]*nipātitam* PS, Śto; *nivāsitaḥ* IS.

No. 8

viṣadigdhasya[1] *bhaktasya*[2] *dantasya calitasya*[3] *ca*,
amātyasya[4] *ca duṣṭasya mūlād*[5] *uddharaṇaṁ*[6] *sukham.*[7]

Clean riddance of poisoned food, of a loose tooth, and of a wicked minister [gives] ease.

HJ 2.128 (cf. 4.98), HS 2.122, HM 2.129, HP 2.115, HN 2.114, HK 2.127, HH 63.5-6, HC 83.17-8, IS 1506; *CRC* 8.69, *CRB* 8.76, *CRP* 8.73, *CRBh I* 8.74, *CRBh II* 8.62; PS 1.59, PN 2.43, PT 1.65, PTem 1.58, PP 1.222, PRE 1.67.

The main editions and various MSs. of H contain minor variants. *CRC* is almost identical with H; it contains three minor variants. Other sources contain minor variants.

Footnotes to No. 8 : [1]*viṣadagdasya C* in HP; *viraktasya ca* HH; *avidagdhasya* HN, N in HP; *vidagdasya ca* HS, HP; *kaṇṭakasya ca* PP; *kaṇṭakasya tu* PT; *kaṇṭakasya CRC*; (cf. fn. 2) [2]*bhuktasya* HK (variant), C in HP; *ca bhuktasya* HP; *ca bhuktasya ca* N in HP; *bhakṣyasya* PS (NBCEI in PS as above); *bhagnasya* PP, PT; *vimārgasya CRC* [3]*galitasyo* HH; *gaṇitasya CRC*; *ca viṣasya* H in PS [4]*amānyasya CRC*, [5]*balād* PS (NABC in PS as above) [6]*uddharaṇāt* HS [7]*varam* HH.

No. 9

jaye[1] *ca*[2] [3]*labhate Lakṣmīṁ mṛtenā'pi*[4] *surāṅganām*,
[5]*kṣaṇa-vidhavaṁsinaḥ kāyāḥ kā cintā maraṇe raṇe.*

And in victory he acquires fortune; by death a celestial bride. Bodies [are] extinct in an instant; what hesitation [should there be] about dying in battle ?

HJ 2.172, HS 2.162, HM 2.172 HK 2.170, HH 69.15-6, IS 2344; *CNP II* 205.

The main editions of H are almost identical; in HS only two minor variants are noted. *CNP II* contains some minor variants.

Footnotes to No. 9 : [1]*jite CNP II* [2]*vā* HS [3]*labhyate Lakṣmī mṛte cai'va surāṅganā CNP II* [4]*vā'pi* HS [5]*kṣaṇa-vidhvaṁsinī kāyā CNP II*

No. 10

na[1] *sā sabhā yatra na santi vṛddhā*[2]
[3]*vṛddhā ne te ye na vadanti dharmam*[4],

[5]*dharmaḥ sa no yatra na* [6]*satyam asti*[7]
[8]*satyaṁ na tad* [9]*yad bhayam abhyupaiti.*[10]

That [is] not a council where there are no elders; those [are] not elders who declare not the law. That [is] not law where truth is not; that [is] not truth which fear influences.

HJ 3.64, HS 3.61, HM 3.61, HP 3.59, HN 3.59, HK 3.61, HH 84.16-7, IS 3483; *CRC* 8.54, *CRB* 8.57, *CRP* 8.54, *CRT*, 8.29, *CRBh II* 8.49; MBh 5.34,59; R 7.59, (3), 33; GP 1.115, 52; BhŚ 568; NMS 1.80; (Also quoted in GMBh 220.1-2 (ascribed to N), DhPS 3.1—35.13 (ascribed to MBh). SC 23.14-5, Apar); PrC 2.129; VA 385, 6-7; cf. KSS 14, 106, 108.

The main editions and various MSs. of H contain some variants. *CRC* contains only three minor variants. Other sources contain several variants, in particular in δ.

Footnotes to No. 10 : [1]*sa CRC* [2]*vīddhāḥ* HH, GP, DhPS [3]*na te vṛ*⁰ tr. MBh, NMS, GMBh, SC [4]*ye pravadantya dharmān* Pp in HS [5]*nā'ste sa dharmo na hi yatra satyaṁ sa*° VA; *nāsau dharmo ya*° MBh, R, NMS, GMBh, DhPS, SC; *dharmo mano ya*° *CRC* [6]*cā'sti satyaṁ sa*° PrC (BP in PrC as above), BhŚ [7]*na cā'sti* (*naivā'sti IS*) *satyaṁ* BhŚ [8]*naitat* (*na tat IS*) *satyaṁ yac chalenā nuviddham* (*chalenā'bhyupetam* IS) GP; *na tacha chalenā-'nuviddham* IS; *na tat satyaṁ* tr. MBh, R, NMS, GMBh, DhPS, SC [9]*yac chalaṁ* HS, HM, HK, AB in HP; *yac chala doṣa yuktam CRC*; *yac chamam* HP, HN; *yac chalenā nuviddham* R, NMS, GMBh, SC, DhPS; *yac chalenā'bhyapetam* MBh; *yat kapaṭanu* (*kṛtakānu* PrC) *viddham* BhŚ; *yat kapaṭena viddham* VA, B in DhPS [10]*anuviddham* IS.

No. 11

[1]*dhanikaḥ*[2] *śrotriyo rājā nadī vaidyas tu*[3] *pañcamaḥ,*[4]
[5]*pañca*[6] *yatra na vidyante* [7]*tatra vāsaṁ*[8] *na kārayet.*

One should not fix one's abode there, where five [things] are not found : a monied man, a divine teacher, a king, a river, and fifthly, a physician.

HJ 1.110, HS 1.100, HP 1.78, HN 1.80, HH 22.13-4, IS 3861; *CVND* 1.9, *CVM* 1.8; *CvW* 1.12, *CvP IV* 1.10, *CvP V* 1.10, *CvGt* 1.10, *CvTb* 1.10, *CvH* 1.10, *CoI* 1.11, *CvL II* 1.10, *CvLd* 1.10, *CRC* 3.23; cf *CRB* 3.22, cf. *CRP* 3.22, cf. *CRBh I* 3.22, cf. *CRBh II* 3.22, cf. *CRCa* 3.15; *CNJV* 36, *CNS* 50, *CNW* 41, *CNF*, 5, *CNPh* 75, *CNPN* 32, *CNG* 292, *CNŚC* 35, *CNŚ* 35, *CNŚL* 21 *CNNM* 30, *CNŚT* 32, *CNŚK* 35, *CNL* 14, *CNI II* 6, *CnT II* 1.9, *CnT III* 1.9, *CnT VI* 9, *CnT V* 10; *GP* 1.110, 26; cf. MP 34.112b-113a; cf. Vi 71.66; cf. No. 12.

In the main editions and in various MSs. of H some minor variants are found. The *CN*, *CV* and *CR* groups are almost identical with H. *CNJV* and *CNW* are almost identical with HS and HH; *CVND* is identical with B in HP. GP contains some minor variants.

Footnotes to No. 11 : [1]*dha*° *pañ*° tr. N in HP, *CVF, CVG, CVK, CVT* (*b*), *CVT*(*c*) *CVGt* [2]*dhaninaḥ* HS, HH, GP, *CŚF, CŚH, CŚW, CŚN*; *prayogī CVG, CVF*; *gaṇakaḥ CVN*; *devajḍaḥ CRC* [3] °*aś ca* HS [4]*pañcakaḥ CVG* [5]*yatra ete na vidyante CŚP* [6]*ete CŚW* [7]*na kuryāt tatra saṁsthitim* (°*sthitiḥ* A in HP; *saṁgatim CVF*) HP, HH, GP, *CVF*; *na tatra divasaṁ vaset* B in HP, *CVND, CVG, CVK, CVN* [8]*vāso CŚF.*

No. 12

[1]*lokayātrā bhayaṁ lajjā*[2] *dākṣiṇyaṁ tyāgaśīlatā*[3],
[4]*pañca yatra*[5] *na vartante* [6]*na kuryāt tatra*[7] *saṁsthitim.*[8]

Where five [things] exist not: traffic, fear, shame, kindness [and] a disposition to liberality,—there one should make no permanent stay.

HJ 1.111, HM 1.104, HK 1.106, HH 22.15-6, HC 30.10-1, IS 3862, *CVND* 1.10, *CVM* 1.9, *CvA* 1.10, *CvṢ* 1.11, *CvW* 1.11, *CvP IV* 1.9, *CvGt* 1.11, *CvTb* 1.11, *CvH* 1.11, *CvI* 1.10, *CvL I* 1.10, *CvL II* 1.11, *CRC* 3.23-4, *CRB* 3.22, *CRP* 3.22, *CRT* 3.22 *cd/ab CRBh I* 3.22, *CRBh II* 3.22, *CRCa I* 3.15; *CSBD* 256, *CSB I* 3.56, *CSJ* 3.64, *CSC I* 3.56, *CSC II* 256, *CSB II*, 256, *CSLd* 3.56; *CNP I* 95, *CNPh* 26, *CNG* 293, *CNT IV* 98, *CNM* 46, *CNMN* 70, *CnT VI* 12; cf. GP 1.110, 26; cf. Vi 71.66; cf. No. 11.

The main editions of H are almost identical, All the *C* groups contain some minor variants, with the exception of *CRC* which is different in γδ. *CVND* is the nearest to H (HM and HK editions).

Footnotes to No. 12 : [1]*lo*° *pañ*° tr. *CV* in IS, *CVA, CVF, CVGt, CVK, CVN, CVW, CRB*; *dhaninaḥ śrotriyo rājā nadī vaidyas tu pañcamaḥ* GP [2]*rājā CVB* (variant) [3]*dharma-śīlatā CVF, CRC, CNH*; °*śitalā CVN*, [4]*tatra deśe na vastavyaṁ yatra nā'sti catuṣṭayam CRC* [5]*yasmin CVB* [6]*vidyante* HM, HK, *GP, CVND* [7]*na tatra divasaṁ vaset CVF* [8]*tena CVB* [9]*saṁgatim CVND, CVB, CVK, CVN, CNH*; *saṁgamam CVB*

No. 13

yasmin deśe na sanmānaṁ[1] [2]*na vṛttir na*[3] *ca*[4] *bāndhavāḥ*[5],
na ca vidyāgamaḥ[6] [7]*kaścit*[8] *taṁ deśaṁ parivarrayet.*

In whatever country [there is] neither respect for the good, nor the means of earning a livelihood, nor friends, nor any advancement of knowledge, that country one should forsake.

HJ 1.109, HS 1.99, HM 1.103, HP 1.77, HN 1.79, HK.

1.105, HH 22.11-2, HC 30.8-9, IS 5352, *CVND* 1.8, *CVM* 1.7; *CvA* 1.8, *CvṢ* 1.9, *CvW* 1.10, *CV* 1.8, *CvP V* 1.9, *CvGt* 1.9, *CvTb* 1.9, *CvH* 1.9, *CvI* 1. 11 *CvL I* 1.8, *CvL II* 1.9, *CvLd* 1.9; *CRC* 2.29, *CRB* 2.27, *CRP* 2.26, *CRT* 2.19, *CRBh I* 2.26, *CRBh II* 2.23, *CRCa I* 2.24; *CNJV* 37, *CNS* 76, *CNW* 75, *CNPh* 14, *CNG* 45, *CNT IV* 127, *CNM* 124, *CNMN* 91, *CNŚC* 36, *CNŚ* 35, *CNŚL* 22, *CNNM* 31, *CNŚT* 33, *CNŚK* 36, *CNL* 8, *CNI II* 52, *CnT II* 1.8, *CnT III* 1.8, *CnT VI* 8, *CnT V* 7; *GP* 1.109, 20; *Śto* 332.22-3.

In the main editions and in various MSS. of H some minor variants are found. The *CN* group is almost identical with H. The *CV*, *Cv* and *CR* groups contain several important variants and changes, in particular in γδ. Similarly Śto. GP contains minor variants.

Footnotes to No. 13 : [1]*samāno* HM, HK, Śto, *CŚF*, *CVND*, *CVG*, *CVK*, *CRC* [2]tr. *na mitrāṇi na bāndhavāḥ* l *na ca vidyāgamo vṛttistaṁ* P in HS [3]*mitrāṇi* HP, HN; *na ca vṛttir CŚF*; *prītir B* in *CŚF*; *prītirna* GP, *CŚH*, *CRC* [4]*na* HP, HN, *CŚF*, *na ca* B in HP; *vā* IS [5]*bāṁdhavaḥ* HM, HC [6]*vidyāgamo* Śto, *CRC*, *CVND*; *cā'tityāgamaḥ* IS [7]*nā'pi dhanaṁ tatra sthitiḥ kathaṁ* Śto; *'py asti tatr vāsaṁ* (*vāsa(ṁ)* *tatra CVND*, *CVN*) *na kārayet CVND*, *CVN*, *CRC*; *na tatra divasaṁ vaset CVF*, *CVG* [8]*vṛttim* IS

No. 14

kṣudraśatrur bhaved yasya[1] *vikramān naiva*[2] *labhyate*[3],
tam āhartuṁ[4] *puras-kāryaḥ sadṛśas tasya*[5] *sainikaḥ.*

If one has an insignificant foe, one will not overcome him by valour, [but] a combatant [that is] a match for him must be employed to take him.

HJ 2.83, HS 2.82, HM 2.84, HP 2.76, HN 2.75, HK 2.84, HH 52.21-2, HC 69. 10.1 IS 2030; (cf. *CSBD* 237. *CSB I* 3.37, *CSJ* 3.45 *CSC I* 3.37, *CSC II* 2.37, *CSB II* 2.37, *CSLd* 3.37).

The main editions and various MS. of H contain minor variants. Other sources contain minor variants.

Footnotes to No. 14 : [1]*yas tu* HS, HM, HP, HN, HK [2]*na sa* IS [3]*namyate* IS [4]*āhaṁtuṁ* HM, HK, HH (cf. HS notes); *nihantuṁ* Boltz 38.11 [5]*ko'pi* A in HP.

No. 15

A similar aphorism to that found in HJ 3.60[1] is also found in *CVND* 11.2 and *CVM* 11.1. It deals with kings.

Footnotes to No. 15 : [1]*ātma-pakṣa-parityāgāt parapakṣeṣu yo rataḥ* /*sa parair hanyate mūḍho nīla-varṇaśṛgāla-vat.*

* * *

Compare also No. 123 below.

16. *Wealth and Poverty*

No. 16

yasyā'rthās[1] *tasya mitrāṇi yasyā'rthās*[2] *tasya bāndhavāḥ,*
yasyā'rthā[3] *sa pumāṁl* [4]*loke yasyā'rthāḥ sa tu*[5] *paṇḍitaḥ.*[6]

He who has riches has friends; he who has riches has relations; he who has riches [is] a man [of consequence] in the world; he who has riches [is] even an oracle of wisdom.

HJ. 1.134. HS 1.118, HM 1.124, HP 1.95, HN 1.96, HK 1.127, HH 25.24-5, HC 35. 3-4, IS 5409 *CVND* 6.5. and 7.15, *CVM* 6.5, *CvA* 6.7, *CvṢ* 6.7, *CvIV* 6.8, *CvP IV* 6.8, *CvP V* 6.6, *CvGt* 6.9 & 6.13, *CvTb* 6.8, *CvL I* 6.7, *CvL II* 6.8, *CvLd* 6.6; *CRC* 4.12, *CRB* 4.12, *CRP* 4.12, *CRBh I* 4.12, *CRBh II* 4.11, *CRCa I* 4.9, *CRCa II* 21; *CNP I* 51, *CNP II* 76, *CNI I* 67, *CNG* 238, *CNT IV* 50, *CnT II* 10.11, *CnT III* 7.21, *CnT V* 37, *CnT I* 19; PS 2.31, PN 1.28, PT 2.52, Pts 1.3, PRE 2.31; VCsr 12.5; Śts 25.11-26. 1, Śto 325.34-5; GP 1.111, 17; cf. KṣB 16.422; MBh 12.8, 19; R 6.83, 35.

The main editions of H contain some minor variants. The *CV* and *Cv* groups are very near to H. *CVND* is identical with some editions of H (HP, HN). Other sources contain minor variants.

Footnotes to No. 16 : [1]*yasyā'rthas* FHE in PS, VC, Śto [2]*yasyā'rthāḥ* HM, HP, HN, HH, PS, PT, Pts, PRE, Śts, Śto, V in VC, MBh, R, GP, *CVND, CVF, CVG, CVN, CRC, CNH, CŚlB* (better); *yasyā'rthas* (*ḥ*) FHE in PS, *CNH CŚlB* [3]*pumān*, MBh, R in Śto, GP, *CRC*; *mupān* B in Śto [4]*yasyā'rthas* (*ḥ*) FHE in PS, VC, MM, H in Śto, *CVF, CVN* [5]*hi* HM, HC; *ca* HS, HP, HN, HK, PS, PT, Pts. PRE, VC, Śts, Śto, MBh, R, GP, *CVND, CVF, CVG, CVN, CRC, CNH, CŚlB* [6]*sa ca jīvati* LO in Śts.

No. 17

brahmahā'pi naraḥ pūjyo yasyā'sti vipulaṁ dhanam,
śaśinas tulya-vaṁśo'pi nirdhanaḥ paribhūyate.

Even a man who has murdered a Brahmaṇ [is] held in respect, provided he has abundant wealth. Although of a race equal to the moon, [if] poor, he is despised.

HJ 2.3, HM 2.3, HP 2.3 & 1.119, HN 2.3, HK 2.3, HH 40.12-3, HC 54. 1-2, IS 4494; *CNJV* 82, *CNS* 68, *CNŚT* 65, *CNL* 87.

The main editions of H are identical The *CN* group is identical with H.

No. 18

ko'rthān[1] *prāpya na garvito*[2] [3]*viṣayiṇaḥ kasyā'pado* [4]*'staṅgatāḥ*[5],
[6]*strībhiḥ kasya na khaṇḍitam bhuvi*[7] *manaḥ*[8] *ko nāma*[9] *rājñām*[10]
priyaḥ[11],
[12]*kaḥ kālasya* [13]*bhujāntaraṁ na ca*[14] *gataḥ*
[15]*ko'rthī*[16] *gato gauravaṁ,*[17]
ko vā durjana-vāgurāsu[18] *patitaḥ kṣemeṇa*[19]
yātaḥ[20] *pumān.*[21]

Who that has acquired riches, [is] not lifted up with pride ? Of what wordling [are] the troubles gone to their setting ? On earth, whose mind [is] not distracted by women ? Who is beloved of princes ? Who enters not into the arms of death ? What beggar [ever] attained respect ? or what man, having fallen into the snares of the wicked, has escaped with safety ?

HJ 2.152, HS 2.144, HM 2.153, HP 2.140, HN 2.139, HK 2.151, HH 66.21-4, HC 88.7-10, IS 1942; *CVND* 16.4, *CRC* 2.28, *CRB* 2.25, *CRP* 2.24, *CRT* 2.17, *CRBh I* 2.24, *CRBh II* 2.21, *CRCa I* 2.22; PS 1.79, PN 2.58, PT 1.90, PTem 1.82, PP 1.109, Pts. I.146, PRE 1.89; VCsr VI.15; Śts 85, 5-9; cf. KSS 10.60, 139; GP 1.109, 18; SR 2.

The main editions and various MSs. of H contain several minor variants. *CRC* contains some minor variants, mostly occurring also in various MSs. of H or in Pañc. Other sources contain some variants.

Footnotes to No. 18 : [1]om LOMM$_1$, HG in Śts. [2]*garhito* N in PS [3]*bhuvi naraḥ* PS (NABC in PS as above), PT, PRE, *CRC*; *vyasaninaḥ* E in VC [4]*'pada* PT (Ptem as above), P in Śts [5]*'staṅ-gataḥ* HJ, P in Śts; *gatā* PT; *'rthāt ga°* IS; *nāgatāḥ* GP, ṢR; *bhuvi madaḥ kasyo'pado'staṁ gataḥ* A in HP [6]*kasyā strībhir akhaṇḍitaṁ bhu°* NABC in PS, V in VC [7]*bhūvi* edd. in HS, HH (wrongly); *bhūja* HC; *nanu* PS, N in VC; *śuci* Q in VC; *vata* *CRC* [8]*ca sumanaḥ* I in PS (cf. fn. 7) [9]*vā'sti* HM, HK, HH, [10]*rāja°* E in VC; *rājya°* *CVND* [11]*mataḥ* A in HP [12]*kaḥ* om. C in Śts; *kālaḥ kasya ca gocare nipatitaḥ* FHO in PS; *kaḥ kālasya bhujāntaraṁ (ca) na* NABC in PS [13]*na gocarāntara gataḥ* HN, PS (NABC in PS as above), PT, PP, Pts, PRE, Śts, GP, ṢR; *na gocaratvam agamat* (*°maḥ* IS) VC, *CVND*; *sukhantaram* *CRC* [14]*hi* HH [15]*na gocarāntara gataḥ* HS, HP [16]*kīrthī* PT (notes); *'rthānagato* P in Śts [17]*gaṁrapaṁ* O in PS [18]*vāgurā ni°* PT, PRE, GP, ṢR; *CRC*; (*vāgurīṁ na* CC_I in Śts; *durjana-durguṇeṣu CVND*); *°vāgrase rase pra°* IS; *durjaya°* A in Śts [19]*kṣameṇa* E in VC [20]*jātaḥ* AB in HP, P in Śts, *CRC* [21]*pathi CVND*.

No. 19

santoṣā'mṛta-tṛptānāṁ[1] *yat sukhaṁ śāntacetasām*[2],
kutas[3] *tad dhana-lubdhānām*[4] [5]*itaś ce'taś*[6] *ca dhāvatām.*

Whence have they, who, greedy of wealth, are running hither and thither, the happiness which those placid spirits enjoy. who are satisfied with the nectar of contentment ?

HJ 1.153, HS 1.136, HM 1.142, HP 1.110, HN 1.111, HK 1.144, HH 27.26-7, HC 37-16-7, IS 6800 *CVND* 7.3, *CVM* 7.3, *CvA* 5.13, *CvṢ* 5.13, *CvW* 5.13, *CvP IV* 5.14, *CvP V* 5.14, *CvGt* 5.13, *CvTb* 5.14, *CvH* 5.13, *CvL I* 5.13, *CvL II* 5.13, *CvLd* 5.12, *CNI I* 130, *CNŚK* 45, *CnT I* 41; PS 2.43, PN 1.39, PP 2.161, Pts. 2.152, PRE 2.48; Skanda Purāṇa, Prabhāṣakhaṇḍa 255.33.

The main editions of H are identical; minor variants are noted in one MS. The *Cv* group, is almost identical with H. Some editions of Pañc. are identical with H., others contain minor variants. Skanda P contains one variant in δ.

Footnotes to No. 19 : [1]*saṁtoṣa-* IS; °*taptānāṁ* Pp in HS, NP in PP; °*cittānāṁ* E in PS [2]*sātma*° IS; *śantir eva ca* IS [3]*na ca CVND* [4]°*luptānāṁ* Pr in PP [5]*sukhaṁ cāśantacetasām* Skanda P °om. M in PP (*contra metrum*).

No. 20

nipānam iva maṇḍūkāḥ[1] *saraḥ pūrṇam ivā'ṇḍajāḥ,*[2]
[3]*sodyogaṁ*[4] *naram*[5] *āyānti*[6] [7]*vivaśāḥ*[8] *sarva-sampadaḥ.*

As frogs to the pool, as fishes to the full lake, [so] to the enterprising man do all riches unresisting come.

HJ 1.185, HS 1.165, HM 1.171, HP 1.133, HN 1.134, HK 1.173, HH 31.10-1, HC 42.11-2, IS 3727; cf. *CvP IV* 3.13, cf. *CvGt* 3.10, cf. *CvTb* 3.18; *CRC* 2. 48 αβ, *CRB* 2.56 αβ, *CRP* 2.53 αβ, *CRBh I* 2.53 αβ, *CRBh II* 2.43 αβ, cf. *CNP II* 217, cf. *CNT IV* 245; PS 2.55, PN 1.52, PT 2.95, PTem 2.84, PP 2.112, PRE 2.59.

The main editions of H and its various MSs. contain minor variants. *CRC* in αβ is almost identical with H (it is identical with PT). Pañc. contains several minor variants.

Footnotes to No. 20 : [1]*maṇḍukāḥ* HH [2]*saraḥ pūrna...*I in PS; *sarā pūrṇnathivā'mdrajāḥ* M in PP [3]*śubhakarmāṇam āy*° PT, *CRC* [4]*bhodyogaṁ* Pr. in PP [5]*svayam* PS, PP, PRE [6]*samupā'yānti* P in HS [7]*sahāyāś ca* (°*yaś ca*) *dhanāni ca* (*va*) PS, PT, PP, PRE, *CRC* [8]*pravaṇāḥ* HP, I in HK; *sanmukhāḥ* A in HP (on the margin); *vivasāḥ* NC Edd in MS.

No. 21

[1]*tathā hy āmiṣam ākāśe pakṣibhiḥ śvāpadair bhuvi,*
[2]*bhakṣyate*[3] *salile*[4] *matsyais*[5] *tathā sarvatra vittavān.*

For as prey is eaten by birds in the air, by beasts on the earth, and by fishes in the water, so [is] a rich man everywhere (liable to be preyed upon).

HJ 1.194, HS 1.174, HM 1.181, HP 1.143, HN 1.144, HK 1.183, HH 32.9-10, HC 43.12-3, IS 5160; *CnT II* 20.3, *CnT III* 53.1; Pts 1.401 and 2.116; MBh 3.2.39.

The main editions and the various MSs. of H contain several variants. Other sources contain some important variants, in particular in $\alpha\beta$.

Footnotes to No. 21 : [1]*yathā* HS, HM, HP, HN, HK, HH, MBh; *yathā miṣaṁ...CnT II, CnT III*; yathā *miṣaṁ jale matsyair bhakṣyate śvā°* (*svā°*) Pts [2]*ākāśe pakṣibhiś cai'vā* P in HK, Pts [3]*bhakṣite* AB in HP [4]*śalilair* A in HP [5]*nakrais* HM, HK, Pp in HS; *matsyaiḥ* A in HP.

No. 22

arthāḥ[1] *pāda-rajo'pamā*[2] [3]*giri-nadī-vego'pamaṁ*[4] *yauvanaṁ,*
mānuṣyaṁ[5] *jala-vindu-lola-capalaṁ*[6] *pheno'pamaṁ*[7] *jīvanam*[8],
[9]*dharmaṁ yo na kuroti*[10] *niścala-matiḥ*[11] [12]*svargā'rgalo 'dghāṭanaṁ,*
paścāt tāpa-hato[13] *jarā-pariṇataḥ*[14] *śokā'gninā*[15] *dahyate.*

Riches [are] like the dust of the feet. Youth [is] like the impetuosity of a mountain torrent. Manhood [is] fickle [and] unsteady as a drop of water. Life [is] like froth. Whoever, with a steady mind, performs not the duties of religion to unbolt the bars of heaven, will when stricken with repentence and weighed down with old age, be consumed by the fire of grief.

HJ 1.164, HS 1.146, HM 1.152, HK 1.54, HH 29.2-5, HC 39.3-6, IS 599; *CRC* 6.4; VCsr 28.4; Vet 23.12; Bhś 383.

The main editions and various MSs. of H contain some minor variants. *CRC* is almost identical with H. Other sources and their various MSs. contain several minor variants.

Footnotes to No. 22 : [1]*arthā* IS; *artha* IS; *arthaṁ* IS [2]*yādo-raco'pamā* V in VC; *yādasvo'pamā* IS; *pāṭa-lajo-'pamā* NNdQ in VC; *pāṭlajo'pamā* M in VC; *pāradacaṁ calāḥ* T in VC; *nadivelo'pamaṁ* IS; *patti°* A in Vet; *°rajaḥ sama* (*samo* IS) BhŚ, *CRC* [3]*guru°* V in VC; *gara°* Q in VC [4]*velo'pamaṁ* P in HS [5]*āyuṣyaṁ* HM, HK, HC, VJ in VC; *mānuṣyo* Q in VC [6]*jalalo-bindu-capalaṁ* HK, *CRC*; *jala-vīci-bindu-capalaṁ* T in VC; *jala-vindur-eva ca°* IS; *jala-bindu-caḍca-lataraṁ* VJ in VC; *kari* (*kaṭi*)-*karṇatāla* (*°tola*)-*taralaṁ* (*talaralaṁ*) Vet; *vaḍca-lataraṁ* IS [7]*pheṇo'pamaṁ* HS (printing error) [8]*jīvitam* HM, HK, HC, VC, (Nd in VC as above), BhŚ [9]*dharmānai'va* Nd in VC [10]*niṁdita°* HM, HK, HC [11]*niścalamanāḥ* N in VC; *ninditamatiḥ* IS

[12]*svargād galod°* Q in VC; *svargāṭanaṁ sarvadā* Nd in VC; *°lādhāraṇaṁ* A in Vet [13] *°yuto* HM, HK, S in HS, T in VC; *°gato* A in Vet; *°vato* IS; *paścāt taṁ praharo* Nd in VC; *°hṛto* BhŚ [13]*vato* IS [14]*parigataḥ* HM, HC, HK; *pariṇatā* Nd in VC; *piraṇato* IS; *janaḥ pari°* N in VC, A in Vet [15]*cārā'gninā* Nd in VC.

Nos. 23, 24

> *āpadarthe*[1] *dhanaṁ rakṣed*[2] *dārān*[3] *rakṣed*[4] *dhanair api,*
> [5]*ātmānaṁ satataṁ*[6] *rakṣed*[7] *dārair api*[8] *dhanair api.*[9]

Let him preserve [his] wealth against misfortune; let him preserve [his] wife even [at the expense] of [his] wealth; let him always preserve himself even [at the expense) of [his] wife and [his] wealth.

HJ 1.43, HS 1.36, HM 1.41, HP 1.31 (cf. 3.122a), HN 1.31, HK 1.42, (cf. 3.126*a*), HH 12.15-6, HC 17.1-2, IS 958; *CVND* 1.6, *CVM* 1.6; *CvA* 1.6, *CvṢ* 1.6, *CvW* 1.7,*CvP IV* 1.6, *CvP V* 1.6, *CvGt* 1.6, *CvTb* 1.6, *CvH* 1.6, *CvI* 1.6, *CvL I* 1.6, *CvL II* 1.6, *CvLd* 1.6; *CRC* 2.1, *CRB* 2.1, *CRP* 2.1, *CRT* 2.1, *CRBh I* 2.1, *CRBh II* 2.1, *CNJV* 29, *CN* 12, *CNW* 8, *CNF* 45, *CNPh* 4, *CNPN* 7, *CNI* I 95, *CNG* 19, *CNT* IV 195, *CNŚ* A 11, *CNHM* 68, *CNŚT* 25, *CNI II* 21; Pts 1.356, & 3.86; VCsr 12.1, VCjr 20.1; Śto 321.12-3, Vet 19.16, MBh 1.160, 27 (also quoted in Dh 3. 1978), 5.36, 18; GP 1. 109, 1; Mn. 7.213 (also quoted in Vīr Rājanīti 413, Rājanītiratnākara 55.11 γδ), BBh (first *pāda* only; identical with HP 3.122a, HK 3.126a); HDh 14.

The main editions of H contain some minor variants, in particular in *a*. HP 3.122*a* and HK 3.126*a* are identical with HJ 1.43*a*. The *CN*, *CV* and *Cv* groups are identical with some editions of H. Pañc. VCsr, VCjr, Śto and Vet are identical with H (changes are noted in MSs. only). Also MBh, GP and Mn are identical with (H changes are noted in MSs. only). Other sources, with the exception of BBh, are also identical with H.

Footnotes to Nos. 23, 24 : [1]*āpadartaṁ* HP, HN, HK, P in HS, VCsr, (VJEND in VCsr as above), GŚ in VCjr, Śto BBh, HDh, MnJ, MnL, Vīr, *CŚH*, *CŚN*, *CVF*, *CVG*, *CVK*; *āpadārthaṁ* A in HP, Pp in HS; *āpadārthe* B in HP [2]*rakṣyaṁ* Ś in VCjr; *rakṣet* HP 3.122, HK 3.126, BBh, *CŚH*, *CŚW*, *CRC* (wrongly) [3]*dārāṁ* HH (corrupt); *dārā* Ś in VCjr [4]*rakṣyā* Ś in VCjr, Vīr, *rakṣet* MnJh (notes), HDh, *CRC* (wrongly) [5]*ātmā tu sarvato rakṣyā*, *rakṣyo CRC*) Ś in *VC*jr, *CRC* [6]*sarvato* Vīr M_9 K in MnJ; *sarvadā* MnJh (notes), G in MnJ; *tu tathā* Nd in MnJ, MnJh (notes) [7]*rakṣet CŚW* (wrongly) [8]*dānair api* KRB in Śto; *rakṣet putradāra* HN; *paśva dārai* IS [9]*apī'ti Rājanīti-ratnākara* (*contra metrum*)

No. 25

dānaṁ bhogo nāśas[1] *tisro gatayo bhavanti vittasya*[2],
[3]*yo na*[4] [5]*dadāti na*[6] *bhuṅkte tasya*[7] *tṛtīyā*[8] *gatir bhavati.*[9]

Distribution,—enjoyment,—loss are the three destinies of wealth; the third doom awaits him who neither imparts, nore njoys.

HJ 1.173, IS 2757; *CRC* 2.41, *CRB* 2.39, *CRP* 2.34, *CRBh I* 2.34, *CRBh II* 2.31, *CnT II* 20.6, *CnT III* 53.4; PS 1.4, (in B MS quoted *ad* line 45), Pts 2.151; VCsr 3.5; BhŚ 50; PrC 264, Pras 11.3; NV 2.11; ŚP 390 (ascribed to BhŚ), VS 478, SRK 6.43.

The main editions of H are identical. *CRC* is almost identical with H. Other sources are identical with H, with the exception of PS which contains a minor variant.

Footnotes to No. 25 : [1]*vināśas* H_2 X in BhŚ; *nāśaś ca* W_{2-4} in BhŚ; *nāśās* G_4 in BhŚ [2]*hi tasya* J_2 in BhŚ; *dravyasya* IS [3]*janna* T_3 in BhŚ [4]om. J_3 in BhŚ [5]*dāti na ca bhu°* F_5 in BhŚ [6]om. D in BhŚ; *na hi* X_1 in BhŚ [7]*taysā'pi* J_1 in BhŚ [8]*tritīyā* PS; *tritayā* J_2 in BhŚ [9]*bhavaty eva* T in VC; *bhavaṁti* X_1 in BhŚ; *nāśaḥ* VS, *CRC*.

No. 26

[1]*aputrasya gṛhaṁ śūnyaṁ* [2]*sanmitrarahitasya ca*
mūrkhasya [3]*ca*[4] *diśaḥ śūnyāḥ sarva-śūnyā*[5] *daridratā.*[6]

Empty [is] the house of a man who has not a son; and of him who is destitute of a true friend. Empty [are all] the regions of the world to an ignorant man. Poverty [is] a total blank.

HJ 1.135, HS 1.120, HM 1.125, HP 1.96, HN 1.97, HK 1.128, HH 25.26-7, HC 35.5-6, IS 444; *CVND* 4.14, *CVM* 4.9; *CvA* 7.12, *CvṢ* 7.12, *CvW* 7.10, *CvP IV* 7.9, *CvP V* 7.7, *CvTb* 7.13, *CvH* 6.21, *CvL I* 7.12, *CvL II* 7.12, *CvLd* 7.7; *CNP I* 24, *CNI I* 150, *CNT IV* 23, *CNM* 23, *CNMN* 23, *CNŚL* 107, *CnT II* 17.1, *CnT III* 7*b* 9, *CnT V* 29; PS 2.32, (PN 1.29), (PT 2.59), PP 2.80, PRE 2.34; VCsr 21.1; Vet 6.2; Skanda Purāṇa, Āvanthyakhaṇḍa, Revākhaṇḍa 103. 128.

The main editions and various MSs. of H contain minor variants. All the groups of *C* contain minor variants, in particular in β. Other sources contain also minor variants.

Footnotes to No. 26 : [1]*śū° apu° gṛ°* tr. PT, PP, PRE [2]*deśaḥ śūnyo'py* (*hy* VC) *abāndhavaḥ* (*'pi bān°* IS) PS, VC; *hṛc chūnyaṁ yasya nā'sti sanmitraṁ* (*manvitram* M in PP, PRE [*contra metrum*]); *dik śūnyā* (*diśaḥ CV in IS*) *'bandhavasya ca* Vet, *CV* in *IS*; *diśaḥ śūnyas* (*diśa śūnyāṁ* AD in Vet) *tv abāndhavāḥ* (*ca bān°* A in Vet; *kubāndhavaiḥ* d in Vet) a in Vet, *CVND*; *diśiḥ śūnyam abāndhavā* IS; *diśaḥ* (*diśāḥ CNH*) *śūnyā* (*śūnyaṁ CVN*) (*hy*) *abāndhavāḥ* (*°vā CVN*; *°ve CVF*, *CVG*, *CNH*) Skanda P. *CVF*, *CVG*, *CVN*, *CNH*; *cira śūnyaṁ yasya nā'sti sanmitram* PT (*contra metrum*); *deśa-śūnyo°* NA in PS; *śūnyadeśo hy* (*'py* MNdV in VC) J in VC [3]*hṛdayaṁ śūnyaṁ* HP, PS, Skanda P, VC, Vet, *CVND*, *CV in IS*, *CVF*, *CVG*, *CVN*, *CNH*; *sarva-śūnyaṁ* B in HP, NA in PS [4]*tu* N in HP; om. PT, PP, PRE (*conta metrum*) [5]*sarvā°* T in VC; *sarvāḥ* N in HP; *sarvaṁ śūnyaṁ* PT, PP, PRE; *sarva-śūnyaṁ* B in HP, Skanda P, AbhNPPrM *ψ* in PP, NNdQ in VC, ABd in Vet, *CVND*; *śarva-sūnyaṁ* ABh *φ* in PP; *sarvaśūna* M in PP; *sarva-śūnyā* IS [6]*daridrasya* PP, PT, PRE; *dāridratā* a in Vet; *daridranaḥ* d in Vet.

No. 27

[1]*arthena hi*[2] *vihīnasya*[3] *puruṣasyā'lpamedhasaḥ*[4],
kriyāḥ sarvā vinaśyanti[5] *grīṣme kusarito*[6] *yathā.*[7]

All the acts of a man deprived of wealth [and] of little understanding, die away like brooks in the summer's heat.

HJ 1.133, HS 1.117, HM 1.123, HP 1.94, HN 1.95, HK 1.126, HH 25.22-3, HC 35.1-2, IS 617; *CvW* 6.10, *CvP IV* 6.10, *CvTb* 6.10, *CvL II* 6.10, *CRC* 4.14, *CRB* 4.13, *CRP* 4.13, *CRBh I* 4.13, *CRBh II* 4.13; PS 2.30; PN 1.27; PT 2.53, PP 2.71, Pts 2.85, PRE 2.32; MBh 12.8,18; cf. 12.8, 16; R 6.83, 33 & 6.62, 29.

The main editions of H contain minor variants. All the *C* groups contain some variants. *CvTb* is nearest to H. Other sources contain some important variants, particularly in γ.

Footnotes to No. 27 : [1]*arthancha* MBh; *artha-hīna CVF* [2]*tu* S in HS, HK, PP; *ca* Pts; [3]*vihīnasya CVF*; *parihīnasya* HS, HH; *vimuktasya* R (6.62, 29) [4] *°syū'lcacetasaḥ* A in PS; *°meghasaḥ* HK (printing error); *'lpacetasaḥ* R (6.62, 29) [5]*vi(c)chidyante* (*ucchidyante* PP, Pts; *pracchidyante* IS; *utsṛjyate CVF*) *kriyāḥ sarvā* PS, PT, PP, Pts, PRE (PMP as above), R (6.62, 29), MBh, *CVF*, *CVN*, *CRC* [6]*°kaṁsarito CVF*; *°tu sari CVN* [7]*grīṣmā kusari yathā* Pr in PP (*contra metrum*).

No. 28

[1]*dhanavān iti hi madas te*[2] *kiṁ gata-*
vibhavo[3] *viṣādam*[4] *upayāsi*[5],
kara-nihita-kanduka-samāḥ[6] *pāto'tpātā*[7]
[8]*manuṣyāṇāṃ.*

Because rich, will you be proud ? When your wealth is gone, will you sink into dependency ? The falls and risings of men [are] like a ball tossed by the hand.

HJ 1.188, HS 1.168, HM 1.175, HP 1.137, HN 1.138, HK 1.177, HH 31.21-2, HC 42.19-20, IS 3053; (cf. *CLA* 8.1); PS 2.64, PN 1.60, PT 2.107, PTem 2.96, PP 2.124, PRE 2.66.

The main editions and various MSs. of H contain minor variants. Other sources contain important variants in αβ and minor variants in γδ

Footnotes to No. 28: [1]*dhanavān īti* (*iti* H in PS) *vibhīvā* (om. in H in PS) *madam api kiṁ* O in PS; *dhanavān aham iti matis te* (*sukhem* A in PS) NA in PŚ; *sadhana iti kiṁ* (*ki* Pr in PP; *ko* PT, PP) *madas* (*madaḥs* ψP in PP; *midas* Pr in PP) *te* PT, PS, PP, PRE [2]*mado* me HM, HC, PS [3]°*vibhavaḥ kiṁ* PP, PRE; *cyutavibhavaḥ kiṁ* PT [4]*viṣāyem* A in PS [5]*upayāmi* HM (cf. fn. 2); *upayāti* Pp in HS, HH; *āyāti* PS [6]°*nihata*° EF in PS PRE; °*kali*° PP; °*samā* HH [7]*bhavanti sampado* HH; *pāto'tpāta* PT (notes) [8]*hi manu*° P in HS.

No. 29

sā tṛṣṇā cet[1] *parityaktā*[2] *ko daridraḥ ka īśvaraḥ,*
tasyāś cet[3] *prasaro datto dāsyaṁ ca śirasi*[4] *sthitam.*

If that thirst were renounced, who [would be] poor, who rich? Let way be but given to it, and slavery stands on the head.

HJ 1.198, HS 1.178, HM 1.185, HP 1.147, HN 1.148, HK 1.187, HH 32.18-9, HC 44.1-2, IS 2598; cf. *CvA* 7.16, cf. *CvṢ* 7.16, *cf. CvW* 7.14, *cf. CvP IV* 7.15, *cf. CvTb* 7.20, *cf. CvL I* 7.16, *cf. CvL II* 7.16.

The main editions and several MSs. of H contain minor variants. The *Cv* group begins like HS and HH.

Footnotes to No. 29: [1]*tṛṣṇāṁ ceha* HM, HK, HC; *tṛṣṇā ceda* B in HP; *tṛṣṇā yadi* HN, N in HN; *tṛṣṇā hi cet* HS, HH, *CVA*; *tṛṣṇayā cet* HP, I in HK; *tṛṣṇā cet sampa*° *C* in HP; *tṛṣṇai'va* P in HS; *tṛṣṇā hi* IS [2]*parityaktvā* HM; *parityakto* HP [3]*ca* HN, N in HP; *tasmatsan* A in HP [4]*samupa* P in HS.

* * *

Compare also Nos. 36, 38, 84, 89, 90, 120, 130 and 132.

17. *Knowledge and Ignorance*

No. 30

vidyā nāma narasya rūpam adhikaṁ vidyā'tiguptaṁ[1] *dhanam*[2]*,*
vidyā bandhur asau[3] *videśagamane*[4] *vidyā'kṣayaṁ saṁbalam*[5]*,*
[6]*vidyā kīrtikarī sabhāvaśakarī*[7] *vidyā paraṁ*[8] *locanam,*
[9]*vidyā jīvanahetur atra bhuvane*[10] *vidyāvihīnaḥ paśuḥ.*[11]

Knowledge [is] truely the chief beauty of a man. Knowledge [is] a well-secured treasure. Knowledge [is] a companion in traveling abroad. Knowledge [is] an unwasting provision. Knowledge [is] the maker of fame,—the captivator of assemblies. Knowledge [is] another eye. Knowledge [is] a means of subsistence here in the world. Destitute of knowledge [one is] a brute.

HH 6.1-4, IS 6089; *CRC* 2.36, *CRB* 2.31, *CRBh I* 2.31; *CNF* 105, *CNI I* 13; VCsr 9.3, VCjr 21.1; Bhś 70; BhG. 3; cf. GP 1.115, 8; Pras 19.4; Sūktāvalī 4; GR 3.

This aphorism is found only in HH. *CNF* and *CRC* contain several important variants and are nearer to Bhś than to H. Other sources contain important variants.

Footnotes to No. 30 : [1]*pra(c)channaguptaṁ* VCsr, VCjr, GR, Pras, BhŚ, *CRC*; *pracchannam antar dhana(m)* V in VCsr, O in VCjr [2]*guptaṁ dhanaṁ vidyayā* M_3 in BhŚ [3]*bandhujano* (°*ne* IX_1 Y_{1AB} in BhŚ; °*nā* W_3 in BhŚ) VCsr (γ), VCjr (γ), GR, Pras, BhŚ, *CRC* [4] °*gamano* T in VCsr; *bandhujanaḥ ṣudeśa* Ś in VCjr [5]*parā devatā* VCsr (γ), Pras; *paraṁ daivataṁ* (*devatāṁ* BhŚ, O in VCjr; *devatāḥ* F in VCjr; *bhūṣaṇaṁ* R in VCjr; *bhaiṣajaṁ* Ś in VCjr), BhŚ $NYW_{1,3}$ in BhŚ GR, VCjr (γ), VJQ in VCsr [6]*vidyā bhogakarī* (*bhagya*° X in BhŚ) *yaśaḥ-sukha* (*śubha*-GR, *CRC*)-*karī vidyā gurūṇāṁ guruḥ* VCsr (β), VCjr (β), GR, Pras, BhŚ, *CRC* [7]better *sabhāvaśakarī* [8]*parā* $F_{1,2}$ $J_3XY_{2,4-8}$TGM in BhŚ [9]*vidyā rājasu pūjyate* (*pujitā* VCjr, TNd in VCsr, Pras, E_2 $F_{1,5}$ $W_{1,2}$ $XG_4M_{4.5}$ in BhŚ; °*ite* Q in VCsr, $F_3J_1Y_7$ in BhŚ; *pūjitaṁ* D in BhŚ; *pujate* Y_2 in BhŚ) *na hi* (*tu* VCjr; *bahu* NNd in VCsr, *CRC*) *dhanam* (°*no CRC*; *pratidinaṁ* O in VCjr, D in BhŚ) VCsr, VCjr, GR, Pras, BhŚ, *CRC* (δ); *śuci dha*° $F_{1,2}tv_{,4}$ in BhŚ; *na tu dha*° Y, in BhŚ; *ca satataṁ* G_1M_3 in BhŚ, *varadhanaṁ* M_4 in BhŚ; *paradhano* M_5 in BhŚ; *vidyā rājasu pūjyate bahudhano vi*° *CRC* [10]*jīvanahelikā tri-bhuvane CŚF* [11]*paśuḥ* VCsr, VCjr, GR, Pras, BhŚ, *CŚF*, *CRC*.

No. 31

paropadeśe pāṇḍityaṁ sarveṣāṁ sukaraṁ[1] *bhavet*[2],
dharme [3]*svayam anuṣṭhānaṁ kasyacit tu*[4] *mahātmanaḥ*.

In giving advice to another, learning may be easy to all persons, but conformity to duty personally [is the characteristic] of one of exalted mind.

HJ 1.108, HS 1.98, HM 1.102, HP 1.76, HN 1.78, HK 1.104, HH 22.7-8, HC 30.3-4, IS 3987; *CNT IV* 139.

The main editions and various MSS. of H contain minor variants.

Footnotes to No. 31 : [1]*nṛṇāṁ* HS, HM, HH [2]*nṛṇām* HP, HN, HK [3]*svīyam*° HM, HK, HC [4]*su* P in HS.

No. 32

[1]*pustakeṣu*[2] *ca nā'dhītaḥ*[3] *nā'dhītaḥ*[3] *guru-sannidhau,*
[4]*na śobhate*[5] *sabhāmadhye jāra-garbhā*[6] *iva striyaḥ.*[7]

What one learned in good faith from books and not from a teacher[8] does not look well in public audience, just as a child received by a woman from [her] paramour.

HH 4.24-5, HC 7.5-6, HS *ad* Intr. 39, IS 4155; *CVND* 17.1, *CVM* 17.17; *CLṢ* 7.10, *CLP V* 7. 10, *CLP IV* 7.14, *CLTb* 7.12, *CLH* 7.6, *CLL I* 7.10, *CLL II* 7.8, *CLLd* 7.10; *CSBD* 38, *CSB I* 1.38, *CSJ* 1.38, *CSC I* 1.38, *CSC II* 38, *CSB II* 38, *CSLd.* 38; *CNN* 54, *CNP II* 283, *CNG* 171, *CNT IV* 221, *CNM* 184, *CNMN* 149, *CnT II* 15.3, *CnT III* 7.74, *CnT V* 114.

The main editions of H are identical. All the groups of *C* contain major variants.

Footnotes to No 32 : [1]*pustakaṁ pratyayā'dhītaṁ nā'dhītaṁ ga°* *CLB, CŚLB*; *pustaka* (°*kaḥ CLD*; °*ke CLM*) *pratyayā'dhītaṁ* (*dhīnam CLM*) *CVND CLC, CLD, CLM* [2]*pustake* IS [3]*nā'dhītaṁ CVND, CLC, CLD, CLM* [4]*śo° na sa°* tr. *CLC*; *sa° na śo° CVND*; *na sobhante sa° CLD*; *bhrājate na sa° CLC, CLD, CLM*; *vrjāte hi idaṁ sarvaṁ jā° CŚLB* [5]*śobhante CLB* [6] °*garbha* IS; *jāla-garbha CVB* [7]*striyā(ḥ) CLC, CLD, CLM*; *jarar-bhamīva kustriyā CLB* (notes); *haṁsamadhye bako yathā CLC* [8]translation from *CVND.*

No. 33

paṇḍite ca[1] *guṇāḥ sarve mūrkhe*[2] *doṣāś*[3] *ca*[4] *kevalam*[5],
[6]*tasmān mūrkha-sahasreṣu*[7] *prājña*[8] *eko viśiṣyate*[9].

And in a learned man are all excellent qualities, but in a blockhead faults only. Therefore, amongst thousands of fools, one wise man is distinguished.

HH 1.17-8, IS 3876; *CvA* 8.10, *CvṢ* 8.10, *CvW* 8.9, *CvP IV* 8.10, *CvP V* 8.7, *CvTb* 8.10, *CvL I* 8.10, *CvL II* 8.11, *CvLd* 8.7; *CRC* 5.36 γδ, *CRB* 5.36, γδ, *CRP* 5.34 γδ, *CRT* 6.1, *CRBh I* 5.34 γδ, *CRBh II* 5.42 γδ, *CRCa I* 5.35 γδ, *CSBD* 66, *CSB I* 1.66, *CSJ* 1.61, *CSC I* 1.66, *CSC II* 66, *CSB II* 65, *CSLd* 1.66; *CNJV* 4, *CNS* 56, *CNW* 20, *CNF* 51, *CNPh* 37, *CNI I* 8, *CNG* 80, *CNT IV* 143, *CNM* 137, *CNMN* 10, *CNŚC* 2, *CNŚ* 2, *CNŚL* 2, *CNNM* 2, *CNŚT* 2, *CNŚK* 3, *CNL* 47, *CNI II* 11; GP 1.113, 1 b; VN 4.

The main editions of H are identical. The *C*N and *Cv* groups contain variants. GP is different in αβ. Other sources contain minor variants.

Footnotes to No. 33 : [1]*paṇḍitasya* GP; *paṇḍiteṣu* VN, *CŚF, CŚW* [2]*mūrkha CVB* [3]*doṣā CŚH, CŚN* [4]*doṣāstu CVB*; *hi CŚH, CŚN* [5]*kevalāḥ*

GP, VN, *CŚW*, *CŚF* [6]*guṇavantaṁ niyuñjīta guṇahīnaṁ vivarjayet* GP αβ [7] °*sahaśrebhyaḥ* VN; °*sahasrāṇi CVB*; °*saharebhyo CŚF*; °*sahasreṇa CŚW* [8]*vijña CŚW*; *dhīra CŚF* [9]*ekaḥ praśasyate CVB*; *na labhyate* IS.

No. 34

ko'tibhāraḥ[1] *samarthānāṁ*[2] *kiṁ dūraṁ*[3] *vyavasāyinām*[4],
ko videśaḥ[5] *savidyānāṁ*[6] *kaḥ paraḥ*[7] *priya-vādinām.*[4]

What burden [is] too great for those who can bear [it]? What is distance to the indefatigable? What country [is] foreign to those who have knowledge? Who [is] a stranger to those who speak kindly?

HJ 2.11, HS 2.11, HM 2.13, HP 2.12, HN 2.12, HK 2.13, HH 41.19-20, HC 55.9-10, IS 1926; *CVND* 3.13, *CVM* 3.21; *CvH* 7.12, *CLṢ* 3.9, *CLB* 3.9, *CLT* 3.9, *CLA* 3.8, *CLP V* 3.8, *CLP IV* 3.8, *CLP II* 3.10, *CLTb* 3.8; *CLH* 3.8, *CLL I* 3.8, *CLLd* 3.8; *CNJV* 73, *CNS* 32, *CNF* 68 *bis*, *CNP I* 19, *CNPh* 41, *CNP II* 19, *CNI I* 57, *CNTI IV* 17, *CNG* 35, *CNM* 18, *CNMN* 18, *CNŚC* 71, *CNŚ* 71, *CNŚL* 84, *CNNM* 47, *CNŚT* 59, *CNŚK* 53, *CNL* 31, *CNI II* 46, *CnT II* 9.5, *CnT III* 7.1, *CnT V* 11, *CnT I* 1; PS 1.20, PN 2.15, PT 1.17, PTem 1.14, PP 1.22, Pts 2.51 & 2.121, PRE 1.19; VCsr 20.9, VCjr 20.4; (cf. KSS 10.61, 118-121).

The main editions of H are identical. The *CN* group is identical with H, with few exceptions. The *CV*, *Cv* and *CL* groups contain minor variants. Other sources contain minor variants.

Footnotes to No. 34: [1]*kopi bhāras* I in PS; *'ti bhāras* PT; *hi bhāraḥ* IS. [2]*samārthāmāṁ CLB* (var), *CLT* (in *C.M.*) [3]*dūre* CO in VCjr, *CLD, CLE, CLM* [4]βδ tr. T in VCsr [5]*videśas* PT [6]*saviryāṇāṁ* O in VCjr; *suvidyānāṁ* PS (*C* in PS as above), PP (α ψ PL_1M in PP as above), Pts 2, 121, PRE, VC (AŚG in VCjr as above) *CŚN, CVND, CLB, CLT*; *samarthānāṁ* T in VCsr [7]*ko'priyaḥ CVND*; *ko'priye CLD.*

No. 35

ajñaḥ sukham[1] *ārādhyaḥ*[2], *sukhataram ārādhyate*[3] *viśeṣajñaḥ*[4]
jñāna-lava-durvidagdhaṁ[5] *Brahmā'pi*[6] *naraṁ*[7] *na rañjayati*[8]

An ignorant man is easy to be conciliated; a man of judgment is conciliated more easily; but an ill-informed mand, with a mere smattering of knowledge, even Brahmā cannot conciliate.

HJ 4.104, HS 4.99, HM 4.100, HP 4.104, HN 4.104, HK 4.105, HH 115. 22-3, HC 155.15-6, IS 105; *CNI I* 271; BhŚ 8.

The main editions and various MSs. of H contain minor variants. BhŚ is identical with H, but its various MSs. contain several variants.

Footnotes to No. 35 : [1]*sukhataram* Y_3 in BhŚ [2]*ārādhya* HH; *ava-bodhyaḥ* $M_{4,5}$ in BhŚ [3]*ārādhya* N in HP; *ārādhyo* IS; *avabodhyate* $M_{4,5}$ in BhŚ [4]*viśepajñaḥ* HK (printing error); *'śeṣajñaḥ* IS [5]*jñānalabdhurvidogdhaṁ* HH; *jñāna-valadvadvidagdhaṁ* Pp in HS [6]*taṁ* edd. in HS [7]om. HN, N in HP; *taṁ* B_1 Y_3 in BhŚ; *taṁ naraṁ* HH, $F_{2,3,5}$ DW_1 Y_1X in BhŚ (*contra metrum*) [8]*bodhayati* $M_{4,5}$ in BhŚ.

No. 36

[1]*lubdham arthena gṛhṇīyāt*[2] *stabdham*[3] *añjali-karmaṇā*[4],
[5]*mūrkhaṁ chando'nuvṛttena*[6] *yāthā*[7] *-tathyena*[8] *paṇḍitam.*

With money one should gain over a covetous man; with hands joined in token of respect, a haughty man; with the humouring of (his) wishes, a silly fellow; [and] with truth, a wise man.

HJ 4.108, HS 4.102, HM 4.104, HP 4.107, HN 4.107, HK 4.109, HH 116. 18-9, HC 156.20-1, IS 5860, *CVND* 6.12, *CVM* 6.11, *CvA* 6.1, *CvṢ* 6.1, *CvW* 6.1, *CvP IV* 6 *CvP V* 6.1, *CvGt* 6.1, *CvTb* 6.1, *CvH* 6.1, *CvL I* 6.1, *CvL II* 6.1, *CvLd* 6.1, *CRC* 2.20, *CRB* 2.17, *CRP* 2.17, *CRT* 2.10, *CRBh I* 2.17, *CRBh II* 2.14, *CRCa II* 14; *CNJV* 33, *CNS* 82, *CNP I* 60 *CNPh* 9, *CNI I* 254, *CNG* 22, *CNT IV* 60, *CNM* 60, *CNMN* 51, *CNSR* A 22, *CNŚL* 17, *CNNM* 69 & 105, *CNŚT* 29, *CNŚK* 32, *CNL* 6. *CNT II* 28; PS 1.26, cf. PP 4,61, cf. Pts 4.109, & 114; GP 1.109, 10; cf. MBh 1.142, 48b-49a, cf. MBh 3.194, 7, cf. MBh 5.38, 73b-74a; cf. Navaratna 1 in KSH.

The various editions and various MSs. of H contain minor variants. The *CN* group is almost identical with H. The *CV*, *Cv* and *CR* groups contain minor variants. GP contains minor variants.

Footnotes to No. 36 : [1]*lubdham artha-pradānena°* GP, *CRC* [2]*gṛhnīyat* IS (printing error); *gṛhīyāt* IS [3]*kruddham CŚH, CŚN, CRC, CVF, CVG, CVN, CNH*; *ślaghyam* GP [4] °*kruddham* I in HK [5]*mūrkha chandā ca vṛtyā ca CVN* [6]*chando'nuvṛttyā ca* AB in HP; *chandā'nurodhena* HK, *CVND*; *chandā-'nuvṛttyā ca* (°*vṛttena* IS) PS, GP, *CVND* (var.) [7]*tathā CŚH, CVF, CVG, CVN, CNH* [8]*yathā tathyena* A in HP, HS (notes); *yātā tāthyena* N in HP; *yādhā tatthyena* I in PS; *yadhā tadhyena* H in PS; *yathā'rthyena ca CVND*; *yathā'rthvena* IS; *yathā' ṛyenai'va* IS. *kathā'nuvṛttyā ca vaśī vaśī kurvanti paṇḍitaḥ CRC.*

No. 37

[1]kusuma-stavakasy eva [2]dve vṛttī[3] tu[4] manasvinaḥ[5],
[6]sarveṣāṁ mūrdhni vā[7] tiṣṭhed [8]viśīryed atha vā vane.

As of a cluster of flowers, the states of the intellectual man [are] two: either he should stand at the head of all, or he should wither away in the forest.

HJ 1.142, HS 1.126, HM 1.131, HP 1.101, HN 1.102, HK 1.134, HH 26, 17-8, HC 36. 3-4, IS 1845; *CRC* 3.11, *CRB* 3. 12, *CRP* 3.12, *CRT* 3.9, *CRBh I* 3.12, *CRBh II* 3.13; GP 1.110, 13; BhŚ 34.

The main editions and various MSs. of H contain several important variants. *CRC* is different in γδ and contains some important variants. Other sources, in particular BhŚ and its various MSS., are quite different.

Footnotes to No. 37 : [1]*mālatī kusumasy eva dve gatī hamanasvinaḥ* (*mahātmanaḥ* IS) IS; cf. F_5 in BhŚ; °*stavakasyai'va* IS [2]*dve tu vṛtte* N in HP, HN; *dvayī vṛttir ma°* BhŚ, *CRC*; *malatī kusumasy eva* F_5 in BhŚ; *dvedhā vṛttir* T_3 in BhŚ; *dve hi vṛttir* G_1 in BhŚ; *dve* (*hi*) *vṛttī* M_2 in BhŚ [3]*gatī* GP, $CT_{icv}M_1$ JY_8 T_2 M_{3-5} W_2 X_1 Y_1 Y_2 in BhŚ [4]ca HP, Pp in HS, W_2 Y_2 in BhŚ; *hi* CT_{icv} M_1 in BhŚ; *su* X_1 in BhŚ; *tu* JY_8 T_2 M_{3-5} in BhŚ; *sto* Y_1 in BhŚ [5]*manasvināṁ* X_1 Y_1 in BhŚ [6]*sarvasya* IS; *sarvalokasya vā mūrdhni viśīryeta venetha vā* (*vanepi vā* N in HP, Pet in HS, HN) HP; *mūrdhni* (*mūrdhani* $W_{2,3}$ in BhŚ) *vā sarvalokasya śīryate vana eva vā* BhŚ, B in HP; *sarvalokasya vā mūrdhni* Pp in HS; *mūrdhni vā sarva lokānaṁ* (°*kasya CRC*) *śīrṣataḥ* (*śīryate, CRC*; *viśīryati* IS) *patito vane* (*vana eva vā CRC*; *vane'tha vā* IS) GP; °*viśīryeta vane'pi vā* HP; *viśīryeda thavā vane* edd., P in HS; °*viśīryeta canetha vā* J_2 F_4 W_1 in BhŚ; °*viśiryeta vane yathā* $W_{1,2,4}$ in BhŚ; *viśīryeta vane'tha vā* HK; °*vīśīryate°* IS, *śīryate°* IS; °*śiryeta°* IS; °*śīyate°* E_{ot} H_2 in BhŚ; °*sthīyate* E_{3t} in BhŚ; °*jīryate* $G_{2,3,5}$ in BhŚ (cf. fn. 8) [7]*hi* IS; *mūrdhnī vā* $W_{2,3}$ in BhŚ; °*lokanāṁ°* E_{3t} F_3 in BhŚ [8]*vana eva vā* IS; °*ca mano'tha vā* IS; *vaneṣv api* IS (cf. fn. 6).

No. 38

ajarāmaravat prājño vidyām arthaṁ ca cintayet[1],
gṛhīta iva keśeṣu mṛtyunā dharmam ācaret.

A wise man should fix his thoughts upon knowledge and wealth as [if he were] undecaying and undying. He should practice duty as if [he were] seized by the hairs of his head by Death [as if he had not an instant to lose].

HJ Intr 3, HS Intr 3, HM Intr 3, HP Intr. 3, HN Intr 3, HK Intr 3, HH 1.7-8, HC 3.5-6, IS 94; *CNW* 11, *CNP II* 255, *CNT IV* 194, *CNŚC* 94, *CNŚ* 93, *CNŚL* 67, *CNNM* 95, *CNŚT* 94; GR 12. In ŚP 669 ascribed to Vyāsa.

The main editions of H are identical. *CNW* and *CNP II* are identical with H. GR is identical with H.

Footnote to No. 38 : [1]*sādhayet* I in HK.

No. 39

ahita-hita-vicāra-śūnya-buddheḥ[1]
śruti-viṣayair[2] [3]*bahubhir bahiṣ-kṛtasya*[4],
udara-bharaṇa-mātra-kevalecchoḥ[5]
[6]*puruṣa-paśoś ca*[7] *paśoś ca ko viśeṣaḥ.*[8]

What [is] the difference between the brute and the beast of a man whose reason is incapable of discriminating between wrong and right, who is a stranger to the many things taught by scripture, and solicitous only about the mere filling of [his] belly.

HJ 2.42, HS 2.42, HM 2.45, HP 2.39, HN 2.39, HK 2.45, HH 46.20-4, HC 62.2-6, IS 826; *CRC* 8.29, *CRB* 8.33 *CRP* 8.32, *CRT* 8.17, *CRBh I* 8.32, *CRBh II* 8.21; PS 1.15, PN 2.11, PT 1.12, PTem 1.9, PP 1.15, PRE 1.14; GP 1.115, 31.

The main editions and various MSs. of H contain minor variants. *CRC* is almost identical with H; it contains two minor variants. Other sources contain several minor variants.

Footnotes to No. 39 : [1] °*vicāraiḥ*° IS; °*buddheś* PT; °*buddhernasya* IS; °*yuddhe* I in PS [2]*śruti-viṣaye* Pp in HS; *śruti-samaye* P in HS, GP; *śruti (a)-samayair* HM, HP, HN, HK, S in HP, PS, PT, PP, PRE, *CRC*; °*samare* IS; *samaye* IS; °*viṣaya* IS [3]°*bahubhis taraskṛtasya* HM, HK; *bahubhiṣ-pariṣ-kṛtasya* PT (PTem as above) [4]*tiras-kṛtasya* HC; *niṣ-kṛtasya* HH; *vitarkitasya* GP; *viramāprīti-sarva-kṣaṇasya* IS; [5] °*kevalaṁ* IS; °*mātre-kevalec-chor CRC*; °*mātra-tuṣṭa-buddheḥ* GP, °*mātram eva lipsoḥ* PP [6]*nānyakarma iti manuja paśor vā ko viśeṣaḥ paśoś ca* IS; (add.) [7]*puruṣapaśoḥ* HH, GP (*ca* om.); *paśoś ca* IS; *manuja paśoś ca CRC* [8]*ko'pi na viśeṣaḥ* Pp in HS.

No. 40

[1]*udīrito'rthaḥ paśunā'pi gṛhyate*[2] *hayāś ca*[3]
nāgāś ca vahanti[4] *deśitāḥ*[5],
anuktam[6] *apy ūhati paṇḍito janaḥ*
[7]*pare'ṅgita-jñāna-phalā*[8] *hi buddhayaḥ.*[9]

A meaning uttered is apprehended even by a brute. Horses and elephants move onward [when] bidden. A wise man guesses even what is not uttered, because [acute] intellects [are] fruitful in the discovery of another's secret intentions.

HJ 2.46, HS 2.46, HM 2.49, HP 2.43, HN 2.42, HK 2.49, HH 47.11-4, HC 63.1-4, IS 1236; *CRC* 2.56, *CRB* 2.63, *CRP*

2.60, *CRBh I* 2.60, *CRCa I* 2.50, *CNP II* 30, *CNI I* 16; PS 1. 19, PN 2. 14, PT 1. 16, PTem 1. 13, PP 1. 20, Pts 1.43, PRE 1.18; VCjr 22.5,1 p. 322; Śts 45, 11-2; Śto 348.27-8; Vct 1.7; GP 1.109, 53; Bhś 427.

The main editions and various MSs. of H contain several minor variants. The *CR* group and *CNP II* are almost identical with H (HP and HN editions). Other sources contain several minor variants.

Footnotes to No. 40 : [1]*udirītā'rthaḥ* GP, *CRC*; *an*° *ud*° tr. GP [2]*budhyate* HN, P in Śts, A in Vct, *CRC*; *vudhyato* NC in HP [3]*ha*° *va*° tr. Śto [4]*vṛddhayaḥ* C in Śts; *vamanti* I in PS; *vadanti* Śto [5]*deśitam* GP; *tāḍitāḥ* B in HP; *coditāḥ* HN, N in HP, PS, PT, Pts, PRE, Śto, *CRC*; *coditaḥ* B in Śto; *noditāḥ* c in HP, PP, G in VC, Śts, Vct (B in Vct as above), BhŚ, *CŚlB*; *budhyate* HS, P in Śts; *yojitāḥ* P in HS; *depreritāḥ śtaḥ* (?) a in Vct; *preritāḥ* IS; *yojitāḥ* IS [6]*anaktam* G in VC [7]*pareta gīta jñīnu phalā* IS; °*ṅgitā*° Pr in PP [8] °*phalaṁ* E in Vct; °*parā* IS [9]*vṛddhayaḥ* C in Śts; *pi CŚlB*.

No. 41

prastāva-sadṛśaṁ vākyaṁ sadbhāva-sadṛśaṁ[1] *priyam*[2],
ātma-śakti-samaṁ[3] *kopaṁ*[4] *yo jānāti*[5] *sa paṇḍitaḥ*.

He [is] a wise man who knows [how to make] a speech suited to the occasion, [how to speak] kindly but in accordance with truth, [and how to manifest] resentment proportioned to his strength.

HJ 2.48, HS 2.47, HM 2.51, HP 2.44, HN 2.43, HK 2.51, HH 47.189, HC 63.8-9. IS 4287; *CVM* 14.19, *CRC* 2.23, *CRB* 2.20, *CRP* 2.20, *CRBh II* 2.17, *CRCa* I 2.18; *CNW* 47, *CNN* 2, *CNP* I 102, *CNI I* 17, *CNG* 135, *CNHU* 9, *CNT IV* 123, *CNM* 120, *CNMN* 87.

The main editions of H are identical. The *CN* and *CV* groups are identical with H. *CVND* contains one minor variant. *CRC* contains two minor variants. Śto contains one minor variant.

Footnotes to No. 41 : [1]*svabhāva*° Śto, *CŚW*, *CRC*; *svabhāta*°, R in Śto; *prabhāvaiḥ CVND*; *prabhāva*° *CVND* (var.) °*sadṛśa* IS; °*sadṛśī* IS [2]*manaḥ CRC* ; *kriyām* IS [3]*ātma-sada*° c in *CLB* [4]*krodhaṁ* Śto [5]*yānāti* IS.

No. 42

yasya yasya hi[1] *yo*[2] *bhāvas tena tena*[3] *hi taṁ naram*[4],
anupraviśya medhāvī kṣipram[5] *ātma-vaśaṁ nayet.*[6]

Whatever [be] the natural disposition of any one, an intelligent person having thereby insinuated himself, [can] quickly bring that man under his power.

HJ 2.51, HS 2.50, HM 2.54, HP 2.47, HN 2.46, HK 2.54, HH 47.25-6, HC 63.16-7, IS 5393; *CvA* 6.3, *CvṢ*. 6.3, *CvW* 6.3, *CvP IV* 6.3, *CvP V* 6.3, *CvGt* 6.3, *CvTb* 6.3, *CvH* 6.3, *CvL I* 6.3, *CvL II* 6.3, *CvLd* 6.3, *CRC* 2.22, *CRB* 2.19, *CRP* 2.19, *CRT* 2.13, *CRBh I* 2.19, *CRBh II* 2.16; *CNPh* 10, *CNI I* 255, *CNG* 25, *CNI II* 50, *CnT II* 8.7, *CnT III* 6.3, *CnT VI* 9.3, *CnT V* 71; PS 1.25, PN 2.22, PT 1.28, PTem 1.25, PP 1.53, PRE 1.29; cf. KSS 10.60, 39; GP 1.109, 13.

The main editions of H are identical. All the *C* groups contain minor variants. PS, PT are identical with H. Other sources and various MSs. of Pañc. contain some minor variants.

Footnotes to No. 42 : [1]*ca* B in PS [2]om. A in PP; (*contra metrum*) [3]*tasya tasya* PP, Pts, GP, *CVF*, *CVG*, *CVN*, *CRC* [4]*naraḥ* PP, Pts, E in PS, *CVF*, *CVG*; *mana CVN*; *karmmaṇā* B in PS; *param* O in PS; *śamāraret* IS; *vibhāvyatām CRC*; *vadan* GP [5]*tan tam* B in PS; *taṁ tam CRC* [6]*bhavet CVN*.

No. 43

mātṛvat para-dāreṣu[1] *para-dravyeṣu*[2] *loṣṭravat*[3],
ātmavat [4]*sarva-bhūteṣu*[5] *yaḥ paśyati*[6] *sa paṇḍitaḥ*[7].

He who looks on the wife of another as a mother, on the goods of another as a clod, and on all beings as himself, [is] a wise man.

HJ 1.13, HS 1.12, HM 1.13, HP 4.132, HN 4.132, HK 1.14 & 4.134, HH 8.17-8, HC 11.15-6 & 159, 12-3, IS 4805, *CVND* 12.14, *CVM* 12.6, *CRCa II* 18; *CNJV* 5, *CNS* 73, *CNF* 27, *CNPh* 72, *CNP II* 145, *CNI I* 25, *CNG* 216, *CNŚC* 3, *CNŚ* 3, *CNNM* 3, *CNŚT* 3, *CNŚK* 4, *CnT II*, 19.6, *CnT III* 52.1; PN 3.32, PT 3.63, PTem 3.49, PP 1.390, Pts. 1.402, PRE 3.52; Vet 16.12; GP 1.111.12; BrDh 2.11,8.

The main editions of H are not completely identical; they contain several minor variants; variants in MSs. are also noted. The *CN* and *CV* groups contain several minor variants. *CNF* and *CNS* are identical with HP, HM and HK. Pañc and Vet contain several important variants.

Footnotes to No. 43 : [1]*paradārāṁś ca* (*tu* PT, PRE) PS, PRE Vet,

CŚlB; °*dravyāṇī* B in HP; °*dārāṇi* B in HP, A in PS, PP, Pts, ABc in Vet; °*dārāṁs tu* PT; °*dravyeṣu* IS; °*dārepi* IS [2] °*draveṣu* HC; °*dravyāni* PS, PT, PP, Pts, PRE, Vet, *CŚlB* [3]*loṣṭavat* HM, HP, HK 1.14, PT, Pts, PRE, Vet, GP, *CŚF*, *CŚN*, *CŚIB*, *CVND*, *CLB*; *loṣṭhavat* HK 4.134, PS; *loṣṭavata* IS (wrongly) [4]*sarvabhūtani yaḥ paśyati sa paśyati* B in *HP* [5]*sarvabhūtāni* PS, PT, PP, Pts, PRE, Vet; *CŚlB*; *bhūtānāṁ* N in PRE [6]*pakṣyati CŚH* [7]*paśyati* A in HP, PS, PT, Pts, PRE, Vet *CŚlB*; *paśyante dharmabuddhayaḥ* d in Vet; *sa buddhimān* B in Vet, *vikṣante dharma buddhayaḥ* PP; *vaiṣṇavaḥ CLB*, B in *CŚF*

No. 44

calaty ekena pādena tiṣṭhaty ekena buddhimān[1],
[2]*nā'samīkṣya paraṁ sthānaṁ pūrvāṁ āyatanaṁ tyajet.*

With one foot a wise man moves, with one he stands still. Without having seen another place [of abode], he ought not to leave a former habitation.

HJ 1.107, HS 1.97, HM 1.101, HP 1.75, HN 1.77, HK 1.103, HH 22. 1-2, HC 29.16-7, IS 2264; *CvA* 1.9, *CvṢ* 1.8, *CvW* 1.5, *CvP* 1.8, *CvGt* 1.8, *CvTb* 1.7, *CvH* 1.8, *CvI* 1.8, *CvL I* 1.9, *CvL II* 1.8, *CvLd* 1.8; *CRC* 2.10, *CRB* 2.10, *CRP* 2.10, *CRT* 2.4, *CRBh I* 2.10, *CRCa II* 12; *CNJV* 32, *CNS* 35, *CNW* 53, *CNF* 12, *CNPh* 8, *CNI I* 203, *CNG* 21, *CNŚC* 98, *CNŚ* 108, *CNŚL* 18, *CNNM* 27, *CNŚT* 28, *CNŚK* 31, *CNI II* 23, *CnT II* 2.7, *CnT III* 1.13, *CnT VI* 14; PP 1.77; GP 1.109, 41.

The main editions of H are identical with the exception of one minor variant in γ. *C* is almost identical with H. The *CN* group is the nearest to H. (*CNF*, *CNH* and *CNS* are identical with H). GP and Pañc. contain some minor variants.

Footnotes to No. 44 : [1]*paṇḍitaḥ* PP [2]*na sa*° *CVG*; *mā'samīkṣya* HS, HM, HK, HH, edd. in HS, *CŚP*; *na parīkṣya* GP; *nā'pa*° *CRC*; *āsam*° *CŚW*; *samīkṣya ca pa*° *CVN*.

No. 45

śucimukhā[1] *durācārā*[2] [3]*mūrkhā*[4] *paṇḍitamāninaḥ*,
[5]*aśaktā gṛha-karaṇe śaktāś ca gṛha-bhañjane.*

Fools fancying themselves wise, with clean faces, but of wicked practice, unable to build a house, but able to demolish a house.

HH 73.20-1, cf *CLB* 1.75, *cf. CNN* 75.

This aphorism is found in HH only. *CLB* and *CNN* contains several important variants.

Footnotes to No. 45 : [1] °*mukhi CLB* [2]*durācare* (°*ri CLB* variant) *CLB* [3]*raṇḍe paṇḍita vādini CLB* [4]*mūrkhaḥ* HJ *ad* line 1673 [5]*asamarthā gṛha-rambhe samarthā gṛ*° *CLB*.

No. 46

[1]rūpa-yauvana-sampannā viśāla-kula-sambhavāḥ,[2]
vidyā-hīnā[3] na śobhante nirgandhā iva kiṁśukāḥ[4].

Possessed of beauty [and] youth, sprung from a noble race, destitute of knowledge, they shine not. They are like scentless *kiṁśuka* flowers [held worthless though beautiful].

HJ Intr 39, HS Intr 38, HM Intr 39, HN Intr 24, HK Intr 39, HH 4.22-3, HC 7.3-4, IS 5795; *CVND* 3.10, and 8.21, *CvM* 3.2; *CvA* 3.2, *CvṢ* 3.2, *CvW* 3.2, *CvP V* 3.3, *CvTb* 3.3, *CvH* 3.3, *CvL I* 3.2, *CvL II* 3.1, *CvLd* 33; *CLP IV* 7.5, *CLH* 8.6; *CRT* 8.44, *CNJV* 7, *CNS* 79, *CNW* 16, *CNF* 4, *CNP I* 9, *CNPh* 83, *CNPN* 50, *CNP II* 257, *CNI I* 5, *CNG* 98, *CNT IV* 4 & 191, *CNM* 8, *CNMN* 8, *CNŚC* 5, *CNŚ* 5, *CNM* 8, *CNNM* 5, *CNŚT* 5, *CNŚK* 6, *CNI II* 5, *CnT II* 4.3, *CnT III* 3, *CnT VI* 41, *CnT V* 10.

The main editions of H are identical. All the *C* groups are identical with H, the only exception being *CLP IV* and *CNH* which contain some minor variants.

Footnotes to No. 46 : [1]*rūpa-lakṣaṇa°* *CNH* [2] *°sambhavā* IS; *°bāndhavāḥ* *CNH* [3] *°hīnaṁ* IS [4]*kiṁśukaḥ* IS; *jāragarbhā iva striyaḥ CLC.*

No. 47

gaṅgā-hīne[1] hato deśo[2] vidyā-hīnaṁ[3] hataṁ[4] kulam[5],
aprasūtā hatā nārī hato[6] yajñas tv[7] adakṣiṇaḥ.[8]

Deprived of the Ganges, a country is stricken. Destitute of knowledge a family is ruined. Without offspring, a woman is undone. Inefficacious is a sacrifice without gifts.

HH 6.5-6, IS 2055; *CNW* 39, *CNF* 69, *CNPN* 85; *cf.* *CNP I* 97; *cf.* Pts. 2.94; *cf.* VCsr 12.12.

This aphorism is found in HH only. The *CN* group is almost identical with H; it contains a few minor variants.

Footnotes to No. 47 : [1] *°hīno* HJ (notes) ; *CNF, CNW* [2]*hīnaṃ hataṁ deśaṁ CNPN* [3] *°hīno CŚF* [4]*hato CNF* [5]*pumān CNF*; [6]*hata CNW* [7]*yajñam* (*tv* om.) *CNW, CNPN* [8]*adakṣiṇam CNW, CNPN.*

No. 48

yasya nā'sti svayaṁ prajñā śāstraṁ[1] tasya karoti kim,
locanābhyāṁ[2] vihīnasya[3] darpaṇaḥ[4] kiṁ kariṣyati.

What can book-learning do for him who has no sense of his own ? What will a mirror do for one deprived of eyes ?

HJ 3.123, HS 3.117, HM 3.119, HP 3.115, HN 3.115, HK 3.119, HH 93.15-6, HC 124.9-10, IS 5380 *CVND* 10.9, *CVM* 10.10, *CvA* 8.12, *CvṢ* 8.12, *CvW* 7.15, *CvP IV* 8.12, *CvLd* 8.9, *CVP IV* 8.12, *CvP* V 8.9, *CvGt* 8.5, *CvTb* 8.12, *CvL I* 8.12, *CRBh II* 3.3, *CNJV* 109, *CNS* 77, *CNW* 61, *CNG* 172, *CNPh*; 122, *CNPN* 45, *CNP II* 214 & 265, *CNN* 60, *CNF* 7, *CNJ I* 9, *CNŚK* 69, *CNŚC* 108, *CNŚ* 104, *CNŚL* 99, *CNNM* 60, *CNŚT* 99, *CNI II* 16;

The main editions of H are identical. The *CN* (with the exception of *CNPN* which contains one minor variant) are identical with H. The *CV*, *Cv* and *CN* groups contain minor variants (*CVND*, *CVF*, *CVP* V are identical with H).

Footnotes to No. 48 : [1]*astraṁ* *CVN* [2]*locanānāṁ* IS [3]*vihīnena* *CŚP* [4]*darpaṇaṁ* IS; *mukuraḥ* *CLB*; *mukuraṁ* *CLB* (variant)

No. 49

araṇya-ruditaṁ[1] *kṛtaṁ*[2] [3]*śava-śarīram udvartitaṁ*[4],
[5]*sthale kamala-ropaṇaṁ* [6]*suciram ūṣare varṣitam*,[7]
[8]*śvapuccham avanāmitaṁ*[9] [10]*badhira-karṇajāpaḥ*[11] *kṛtas*[12],
[13]*tad andha-mukha-maṇḍamaṁ yad abudhe*[14] *jane*[15] *bhāṣitam*[16].

What is spoken to a stupid person [is as] a cry made in the wilderness, a corpse perfumed, planting a lotus in dry soil, raining a long while on salt land, a cur's tail bent down, a whisper made in the ear of the deaf, adorning the face of the blind.

ad HJ 2.162, IS 570; *CRC* 5.43, *CRB* 5.42; PS 1.92, PN 2.71, PT 1.105, PTcm 1.97, PP 1.245, PRE 1.104.

CRC contains minor variants, mostly occurring also in Pañc. Other sources, as well as *CRC*, transfer some *pādas*, but do not contain important variants.

Footnotes to No. 49 : [1]*araṇye-ru°* N in PP; *°rudinaṁ* ψP in PP [2]*gata* PN [3]*śava°* om. M in PP; *śaba°* NAψ PPrpBh in PP; *svaśa°* *CRC* (*contra metrum*) [4]*udvartitaṁ* PP, *CRC*; *udvartanaṁ* O in PS [5]*sthale'bjam avaropitaṁ* NABC in PS, PT, PRE, *CRC* [6]*suciram ūkhare var°* IS; *badhira-karṇa-jāpaḥ kṛtaḥ* (*°karṇayor jalpitaṁ* FHO in PS) PS (NABC in PS as above) PT, PRE, (tr. *su° ba°* PT, PRE) (cf. fns. 11-13) [7]*varṣaṇam* PP; *varṣaṇaḥ* M in PP [8]*śva°* PS, PT, PP, PRE, *CRC*; *śvapuccham iva nāmitaṁ* C in PS, (cf. fn. 10); *kṛto dhṛto'ndha-mukha-darpaṇe yad abudhajanaḥ sevitaḥ* IS [9]*iva nāmitaṁ* bhNBh in PP [10]*satatam ūṣare varṣitam* PS (NABC in PS as above); tr. *su° ba°* PT, PRE (cf. fns. 7-8) [11]*jāpaṁ* *CRC* [12]*kṛtaṁ* *CRC* [13]*kṛto'ndha-mukha-darpaṇo* PS; *kṛtā'ndha-mukha-maṇḍanā* (*°naṁ* AC in PS) NAC in PS, PT, PRE, *CRC* [14]*abudho* PS, PT, PRE; *abudha* IS; *°yādhamo* *CRC* [15]*janaḥ* (*s*) PS, PT, PRE, *CRC* [16]*sevitaḥ* PS, PT, PRE, *CRC*.

No. 50

ayaṁ nijaḥ[1] *paro ve*[2] *'ti* [3]*gaṇanā*[4] *laghu-cetasām*[5],
[6]*udāra-caritānāṁ* [7]*ca* [8]*vasudhai'va kuṭumbakam.*[9]

"This is this one of our clan or a stranger" Such is a calculation of a narrow-minded, but to those of a generous disposition, the earth itself is one family.

HJ 1.72, HS 1.64, HM 1.69, HP 1.53 & 4.131, HN 1.54 & 4.131, HK 1.71 & 4.133, HH 17.11-2, HC 23.13 & 159.10-1, IS 550; *CNP I* 69, *CNI I* 128, *CNT IV* 70; Pts 5.38; VCsr 3.1, VCjr 17.4; BhŚ 376.

The main editions of H are almost identical. *CNP I* is almost identical with H (i. e. with all editions with the exception of HJ).Pañc., VCjr are identical with H. VCsr, BhŚ contain some minor variants.

Footnotes to No. 50 : [1]*bandhuḥ* VS 498 [2]*paraś ce* T in VCsr [3]*kalpo bahu-cetasām* IS [4]*vikalpo* VCsr [5]*bhrānta-cetasām* J in VCsr; *bahu°* V in VCsr; *°tasaḥ CNP I* [6]*punas tū'dāracittānām* VCsr; *puṁsām udāracittānāṁ* VS 498 [7]*tu* HS, HM, HP, HN, HK, HH, Boltz 8.41-2, VCjr., BhŚ, ŚP 273, *CNP I* [8]*tathā nā'sti mahātmanām* E in VCsr; *vasudhe'va* IS [9]*kuṭumbakaḥ* B in HP *ad* 1.53, Nd in VCsr; *kutum°* HH (printing error); *°binī* T in VCsr

No. 51

mūrkho'pi[1] *śobhate* [2]*tāvat sabhāyāṁ vastra-veṣṭitaḥ,*
tāvac ca śobhate mūrkho yāvat kiñcin na bhāṣate.

Even a blockhead shines in an assembly as far as [he is] dressed in [fine] clothes; and so long shines a fool, as he speaks not anything.

HJ Intr 40, HS Intr 39, HM Intr 40, HK Intr 40, HH 4.26-7, IS 4920, and 2901; *cf. CNJV* 15, *cf. CNS* 48, *cf. CNW* 52, *cf. CNŚC* 13, *cf. CNŚ* 13, *cf. CNŚL* 7, *cf. CNNM* 13, *cf. CNŚT* 13, *cf. CNŚK* 17, *cf. CNL* 75.

The main editions of H are identical. αβ are different in the *CN* group.

Footnotes to No. 51 : [1]*dūrataḥ CNJV, CNW, CNS.* [2]*mūrkho lambaśāṭa* (*°māna CNS*) *paṭāvṛtaḥ CNJB, CNW, CNS.*

No. 52

[1]*kāvyaśāstra-vinodena kālo gacchati*[2] *dhīmatām,*
vyasanena ca[3] *mūrkhāṇāṁ nidrayā kalahena vā.*[4]

In the enjoyment of poetical writings, the time of the wise

passes away, but (that)of fools in dissipation, slumber or strife.

HJ Intr 48, HS Intr 48, HM Intr 48, HP Intr 32, HN Intr 32, HK 1.1, HH 6.7-8, HC 8.13-4, IS 1711; *CNN* 7, *CNP II* 193, *CNI I* 1 230, *CNG* 179, *CNT IV* 189, *CnT II* 14.6, *CnT III* 7.65, *CnT V* 105; PP 2.171; Vet Intr 32.

The main editions of H are almost identical; HS, HP and HN contain one minor variant which is also found in Vet. *CNP II* is almost identical with H. PP and Vet contain some minor variants.

Footnotes to No. 52 : [1]*gītaśāstra°* (*gītavādya°*) CEbc in Vet; AP in PP; *CKl*; *kāvya-gīta-vinodena* MPr in PP, *kāvya-(gī)ta-śāstra vinodena* ψ in PP (*contra metrum*) [2]*gachati* HS [3]*tu* HS, HP, HN, Vet; *hi* PP, D in Vet [4]*ca* ψPMBhφ in PP, *CNP II*.

* * *

Compare also Nos. 3, 5, 20, 26, 83, 84, 90, 92, 93, 126 and 141.

18. *Virtue and Vice*

No. 53

tribhir varṣais tribhir māsais tribhiḥ pakṣais tribhir dinaiḥ,
[1]*aty-utkataiḥ pāpa-puṇyair*[2] *ihaiva phalam aśnute.*[3]

Within three years, within three months, within three fortnights, (or) within three days, one reaps, even here, the fruit of extraordinary vices or virtues.

HJ 1.85, HS 1.78, HM 1.82, HP 1.60, HN 1.61, HK 1.84, HH 19.17-8, HC 26. 16-7, IS 2642; *CnT II* 12.3, *CnT III* 7.37, *CnT V* 63; PrC 4.211.

The main editions of H contain some minor variants. PrC contains some minor variants.

Footnotes to No. 53 : [1]*aty-ugrapuṇya* HP, PrC; *aty-utkataiḥ puṇya pāpaiḥ* N in HP [2]*pāpānām* HP, PrC; *puṇyo-pāpair* HN [3]*ucyate* Pp in HS.

No. 54

[1]*na sthātavyaṁ na gantavyaṁ kṣaṇam*[2] *apy asatā*[3] *saha,*
[4]*asatāṁ saṅgamo mṛtyuḥ satāṁ saṅgo hi bheṣajam*[5].

One ought not live together or walk even for a moment with a wicked man. Relationship with a wicked [person] is death; association with a good [person] medicine.

HH 74.26-7, IS 3499; *CNN* 43 αβ, *CNI II* 96 α β, (cf. HJ 3.23 α and IS 3498).

The main editions of H are identical. *C* is identical in αβ only; that part contains minor variants.

Footnotes to No. 54 : [1]*nā'sthā°* IS [2]*kṣanāṁ CNN* [3]*asatāṁ* IS; *adhamaiḥ CNN* [4]*payo'pi śauṇḍinīhaste* (*śoṇḍini°* IS; *śoḍinī° CNN* var.; *sau°* IS) *madirāṁ manyate janaḥ CNN* [5]*vāruṇīty abhidhīyate* IS.

No. 55

tyaja durjana-saṁsargaṁ bhaja sādhusamāgamam
kuru puṇyam aho-rātraṁ smara nityam anityatām.[1]

Forsake the society of the wicked. Cultivate the society of the good. Practise virtue day and night. Remember always [your] transitory state.

HJ 3.24; HH 77.20-1, IS 2621; *CvND* 14.20, *CvM* 14.12, *CvA* 6.16, *CvṢ* 6.16, *CvW* 6.16, *CvP IV* 6.17, *CvP V* 6.16, *CvTb* 6.18, *CvL I* 6.16, *CvL II* 6.18, *CvLd* 6.16, *CRC* 2.12, *CRB* 2.12, *CRP* 2.11, *CRBh I* 2.11, *CRBh II* 2.8, *CSBD* 100, *CSB I* 1.100, *CSJ* 1.100, *CSC I* 1.100, *CSC II* 100, *CSB II* 99, *CSLd* 1.100; *CNN* 57, *CNP II* 140, *CNG* 4, *CNT IV* 130, *CNM* 131, *CNMN* 97, *CNŚC* 25, *CNŚ* 25, *CNŚL* 34, *CNNM* 103, *CNŚT* 78, *CNŚK* 29, *CnT II* 9.4, *CnT III* 6.12, *CnT VI* 102, *CnT V* 42, *CnT I* 24; GP 1.108.26; BhŚ 519.

The main editions of H are identical . The *CV* and *Cv* groups are identical with H; the *CR* and *CS* groups contain minor variants. Other sources are almost identical with H.

Footnotes to No. 55 : [1]*anityataḥ* IS; *°tāḥ* BhŚ; *bhaja nitya* BhŚ (notes); *najīvitam CNN*; *anāmayam CRC*

No. 56

saṅgaḥ sarvā'tmanā tyājyaḥ sa cet[1] *tyaktuṁ na śakyate,*
sa sadbhiḥ saha kartavyaḥ [2]*satāṁ saṅgo hi bheṣajam.*

Society ought to be shunned with all the soul, but if it cannot be relinquished, it should be formed with the virtuous; for the company of the virtuous [is] a [healing] medicine.

HJ 4.93, HS 4.89, HM 4.90, HP 4.93, HN 4.93, HK 4.95, HH 113.19-20, HC 152.10-1, IS 6674; *CNP II* 268; MP 37.23.

The main editions and various MSs. of H are almost identical, *CNP II* contains one minor variant. MP is identical with H.

Footnotes to No. 56 : [1]*ca* HM, HC [2]°*santaḥ saṅgasya* *CNP* II.

No. 57

vipadi dhairyam athaubhyudaye kṣamā[1]
sadasi[2] *vākpaṭutā yudhi vikramaḥ,*
yaśasi cā'bhirucir[3] *vyasanaṁ*[4] *śrutau*[5]
prakṛtisiddhir[6] *iyaṁ*[7] *mahātmanām.*

The perfection of the nature of great souls [is] this—fortitude in adversity, moderation in prosperity, eloquence in the assembly, valour in war, ambition for fame, perseverance in study.

HJ 1.32, HS 1.28, HM 1.31, HP 1.24, HN 1.25, HK 1.32, HH 10.21-2, HC 14.12-3, IS 6147; *CRC* 7.60, *CRB* 7.53, *CRP* 7.51, *CRBh I* 7.51, BhŚ 14.

The various editions of H contain several minor variants. *CRC* is identical with HH and HN. BhŚ contains some minor variants.

Footnotes to No. 57 : [1]*kṣamāḥ* $A_{1,3}$ H_2 in BhŚ [2] °*hasi* IS; *rahasi* IS [3]*cā'bhiratir* HN, BhŚ (DE_2 H_1 $F_{2,4,5}$ J_2 $IXY_{1A,3}$ as above) [4]*vinayaḥ* Y_7 in BhŚ [5]*śrute* I in BhŚ [6] °*siddhim* HS, HM, HP, HK, BhŚ; °*siddham* HN, HH, *CRC* [7]*idaṁ hi* HS, HM, HP, HN, HK, HH, BhŚ, *CRC* (better; *metri causa*).

No. 58

nārikela-samā'kārā[1] *dṛśyante'pi hi*[2] *sajjanāḥ*[3],
anye badarikā'kārā[4] *bahir eva manoharāḥ.*[5]

For good men are seen formed like the cocoanut; others [are] like the fruit of jujube, charming enough externally.

HJ 1.96, HM 1.93, HK 1.95, HH 20.18-9, HC 28.8-9, IS 3644; *CvA* 7.13, *CvṢ* 7.13, *CvW* 7.11, *CvP IV* 7.10, *CvP V* 7.8, *CvTb* 7.14, *CvL I* 7.13, *CvL II* 7.13, *CvLd* 7.8, *CSD* 2.12, *CSJ* 3.20, *CSC I* 3.12, *CSC II* 212, *CSLd* 3.11, *GSB II*; 2.12, *CNN* 59.

The main editions of H are identical with the exception of HK which contains one minor variant in β The *CV* and *CV* groups contain several important variants.

Footnotes to No. 58 : [1] °*kālo CVB*; *kela phalākālā* *CVB* (var.); *nālikera*° *CVF, CVG, CVN, CVA* [2]*ke'pi* *CVB*; *viralāḥ ke'pi* *CVF, CVG* [3]*dṛśyante hi sṛhṛjjanāḥ* HK; *sajjana janā CVN* [4] *'pi badarā'kārā CVB*; *itare* (°*rā CVG*) *badarā'kārā CVF, CVG, anye tu badirā'kārā CVN* [5]*manoramāḥ CVN*, *manoramā CVB* (var).

No. 59

[1]*sthānam*[2] *utsṛjya gacchanti*[3] *siṁhāḥ satpuruṣā*[4] *gajāḥ*[5],
tatraiva[6] *nidhanaṁ*[7] *yānti kākāḥ*[8] *kāpuruṣā*[9] *mṛgāḥ*.[10]

Lions, good men [and] elephants, abandoning a place, depart; crows, cowards [and] deer, find their death in the same spot.

HJ 1.105, HS 1.95, HM 1.169, HP 1.131, HN 1.132, HK 1.171, HH 21.24-5, HC 42 3.4, IS 7224, *CNP II* 203, *CNI I* 204; PS 2.53, PN 1.50, PP 5.27, Pts 1.321.

The main editions of H, with the exception of HP, HN and HH which contain minor variants, are identical; minor variants are noted in different MSs. of H. *C* contains some minor variants. Pañc. contains some important variants.

Footnotes to No. 59 : [1]*subhālaḥ paradeśebhyo bahvālasyāḥ pramādinaḥ* PP; *paradeśa bhāyād bhīta bahumāyā napuṁsakāḥ* Pts; *sthāna-tyāgaṁ kariṣyanti CNI, CŚlB* [2]*deśam* HP, PS; *deśān* AN in HP, HN; *deśān saṁtyajya* B in HP [3]*gachanti* HS; *gacchanto* N in PS; *jīvanti* HO in PS; °'*bhraṣṭāḥ na* (*su* ?) *śobhante* IS [4]*satpuruṣāḥ* IS [5]*haṁsās satpuruṣā narāḥ* NA in PS [6]*svadeśe* PP, Pts [7]*prabhītāh* Bh in PP; *niyanaṁ CŚIB* [8]*kāḥ* M in PP (*contra metrum*); *kākā* HH [9]*kāpuruṣāḥ* IS [10]*mṛtāḥ* N in PP.

No. 60

āhāra-nidrā-bhaya-maithunaṁ ca[1]
[2]*sāmānyam*[3] *etat paśubhir narāṇām,*
[4]*dharmo hi teṣām adhiko*[5] *viśeṣo*[6]
[7]*dharmeṇa*[8] *hīnāḥ*[9] [10]*paśubhiḥ samānāḥ.*

Food, sleep, fear, copulation—each [is] the common property of men with brutes. Virtue [is] really their superior distinction. Devoid of virtue, [they are] equal with brutes.

HJ Intr 25, HS Intr 24, HM Intr 25, HK Intr. 25, HH 3.17-8, HC 5.17-8, IS 1077; *CVND* 17.17; *CRC* 8.30, *CRB* 8.34, *CRP* 8.33, *CRBh I* 8.33, *CRBh II* 8.32; PD 300.18; *Śto* 348. 29-30, Bhś 407.

The main editions of H are identical. The *CV* and *CR* groups contain some important variants. PD, Śto and BhŚ contain some important variants. *CV* is nearer to Śto than to H.

Footnotes to No. 60 : [1]*maithunāni CVND* [2]*samāni caitāni nṛṇāṁ paśūnāṁ CVND* [3]*samānam* IS; *samānim* IS [4]*jñānaṁ narāṇām* PD, Śto, *CVND*; *jñāne narāṇām* BhŚ; *jñānaṁ viśeṣaṁ khalu manuṣāṇām* IS; *eko vivekastv CRC* [5]*adhikaṁ* IS [6]*viśeṣaḥ* K in Śto; *manuṣye CRC* [7]*jñānair viddhinā* IS [8]*jñānena* PD, Śto, BhŚ, *CVND*; *jñenena* H in Śto; *tenaiva CRC* [9]*hīnaḥ* Śto [10]*paśubhis* PD; *paśavo manuṣyāḥ* IS; *samaḥ syāt CRC.*

No. 61

durjanaḥ parihartavyo[1] [2]*vidyayā'laṅkṛto'pi san.*[3]
maṇinā bhūṣitaḥ[4] *sarpaḥ*[5] *kim asau na bhayaṅkaraḥ.*

A bad man ought to be shunned, although being adorned with knowledge. The serpent [is[adorned with a jewel, [still] is he not dangerous ?

HJ 1.91, HS 1.75, HM 1.88, HK 1.90, HH 20.5-6, HC 27.14-15, IS 2850; *CRB* 3.31, *CRP* 3.30, *CRT* 5·16,*CRBh I* 3.30, *CRBh II* 3.30, *CRT* 5.16, *CRCa I* 3.21; *CSBD* 235, *CSB I* 3.35, *CSJ* 3.43, *CSC I* 3.35 *CSC II*235, *CSB II* 235, *CSLd* 3.35; *CNJV* 25, *CNS* 43, *CNF* 90, *CNP II* 156, *CNG* 82, *CNT IV* 146, *CNM* 144, *CNŚC* 23, *CNŚ* 23, *CNŚL* 13, *CNNM* 23, *CNŚT* 22, *CNŚK* 25, *CNI II* 69, *CnT II* 15.12, *CnT III* 7.84, *CnT V* 126; *BhŚ.* 2, *GP* 1 .112, 15.

The main editions of H are identical All the *C* groups contain some variants. The nearest to H is the *CN* group. BhŚ is identical with H; variants in different MSs. are noted.

Footnotes to No. 61 : [1]*parihartavyo* IS; *parihartavyaḥ CVB* [2]*vidyayā'pi samanvataḥ* IS; °*bhūṣito'pi* BDEF$_2$ HIW in BhŚ; °*kṛto'py asan* X$_1$ in BhŚ; *śāstreṇā'laṅkṛto yadi CVB*; *'laṅkārito yadi CŚIB* [3]*sat* IS; *saḥ CŚH*; *yadi* F$_{4,5}$ in BhŚ, *CŚF* [4]*'laṅkṛtaḥ CŚF* [5]*nāgaḥ* F$_5$ in BhŚ; *sarpa* IS.

No. 62

durjana-dūṣita-manasaḥ[1] *sujaneṣv api nā'sti*[2] *viśvāsaḥ,*
[3]*bālaḥ*[4] *pāyasa-dagdho*[5] [6]*dadhy api* [7]*nanu phut-kṛtaṁ bhuṅkte.*

A mind which has been poisoned by the wicked, has no confidence even in the good. Does not a child that has been scalded with porridge, eat curd [only after it has been] blown upon [to cool it] ?

HJ 4.107, HM 4.103, HK 4.108, HC 156. 12-3, IS 2855; *CRC* 3.70, *CRB* 3.69, *CRP* 3.63, *CRBh I* 3.62, *CRBh II* 3.56, *CRCa I* 3.50; AIR 166 & 187 (attributed to Vimarśinī).

The main editions of H are almost identical. Pā in HK is however different in γδ. *CRC* contains minor variants. Other sources contain minor variants.

Footnotes to No. 62 : [1]*durjana-duḥkhita-manasāṁ* Pā in HK, AIR, *CRC* [2]*puṁsāṁ sujane'pi* (°*neṣu CRC*) *nā*° Pā in HK, AIR, *CRC*; *hi* IS add. [3]*paṇau pāyasadagdhe takraṁ phut-kṛtya pāmaraḥ pivati* Pā in HK [4]*pāṇi* IS [5]*payasā-dagdho* IS [6]*dadhv api yat kṛtya* IS [7]*phut-kṛtya bhakṣayati* (°*yate CRC*; *bhuñjita* IS add; *yat pibati* IS) HM, HK, AIR, *CRC*.

No. 63

[1]*poto dustara-vārirāśi-taraṇe*
[2]*dipo'ndhakārāgame*
nirvāte[3] *vyajanaṁ*[4] *madā'ndha-kariṇo*[5]
darpo'paśāntyai[6] *sṛṇiḥ*[7],
itthaṁ tad[8] *bhuvi nā'sti yasya*[9]
vidhinā no'pāyacintā[10] *kṛtā*
manye[11] *durjana-citta-vṛtti-haraṇe*
dhātā'pi[12] *bhagnodyamaḥ.*[13]

A barque [serves] in crossing the mass of waters difficult to be crossed; a lamp at the approach of darkness; a fan in a calm; a hook for curbing the fury of an elephant blind with passion;—thus there is nothing upon earth for which a thought of an appliance has not been bestowed by the Creator, but I believe the Creator himself [would be) baffled in his efforts to check the course of the thoughts of the wicked.

HJ 2.165, HS 2.155, HM 2.165, HP 2.151, HN 2.150, HK 2.163, HH 68.19-22, HC 90.19-91.2, IS 4189; *CRC* 3.71, *CRB* 3.70, *CRP* 3.64, *CRBh I* 3.63, *CRBh II* 3.58, *CRCa I* 3.51; PS 1.97, PN 2.75, PR 2.

The main editions and various MSs. of H contain some minor variants. *CRC* contains some important variants. Pañc. and its various MSs. contain several variants. PR is almost identical with H.

Footnotes to No 63 : [1]*po° nir°* tr. IS; *durbhara-vāri°* N in PS [2]*dīpā-'ndha°* IS; *doṣa* O in PS; *°kārodadher* N in PS; *°kārodaye* AB in PS; *°karo-dgame* I in PS [3]*nirvāti* I in PS; *niryāto* O in PS [4]*vyajane* A in PS [5] *°kariṇaḥ CRC*; *°kāriṇāṁ (kariṇāṁ)* HS, HM, HK, HH, PS, PR; *°kariṇo* B in PS; *vadā'ndha* IS [6] *°paśāntau* HP (edd. and Pp in HS as above), B in HP, PS; *varṣo paśāntau* H in PS [7]*sṛṇi* HH; *°sāntyai śirasyaṅkuśaḥ CRC* [8]*ithan tat* B in PS [9]*yatra* HS (edd. in HS as above), C in PS; *tena* A in HP; *bhuvanan na yamya* B in PS; tr. *ya° nā°* ANI in PS [10]*'pāyasṛṣṭiḥ CRC* [11]*prāyo* codd in HS; *kaṣṭaṁ CṚC* [12]*dhātā'sti* PR; *vṛttiśamane dhā°* N in PS [13]*bhagnodyaḥ* IS (*contra metrum*)

No. 64

durjanaḥ[1] *priya-vādī ca naitad*[2] *viśvāsa-kāraṇam,*[3]
[4]*madhurayati jihvāgre*[5] [6]*hṛdi hālāhalaṁ viṣam.*

One of evil character]may be] a kind speaker, that [is] no reason for trusting [him]. He carries sweetness on the tip of [his] tongue; poison the most deadly [lurks] in [his] heart.

HJ 1.84, HS 1.77, HM 1.81, HK 1.83, HH 19.6-7, HC 26. 5-6, IS 2852; *CSBD* 227, *CSB I* 3.28, *CSJ* 3.36, *CSC I* 3.28, *CSC II* 228, *CSB II* 228, *CSLd* 3.28; *CNJV* 24, *CNS* 44, *CNF* 87, *CNP II* 159, & 226, *CNI I* 108, *CNG* 91, *CNT IV* 151, *CNM* 149, *CNMN* 115, *CNŚC* 22, *CNŚ* 22, *CNŚL* 12, *CNNM* 22, *CNŚT* 21, *CNŚK* 24.

The main editions of H are almost identical; one variant in noted in γ in HS, HM, HK and HH. All groups of *C* contain some minor variants.

Footnotes to No. 64 : [1]*durjana* IS [2]*nai'va CVB*; *ye ca CŚlB*; *ceto CŚlB* (variant) [3]*kārakāḥ CVB*; *kārayet CVB* (variant) [4]*madhu tiṣṭhati* HS, HM, HK, HH, Boltz 14.134, *CŚH*; *madhurvasati CVB*, *CŚlB*; *madhu śravanti CVB* [5]*jivhāgre* HK (printing error) [6]*hṛdaye tu halāhalam CŚH, CŚlB*

No. 65

durjanair ucyamānāni [1]*sasmitāni priyāṇy api,*
akāla-kusumānī'va bhayaṁ saṁjanayanti me[2].

Even kind [words] accompanied with smiles, being spoken by evil persons excite my fears, like (the scent of) flowers out of season.

HJ 3.25, HS 3.23, HM 3.23, HP 3.24, HN 3.24, HK 3.24, HH 78.4-5, HC 103.8-9, IS 2800; *CNN* 1.13.

The main editions and various MSs. of H are almost identical. *CNN* is almost identical with the HM edition.

Footnotes to No. 65 : [1]*saṁmatāni* HM, I in HK, L in HS, *CNN*; *sammitāni* N in HP, Pp in HS; *sammatānya* A in HP [2]*hi* HM, HK; *ca CNN*.

No. 66

khalaḥ karoti durvṛttaṁ[1] *nūnaṁ*[2] *phalati*[3] *sādhuṣu,*
daśānano haret[4] *sītām bandhanaṁ syān*[5] *mahodadheḥ.*[6]

A villain does a bad action; it produces its effect amongst the good. Should the ten-headed one (Rāvaṇa) carry off Sītā, the binding of the ocean might ensue.

HJ 3.22, HS 3.21, HM 3.21, HP 3.21, HN 3.21, HK 3.21, HH 77.7-8, HC 102.6-7, IS 2044; *CNF* 99, *CNW* 82, *CNL* 42, *CNI II* 95; cf. VCsr 18.1; Mahānāṭaka 409.

The main editions and various MSs. of H are almost identical. The *CN* group contains minor variants.

Footnotes to No. 66 : [1]*durvṛttiṁ* HP [2]*phalaṁ CNW* [3]*patati AB* in HP [4]'*harat CNW* [5]*tan CNF* (variant); *ca CNW* [6]*mahodadhau* Mahān, *CNF*.

* * *

Compare also Nos. 87, 89, 92 and 98 .

19. *Women in General and as Wives*

No. 67

pitā rakṣati kaumāre bhartā rakṣati yauvane[1],
[2]*putrāś ca sthavire*[3] *bhāve*[4] *na* [5]*strī svātantryam arhati.*[6]

The father protects [her] in maidenhood; the husband protects [her] in youth, and [their] sons in old age. A woman is never fit to be free from control.

HJ 1.128, HS 1.113, HM 1.119, HP 1.91, HN 1.92, HK 1.122, HH 24.26-7, HC 33.17-8, IS 4067, *CRB* 8.68, *CRP* 8.65, *CRT* 8.33, *CRBh I* 8.66, *CRBh II* 8.55, *CNF* 58, *CNPh* 92, *CNI I* 155, *CNG* 180, *CNL* 46; Mn 9.3, (also quoted in DhPS 2.1, 38.2, 355.6, SC 2.240, 16; VyPr 406, 16; VT 821, VRV 281, U 2.14,2; VyB Vyavahāra Prakāśa 195.33; Vivāha Prakāśa 342.24-5, 211.17, Saṁskāra-ratnamālā 674; Dharmattva-nirṇayapariśiṣṭam 2.50, VR 1191, Vyavahārakalpataru 128, Vyavahāraprakāśa 406, Vyavahārārthasamuccaya 120, Smṛti-cintāmaṇi 27, Vivādārṇavasetu 281, Vivādabhaṅgārṇavaḥ 2.53, Nṛsiṁhaprasāda, Saṁskara 66 (b)[2]; cf. Mn 5.146; Gautama; Mitākṣara, Haradatta 3.10-1, cf. 18.1; B 2.2, 3, 45; Vās 5.3; N. 13.31; Nāradīyamanusaṁhitā 13.31; Cf. Y 1.85-6; cf. Vi 25.13; MBh 13.20, 21 (also quoted in Dh 2.1031), 13.46, 14; GP 1.115, 63; R 2.39, 32; Padma Purāṇa, Sṛṣṭikhaṇḍa 54.23; cf. Mahānirvāṇatantra 8.106.

The main editions of H and its various MSs. contain some minor variants. The *CN* groups is almost identical with H. The Dharmaśāstra sources and MBh contain several important variants. GP is almost identical with H.

Footnotes to No. 67 : [1]*yāvane* IS [2]*putrās* (*putras*) *tu* N in HP, HN, P in HS, MBh in Dh, GP, B, N, RNd in MnJ, Gautama Mit. Haradatta, U, Vīr Vyavahāra Prakāśa, Vyavahārārthasamuccaya, Vyavahāra Prakāśa, DhPS 2.1; 355, Dharmattvanirṇayaparisiṣṭa, VR, *CNF*; *putraś ca* Vās (FH in Vās as above); *putrā ṛakṣanti vārdhake* R in Dh; *putraḥ sthāvira bhāve tu na*° DhPS 2.1; 38; *rakṣanti stha*° HK, Mn (all editions), SC, SCM, VyB, VBh, Vyavahārārthasamuccaya; *rakṣanti vārdhake putra* NMS [3]*sthāvire* HM, HC, U, *CNF*; *sthavirī GMH* U, B (ed in B as above; *sthāvire co* in B, B in KSS 2.3, 46, B in ĀnSS 2.2, 52) [4]*kāle* Pp in HS, GP, MBh 13. 20, 21, *CNF*; *putrā* HK, Mn (all editions and most digests quoting Mn; differently GMH, U, Vīr Vyavahāra Prakāśa, Dharmattvanirṇayapariśiṣṭa, VR, Vyavahāra Prakāśa, Vyavahārāthasamuccaya) [5]*svātantryaṁ kvacit striyāḥ* Saṁskāraratnamālā; *nā'sti striṇāṁ svātantratā* MBh 13. 20, 21 [6] °*arhatī'ti* B (BS in B as above), G, Vās [7]cf. above Study XX para 4.

Nos. 68, 69

[1]*ahāro* [2]*dviguṇaḥ strīṇāṁ buddhis*[3] *tāsāṁ*[4] *caturguṇā*[5],
[6]*ṣaḍguṇo vyavasāyaś ca kāmaś cā'ṣṭaguṇaḥ smṛtaḥ*[7].

Women's appetite is stated [to be] two-fold, their wit four-fold, [their] ingenuity six-fold, and passion eight-fold.

HJ. 2.118 & 4.8, HS 2.113, HM 2.119, HP 2.105 & 4.8, HN 2.104, & 4.8; HK 2.117, & 4.8, HH 60.22-3, HC 80.5-6. IS 1082, and 7204; *CVND* 1.17, *CvM* 1.14; *CvA* 1.17, *CvṢ* 1.18, *CvW* 1.18, *cf. CvP IV* 1.16, *CvP V* 1.16, *CvGt* 1.17, *CvTb* 1.18, *CvH* 1.18, *CvI* 1.18, *CvL I* 1.17, *CvL II* 1.18, *CvLd* 1.17; *CRB* 2.46, αβ, *CRP* 2.41, αβ, *CRBh I* 2.41 αβ, *CRBh II* 2.35 αβ, *CRT* 2.26 *CRCa I* 2.35, αβ; *CVND* 78, *CNS* 15, *CNW* 81, *CNF* 35, *CNPh* 17, *CNPN* 9, *CNP II* 167, *CNI I* 152, *CNG* 48, *CNT V* 167, *I CNM* 162, *CNMN* 128, *CNL* 10, *CNI II* 29, *CnT II* 2.8, *CnT III* 1.20, *Cn*T *VI* 21, GP 1.109, 33; BP in śabdakalpadruma (*nāri*), cf. NPR 1.14, 96 & 1.14, 112.

The main editions of H are identical. The *CN* group is almost identical with H. with the exception of *CNW* which contains two minor variants. The *CV* and *CN* groups contain some minor variants. GP contains minor variants. Other sources are often different.

Footnotes to Nos. 68-69 : [1]*strīṇāṁ dviguṇa*(*m*) *āhāro* (*āhāraḥ* GP) GP, *CV* in IS *CVF*, *CVG*, *CVK*, *CVN*, *CŚlB* [2]*dviguṇas tāsāṁ* NPR; *dviguṇo nityaṁ naiṣṭhuryaṁ ca caturgaṇam* BP [3]*lajjā CV* in IS, *CVF*, *CVG*, *CVK*, *CVN*, *CŚlB*; cf. fn. 4 [4]*buddhiḥ strīṇāṁ CŚW*; *buddhiś cā'pi CV* in IS; *lajja cā'pi CVND*; *prajđā cai'va* GP [5]*caturguṇaḥ* IS 7204 [6]*sāhasaḥ* (°*saṁ*) *ṣaḍguṇaś* (*ñ*) *cai'va CVND*; *ṣaḍguṇā mantranā tāsāṁ* NPR; *kpaḥ puṁsaḥ ṣaḍguṇaś ca vyavasāyaś ca niścitan* BP; om. in HP 4.8 [7]*striyaḥ CŚW*; *kāmo'ṣṭaguṇa ucyate* IS 7204 (*CV* in IS as above).

No. 70

kūpo'dakaṁ vaṭac-chāyā[1] [2]*śyāmā strī iṣṭakā-gṛham*[3],
śīta-kāle bhaved uṣṇam uṣṇa-kāle[4] *ca śītalam.*

Well-water, the shade of a Baṭa-tree (fig tree), a swarthy woman, a brick-house,—in cold weather should be warm and in warm weather cool.

HJ 1.206, HS 1.186, HH 33.25-6, IS 1850; *CRC* 7.37 γδ, *CRB* 7.27 γδ, *CRP* 7.27 γδ, *CRBh I* 7.26 γδ, *CRBh II* 7.22 γδ, *CRCa I* 7.23; *CNJV* 96, *CNS* 30, *CNL* 41, *CnT II* 14.3, *CnT III* 7.62, *CnT V* 100; GP 1.114, 32.

The main editions of H contain minor varīants. The *CN* group contains some minor vasiants. In *GP* β is different.

Footnotes to No. 70 : [1]*vaṭa-chāyā* HS, HH [2]*nāriṇāṃ ca payodharaḥ* GP [3]*iṣakā-gṛham* HH; *ce'ṣṭakā'layam CNJV CNN* [4]*grīṣma-kāle CNJV, CNS*.

No. 71

[1]*asatyaṁ sāhasaṁ māyā mātsaryaṁ*[2] *cā'ti-lubdhatā*[3],
[4]*nirguṇatvam aśaucatvaṁ strīṇāṁ doṣāḥ svabhāvajāḥ.*

Falsehood, precipitancy, guile, envy and extreme avariciousness, want of principle, [and] impurity, [are] the inbred faults of women.

HJ 1.210, HM 1.194, HK 1.196, HH 34.26-7, IS 328; *CVND* 2.1, *CvM* 2.1; *CvA* 2.1, *CvṢ* 2.1, *CvW* 2.1, *CvP IV* 2.1, *CvP V* 2.1, *CvGt* 2.1, *CvTb* 2.1, *CvH* 2.1, *CvI* 2.1, *CvL I* 2.1, *CvL II* 2.1, *CvLd* 2.1, *CRC* 1.51; *CNP II* 165, *CNG* 49, *CNT IV* 157, *CNM* 154, *CNMN* 120, *CnT II* 2.9, *CnT III* 2.1, *CnT VI* 2.2, *CnT V* 129, *CnT VII* 14; PP 1.143, Pts 1.195; Vet 3.6; Bhś 368 v.l.

The main editions of H are identical with H. The *CV*, *Cv* and *CN* groups contain several minor variants, almost identical with those found in Pañc., Vet and Bhś.

Footnotes to No. 71 : [1]*anṛtaṁ* PP, Pts, Vet, BhŚ, *CVND, CV* in IS, *CVF, CVG, CVK, CVN, CŚlB*; *anṛta sāhasaṁ dhairyam* D in Vet [2]*mūrkhatvaṁ* PP, Pts, Vet, BhŚ, *CVND, CV* in IS, *CVF, CVG, CVK, CVN, CŚlB* [3]*ati-lobdhatā* (°*lobhitā*) PP, Pts, Vet, BhŚ, *CVND, CVF, CVG, CVK, CVN, CŚlB*; '*ti-lobhataḥ* BhŚ (notes) [4]*nirghṛṇatvam* b in Vet; *aśaucaṁ* (*aśaucatvaṁ CVND* (var.), *CV* in IS, *CVF, CVG, CVK, CŚlB*; *aśocaṁ CVN*; *aśaucyaṁ* IS) *nirdayatvaṁ* (*nirghṛṇatvaṁ CVN*) *ca* (om. *CVND*) PP, Pts, Vet, BhŚ, *CVND, CV* in IS, *CVF, CVG, CVK, CVN CŚlB*; *nirdayatvam aśaucatvaṁ* (*ahaṁkāraṁ* IS) a in Vet.

No. 72

[1]*nadīnāṁ śastra-pāṇīnāṁ nakhināṁ*[2] *śṛṅgināṁ*[3] *tathā,*
viśvāso[4] *nai'va kartavyaḥ*[5] *strīṣu rājā-kuleṣu ca.*

Confidence ought never be put in rivers, in those with weapons in their hands, in those having claws or horns, in women and in kings' families.

HJ 1.18, HS 1.17, HM 1.18, HK 1.19, HH 9.6-7, HC 12. 13-4, IS 3214, *CVND* 1.15; *CVM* 1.12; *CvA* 1.15, *CvṢ* 1.16, *CvW* 2.7, *CvP IV* 2.7, *CvGt* 2.7, *CvTb* 1.15, *CvH* 1.15, *CvI* 1.16, *CvL I* 1.15, *CvL II* 1.16, *CvLd* 1.13; *CRC* 2.24, *CRB* 2.22, *CRP* 2.21, *CRT* 2.14, *CRBh I* 2.21, *CRBh II* 2.18, *CRCa I* 2.20; *CSBD* 2.48, *CSB I* 3.48, *CSJ* 3.56, *CSC I* 3,48, *CSC II* 248, *CSB II* 248,

CSLd 3.46, *CNJV* 27, *CNS* 52, *CNW* 31, *CNPh* 11, *CNI I* 104, *CNG* 26, *CNŚ* 107, *CNNM* 66, *CNŚK* 27, *CNL* 7, *CNI II* 7, *CnT II* 2.6, *CnT III* 1.18, *CnT VI* 19; PP 1.52, VCsr VII 8, VCjr VII 1; GP 1.109, 14.

The main editions of H are identical. The *CN*, *Cv*, *CV* and *CR* groups contain several minor variants. *CNW* is identical with H; *CNJV* is very near to H (it is identical with PP). Pañc., VC, its various MSs. and GP contain several minor variants.

Footnotes to No. 72 : [1]*nakhinām ca nadīnāṁ ca śṛṅgināṁ śastra-dhāriṇāṁ* (°*pāṇinām CŚH, CŚN*; *śastriṇāṁ dviṣām Ś in* VCjr, *CRC*) PP, *CŚH*, *CŚN*, *CRC*; *nadīnām ca nakhināṁ ca śṛṅgināṁ* (*śṛṅgīnāṁ* IS) *śastra-paṇināṁ* (*śāstra*° IS—wrongly) VCsr; VCjr, GP, *CVND*, *CVK*, *CVN*; *nakh*° *nad*° tr. Q in VCsr, PBGKR in VCjr; *nadīnāṁ nakhinām cai'vā* M in VCsr, Ś in VCjr; *śastra-dhāriṇām* ME in VCsr; *śṛṅgināṁ ca nadināṁ ca nakhināṁ śastra-paṇinām* IS [2]*nakhiṇāṁ CVND* [3]*śṛṅgiṇāṁ* HM; *śṛṅgiṇāṁ bhūbhujām CVF* [4]*āśvāso* Ś in VCjr [5]*no'pagantavyaḥ* PP, VQ in VCsr; *kartavyaṁ* IS.

No. 73

na dānenana namānena nā'rjavena na sevayā
na śastreṇa na śāstreṇa [1]*viṣamāḥ* [2]*sarvathā*[3] *striyaḥ.*

Neither by gifts, nor by honours, nor by uprightness, nor by devotedness, nor by punishment, nor by precept, [are] women [to be rendered faithful; they are] altogether dishonest.

HJ 2.115, HS 2.112, HM 2.116, HP 2.104, HN 2.103, HK 2.114, HH 60.6-7, HC 79.11-2, IS 3283; *CRC* 1.49, *CRB* 1.39, *CRP* 1.44, *CRBh I* 1.45, *CRBh II* 1.46, *CRCa II* 20; GP 1.109, 45.

The main editions of H contain minor variants. *CRC* is identical with H (HS, HM, HP, HK, HH editions); GP is also identical with some editions of H.

Footnotes to No. 73 : [1]*sarvasthā kim api striyaḥ* HN (cf. fn. 2) [2]*kim api* HP, *ad* HK (cf. fn. 1) [3]*vi*° *sa*° tr. HS, HM, HP, HK, HH, GP, *CRC*.

No. 74

[1]*sthānaṁ*[2] *nā'sti kṣaṇo*[3] *nā'sti* [4]*nā'sti prā'rthayitā*[5] *naraḥ,*[6]
[7]*tena*[8] *nārada*[9] *nārīṇāṁ satītvam upajāyate*[10].

There is no place,—there is not a (favourable) moment,—there is no man a suitor,—through that, O Nārada, does the chastity of women arise.

HJ 1.123, HS 1.109, HM 1.115, HP 1.88, HN 1.89,

HK 1.117, HH 24.14-5, HC 33.7-8, IS 7222; *CRB* 7.7, *CRP* 7.7, *CRBh I* 7.7, *CRCa I* 7.7; *CNF* 39, *CNPN* 54, *CNI I* 157, *CNG* 138; PP 1.107, Pts 1.138; VCsr VI.11; Vet 24.2; GP 1.14, 9; NPR 1.14, 76; cf. MBh. 13.38 23.[11]

The main editions of H. are almost identical. The *CN* group is identical with H. The other *C* groups contain minor variants. Pañc., VC and GP contain minor variants. Vet is almost identical with H. NPR is different in βγ.

Footnotes to No. 74 : [1]*sthā*° *te*° tr. B in HP; *kṣa*° *nā*° *raho* GP [2]*raho* PP (M in PP as above), Pts,. VCsr, Vet, GP, *CRB*, *CNI* [3]*kṣaṇaṁ* HS, HM, HP, HN, HK, HH, NPR, a in Vet; *kṣane* IS; *raho* Q in VC; *aho* VN in VC; *ahar* Q in VC; *dhakṣo* M in VC; *pakṣo* Nd in VC; *sthalaṁ* a in Vet; *sthānaṁ* A in Vet [4]*nā'sti dūtī tad uttamā* NPR [5] °*yito* Pp in HS (wrongly); °*yatā* Pr in PP [6]*janāḥ* VC, GP [7]*tenai'va yuvatīnaṁ ca* NPR [8]*itthaṁ* VC; *evaṁ* a in Vet; *aho* b in Vet. [9]*śaunaka* GP [10]*upajayate* HK; *upajñāyate* M in PP; *pātivratyaṁ prakalpyate* (*hi kal*° VJ in VC; °*kalpayet* Nd in *VC*; °*kalpate* MNVJ in VC) VC (Q in VC as above) [11]cf. JSAIL 22 par. 20.

No. 75

[1]*nīcam āśrayate lakṣmīr*[2] [3]*akulena*[4] *sarasvatī,*

apātraṁ[5] *bhajate*[6] *nārī girau*[7] *carṣati vāsavaḥ.*[8]

Lakṣmī patronizes the base. Sarasvatī [consorts] with the plebeian. A woman pays court to the unworthy. The cloud rains on the mountain.

HJ 2.156, HH 67, 14-5, HC 89. 7-8, *IS* 3793; *cf. CRC* 7.65, *cf.CRBh II* 7.32; *cf. CSBD* 181, *cf. CSB I* 2.82, *cf. CSJ* 2.80, *cf. CSC I* 2.81, *cf. CSC II* 181, *cf. CSB II* 180, cf. *CSLd* 2.80; *CNF* 84, *CNI I* 169, *CNG* 115, *CNL* 80, αβ, *CNI II* 62, *cf. CNP II* 169, (189), *cf CNM* 165, *cf. CNMN* 131, *cf. CnT II* 103, *cf CnT III* 7.11, *cf. CnT V* 26, *cf. CnT I* 11.

The main editions of H are almost identical. The *CN* and *CS* groups contain important variants. *CŚlB*, *CNP* II is different in αβγ.

Footnotes to No. 75 : [1]*nī*° *apa*° tr. *CŚF*; *lakṣmī rakṣaṇa hiṇyaś ca CVB*; *lakṣaṇa hīnasya* IS; °*jāti hīnasya bhārati* IS; *lakṣmi*(*r*) *lakṣaṇa-hīne* (°*nā*) *ca jāti-hīne* (°*nā kula-hīne CKI*; °*nya* IS) *sarasvatī CŚlB* [2] °*mīḥ CŚF*; °*mī CVB* [3]*prajñaḥ prayeṇa nirdhanaḥ CŚF* [4]*akulīnaṁ* IS [5]*apātre CŚF, CKI*; *kupātre CŚlB* [6]*ramate CVB, CŚlB, CKI*; *kupātre* IS [7]*śaile CŚF* [8]*mādhavaḥ CŚlB*.

Nos. 76, 76*A*

na strīṇām[1] *apriyaḥ kaścit priyo vā'pi na vidyate,*
[2]*gāvas tṛṇam ivā'raṇye prārthayanti navaṁ navam.*

To women no one soever is found disagreeable or agreeable; as cattle in a forest [they are ever seeking] fresh pasture.

HJ 1.124 & 4.7, HS 1.189, HM 1.116, HP 1.155 & 4.7, HN 1.156, & 4.7, HH 24.16-7, HC 33.9-10 & 133, 10-1, IS 3496; *CNF* 40, *cf. CNPN* 55; *cf.* MBh. 13.39, 5; *cf.* R in VR 1204; 414, 15-6; cf. IS 3235, 3531.

The main editions and various MSs. of H are almost identical. *CNF* is identical with H. *CNPN* is different in γ.

Footnotes to Nos. 76, 76 A: [1]*nāriṇām* B in HP 4.7 [2]*purātanaṁ nivarante CNF.*

No. 77

mātrā svasrā duhitrā vā[1] [2]*na*[3] *viviktāsano bhavet,*[4]
balavān indriya-grāmo[5] *vidvāṁsam*[6] *api karṣati.*

One should not sit in a lonely place near to mother, or sister, or daughter; for powerful is the assemblage of sense organs which overcomes even a learned man.

HJ 1.129, HH 25.1-2, *ad* HS 1.113, IS 4809; *CRC* 7.9, (7.76), *cf. CRB* 7.66, *cf. CRP* 7.66, cf. *CRT* 8.42, *cf. CRBh I* 7.65, *cf. CRBh II* 7.65; GP 1.114, 6; BhP 9.19, 17; Bhaviṣya Purāṇa, Brāhmaparvan 4.184; Mn 2.215; ŚŚ 3.18 a, (cf. MBh 13.48, 37-8; B 1.2, 3, 23 and 33; Āp 1.2, 7, 3 and 7, 11 and 1.1, 3, 16).

The main editions of H are identical with the exception of one minor variant. *CRC* 7.9, contains one minor variant. Other sources are almost identical with H.

Footnotes to No 77: [1]*ca* IS [2]*nātyantaikāntikaṁ vaset* ŚŚ [3]*no* HH, *ad* HS [4]*vaset CRC*; *viśat* IS [5]*indriyaḥ grāmaṁ* IS [6]*vidhvāṁsam* BhP.

No. 78

nā'gnis tṛpyati[1] *kāṣṭhānāṁ*[2] *nā'pagānāṁ*[3] *mahodadhiḥ,*
nā'ntakaḥ sarvabhūtānāṁ[4] [5]*na puṁsāṁ*[6] *vāma-locanāḥ.*[7]

Fire is not satisfied with fuel, nor the ocean with rivers, nor death with all creatures, nor bright-eyed women with men.

HJ 2.114, HS 2.111, HM 2.115, HP 2.103, HN 2.102,

HK 2.113, HH 60. 4-5, HC 79. 9-10, IS 3547; *CvA* 7.10, *CvṢ* 7.10, *CvW* 7.8, *CvP IV* 7.7, *CvP V* 7.6, *CvGt* 7.4, *CvTb* 7.12, *CvH* 7.9, *CvL I* 7.10, *CvL II* 7.10, *CvLd* 7.6, *CRB* 2.51, *CRP* 2.48, *CRT* 2.27, *CRBh I* 2.48, *CRCa I* 2.41, *CRCa II* 16; *CNF* 41, *CNP I* 13, *CNI I* 172, *CNT IV* 12, *CNM* 12, *CNMN* 12, *CnT II* 16.9, *CnT III* 7.b 5, and 53.17, PP 1.106, Pts 1.137; VCsr VI 10; MBh 5.39, 7 and 13.38, 25; R 5.50, 12; GP 1.109, 40; Bhś 571; NPR 1.14, 99.

The main editions and the MSs. of H are almost identical, with the exception of two minor variants. The *CŚ*, *CN* groups and most of the *Cv* group are identical with H, *CNF*, *CvTb*, with HM, HP, HN, HK editions). Other sources contain minor variants, with the exception of NPR which is different in δ.

Footnotes No. 78 : [1]*tapyati* Pp in HS [2]*kāṣṭhaughair* J in *CV*; *kāṣṭhena CVG* [3]*'pagābhir* J in *VC*, *CVG* [4] °*bhutaiś ca* J in VC [5]*nāśa tṛpyatī sampadāṁ* NPR [6]*pumbhir* J in *VC* [7]*locanā* HM, HP, HN, HK, Pts, bhNPr in PP, MBh 5.39, 7, GP; J in VC; °*locana*, IS.

No. 79

ghṛta-kumbha-samā nārī[1] *taptā'ṅgāra-samaḥ pumān,*
[2]*tasmād ghṛtaṁ ca vahniṁ ca* [3]*naikatra sthāpayed budhaḥ.*

A woman [is] like a jar of ghee. A man [is] like a glowing coal. A prudent person, therefore, should not place ghee and fire together.

HJ 1.127, HS 1.112, HM 1.117, HP 1.90, HN 1.91, HK 1.120, HH 24.24-5, HC 33.13-4, IS 2217; *CNJV* 77, *CNS* 34, *CNF* 101, *CNPh* 112, *CNPN* 52, CNI *II* 18; *cf.* *CNP II* 263[4]; Vet Intr 1 (cf. Vet 3.10) Padma Purāṇa, Śṛṣṭikhaṇḍa 54.21; cf. BhP 7.12, 9; cf. Mn 2.94.

The main editions of H are identical. The *CN* group, with the exception of *CNPN* which contains one minor variant, is identical with H. Vet is different in γδ. Padma P is different in γ.

Footnotes to No. 79 : [1]*puruṣaś cā'gnivarcasaḥ* Vet 3.10 [2]*tasmāt* HH; *saṁśleṣād dravate* (*sasneho dravate* IS) *kumbhaḥ tadvat strī-puṁsa-bhāvitā Vet* Intr [3]*pṛthak-sthānena dhārayet* HP, *tad vatstrīpuṁsa* (*puṁsi* IS) *bhāvatā* (*bhuvatā* IS; *bhāṣitaṁ* IS; *bhāṣite* IS; *yogataḥ* IS) IS; *naikasthāne na dharayet* Padma P; *naiva*...... (illegible) *CŚP* [4]*CŚlB* 263 (αβ are similar in BhP 7.12, 9) reads :

agni-kumbha-samā nārī ghṛta-kumbha-samo naraḥ
ubhayor api saṁyogaḥ kasya viśvāsa-kārakaḥ (*viśvāsa te naraḥ* var.).

No. 80

surūpaṁ[1] *puruṣaṁ*[2] *dṛṣṭvā bhrātaraṁ*[3] [4]*yadi vā sutam,*
[5]*yoniḥ klidyati*[6] *nārīṇāṁ* [7]*satyaṁ satyaṁ hi nārada*[8].

Feminae virum pulchrum, sive fratrem, sive filium intuitae pudendum madescit; vero, Nārada, vero !

HP 1.87, HS 1.110, HK 1.116, HH 24. 18-9, HC 33. 10-1, IS 7135 & 7107; *cf. CRP* 2.45, *CRBh I* 2.45, *cf. CRCa I* 2.39, *CNF* 38, *CNPN* 53, *cf. CNI I* 159, *cf. CnT II* 23.9, *cf. CnT III* 57.3, GP 1.109, 37; cf. Vct 3.9; cf. NPR 1.14, 77; cf. MBh 13.38, 26.

The main editions and various MSs. of H contain minor variants. The *CN* group is almost identical with H. Other sources contain major variants. NPR is quite different.

Footnotes to No. 80 : [1]*suveśam* HS, HH, GP, *CŚP*; *suveṣaṁ CŚF*; *svarūpaṁ* A in HP (B in HP as above); *sundaraṁ* IS 7107 [2]*kāmukaṁ* NPR [3]*kāmanī* NPR [4]*pitaraṁ* IS 7107; *madanāturā* NPR [5]om. HK; *yonir dravati* IS 7107; *tad gātraṁ ca pulakitaṁ yonau kaṇḍūyanaṁ paraṁ* NPR [6]*krīḍati* B in HP; *syadati CŚF* [7]*āmapātram ivāmbhasā* HP (B in HP as above) *tathyaṁ me brūhi* IS 7101 [8]*śaunaka* GP; *janārdana* IS 7107.

No. 81

sā bhāryā yā gṛhe dakṣā[1], *sā bhāryā yā prajāvatī*[2],
sa bhāryā yā patiprāṇā[3], *sā bhāryā yā pativratā.*[4]

She [is] a wife who in the house [is] clever. She [is] a wife who [is] prolific. She [is] a wife who lives in her lord (or who is the life of her lord). She [is] a wife who [is] faithful to [her] husband.

HJ 1.211, HS 1.190, HM 1.195, HP 1.156, HN 1.157, HK 1.197, HH 35. 3-4, HC 46.19-20, IS 7004; *cf. CVND* 4.13, *cf. CVM* 4.17, *cf. CvA* 7.5, *cf. CvW* 7.5, *cf. CvP IV* 7.4, *cf. CvP V* 7.4, *cf. CvTb* 7.5, *cf. CvL I* 7.50, *cf. CvL II* 7.5; *CRC* 1.28, *CRB* 1.25, *CRP* 1.27, *CRT* 1.14 *CRBh I* 1.27, *CRBh II* 1.28, *cf. CNP I* 23, *cf. CNT IV* 22, *cf. CNŚ* 87, *cf. CnT II* 12.9, *cf. CnT III* 7.43, *cf. CnT V* 70.

The main editions and various MSs. cf. H contain minor variants. The *CV*, *Cv* and *CR* groups contain minor variants. GP contains minor variants, MBh. is identical with H.

Footnotes to No. 81 : [1]*śucir-dakṣā CVND*; *priyaṁ brūyāt CNH* [2]*pativratā* B in HP, *CVND*, *priyaṁvadā* GP, *CVF*, *CRC* [3]*pratiprāṇā* Boltz 30.27, GP; *patipritā CVND*; *priyaṁvādinī CNH*; *vacaḥstokā CVN* [4]*priyaṁvadā* B in HP; *yat* (*sat*) *yavādini CVND*; *prajāvati CRC*; *ca putriṇī CVG*, *CVN*.

No. 82

duṣṭā bhāryā śaṭhaṁ[1] *mitraṁ bhṛtyaś*[2] *co'ttaradāyakaḥ,*[3]
[4]*sasarpe ca gṛhe vāso mṛtyur eva na saṁśayaḥ.*

A wicked wife, a false friend, a servant that gives [saucy] answers, and a residence in a house infested by serpents, [is] death beyond a doubt.

HJ 2.120, HS 2.115, HM 2.121, HP 2.107, HN 2.106, HK 2.119, HH 61.7-8, HC 80.17-8, IS 2891; *CVND* 1.5, *CVM* 1.5, *CvA* 1.5, *CvṢ* 1.5, *CvW* 1.5, *CvP IV* 1.5, *CvP V* 1.5, *CvGt* 1.4, *CvTb* 1.5, *CvH* 1.5, *CvI* 1.5, *CvL I* 1.5, *CvL II* 1.5, *CvLd* 1.5, *CRC* 1.45, *CRB* 1.38, *CRP* 1.43, *CRT* 1.22, *CRBh I* 1.44, *CRBh II* 1.45, *CRCa II* 9; *CNJV* 43, *CNS* 7, *CNW* 7, *CNF* 8, *CNPh* 3, *CNPN* 3, *CNP II* 162, *CNI I* 111, *CNG* 18, *CNT IV* 156, *CNŚC* 43, *CNŚ* 41, *CNŚL* 105, *CNNM* 35, *CNŚT* 38, *CNŚK* 40, *CNL* 3, *CnT II* 1.6, *CnT III* 1.6, *CnT VI* 63, *CnT V* 5; *cf.* PtsK 1.235; GP 1.108, 25.

The main editions of H are almost identical. All groups of *C* are identical with H with the exception of *CNP II* and *CvP V*; each of them contains one minor variant. GP is identical with H. PtsK is almost identical in γδ, while αβ are different.

Footnotes to No. 82 : [1]*saṭhaṁ* IS [2]*bhṛtyāś* Boltz 46.12; *bhṛtyo(ś)* IS (add.) [3] °*ttaradāyakāḥ*, HS, HM, Boltz 46.12, *CŚW*; °*ttaradāyakaṁ* IS; *'haṁkārasaṁyutah IS (add.), cā'ṁtara*⁰ *CSLB, co'mtara*⁰ *CVG* [4]*sarpayukte gṛhe* PtsK.

No. 83

kokilānāṁ svaraṁ[1] *rūpaṁ* [2]*nārī-rūpaṁ*[3] *pativratam*[4],
vidyā rūpaṁ kurūpaṇāṁ kṣamā[5] *rūpaṁ*[6] *tapasvinām*[7].

The beauty of cuckoos [is their] note. The beauty of a woman (wife) [is] constancy to her husband. The beauty of the ill-favoured [is] knowledge, The beauty of the pious [is] patience.

HJ 1.212, HH 35.7-8, IS 1919; *CVND* 3.9, *CVM* 3.1; *CvH* 7.11, *CLB* 7.3, *CLT* 7.3, *CLI* 7.3, *CLP V* 7.5, *CLP IV* 7.9, *CLTb* 7.7, *CLH* 8.7, *CLL II* 7.3, *CLLd* 7.5; *CRC* 7.23; *CSBD* 12, *CSB I* 1.12, *CSJ* 1.12, *CSC I* 1.12, *CSC II* 12, *CSB II* 12, *CSLd* 1.12; *CNJV* 46, *CNS* 31, *CNW* 18, *CNP I* 17, *CNPN* 44, *CNI I* 153, *CNG* 140, *CNHU* 15, *CNT IV* 15, *CNM* 16, *CN-MN* 16, *CNŚC* 45, *CNŚ* 45, *CNŚL* 78, *CNNM* 37, *CNŚT* 40, *CNŚK* 42, *CNL* 77, *CNI II* 65; Vet 9.17, Śto 324.21-2 αβδ, Pras 5.11

The main editions of H, with the exception of HN and HH, which contain one minor variant, are identical. The *CN* *CV*, *Cv* and *CL* groups contain minor variants. The *CS* group is different in β. The *CRC* is identical with H in *a* only. Other sources contain minor variants.

Footnotes to No. 83: [1]*svaro* Pras, Vet, *CŚH*, *CŚW*, *CŚN*, *CŚP*, *CVND*, *CV* in IS, *CRC*, *CLB*, *CLT*, *CLC*, *CLD*, *CLI*, *CLM*, *CNH* [2]*pātivratyaṁ tathā strīyaṁ* IS; *pātivratyaṁ tu yoṣitām CVB* [3]*strīṇāṁ rūpaṁ* Pras, *CVND*; *strī-rūpāṁ ca* c in Vet [4]*Pativratā* HN, HH, ABacd in Vet *CLB*, *CLT*, *CŚH*, *CŚN*; °*vṛtā* D in Vet; *pavitratā CŚN*; *pativratyaṁ tathā striyām* IS [5]*śāntī CLB*, *CLT* [6]*virūpāṇāṁ CVB* [7]*tapasvinaḥ CŚN*.

No. 84

anabhyāse[1] *viṣaṁ vidyā*[2] *ajīrṇe*[3] *bhojanaṁ viṣam*[4],
[5]*viṣaṁ sabhā*[6] *daridrasya vṛddhasya taruṇī viṣam.*

In the absence of practice, knowledge [is] poison. In indigestion, food [is] poison. A court [is] the bane of a poor man. To an old man, a young wife [is] poison.

HJ Intr 22, HS Intr 21, HM Intr 22, HK Intr 22, HH 3.10-1, IS 2836; *CVND* 4.15, *CVM* 4.10, *cf. CvH* 8.15, *cf. CvL I* 8.24, *cf. CvL II* 8.18; *CSBD* 15, *CSB I* 1.15, *CSJ* 1.15, *CSC I* 1.15, *CSC II* 15, *CSB II* 15, *CSLd* 1.15; *CNJV* 98, *CNS* 47, *CNW* 78, *CNF* 11, *CNP I* 26, *CNPh* 56, *CNPN* 21, *CNP II* 69, *CNI I* 229, *CNG* 144, *CNT IV* 25 *CNM* 25 *CNMN* 25, *CNM* 97, *CNL* 21, *CNI II* 13, *CnT V* 44, *CnT VII* 58, *CnT II* 27.9,

The main editions of H are identical. The *CN*, and *CV* groups contain several variants, some of them are important.

Footnotes to No. 84: [1]*anabhyāsaṁ CNH* (°*se CŚlB*); *duradhītā CŚF*, *CŚH*, *CŚW*, *CŚN*, *CŚP* [2]*śāstraṁ CVND*, *CNH*, *CŚlB* [3]*ajīrṇaṁ CŚF*, *CVB*; (°*ne CVND*) [4]*bho*° *vi*° tr. *CNH*, *CŚlB* [5]*daridrasya viṣaṁ goṣṭhī CVND* [6]*goṣṭhī CŚF*, *CŚH*, *CŚW*, *CŚN*, *CŚP*, *CNH*, *CŚlB*. See fn. 5 (*CVND*).

* * *

Compare also Nos. 3, 5, 18, 47, 94 and 98.

20. *Sons*

No. 85

[1]*sa*[2] *jāto yena jātena*[3] *yāti vaṁśaḥ*[4] *samunnatim*[5],
[6]*parivartini*[7] *saṁsāre* [8]*mṛtaḥ*[9] *ko vā*[10] *na jāyate.*[11]

He [is] born, by whom [when] born, the family attains exaltation. In the revolving world, who, [when] dead, is not born again ?

HJ Intr 14, HS Intr 13, HM Intr 14, HP Intr 13, HN Intr 12, HK Intr 14, HH 2.18-9, HC 5.3-4, IS 6681; *CRC* 8.35, *CRB* 8.35, *CRP* 8.34, *CRBh I* 8.34, *CRBh II* 8.33; Pts 1.27a; BhŚ 74.

The main editions of H are identical. *CRC* is identical with H with the exception of δ. Pts is different in αβ. BhŚ is identical with H; changes are noted in MSs. only.

Footnotes to No. 85 : [1]*sa pa°* tr. in BhŚ; αβ different Pts in [2]*na* F_3J_2 in BhŚ [3]*yātena* B_{1t} in BhŚ [4]*jāti vaṁśaḥ* A_2 in BhŚ; *magnaḥ* J_2 in BhŚ; *vaṁśa°* J_2 W_1 X_1 in BhŚ; *vaṁśo yāti* T_3 in BhŚ; *mānaḥ* M_4 in BhŚ [5]*samunnatīḥ* X_1 in BhŚ; *samunnatīṁ* M_5 in BhŚ [6]γδ identical in Pts [7]*parivartani* IY_{1A} in BhŚ; *parivṛttini* J_1 in BhŚ; *parivartmani* Y_3 in BhŚ [8]*parairjātairmṛtaiś ca kim CRC* [9]*martyaḥ* B_2 F_4 HI in BhŚ; *naraḥ* Y_7 in BhŚ; *madaḥ* M_4 in BhŚ; *mṛto* IS; *śrutaḥ* F_3 in BhŚ [10]*ko'pi* E_2 F_5 in BhŚ; *ko'pān* M_4 in BhŚ; *vā ko* IS [11]*janāyate* F_1 in BhŚ; *jāyati* G_2 in BhŚ.

No. 86

āyuḥ[1] *karma*[2] *ca vittaṁ*[3] *ca vidyā*[4] *nidhanam*[5] *eva ca,*
[6]*pañcai* [7]*'tāny api*[8] *sṛjyante*[9] [10]*garbhasthasyai'va*[11] *dehinaḥ.*[12]

Age, actions, wealth, knowledge, and also death; these five are created for the embodied spirit even whilst existing in the embryo state.

HJ Intr 27, HS Intr 26, HM Intr 27, HP Intr 17, HN Intr 16, HK Intr 27, HH 3.21-2, HC 6.1-2, IS 992; *CVND* 4.1 and 13. 14, *CVM* 4.1; *CLP V* 8.7, *CLP IV* 8.5, *CLTb* 8.7, *CLH* 8.12, *CLL II* 8.9, *CLLd* 8.7, *CNP I* 82, *CNP II* 58, *CNI I* 180, *CNG* 308, *CNT IV* 83, *CNM* 80, *CNMN* 65, *CnT II* 24.7, *CnT III* 58.5, *CnT V* 80; PP 2.64, Vet 8.8; GP 1.115, 23 (cf. Mn 2.136, Y 1.116, Vās 13.56-7, Vi 32.16).

The main editions of H are identical with the exception of one minor variant in HH. The *CV*, *CL* and *CN* groups are identical with H, with the exception of two very minor variants. PP is identical with H, with the exception of one minor variant. Vet, and in particular its various MSs. and GP contain some variants and show differences in the text.

Footnotes to No. 86 : [1]*āyus* B in Vet [2]*karmaṁ* AD in Vet; *karmāṇi* (*ca* om.) *CŚlB* [3]*caritraṁ* GP [4]*vidyāti* c in Vet [5]*āyuḥ karma ca vidyā ca saukhyaṁ nidhanam* e in Vet; *vinayam* IS [6]*āy⁰ pañ°* tr. *CLM* [7]*'tāni visṛjyante* Vete [8]*'tāni hi* (*ca*) PP, *CVND* [9]*sūjyante* HH; *sṛjyante* B in Vet; *'tāni prapadyanti* IS; *'tāni vivicyante* GP; *vilikhyante* De in Vet [10]*jāyamānasya dehinaḥ* GP; *°stasya* B in Vet [11] *°sy'eva* D in Vet [12]*dehināṁ CŚlB*.

No. 87

avaśyaṁ bhāvino[1] *bhāvā bhavanti mahatām*[2] *api,*
[3]*nagnatvaṁ nīlakaṇṭhasya mahāhi-śayanaṁ hareḥ.*

Inevitably, the conditions that are to be, happen, even of the mighty. Nakedness [is the fate] of Nīlakaṇṭha (Śiva); sleep upon the great serpent [that] of Hari (Viṣṇu).

HJ Intr 28, HS Intr 27, HM Intr 28, HP Intr 18, HN Intr 17, HK Intr 28, HH 3.23-4, HC 6.3-4, IS 671; *CNP II* 248, *CNG* 227, *CNT IV* 256.

The main editions of H are identical. *CNP II* contains important changes in γδ.

Footnotes to No 87 : [1]*bhāvito* IS [2]*sarvatām CŚlB* [3]*maheśvarasya nagnatvaṁ samudraśa°* *CŚlB*.

No. 88

yasya tasya[1] *prasūto'pi*[2] *guṇavān pūjyate naraḥ,*
dhanur vaṁśaviśuddho'pi nirguṇaḥ kiṁ kariṣyati.[3]

Of whomever the son [is] endowed with good qualities, the man is honoured. A bow,—though faultless as to the cane (lineage)—is without the bowstring (without virtue), what will it accomplish ?

HJ Intr 23, HS Intr 22, HM Intr 23, HK Intr 23, HH 3.12-3, IS 5369; *CNW* 14, *CNPN* 48, *CNG* 29.

The main editions of H are identical with the exception of HK which contains one minor variant. *CNW*, *CNPN* and *CNG* contain minor variants.

Footnotes to No. 88 : [1]*kasya* HK; *yasyaṁ tasyaṁ* *CŚW*; *putra CSP* [2]*hi CŚW*; *prasūtas tu CŚP* [3]*paribhūyate CŚW*.

No. 89

dharmā'rtha-kāma-mokṣāṇāṁ[1] *yasyai*[2]*'ko'pi na vidyate*[3],
[4]*aja-gala-stanasye'va tasya*[5] *janma nirarthakam.*[6]

Virtue, wealth, pleasure, liberation,—he in whom not one is found, his birth [is] useless, like the pendulous excrescence on a goat's neck.

HJ Intr 26, HS Intr 25, HM Intr 26, HK Intr 26, HH 3.19-20, HC 5.19-20, IS 3120; *CVND* 13.10, *cf. CVND* 3.20, *cf. CVM* 3.6, *CvA* 3.6 (*cf.* 3.4), *CvṢ* 3.6, (*cf.* 3.4), *CvL I* 3.6 (*cf.* 3.4), *CvLd* 3.9, *cf. CvH* 3.7, *cf. CvP IV* 3.12, *cf. CvP V* 3.9, *cf. CvGt* 3.8, *cf. CvTb* 3.12, *cf. CvH* 3.10; *CSBD* 196, *CSB I*

1.97, *CSJ* 3.3, *CSC I* 2.96, *CSC II* 196, *CSB II* 196, *CSLd* 1.95; *CNP I* 86, *CNP II* 123, *CNI I* 26, *CNG* 195, *CNT IV* 87, *CNM* 85, *CNMN* 68, *cf. CnT II* 48, *cf. CnT III* 3.8, *cf. CnT* VI 46; Vet 22.11, BhŚ 544.

The main editions of H are identical with the exception HK and HC which contain one minor variant. The *CN* group and *CV* are identical with H. (*CVND* with the HK and HC editions). Other *CV* and *Cv* editions contain important variants in γδ. Vet contains important variants in β. BhŚ is identical with H, viz. with the HK and HC editions.

Footnotes to No. 89 : [1]*mokṣeṣu CV* in IS; *mokṣaś ca CVB* [2]*yasya CV* in IS; *yasyaiṣo CVN* [3]*mokṣaṁś ca yo na sādhyate naraḥ* D in Vet [4]*ajā°* HK, HC, ABDd in Vet, BhŚ, *CVND* (better); *mṛtatulyaḥ sa vijñeyas° CV* in IS; *janma-janmani martyeṣu maraṇaṁ tasya kevalaṁ CV* in IS; *ajāgaranamaḥ mo'pi nirartha tasya jīvitam CVB*; *janma janma mahad duḥkhaṁ CVF*; *janma janma manuṣyasya CVN* [5]*gataṁ CVG* [6]*nirarthakaḥ CNH*; *naraṇāṁ tasya kevalam CVF, CVN*.

No. 90

dāne tapasi śaurye[1] *ca*[2] *yasya na prathitaṁ*[3] *manaḥ*[4],
vidyāyām arthalābhe ca[5] [6]*mātur uccāra eva saḥ.*

He, whose mind [is] not intent on liberality, on piety and on heroism; on knowledge and on the acquisition of wealth, [is] verily but [his] mother's excrement.

HJ Intr 16, HS Intr 15, HM Intr 16, HK Intr 16, HH 2.23-4, HC Intr 5.7-8, IS 2761; *cf. CVND* 14.8, *cf. CVM* 14.6; *CRC* 8.36, *CRB* 8.36, *CRP* 8.35, *CRBh I* 8.35, *CRBh II* 8.34; *CNG* 110, *cf. CNP II* 142, *cf. CNT IV* 113, *cf. CNM* 110, *cf. CNMN* 79, *cf. CnT II* 11.6 & 17.2, *cf. CnT III* 7.28, *cf. CnT V* 46 & 7b 21. MBh. 5.132, 23b-24a; GP 1.115, 32; (ŚP 1477, SV 2731).

The main editions of H are identical with the exception of HK which contains one minor variant. The *CR* group is identical with H with the exception of two minor variants. The *CV* group contains a similar, but not identical aphorism (IS 2760). MBh, GP and ŚP contain a few minor variants. The H text is the nearest to *CRC*.

Footnotes to No. 90 : [1]*satye* MBh; *śau° ta° dā°* GP [2]*vā CRC* [3]*noccāritaṁ* MBh [4]*yaśaḥ* HK, MBh, GP, ŚP, *CRC* [5]*vā* MBh, GP, ŚP [6]*tasya janma nirarthakam* ŚP.

No. 91

[1]*ko dhanyo bahubhiḥ putraiḥ* [2]*kuśūlapūraṇāḍhakaiḥ,*
[3]*varam ekaḥ kulālambī yatra viśrūyate*[4] *pitā.*[5]

Who [is] fortunate by many sons, [mere empty] measures filling up a granary ? Better is one the supporter of his family, by whom the father is renowned.

HJ Intr 20, HS Intr 19, HM Intr 20, HK Intr 20, HH 3.6-7, HC 5.15-6, IS 1928, *cf. CVND* 3.17, *cf. CVM* 3.17, *cf. CvH* 3.11, *cf. CvL II* 3.3; *cf. CLA* 7.6, *cf. CLP V* 74, *cf. CLP IV* 7.8, *cf. CLTb* 7.6, *cf. CLH II* 9.4, *cf. CLL I* 7.6, *cf. CLLd* 7.4; *cf. CSBD* 186, *cf. CSB I* 2.87, *cf. CSJ* 2.93, *cf. CSC I* 2.86, *cf. CSC II* 186, *cf. CSB II* 185, *cf. CSLd* 2.85; *cf. CNP II* 281, *cf. CNI I* 177, *cf. CNG* 103.

The main editions of H and its various MSs. contain minor variants. *C* is identical with H in γδ only; this part contains some minor variants.

Footnotes to No. 91 : [1]αβ different in *C* [2]*kuśulā°* HM; *kuśūla°* IS; *kuśala°* HS (notes); *kūśalā°* HH; *kuśalā°* IS; [3]*eka eva ku° CLM* [4]*viśrāmyate CVND*; *viramate CŚlB* [5]*kulam CVND.*

No. 92

[1]*ko'rthaḥ* [2]*putreṇa jātena yo na vidvān na dhārmikaḥ,*[3]
[4]*kāṇena cakṣuṣā kiṁ vā cakṣuḥpīḍai'va kevalam.*[5]

What benefit [accrues] by a son born, who [is] neither learned nor virtuous ? Or what [is the use of] a sightless eye ? Indeed [such] an eye [is] trouble merely.

HJ Intr 12, HS Intr 11, HM Intr 12. HP Intr 12, HN Intr 11, HK Intr 12, HH 2.14-5, HC 4.14-5, IS 1941; *CVND* 4.9, *CVM* 4.5, *CRC* 7.68, *CRB* 7.63, *CRP* 7.62, *CRBh I* 7.61; PS Intr 4, PN Intr 3,PP Intr 3,Pts Intr 4, PRE Intr 3; VCsr 21.2; GP 1.114, 55; Bṛh 26.36b; NV 27.16.

The main editions of H are identical, with the exception of HN. αβ are only identical in H and other sources. The *CV* group contains in αβ one variant only.

Footnotes to No. 92 : [1]In PP, Pts, GP, *C* αβ are γδ cf. fn. 4 [2]*tena tu putrena* VyN 300 in Bṛh; DāBh 101 in Bṛh [3]*vidvān adhārmnikaḥ* B in PS; *bhaktimān* PP, Pts, *CVND*; (*śa*)*ktimān* M in PP [4]*tayā gava kiṁ kriyate* (*śriyate* E in PS) *yā na doghdrī na garbhiṇī* PS, PRE, VC, GP, Bṛh, *CRC*; *kiṁ tayā kriyate dhenvā yā sute na dugdhadā* (*na doghdrī na garbhiṇī CVND*) PP, Pts, NV [5]*yat phalam* HN, N in HP.

No. 93

[1]*varam eko guṇī putro* [2]*na ca mūrkha-śatair api*[3],
ekaś candras[4] *tamo hanti na ca tārā-gaṇair api.*[5]

Better one accomplished son. [There is] no [benefit] even by hundreds of fools. One moon dispels the darkness. [It is] not [dispersed] even by hosts of stars.

HJ Intr 17, HS Intr 16, HM Intr 17, HK Intr 17, HH 2.25-6, HC 5.9-10, IS 5971; *CVND* 4.6, *CVM* 4.4, *cf. CLA* 7.5, *cf. CLL I* 7.5, *CRC* 7.74, *CRP* 7.65, *CRBh I* 7.64, *CRBh II* 7.34, *CNJV* 10, *CNW* 23, *CNPN* 89, *CNMN* 8, *CNŚC* 8, *CNŚ* 8, *CNŚT* 8, *CNŚK* 10, *CNL* 48, *CnT I* 31 v.l.; GP 1.114, 58; cf. BhP 10. 114, 58.

The main editions of H are almost identical; variants are noted in HS and HK. The *CN* group contains only a few minor variants. *CNJV* is identical with the main editions of H. β is different in *CRC*, while γδ are different in the *CV* and *CL* groups. The H text is nearest to the *CN* group. GP is very different from the H and *C* texts and may be considered as a different aphorism.

Footnotes to No. 93: [1]*eko'pi guṇavān putro nirguṇaiś ca* (°*ṇena śatena kim* GP) *śatair varaḥ* GP, *CVND* [2]*nirguṇena śatena kim CRC* [3] °*śatany api* HK, *CŚW*, *CŚN* [4]*candro* HS [5] °*gaṇo'pi ca* HK, *CŚN* (*ca* om. in *CŚN*; better); *gaṇas tathā CŚW*; *tārā-śatair api CŚP*; *tārā-sahasraśaḥ CRC*; *tārāḥ sahasraśaḥ CVND*; *candro hanti tamāṁsy eko na ca jyotiḥ sahasraśaḥ* GP.

No. 94

[1]*ṛṇa-kartā pitā śatrur mātā ca vyabhicāriṇī*[2],
[3]*bhāryā rūpavatī*[4] *śatruḥ putraḥ śatrur apaṇḍitaḥ.*[5]

A father who contracts debts [is] an enemy and [so is] an unchaste mother. A beautiful wife [is] an enemy. An unlearned son [is] an enemy.

HJ Intr 21, HS Intr 20, HM Intr 21, HK Intr 21, HH 3.8-9, IS 1330; *CVND* 6.11, *CVM* 6.3; *CNJV* 43, *CNS* 19, *CNW* 29, *CNF* 92, *CNP I* 57, *CNT IV* 57, *CNM* 57, *CNMN* 50; *cf. CR* 1.25.

The main editions of H are identical, *CNJV*, *CNS* and *CVND* are identical with H.; minor variants are noted in *CNF*, *CNW* and *CRC*; important differences are noted in *CNP I*.

Footnotes to No. 94: [1]*ṛṇaṁ* IS; *pitā ca ṛṇavān CRC* [2]*dvicāriṇī* IS; *duścāriṇī tathā CŚF*; *śatrur vicāriṇī CŚW*; *śatrur aśīlinī CRC*; *duścāriṇī ripuḥ CNH* [3]*avinītā ripur bhāryā putro ripur apaṇḍitaḥ CNH* [4]*pararatā CŚF* [5]*śatruḥ kupaṇḍitaḥ CŚF*.

No. 95

[1]*mātā śatruḥ*[2] *pitā* [3]*vairī yena bālo*[4] *na pāṭhitaḥ*[5],
[6]*na śobhate sabhā-madhye haṁsa-madhye vako*[7] *yathā.*

The mother [is] an enemy, the father a foe, by whom a child [is] not instructed. He shines not in company. [He is] as a heron amongst swans.

HJ Intr 38, HS Intr 37, HM Intr 38, HP Intr 25, HN Intr 23, HK Intr 38, HH 4.20-1, HC 7.1-2, IS 4800; *CVND* 2.11, *CVM* 2.11; *CvA* 2.15, *CvṢ* 2.15, *CvW* 2.14, *CvP IV* 2.15, *CvP V* 2.14, *CvGt* 2.18, *CvTb* 2.15, *CvL I* 2.15, *CvL II* 2.15, *CvLd* 2.15; *cf. CRC* 7.76, *cf. CRB* 7.66, *cf. CRP* 7.66, *cf. CRT* 8.42, *cf. CRBh I* 7.65, *cf. CRBh II* 7.65; *CNJV* 9, *CNS* 72, *CNW* 17, *CNPN* 181, *CNG* 93, *CNT IV* 159, *CNM* 156, *CNMN* 122, *CNŚ* 41, *CNNM* 7, *CNŚT* 7, *CNŚK* 9, *CNI II* 94, *CnT II* 3.11, *CnT III* 2.15, *CnT VI* 37.

The main editions of H are identical with the exception of HP and HN where two words are transferred in β. The *CN* group, with few exceptions is identical with H. The *CV* and *Cv* groups (with the exception of *CvP IV* and *CvP V* which are identical with H) and *CR* groups contain several important variants.

Footnotes to No. 95 : [1]*dviṣantau pitarau manye putro yābhyāṁ na pāṭhitaḥ CRC*; *mā° vai° pi° śa°* tr. IS [2]*ripuḥ CVND* ; *vairī CVND* in *CKr* [3]*śatrur bālo yabhyāṁ na* (*yena na* IS) *pāṭhyate CVND*; *°rī yabhyām CVND* (var.) [4]*ye° bā°* tr. HP,HN [5]*bālo yena na pāṭhita CVN*; *pāṭhyate CVND* (var.) [6]*sabhāmadhye na śobhante* (*sobhante* IS) *CŚH* [7]*vakā CŚH*.

No. 96

A similar aphorism to that found in HJ Intr 13[1] is also found in some *C* aphorisms (*cf.* IS 4907); it deals with sons.

Footnotes to No. 96 :
[1]*ajāta-mṛta-mūrkhāṇāṁ varam ādyau na cā'ntimaḥ,*
sakṛd duḥkha-karāv ādyāv antimas tu pade pade.

* * *

Compare also Nos. 26, 46, 47 and 109.

21. *Friends, Foes and Various Types of Association*

No. 97

[1]*śokārāti-bhaya-trāṇaṁ*[2] *prīti-viśrambha-bhājanam,*[3]
[4]*kena ratnam idaṁ*[5] *sṛṣṭaṁ*[6] *"mitram" ity akṣara-dvayam.*

By whom was created this jewel—"*mitram,*" a word of

two syllables, the preserver from sorrows, enemies and danger, the depository of affection and confidence ?

HJ 1.225, HS 1.203, HM 1.208, HP 1.169, HN 1.170, HK 1.210, HH 38.2-3, HC 50.18-9, IS 6527; *CRC* 7.2, *CRB* 7.2, *CRP* 7.2, *CRV* 7·2, *CRBh I* 7.2, *CRB*; *II* 7.2, *CRCa I* 7.2, *CRCa II* 49; *CNG* 134; PS 2.83 & 4.3, PN 1.79 & 4.3, PT 2.170 & 4.7, PTem 2.152, PP 2.195, Pts 2.179, PRE 2.95 & 4.7, GP 1.114,2.

The main editions and various MSs. of H. contain minor variants. *CRC* is identical with H. GP contains one minor variant. Pañc. contains important variants.

Footnotes to No. 97 : [1]*śokārati* B in HP, IP in HK, PT, PP, PRE; *śokārti-bhayasaṁ-trāṇaṁ* HP; *prāpte bhaye paritrāṇaṁ* Pts; *śoka-trāṇaṁ* GP [2]*paritrāṇaṁ* HS, BBh; °*ṇama* A in PS 4.3 [3]*bhājana* A in PS; *kājanam* P in His; *kāraṇam* IS; °*visra*° PT, PRE, BBh [4]*kenedam* (*nedam* A in PS) *sṛṣṭam amṛtaṁ mitra* (*mitram* A in PS) *ity ak*° NA in PS [5]*sarvaṁ* add. *ψ* in PP (*contra metrum*) [6]*syṛṣṭaṁ* M in PP.

No. 98

āpatsu mitraṁ jānīyāt[1] *yuddhe*[2] *śūram ṛṇe*[3] *śucim,*
[4]*bhāryāṁ kṣīṇeṣu vitteṣu vyasaneṣu ca bāndhavān.*

In misfortunes one may know a friend; in battle a hero; in a debt, an honest man; a wife, in reduced fortunes; and kinsmen in afflictions.

HJ 1.74, HS 1.66, HM 1.71, HP 1.54, HN 1.55, HK 1.73, HH 18.1-2, HC 24.10-1, IS 954; *CRC* 2.18, *CRB* 2.15, *CRP* 2.15, *CRT* 2.8 *CRBh I* 2.15, *CRBh II* 2.12, GP 1.109, 8.

The main editions of H are almost identical. *CRC* is different in γδ; it is nearer to GP than to H.

Footnotes to No. 98 : [1]*jānīyād* HM, HP, HN, HS, HK, Boltz 10.78, *CRC* (better) [2]*dhane* HP, HN; *vane* IS; *raṇe* GP, *CRC* [3]*rahaṁ* GP, *CRC* [4]*bhāryāñ ca vibhave* (°*va CRC*) *kṣīṇe durbhikṣe ca priyātithim* GP, *CRC*.

No. 99

na [1]*mātari na dāreṣu*[2] *na so'darye na cā'tmaje*[3],
viśvāsas[4] *yadṛśaḥ puṁsāṁ yādṛṅmitre*[5] *svabhavaje.*[6]

Men have not such a confidence in a mother, or in a wife, or in a brother, or in a son, as they have in a friend by natural disposition.

HJ 1.222, HS 1.200, HM 1.205, HP 1.166, HN 1.167, HK 1.207, HH 37.19-20, HC 50.8-9, IS 3370; *CRC* 7.3, *CRB* 7.3,

CRP 7.3, *CRBh I* 7.3, *CRCa I* 7.3; PS 2.79, PN 1.75, PP 2.190, PRE 2.89; GP 1.114,4.

The various editions of H are almost identical. GP is identical with H. P contains minor variants. *C* contains very important variants; αβ are different.

Footnotes to No. 99 : [1]*mātā-pitṛ-dāreṣu sodareṣu na bandhuṣu CRC, CRB* [2]*na dāre vā* E in PS [3]*cātmani* HP, HN [4]*viśrāmas* PRE; *viśrambhas* PP; *visrambhas CRC* [5]*yādṛg mitre* HM, HP, HN; *yāvan mitre* HH [6]*nirantare* NA in PS, PP, PRE; *nirantaram* PS, *CRC*.

Nos. 100, 100A

[1]*utsave vyasane*[2] *cai'va*[3] *durbhikhṣe rāṣṭra-viplave,*[4]
rāja-dvāre śmaśāne[5] *ca*[6] *yas tiṣṭhati*[7] *sa*[8] *bāndhavaḥ.*[9]

He who stands [by one] at a feast, and also in affliction, in famine, in an invasion of the country, at the king's gate, and at the cemetery, is a kinsman.

HJ 1.75 & 4.66, HS 1.67, HM 1.72, & 4.62, HP 4.66, HN 4.66, HK 1.74 & 4.67, HH 18,3-4, HC 24.12-3 & 149.3-4, IS 1221; *CVND* 1.12, *CVM* 1.15, *CvA* 1.12, *CvṢ* 1.12, *CvW* 1.14, *CvP IV* 1.12, *CvP V* 1.12, *CvGt* 1.13, *CvTb* 1.13, *CvH* 1.13, *CvI* 1.14, *CvL I* 1.12, *CvL II* 1.13, *CvLd* 1.12, *CSBD* 84, *CSB I* 1.84, *CSJ* 1.84, *CSC I* 1.84, *CSC II* 84, *CSB II* 83, *CSLd* 1.84, *CNJV* 17, *CNS* 17, *CNF* 16, *CNPh* 15, *CNPN* 19, *CNP II* 161, *CNI I* 131, *CNT IV*, 155,*CNM* 153, *CNMN* 119, *CNŚC* 15, *CNŚ* 15, *CNŚL* 72, *CNG* 47, *CNNM* 15, *CNŚT* 15, *CNŚK* 20, *CNL* 9, *CNI II* 25, *CnT II* 25, *CnT III* 1.15, *CnT VI* 16; Pts 5.41.

The main editions of H contain minor variants. *C* contains several minor variants; *C* is nearer to Pts than to H. The *CN* group is the nearest to H. Pts contains several minor variants.

Footnotes to Nos. 100-100A : [1]*āture* Pts; *CVND, CVB CVF, CVG, CVK, CVN, CŚlB*; *ātulya vāmaśaṁpāpte CVB* (var.); *āhave* HJ 4.66, HN, HK (Pā in HK as above); *āhāra sparśane* L in HP [2]*vyasanaṁ CVN*, *visanaṁ CVG* [3]*prāpte* Pts, *CVND, CVB, CVF, CVG, CVK, CVN, CŚlB*; *vyāpte* IS; *yuddhe* HM 4.62 [4]*rāṣṭrasaṁplave* HS; *rājavigrahe* A in HP; *śatru-saṅkaṭe* Pts, *CVND, CVK*; *śatru-vigraha* HJ 4.66, HP, HN, *CŚF, CŚH, CŚN, CŚP, CVB, CVF, CVG, CVN, CŚlB*; *śatrusaṅgrahe* IS [5]*śmasane CŚH* [6]*vā CVB* [7]*tiṣṭhayaste* N in HP; *tiṣṭheyus te* HN [8]*hi* N in HP, HN [9]*bāndhavāḥ* N in HP, HN.

No. 101

parokṣe kārya-hantāraṁ pratyakṣe priyavādinam,[1]
varjayet[2] [3]*tādṛśaṁ mitraṁ viṣa-kumbhaṁ*[4] *payo-mukhaṁ*[5].

One should avoid such a friend as mars [one's] business behind [one's] back, [and] speaks kindly to [one's] face. He [is] a jar of poison with milk on the surface.

HJ 1.79, HS 1.71, HM 1.76, HK 1.78, HH 18. 19-20, HC 25.9-10, IS 3979; *CVND* 2.5, *CVV* 2.5, *CVM* 2.1, *CvA* 2.5, *CvṢ* 2.5, *CvH* 2.5, *CvP V* 2.5, *CvP IV* 2.5, *CvGt* 2.5, *CvTb* 2.5, *CvI* 2.5, *CvL I* 2.5, *CvL II* 2.5, *CvLd* 2.5, *CRC* 8.50, *CRB* 8.53; *CRP* 8.50, *CRBh I* 8.50, *CRT* 8.26 *CSBD* 261, *CSB I* 3.61, *CSJ* 3.69, *CSC I* 3.60, *CSC II* 261, *CSB II* 261, *CSLd* 3.61, *CNJV* 18, *CNS* 58, *CNW* 74, *CNF* 42, *CNN* 49, *CNPh* 123, *CNPN* 11,*CNP II* 222, *CNI I* 87, *CNG* 164, *CNT IV* 152,*CNM* 150, *CNMN* 116, *CNŚC* 16, *CNŚ* 16, *CNŚL* 73, *CNNM* 16, *CNŚT* 16, *CNŚK* 21, *CNI II* 19, *CnT II* 3.1, *CnT III* 25, *CnT VI* 26; PM 1.78; GP 1.115, 48; Bhś 597, in Sūrya's Sūktiratnākara (89.6) attributed to Kauṭilya.

The main editions of H are almost identical. The *CN CV*, *Cv*, and *CS* groups are identical with H; the *CR* group contains one variant in γ. PM and Bhś are identical with H. GP is different in δ.

Footnotes to No. 101 : [1] °*vāditaḥ* IS [2]*varjaye* IS (printing error) [3]*kuṭilaṁ bandhuṁ CRC* [4]*viṣakumbha* edd. in HS, HH [5]*viṣargabha payo yathā* IS; *māyāmayarin tathā* GP.

No. 102

paro'pi hitavān[1] *bandhur bandhur apy ahitaḥ*[2] *paraḥ*[3],
ahito dehajo vyādhir hitam āraṇyaṁ[4] *auṣadham.*

Even an enemy, [if] kind, [is] a friend. A kinsman, [if] unkind, [is] an enemy. A distemper, though bred in the body, [is] malignant. A drug [though] grown in the woods, [is] healing.

HJ 3.101, HS 3.98, HM 3.98, HP 3.96, HN 3.96, HK 3.98, HH 88.14-5, HC 117.13-4, IS 3988; *CRC* 1.20, *CRB* 1.18, *CRP* 1.20, *CRT* 1.11 *CRBh I* 1.20, *CRBh II* 1.20, *CRCa II* 5; *CNF* 43, *CNN* 45, *CNPh* 91, *CNI I* 133, *CNG* 13, *CNT IV* 154, *CNM* 152, *CNMN* 118; GP 1.108, 14; BhŚ 598; cf. *NV* 27.9, (273. 18-9; attributed to *C*) and 29.76 (334.9-10; attributed to Śukra).

The main editions and various MSs. of H contain only one minor variant. The *CN* and *CR* groups are identical with H; *CNN* contains one minor variant. GP, BhŚ and NV 27.9 are identical with H; NV 29.76 contains one minor variant.

Footnotes to No. 102 : [1]*hi hito* HP, HN, Pp in HS; *api hitaḥ CNN*. (var.) [2]*ahita* NV 29.76 [3]*svayaṁ CNN* [4]*araṇaṁ CNN* (var.)

No. 103

na kaścit kasyacin[1] *mitraṁ na kaścit kasyacid*[2] *ripuḥ,*[3]
[4]*vyavahāreṇa mitrāṇi jāyante*[5] *ripavas tathā.*

No one [is] the friend of any one, no one [is] the enemy of any one. By behaviour, friends as well as enemies are produced.

HJ 1.73, HS 1.65, HM 1.70, HK 1.72, HH 17.15-6, HC 23.17-8, IS 3189; *cf. CRC* 7.1, *cf. CRB* 7.1, *cf CRP* 7.1, *cf. CRT.* 7.1, *cf. CRBh I* 71., *cf. CRBh II* 7.1, *II cf. CRCa I* 7.1; *cf. CSBD* 77, *cf. CSB I* 1.77, *cf. CSJ* 1.77, *cf. CSC I* 1.77, *cf. CSC II* 77, *cf. CSB II* 76, *cf. CSLd* 1.77, *cf. CNJV* 23, *cf. CNS* 51, *cf. CNI I* 58, *cf. CNG* 133, *cf. CNNM* 107, *cf. CNŚC* 21, *cf. CNŚ* 21; *cf. CNŚL* 11, *cf. CNNM* 24, *cf. CNŚT* 20; GP 1.114,1.

The main editions of H are almost identical. All groups of *C* are different in γδ; they are nearer to GP than to H.

Footnotes to No. 103 : [1]*kasyacid* Boltz 8.48 [2]*kasyacit* Boltz 8.48, *CVB* [3]*priyaḥ CVB* [4]*kāraṇad eva jāyante mitrāṇi ri°* GP, *CVB*; *kāraṇena hi jānāti mitrāṇi ca ripūṁs tathā CŚH, CŚN*; *avasthātaḥ prajāyante mitrāṇi ri° CRC, CRB* [5]*jayanti* HH.

No. 104

[1]*sakṛd duṣṭaṁ*[2] [3]*yo tu mitraṁ* [4]*punaḥ* [5]*saṁdhātum icchati*[6],
[7]*sa mṛtyum*[8] *eva*[9] *gṛhṇāti*[10] *garbham*[11] *aśvarari*[12] *yathā*[13].

He who consents to re-admit to friendship a friend who has once offended, receives death like a she-mule an embryo.

HJ 2.147, HS 2.140, HM 2.148, HP 2.135, HN 2.134, HK 2.146, HH 65.11-2, HC 86.9-10, IS 6656; *CRP* 3.15, *CRT* 3.15, *CRC* 3.15, *CRB* 3.15; *CRBh I* 3.15, *CRBh II* 3.16, *CRCa I* 3.12; *CNJV* 19, *CNS* 92, *CNPh* 22, *CNP II* 225, *CNI I* 114, *CNT IV* 150, *CNM* 148, *CNMN* 114, *CNŚ* 105, *CNNM* 17, *CNŚK* 78; PS 2.19, PN 1.17, PT 2.29, PTem 2.29, PP 2.27 & 4.13, Pts 2.32 & 4.14, PRE 2.19; GP 1.110, 19; cf. MBh 12.140, 30, cf. *MBh* 1.142, 81b-82a,

The main editions contain several minor variants. The *CN* and *CR* groups contain some minor variants. *CNP II* is quite different and corrupt. Other sources contain minor variants.

Footnotes to No. 104 : [1]*sakṣad CŚlB*; *daṇḍeno'panataṁ śatruṁ yo rājā na niyacchati* MBh 12.140, 30; °*rum anugṛhṇāti yo naraḥ* MBh 1.142, 81b (cf. SV 2757) [2]*dṛṣṭan* A in PS [3]*tu yo* HS, HM, HK, PS, PT, PRE, *CRC*; *ca yo* Pts 4.14, PP, GP; *ta yo CNP II* ; *hi tu* IS; *ya ca* codd, in HS; *tu yan* HP, HN, HH; *ca mitraṁ yaḥ CŚH, CŚN*; *yan mi°* IS; *apīṣṭaṁ yaḥ pu°* Pts 2.32; *apoṣṭaṁ* IS [4]*dhānam itsati* (*sic* !) *CNP II* [5]*punas* PT (PTem as above) [6]*ichati* HS; *icchasi* I in PS; *arhati* Bh in PP; *arhasi* ϕ in PP [7]*yathā sa mṛtyu CNP II* [8]*mṛtyur* P in HS; [9]*upa°* PS, PT, PP 4.13, Pts, PRE MBh, *CŚH, CŚN, CRC* [10]*gṛhṇīyāt* N in PS, GP; *gṛṇiyād* MBh 1.142, 82a (MBh 12.140, 30 as above); *gṛṇhīyāt* A in PS [11]*garbhad* PP 2.27 (Bh ϕ in PP as above); *gebham CNP II*; *gabhām* MBh 1.142, 82 [12]*aśvataro* PTem (printing error); *karkaṭikā* IS; *karkaṭakī CŚN* [13]*tathā CNP II*.

No. 105

rahasya-bhedo yācñā ca naiṣṭhuryaṁ[1] *cala-cittatā,*
krodho[2] *niḥsatyatā*[3] *dyūtam*[4] *etan mitrasya dūṣaṇam.*

Betraying a secret, importunity, harshness, fickleness of mind, anger, falsehood, gaming—these [are] the faults of a friend.

HJ 1.100, HS 1.91, HM 1.97, HP 1.72, HN 1.74, HK 1.99, HH 21.6-7, HC 29. 1-2, IS 5722, *cf. CRB* 1.6, Nepalese MS 243 transcribed by Klatt, quoted in *CKr.*

The main editions of H contain some minor variants; variants are noted in different MSs.

Footnotes to No. 105 : [1]*caiśaryaṁ* Pp in HS [2]*krodha* B in HP [3]*niḥsattvatā* HP, HN, P in HS [4]*dyutam* HH (wronglty).

No. 106

yathā kāṣṭhaṁ ca kāṣṭhaṁ ca sameyātām maho'dadhau[1],
[2]*same'tya cā*[3] *vyapeyātāṁ* [4]*tadvad bhūta-samāgamaḥ.*

As a piece of drift wood and [another] piece of drift wood may come together in the mighty receptacle of waters, and having met, may part company; even such [is] the meeting of human beings.

HJ 4.72, HS 4.66, HM 4.69, HP 4.73, HN 4.73, HK 4.74, HH 111. 21-1, HC 149.19-20, IS 5093, *CRC* 6.54, *CRB*

6.43, *CRP* 6.39, *CRBh I* 6.40; MBh 12.28,36 & 12.174, 16; R 2.105, 26.

The main editions and various MSs. of H are almost identical. *CRC* is identical with H. MBh is identical with H. R contains some variants, particularly in δ.

Footnotes to No. 106 : [1]*mahārṇave* R [2]*sameta* N in HP; °*sma*° P in HS [3]*tu* R [4]*kālamā sādya kañcana* R; *sthitvā kiñcit kṣaṇāntaram* RG.

No. 107

saṁsāra-viṣa-vṛkṣasya[1] *dve* [2]*eva madhure*[3] *phale,*
[4]*kāvyā'mṛtarasā'svādaḥ* [5]*saṅgamaḥ*[6] *sajjanaiḥ*[7] *saha.*

The poisonous tree of the world bears indeed two sweet fruits; enjoyment of the taste of the nectar of poetry [and] association with the good.

HJ 1.62, HS 1.145, HM 1.151, HP 1.117, HN 1,118, HK 1.153, HH 28.23-4, HC 39.1-2, IS 6636; *CVND* 16.18, *CVM* 16.3; *CLṢ* 8.11; *CNP II* 289, *CNG* 258, *C NT IV* 215, *CNM* 178, *CNMN* 143, *CnT II* 28.8, *CnT VII* 69; VN 3.

The main editions of H contain some variants in β and δ. *CVND* is different in γδ. *CNP II* contains minor variants. Other sources contain minor variants.

Footnotes to No. 107 : [1] °*kūṭā-vṛ* *CVND*; °*kaṭu-vṛ* *CVND* (var.), *CNP II*; *kaṭukā-rakṣasya* IS [2]*atra HM, HC*; *amṛtopame* HP, HC; *phale amṛtopame* I in HK, VN, *CVND*, *CNP II*; *evā'mṛtavat* B in HP; *phale cā'mṛtopame* HH; *eva rasava-phatle* HK (printing error?) ; *yamṛtopame* IS [3]*rasavat* HM, HP, HN, HC, Pp in HS [4]*subhāṣitaṁ ca sukhādaṁ saṅgatiḥ sujane jane* (°*naiḥ saha*) *CVND*; *subhāṣitaṁ ca susvādu* IS; *subhāṣita* (°*tā* IS) *rasāsvāda* *CNP II*; °*svāda* VN [5]*saṅgatiḥ sujane jane* IS (cf. fn. 4) [6]*ālāpaḥ* VN, *CNP II*, *saṅgamaḥ* IS [7]*sujanaiḥ* HM, HN, HC; *svajanaiḥ* Pp in HS.

No. 108

hīna-sevā na kartavyā kartavyo mahad-āśrayaḥ[1],
[2]*payo'pi śauṇḍiki-haste*[3] [4]*vāruṇī'ty abhidhīyate.*

Court should not be paid to the base. To the great must resort for protection be made. Even water in the hand of the mistress of a dram-shop, is called spirituous liquor.

HJ 3.11, HS 3.11, HM 3.11, HP 3.11, HN 3.11, HK 3.11, HH 74.24-5, HC 98.20-1, IS 7402; *CNW* 93, *CNPN* 66, *CNL* 53.

The main editions and various MSs. of H are identical,

with the exception of HS which is different in γδ. The *CN* group is almost identical with the HS edition.

Footnotes to No. 108 : [1]*mahat-aśrayaḥ* N in HP [2]*ajā* (*ajaḥ CŚP*) *siṁha-prasadena vane carati nirbhayam* (°*bhayā CŚW*; °*bhayaḥ CŚP*) HS, *CŚW*, *CŚP* [3]*śauṇḍinī*° HS (notes), HP, HN; *sauṇḍinī*° IS [4]*madyam ity* N in HP, HN.

No. 109

guṇāguṇajñā guṇino[1] *bhavanti*
te nirguṇaṁ[2] *prāpya bhavanti doṣāḥ,*
[3]*āsvādya-toyāḥ prabhavanti nadyaḥ*
samudram āsādya bhavanty apeyāḥ.[4]

Those possessed of excellent qualities become judges of merit and demerit. Falling in with vicious [company], they become vitiated. Rivers rise having their waters sweet, but having reached the sea, they become undrinkable.

HJ Intr 47, HS Intr 47, HM Intr 47, HK Intr 47, HH 5.22-3, IS 2130, *cf. CRC* 8.127, *cf. CRP* 8.118, *cf. CRT* 8.64, *cf. CRBh I* 8.129, *cf. CRBh II* 8.76, *cf. CNI I* 44; PS 1.87, PN 2.66, PT 1.100, PTem 1.92, PRE 1.99; GR 5.

The main editions of H are identical with the exception of HM and HK which contain some minor variants in *a*. *CRC* is almost identical with H but is nearer to PT. Pañc. and GR contain some minor variants.

Footnotes to No. 109 : [1]*guṇāguṇajdeṣu guṇā* (*guṇī* PT, PRE, NAB in PS) HM, HK, PS, PT, PRE, GR, *CRC* [2]*nirguṇān* PS (NABC in PS as above) [3]*susvādutoyaḥ* GR; *susvādutoya prabhavā* (*pravahā* PT, PRE, B in PS, *CRC*) *hi* PS, PT, PRE, *CRC*; *svasādutoya* N in PS [4]*apeyaḥ* B in PS.

Compare also Nos. 26, 55, 56, 71 and 82.

22. *Guests and Hosts*

No. 110

uttamasyā'pi [1]*varṇasya nico'pi*[2] *gṛham āgataḥ,*[3]
[4]*pūjanīyo yathāyogyaṁ*[5] [6]*sarva-deva-mayo'tithiḥ.*

Even one of low caste, when come to the house of one of high caste, ought to be suitably entertained. A guest is an impersonation of all the deities.

HJ 1.65, HS 1.57, HM 1.62, HK 1.64, HH 16.7-8, HC 22.3-4, & 31.3-4, IS 1177; *CvW* 4.19, *CvGt* 4.7, *CvL* 4.7

v.l., *CvLd* 4.18; *CSBD* 90, *CSB I* 1.90, *CSJ* 1.90, *CSC II* 90, *CSB II* 89, *CSLd* 1.90; *CNW* 50, *cf. CNP II* 54, *cf CNI I* 34, *cf. CNG* 114, *CnT II* 5.8, *CnT III* 4.3, *CnT VI* 58; Vet 19.2.

The main editions of H are identical. *C* contains important variants and in all groups is nearer to Vet than to H. Vet contains important variants.

Footnotes to No. 110 : [1] *'tha* e in Vet [2]*nicā'pi CVB*; *vā CVN* [3]*āgata CVB* [4]*tasya pūjā vidhātavyā* B in Vet, *CŚW*; *vipro vā yadi vā śudraḥ* e in Vet; *bālo vā yadi* (*vātha CŚlB*) *vā vṛddhaḥ* (*vālo vā taruṇo vṛddha CVN*) *sarvasyā'bhyāgato guruḥ CVG, CVN, CSlB* [5]*yathā-nyāyaṁ* Vet, *CVB* [6]*sarvasyābhyāgato guruḥ* Vet, *CVB*; *sarvatrābhyāgato CŚW* (cf. fn. 4).

No. 111

[1]*gurur*[2] *agnir*[3] *dvijātīnāṁ*[4] *varṇānāṁ brāhmaṇo guruḥ,*
patir eko[5] *guruḥ*[6] *strīṇāṁ sarvatrā*[7] *'bhyāgato*[8] *guruḥ*[9].

Fire [is] the superior of the twice born. Of the [four] classes, the Brahmaṇ [is] the superior. The husband [is] the sole superior of wives. Everywhere the guest [is] the superior.

HJ 1.113, HS 1.101, HM 1.107, HP 1.47, HK 1.62, HH 16.3-4, HC 21.18-9 & 31-2, IS 2172; *CVND* 5.1, *CVM* 5.1, *CvA* 4.5, *CvṢ* 4.5, *CvW* 4.5, *CvP IV* 4.6, *CvP V* 4.5, *CvGt* 4.6, *CvTb* 4.6, *CvL I* 4.5, *CvL II* 4.5, *CvLd* 4.5, *CSBD* 89, *CSB I* 1.89, *CSJ* 1.88, *CSC I* 1.89, *CSC II* 89, *CSB II* 88, *CSLd* 1.89, *CNJV* 49, *CNS* 33, *CNW* 48, *CNF* 77, *CNPh* 97, *CNPN* 39, *CNP II* 232, *CNI I* 33, *CNŚC* 48, *CNŚ* 47, *CNŚL* 80, *CNNM* 39, *CNŚT* 43, *CNŚK* 43, *CNL* 16 & 98, *CNI II* 81, *CnT II* 5.11, *CnT III* 4.6, *CnT VI* 61; PP 1.257, PD 305. 84; Śto 325.4-5.

The main editions of H are almost identical. The *CN* group contains only a few minor variants (*CNW*, *CNH*, *CNS*, *CNP II*, *CvP V*, *CvTb*, and *CSB I* & *II* are identical with H). The *CN* group is the nearest to H. Other sources contain some minor variants.

Footnotes to No. 111 : [1]*gu° pa°* tr. *CVND* [2]*garur* H in Śto (wrongly) [3]*vahnir CŚP* [4]*dvijatīnāṁ CŚF* (wrongly) [5]*eka* Pr in PP; *eva CŚF. CVND* [6]*gurus* PD [7]*sarvasyā°* HS, Śto, PP, PD, *CŚN*, *CVND* [8]*bhagavato CŚF* (var.) [9]*ripu CVF.*

No. 112

[1]*nirguṇeṣv api sattveṣu*[2] *dayāṁ kurvanti sādhavaḥ,*
[3]*na hi saṁharate jyotsnāṁ*[4] [5]*candraś cāṇḍāla-veśmani*[6].

The good show pity even to worthless beings. The moon withholds not its light from the hovel of the Cāṇḍāla.

HJ 1.63, HS 1.55, HM 1.60, HP 1.46, HN 1.48, HK 1.61, HH 16.1-2, HC 21.16-7, IS 3755; *CRC* 3.50, *CRBh II* 8.43; *CNPh* 162, *CNŚC* 18, *CNŚ* 18, *CNŚT* 79; NM 1.42; Pras 7.3.

The main editions of H are almost identical; variants are noted in various MSs. *CRC* is identical with H (HK edition). Other sources contains some important variants.

Footnotes to No. 112 : [1]*durjaneṣv api* P in HS [2]*prāṇiṣu* Pras (notes); *saṁteṣu* IS [3]*aśvibhyāṁ mocitā grastā pakṣinī* (*pakṣistrī* g in NM) *varttikā śubhā* (*śunā* g in NM) NM [4]*jyetsnāṁ* HC (wrongly); *jyosnā* IS; *jyotsnāś* IS; *jyetsnāṁ* IS [5]*candraḥ ścāṇḍa°* IS [6] *°veśmanaḥ* HK, *CRC*; *veśmasu* Pras ; *°caṇḍāla°* IS.

* * *

Compare also No. 50.

23. *Servants; Service*

No. 113

maunān[1] *mūrkhaḥ*[2] *pravacana-paṭur vātulo*[3] *jalpako*[4] *vā*[5],
[6]*kṣāntyā bhīrur yadi na sahate prāyaśo nā'bhijātaḥ,*[7]
[8]*ghṛṣṭaḥ pārśve* [9]*vasati niyataṁ* [10]*dūrataś cā'pragalbhaḥ*[11],
-sevā-dharmaḥ parama-gahano yogināṁ apy agamyaḥ.[12]

For [his] silence [he is thought] a fool; [if] fluent in speech, [he is] crazy or a babbler; by patient submission [he is regarded as] timid; if he cannot endure [bad treatment, he is] for the most part [considered] ill-bred. Does he sit at [your] side ?—[he is] sure to be intrusive; at a distance ? —diffident. The duty of service [is] extremely difficult, [if not] unattainable, even to those who have acquired superhuman power.

HJ 2.25, HS 2.26, HM 2.26, HK 2.26, HH 43.18-21, HC 57.17-20 & 98.9-12, IS 4987; *cf. CNI* 253; PD 306. 98; Vet 4.6; Bhś. 35.

The main editions of H are identical. PD, Vet and in particular Bhś and their various MSs. contain minor variants.

Footnotes to No. 113 : [1]*maṁdān* J_2 in BhŚ [3]*mākhaḥ* PD, Vet (D in Vet as above); *mūkaḥ* BhŚ; *paṭu vaṭiko* c in Vet [3]*vātalo* BhŚ; *vācako* PD, F_3 $Y_{3,6,8}$ $TG_{1,4}$ M in BhŚ; *vātako* H_{1t2} Ic in BhŚ, *vātakī*, A_3 H_{1c} It in BhŚ; *vātuki* D in BhŚ; *vādako* $Y_{2,4,5,7}$ in BhŚ; *vātiko* $G_{2\cdot3,5}$ in BhŚ; *pittako* $J_{1,2}$ in BhŚ; *cāṭulo* XY_1 in BhŚ [4]*vātalo* E_2 in BhŚ *vātulo* F_4 in BhŚ [5]*jalpavo vātulo vā* IS [6]*kṣa° se°* tr. B in Vet, PD; *kṣā° gṛh°* tr. BhŚ; *pārśve dhṛṣṭah kiṁ uparathavā dūrato'py apragalbhaḥ* β (var.) [7]*prāyaso* A_{01} E_{01-3} in BhŚ; *nā'tijātaḥ* E_3 in BhŚ; *nā'bhijāne* T_3 in

BhŚ [8]*dṛṣṭaḥ* H_1m,v J_3 Y_7 T_3 M_2 in BhŚ; *dhṛṣṭaḥ* Vets, BhŚ; *duṣṭaḥ* J_1 in BhŚ; *ghṛṣṭaḥ* W_4 in BhŚ; Vet; *dhṛṣṇuḥ* $Y_{4,5}$ $G_{2,3}$ in BhŚ; *pṛṣṭaḥ* e in Vet [9]*nivasati yadā* Vet; *vasati vicaran* A in Vet; *bhavati nitarāṁ* D in Vet; *prabhavati hi cirād* d in Vet; *bhavati ca tathā* BhŚ, c in Vet; *vasati ca* $BY_{1,7,8}$ G_1 M_{1-3} in BhŚ; *bhavati na C* in BhŚ; *prabhavati* W_{1-3} in BhŚ; *bhavati nivasan* G_4 in BhŚ; *bhavati tadā* (*sadā* Y_1 in BhŚ; *vasan* $Y_{2,4-6,8}$ $TG_{2,3,5}$ $M_{4,5}$ in BhŚ) W_{1-3} J_3 $Y_{1,2,4-6,8}$ $TG_{2,3,5}$ M_{4-5} in BhŚ [10]*dūrato'pi pramattaḥ* (*'pragalbhaḥ* BDcd in Vet) Vet; *dūrataś ca* BCce in Vet; *dūrato'py apragalbhaḥ* BhŚ; *dūrataś cā'pra°* $BCDE_3$ F_5 HWY_3 in BhŚ; *dūrataś ca pramādī* $E_{0-2.5}$ in BhŚ; *dūrataś cā'pramādi* IX (X_2 lacuna) in BhŚ; *dūratasya pragalbhaḥ* M_4 in BhŚ; *durago'pi apragalbhaḥ* M_5 in BhŚ; [11]*pramādī* e in Vet [12]*apragamyaḥ* B in Vet.

No. 114

[1]*pṛṣṭhataḥ sevayed arkaṁ jaṭhareṇa hutā'śanam*[2],
[3]*svāminaṁ* [4]*sarva-bhāvena para-lokam amāyayā.*

With the back one should serve the sun; with the breast, fire; a master, with all the soul; the next world with sincerity.

HJ 2.32, HS 2.33, HM 2.34, HP 2.30, HN 2.30, HK 2.34, HH 45.12-3, HC 60.6-7, IS 4188; *CRC* 8.53, *CRB* 8.56; *CRP* 8.53, *CRBh I* 8.53; *CNP II* 103.

The main editions of H are identical; one MS in HP contains one minor variant. The *CR* group contains variants in *a*. *CNP II* contains minor variants.

Footnotes to No. 114 : [1]*pṛṣṭhato'rkaṁ niṣeveta ja° CRC, CRB* [2]*hutāśanaḥ CŚlB* [3]*svāminaḥ sarvabhāveṣu paraloke mayā tvayā CŚlB* [4]*svāmino* A in HP.

No. 115

[1]*jīvite yasya jīvanti viprā mitrāṇi bāndhavāḥ*[2],
saphalaṁ jīvitaṁ tasya ātmā'rthaṁ[3] *ko na jīvati.*

Useful [is] the life of him, in whose life Brahmaṇs, friends [and] relations live. Who lives not for himself ?

HJ 2.34, HM 2.36, HK 2.36, HH 45.23-4, HC 60,17-8, IS 2439. Regarding *C* See No. 116.

The main editions contain only one minor variant. See No. 116.

Footnotes to No. 115 : [1]*yasya jīvati* (°*anti*) *CVB*; *yasmin jīvati CKl*; *yasya jīvena CVF, CVG, CVN* [2]*mitrāś ca° CVB, CKI*; *mitrāḥ svajana bāndhavā CVN* [3]*ātmā'rthe* HM, HK; *hy ātmā'rthaṁ CVB.*

No. 116

yasmin[1] *jīvati*[2] *jīvanti bahavaḥ sa tu*[3] *jīvatu,*[4]
kāko'pi[5] *kiṁ na*[6] *kurute*[7] *vañcvā*[8] *svo'dara-pūraṇam.*[9]

But let him live, in whom living, many live ? For does not even the crow fill his crop with [his] beak ?

HJ 2.35, HS 2.35, HM 2.37, HP 2.32, HN 2.32, HK 2.37, HH 45.25-6, HC 60. 19-20, IS 5348; *CvA* 7.17, *CvṢ* 7.17, *CvW* 7.16, *CvP IV* 7.16, *CvP V* 7.12, *CvGt* 7.8, *CvTb* 7.21, *CvH* 3.15, *CvL I* 7.17, *CvL II* 7.17, *CvLd* 7.12; *CSBD* 193, *CSB I* 2.94, *CSJ* 2.100, *CSC I* 2.93, *CSC II* 193, *CSB II* 193, *CSLd* 2.92; *CNG* 316, *cf. CnT II* 17.2, *cf. CnT III* 7 *b* 10; PS 1.9, PN 2.6, PP 1.10, Pts 1.23, PRE 1.8; VCsr II.3; cf. KSS 10.60, 34; Bhś 680.

The main editions and various MSs. of H contain some minor variants. Other sources and their various MSs. contain several minor variants.

Footnotes to No 116 : [1]*yasmiñ* HM, HP, HN, HK, PS, PP, Pts, PRE, VC, BhŚ (better); *sa tu* ABCN in PS [2]*jivati* IS; *jivanaṁ* N in PS [3]*so'tra* Pts [4]*jī(i)vati* HK, HN, H in HP, PP, Pts, PRE, VC (MNTQE in VC as above), BhŚ [5]*vāko'pi* HP; *bako'pi* HN, PS, PRE, VC, BhŚ; *eko* E in PS; *vayāṁsi* PP, Pts, VJQE in VC [6]*nityaṁ* N in PS; om. IS [7]*kurvanti* PP. Pts, JQE in VC; *jīvanti* V in VC [8]*cañcvā* HN, HH, PS, PP, Pts, PRE, VC (better); *cvaṁcā* IS; *hiṁsā* BhŚ [9]*so'dara* N in HP; *s(ś)vo'dara-poṣaṇam* PS (OFIABC in PS as above) ; °*pūraṇāt* Q in VC; °*pūraṇaiḥ* V in VC

No. 117

[1]*sthāna eva hi*[2] *yujyante*[3] *bhṛtyāś cā'bharaṇāni*[4] *ca,*
[5]*na hi cūḍāmaṇiḥ pāde* [6]*nūpuro na ca mūrdhani.*[7]

Servants and ornaments in their proper place are becoming. A crest-jewel [is] not worn on the foot, nor an ankle-ring on the head.

HJ 2.70, HS 2.70, (cf. HS 4.11), HM 2.71, HP 2.64, HN 2.63, HK 2.71, HH 50.16-7, (cf. HH 102.3-4) HC 66. 10-1, IS 7221; *CRC* 3.10, *CRB* 3.10, *CRP* 3. 10, *CRT* 3.8, *CRBh I* 3.10, *CRBh II* 3.11, *CRCa I* 3.10; *CNG* 56; PS 1.34, PT 1.35, PTem 1.31, PP 1.60, Pts 1.72, PRE 1.35, GP 1.110, 11.

The various editions of H contain several minor variants. A in HP is different in $\gamma\delta$. *CRC* is different in $\alpha\delta$; it is nearer to Pañc. than to H. Pañc. and GP are different, in particular in $\alpha\delta$.

Footnotes to No. 117 : [1]*sthāneṣv* (*sthāneṣu* NB in BS) *eva niyoktavyā prayoktavyā* GP; *niyojyante* HIO in PS; *piyojyāni* PP, *CRC*; *niyujyante* PS; *viniyojyante* B in PS; *viniyujyante* N in PS) PS, PT, PP, Pts, PRE, GP, *CRC* [2]*ni* IS [3]*niyojyante* HS, HM, HP, HN, HK (cf. fn. 1) [4]*vā'bha°* HP, I in PS [5]*cuḍamaṇis tathā pāde svabhāvāt pratibudhyate* A in HP [6]*prājñaiḥ CRC*; om. IS [7]*nūpuraṁ mūrdhani dhāryate* HK; *nūpuraṁ* (°*re* IS) *śirasā kṛtam* HM, HC; *prabhavāmī'ti* (°*vān iti* NB in PS; °*vamie'ti* PT (variant) ; °*vād vini°* A in PS; °*vād api* PS; °*venā'pi* C in PS; *prabhunā'pī'ti* IS) *badhyate* (*budhyate* B in PS) HP, HN, PS, PT, PP, Pts, PRE; *pādādau pratibadhyate CRC* ; *śobhate vai kadācana* GP.

No. 118

kanaka-bhūṣaṇa-saṁgrahaṇo'cito[1]
[2]*yadi maṇis*[3] *trapuṇi*[4] *praṇidhīyate*[5],
[6]*na sa*[7] [8]*virauti* [9]*na cā'pi*[10],[11] *sa śobhate*[12]
[13]*bhavati* [14]*yojayitur vacanīyatā*[15].

If a gem, worthy of being set in an ornament of gold, be set in lead, it neither tinkles nor glitters. The blame, however, attaches to the setter.

HJ 2.71, HS 2.71, HM 2.72, HP 2.65, HN 2.64, HK 2.72, HH 50, 18-21, HC 66. 12-3, IS 1526; *CRC* 3.54, *CRB* 3.53, *CRP* 3.48, *CRBh I* 3.48; PS 1.35, PN 2.26, PT 1.36, PTem 1.32, PP 1.63, Pts 1.75, PRE 1.36; GP 1.110, 14.

The main editions and the various MSs. of H contain some minor variants. *CRC* is almost identical with H. Other sources and its various MSs. contain several variants.

Footnotes to No. 118 : [1] °*saṁśrayaṇo°* PS (NAB) in PS as above) ; °*saṁkramaṇo'cito* EJ in PS; *karṇabhūṣaṇa-saṁgraho'cito* GP [2]*yavi maṇi pratibudhyate* M in PP [3]*maṇes* H in PS [4]*triguṇī CRC*; *tu pāde* GP [5]*pratibudhyate* A in HP, P in HS; *pratibāddhyate* H in PS; *pratibadhyate* PS, PT, PP, Pts, PRE, GP, *CRC*; *pranidhīyate* IS; *tripuṇīṁ prati vidyate* C in PS [6]*kiṁ maṇir nahi śobhate tataḥ* GP; *sa* N in PS [7]*ca* PS; *na* NABC in PS [8]*virocayati* (°*yati* I in PS) *ha na* PS; *virodhi na* (*ni* A in PS; *sa* B in PS) *cā'pi hi* (*na* B in PS) NABC in PS; *vibhāsate* A in PP [9]*tathā'pi na śo°* C in HP; *na* HH [10]*viśobhate* HS, HM, *CRC*; ; *na śo°* HP, HK, *ca śo°* B in HP; *cā'py* IS; *cāti* IS [11]*na* HK, P in HS, PT, PP, PRE; om. HH; *upa°* IS [12]*vibhāsate* IS (cf. fn. 11) [13]*ayaṁ bhaktoyam ayaṁ jaḍaḥ* N in PP [14]*yojayituṁ vyasanīyyatām* B in PS; *joyitur* M in PP [15]*vacanīkṛtan* A in HP

* * *

Compare also Nos. 71 and 82.

24. *Miscellanea*

No. 119

[1]*tyajed*[2] *ekaṁ*[3] *kulasyā'rthe grāmasyā'rthe*[4] *kulaṁ tyajet*[5].
grāmaṁ[6] *jana-padasyā'rthe*[7] *ātmā'rthe*[8] *pṛthivīṁ*[9] *tyajet.*

[A man] should leave an individual for the sake of a family, for the sake of a village he should abandon a family; a village he should renounce for the sake of a country; for the sake of the soul, the world.

HJ 1.159, HS 1.141, HM 1.148, HP 1.115, HN 1.116, HK 1.150, HH 28.12-3, HC 38.12-3, IS 2627; *CVND* 3.10, *CVM* 3.3, in *CvA* 1.7, *CvṢ* 1.7, *CvW* 1.8, *CvP IV* 1.7, *CvP V* 1.7, *CvGt* 1.7, *CvTb* 1.8, *CvH* 1.7, *CvI* 1.7, *CvL I* 1.7, *CvL II* 1.7, *CvLd* 1.7, *CRB* 2.2, *CRP* 2.7, *CRBh I* 2.7, *CRT* 2.2 *CRBh II* 2.3, *CRCa II* 10; *CNJV* 31, *CNS* 41, *CNF* 14, *CNN* 58, *CNPh* 6, *CNP II* 84, *CNI I* 94 & 316, *CNG* 20, *CNT IV* 58, *CNM* 58, *CNŚ* A 10; *CNNM* 26, *CNŚT* 27, *CNI II* 24, *CnT II*, 1.12, *CnT III* 1.12, *CnT VI* 13; PS 1.105, PN 2.83, PT 1.118, PTem 1.107, Pts 1.355 & 3.84, PRE 1.117; Kathārṇava (ZDMG 14.574); VCjr 28.3; Śts 21.4-5; MBh 2.61, 11 & 5.36,17.

The main editions of H are almost identical with H. The *CN* group is identical with H (*CNF* contains however two scribe's errors). The *CV* and *Cv* groups contain some minor variants (*CVND*, *CvP IV*, *CvTb* and other are identical with H). Pañc. contains some minor variants. (PS and PT are identical with H). Other sources contain some minor variants.

Footnotes to No. 119: [1]*tyajet kulā'rthe paruṣaṁ* MBh; *tyajed ekaṁ* om. AG in Śts [2]*tyajad* PT (notes) [3]*doṣam CNH* [4]*grāmasyarthe CŚF* (wrongly) [5]*bhavet CNH* [6]*kulaṁ* PT [7]*janāsyā'rthe* N in HP (*contra metrum*); *'rtha* VC, Pts. [8]*svā'tmā'rthe* HK, HS, HC, PT, PRE, ŚR in VC; *cā'tmā'rthe* PS (notes); *ātmā'rthe CŚF* (wrongly); °*'rthaṁ CVK* [9]*sakalam CVF*.

No. 120

jala-bindu-nipātena kramaśaḥ pūryate[1] *ghaṭaḥ,*
sa hetuḥ sarva-vidyānāṁ dharmasya[2] *ca dhanasya ca.*[3]

By the fall of drops of water, the jar is gradually filled; this [is] the cause of all sciences, of religion, and of wealth.

HJ 2.10, HS 2.10, HM 2.10, HP 2.11, HN 2.11, HK 2.11, HH 41.15-6, HC 54.13-4, IS 2357; *CVND* 12.22, *CVM* 12.1; *CNN* 6, *CNP I* 73, *CNPh* 129, *CNPN* 106, *CNT IV* 74, *CNM* 72, *CNMN* 61.

The main editions of H are identical. All the *C* groups are almost identical with H.

Footnotes to No. 120 : [1]*pūrṇate* IS; *pūrayed CNI I* [2]*svarkṣasya* (or better *mokṣasya*) *CŚH* [3]*ca* om. *CVND* (*contra metrum*; in other editions as above).

No. 121

[1]*payaḥ-pānaṁ bhujaṅgānāṁ kevalaṁ viṣa-vardhanam,*
[2]*upadeśo hi mūrkhāṇāṁ prakopāya*[3] *na śāntaye.*

A draught of milk only increases the serpent's venom; thus, good advice [ministers] to the exasperation, not to the conciliation, of fools.

HJ 3.4, HS 3.4, HM 3.4, HP 3.4, HN 3.4, HK 3.4, HH 73.6-7, HC. 96. 17-8, IS 1287 and 7482; *CvA* 4.15, *CvṢ* 4.15, *CVW* 4.18, *CvP V* 4.17, *CvTb* 4. 23, *CvL I* 4.15, *CvL II* 4.17, *CvLd* 4.17, *CNW* 73, *CNN* 55, *CNP II* 153, *CNI I* 85, *CNG* 142, *CNT IV* 141, *CNM* 139, *CNMN* 105, *CNŚC* 107, *CNL* 5, *CnT II* 19.8, *CnT III* 52.3, *CnT VII* 88, *CnT I* 36; Pts 1.389; BhŚ 431; cf. BhP 4.14, 9.

The main editions of H are identical. The *Cv* and *CN* groups are almost identical with H; (*CNP II* is identical with H); similarly Pts.

Footnotes to No. 121 : [1] °*pa* °*upa* tr. Pts, BhŚ *CVG, CVN, CLB, CŚlB* [2]*upakāraṇa nīcanām upakāro hi jayate* IS (7482); *upakāro nīcānām* BhŚ (v. l.) [3]*virūpāya CSW*; *prakāśāya CLB.*

No. 122

[1]*roga-śoka-paritāpa-bandhana*[2] *vyasanāni ca*
ātmā'parādha-vṛkṣasya[3] *phalāny etāni*[4] *dehinām.*

Sickness, sorrow, anguish, bonds and afflictions —these [are] the fruits of the tree of the personal transgressions of corporeal beings.

HJ 1.42, HS 1.35, HM 1.40, HN 1.30, HK 1.41, HH 12.5-6, HC 16.12-3, IS 5803 and 2777; *cf. CVND* 14.12, *cf. CVM* 14.8; *cf. CRC* 7.14, *cf. CRB* 7.10, *cf. CRP* 7.10, *cf. CRT* 2.4, *cf. CRBh I* 7.10, *cf. CRBh II* 7.10, *cf. CRCa I* 7.10; *cf. CNP II* 148, *cf. CNT IV* 106 & 116, *cf. CNM* 113; PP 3.139.

The main editions of H contain some minor variants. *C* contains variants. Pañc. contains some minor variants.

Footnotes to No. 122; [1]*roga-śoka-parītāpa*° HM, HN, HS; *dāridrya-roga-duḥkhāni* (*dāridrya-roga-dukhāni* Pr in PP; *dāridra-rodukhāṇi* M in PP) PP, *CVND* (var. γδ) [2] °*naṁ* HN, *CV* in IS (better); °*parītāpa*° HS (cf. fn. 1) [3] °*vṛkṣāṇāṁ* HS, HN, HK, HH [4]*eva hi* P in HS.

No. 123

anucita-karmā'rambhaḥ[1] *svajana-virodho balīyasā spardhā,*
[2]*pramadā-jana-viśvāso mṛtyor*[3] *dvārāṇi catvāri.*

Undertaking an inproper business, opposition to one's own folk, rivalry with a stronger, [and] reliance on the fair sex, [are] four avenues to death.

HJ 2.150, HM 2.151, HK 2.149, HH 65.25-6, HC 87.7-8, IS 316; *CNP II* 164, *CnT II* 23.6, *CnT III* 56.11,

The main editions of H contain some minor variants. *CNP II* is almost identical with H; it contains one minor variant only.

Footnotes to No. 123 : [1] °*kāryā'rambhaḥ* HM, HK, HH [2]*pramada*° HH [3]*mṛtyu CNP II.*

No. 124

[1]*pullava-grāhi pāṇḍityaṁ kraya-krītaṁ*[2] *ca maithunam,*
bhojanaṁ ca parādhīnaṁ[3] *tisraḥ puṁsāṁ viḍambanāḥ.*[4]

Superficial learning, sexual pleasure purchased with a price and subsistence at the will of another [are] the three ways men are cheated.

HJ 1.148 HS 1.131, HM 1.137; HP 1.106, HN 1.107, HK 1.140, HH 27.13-4, HC 37.5-6, IS 4000; *CLṢ* 1.7, *CLB* 1.7, *CLT* 1.7, *CLA* 107, *CLI* 1.7, *CLP V* 1.7, *CLP IV* 1.7, *CLP II* 1.7, *CLTb* 1.7, *CLH* 1.7, *CLL I* 1.7, *CLLd* 1.7; *CRC* 8.7, *CRB* 8.5, *CRP* 8.5, *CRBh I* 8.5, *CRBh II* 8.5, *CNP II* 286, *CNT IV* 222, *CNM* 185, *CNMN* 150, *CnT II* 13.4, *CnT III* 7.50, *CnT V* 86.

The main editions of H are almost identical. All the groups of *C* contain variants in *a.*

Footnotes to No. 124 : [1]*khaṇḍe khaṇḍe ca* (*tu CLE*; *su CLD*; *ṣu CLI, CLM*) *pā*° *CLT, CLT* (cod. nap.), *CLC, CLD, CLE, CLI, CLM*; *khaṇḍa khaṇḍeṣu paṇḍitya CLT* (*var*); *khaṇḍaṁ khaṇḍaṁ ca CRC*; *vallavārāhi CNP II* [2]*kreyo-krītaṁ* HC (wrongly) [3]*parāyattaṁ CRC* [4]*viḍhambanāḥ* HK (printing error); *viṭambanā CLT* (cod. nap.); *viṭambanāḥ CLT* (var.)

No. 125

[1]*kadarthitasyā'pi ca*[2] *dhairya-vṛtter*[3]
[4]*buddher*[5] *vināśo na hi śaṅkanīyaḥ,*
[6]*adhaḥ kṛtasyā'pi tanūnapāto*[7]
[8]*nā'dhaḥ*[9] *śikhā yāti*[10] *kadācid*[11] *eva.*

Loss of understanding is not to be apprehended in one of resolute habits, although calumniated. The flame of fire which may have been overturned, never goes downwards.

HJ 2.67, HS 2.66, HM 2.67, HP 2.61, HN 2.60, HK 2.68, HH 50.9-10, HC 66.1-2, IS 1519; *CRC* 3.40, *CRB* 3.43, *CRP* 3.41, *CRT* 3.11 *CRBh I* 3.41; PS 1.32, PN 2.24, PT 1.31, PTem 1.28, PRE 1.31; GP 1.110, 16; BhŚ 226.

The various editions of H are almost identical. *CRC* contains some important variants; it is nearer to Pañc. than to H. Pañc. and other sources and their various MSs. contain several important variants.

Footnotes to No. 125: [1]*kadār°* HH [2]*hi* PS, PT, PRE, GP, BhŚ *CRC*; *ha* EoW in BhŚ; *na* T_3 in BhŚ (T_2 in BhŚ as above) [3] *°vṛttair* D in BhŚ; *vṛtte* NA in PS, Y_3 M_4 in BhŚ; *°guṇaṃ* I in PS; *dainya-vṛtter* *CRC* [4]*na śakyate dhairya-guṇah* (*°ṇaṁ* PT) *pramārṣṭum* (*pramāṣṭum* A in PS) PS, PT, PRE, BhŚ (HMP in BhŚ as above); *na śakyate sarva-guṇa* (*dhairya-guṇaṁ* PT, E_{2t3t} F_5 I_1 $XY_{1,3}$ G_{1-3} M_{1-4} in BhŚ; *°guṇān C* in BhŚ; *°guṇa* J_1 in BhŚ; *°guṇaḥ* IS; *sattvaguṇān* $J_{2,3}$ in BhŚ *pramāthaḥ* GP; *na śakyate sarvaguṇām pramārṣṭaṁ* *CRC* [5]*buddhe* HH [6]*adho mukhasyā'pi kṛtasya vahner* PS, PT, PRE, BhŚ, *CRC*; *adhaḥ khalenā'pi kṛtasya vahner* GP; *adhaḥ kṛtāsyā'pi tanūpāto* X in BhŚ; *°pi hi tasya* IS; *tanūpato* Y_1 in BhŚ; *kṛśasya vahneḥ* G_4 in BhŚ [7] *°pādo* HS; *°pātaḥ* HM [8]*na* om. J_3 in BhŚ; *nā'dho mukhā jvālaśikhāḥ prayānti* IS [9]*'dhaś* PT (PTem as above) [10]*yānti* HP, HC, PS (ABCI in PS as above), PT, PRE, B_2 $DCEF_{1-3}$ $IJXY_{1,6,7}$ $TG_{1-3,5}$ M in BhŚ [11]*kathaṁcid* $BEo_{1,5}$ I in BhŚ.

No. 126

[1]*ākārair iṅgitair*[2] *gatyā ceṣṭayā bhāṣaṇena*[3] *ca*[4],
netra-vaktra-vikāreṇa[5] *lakṣyate*[6] *'ntargataṁ manaḥ*[7].

By external appearances, by motions, by the gait, by gestures and by speech; by changes in the eye [or] of the face the inward thought is discovered.

HJ 2.47, (cf. 3.35), HS *ad* 2.46, HM 2.50, HK 2.50, HH 47.15-6, HC 63.5-6 & 106. 3-4, IS 848; *CRC* 2.55, *CRB* 2.62, *CRP* 2.59, *CRBh I* 2.59, *CRBh II* 2.49, *CRCa I* 2.49; *CNG* 259, *CnT II* 27.8, *CnT VII* 57; PP 1.21, Pts 1.44; Vet 1.8; GP 1.109, 52; NV 10.27 (117.10-1); Mn 8.26 (also quoted in DhPS 3.1—55.12, SC 49. 17, GMBh 186. 12-3, Apar 620.21-2, SV 104. 8-9, VyMā 313, Vyavahāranirṇaya of Varadarāja wrongly ascribed to N—70. 2-4, Gautama Mitākṣara Haradatta 11.23, Vīr. Vyavahāra Prakāśa 71.13-4, Vyavahārārthasamuccaya 24, Vyavahāraprakāśa 21, 31, Vyavahārakalpataru 32, Vyavahārasaukhya 31, Vivādavyavahāra 10, Govindarājīyā in Dh, Smṛticintāmaṇi 41.42); cf. Mn 8.25, cf. Y 2. 13-5; cf. Vi 8.18; cf. N 1.193-6, Pariśiṣṭa 10.1; cf. Bṛh 5.43a; cf. R. in Vyavahāratattva 31.

The main editions of H are identical. *CRC* is alsmo identical with H; it contains only three minor variants. Other sources contain several minor variants.

Footnotes to No. 126 : [1]*ākaraṇe'ṅgitair* Apar, SV, Vyavahārakalpataru [2]*aṅgitair* NψPL$_1$ PrMBh in PP [3]*bhāṣitena* ψPL$_1$ Pr in PP, Mn and digests quoting Mn with the exceptions of GMBh and Vyavahāranirṇaya (k, ch in Vyavahāranirṇaya have also *bhāṣitena*), GP; *harṣitaja* GMBh [4]*tu* HP [5]*cak(t)ra-vikārais ca* A in PP; °*vikārais ca* Pts, Vet, Mn and digests quoting Mn, with the exception of SV; *vikāreṇa* BDce in Vet; *vikārais tu* a in Vet; *vikārabhyām* A in Vet, GP, SV, *CRC* [6]*gṛhyate* PP, A in Vet (d in Vet as above), Mn and digests quoting Mn with the exception of SV, Vīr. Vyavahāra Prakāśa, Govindārājiyā and Vyavahārakalpataru, NV; *jñāyate* A in PP, Vet, G in MnJ (also quoted in MnJh), SV, Vīr. Vyavahāra Prakāśa, *CRC*; *śaya*° Govindarājiyā; *lakṣya*° Vyāvahārakalpataru [7]*nṛṇām CRC.*

No. 127

[1]*nā'kāle mriyate*[2] *jantur*[3] *viddhaḥ śara-śatair api,*
[4]*kuśā'greṇai'va*[5] *saṁspṛṣṭaḥ prāpta-kālo na jīvati.*

Though pierced by hundreds of arrows at the wrong time, a creature dies not; touched only by the point of a blade of grass, when he has reached his hour, he lives no longer.

HJ 2.15, HS 2.16, HM 2.17, HK 2.17, HH 42.8-9, HC 56.7-8, IS 3595; *CRC* 6.87, *CRB* 6.48, *CRP* 6.43, *CRBh I* 6.44, *CRBh II* 6.44, *CRCa I* 6.37, *CRCa II* 39; *CNG* 232; GhN 19; GP 1.113, 48; NPR 1.3, 20; MBh 13.163, 11; Cf. BhP 7.2, 40; cf. VCsr 14.9.

The main editions of H contain minor variants. *CRC* is different in a, otherwise is identical with H, with one minor variant. Other sources contain minor variants.

Footnotes to No. 127 : [1]*nāprāpta* (*na prā*° *CRC*) *kālo mriyate vi*° MBh, GP, NPR, *CRC* [2]*mṛyate* HH [3]*kaścid* IS (*add.*) [4]*kuśa-kaṇṭa kaviddho'pi prā*° GhN; *tṛṇāgreṇā'pi* MBh, NPR; *spṛṣṭaḥ kuśā'gramātreṇa* IS (add.) [5] °*ṇā'pi* HM, HK, *CRC*; °*ṇa tu* GP.

No. 128

āpadāṁ kathitaḥ panthā indriyāṇaṁ asaṁyamaḥ,
tajjayaḥ sampadāṁ mārgo yeneṣṭaṁ tena gamyatām.

The want of control over the senses has been called the

road to ruin, the victory over them the path to fortune. Go then by whichever you please.

HJ 1.29, *ad* HS 1.25, HH 10.12-3, HC 14.3-4, IS 960; *CNJV* 74, *CNS* 13, *CNŚC* 72, *CNŚ* 72, *CNŚL* 56, *CNNM* 48, *CNŚT* 60, *CNŚK* 54.

The main editions of H are identical. *CNV* is identical with H.

No. 129

[1]*anāgata-vidhātā ca pratyutpanna-matis tathā*[2],
dvāv etau[3] *sukham*[4] *edhete*[5] *yad-bhaviṣyo*[6] *vinaśyati.*[7]

Anāgata-vidhātṛ and likewise Pratyutpanna-mati, these two happily escaped but Yad-bhaviṣya perished.

HJ 4.5, HS 4.5, HM 4.6, HP 4.5, HN 4.5, HK 4.5, HH 99.7-8, HC 132.17-8, IS 268, *CVND* 13.7, *CVM* 13.15, *CNP I* 85, *CNPh* 154, *CNP II* 122, *CNT IV* 86; PS 1.118, PN 2.95, PT 1.128, PTem 1.117, PP 1.326, Pts 1.318, PRE 1.127, cf. KSS 10.60, 178; cf. KṣB 16.336; MBh 12.137.1 & 12. 137, 20.

The main editions of H are identical, but some MSs. of H contain two minor variants. The *CV* group is identical with H; the *CN* group contains, some minor variants, particularly *CNP II*. Pañc. and in particular various MSs. of Pañc. contain several minor variants. MBh contain few minor variants.

Footnotes to No. 129 : [1]*anāgati°* *CNP II* .[2] *°tiś ca yaḥ* (*saḥ* B in PS) PS, PT, PP, (ψPPrMp in PP as above), PRE, MBh [3]*imau* ABC in PS; *ete* bhN in PP; *eva* MBh, *CNP I*, *CNP II*. [4]*mukham* P in PP [5]*edhanyte* A in HP [6] *°bhaviṣyati* *CNP II*; *dīrghasūtro* MBh, *CNP I*; *dīrghasūtrī* IS [7]*vināśitaḥ* B in PS; *viśeṣyati* H in PS; *bhaviṣyati* Pp in HS; *bhāvi ca* *CNP II*.

No. 130

artha-nāśaṁ[1] *manas-tāpaṁ*[2] [3]*gṛhe*[4], *duścaritāni ca,*
[5]*vañcanaṁ*[6] *cā'pamānaṁ*[7] *ca*[8] *matimān na prakāśayet*[9].

A prudent person should not divulge the loss of property, distress of mind, malpractices at home, being cozened, and disgrace.

HJ 1.138, HS 1.122, HM 1.127. HP 1.98, HN 1.99, HK 1.130, HH 26.9-10, HC 35. 13-4, IS 583; *CVND* 7.1, *CVM* 7.1; *CvA* 5.11, *CvṢ* 5.11, *CvW* 5.11, *CvP IV* 5.11, *CvP V* 5.11, *CvGt* 5.10, *CvH* 5.11, *CvL I* 5.11, *CvL II* 5.11, *CvLd* 5.11, *CRC* 2.25, *CRB* 2.25, *CRP* 2.22, *CRT* 2,15, *CRBh I* 2.22, *CRBh II* 2.19,

CRCa II 15; *CNJV* 34, *CNS* 5, *CNPh* 12, *CNI I* 88, *CNG* 27, *CNT IV* 133, *CNM* 128, *CNMN* 95, *CNŚC* 33, *CNŚ* 32, *CNŚL* 19, *CNNM* 28, *CNŚT* 30, *CNŚK* 33, *CNI II* 51, *CnT II* 7.11, *CnT III* 5.11, *CnT VI* 85, *CnT V* 22; Śts 40.10-1 & 63.7-8, Vet 1.26; GP 1.109, 15; ŚB 2.618.

The main editions and various MSs. of H contain minor variants. The *CN* group is identical and the *CV*, *Cv* and *CR* groups are almost identical with H (*CVND*, *CvP IV*, *CvP I* are identical with H). GP is identical with H. Other sources and its various MSs. contain minor variants.

Footnotes to No. 130 : [1]*arthanārthaṁ* L in Śts 40.11; *artha-nāśam ity ādi* LO in Sts 63.7 [2]*mana(ḥ)-sthairyaṁ* E in Vet [3]*gṛhini caritāni ca CV* in IS [4]*ity ādi* O in Śts (cf. fn. 1); [5]*vacanaṁ* E in Vet; *gṛñjanaṁ* AB in Vet; *nicavākyaṁ* ŚB; *mānaṁ cai'vā CRC* [6]*vañjanaṁ* HN; *vacanaṁ* N in HP (corrupt); *gañjanaṁ* HP, Pp in HS, P in Śts 63.8; *gajjanañ* P in Śts 40.11; *nīcavākyam* IS [7]*mānam* d in Vet (*contra metrum*, instead of *amanaṁ*) [8]*ca* om. ŚB. [9]*prakārayet* P in Śts 40.11.

* * *

No. 131

A similar aphorism to that found in HJ 1.139[1] is also found in *CVND* 14.17, *CNP II* 36, *CNI I* 92, *CNG* 28, *CNT IV* 128, *CNM* 131, *CNMN* 96, *CnT II* 24.9, *CnT III* 58.7; it deals with different things to be concealed (cf. No. 130).

Footnote to No. 131 :
[1]*āyur-vittaṁ gṛhac-chidraṁ mantra-maithuna-bheṣajam,*
tapo-dānā'pamānaṁ ca nava gopyāni yatnataḥ.

No. 132

[1]*sarvāḥ sampattayas*[2] *tasya saṁtuṣṭaṁ yasya mānasam,*[3]
upānad-gūḍha-pādasya[4] *nanu*[5] *carmā'vṛte'va*[6] *bhūḥ.*

Whoever has a contented mind, has all riches. To him whose foot is enclosed in a shoe, is not the earth, as it were, carpeted with leather ?

HJ 1.152, HS 1.135, HM 1.141, HP 1.109, HN 1.110, HK 1.143, HH 27.24-5, IS 6918; *CRC* 8.72, *CRB* 8.79, *CRP* 8.76, *CRBh I* 8.77; PS 2.42, PN 1.38, PT 2.79, PTem 2.68. PP 2.97, PRE 2.47; ŚP (ascribed to Vyāsa) 316; VS 3347,

The main editions and various MSs. of H contain minor variants. *CRC* is identical with H. Pañc. contains minor variants.

Footnotes to No. 132 : [1]*sarvāś ca* PS; *sarvās tu* NA in PS; *sarvās* PT, *sarvatra* ŚP, VS; *sarvataḥ* C in VS [2]*saṁpadas* PS, ŚP, VS; *saṁpadayas* PT (var.) [3]*mānasyaṁ* Pr in PP [4] °*pānasya* bhN in PP, °*vūṭa*° ψ P in PP; *ūpanaḍūḍha*° M in PP [5]*na tu* edd. in HS, HH; *sarvā* PT; *sarva* PT (var.) [6]*carma*° HM; *carmāstṛte'va* B in HP; *carmāstṛtai'va* PS; *carmāstṛtei'va* N in PS; *caḥmās*° A in PS; *carmāvṛttai(ḥ)'va* PT, PP, PRE, ŚP, VS.

No. 133

yo[1] *dhruvāṇi parityajya* [2]*adhruvāṇi*[3] *niṣevate*[4],
dhruvāṇi tasya[5] *naśyanti adhruvaṁ*[6] [7]*naṣṭam eva hi.*[8]

Whoever, quitting certainties, pursues things uncertain, loses his certainties. What is uncertain, [is] already lost.

HJ 1.227, HS 1.205, HM 1.210, HP 1.171, HN 1.172, HK 1.212, HH 38.20-1, HC 51.16-7, IS 5600; *CVND* 1.3, *CVM* 1.13, *CvA* 1.13, *CvṢ* 1.14, *CvW* 1.15, *CvP IV* 1.3, *CvP V* 1.13, *CvGt* 1.14 *CvTb* 1.14, *CvH* 1.14, *CvL I* 1.13, *CvL II* 1.14, *CvLd* 1.14; *CRC* 3.1, *CRB* 3.1, *CRP* 3.1, *CRT* 3.1, *CRBh I* 3.1, *CRBh II* 3.1, *CRCa I* 3.1, *CRCa II* 17, *CNJV* 63, *CNS* 78, *CNF* 78, *CNPh* 7, *CNI I*, *CNŚC* 61, *CNŚ* 61, *CNŚL* 46, *CNNM* 46, *CNŚT* 51; *CNŚK* 49, *CNF* 78, *CNPh* 7, *CNII* 202, *CnT II* 2.4, *CNT III* 1.16, *CnT VI* 17; PP 2.143, Pts 2.137; GP 1.110, 1.

The main editions and various MSs. of H are almost identical. All the *C* groups contain minor variants only, in particular *CNJV* , *CVND* and *CRC*. Other sources contain minor variants.

Footnotes to No. 133 : [1]*ke CVG* [2]*adhruvaṁ* (*cā'dhru*° *CŚF*) *pariṣevate CŚF, CŚH, CŚN, CVND*; *adhruvāṇy eva se*° *CVN* [3]*hy adhruvāṇi* GP, *CRC*; *adhruvaṁ CŚH, CVND*; *hy adhruvaṁ* IS [4]*ca sevyate* Pp in HS; *ca sevate CRC*; *ca sevete* IS; *pariṣevate CŚH, CVND* [5]*teṣām CVG* [6]*cā'dhruvaṁ* IS [7]*ca vinaśyati CVG*; *naṣṭa naiva ca CVF* [8]*ca* HN, ABN in HP, Pp in HS, PP, Pts, GP, *CŚF, CŚH, CŚN, CVN*.

No. 134

maṇir luṭhati[1] *pādeṣu*[2] *kācaḥ śirasi dhāryate,*
[3]*kraya-vikraya-velāyāṁ kācaḥ kāco*[4] *maṇir maṇiḥ.*

A gem may play about the feet (as in an anklet). Glass may be raised upon the head. At the time of buying and selling, glass [is] glass, a gem [is] a gem.

HJ 2.66, HS 2.67, HM 2.68, HP 2.60, HN 2.59, HK 2.67, HH 50.7-8, HC 66.4-5, IS 4656; *CVND* 15.9, *CVM* 15.9, *CvTb* 8.19, *CNF* 49, *CNPN* 64; VN 12.

The main editions and the various MSs. of H contain minor variants. The *CV* and *CN* groups contain minor variants. The *CV* group is nearer to the HJ and HH editions, while the *CN* group is nearer to the HM, HN and HK editions. VN is identical with the HM and HK editions.

Footnotes to No. 134 : [1]*lumṭhaṭi* A in HP; *luṭhatu* HN, N in HP [2]*pādena CNF*; *pāde* IS (*contra metrum*); *pādāgre CVND*, *CNF* (var.), *CNPN CvTb* [3]*yathai-vā'ste* (*vā'sti* HS, P in HS; *vā'stu* IS) *tathaivā'staṁ* (*vā'sti* P in HS; *vāsi* IS) HM, HK, S in HP, P in HS, VN, *CNF*, *CNPN*, *CvTb*; *yathai-vā'stu* (*vā'sti* HS) *tathai-vā'stu* HS, HP, HN, I in HK, Pp in HS; *yathai vāṁstāsti CNF* (var.) [4]*kācau* HK

No. 135

[1]*vāji-vāraṇa-lohānaṁ*[2] *kāṣṭha-pāṣāṇa-vāsasām*,[3]
[4]*nārī-puruṣa-tayānām antaraṁ*[5] *mahad antaram.*[6]

The difference between a horse, an elephant and iron [utensils]; between wood, stone and raiment; between women, men and water [is] a great difference.

HJ 2.38, HS 2.38, HM 2.40, HP 2.35, HN 2.35, HK 2.40, HH 46.5-6, HC 61.5-6, IS 6029; *CvA* 8.10 *CvŚ* 8.10, *CvW* 8.9, *CvP IV* 8.10, *CvP V* 8.7, *CvTb* 8.10, *CvL I* 8.10, *CvL II* 8.11, *CvLd* 8.7, *CRC* 3.13, *CRB* 3.13, *CRP* 3.13, *CRT* 3.10, *CRBh I* 3.13, *CRBh II* 3.14, *CNI I* 222, *CNG* 57, *CNHJ* 18, *CNT VI* 246, *CnT V* 45; PT 1.40, PTem 1.36, PP 1.328, PRE 1.41; VCsr 26.4; Śts 172. 11-2, Vet 3.7; Padma Purāṇa, Śṛṣṭikhaṇḍa 18.92; GP 1.110, 15.

The main editions of H contain minor variants. The *CR* group and some editions of the *Cv* group (*CvP IV*, *CvP V*, *CvTb*) are identical with H. Pañc., Vet, Padma P. are indentiwith H. Other sources and their various MSs. contain minor variants.

Footnotes to No. 135 : [1]*vāji* (°*ī* IS) *vānara* T in VC; *vāṇi-vāriṇa* c in Vet [2]*lauhānāṁ* HS, HP, HH, GP, J in VC [3]*vāsanām* T in VC [4]*nārā* P in Śts [5]*antarā* VC (VJE in VC as above); *vā'ntaraṁ* P in Śts; *dṛśyato* PP [6]*maha antaram* IS; *bahu vidyate* Śts; *vahu vighnate* P in Śts.

No. 136

[1]*viśvāsa*[2]*-pratipannānāṁ*[3] *vañcane*[4] *kā*[5] *vidagdhatā*[6],
aṅkam āruhya suptānāṁ[7] *hantuḥ*[8] *kiṁ*[9] *nāma*[10] *pauruṣam.*

What great art [is there] in the deceiving of those who are inspired with confidence ? What, forsooth, [is] the manliness of the slayer of those who have climbed into the lap [and] fallen asleep [there] ?

HJ 4.56, HS 2.166, HM 4.52, HP 4.55, HN 4.55, HK 4.57, HH 108.17-8, HC 145.5-6, IS 6206; *CNP II* 264; PD 302.42 (only αβ); VCsr VII.14, VCmr VII. 139-40, VCjr VII 3 (p.43); Śts. 35.4-5; Purātana Prabandha saṅgraha 262.

The main editions of H contain some minor variants. *CNP II* contains several minor variants. Other sources contain minor variants.

Footnotes to No. 136 : [1]*viś*° *aṅk*° tr. *CNP II* [2]*sadbhāva*° HS, VCmr, JE in VCsr; *subhāvaṁ* VCsr, Gr in VCmr [3]*pratipaṁnnā*° *CNP II*; *pratiprannā*° CC_1 O in Śts [3]*vañcanaṁ* PD; *vañcanaiś* *CNP II* ; *vacane* P in Śts; *ca cenckā* O in Śts [5]*ca* *CNP II*; cf. fn. 4 [6]*pidagdhatā* P in Śts; *vidagdhatāḥ* O in Śts; *vicitratā* HH; *viduścitāḥ* *CNP II* [7]*suptaṁ hi* HS, HM, HP, HN, HK, HH, Śts (CC_1 in Śts as above); *suptasya* QE in VCsr, Purātana P; *suptaśya* P in Śts; *āruhya guptasya* *CNP II* [8]*hantuṁ* VN in VCsr, PAŚRHY in VCjr, Śts; *hi hantuṁ* IS; *hantu* GK in VCjr; *hatiḥ* E in VCsr; *haṁti* *CNP II*; *hatvā* HS, HM, HP, HN, HK, HH; *hanane* VCmr, T in VCsr; *pātane* Gr in VCmr [9]*kā* *CNP II*; cf. fn. 8 [10]*nu* VCsr, T in VCsr.

No. 137

[1]*varaṁ vanaṁ*[2] *vyāghra-gajendra-sevitaṁ*[3]
[4]drumālayaḥ[5] *[6]pakva-phalā'mbu-bhakṣaṇam*[7],
tṛṇāni[8] *śayyā paridhāna-valkalaṁ*[9]
na bandhu-madhye dhana-hīna-jīvanam.[10]

A forest haunted by tigers and huge elephants, with trees for a habitation, ripe fruits and water for food, grass for a bed, bark for clothing—is preferable to living, deprived of wealth, amongst relations.

HJ 1.161, HS 1.144, HM 1.150, HK 1.152, HH 28. 19-20, HC 38. 17-8, IS 5949; *CVND* 10.12, *CVM* 10.15; Pts 5.23; VCjr 12.7; BhŚ 737; VN 14.

The main editions of H are identical. The *CV* group contains some minor variants. Other sources contain minor variants.

Footnotes to No. 137 : [1]*vanaṁ vyāghra-gajādi-sevitaṁ* IS; *vanaṁ vyāghra-gajaiḥ samanvitaṁ* IS [2]*vane* R in VC, *CVM* [3] °*gajādi-sevitaṁ* Pts; °*sevite* R in VC; °*sevanaṁ* IS [4]*jalena* (*janena* IS) *hīnaṁ bahukaṇṭakāvṛtam* Pts [5] °*ālaye* ABŚR in VC; °*ālayaṁ* BhŚ, *CVND* [6]*puṣpa*° K in VC; *mūla*° A in *VC*; *pat(t)rā*° VC, BhŚ, VN; *pakta*° HH; *yatra*° IS [7]*bhojanam* HM, HK, HC, VC, VN; *sevanam* *CVND*; [8]*tṛṇaiś ca* VC (O in VC as above); *tṛṇaś ca* H in VC; *tṛṇe ca* H in VC; *tṛṇeṣu* AY in VC, BhŚ, *CVND* [9]'*vara-jīrṇa-val*° VC, BhŞ (*pari°* O in *VC*); *varaṁ jīrṇa* IS; *vava-jīrṇa* IS; *jana-jīrṇa* Ś in VC; *śata-jīrṇa* *CVND* (in some editions); *śatar-jīrṇa* IS; *vasanaṁ ca* VN [10]*jīvitaṁ* Pts, VC (ŚR in VC as above)

No. 138

vane'pi[1] *doṣāḥ prabhavanti rāgiṇāṁ*
gṛhe'pi[2] *pañce'ndriya-nigrahas*[3] *tapaḥ*[4],
akutsite[5] *karmaṇi*[6] *yaḥ pravartate*
nivṛtta-rāgasya[7] *gṛhaṁ*[8] *tapovanam.*

Even in a forest, evils prevail over the passionate; whilst in the house the restraining of the five senses is a penance. The home of one free from passions, who is occupied in irreproachable acts, [is as] a forest dedicated to a course of] penance.

HJ 4.87, HS 4.83, HM 4.84, HP 4.87, HN 4.87, HK 4.89, HH 113.1-4, HC 151.13-4, IS 5929; *CRC* 5.47, *CRB* 5.47, *CRP* 5.43, *CRT* 6.5, *CRBh I* 5.43, *CRBh II* 5.49, *CRCa I* 5.43; PS 4.6, PN 4.2, PRE 4.14, GP 1.113, 9; Padma Purāṇa Sṛṣṭikhaṇḍa 19.317; Śānt 2.23.

The various editions of H contain minor variants. *CRC* is identical with H. PRE, Padma Purāṇa and Śānt. are identical with H. PS and various MSs. of Pañc. and Śānt. contain minor variants.

Footnotes to No. 138 : [1]*vane ca* T in Śānt; *vaneṣu* PS (NA in PS as above), $\kappa\gamma_3$ in Śānt [2]*gṛheṣu* P in HS, $\gamma\gamma_2 v\kappa$ in Śānt, E in PS; °*nigrahaṁ* IS, AN in PS [3] °*grahaṁ* HP, HN, N in PS; °*grahan* A in PS [4]*pañce'ndriyā'nagrahara tapaḥ* HK [5]*akutsate* A in PS; *akutsitaḥ* IS [6]*vartmani* P in Śānt [7] °*rāgo'sya* HS, Śānt (notes); *nivṛta* HH; *nivarta-rāgasya* B in Śānt [8]*gṛhe* IS.

No. 139

sevitavyo mahā[1]*vṛkṣaḥ* [2]*phalac-chāyā-samanvitaḥ*[3],
yadi daivāt phalaṁ nā'sti chāya[4] *kena nivāryate*[5].

A great tree yielding fruit and shade, is to be had in honour. If, by heaven's will, there be no fruit, why must the shade be forbidden ?

HJ 3.10, HS 3.10, HM 3.10, HP 3.10, HN 3.10, HK 3.10, HH 74.22-3, HC 98. 18-9, IS 7171; *CLṢ* 1.10, *CLB* 1.10, *CLT* 1.10, *CLA* 1.9, *CLP V* 7.10, *CLP IV* 1.10, *CLP II* 1.10, *CLTb* 1.10, *CLĹ I* 1.9, *CLI* 1.10, *CLLd* 1.10; *CNJV* 92, *CNS* 104, *CNPN* 88, *CNŚC* 90, *CNŚ A* 4, *CNŚL* 64, *CNNM* 58, *CNŚT* 74, *CNŚK* 66, *CNI II* 79, *CnT I* 40.

The main editions of H are almost identical. The *CN* group is identical with H. The *CL* group contains minor variants and in some cases (*CLT*, *CLA*) is almost identical with H.

Footnotes to No. 139 : [1]*mahān CLT* [2]*phala-chā°* HS, HH, *CNW* [3] *°ṣaś chāyā bhavati śitalā CLC, CLD, CLI, CLM* [4]*cchāyā* HM, HK, *CLT* [5]*nivāritā CLC, CLM*; *nivāritaḥ CLI*; *nivārayet CLE.*

No. 140

[1]*duḥkham evā'sti na sukhaṁ yasmāt*[2] *tad upalakṣyate*[3],
[4]*duḥkhārtasya pratikāre sukha-saṁjñā vidhīyate.*[5]

Pain exists positively; ease negatively. That is evident, since the term ease is employed in [the case of] alleviation of one oppressed with pain.

HJ 4.92, HS 4.88, HM 4.89, HP 4.92, HN 4.92, HK 4.94, HH 113.14-5, HC 152.5-6, IS 3487; *cf. CvP IV* 3.4, *cf. CvGt* 3.2, *cf. CvTb* 3.4, *cf. CvH* 3.2; *cf. CnT II* 4.6, *cf. CnT III* 3.6, *cf. CnT VI* 44; MBh 12.25, 22.

The main editions and various MS. of H. contain minor variants.

Footnotes to No. 140 : [1]*na su° duḥ°*tr. HS (edd. in HS as above), *CVT CVGt* [2]*tasmāt* MBh [3]*upalabhyate* HS (edd. in HS as above), MBh [4]*tṛṣṇārtiprabhavaṁ duḥkhaṁ duḥkharti prabhavaṁ sukham* MBh [5]*'bhidhīyate* Pp in HS.

No. 141

asambhavaṁ[1] *hema-mṛgasya*[2] *janma*[3]
tathā'pi rāmo lulubhe mṛgāya,
prāyaḥ [4]*samāpanna-vipatti-kāle*
dhiyo[5]*'pi* [6]*puṁsāṁ malinā*[7] *bhavanti.*[8]

The birth of a golden deer [is] an impossibility; nevertheless Rāma was tempted by desire for such a deer. Generally the minds of men are clouded when the time of their destruction has arrived.

HJ 1.27, *ad* HS 1.24, HM 1.27, HK 1.28, HH 10.6-7, IS 766; *CNPN* 97; Mahānataka 179; cf. PP 2.3, cf. Pts 2.4; cf. VCsr VII.3; cf. Vet 1.31; cf. Śts 29.9-12; MBh 2.67, 4b (583*).[9]

The main editions of H are identical. *CNPN* contains only two minor variants. Other sources contain some variants.

Footnotes to No. 141 : [1] *°bhave* MBh [2]*hemamayasya* MBh [3]*jantos* MBh [4]*samāsanna°* Mahān; *samāpanna-parābhavāṇaṁ dhi°* MBh; *samāpanna-*

vipatya-kāle CNPN [5]*viparyastataya* MBh [6]*hi* Mahān [7]*malinī°* Mahān; *mulino CNPN* [8]*bhavānām* MBh ($D_{4,5}$) [9]in K_4 Dn$D_{4,5}$ MSs, of the critical Bhandarkar edition and noticed by Nilakaṇṭha.

No. 142

nā'bhiṣeko na saṁskāraḥ[1] [2]*siṁhasya kriyate mṛgaiḥ*[3],
vikramā'rjita-rājyasya[4] *svayam eva mṛgendratā.*

No sprinkling with holy water, no rite of consecration is performed by the beasts for the lion. The sovereignty of the ferine species is naturally the right of him who has acquired the dominion by [his] prowess.

HJ 2.17, HS 2.18, HM 2.19, HP 2.16, HN 2.16, HK 2.19, HH 42.17-8, HC 56.11-2, IS 3601; *CRC* 8.13, *CRB* 8.13, *CRP* 8.14, *CRBh I* 8.14, *CRBh II* 8.16; *CNN* 12, *CNI I* 55; PS 1.5, PN 2.3, PP 1.6, PtsK 1.25, PRE 1.5; cf. KSS 10.60, 18, GP 1.115, 15.

The main editions and various MSs. of H are almost identical. The *CR* and *CN* groups are almost identical with H. Pañc. is almost identical with H. GP contains one important variant in γ.

Footnotes to No. 142 : [1]*satkāraḥ CNN* [2]*saṁskā......vane* A in PS [3]*vane* NABC in PS, GP, *CRC* [4]*vittasya* HP, HN, codd. in HS, PP, PtsK, PRE, *CNN*; *cittasya* P in PP; *sattvasya* PS, *CRC*; *nityam-ūrjita-sattvasya* GP.

Nos. 143, 144

upāyena hi[1] [2]*yac chakyaṁ*[3] *na tac chakyaṁ*[4] *parākramaiḥ*[5],
kākī[6] *kanaka-sūtreṇa kṛṣṇa-sarpam*[7] *aphātayat.*[8]

That which could not be accomplished by prowess may be effected by stratagem. A hen crow, by [means of] a gold chain, caused a black serpent to be put to death.

HJ 2.119 & 1.214αβ. HS 2.114 & 1.192αβ, HM 2.120 & 1.197 αβ, HP 2.106 & 1.158 αβ, HN 2.105 & 1.159 αβ, HK 2.118 & 1.199αβ, HH 61.1-2 & 35.16, HC 80.1 & 47.10, IS 1305; *CNW* 100; PS 1.50, PN 2.36, PT 1.59, PTem 1.52, PP 1.159, Pts 1.207, PRE 1.60; Tant 7.1; cf. KSS 10.6, 78; cf. KṣB 16. 283-4.

The main editions and various MSs. of H contain minor variants. *CNW* is almost identical with H (HM, HC editions). Other sources contain minor variants.

Footnotes to Nos. 143-144 : [1]*tu* NABC in PS, Tant [2]*yat kuryāt tan na śakym pa°* Pts; *tat kuryād yan na śakyaṁ pa°* PP [3]*yac śakyaṁ* Boltz 50.86 [4]*nac śakyaṁ* Boltz 50.86 [5]*balair api* Tant [6]*kākaḥ* HK, B in HP, PS (NBC in PS as above), Tant; *kākaiḥ* A in HP; *kākyā* HM, HC, PP, Pts, Tant [7] °*sarpo* HM, A in HP, A in HK, HC, PP, Pts, Tant; *kāla-sarpo CNW* [8]*atāḍayat* B in HP; cf. HS notes; *amārayat* (°*yet*) PS, PT, PRE; *vināśitaḥ* N in PP; *nipātitaḥ* HM, I in HK, A in HP, HC, PP, Pts, Tant, *CNW*.

Nos. 145, 146

[1]*tāvad bhayasya*[2] *bhetavyaṁ yāvad bhayam anāgatam,*[3]
[4]*āgataṁ ca*[5] *bhayaṁ*[6] [7]*vīkṣya*[8] [9]*naraḥ kuryād yatho'citam.*

As long as danger [is] not imminent, so long is fear of danger to be entertained, but when a man perceives danger at hand, he should act becomingly.

HJ 1.58 & 4.17, HS 1.50, HM 1.56, HP 4.17, HN 4.17, HK 1.57, & 4.17, HH 15.6-7, HC 20. 16-7 & 138.5-6, IS 2550; *CVND* 5.3, *CVM* 5.3, *CRC* 8.43, *CRB* 8.46, *CRP* 8.44, *CRBh I* 8.44, *CRBh II* 3.42, *CNP II* 185, *cf. CNI I* 189, *CNG* 177, *CNT IV* 250, *CnT II* 17.11, *CnT III* 7b20 & 5.35; PP 1.170, PD 307. 109-10; Vet 11.7 (203); MBh 1.142, 80b-81a & 12.140,33; GP 1.115, 43; ŚB 2.585.

The main editions of H are almost identical. All the *C* groups contain several important variants. Other sources are quite different, in particular in αβγ and GP in γδ.

Footnotes to Nos. 145-146 : [1]*bhītavat saṁvidhātavyaṁ yāvad bhayam anāgatam* MBh [2]*bhayac ca* d in Vet; *bhayeṣu* IS; *bhayāt tu* HJ 4.17, HK 4.17; *CNP II*; *bhayād vi° CRC*; *bhayād dhi* ŚB; *bhayena CVND* [3]*yāvan na bhayam āgatam* HP 4.17, HN 4.17; *yāvad anāgatam bhayam* A in HP 4.17; *bhayasam āgatam* c in Vet; *bhayasam āgamam CNP II* [4]*utpanne tu bhaye tīvre sthātavyaṁ vai hy abhītavat* (*tairabhi°*) GP; *bhayam āgatam ālokya* A in HP 4.17 [5]*tu* HJ 4.17, HM, HK, HP 4.17, HN, 4.17, PP. PD, Vet (c in Vet as above), ŚB, MBh, *CVND*, *CRC*, *CNP II* [6]*bhayasam āgatam* Vet; *bhaya* IS [7]*dṛṣṭvā tat kāle ca bhayaṁ tyajet* PD [8]*dṛṣṭvā* PP, Vet, MBh, *CVND*, *CRC*, *CNP II* [9]*praha*(*va*)*rtayam aśaṅkayā* (*abhītavat* (*CRC*) ; *prahan*(*ṛ*)*tavyam abhītavam* HJ 4.17, HP 4,17, HN 4.17; °*tavat* HK 4.17, MBh, ŚB, *CNP II* °*tavan* IS; °*gṛhītavyam* IS; *pahartavyam* D in Vet; *aśaṅkitaḥ* b in Vet; *aśaṅkita* Din Vet, *aśaṅkayā* IS

No. 147

pānīyaṁ vā nirāyāsaṁ svādv annaṁ[1] *vā*[2] *bhayottaram*[3],
vicārya khalu paśyāmi [4]*tat sukhaṁ yatra nirvṛtiḥ.*

Either water without labour, or dainty food attended with

danger;—having duly deliberated, I plainly perceive that [to be] happiness where [there is] repose.

HJ 1.160, HS 1.143, HM 1.149, HP 1.116, HN 1.117, HK 1.151, HH 28.16-7, HC 38.14-5, IS 4047; *CRC* 6.96, *CRB* 6.59, *CRP* 6.51, *CRBh I* 6.52, *CRCa I* 6.43; MBh 12.111, 32; GP 1.113, 57 γδ.

The main editions of H are almost identical. *CRC* is different in δ only. MBh is identical with H. GP is different in αβ[5].

Footnotes to No. 147 : [1]*svādā'nnaṁ* HH [2]*ca* Pp in HS [3]*'bha°* IS [4]*pāniyaṁ nirbhayaṁ sukham CRC* [5]*rāgadveṣā 'diyuktānāṁ na sukhaṁ kutracid dvija* GP αβ.

No. 148

[1]*upārjitānāṁ vittānāṁ*[2] *tyāga eva*[3] *hi rakṣaṇam*[4],
[5]*taḍāgo'dara-saṁsthānāṁ*[6] *parīvāha*[7] *evā'mbhasām.*

Liberality (generosity) [is] truly a preservation of accumulated treasures, as a pipe for carrying off the waters impounded in a tank.

HJ 1.165, HS 1.147, HM 1.153, HP 1.118, HN 1.119 HK 1.155, HH 29.7-8, HC 39.8-9, IS 1307; *CVND* 7.14, *CVM* 7.12; *CvA* 6.6 *CvŚ* 6.6, *CvW* 6.7, *CvP IV CvP V* 6.7, 6.7, *CvTb* 6.7, *CvL I* 6.6, *CvL II* 6.2, *CvLd* 6.7; *CnT* 8.10, *CnT III* 66, *CnT VI* 96; PS 1.3, PN 2.2, PT 1.3, PP 1.2, Pts 1. 2.150, PRE 1.3; VCsr 3.8; NV 30.30 (Viṣṇuśarman).

The main editions and various MSs. of H contain minor variants. *CVND* is identical with H; the *Cv* group is almost identical with H. Other sources contain minor variants or are identical with H.

Footnotes to No. 148 : [1]*upārjjiṛ......tthānān* A in PS [2]*arthānāṁ* HP, HN, Pp in HS, PS, PT, PP, Pts, PRE, M in VC, *CV* in IS, *CVF*, *CVG*, *CVN*; *vastūnāṁ* P in HS; *dravyānāṁ* NCO in PS [3]*tyāgāyai'va* J in VC; *eko* IS [4]*kāraṇaṁ* MJ in VC [5]*taḍako°* PT; *taṭāgo°* *CVF*, *CVG*, *CVN*; *taṭāko°* PS, A in PP; VC, *CV* in *IS* [6] *°saṁthānaṁ CVF* [7]*parivāha* ABE in PS, *CVN*; *parivāhair*, *CVF*, *CVG*.

No. 149

[1]*añjnasya*[2] *kṣayaṁ dṛṣṭvā valmīkasya*[3] *ca*[4] *saṁcayam*[5],
avandhyaṁ[6] *divasaṁ*[7] *kuryāt*[8] [9]*dānā'dhyayana-karmabhiḥ.*[10]

Having observed the [almost imperceptible] decrease of a collyrium, and the [gradually] raised hillock of the white ant, [a man] should make [each day] fruitful by liberality, study [and other good] works.

HJ 2.9, HS 2.9, HM 1.12, HP 2.10, HN 2.10, HK 2.10, HH 41.13-4, HC 55.7-8, IS 115 and 6594; *CvA* 6.14, *CvṢ* 6.14, *CvP V* 6.12, *CvTb* 6.15, *CvL I* 6.14, *CvL II* 6.15, *CvLd* 6.12, *CRC* 5.44, *CRB* 5.44, *CRP* 5.40, *CRBh I* 5.40, *CRCa I* 25; *CNŚK* 75, GP 1.113.8.

The main editions and various MSs. of H contain minor variants. Most of the *CV* group is different in αβ. The nearest to H are *CvP V* and *CvTb*. Some of the variants could be considered as different aphorisms.

Footnotes to No. 149: [1]*nasya kṣyaṁ dadā* *CVG*; *ślokena vā* (*ca CVF*; *ślokenā'pi CVN* 2.17) *tadardhena* (*tathārthena CVF*) *tadardhārdhā'kṣaraṇa ca CVND*; *ślokārdhaṃ ślokapādaṁ vā samastaṁ ślokam eva ca* *CVG* 2.15; *ślokena vā tadardhena* (*pādenai-kākṣareṇa CVN* 2.17; *pādainai vakṣa CVF*) *vā CV* in IS, *CVB*, *CVN* 2.17 [2]*aṁjanakṣayaṁ* N in HP [3]*vālmikasya* N in HP, *CVN* (wrongly) [4]*tu* HS, HH, GP, *CVG*; *vā* *CVN* [5]*vardhananam* CVG_1 *CVN* [6]*abandhya* IS; *navandhyaṁ CVN* [7]*divasa CV* in IS, *CVB* [8]*kuryād* HS, HM, HP, HK, HH, GP, *CVND*, *CV* in IS, *CVF*, *CVG* 2.15, *CVN* 2.17, *CRC* (better) [9]*yadīcched vipulāṁ mati*(*ṁ mati*(*ṁ*) *CVG* 2.15, *CVN* 2.17 [10]*karmasu* HS, HM, HP, HN, HK, HH, GP, *CVN*, *CVF* 2.16; *karmaṇā* P in HS; *dānā'dhyeyona-karmanāt CVB*

No. 150

[1]*yaj jīvyate*[2] *kṣaṇam api prathitaṁ*[3] *manuṣyair*[4]
[5]*vijñāna-vikrama-yaśobhir abhajyamānam*[6],
[7]*tan nāma jīvitam*[8] *iha*[9] *pravadanti tajjñāḥ*[10],
[11]*kāko'pi jīvati cirāya*[12] *baliṁ ca*[13] *bhuṅkte.*

Real life in this world, the wise say, is only that which is lived, perchance only for a brief season, yet known to fame among men, and not lacking in wisdom, prowess, or glory. A very crow lives a long time and devours the food that is thrown to it.[14]

HJ 2.41, HS 2.41, HM 2.43, HP 2.38, HN 2.38, HK 2.43, HH 46.16-9, HC 61. 15-8, IS 5023; *CRC* 8.38, *CRB* 8.37, *CRP* 8.36, *CRBh I* 8.36, *CRBh II* 8.35; PS 1.13, PN 2.9, PT 1.10, PTem 1.7, Pts 1.24, PRE 1.12; VCsr II. 1; GP 1.115 33; cf. Mn 7.21; cf. VCsr II 2.

The main editions of H contain minor variants; the various editions of Pañc. contain some important variants which are sometimes reflected in VC and *CRC*.

Footnotes to No. 150 : [1]*yo jīvati* PS (N in PS as above); *yo* NQE in VC; *yarj jī°* A in PS [2]*jīvate* edd. in HS; *jīvati* HM; *jīvanaṁ* B in HP; *jīvitam* GP, *CRC* [3]*prathito* PS (NBC in PS as above), JQ in VC (V in VC as above); *prathitair* VC; *prathanam* A in PS [4]*manuṣyo* PS, VC (VN in VC as above) [5]*vijñāta* Pp in HS; *°vidruma°* N in PS; *°śauryavibhavāryaguṇaiḥ* (*°vādigu°* IS) *sametam* (*°taḥ* VC; N in VC as above) Pts, VC [6]*abhagnamānam* HP, HN, HH, AB in PS, PT, Pts, PRE; *abhagnamānaḥ* NC in PS; *abhagnamānaiḥ* GP; *alaṅghyamānaḥ* PS; *amyamānam* *CRC* [7]*tat tasya* (*tat teṣu* IS) *jīvitaphalaṁ p* [2]*a°* VC [8]*jīvanam* B in PS [9]*iti* PS (NA in PS as above), GP [10]*tajjñā* HH; *pravada...tajñāḥ* A in PS; *santaḥ* C in PS, VC, *CRC*; *loke* PT [11]*kālo'pi* H in PS [12]*ciraṁ ca* N in HP, HN, AC in PS, PRE, VC (NQE in VC as above); *cireṇa* B in PS; *cirāt tu* T in VC [13]om. A in PS; *baliś ca* HH; *ciraṁ balim eva* IS [14]According to F. Edgerton's translation in PRE.

No. 151

tāmbūlaṁ kaṭu-tikta-miśra-madhuraṁ[1] *kṣāraṁ kaṣāyā'nvitaṁ,*
vātaghnaṁ[2] *kapha-nāśanaṁ kṛmiharaṁ daurgandhi-doṣāpaham.*[3]
vaktrasyā'bharaṇaṁ[4] *malā' paharaṇaṁ*[5] *kāmā'gni-saṁdīpanaṁ,*
tāmbūlasya[6] *sakhe trayodaśa guṇāḥ svarge'py amī*[7] *durlabhāḥ.*[8]

Betel [is] pungent, bitter, spicy, sweet, alkaline, astringent, a carminative, anti-phlegmatic, a vermifuge; a sweetener of the breath, an ornament of the mouth, a detergent, and a kindler of the flame of love. O friend ! These thirteen properties of betel [are] hard to be met with, even in paradise.

HJ 3.103, HH 89.3-6, IS 2536; *CRC* 7.45, *CRB* 7.39, *CRBh I* 7.36 *CRBh II* 7.61, *CRCa* I 33; Vet 1.18.

The main editions of H are identical. *CRC* contains some minor variants. Vet. contains some minor variants.

Footnotes to No. 151 : [1]*uṣṇa°* Vet; *uṣka°* c in Vet; *iṣṭa°* LB in Vet [2]*pittaghnam* *CRC* [3]*durghandi* (*°gān°* d in Vet; *gandha* ce in Vet) *nirnāśanam* Vet, *CRC* [4]*carkrasyābha°* IS [5]*viśuddhi* (*°dha* IS) *karaṇam* Vet, *CRC* [6]*tāmbūle hi* c in Vet [7]*'pi tu* Vet; *'pi tad* B in Vet, *CRC* [8]*durlabham* *CRC* [9]According to CKr *CRB* has been marked as identical with IS 2535, instead of 2536.

No. 152

pañcabhiḥ[1] *saṁbhṛtaḥ*[2] *kāyo yadi pañcatvam āgataḥ*[3]*,*
karmabhiḥ svaśarīrotthais tatra[4] *ka paridevanā.*

Why lament, if the body, which is composed of five elements, reverts to the five elements, because of acts performed by one's own body ?

ad HS 4.71 (in codd.), IS 3854; *CRC* 6.56, *CRB* 6.45, *CRP* 6.41, *CRBh I* 6.42, *CRBh II* 6.42; Y 3.9.

The text of Y is identical with that of H with the exception of one minor variant in *a*. *C* contains three important variants.

Footnotes to No. 152 : [1]*pañcadhā* Y [2]*sambhūtaḥ pañcadhā CRC* [3]*pañcatvamāpnuyāt CRC* [4]*svatmacaritaist CRC*

* * *

Compare also Nos. 3, 4, 7, 18, 19, 22, 34, 36, 39, 40, 47, 50, 53, 54, 55, 57, 60, 62, 63, 68-9, 82, 84, 87, 91, 100-100 A, 102, 106, 113, 116 and 118.

* * *

POST SCRIPTUM

Long after this study was published the author came across MSs. and reconstructions of Cāṇakya's compendia previously unknown to him.[1] He has found in these sources that the following additional stanzas of the Hitopadeśa correspond to stanzas of Cāṇakya's compendia, namely :

No. 153. HJ Intr 10 corresponds to *CNŚC* 96, *CNŚ* 96, *CNŚL* 6 and (Cāṇakya-śloka-saṁgraha, Rudra Printing Press, Calcutta, 1918) 96.

No. 154. HJ Intr 29 is similar to *CNL* 91, *CR* (as published by the author in the Vishveshvaranand Indological Studies, 28) 6.41-2, *CNG* 232, *CNP II* 38, *CnT* II 19.1, *CnT III* 87, *CNI I* 78 and *CL* (as published by the author in the Vishveshvaranand Indological Studies, 28) 8.10.

No. 155. HJ Intr 31 corresponds to *CNŚC* 110 and *CNŚl* 110.

No. 156. HJ Intr 36 is similar to *CNN* 49.

1. Additional references : *CNB*, Bṛhat-Cāṇakya-ślokaḥ with Utkala Padyānuvāda by Śrī Arjuna Mahārānaṅka, Utkal Press, Calcutta; *CNŚIV*-Cāṇakya-ślokaḥ by Vijayakṛṣṇanātha. Second edition. Girīśa Printing Works, Calcutta 1320 (1914). *CRT*-Cāṇakya-rāja-nīti-śāstra, edited by Suniti Kumar Pathak, Sanskrit and Tibetan, *Viśva Bhārati Annals,* VIII.

No. 157. **H J Intr 46** corresponds to *CNPh* 156.

No. 158. **H J 1.2** corresponds to *CNŚC* 103, *CNŚ* 101, *CNŚL* 89 and Cāṇakya-Śloka-Saṁgraha, (Rudra Printing Press, Calcutta, 1918) 89.

No. 159. **H J 1.10** corresponds to *CNG* 288.

No. 160. **H J 1.24** corresponds to *CSC I* 3.73, *CVM* 17.22.

No. 161. **H J 1.26** is similar to *CNMN* 132.

No. 162. **H J 1.34** corresponds to *CNŚC* 109 and Cāṇakya-Śloka-Saṁgraha, (Rudra Printing Press, Calcutta, 1918) 109.

No. 163. **H J 1.35** is similar to *CRC* 7.85, *CRB* 7.80 and *CRBh II* 7.37.

No. 164. **H J 1.36** is similar to *CR* (as published by the author in the Vishveshvaranand Indological Studies, 28) 7.69. *CVGt* 4.17, *CvTb* 4.18 and *CNW* 101.

No. 165. **H J 1.45** corresponds to *CN* (as published by the author in the Vishveshvaranand Indological Studies, 27) "*C*" and *CNB* 145.

No. 166. **H J 1.49** corresponds to *CN* (as published by the author in the Vishveshvaranand Indological Studies, 27) "F".

No. 167. **H J 1.52** corresponds to *CRC* 6.26.

No. 168. **H J 1.62** corresponds to *CNPh* 137.

No. 169. **H J 1.66** corresponds to *CNB* 143.

No. 170. **H J 1.67** corresponds to *CNŚ A* 17, *CNŚL* 47 and *CNMN* 80.

No. 171. **H J 1.68** corresponds to *CNŚ A* 14 and *CNMN* 74.

No. 172. **H J 1.70** corresponds to *CNPh* 164, *CNŚ A* 18 and *CNMN* 81.

No. 173. **H J 1.71** is similar to *CNF* 83 and *CNI II* 61.

No. 174. **H J 1.81** corresponds to *CR* (as published by the author the Vishveshvaranand Indological Series, 28) 5.40, *CVM* 10.22, *CNG* 119, *CNT IV* 104, *CNM* 50, *CnT II* 27.12 and *CnT VII* 61.

No. 175. **H J 1.82** corresponds to *CNB* 119.

No. 176. **H J 1.103** corresponds to *CN* (as published by the author in the Vishveshvaranand Indological Series, 27) "Z".

No. 177. **H J 1.126** corresponds to *CNB* 130.

No. 178. *ad* **H J 1.135** corresponds to *CNPh* 78 and *CNI II* 73.

No. 179. **H J 1.150** corresponds to *CNŚIV* 65.

No. 180. **H S 1.142** is similar to *CNN* 18.

No. 181. **H J 1.163** is similar to *CS* (as published by the author in the Vishveshvaranand Indological Series, 27) 3.100

No. 182. *ad* **H J 1.165** corresponds to *CNT IV* 206.

No. 183. **H J 1.169** is similar to *CR* (as published by the author in the Vishveshvaranand Indological Series, 28) 8.35.

No. 184. **H J 1.176** corresponds to *CNB* 144.

No. 185. **H J 1.177** corresponds to *CR* (as published by the author in the Vishveshvaranand Indological Series, 28) 6.43.

No. 186. **H J 1.181** corresponds to *CNŚC* 99, *CNŚ* 98,*CNŚL* 98 and Cāṇakya-Śloka-Śaṁgraha, Rudra Printing Press, Calcutta, 1918) 99.

No. 187. **H J 189** corresponds to *CNPN* 141 and *CNHU* 12; it is similar to *CNW* 45.

No. 188. **H J 1.192** corresponds to *CNB* 114.

No. 189. *ad* **H S 1.180** corresponds to *CR* (as published by the author in the Vishveshvaranand Indological Series, 28) 8.59, *CNI I* 186 and *CNG* 329.

No. 190. **H J 1.217** corresponds to *CRT* 3.23.

No. 191. *ad* **H J 2.11** corresponds to *CS* (as published by the author in Vishveshvaranand Indological Series, 27) 3.74, *CL* (as published by the author in Vishveshvaranand Indological Series, 28) "D", *CNPh* 96, *CNI I* 182, *CNG* 37, *CvGt* 8.8, *CvP IV* 7.14, *CvP V* 7.11 and *CvTb* 7.19.

No. 192. **H J 2.33** corresponds to *CvL I* 8.43 and *CRT* 8.18.

No. 193. **H J 2.61** is similar to *CNPh* 159.

No. 194. *ad* **HJ 2.67** corresponds to *CNI I* 333.

No. 195. **H J 2.69** corresponds to *CRT* 5.11 and is similar to *CS* (as published by the author in Vishveshvaranand Indological Series, 27) 1.73, *CNI I* 267, *CNG* 79 and *CR* (as published by the author in Vishveshvaranand Indological Series, 28) 5.1.

No. 196. **H J 2.132** corresponds to *CNL* 88.

No. 197. **H J 2.137** corresponds to *CNB* 112.

No. 198. **H J 2.157** is similar to *CNN* 70.

No. 199. **H J 2.163** is similar to *CNN* 10.

No. 200. **H J 3.5** is similar to *CNN* 73.

No. 201. **H J 3.6** is similar to *CNN* 74.

No. 202. **H J 3.19** is similar to *CNW* 87, *CNF* 91, *CNPN* 63 and *CNI II* 75.

No. 203. **H J 3.27** corresponds to *CNB* 122.

No. 204. **H J 3.58** corresponds to *CNB* 124.

No. 205. **H J 3.81** corresponds to *CNB* 125.

No. 206. **H J 3.104**=H J 1.45 (No. 170).

No. 207. **H J 3. 108** corresponds to *CNB* 132.

No. 208. **H J 3.116** corresponds to *CNB* 128.

No. 209. **H J 3.132** corresponds to *CNB* 129.

No. 210. **H J 3.144** corresponds to *CNI I* 275 and *CnT II* 26.6; it is similar to *CNG* 234.

No.211. **H J 3.148** corresponds to *CNB* 130.

No. 212. **H J 4.11** is similar to *CR* (as published by the author in Vishveshvaranand Indological Series, 28) 7.44, *CS* (as published by the author in Vishveshvaranand Indological Series, 27) 1.8 and *CNG* 152.

No. 213. **H J 4.14** corresponds to *CNL* 90.

No. 214. **H J 4.33** corresponds to *CNŚC* 96 *CNŚ* 96, *CNŚL* 6 and Cāṇakya-Śloka-Saṁgraha (Rudra Printing Press, Calcutta, 1918) 96.

No. 215. **H J 4.59** is similar to *CvL I* 8.25 and *CvL II* 8.19.

No. 216. **H J 4.65** is similar to *CS* (as published by the author in Vishveshvaranand Indological Series, 27) 2.10, *CR* (as published by the author in Vishveshvaranand Indological Series, 28) 5.28 and *CNI I* 122.

No. 217. **H J 4.74** is similar to *CR* (as published by the author in Vishveshvaranand Indological Series, 28) 6.39.

No. 218. **H Ś 4.71** corresponds to *CvGt* 4.18.

No. 219. **H J 4.99** is similar to *CRC* 6.63.

No. 220. **H J 4.135** corresponds to *CNNM* 65.

In the meantime the author has also had the opportunity to study several MSS of Cāṇakya previously unknown to him. After careful study of the material additional to that examined before, he reached the conclusion, mentioned already in paragraph 11 above, that Cāṇakya's compendia should be divided into six versions which could be titled: (a) the Vṛddha Cāṇakya *textus ornatior* (comprising *CVND* and *CVV*); (b) the Vṛddha Cāṇakya *textus simplicior* comprising *inter alia CVA, CVF, CVG, CVGt, CVK, CVN*, and *CVW*); (c) the Laghu

Cāṇakya (comprising *inter alia CLA*, *CLB* (second part), *CLC*, *CLD*, *CLE*, *CLI*, *CLM* and *CLT*); (d) the Cāṇakya-rāja-nīti-śāstra (comprising inter alia *CRB*, *CRC* and *CRP*); (e) the Cāṇakya-sāra-saṁgraha (comprising inter alia *CVB*); and (f) the Cāṇakya-nīti-śāstra (comprising inter alia the classical source *CSH*, and different subhāṣita-saṁgraha-s, partly composed of authentic Cāṇakya's sayings i. e. *CŚF*, *CŚN*, *CŚP*, *CŚW*, *CNI*, *CNH*, *CŚIB*, *CLB* (first part) and *CVT*). The writer elaborated on this subject in greater detail at the Twenty-fourth International Congress of Orientalists in Munich, in August 1957.[2]

2. Following is the text of his contribution to the XXIV International Congress of Orientalists in Munich, as published in the Akten des XXIV Internationalen Orientalisten Kongresses, München, 1957, pp. 544-546. Ŝternbach, Ludwik (New York); *Various Versions of Cāṇakya's Compendia*

In many parts of the world and more particularly in India, we find a great number of MSs containing collections Cāṇakya's sayings. Some of them are very much alike but many, at least at first sight, are complctely different. This is probably the reason why at the beginning of the twentieth century almost each MS was considered as a new version. So, O. Kressler, who in 1907 wrote a long dissertation about Cāṇakya's aphorisms, fixed the number of Cāṇakya's compendia at 17 versions. This number was then generally accepted (M. Winternitz, S. N. Dasgupta and S. K. De, A. B. Keith, L. Renou).

The author, after having studied seventy five editions and MSs of Cāṇakya came to the conclusion that collections of Cāṇakya's sayings can be divided into six version only :

1. *The Vṛddha-Caṇakya, textus ornatior* (several editions) divided into 17 *adhyāya-s* and containing usually 340 stanzas.

The first three stanzas beginning with the word *praṇamya śirasā Viṣṇuṁ...*, *adhiiyedaṁ yathā śāstram...*and *tad ahaṁ sampravaṣyāmi...*are always identical. This version is the best known and has been published several times in India under the name : Vṛddha Cāṇakya or Cāṇakya-nītidarpaṇa.

2. *The Vṛddha-Cāṇakya, textes simplicior* (2 edition and many MSs) divided into eight *adhyāya-s* and containing from 109 to 173 stanzas. The first three stanzas are always identical with the three introductory stanzas of the Vṛddha-Cāṇakya, *textus ornatior* version. The first, second, fifth and sixth *adhyāya-s* usually correspond closely to the same *adhyāya-s* of the Vṛddha-Cāṇakya, *textus ornatior* version. The third, sixth, seventh and eighth *adhyayas* correspond only partly to the same *adhyaya-s* of the Vṛddha-Cāṇakya, the *textus ornatior* version. *Adhyāya-s* nine to seventeenth of the Vṛddha-Cāṇakya, *textus ornatior* are only found in fragments in this version.

3. *The Laghū-Cāṇakya* (4 editions, and several MSs) divided into eight *adhyaya-s* and containing 83 to 97 stanzas. Differences between MSs are slight. The first three stanzas beginning with the words *praṇamya Śaṅkaraṁ*

devaṁ..., *Cāṇakyena svayaṁ prokto...*, *jñānārthaṁ* (*ato'rthaṁ*) *paṭhyate śāstraṁ...*are always identical.

4. *The Cāṇakya-rāja-niti-śāstra* (2 edition and several MSs.) divided into eight *adhyāya-s* and containing from 472 to 658 stanzas. The seventh and eighth *adhyayas* particularly the eighth, are long. A great number of stanzas correspond to the Bṛhaspati-Saṁhitā of the Garuḍa-Purāṇa.

The five introductory stanzas and the fourteenth (or in some MSs the sixteenth) stanza as well as the last stanza, beginning with the word *Cāṇakya* (*Cāṇikya*)-*māṇikyam idaṁ...*are always identical. The first stanza begins with the words *ekadantaṁ trinayanaṁ...*the second stanza begins with the words *praṇamya śirasā Viṣṇuṁ...*and is identical with the first stanza of the *CV* and *Cv* versions. The third to fifth introductory stanzas begin with the words *yena samyagadhitena......*, *paṭhitvaivaṁ śubhaṁ......*and *tad ahaṁ sampravakṣyāmi yaj...*The fourteenth (or sixteenth) stanza (and the sixth introductory stanza) always begins with the words *mūlasūtraṁ pravakṣyāmi* and in αβγ is dentical with the second introductory stanza of the *CN* version. The language of this version is quite beautifully polished and the stanzas tend to become highly refined *kāvya* stanzas.

5. *The Cāṇakya-sāra-saṃgraha* (1 edition and several MSs) divided into three *śataka-s* and containing, as a rule, 300 stanzas.

The four introductory stanzas beginning with the words *praṇamya śirasā Viṣṇuṁ...*, *adhityedaṁ yathā śāstraṁ...*, *tad ahaṁ sampravakṣyāmi...*and *mūlasūtraṁ pravakṣyāmi...*are always identical. (The two first introductory stanzas are identical with the first two stanzas of the *CV* and *Cv* version; the third introductory stanza is a variant of the third introductory stanza of the *CV* and *Cv* versions; the fourth introductory stanza is the second introductory stanza of the *CN* version). This version is most common in Nepāl.

These five versions of Cāṇakya's compendia are clearly definable.

6. The last version, which could be termed the *Cāṇakya-nīti-śāstra*, is a version containing collections of Cāṇakya's sayings composed of a number of identical stanzas arranged in varying orders and of a number of stanzas which are new and peculiar to each separate MS. Some of these stanzas, particularly those belonging to the first group, seem—as far as possible—authentic, but a great part of them are but currently known maxims, the authorship of which was merely attributed in *majorem gloriam* to Cāṇakya. The added maxims are often congruous with the preceding or subsequent ones, but they sometimes deal with unrelated subjects.

This version of Cāṇakya's saying is, as a rule, prefaced by two introductory stanzas beginning with the words *nānāśāstroddhṛtaṁ vakṣye...*and *mūlasūtraṁ pravakṣyāmi...*which state that the author teaches worldly wisdom "from selected various *śāstra-s*", the knowledge of which enables a foolish man to become wise. These introductory stanzas already show that in this version the maxims contain not necessarily original Cāṇakya's sayings, but many others picked from various sources.

The compiler of these sayings chose the best known maxims, usually attributed to Cāṇakya, but added maxims that he liked himself or believed to be liked by the reader. Therefore, with one or two exceptions, all MSs belonging to this group are different. The only important exception is the Cāṇakya-śataka (Haeberlin's edition) which was printed and reprinted several times with very few variants.

MSs in this version are not, as a rule, divided into *adhyāya-s* . They contain from 78 to 343 maxims but most contain 108 to 110 maxims. There are in existence a number of MSs which have the appearance of note books of students in Sanskrit written probably by children or adolescents. They correspond in substance to the version defined here as the sixth version. They do not merit however, any special attention or analysis.

There are many editions of this version, most of them being the text of the Cāṇakya-śataka mentioned above and sixteen or more well-known MSs. Most of the texts are different, but a great part of the maxims contained in these editions and MSs. in particular in their first part, are maxims found in one or another Cāṇakya's compendia.

While the evidence leading to the establishment of the first five versions seems to be unequivocal, it is not unlikely that the evidence leading to the narrowing down of the other manuscripts to the version called here Cāṇakya-nīti-śāstra may cause apprehension in the minds of some scholars. A further analysis offers the possibility of dividing the sixth version in two groups. By such division the Cāṇakya'śātaka (several editions and MSs) would comprise the actual Cāṇakya's version, while the Cāṇakya-nīti-śāstra would in reality be composed of several *subhāṣita-saṁgraha-s*. Each of them, while containing a great number of actual Cāṇakya's sayings, would also include a considerable number of other currently known maxims. These *subhāṣita-saṅgraha-s*, being collections of maxims composed by individual scribes or authors, would consequently differ from each other in individual cases. The only common feature of the *subhāṣita-saṁgraha-s* as such, and the *subhāṣita-saṁgraha-s* and the Cāṇakya-śatakas taken jointly, would be their attribution to Cāṇakya and the existence of the two introductory stanzas mentioned above. This group would also comprise the note book MSs. which, anyway, could not be regarded as MSs of collection of Cāṇakya's maxims.

TABLE SHOWING THE RELATIONSHIP BETWEEN THE HJ EDITION OF THE HITOPADEŚA AND THE STANZAS QUOTED IN THIS STUDY AS NUMBERS 1 TO 226

HJ Intr 3	No. 38	HJ 1.13	No. 43	HJ 1.82	No. 175
HL **1.17-8**	No. 33	HJ 1.18	No. 72	HJ 1.84	No. 64
HJ Intr 10	No. 153	HJ 1.24	No. 160	HJ 1.85	No. 53
HJ Intr 12	No. 92	HJ 1.26	No. 167	HJ 1.91	No. 61
HJ Intr 13	No. 96	HJ. 127	No. 141	HJ 1.96	No. 58
HJ Intr 14	No. 85	HJ 1.29	No. 128	HJ 1.100	No. 105
HJ Intr 16	No. 90	HJ. 1.32	No. 57	HJ 1.103	No. 176
HJ Intr 17	No. 93	HJ 1.34	No. 162	HJ 1.104	No. 6
HJ Intr 20	No. 91	HJ 1.35	No. 163	HJ 1.105	No. 59
HJ Intr 21	No. 94	HJ 1.36	No. 164	HJ 1.107	No. 44
HJ Intr 22	No. 84	HJ 1.42	No. 122	HJ 1.108	No. 31
HJ Intr 23	No. 88	HJ 1.43	Nos.23-4	HJ 1.109	No. 13
HJ Intr 25	No. 60	HJ 1.45	No. 165	HJ 1.110	No. 11
HJ Intr 26	No. 89	HJ 1.49	No. 166	HJ 1.111	No. 12
HJ Intr 27	No. 86	HJ 1.52	No. 167	HJ 1.113	No. 111
HJ Intr 28	No. 87	HJ 1.58	Nos.145-6	HJ 1.123	No. 74
HJ Intr 29	No. 154	HJ 1.62	No. 168	HJ 1.124	No. 76-
HJ Intr 31	No. 155	HJ 1.63	No. 112		76 A
HJ Intr 36	No. 156	HJ 1.65	No. 110	*HP* **1.87**	No. 80
HJ Intr 38	No. 95	HJ 1.66	No. 169	HJ 1.126	No. 183
HJ Intr 39	No. 46	HJ 1.67	No. 170	HJ 1.127	No. 79
HL **4.24-5**	No. 32	HJ 1.68	No. 171	HJ 1.128	No. 67
HJ Intr 40	No. 51	HJ 1.70	No. 172	HJ 1.129	No. 77
HJ Intr 46	No. 157	HJ 1.71	No. 173	HJ 1.133	No. 27
HJ Intr 47	No. 109	HJ 1.72	No. 50	HJ 1.134	No. 16
HL **6.1-4**	No. 30	HJ 1.73	No. 103	HJ 1.135	No. 26
HL **6.5-6**	No. 47	HJ 1.74	No. 98	*ad HJ* **1.135**	No. 178
HJ Intr 48	No. 52	HJ 1.75	No. 100-	HJ 1.138	No. 130
*	*		100A	HJ 1.139	No. 131
HJ 1.2	No. 158	HJ 1.79	No. 101	HJ 1.142	No. 37
HJ 1.10	No. 159	HJ 1.81	No. 174	HJ 1.148	No. 124

HJ 1.150	No. 179	HJ 2.15	No. 127	HJ 2.172	No. 9
HS **1.142**	No. 180	HJ 2.17	No. 142	*	*
HJ 1.152	No. 132	HJ 2.25	No. 113	HJ 3.4	No. 121
HJ 1.153	No. 19	HJ 2.32	No. 114	*HL* **73.20-1**	No. 45
HJ 1.159	No. 119	HJ 2.33	No. 192	HJ 3.5	No. 200
HJ 1.160	No. 147	HJ 2.34	No. 115	HJ 3.6	No. 201
HJ 1.161	No. 137	HJ 2.35	No. 116	HJ 3.10	No. 139
HJ 1.162	No. 107	HJ 2.38	No. 135	HJ 3.11	No. 108
HJ 1.163	No. 181	HJ 2.41	No. 150	*HL* **74.26-7**	No. 54
HJ 1.164	No. 22	HJ 2.42	No. 39	HJ 3.19	No. 202
HJ 1.165	No. 145	HJ 2.46	No. 40	HJ 3.22	No. 66
ad HJ **1.165**	No. 182	HJ 2.47	No. 126	HJ. 3.24	No. 55
HJ 1.169	No. 183	HJ 2.48	No. 41	HJ 3.25	No. 65
HJ 1.173	No. 25	HJ 2.51	No. 42	HJ. 3.27	No. 203
HJ 1.176	No. 184	HJ 2.61	No. 193	HJ 3.58	No. 204
HJ 1.177	No. 185	HJ 2.66	No. 134	HJ 3.60	No. 15
ad HS **1.162**	No. 5	*adHS* **2.67**	No. 194	HJ 3.64	No. 10
HJ 1.181	No. 186	HJ 2.67	No. 125	HJ 3.67	No. 4
HJ 1.185	No. 20	HJ 2.69	No. 194	HJ 3.81	No. 205
HJ 1.188	No. 28	HJ 2.70	No. 117	HJ 3.101	No. 102
HJ 1.189	No. 187	HJ 2.71	No. 118	HJ 3.103	No. 151
HJ 1.192	No. 188	HJ 2.81	No. 1	HJ 3.104	No. 206
ad HS **1.180**	No. 189	HJ 2.84	No. 3	HJ 3.108	No. 207
HJ 1.194	No. 21	HJ 2.114	No. 78	HJ 3.116	No. 208
HJ 1.198	No. 29	HJ 2.115	No. 73	HJ 3.123	No. 48
HJ 1.206	No. 70	HJ 2.118	Nos.68-9	HK 3.126	Nos.23-4
HJ 1.210	No. 71	HJ 2.119	Nos.143-4	HJ 3.132	No. 209
HJ 1.211	No. 81	HJ 2.120	No. 82	HJ 3.144	No. 210
HJ 1.212	No. 83	HJ 2.121	No. 7	HJ 3.148	No. 211
HJ 1.214	Nos. 143-4	HJ 2.128	No. 8	*	*
HJ 1.217	No. 190	HJ 2.132	No. 196	HJ 4.5	No. 129
HJ 1.222	No. 99	HJ 2.137	No. 197	HJ 4.7	No.76-76A
HJ 1.225	No. 97	HJ 2.147	No. 104	HJ 4.8	Nos.68-9
HJ 1.227	No. 133	HJ 2.150	No. 123	*HL* **98.21-4**	No. 2
*	*	HJ 2.152	No. 18	HJ 4.11	No. 212
HJ 2.3	No. 17	HJ 2.156	No. 75	HJ 4.14	No. 213
HJ 2.9	No. 149	HJ 2.157	No. 198	HJ 4.17	Nos. 145-6
HJ 2.10	No. 120	*ad HJ* **2.162**	No. 49	HJ 4.33	No. 214
HJ 2.11	No. 34	HJ 2.163	No. 199	HJ 4.56	No. 136
adHJ **2.11**	No. 191	HJ 2.165	No. 63	HJ 4.59	No. 215

HJ 4.65	No. 216	*HS* **4.71**	No. 218	HJ 4.104	No. 35
HJ 4.66	No. 100-	*ad HS* **4.71**	No. 152	HJ 4.107	No. 62
	100A	HJ 4.87	No. 138	HJ 4.108	No. 36
HJ 4.72	No. 106	HJ 4.93	No. 56	HJ 4.135	No. 220
HJ 4.74	No. 217	HJ 4.99	No. 219		

XXV

CĀṆAKYA'S APHORISMS IN THE PAÑCATANTRA*

1. In the Journal of the American Oriental Society, Vol. 76, No. 2 and Vol. 77 Nos. 1, 2, and 3 the author's twenty-fourth study in the series *Juridical Studies in Ancient Indian Law* entitled *C(āṇakya's) A(phorisms in the) H(itopadeśa)* appeared.[1] This study contains an introduction and the texts of 152 H(itopadeśa) stanzas which are identical with (Cāṇakya's Aphorisms).[2]

It was emphasized in this study that any identity of stanzas "does not always imply direct borrowing one from another in view of the fact that earlier works or the floating mass of oral traditions may serve as common depositories for the borrowing." The same remark is also applicable to the aphorisms found both in the P(añcatantra) and among the Cāṇakya's compendia (C.c). There is no doubt that the H. borrowed from the P. and not vice-versa and that fifty-seven stanzas which are also found in the C. are found both in the P. and in the H.; thus, if there was any borrowing in these 57 cases, the original source was either the P. or one of the C.c. but not H.

2. The preparation of the correlation of Cāṇakya's aphorisms with the various versions of the P. was more difficult for the P. than for the H., since for all practical purposes there exists only one version of the H., though many different texts are known[3], while the number of versions of the P. is quite numerous. This study, however, because of lack of space, does not contain the texts of the aphorisms with the critical apparatus, as was done for the H., but only a table containing the correlation of one hundred sixty-nine aphorisms found in at least one, version of P. and in at least, one, text of Cc.

3. As the basis for the correlation the following P. versions and texts were studied : the Pūrṇabhadra (PP.) ed. by J.

*. Previously appeared as JSAIL 29 in the Festschrift Prof. Dr Ernst Dier, Istambul.

1. It appeared also as No. 28 of the American Oriental Society Offprint Series.

2. With addenda 220 texts. See Post-Scriptum to study XXV.

3. L. Sternbach, *The Hitopadeśa and its Sources*, American Oriental Series Vol. 44, par. 3.

Hertel in H(arvard) O(riental) S(eries) 11-2; the *textus simplicior* (Pts), ed. by F. Kielhorn and G. Bühler in Bombay Sanskrit Series 1, 3, 4; and ed. by I. G. L. Kosegarten (PtsK), Bonnae ad Rhenum 1848; the Reconstructed text (PRE.) by F. Edgerton in American Oriental Series 2-3; the Tantrākhyāyikā (PT.) ed. by J. Hertel in the Abh(andlungen d. phil.-hist. Klasse der kön.) Sächsischen Ges. d. Wiss (enschaften) XXII. 5; and in HOS 14, ed. by J. Hertal (PTem.); the Southern Recension (PS.), ed. by J. Hertel in the Abh. Sächsischen Ges. d. Wiss. XXIV.5; and the Nepāli Text (PN.), as quoted in PRE 3.190-253; as well as the P. of Durgasiṁha by Veṅkasubbiah (PD.) in the Zeitschrift für Indologie und Iranstik 6.255; and the Meghavijaya (PM.) in ZDMG 64.62.

The Cāṇakya's stanzas were taken from two hundred thirty-three printed texts and MS. In 1956 the author divided these texts into six versions[4], viz. The Vṛddha Cāṇakya, *textus ornatior* (*CV.*), the Vṛddha Cāṇakya, *textus simplicior* (*Cv.*), the Cāṇakya-rāja-nīti-śāstra (*CR*), the Cāṇakya-nīti-śāstra (*CN*), the Cāṇakya-sāra-saṁgraha (*CS*) and the Laghu Cāṇakya (*CL*). Reconstructed texts of these six versions are now being published by the Vishveshvaranand Vedic Research Institute.[5]

The numbers of the stanzas in the table of correlation refer to these reconstructed texts. In order to make use of the present study possible, in each case underneath the numbers showing the stanzas of the reconstructed text, numbers in brackets are added; they refer to the available printed editions as follows: for *CV.* the texts of the Cāṇakya-nīti-darpaṇa; for Cv, Śrī-atha-ṣodaśa-Cāṇakya-prārambhaḥ. Jñāna Sāgara Press, Saṁvat 1932; for *CR.* Cāṇakya-rāja-nīti-śāstram, ed. by Pt. Iśvara Chandra Śāstri...Calcutta. Calcutta Oriental

4. Akten des XXIV Internationalen Orientalisten-Kongresses, München, herausg. von Herbert Franke, Deutsche Morgenlsdische Gesellschaft, Wiesbaden 1959, pp. 544-6. Cf. above pages 2892-91.

5. The Aphorisms attributed to Cāṇakya (Reconstructed) including the six Versions of Cāṇakya Compendia. (The Vṛddha-Cāṇakya, *textus ornatior*; the Vṛddha Cāṇakya, *textus simplicior*, the Laghu-Cāṇakya; the Cāṇakya-nīti-śāstra; the Cāṇakya-sāra-saṁgraha; and the Cāṇakya-rāja-nīti-sāra) for the first Time Collected and Critically edited with principal Variants and an Introduction, by Ludwik Sternbach LL.D. Vishveshvaranand Indogical Series, Nos. 27-28.

Series, No. 2 (*CRC.*), for *CN.* Cāṇakyaśatakam, ed. by Jīvānanda Vidyāsāgara, Calcutta 1926; for *CS.* Bodhi Cāṇakyam. athāvā Cāṇakya-sāra-saṁgrahaḥ...by Bh.C. Dutt. Calcutta 1888; for *CL.* Śrī-atha-ṣodaśa-Cāṇakya-prārambhaḥ, Jñana-Sāgara Press, Saṁvat 1932; where no printed texts exists the abbreviation MS. (manuscript) was used.

In ninety two cases the P. stanzas refer to Cāṇakya's aphorisms not found in the reconstructed texts of *C.* but in one or more texts only. These texts are marked in italics either in the table given below or in the footnotes to the table. (The abbreviations are found in footnote 44 to the Table of Correlations).

4. When analysing this table of correlation we find that one hundred-sixty-nine aphorisms of various versions of P. are found in the *Cc.* In thirty-three cases they are found in the reconstructed text of *CV* and in three cases in some other texts of this version. In twenty-three cases they are found in the reconstructed text of the *Cv* and in ten cases in some other texts of this version. In sixty cases they are found in the reconstructed text of *CR* and in thirteen cases in some other texts of this version. In sixteen cases they are found in the reconstructed text of *CN* and in seventy-one cases in some other text of this version. In twelve cases they are found in the reconstructed text of *CS* and in one case in another text of this version. In six cases they are found in the reconstructed text of *CL* and in one case in another text of this version.

This shows clearly (no such deduction could have been made as far as H. is concerned) that most stanzas found in P. are also found in the *CR.* version which could not have been composed after the tenth century A.D. (it was translated into Tibetan by Rin-chen-bzoṅ-po of Zhu hen who was born in 955 A. D.),[6] while most stanzas found in *CN.* are not found in the reconstructed version of *CN.* but in eighteen different texts belonging to this version; the latter texts are not representative of *Cc.* and therefore it is most likely that they were borrowed from the P. by the compilors of the *CN.* texts and included in these texts and not vice-versa.

5. In some cases it can be proved that the aphorisms

6. The Tibetan Cāṇakya-rāja-nīti-śāstra by L. Sternbach in ABORI.

originated in the P. and were borrowed from the P. by the author (s) of a Cc. That is for instance the case of PP. 1.159, 1.172, 1.326, 2 27; these aphorisms originally formed the prefatory or concluding stanzas of P.'s frame-stories.[7]

6. However, in general, it is not possible to prove whether a particular aphorism was borrowed by the author(s) of the P. from a Cc. or by the author (s)of a *Cc.* from the P. As long as the ur-text of *C.* is not found this question will remain unsolved.

7. Only in some cases it can be proved that the maxims which appear both in the P. and in a *Cc.* were borrowed from a third source. This for instance is the case of aphorisms found alsa in the Mahābhārata, the Rāmāyaṇa, the Mānava-dharma-śāstra, etc., for these sources are, no doubt older and are primary sources (e. g. Pts 1.356, 1.401, or PRE 3.50).

7. Cf. CAH. (Study XXIV above) par. 4.

PP	Pts	PtsK	PRE	PT	PTem	PN	PS	Other	*CV*	*Cv*	*CR*	*CN*	*CS*	*CL*	Other
1.2	2.150	2.157	1.3		1.3	2.2	1.3		7.14 (7.14)	6.7 (6.6)					
	1.3	1.3	2.31		2.52	1.28	2.31		7.15 (6.5 & 7.15)	6.8 (6.7)	4.12 (4.12)	[1]			H.16
1.6		1.25	1.5			2.3	1.5				8.13 (8.13)	[2]			H.142
1.9	1.22	1.27	1.7	1.6	1.3	2.5	1.8			*CvL I* 8.43	*CRT* 8.18				H
	1.24	1.29	1.12	1.7	1.10	2.9	1.13				8.34 (8.38)				H.150
1.15			1.14	1.9	1.12	2.11	1.15				8.30 (8.29)				H.39
	1.27ab	1.33ab									8.32 (8.35)				H.85
1.20	1.43	1.49	1.18	1.13	1.16	2.14	1.19				2.60 (2.56)	[3]			H.40
1.21	1.44	1.50									2.59 (2.55)	[4]			H.126

PP	Pts	PtsK	PRE	PT	PTem	PN	PS	Other	*CV*	*Cv*	*CR*	*CN*	*CS*	*CL*	Other
1-22	2.51 &2.121	1.22	1.14	1.19	1.17	2.15	1.20		3.13 (3.13)			71 (73)		3.8 (3.9)	H.43
1.23	1.63		1.24	1.22	1.19	2.19	1.28					*CNPh* 158.1			
1.30	1.45	1.51								[5]	8.75 (8.73)	[5]			
1.52									1.15 (1.15)	1.16 (1.16)	2.21 (2.24)	25 (27)			H.72
1.53	1.68	1.78	1.29	1.25	1.28	2.22	1.25			6.3 (6.3)	2.19 (2.22)	[6]			H.42
1.56	1.33	1.39								[7]					
			1.31	1.28	1.31	2.24	1.32				3.39 (3.40)				H.125
1.60	1.72	1.82	1.35	1.31	1.35		1.34				3.10 (3.10)	[8]			H.117
1.63	1.75	1.85	1.36	1.32	1.36	2.26	1.35				3.46 (3.54)				H.118
—	—	1.88								*CvTb* 7.11					

PP	Pts	PtsK	PRE	PT	PTem	PN	PS	Other	*CV*	*Cv*	*CR*	*CN*	*CS*	*CL*	Other
1.71	1.95	1.109	1.47	1.46	1.42						*CRC* 7.70				
1.77										1.8 (1.8)	2.9 (2.10)	30 (32)			H.44
1.105	1.135	1.151							16.2 (16.2)		*CRC* 1.50	*CNPII* 174			
1.106	1.137	1.153								7.8 (7.10)	2.48 (MS)	9			H.78
1.107	1.138										7.6 (MS)	10			H.74
1.109	1.146	1.162	1.89	1.82	1.90	2.58	1.79		16.4 (16.4)		2.24 (2.28)				H.18
1.110	1.147	1.163										11			
1.124 &2.37	1.164	1.180							5.5 (5.5)			12			
1.143	1.195								2.1 (2.1)	2.1 (2.1)	*CRC* 1.51	13			H.71

PP	Pts	PtsK	PRE	PT	PTem	PN	PS	Other	CV	Cv	CR	CN	CS	CL	Other
	1.204 &3.87	1.229 &3.83							9.10 (9.10)			14			
	1.206	1.219									CRC4.53 CRB4.53 CRBH 4.37	*CNI I* 200			
1.159	1.207	1.236 & 243	1.60	1.52	1.59	2.36	1.50					*CNW* 100			H.143-4
1.161															*CnT V* 96
1.162	1.208	1.234										*CNG* 42			
1.172	1.214	1.245 &268	1.63	1.55	1.62	2.39	1.54					15			
1.210	1.101											*CN II* 235			
	1.142	1.158									8.87 (8.96)				
1.212		1.226									8.93 (8.103)				

PP	Pts	PtsK	PRE	PT	PTem	PN	PS	Other	*CV*	*Cv*	*CR*	*CN*	*CS*	*CL*	Other
		1.227									2.46 (2.42)				
		1.235*							1.5 (1.5)	1.5 (1.5)	1.45 (1.52)	41 (43)			H.82
1.222			1.67	1.58	1.65	2.43	1.59				8.71 (8.69)				H.8
			1.99	1.92	1.100	2.66	1.87				8.114 (8.127)				H.109
1.245			1.104	1.97	1.105	2.71	1.92				16				H.49
						2.75	1.97				3.60 (3.71)				H.63
1.248 &4.10	4.10	4.11									7.72 (7.89)				

PP	Pts	PtsK	PRE	PT	Tem	PN	PS	Other	*CV*	*Cv*	*CR*	*CN*	*CS*	*CL*	Other
1.257								PD 305.84	5.1 (5.1)	4.5 (4.5)		4.7 (49)	1.89 (89)		H.111
	1.248	1.278									5.21 (5.22)	17			
	1.257	1.287										18			
1.264	1.266	1.298										19			
1.280*	1.312*									*CvL I* 8.42	*CRC* 2.7	*CNI I* 72			
1.288 &3.190	1.281 &2.27	1.313 &2.28	3.75	3.89	3.78	3.47	3.53				3.6 (3.5)				
	1. 282	1.314									8.129 (8.147)				
1.326	1.318	1.361 &367	1.127	1.117	1.128	2.95	1.118		13.6 (13.7)			20			H.129
1.328			1.41	1.36	1.40							*CNPN* 94			H.135

PP	Pts	PtsK	PRE	PT	PTem	PN	PS	Other	*CV*	*Cv*	*CR*	*CN*	*CS*	*CL*	Other
1.331	1.328	1.372							*CVNS* 10.23[21]						
		1.373							11.3 (11.3)						
1.334	1.331	1.376									[22]				
1.336	1.333	1.378										*CNT IV* 132			
	1.335 &3.84	3.81	1.117	2.83	1.118	2.83	1.105		3.10 (3.10)	1.7 (1.7)	2.3 (MS)	29 (31)			H.119
	1.356 &3.86								1.6 (1.6)	1.6 (1.6)	2.1 (2.1)	27 (29)			H.23-24
	1.361 &2.130											*CNŚC*, *CNŚL* 110			
	1.373	1.418								[23]		[23]			
	1.389	1.434								4.17 (4.15)			[24]		H.121

PP	P t	PtsK	PRE	PT	PTem	PN	PS	Other	*CV*	*Cv*	*CR*	*CN*	*CS*	*CL*	Other
	1.401& 2.116	1.449& 2.124													[25]H.21
1.390	1.402	1.450	3.52	3.49	3.63	3.32	3.39		12.14 (12.14)		*CRCaII* 18	3 (5)			
1.418 &1.421	1.417											*CNN* 20			
	1.421											[26]			
2.3	2.4											*cf.* *CNPN* 97			*cf.* H.141
2.6	5.101-102	5.86											2.30 (132)		
		2.16									*CRC* 2.44	*CNPII* 194 *CNG* 202*			
2.15	2.19	2.20	2.5	2.8	2.8	2.5	2.5				*CRC* 6.26				

PP	Pts	PtsK	PRE	PT	PTem	PN	PS	Other	*CV*	*Cv*	*CR*	*CN*	*CS*	*CL*	Other
2.27	2.32& 4.14	2.33& 4.15	2.19	2.29	2.29	1.17	2.19				3.15 (3.15)	17 (19)			H.104
2.39 & 4.11	2.45& 4.12	2.49& 4.13								*CvL I* 8.34		27			
2.43& 5.58	5.78	5.65									8.3 (8.5)*				
2.52	2.56& 2.129											1 (3)	1.46 (46)	6.9 (6.9)	
								Pts Ham-burg MS 2.147						6.7 (6.7)	
2.64		2.82												8.7 (8.7)	H.86
		2.88									8.132 (8.149)				
2.71	2.85	2.92	2.32		2.53	1.27	2.30			6.10 (MS)	4.13 (4.14)				H.27

PP	Pts	PtsK	PRE	PT	PTem	PN	PS	Other	*CV*	*Cv*	*CR*	*CN*	*CS*	*CL*	Other
2.80			2.34		(2.59)	(1.29)	2.32		4.14 (4.14)	7.9 (7.12)		[28]			H.26
		2.102									2.15 (2.19)	*CNP II* 23			
2.93	2.105-6&109	2.113& 119										*CNP II* 38		8.10 (8.13)	
2.97			2.47	2.68	2.79	1.38	2.42				8.74 (8.72)				H.132
2.112			2.59	2.84	2.95	1.52	2.55				2.53 (2.48)				H.20
2.118			2.57	2.81	2.92	1.49	2.52			*CvA & CvṢ* 8.18		[29]			H.5
	2.117	2.125													*CnT II* 20.4 *CnT II* 53.2
	2.132											*CNN* 46*			

PP	Pts	PtsK	PRE	PT	PTem	PN	PS	Other	CV	Cv	CR	CN	CS	CL	Other
	2.134 &5.37	2.141							16.12 (16.12)						
2.131	2.158	2.168	2.72	2.141	2.123	1.65	2.69				*CRBh* 8.79	*II*			
2.135	2.125								13.14 (13.15		6.47 (6.94)	[30]			
2.150	2.147	2.154								8.4 (8.4)	3.4 (3.3)	[31]	3.88 (2.88)	[31]	
	2.151	2.159					1.4 [32]				2.34 (2.41)				H.25
		2.161										*CNPII* 34			
2.161	2.152	2.162	2.48			1.39	2.43		7.3 (7.3)	5.13 (5.13)		*CNI I* 130 *CNŚK* 45			H.19
2.171												[33]			H.52

PP	Pts	PtsK	PRE	PT	PTem	PN	PS	Other	CV	Cv	CR	CN	CS	CL	Other
	2.173	2.183											3.70 (2.70)		
2.190		2.190	2.89			1.75	2.79				7.3 (7.3)				H.99
2.193	2.137	2.144							1.13 (1.13)	1.14 (1.14)	3.1 (3.1)	61 (63)			H.133
2.195	2.179	2.194	2.95& 4.7	2.152	2.170 & 4.7	1.79& 4.3	2.83& 4.3				7.21 (7.2)	*CNG* 134			H.97
3.1	3.1	3.1	3.1	3.1	3.1	3.1	3.1				7.43 (7.29)				
3.12										6.15* (6.14)	5.39* (5.44)	*CNŚK* 75*			
3.48	3.56	3.54										*CNP II* 276*			
3.53	3.67	3.67										*CNP II* 117			
3.66	3.76	3.73							5.21 (5.21)			34			

PP	Pts	PtsK	PRE	PT	PTem	PN	PS	Other	*CV*	*Cv*	*CR*	*CN*	CS	*CL*	Other
		3.96							12.12 (19.12)			"T" (*CNF* 81)			
2.88	3.96	3.97									8.35 (8.37)				H.154*
			3.50	3.47	3.61	3.30	3.37					*CNŚA* 17			
3.90	3.98	3.99											1.99 (99)		
	3.103	3.104									1.7 (1.7)	35			
	3.109	3.123										*CNI I* 209			
3.99	3.111	3.112										*CNT IV* 216			
	3.156											*CNP II* 220 *CNT IV*175			

PP	Pts	PtsK	PRE	PT	PTem	PN	PS	Other	*CV*	*Cv*	*CR*	*CN*	*CS*	*CL*	Other
3.139		3.161							14.2 (14.2)			*CNP II* 148, *CNT IV* 106			H.122
3.162	3.162											*CNI I* 183, *CNG* 36			
	3.172	3.200							9.2 (9.2)						
3.173		3.202										*CNN* 125 *CNMN*92			
		3.246						Pts. Hamburg MS 3.164				36			
3.217		3.253	3.97	3.112		3.58	3.68	Pts. Hemburg MS. 3.166					3.41 (241)		

PP	Pts	PtsK	PRE	PT	PTem	PN	PS	Other	*CV*	*Cv*	*CR*	*CN*	*CS*	*CL*	Other
	3.182										6.25 (6.37)				
	3.233	3.270													*CnT II* 24.12 *CnT VII* 86
4.5	1.390& 4.97& 101	1.435& 4.39										*CNW* 73			
4.6			4.14			4.2					5.42 (5.47)				H.138
4.12	2.39& 4.13	2.43& 4.14											3.47 (247)		
4.14 & 28	4.15& 30	4.16& 32								*CvL I* 8.25 *CvL II* 8.19					
4.19	4.22	4.22										*CNT IV* 251			

PP	Pts	PtsK	PRE	PT	PTe.n	PN	PS	Other	*CV*	*Cv*	*CR*	*CN*	*CS*	*CL*	Oher
4.24	4.27& 5.42	5.34										*CNP II* 216, *CNG* 296			
4.29	4.32	4.34									*CRC* 8.90	*CNP II* 175			
4.42	4.44	4.51												2.3 (2.3)	
	4.62-3	4.62										*CNPII* 282			
	4.66								4.19 (4.19)	4.3 (4.3)		[37]	(19) 1.19		
4.44	4.83	4.54										42 (44)			
4.60	1.247& 4.108	1.277& 4.108							*CVM* 10.32		5.40 (5.45)	[38]			
4.61v.l.	4.109v.l. &114v.l.	4.74v.l. &80v.l.					1.26		6.11 (6.12)	6.1 (6.1)	2.16 (2.20)	31 (33)			H.36

PP	Pts	PtsK	PRE	PT	PTem	PN	PS	Other	*CV*	*Cv*	*CR*	*CN*	*CS*	*CL*	Other
		4.75								*CvTb* 7.27		*CNP II* 33, *CNI I* 290			
	5.23	5.21							10.12 (10.12)						H.137
5.18		5.24									8.1(6 (8.116)				
5.27	1.321					1.50	2.53					*CNT IV*228*			H.59
	5.38											*CNP I* *CNI I* 128 *CNT IV* 70	65		H.50
	5.39	5.31										*CNN* 26, *CNP II* 92			
	5.41								1.12 (1.12)	1.13 (1.12)	2.27 (2.17)	15 (13)	1.84 (84)		H.100

PP	Pts	PtsK	PRE	PT	PTem	PN	PS	Other	CV	Cv	CR	CN	CS	CL	Other
5.35	5.48	5.37	5.37						*CVNS* 10·20						
5.64.	5.84	5.7							17.2 (17.2)			40			
	5.90	5.76									6.13 (6.19)				
	5.105	5.91												"*C*" (MS)	
								PD 300.18			8.31* (8.30)				H.60
								PD 302.42				*CNP II* 264*			
								in Gött gel.Anz. 1862 p.1365[41]			8.59 (8.59)	*CN II* 186 *CNG* 329			
								PD 306.98				*CR II* 253*			H.113

PP	Pts	PtsK	PRE	PT	PTem	PN	PS	Other	*CV*	*Cv*	*CR*	*CN*	*CS*	*CL*	Other
									PD 307. 109-10[42]	5.3 (5.3)		8.42 (8.43)	[42]		H.145-6
									Pts. Hamburg MS in ŚP[43]			2.7 (2.6)			
									PM 1.78	2.5 (2.5)	2.5 (2.5)	8.49 (8.50)	16 (18)	3.61 (2.61)	H.101
									Bühler *ad* V p.58[44]						*CnT II* 13.9 *CnT III* 7.56

Footnotes to Table of Correlation

(for abbreviations see footnote 44)

1. CNP I 51, CNP II 76, CNI I 67, CNG 238, CNT IV 50.
2. CNN 12, CNI I 55.
3. CNP II 30, CNI I 16.
4. CNG 259.
5. CvTb 4.20, CNP II 126, CNI I 53, CNT IV 97.
6. CNPh 10, CNI I 255, CNG 25, CNI II 50.
7. CvW 8.16, CvP V 8.11, CvLd 8.11.
8. CNG 56.
9. CNF 41, CNI I 172, CNP I 13, CNT IV 12, CNM 12, CNMN 12.
10. CNF 39, CNPN 54, CNI I 157, CNG 138.
11. CNP II 25, CNI I 236, CNG 325.
12. CNP I 28, CNP II 217, CNG 167, CNT IV 27, CNM 27, CNMN 27.
13. CNP II 165, CNG 49, CNT IV 157, CNM 154, CNMN 120.
14. CNP II 37 CNI I 196.
15. CNW 64, CNPN 58, CNP II 201.
16. CRC 5.43, CRB 5.42, CRCa I 5.40.
17. CNPh 108, CNP II 197, CNI I 257, CNG 83, CNT IV 232.
18. CNP I 93, CNT IV 95 v. l., CNM 93.
19. CNP II 120, CNI I 149, CNT IV 253, CNL 69.
20. CNP I 85, CNP II 122, CNPh 154, CNT IV 86.
21. Interpolation.
22. CRC. 7.85, CRB 7.80, CRBh II 7.37.
23. CvP IV 7.8, CvI 7.10, CvL II 7.11, CNG 242.
24. CNW 73, CNN 55, CNP II 153, CNI I 85, CNG 142, CNT IV 141, CNM 139, CNMN 105, CNŚC 107, CNŚI 107, CNL 5.
25. CnT II 20.3, CnT III 53.1.
26. CNP II 186, CNT IV 252.
27. CNI I 135, CNG 294, CNT IV 234.
28. CNP I 24, CNI I 150, CNT IV 23, CNMN 23, CNŚL 107.
29. CNP II 202, CNII 205, CNG 271.
30. CNP II 247, CNG 233, CNT IV 261.
31. CNP II 9, CNG 54, CNF 106, CNPh 19, CNI II 78, CLṢ 3.2.
32. In B MS. quoted *ad* line 45.
33. CNP. II 193, CNI I 230, CNG 179, CNT IV 242, CNM 189.
34. CNP I. 46, CNP II 190, CNT IV 45, CNM 45.
35. CNP II 23, CNG 6, CNŚ 17, CNŚL 69.
36. CNI I 73, CNT IV 127 and 172, CNM 94 and 137.
37. CNI I 35, CNG 113, CNT IV 243, CNM 190, CNMN 154, CNŚK 73.
38. CNG 119, CNT IV 104, CNM 50.
39. CNP I 6, CNI 256, CNG 24, CNT IV 5, CNM 6, CNMN 5.
40. CNP II 206, CNI I 123, CNG 175, CNT IV 231, CNM 54.
41. Böhtlingk's Indische Sprüche 6948. Cf. PT 2.165, PTem 2.147.
42. Cf. PP. 1.170, CNP II 185, CNI 189, CNG 177, CNT IV 250.

43. Böhtlingk's Indische Sprüche 5937. Cf. Pts. 1.280.

44. Abbreviation to the Table of Correlation; For CV; CVNS (Vṛddha-Cāṇakya-nīti-sumuccaya, Ahmedabad 1913); CVM (Vṛddha Cāṇakhyanum, Nirṇaya Sāgara Press, Bombay 1874). For Cv; CvA (Rāja-niti. Cāṇakya-muni-viracitam, Agra 1920); CvI (MS 2411 in the Library of the India office, London; CvL I and II (MSs A.445 and A. 446 in the Karl-Marx Universitāt. Universitätsbibliothek, Leipzig); CvLd (MS Cod. or. 8859; UB/128 in the University Library, Leiden); CvP IV and V (MSs 17072-4 and 17072-5 in the Universitẻ de Paris Institut de Civilisation Indienne), CvṢ (Śri atha-ṣodaśa-Cāṇakya-prārambhaḥ. Jñāna Sāgara Press, Saṁvat 1932); CvTb MS or. fol. 1037 in the Universitätsbibliothek Tūbingen), CvW (MS Walker 205c in the Bodleian Library Oxford) For CR; CRB (MS sansk. f. 15 in the Bodleian Library, Oxford) CRBh II (MS 348 of 1892-95 in the Bhandarkar Oriental Research Institute Collection, Poona), CRCa I and III (MSs Add. 2525 and Add. 1040 in the University Library, Cambridge), CRT Cāṇakyarājanītiśāstram by Sunitikumar Pathak. Viśva-Bhārati Anuals, VIII). For CN; CNF (Cāṇakyam. Codice Indiano edito dal Dre Emilio Bartoli. Napoli 1911), GNG (The Recension of Cāṇakya used by Galanos ...by G. M. Bolling in Studies in Honor of Maurice Bloomfield. New Haven 1920); CNI I and II (MSs 1518 Eggeling 8990 and Keith 7204, Tagore 40b, in the Library of the India Office, London,) CNL (MS A in the Universitätsbibliothek of the Karl Marx Universität, Leipzig CNM (Rājanitau Cāṇakya-mūni-viracitam; no place, on date); CNMN (Cāṇakya-mūni-kṛtam-nīti-sāra, Allahabad 1880), CNN (E. Bartoli, Un secondo codice fiorentino inedito di Cāṇakya in *Rivista Indo-greco-italica di Filologia* Vol. 3, fasc. 3-4), CNP I and II (MSs 17072-3 and 17072-1 in the Universitẻ de Paris, Institut de Civilisation Indienne), CNPh (MSs 1566 in the University of Pennsylvania Library, Philadelphia, Pa), Cāṇakya-ślokaḥ...Śrīrāma Śāstri Bhaṭṭacāryyeṇa saṁpāditah. Ghose Press, Calcutta 1918). CNŚC Cāṇakya-śloka-saṁgraha...Publ. by Tārāsanna Mṛtyunjay, Calcutta 1915), CNŚK Cāṇakya-śloka. New Sanskrit Press, Calcutta 1887) CNŚL (Aṣṭottara-śata-Cāṇakya-ślokaḥ. Lakṣmī Printing Works, Culcutta 1322) CNŚI Cāṇakya-śloka-saṁgrahaḥ (Hindi gadya anuvāda sahita). Saṁgrahakarttā tathā anuvādaka Śrī Nārāyaṇachandra caṭṭopādhyāya, Rudra Printing Press, Calcutta 1918), CNT IV MS No. 5119, as quoted in O. Kressler's *Stimmen indischer Lebensklugheit* as TjD); CNW (A. Weber, Über 100 Sprüche des Cāṇakya, in Mona sberichte der kön. Ak. d. Wiss. zu Berlin aus dem Jahre 1864, Berlin 1865); For CL; CLṢ (Śrī-atha-ṣoḍaśa-Cāṇakya-prārambhaḥ. Jñāna-Sāgara Press, Saṁvat 1932); for other texes: CnT II, III, V and VII (MSs 5117, 5118, 5120, 5122 in Tanjore, as quoted in O. Kressler's *Stimmen indischer Lebensklugheit* as TjB, TjC, TjE and TjG)

XXVI

MĀNAVA-DHARMAŚĀSTRA VERSES IN CĀṆAKYA'S COMPENDIA[1]

I. INTRODUCTORY NOTE

1. Aphorisms and maxims found in Cāṇakya's compendia are very numerous. The author has been able to collect 2433 different aphorisms and maxims which he found in 171 editions and manuscripts.[2] This large number of aphorisms and maxims suggests that it could not have been possible for one man—Cāṇakya—to compose all of them.

The origin of the aphorisms and maxims is in most cases unknown. They passed orally from one person to another, just as today "golden rules" and proverbs float among people of different nations. But in India this floating mass of oral tradition and wisdom was very often *in majorem gloriam* attributed to one man; Cāṇakya—the moralist, Cāṇakya—the idealized minister of Candragupta Maurya. Others were incorporated in the classical Sanskrit literature, in particular the *kathā* literature, the Pañcatantra, the Hitopadeśa, the Vetālapañcaviṁśatikā, the Śukasaptati, the Vikramacarita, etc., and before in the epics and the dharmaśāstra-s, in particular theMānava-dharmaśāstra (Mn).

The aim of this study is to show which of the maxims attributed to Cāṇakya originated in the Mānava-dharmaśāstra. Since the Mānava-dharmaśāstra was composed before the Cāṇakya-compendia were compiled, the compiler had to borrow from the Mānava-dharmaśāstra and not vice-versa. However in some cases he, similarly, as the compiler of the Mānava-dharmaśāstra, could have drawn independently from the floating wealth of common wisdom or from other sources.

2. On the basis of the analysis of over 171 MSs and edi-

1 Previously appeared as JSAIL 27 in the *Journal of the American Oriental Society*, Vol. 79, N 4, pp. 233-254.

2. L. Sternbach, "Cāṇakya's Various Versions of Aphorisms with a *pratīka* Index of aphorisms attributed to Cāṇakya. (An attempt at a revised analysis.)"

tions of Cāṇakya's compendia it was possible to conclude that they should be divided into six versions, viz., the Vṛddha Cāṇakya, *textus ornatior*, represented by the well-known text of the Cāṇakya-nīti-darpaṇa and divided into 17 adhyāya-s (*CV*); the Vṛddha Cāṇakya, *textus simplicior*, represented by texts usually called Vṛddha Cāṇakya and divided into eight adhyāya-s; some of the maxims of this version are identical with those found in the Vṛddha Cāṇakya, *textus ornatior* version; the Laghu Cāṇakya represented by several texts called Laghu Cāṇakya and divided into eight short adhyāya-s; the Cāṇakya-rāja-nīti-śāstra represented by texts usually called Cāṇakya-rāja-nīti and divided into eight long adhyāya-s of which the seventh and eighth are particularly long and in which a great number of maxims correspond to the Bṛhaspati-saṁhitā of the Garuḍa-purāṇa; the Cāṇakya-sāra-saṁgraha represented by texts of the same title and divided into three śataka-s; and the Cāṇakya-nīti-śāstra represented by numerous editions and MSs entitled Cāṇakya-nīti and the like, not divided into adhyāya-s or śataka-s and containing usually 108 stanzas (*aṣṭottaraśata*) but often more; they are very often general collections of maxims and aphorisms—*Subhāṣita-saṁgraha-s in majorem gloriam* attributed to Cāṇakya.

Of these six versions the most homogenous are the Laghu Cāṇakya, the Cāṇakya-nīti-śāstra, if represented by the *aṣṭottaraśata-s*, and the Vṛddha Cāṇakya, *textus ornatior* (the Cāṇakya-nīti-darpaṇa text). This fact seems to be also reflected in this study. Out of the twenty-nine maxims the origin of which can be traced to the Mānava-dharmaśāstra, none is found in the Laghu Cāṇakya version, only one in the Cāṇakya-nīti-śāstra (*aṣṭottaraśata*) version and only two in the Vṛddha Cāṇakya, *textus ornatior* version; one of the maxims found in the Cāṇakya-nīti-śāstra version and in the Vṛddha Cāṇakya, *textus ornatior* version is the same maxim.

The maxims which we find in the Mānava-dharmaśāstra and the Vṛddha Cāṇakya, *textus ornatior* and Cāṇakya-nīti-śāstra versions (Nos. 7, 18 and 24), were very well-known maxims in classical India; they were incorporated in many Sanskrit works such as the Mārkaṇḍeya-purāṇa, the Śukasaptati, *textus simplicior* (No. 18), and the Mahābhārata, the Pañcatantra, the Hitopadeśa, the Vikramacarita, the Śukasapatati, the Vetālapañcaviṁśatikā, the Dharmaviveka, the Bhojaprabandha, the Garuḍa-purāṇa (No. 24), etc. Probably as such they were incorporated in Cāṇakya's compendia and Cāṇakya was labeled as the author. The second of them which also occurs in the Mahābhārata could have been borrowed from that source and not necessarily from the Mānava-dharmaśāstra. Many so-called Cāṇakya's aphorisms were borrowed from the Mahābhārata.

3. In order to be able to conclude whether the compiler of Cāṇakya's compendia borrowed from the Mānava-dharmaśāstra directly or not, it was necessary to analyse each stanza occurring in any of Cāṇakya's compendia as well as in the Mānava-dharmaśāstra separately and to give all variants of this stanza. This has been done in the second part of this study.

On the basis of this analysis it was possible to conclude that the compiler of the Cāṇakya's compendia could not have used the Mānava-dharmaśāstra text used by Medhātithi (see No. 11 below) nor by Nandana nor the anonymous Kaśmīrian commentary (see No. 16 below) but probably used the same text as was used by Govindarāja (see No. 13 below). It has also been possible to conclude in some cases, when Cāṇakya's compendia included a maxim the origin of which could be traced to more than one primary source (e. g. the Mahābhārata or the Mārkaṇḍeya-purāṇa and the Mānava-dharmaśāstra), from which of them it was borrowed. And so, it has been possible to conclude that maxims Nos. 5, 19, 20 and 22 were not borrowed from the Mahābhārata but from the Mānava-dharmaśāstra and that the maxim No. 18 was not borrowed from the Mārkaṇḍeya-purāṇa but from the Mānava-dharmaśāstra. In the case of No. 24, however, it has not been possible to conclude whether it was borrowed from the Mahābhārata or the Mānava-dharmaśāstra and in the case of maxims Nos. 15, 17, 26 and 27 the exact source from which the four Cāṇakya-maxims originated could not be traced so far, although it is certain that they were influenced by the Mānava-dharmaśāstra.

It was also possible to conclude whether the compiler of Cāṇakya's stanzas used the pure text of the Mānava-dharmaśāstra or the vulgata. And so, Nos. 6, 13, 14 and 28 were based, not on the classical Mānava-dharmaśāstra text, but on the Vulgata of the Mānava-dharmaśāstra, or contained changes made by the compiler of one or other of Cāṇakya's compendia. The text of the vulgata of the Mānava-dharmaśāstra, as used in maxims Nos. 6, 13, and 14, and particularly of No. 28, should be of great interest to a student of the Mānava-dharmaśāstra.

Some of the Cāṇakya's stanzas printed in the Vṛddha-cāṇakya-nīti-samuccaya edition, or found in some MSs contain a number of spelling mistakes. They are not variants and are of no importance for the analysis of the maxims. A special note of these errors has been made at the end of the analysis of each maxim.

4. Most of the maxims which were borrowed by Cāṇakya from the Mānava-dharmaśāstra are well known; they often occur also in the Mahābhārata, the Rāmāyaṇa, the Harivaṁśa, the Bhāgavata-purāṇa, the Mākaṇḍeya-purāṇa, the Matsya-purāṇa, the Bṛhaspati-saṁhitā of the Garuḍa-purāṇa, the Bhaviṣya-purāṇa, as well as the Pañcatantra, the Hitopadeśa, the Vetālapañcaviṁśatikā, the Śukasaptati, the Vikramacarita, etc. These are mostly moral stanzas and, therefore, are not quoted often in other dharmaśāstra-s, their commentaries and the nibandha-s. Wherever the stanzas borrowed were of a less general nature and were closely connected with *dharma* and *nīti*, they were also quoted in other dharmaśāstra-s, such as the Viṣṇu-smṛti, the Gautamīya-dharmasūtra, the Baudhāyana-dharma-sūtra, the Nārada-smṛti, the Vāsiṣṭha-dharmaśāstra-s, the Devalasmṛti and in numerous nibandha-s and commentaries. In the second part of this study special attention has been paid to this fact.

5. Usually the stanzas which were borrowed from the Mānava-dharmaśāstra were not incorporated in one particular compendium but were incorporated in all, or nearly all editions or MSs belonging to the same version. That is particularly true if a maxim was borrowed by the Cāṇakya-rāja-nīti-śāstra, Cāṇakya-sāra-saṁgraha or the Vṛddha Cāṇakya, *textus simplicior* versions. This rule does not apply, however, to the Cāṇakya-nīti-śāstra version and to one edition of the Vṛddha Cāṇakya, *textus ornatior* version. As stated above, the Cāṇakya-nīti-śāstra version, if the edition or MS is not an *aṣṭottaraśata*, is a collection of various maxims, a Subhāṣita-saṁgraha, *in majorem gloriam*, attributed to Cāṇakya. The so-called "longer" MSs add to the main body of their collections many maxims from various sources and *eo ipso* also from the Mānava-dharmaśāstra. And so, MS. 1518a (Eggeling 3990), in the India Office Library in London, incorporated from the Mānava-dharmaśāstra maxims Nos. 13 and 28; MS. 1566 in the Library of the University of Pennsylvania, maxim No. 17; the edition entitled Cāṇakya-ślokaḥ, Calcutta, 1319 (A. D. 1913), maxim No. 25; the edition entitled "The Recension of Cāṇakya used by Galanos" by G. M. Bolling in *Studies in Honor of Maurice Boomfield*, New Haven, maxims Nos. 26 and 28; and MS. A 447 in the Universitätsbibliothek of the Karl-Marx Universität in Leipzing, maxim No. 28.[3] The genuine Vṛddha Cāṇakya, *textus ornatior* version, borrowed from the Mānava-dharmaśāstra three maxims, viz., Nos. 7, 18, and 24,[4] all of which are well-known maxims. They are found in many editions or MSs of Cāṇakya.

In addition to these maxims we find twelve maxims (Nos. 3, 4, 5, 8, 9, 10, 11, 12, 19, 20, 21, and 29) borrowed from the Mānava-dharmaśāstra which are incorporated only in one edition belonging to the Vṛddha Cāṇakya, *textus ornatior* version. This edition is entitled *Vṛddhacāṇakya-nīti-samuccaya...... Taiyātra-karanāra Maṇilāla Chappārāma Bhaṭṭa* (pp. 4, 77)+(i) covers, Granthodaya Printing Press, Ahmedabad, 1913). It contains an introduction in Gujarātī and a Gujarātī translation of each verse. It further contains the text of the Cāṇakya-nīti-darpaṇa with several additions. And so, at the end of the tenth *adhyāya* it adds four maxims, the first, third and fourth of which were borrowed from Bhartṛhari's *Śataka-s*. At the end of the eleventh *adhyāya* it adds six maxims, some from the Mahābhārata, the Cāṇakya-nīti-śāstra version and other sources. Beginning from the eleventh adhyāya it adds Mānava-dharmaśāstra stanzas: after the tenth stanzas it adds five stanzas which were borrowed from the second book of the Mānava-dharmaśāstra, viz., stanzas Nos. 3, 4, 5, 8 and 9 and after the thirteenth stanza one maxim borrowed from the Mahābhārata. In the fourteenth adhyāya it adds after the twelfth stanza five stanzas, three of which were borrowed from the third book of the Mānava-

3. Maxim No. 28, a well-known one, was incorporated in three different Cāṇakya-compendia belonging to the Cāṇakya-nīti-śāstra version. Other Cāṇakya stanzas borrowed from the Mānava-dharmaśāstra and incorporated in the Cāṇakya-nīti-śāstra version are represented by several editions and MSs belonging to this version, viz., Nos. 7, 18 and 24.

4. See paragraph 3, above.

dharmaśāstra, viz., maxims Nos. 10, 11, 12 and the fourth from the eleventh book of the Mānava-dharmaśāstra, viz., No. 29. At the end of the fifteenth adhyāya it adds four stanzas borrowed from Bhartṛhari's *Śataka-s* and at the end of the sixteenth *adhyāya* four stanzas, three of which were borrowed from the seventh book of the Mānava-dharmaśāstra, viz., Nos. 19, 20 and 21 and one maxim (16.24), the origin of which could not be traced, with the exception of $\alpha\beta$ which are almost identical with $\gamma\delta$ of Mn 1.96. Finally at the end of the seventeenth *adhyāya* it adds five maxims borrowed from the Mahābhārata. All the maxims borrowed from the Mānava-dharmaśāstra were incorporated into this edition without any changes.

It may be also added that one Mānava-dharmaśāstra maxim, viz., No. 2, was incorporated into the Vṛddha-cāṇakyaḥ, Cāṇakya-praṇītaḥ, by Pt. Śrī Rāma Śāstri-Sampaditaḥ, Calcutta, 1332 (A. D. 1916) edition, which is a Subhāṣita-saṁgraha composed exclusively of Cāṇakya's stanzas. It contains 991 aphorisms and maxims attributed to Cāṇakya, of which 22 could not be traced to any of the 171 editions and MSs of Cāṇakya's compendia. One of these 22 aphorisms (377.16) is maxim No. 2 borrowed from the second book of the Mānava-dharmaśāstra.

All the borrowed stanzas which are found only in one edition of MS are of lesser value to a student of Cāṇakya's aphorisms and of the Mānava-dharmaśāstra; those maxims which are found in the two editions mentioned above are of no particular interest.

6. Usually the maxims borrowed from the Mānava-dharmaśāstra and incorporated in one or the other Cāṇakya's compendia were genuine and well-known maxims, but sometimes they were taken out of context and incorporated in one of the Cāṇakya-compendia. This was the case of stanzas Nos. 21, 26 and 29.

Maxim No. 21 deals with the obligation to shun vices proceeding from love of pleasure and from wrath but does not describe them, though they are enumerated in the following stanzas of the Mānava-dharmaśāstra. The quotation of only one of these stanzas is incomplete and valueless.

Maxims No. 29 deals with the bestowing of gifts for purposes of reward to the detriment of persons who, according to law, had to be maintained. The following stanza enumerates these persons. Also in this case the quotation is incomplete and valueless.

Both these incomplete quotations (Nos. 21 and 29) were incorporated in the non-critical edition, the Vṛddhacāṇakya-nīti-samuccaya. That may be the explanation of this unfortunate choice from the Mānava-dharmaśāstra.

Maxim No. 26 deals with false witnesses and the external marks which makes it possible to recognize a false from a true witness. This stanza, as Medhātithi has stated, is a "supporting stanza" of the preceding one which deals with the same subject. It was illogical to quote only Mn. 8.26 without the preceding stanza but this has happened in classical Indian literature several times. The same maxim (No. 26) was quoted without the preceding one in the Pañcatantra (Pañcakhyānaka, 1.21; Keilhorn and Bühler's edition, 1.44), the Hitopadeśa (Johnson's edition, 2.47 and others), the Vetālapañcaviṁśatikā (1.8) and the Bṛhaspati-saṁhitā of the Garuḍa-purāṇa (1.109, 52). It is difficult to give an explanation for the unfortunate choice of this particular maxim and the incomplete quotation; it could have lost its specific meaning at the time it was incorporated into these sources.

7. The detailed analysis of each stanza borrowed from the Mānava-dharmaśāstra and incorporated in one or other Cāṇakya's compendium bears out in detail the general remarks given above in paragraphs 1 to 6.

The detailed analysis of stanzas gives, first, the text of each Mānava-dharmaśāstra stanza, as found in Jolly's text of Manu[5] with various readings in the footnotes, then a new English translation of the stanza is given. In the paragraphs that follow the appropriate places are given showing in which of Cāṇakya's compendia, and other sources, including the *nibandha-s*, commentaries and *Subhāṣita-saṁgraha-s*, the maxim is found. Finally a detailed analysis of each stanza is given.

The maxims are arranged according to the order in which they appear in the Mānava-dharmaśāstra.

5. Only stanzas Nos. 8, 9 and 24, were quoted according to Jhā's or other editions.

II. *Detailed Analysis of Stanzas*

No. 1. *Mn* 1.96.

bhūtānāṁ[1] *prāṇinaḥ śreṣṭhāḥ*[2] *prāṇināṁ buddhi-jīvinaḥ,*
buddhimatsu narāḥ[3] *śreṣṭhā*[4] *nareṣu brāhmaṇāḥ*[5] *smṛtaḥ.*[6]

"From among living beings, the animated ones are considered to be the best; from among the animated beings, those which subsist by intelligence, (are considered to be the best); from among those which subsist by intelligence, human beings (are considered to be the best); and from among them, the Brāhmaṇs (are considered to be the best)".

This maxim occurs in the Cāṇakya-rāja-nīti-śāstram edition (*Calc. Or. Ser.* 2), 3.27 (*CRC*); MS. sansk. f. 15 in the Bodleian Library in Oxford, 3.28 (*CRB*); MS. 1559 in the Library of the University of Pennsylvania in Philadelphia, 3.26 (*CRP*); MS. No. 347 of 1892-95 in the Bhāṇḍārkar O. R. Institute in Poona, 3.26 (*CRBh I*); MS. No. 348 of 1892-95 in the Bhāṇḍārkar O. R. Institute in Poona, 3.26 (*CRBh II*); MS. Add. 2525 in the University Library in Cambridge, 3.18 (*CRCa*); and in the Vṛddha Cāṇakyaḥ, Cāṇakya-praṇītaḥ, Calcutta, 1332 edition, 63.36 (*CPS*).

It is also quoted in the Smṛtimuktāphalam, 70.6 (SMPh).

The Mānava-dharmaśāstra text is found only in the Cāṇakya-rāja-nīti-śāstra version from which it was incorporated in the Vṛddha Cāṇakyaḥ, Cāṇakya-praṇītaḥ edition. The maxim deals in the first place with Brāhmaṇs; it is not well-known. It is only quoted in one *nibandha*, viz., the Smṛtimuktāphalam.

No variants occur in the Manu text. The Cāṇakya texts follow closely the Manu text and contain only unimportant variants.

The Cāṇakya text was undoubtedly borrowed directly from the Mānava-dharmaśāstra.

αβ of the 16.24 stanza found in the Vṛddha-cāṇakya-nīti-samucaya edition is similar to γδ of this stanza.

[1] *bhūtānā CRBh II.* [2]*śreṣṭhā CRBh I.* [3]*narā CRBh I, CRBh II, CRCa.* [4]*śreṣṭāḥ CRCa, CPS.* [5]*brāmaṇā CRP, CRBh I, CRBh II, CRCa.* [6]*smṛtā CRBh I; varāḥ CRBh II, CRCa.*

No. 2. *Mn* 2.94.

na jātu kāmaḥ kāmānām upabhogena śāmyati,
haviṣā kṛṣṇavartmeva bhūya evābhivardhate.

"Desire is never supposed by the enjoyment of the object desired; it only becomes stronger like fire by clarified butter."

This maxim occurs in the Vṛddha Cāṇakyaḥ, Cāṇakya-praṇītaḥ, Calcutta, 1332, edition, 377.16.

It also occurs in the Mahābhārata (Roy's edition), 1.75, 49 and 1.85, 12; the Harivaṁśa, 1639; the Brāhmadharma, 2.13, 3; and the Bhāgavata-purāṇa, 9.19, 14.

It is also quoted in Vallabahadeva's Subhāṣitāvalī, 3352; the Subhāṣita-ratna-bhāṇḍāgāra, 166.609 where it is ascribed to the Vāyu-purāṇa (93. 95); and Böhtlingk's *Indische Sprüche*, 3241.

Similarly Pañcarātra, 1.14, 97.

The Mānava-dharmaśāstra text is found in one Cāṇakya source, i. e., in the Vṛddha Cāṇakyaḥ, Calcutta, 1332, edition, which is a subhāṣita-saṁgraha composed of Cāṇakya's sayings.

The maxim deals with desire and enjoyment and is a well-known one. It occurs in the Mahābhārata, the Harivaṁśa, the Bhāgavata-purāṇa, the Vāyu-purāṇa, the Brāhmadharma and in several Subhāṣita-saṁgraha-s.

Neither the Manu text nor the Cāṇakya text contain any variants.

The text has been incorporated in the Vṛddha Cāṇakyaḥ edition either directly from the Mānava-dharmaśāstra or from the Mahābhārata. There is no doubt that it is not an original Cāṇakya stanza.

No. 3. *Mn* 2.121.

abhivādanaśīlasya nityaṁ vṛddhopasevinaḥ,
catvāri tasya[1] *vardhanta*[2] [3]*āyuḥ*[4] *prajñā yaśo balam.*

"He who usually salutes and constantly pays reverence to elders obtains an increase of four things; longevity, merit, fame and strength."

This maxim occurs in the Vṛddhacāṇakya-nīti-samuccaya, Ahmedabad, 1913 edition, 12.11.

It also occurs in the Mahābhārata (Roy's edition), 5.38, 74γδ-75αβ (MBh).

It is also quoted in Vīramitrodaya, Saṁskāraprakāśa, 460.23-4 (VRS); Vidhāna-pārijāta, 1. 501. 14-5 (VP); Parāśara-dharma-saṁhitā, 1.1; 336, 5-6 (PS); Smṛti-candrikā (Ghārpure's edition, 37.7) (SMC), and Smṛtimuktāphalam, 108.34 (SMPh).

The Mānava-dharmaśāstra text is found only in one Cāṇakya-compendium belonging to the Vṛdha Cāṇakya, *textus ornatior* version, viz., the Vṛddhacāṇakya-nīti-samuccaya edition.

The maxim deals with the duty to pay reverence to elders and describes the reward for saluting one's superiors (Vidhāna-pārijāta), or eulogies the act of saluting one's superiors (Parāśara-dharma-saṁhitā). It is a well-known maxim. It also occurs in the Mahābhārata. Similar thoughts are also expressed in the Āpastambhīya-dharmasūtra (1.5, 15). The maxim is often quoted in the *nibandha-s* and commentaries. It was also quoted by Böhtlingk in his *Indische Sprüche*, 504 (IS).

Some variants occur in the Manu text, in particular in β. Medhātithi (M) and Govindarāja (G) use *āyur dharmo* while other texts use *āyur prajñā*, or *āyur vidyā*. The Cāṇakya text is identical with most common Manu texts. The *nibandha-s* contain some unimportant variants.

The text of Cāṇakya was borrowed probably directly from the Mānava-dharmaśāstra and not from the Mahābhārata, since the latter text contains a variant in β which is not found in the Cāṇakya text.

[1]*sampra* IS; *samyag* (*k*) VRS, SMPh. [2]*vardhante CV*, PS, SMPh; *sampravardhante* Mn (Jhā's edition), MBh. [3]*āyur vidyā ya°* Mn (M), *CV*, Mn (*vulgata*); *āyur dharmo* Mn (M, G), Mn (Jhā's edition); *āyur prajnā* VRS; *kīrtir āyur ya°* MBh; *vardhante* VRS, VP. [4]*hy āyuḥ* PS.

No. 4. *Mn* 2.129.

parapatnī tu[1] *yā strī syād asaṁbaddhā*[2] *ca yonitaḥ*,[3]
tāṁ brūyād bhavatī'ty evaṁ[4] *subhage* [5]*bhaganī'ti ca.*[6]

"He should address a woman who is a wife of another and not related by blood as 'lady' or 'blessed sister'."

This maxim occurs in the Vṛddhacāṇakya-nīti-samuccaya, Ahmedabad, 1913 edition, 12. 12.

It is also quoted in Vīramitrodaya, Saṁskāra-prakāśa

467.2-3, (VRS); Parāśara-dharmasaṁhitā, 1.1; 325, 10-1; Smṛti-candrikā (Ghārpure's edition), 38.11 (SCM); Smṛti-muktāphalam, 110. 20 (SMPh); and Bālambhaṭṭi, Brahma-cāri-prakāraṇa (Ghārpure's edition), 148.19 (BBh).

The Mānava-dharmaśāstra text is found in one Cāṇakya's compendium belonging to the Vṛddha Cāṇakya, *textus ornatior* version, viz., the Vṛddhacāṇakya-nīti-samuccaya edition.

The maxim deals with salutation of not one's own wife. The maxim is not well known but occurs in several *nibandha-s* and commentaries. A similar thought is also expressed in the Viṣṇu-smṛti (32.7).

Some variants occur in the Manu text, in particular in β and δ. The Cāṇakya text is identical with most of the Manu texts, with the exception of one variant in β. The *nibandha-s* contain some variants which in β are identical with the Kullūka's and Rāghavānanda's commentaries and with the *vulgata* text of the Mānava-dharmaśāstra.

The stanza was taken somewhat out of context and no reason is seen why it has been borrowed by a Cāṇakya text. It was undoubtedly borrowed directly from the Mānava-dharma-śāstra.

[1]*ca*, in Haughton's MSs VI and VII in the India Office Library, in Haughton's MS II of Kullūka's commentary and in the anonymous Kaśmīrian commentary. [2]*asaṁbandhā* in Kullūka's and Rāghavananda's commentaries and in the *vulgata* text of Mn, VRS, SCM, SMPh. [3]*jātitaḥ CV*. [4]*eva* SCM. [5]*bhaginī tu vā* SCM. [6]*vā* variant in Mn (Jhā's edition), SMPh.

No. 5. *Mn* 2.156.

na tena vṛddho bhavati[1] *yenāsya palitaṁ śiraḥ,*
[2]*yo vai yuvā'py adhiyānas taṁ devāḥ*[3] *sthaviraṁ viduḥ.*

"One is not considered venerable because his head became gray ; (however) he who, though young in years, is learned in the Vedas is considered venerable."

This maxim occurs in the Vṛddhacāṇakya-nīti-samuccaya, Ahmedabad 1913 edition, 12.13.

It also occurs in the Mahābhārata (Roy's edition), 3.133, 11 (MBh); and the Brāhamadharma, 2.4,11.

It is also quoted in the Smṛtimuktāphalam, 104.27 (SMPh).

The Mānava-dharmaśāstra text is found only in one Cāṇakya's compendium belonging to the Vṛddha Cāṇakya, *textus ornatior* version, viz., the Vṛddhacāṇakya-nīti-samuccaya edition.

The maxim deals with wisdom and tribute paid to it. It is a quite well-known maxim. It occurs also in the Mahābhārata and in the Brāhma-dharma. Böhtlingk quotes it also in his *Indische Sprüche* (3275). It is also quoted in one *nibandha*, viz., the Smṛtimuktāphalam. Similar thoughts are expressed in another place of the Mahābhārata (5.167, 16).

The Manu text contains some variants. In *a* the text, as quoted above, is found in the commentaries of Medhātithi, Govindarāja, Rāghavānanda, Kullūka and in the *vulgata*; the commentary of Nandana and the Beṅgālī MS, dated Śakasaṁvat 1453, as well as the Mahābhārata and the Smṛtimuktāphalam have *sthaviro bhavati*; finally the anonymous Kaśmīrian commentary has *sthaviro jñeyo*. The Cāṇakya text follows the commentaries of Medhātithi, Govindarāja, Rāghavānanda, Kullūka and the *valgata*, but contains an unimportant variant in δ.

The text of Cāṇakya was undoubtedly borrowed directly from the Mānava-dharmaśāstra and not from the Mahābhārata since the latter text has a different third *pāda*.

[1]*sthaviro bhavati* Nandana, Beṅgālī MS dated Śakasaṁvat 1453, MBh, SMPh; *ṣthaviro jñeyo* anonymous Kaśmīrian commentary. [2]*bālo'pi yaḥ prajānāti* MBh. [3]*devā CV*.

No. 6. *Mn.* 2.215.

mātrā svasrā duhitrā vā[1] [2]*na*[3] *vivaktāsano*[4] *bhavet*,[5]
[6]*balavān indriya*[7]*-grāmo* [8]*vidvāṁsam api karṣati*.

"One should not sit in a lonely place near to his mother, sister or daughter; the assemblage of sense organs overpowers even a wise man."

This maxim occurs in the Cāṇakya-rāja-nīti-śāstram edition (*Calc. Or. Series* 2), 7.9 (*CRC*); and in the Vṛddha Cāṇakyaḥ, Cāṇakya-praṇītaḥ, Calcutta, 1332, edition, 188.36 (*CPS*).

It also occurs in the Bhāgavata-purāṇa, 9.19, 17 (BhP); Garuḍa-purāṇa, 1.114, 6 (GP); Bhaviṣya-purāṇa, Brahmaparvan, 4.184; the Hitopadeśa (Johnson's edition, 1.129; Hamilton's edition, 25.1-2 (HH); Schlegel's and Lassen's edition, vol. II, *ad* 1.113) and the Śukranītisāraḥ, 3.18 *αβ* only (ŚS).

It is also quoted in Vallabhadeva's Subhāṣitāvali, 2780 (SV); Subhāṣita-ratna-bhāṇḍāgāra, 154.45 (SRBh); and Śārṅgadharapaddhati, 654 (ŚP).

The Mānava-dharmaśāstra text is found in the Cāṇakya-rāja-nīti-śāstra version in one MS only, i.e., that which was used for the Cāṇakya-rāja-nīti-śāstram edition. It was incorporated from it into the Vṛddha Cāṇakyaḥ, Cāṇakyapraṇītaḥ edition.

The maxim deals with sense organs and libido. It is a well-known maxim but since it is not closely connected with *dharṁa* and *dharmaśāstrā* it is not quoted in any *nibandha-s*. However, it is quoted in the *purāṇa-s*, in particular in the Bṛhaspati-saṁhitā of the Garuḍa-purāṇa from which it was probably incorporated in the Cāṇakya-rāja-nīti-śāstra version (or vice versa), the Bhāgavata-purāṇa, the Bhaviṣya-purāṇa, as well as the Hitopadeśa and the Śukranītisāraḥ (αβ only). Several Subhāṣita-saṁgraha-s also quote this maxim; Böhtlingk quotes it in *Indische Sprüche*, 4809 (IS). Similar thoughts are expressed in the Mahābharata (13.48. 37-8), the Baudhāyana-dharmasūtra (1.2, 3, 23, and 33). and the Āpastambīya-dharmasūtra (1.2, 1, 3 and 7.11 and 1.1, 3, 16).

No variants occur in the Manu text. The Cāṇakya texts are identical with the Manu text with the exception of one unimportant variant in δ. Variants in other texts are unimportant, with the exception of the Vallabhadeva's Subhāṣitāvali text in γδ.

The text of Cāṇakya was undoubtedly borrowed from the Mānava-dharmaśāstra text but not in the purest form.

[1]*ca* ŚP. [2]*nātyantaikāntikaṁ vaset* ŚŚ; *naikaśay-yāsano* SRBh. [3]*no* HH Mn, Nirṇaya Śāgara Press, Bombay 1846 (variant). [4]*viviktāsane* GP; *naikaśāyāsano* VS. [5]*vaset CRC, CPS,* GP (see fn. 1); *viśat* IS. [6]*balavān indriyaḥ grāmaṁ* IS; *yathā sambandhamā-hūyādābhāṣyāśvasya vai striyam* ŚŚ. [7] *°grāmaḥ paṇḍitopy atra muhyati* VS. [8]*vivāṁsam api* BhP.

No. 7. *Mn* 2.218.

yathā khanan[1] *khanitreṇa* [2]*naro*[3] *vāry*[4] *adhigacchati,*[5]
[6]*tathā*[7] *guru-gatāṁ*[8] *vidyāṁ*[9] [10]*śuśruṣur*[11] *adhigacchati.*[12]

"Similarly as one obtains water who digs (deep) with the spade, the student obtains knowledge that (lies deep) in the teacher's mind."

This maxim occurs in all editions of the Cāṇakya-nīti-darpaṇa, 13.17 (*CVND*), including the Vṛddha-Cāṇakhyanuṁ (Nirṇaya Sāgara Press, Bombay, 1874) edition, 13.6 (*CVM*); the MS. H. 250 in the Harvard University Library, Cambridge, Mass., 8.23 (*CvH*); MS. 445 in the Karl-Marx Universität, Universitätsbibliothek, Leipzig, 8.23, (*CvL* I); MS. 446 in the Karl-Marx Universität, Universitätsbibliothek, Leipzig, 8.17 (*CvL II*); MS. 17072-3 (A) in the Université de Paris. Institut de Civilisation Indienne, 94 (*CNP I*); MS. No. 5119 from Tanjore, 96 (*CNT IV*); Cāṇakya-śloka-saṁgraha, Calcutta, 1915, edition, 78 (*CNŚC*); Cāṇakya-śloka-saṁgraha, Calcutta, 1918, edition, 78 (*CNŚI*); Cāṇakya-ślokaḥ, Calcutta, 1919, edition 78 (*CNŚ*); and the Vṛddha Cāṇakyaḥ, Cāṇakya-praṇītaḥ, Calcutta, 1332, edition, 315.25 (*CPS*).

It is quoted in Vīramitrodaya, Saṁskāra-prākāśa 525. 20-1; Smṛti-candrikā (Ghārpure's edition), 52.2; and the Subhāṣita-ratna-bhāṇḍāgāra, 167.616.

The Mānava-dharmaśāstra text is found in three versions of Cāṇakya, viz., the Vṛddha Cāṇakya, *textus ornatior* (Cāṇakya-nīti-darpaṇa, *CVM*), and the Vṛddha Cāṇakya, *textus simplicior* (*CvH I, CvL II*) and the Cāṇakya-nīti-śāstra (*CNP I, CNT IV, CNŚC, CNŚI, CNŚ*). From the Vṛddha Cāṇakya, *textus ornatior* version, it was incorporated in the Vṛddha Cāṇakyaḥ, Cāṇakya-praṇītaḥ edition.

It deals, similarly as No. 4 with wisdom and is also not well-known. The text is quoted in two *nibandha-s* and one Subhāṣita-saṁgraha. Also Böhtlingk quotes it in *Indische Sprüche*, 5095 (IS).

The Mānava-dharmaśāstra text contains only one variant in γ. Rāghavānanda's commentary has *evaṁ guru-taraṁ* instead of *tathā guru-gatāṁ*. The *nibandha-s* usually follow the Manu text, but the various MSs, and editions of Cāṇakya-contain numerous variants, some of which are quite important (in particular in γ), while others are rather misspellings than variants. The Vṛddha Cāṇakya, *textus ornatior* version, and the Cāṇakya-nīti-śāstra version are different from the Manu text in β.

The text of Cāṇakya was undoubtedly borrowed directly from the Mānava-dharmaśāstra, but not in its purest form.

[1]*khanitvā CVND, CNŚ*; *khatvā CNŚC*; *khaniḥ CvH*; *khana CvL II*; *khātā CVM, CNP I*; *yathā sanim CvL I*. [2]*bhūtale vāri vindati* (*bindati*) *CVND, CVM,*

CNŚ, *CNŚC*; *CNP I*; *tiṣanatreṇa CvL II*. [3]*naraḥ CvH*; *naro CvL II*, [4]*vāhy CvL I*; *vāri CVM*. [5]*khanitum ichati CvH*; *ārtha gachati CvL I*; *arghagattachati* (?) *CvL II*. [6]*evaṁ guru-taraṁ* Rāghavānanda's commentary (see fn. 7). [7]*yathā* IS; *evaṁ* VRS, SCM (see fn. 6). [8]*taṣa* (?) *CvL I*; *tarā* (?) *CvL II*. [9]*vidyā CvL I*; *bhūtala CVM*. [10]*dhīmānādatum ichati CvH*. [11]*śusarṣam CvL I*; *śuśruṣam CvL II*. [12]*adhigacchanti CNP I*; *vā'dhi°* VRS.

No. 8. *Mn* 2.223.

yadi strī yady avarajaḥ śreyaḥ kiñcit samācaret[1],
tat sarvamācared yukto yatra vā'sya[2] *ramen-manaḥ*.

"If a woman or a junior[3] perform a good act (conducing to religious merit, worldly prosperity and pleasure), they should perform it with perseverance as well as any other (permissible) act in which they find self-satisfaction."

This maxim occurs in the Vṛddhacāṇakya-nīti-samuccaya edition, Ahmedabad, 1913, 12.14.

The Mānava-dharmaśāstra text is found only in one edition belonging to the Vṛddha Cāṇakya, *textus ornatior* version, viz., the Vṛddhacāṇakya-nīti-samuccaya edition.

The maxim deals with acts performed by women or juniors; it is not well-known. It does not occur in Subhāṣita-saṁgraha-s or *nibandha-s*.

The Mānava-dharmaśāstra text contains only two unimportant variants. The Jolly's text has in β *sasācaret* while all other texts have *samācaret*. The Cāṇakya text has also corectly *samācaret*. In addition in δ most texts have *cā'sya* while some Medhātithi texts and the anonymous Kaśmīrian commentary has *vā'sya*. The Cāṇakya text has also *vā'sya*.

The text of Cāṇakya was undoubtedly borrowed directly from the Mānava-dharmaśāstra.

[1]*sasācaret* Mn (Jolly's edition). [2]*cā'sya* in some Mn commentaries. [3]or a person of lower class, a Śūdra (Medhātithi).

No. 9. *Mn* 2.240.

[1]*striyo ratnāny atho*[2] *vidyā dharmaḥ śaucaṁ subhāṣitam*,
[3]*vividhāni cāpyaduṣṭāni samādeyāni*[4] *sarvataḥ*.[5]

"Wives like gems[6], wisdom, purity, wise sayings and various arts may be acquired from all sources."

This maxim occurs in the Vṛddhacāṇakya-nīti-samuccaya edition, Ahmedabad, 1913, 12.15.

It also occurs in the Devala-smṛti quoted in Vīramitrodaya, Saṁskāra-prakāśa (VRS), 514. 1-2.

It is also quoted in A. W. Carr's, *A Collection of Telugu Proverbs*, 147.

The Mānava-dharmaśāstra text is found only in one Cāṇakya's compendium belonging to the Vṛddha Cāṇakya, *textus ornatior* version, viz., the Vṛddha Cāṇakya-nīti-samuccaya edition.

The maxim deals with the sources of acquisition of wisdom, *dharma*, etc. from different sources. It is not well-known, although similar thoughts are expressed also in different sources, viz., by Ujjavaladatta *ad* Uṇādisūtra (3.14); Mallinātha *ad* Kumārasambhava (6.30); in the Brahmavaivartapurāṇa (2.56, 22); the Mahābhārata (12.165, 31-2); as well as in other Cāṇakya's compendia, such as the Cāṇakya-nīti-darpaṇa (1.16) and other editions and MSs of the Vṛddha Cāṇakya, *textus simplicior* version, which are indentical with the Cāṇakya-nīti-darpaṇa stanza; the Cāṇakya-rāja-nīti-śāstram edition (3.7); the Bodhi Cāṇakyam, Calcutta edition (163); and other MSs of the Cāṇakya-sāra-saṁgraha version which repeat this maxim, the Cāṇakyaśatakam edited by J. Vidyāsāgara (Calcutta, 1926) (16) and numerous other editions and MSs belonging to the Cāṇakya-nīti-śāstra version. It is also found in the Devala-smṛti and in one Subhāṣita-saṁgraha. Also Böhtlingk quotes it in his *Indische Sprüche* (7194).

The first *pāda* of this maxim can be interpreted in two different ways. And so, Rāghavānanda understands this *pāda* as meaning "wives like gems," while Medhātithi and Govindarāja "wives, gems......"

The Mānava-dharmaśāstra text contains one important variant in γ: commentaries by Medhātithi, Govindarāja, Sarvajña-Nārāyaṇa, Kullūka and Rāghavānanda have *śilpāni cāpyaduṣṭāni*, while Nandana's commentary and the *vulgata* have *vividhāni ca śilpāni*, The Cāṇakya text and the Devala-smṛti follow the *vulgata* and the Nandana's commentary. The Devala-smṛti has also some variants in α and δ, while the Cāṇakya text in δ. The Nītisāra in Telugu is different in α.

The text of Cāṇakya was undoubtedly borrowed from the *vulgata* text of the Mānava-dharmaśāstra or from the Nandana's commentary of Manu.

[1]*ratnaṁ nāma striyo* Devala-smṛti. [2]*adho* Nītisāra. [3]*vividhāni ca śilpāni* commentaries of Nandana, *vulgata*, Mandlik's edition, and some other editions based on these texts, *CV*, Devala-smṛti. [4] °*devāni CV*. [5]*sarvaśaḥ* Devala-smṛti. [6]Rāghavānandana's commentary; Medhātithi and Govindarāja—"wives, gems."

Nos. 10, 11, 12. *Mn* 3.55, 56, 57.

pitṛbhir bhātṛbhiś caitāḥ patibhir devarais tathā,
pūjyā bhūṣayitavyāś[1] *ca bahu kalyāṇamīpsubhiḥ.*
yatra nāryas[2] *tu pūjyante ramante*[3] *tatra devatāḥ,*
[4]*yatraitās tu na*[5] *pūjyante*[6] *sarvās tatrā'phalāḥ*[7] *kriyāḥ.*
śocanti jāmayo[8] *yatra vinaśyatyāśu*[9] *tat kulam,*
[10]*na śocanti*[11] *tu yatraitā vardhate taddhi*[12] *sarvadā.*

"They should be honoured and adorned by their fathers and brothers, husbands, brothers-in-law who are desirous (of their own) well-being.

"Where women are honoured, there the gods rejoice, but where they are not honoured, there all religious rites are ineffectual.

"Where female relations are made pitiable, the family (of those responsible) soon perishes completely, but that family who does not do so prospers always."

These three maxims occur in the Vṛddha-cāṇakya-nīti-samuccaya edition, Ahmedabad, 1913, 14.13-5.

The first of these maxims is also quoted in the Parāśara-dharma-saṁhitā, 1.2; 111.16-7 (PS); Smṛti-candrikā (Ghārpure's edition), 243.9; Smṛtimuktāphalam, 143.23 (SMPh); Bālambhaṭṭi, Vivāha-prakaraṇa (Ghārpure's edition), 230.21 (γδ only) (BBh); and Vyavahārārtha-samuccaya, 121.

The second of these maxims occurs in the Mahābhārata (Roy's edition), 13.46, 5-6 (MBh). It is also quoted in the Parāśara-dharma-saṁhitā, 1.2; 111.18-9; Smṛtimuktāphalam, 143.24; Bālambhaṭṭi, Vivāha-prakaraṇa (Ghārpure's edition), 212.22 and 230.23; Vivādaratnākara (in *Bibl. Ind.*), 418.1211 (VRK); and Vyavahārakalpataruḥ, Prajñāpasthala, 130 It is farther quoted in the Subhāṣita-ratna-bhāṇḍāgāra, 389. 493.

The third of these maxims is also quoted in the Parāśara-dharma-saṁhitā, 1.2; 112.1-2; Smṛtimuktāphalam, 143.25; Bālambhaṭṭi, Vivāha-prakaraṇa (Ghārpure's edition), 212.23; Vivāda-ratnākara (in *Bibl. Ind*), 418. 1211; and Vyavahārakalpataruḥ, Prajñapasthala, 130.

The Mānava-dharmaśāstra texts of these three maxims are found only in one Cāṇakya's compendium belonging to the Vṛddha Cāṇakya *textus ornatior* version, viz, the Vṛddha Cāṇakya nīti-samuccaya edition.

The three maxims deal with women and their duty to

honour them. The maxims form a part of a longer extract from Manu (3.55-62). It is a possible that all these maxims, or some of them, were a later addition to Manu, the more so as the corresponding section in the Mahābhārata (13.46) stops right here (Hopkins) and stanzas 57 to 66 were omitted by Medhātithi. Despite that, the three maxims were well-known.

As to the first one, similar thoughts, are expressed in the Mahābhārata (13.46, 3) and the Yājñavalkya Smṛti (1.82). This maxim is often quoted in the *nibandha-s*. No variants occur in the Manu text. This text is also found without any changes in the *nibandha-s* and in the Cāṇakya text. Only one variant occurs in some MSs of the Parāśara-dharma-saṁhitā.

The second maxim also occurs in the Mahābhārata. It is often quoted in the *nibaudha-s* and in Subhāṣita-saṁgraha-s. Also Böhtlingk quotes it in *Indische Sprüche*, 5063. Some variants occur in the Manu text. The anonymous Kaśmīrian commentary has in *a yatraitā na hi* while the other texts have *yatraithās tu na*; Govindarāja's commentary has in β *ramanti*, while the other texts have *ramante*; and in δ *Nandana's* commentary has *tasyā'phalaḥ*, while the other texts have *tatrā 'phalāḥ*. The Smṛtimuktāphalam follows the text used in Nandana's commentary. Cāṇakya's text follows the common Manu text. Some variants occur also in the Mahābhārata and some *nibandha-s*.

Similar thoughts as those expressed in the third maxim are also found in the Mahābhārata (13.46, 6), i. e., the next one to that identical with the second maxim. This maxim is also often quoted in the *nibandha-s*.

The texts of the three Cāṇakya's maxims, which form an entirety, were undoubtedly borrowed directly from the Mānava-dharmaśāstra, but not from the Medhātithi's text. They were also incorporated in the Cāṇakya text one after the other as they occur in Manu.

[1] *poṣayitavyāś* PS (variant). [2]*striyo yatra ca* MBh. [3]*ramanti* Govindarāja's commentary. [4]*yatraitā na hi* anonymous Kaśmīrian Commentary; *apūjitāś ca* MBh; *yatraitā na propūjyante* VRK. [5]*na pra°* VRK. [6]*yatraitāḥ* MBh; *yatremās* PS (variant). [7]*tasyā'phalāḥ* Nandana's commentary SMPh. [8]*yāmayo* BBh, VRK. [9]*praṇaśyatyāśu* VRK. [10]*na ca śocanti* PS (variant). [11]*śocanti* PS (variant). [12]*tāddhi* BBh.

No. 13. *Mn* 4.85.

daśa-sūnā-samaṁ[1] *cakraṁ*[2] *daśa-cakra-samo*[3] *dhavajaḥ*,[4]
[5]*daśa-dhavaja-samā veśyā daśa-veśyā-samo nṛpaḥ.*[6]

"One oil-press is as bad as ten slaughter-houses, one liquor-seller's shop as bad as ten oil-presses; one prostitute (brothel) as bad as ten liquor-seller's shops, one king as bad as ten prostitutes (brothels)."

This maxim occurs in MS. 1518 a (Eggeling 3990) in the India Office Library in London, 305.

It is also quoted in Smṛtimuktāphalam, 55.20 (SMPh); and Bālambhaṭṭi, Snātaka-prakaraṇa (Gharpure's edition), 401.6.

The Mānava-dharmaśāstra text is found in only one Cāṇakya's compendium belonging to the Cāṇakya-nīti-śāstra version; this MS is one of the "longer" MSs and not an *aṣṭottaraśata.* The MS contains many interpolations.

The maxim deals with places considered to be of bad reputation and with the bad king. It is a well known maxim. Similar thoughts are also expressed in the preceding stanza of the Mānavā-dharmaśāstra (4.84) and in the Yājñavalkya-smṛti (1.141).[7] The maxim is also quoted in some *nibandha-s.*

The Manu text contains some important variants. The commentaries of Medhātithi, Govindarāja, Rāghavānanda, Nandana, Sarvajña-Nārāyaṇa and of the anonymous Kaśmīrian have in γδ °*samā veśyā daśa-veśyā-samo*, while the commentary of Kullūka, some MSs of Rāghavānanda's and of the anonymous Kaśmīrian commentaries and the *vulgata* have °*samo veśo daśa-veśa-samo.* In the first case the liquor-seller's shops and the bad king are compared with prostitutes and in the second with brothels. The latter comparison seems to be nearer to the original thought of the author because the maxim deals mostly with "places" and not "persons" of bad reputation. The Cāṇakya text follows closely the text used in the first group of commentators. This text is also used in the *nibandha-s* which, however, contain some other unimportant variants which are sometimes rather misspellings than variants; the same remarks refers also to the Cāṇakya text.

The text of Cāṇakya was undoubtedly borrowed directly from the Mānava-dharmaśāstra, but probably not from the original text of Manu.

[1]*samaś* SMPh. [2]*cakrī* *CNI*, SMPh. [3]*cakrī*° *CNI*, SMPh. [4]*dhvaji* SMPh. [5] °*samo veśo daśa-veśa-samo* Kullūka's commentary, some other MSs of Rāghavānanda's and of the anonymous Kaśmīrian commentaries and the *vulgata*. [6]*nṛpa* *CNI*. [7]Cf. L. Sternbach, Gaṇikā-vṛtta-saṁgrahaḥ, *Viśveśvarānand Indological. Series* 4.

No. 14. *Mn* 4.160.

sarvaṁ[1] *para-vaśaṁ*[2] *duḥkhaṁ sarvam*[3] *ātma-vaśaṁ*[4] *sukham,*
[5]*etad*[6] *vidyāt*[7] *samāsena*[8] *lakṣaṇaṁ*[9] *sukha-duḥkhayoḥ.*[10]

"In a few words the definition of pleasure and pain is as follows: all that depends on others is painful; all that depends on oneself is pleasing."

This maxim occurs in the Cāṇakya-rāja-nīti śāstram edition (*Calc. Or. Ser.* 2), 6.97 (*CRC*); MS. Sansk. 15 in the Bodleian Library in Oxford, 6.60 (*CRB*); MS. 1559 in the Library of the University of Pennsylvania in Philadelphia, 6.52 γδ (αβ are missing) (*CRP*); MS. No. 347 of 1892-95 in the Bhāṇḍārkar O. R. Institute in Poona, 6.53 (*CRBh I*); MS. No. 348 of 1892-95 in the Bhāṇḍārkar O. R. Institute in Poona, 6.55 (*CRBh II*); MS. Add. 2525 in the University Library in Cambridge, 6.44 (*CRCa*); the Bodhi Cāṇakyam edition by Bhoobhun Chaund Dutt, Calcutta, 147 (*CSBD*); MS. or. fol. 598 in the Universitätsbibliothek in Tübingen (Weber No. 1591), 2.49 (*CSB I*); MS. belonging to Professor J. W. de Jong in Leiden, 2.47 (*CSJ*); MS. Add. 1539 in the University Library in Cambridge, 2.48 (*CRC* I); MS. Add. 1346 in the University Library in Cambridge, 147, (*CSC II*); MS. Cod. or. 8857, Lub/D 122 in the University Library in Leiden, 2.47 (CSLd); and the Vṛddha Cāṇakya, Cāṇakya-praṇītaḥ, Calcutta, 1332 edition, 153.51 (*CPS*).

It also occurs in the Garuḍa-purāṇa, 1.113, 60; and the Brāhmadharma, 2. 4, 4.

It is also quoted in Mandana-pārijāta (in *Bibl. Ind.*), 14.9-10 (MP); and Aparārka's commentary on the Yājñavalkya-smṛti, 223. 3-4 (Apar.).

The Mānava-dharmaśāstra text is found in thirteen Cāṇakya's compendia belonging to the Cāṇakya-rāja-nīti-śāstra and Cāṇakya-sāra-saṁgraha versions. Some of these texts are corrupt (viz., *CSJ*) and some are incomplete (viz., *CRP*; this text has α and β only). The text was incorporated into the *CPS* text from the Cāṇakya-rāja-nīti-śāstra version.

The maxim deals with pleasure and pain and is well-known. It is also quoted in the Bṛhaspati-saṁhitā of the Garuḍa-purāṇa from which it was probably incorporated into the Cāṇakya-rāja-nīti-śāstra version (or *vice-versa*) and in the Brāhma-dharma. Also one *nibandha* and one commentary quotes this maxim. It is also quoted by Böhtlingk in his *Indische Sprüche*, 5272 IS).

No variants occur in the different Manu texts but some important variants from the Manu text are noted in particular in one of the MSs of the Cāṇakya-rāja-nīti-śāstra version (*CRBh II*) and in all the texts of the Cāṇakya-sāra-saṁgraha version, particularly in the *CSJ* MS.

The Mānava-dharmaśāstra maxim is very close to the Cāṇakya-rāja-nīti-śāstra text and it was most probably borrowed directly from Manu but not in its purest form.

[1]*sarva CSC I.* [2]*paravasaṁ CSJ.* [3]*vasam CSJ.* [4]*ātmavasaṁ CSJ; atma° CSC II.* [5]*susvahaḥ svamanuṣyāṇāṁ ca kravat parivartatenam* (?) *CRBh II.* [6]*yetad CSJ; aitad CSB II.* [7]*vidyā CSJ; vidyāḥ* IS; *vindyāt* IS; *viprāt CSB II.* [8]*samāsenaṁ CSJ; samānena* IS. [9]*lakṣaṇe CSJ.* [10] *°duḥkyo CSJ, CSC I, CSC II; sukha-duḥkhayo CSB I.*

No. 15. *Mn* 5.56.

na māṁsa-bhakṣane[1] *doṣo*[2] *na madye*[3] *na ca maithune*[4],
pravṛttir eṣā[5] *bhūtānāṁ*[6] *nivṛttis tu mahāphalā.*[7]

"It is no sin to eat meat, to drink spirituous beverages, or to have sexual intercourse, since that is the natural disposition of men; but abstention from them brings great reward."

This maxim occurs in the Boddhi Cāṇakya edition by Bhoobhun Chaund Dutt, Calcutta, 292 (*CSBD*); MS. or. fol. 598 in the Universitäts-bibliothek in Tübingen (Weber No. 1591), 3.91 (*CSB I*); MS. or. fol. 599 in the Universitäts-bibliothek in Tübingen (Weber No. 1592), 3.92 (*CSB II*); MS. belonging to Professor J. W. de Jong in Leiden, 3.92 (*CSJ*); MS. Add. 1539 in the University Library in Cambridge, 3.93 (*CSC I*); MS. Add. 1346 in the University Library in Cambridge, 292 (*CSC II*); MS. Cod. or. 8857 Lub/D 122 in the University Library Leiden, 2.92 (*CSLd*).

It is also quoted in the Parāśara-dharmasaṁhitā, 1.2;

389.11-2 (PS); Vīramitrodaya, Ahnikaprakāśa, 537.3-4 (VRĀ); Bālambhaṭṭi, Bhakṣyābhakṣya-prakaraṇa (Ghārpure's edition), 447.25 (BBh); Prāyaścittaviveka, 277 (PV); and Śūlapāṇi's Dīpakalikā, 22.14 (ŚD).

The Mānava-dharmaśāstra text is found in the Cāṇakya-sāra-saṁgraha version in seven texts, of which one (viz., *CSB II*) is corrupt.

The maxim deals with abstention from worldly pleasures. It is very well known. The maxim is quoted in many *nibandha-s* and commentaries.

No variants occur in Manu and *nibandha-s* text (with one exception) and in the commentaries. However the MSs and the only edition of the Cāṇakya-sāra-saṁgraha version contain several variants from the Manu text; they are however unimportant.

It is difficult to conclude what was the exact source of the maxim as found in the Cāṇakya-sāra-saṁgraha version. It is certain, however, that the text of Cāṇakya was borrowed from Manu, though it does not correspond to it word by word.

[1]*bhakṣaṇaṁ CSBD, CSJ, CSC II*; *bhakṣaṇa CSLd*; *bhakṣaṇo CSB I.* [2]*doṣā CSJ*; *doṣaṁ CSC I, CSC II, CSB II*; *doṣaiś CSB I.* [3]*madyaṁ CSBD, CSJ, CSLd*; *madya CSB I.* [4]*maittunam CSBD, CSC I, CSC II, CSB I, CSLd.* [5]*eva CSBD, CSC I, CSC II, CSB I, CSB II*; *evtā CSJ.* [6]*bhūtā CSJ*; *karttavyaṁ CSB I.* [7]*mahāphalam CSLd, CSC I, CSC II, CSB I*; *mahāphalaḥ* BBh.

No. 16. *Mn* 5.106.[1]

sarveṣām[2] *eva śaucānām*[3] *artha-śaucaṁ*[4] *paraṁ*[5] *smṛtam,*[6]
[7]*yo'rthe* [8]*śucir hi sa śucir na mṛdvāri*[9] *śuciḥ śuciḥ.*

"Of all pure things, purity of acquiring wealth is considered to be the best; he who gains wealth with clean hands is really pure; not he who purifies himself with earth and water."

This maxim occurs in the Cāṇakya-rāja-nīti-śāstram edition (*Calc. Or. Ser.* 2), 6.40 (*CRC*); MS. Sansk. f. 15 in the Bodleian Library in Oxford, 6.33 (*CRB*); MS. 1559 in the Library of the University of Pennsylvania in Philadelphia, 6.29 (*CRP*); MS. No. 347 of 1892-95 in the Bhāṇḍārkar O. R. Institute in Poona, 6.30 (*CRBh I*); MS. No. 348 of 1892-95 in the Bhāṇḍārkar O. R. Institute in Poona, 6.27 (*CRBh II*); MS. Add. 2525 in the University Library in Cambridge, 6.26 (*CRCa*); MS. No. 5119 from Tanjore, 235 (*CNT IV*); MS.

5122 from Tanjore, 9 (*CnT VII*); and the Vṛddha-cāṇakyaḥ, Cāṇakya-praṇītaḥ, Calcutta, 1332 edition, 164.83 (*CPS*).

It also occurs in the Viṣṇu-smṛti, 22.89 (Vi); and the Garuḍa-purāṇa, 1.113.36 (GP).

It is also quoted in Hemādri's Caturvarga-cintāmaṇī, Pariśeṣakhaṇḍa, 3.1; 792.14-5 (Hem); Smṛtisāroddhāra, 249. 10-2 (SSar); and Nṛsiṁha-prasāda, Śrāddha-sāra, 90.1-2 (NṛPr).

The Mānava-dharmaśāstra text is found in the Cāṇakya-rāja-nīti-śāstra and the Cāṇakya-nīti-śāstra versions. It was incorporated in the Vṛddha-cāṇakya, Cāṇakya-praṇītaḥ edition from the Cāṇakya-rāja-nīti-śāstra version.

The maxim deals with purity in the acquisition of wealth and is a very well-known stanza. It also occurs in the Viṣṇu-smṛti and is quoted in several *nibandha-s*. The Bṛhaspati-saṁhitā of the Garuḍa-purāṇa from which it was probably incorporated into the Cāṇakya-rāja-nīti-śāstra version (or *vice-versa*) quotes this maxim also, but is different in γδ. It is also quoted by Böhtlingk in his *Indische Sprüche*, 6957.

The Manu texts contain some variants. The commentaries of Nandana and of the anonymous Kaśmīrian have in *a* *varṇānām* instead of *śaucānām*. Otherwise there are no variants in the Manu text. The Cāṇakya-rāja-nīti-śāstra texts contain several minor variants from the Manu text, of which one is also found in the Viṣṇu-smṛti.

The Cāṇakya text was undoubtedly borrowed directly from the Mānava-dharmaśāstra, but not from the texts used in the commentaries of Nandana and of the anonymous Kaśmīrian.

[1]In some other editions, e.g., Jhā's edition, 5. 105. [2]*sārvaṣām* *CRP*. [3]*varṇānām* Nandana's and anonymous Kaśmīrian's commentaries. Also quoted in Jhā's edition as a possible variant. [4]*anna-śaucam* GP; *antaḥ śaucam* SSar. [5]*para* *CRCa*. [6]*praśasyate* *CRC*, *CPS*; *viśiṣyate* GP. [7]*yo'nnārthair* (*a*) *śuciḥ śaucāt na mṛdā vāriṇā śuciḥ* GP; *yo'ntaḥ* SSar; *yo'nne* Vi. [8]*śuci* (*ḥ*) *sa hi* *CRC*, *CRB*, *CRBh I*, *CRBh II*, *CRCa*, *CPS*, Vi. [9]*mṛdbhāraih* *CRC*; *na mṛdbhāra* *CRP*, *CRBh I*, *CRBh II*, *CRCa*.

No. 17. *Mn* 5.155.[1]

nāsti strīṇaṁ pṛthag[2] *yajño*[3] *na vrataṁ*[4] *nā'py upoṣaṇam,*[5]
[6]*patiṁ*[7] *śuśrūṣate*[8] *yena*[9] *tena svarge mahīyate.*

"No sacrifice, no (religious) observance, no (religious)

fasting is allowed to women separately from their husbands; it is only by honouring his husband that the wife is exalted in heaven."

The maxim occurs in MS. 1566 in the Library of the University of Pennsylvania, 93 (*CNPh*).

It also occurs in the Viṣṇu-smṛti, 25.15 (Vi).

It is also quoted in Smṛti-candrikā (Ghārpure's edition), 252.10 (SC); Bālambhaṭṭi, Vivāhaparakaraṇa (Ghārpure's edition), 213,14 (BBh); Gadādhara-paddhati, Kāla-sāra, 52.5 (αβ), 129.15 (αβ) (GaP); Saṁskāraratnamālā, 675.13-4 (SRM); Varṣa Kriyā Kaumundī 579.11-2 (VKK); Puruṣārthacintāmaṇi (Nirṇaya Sāgara Press), 201.7-8 (αβ) (PC); Smṛtisāroddhāra, 101.22 (αβ); Madana-pārijāta, 193.9-10 (MaP); Vidhāna-pārijāta, 2.729, 2-3 (VP); Vyavahārakalpataruḥ, Prajñapasthala, 135 (VyK); Vivādabhaṅgarṇavaḥ, 21 (VBh); Vyavahārārthasamuccaya, 124 (VyS); and Subhāṣitaratna-bhāṇḍāgāra, 351.16 (SRBh).

The Mānava-dharmaśāstra text is found only in one Cāṇakya MS. belonging to the Cāṇakya-nīti-śāstra version. It is one of the longer MSs of this version.

The maxim deals with the duty of the wife to honour her husband. It is a well-known maxim which also occurs in the Viṣṇu-smṛti. It is also quoted in numerous *nibandha-s* and in some Subhāṣita-saṁgraha-s. Böhtlingk also quotes it in his *Indische Sprüche*, 3686 (IS). Similar thoughts are expressed in the Mahābhārata (13.46, 13; 3. 204, 22-3), the Rāmāyaṇa (2.24, 26-7), in another place of the Mānava-dharmaśāstra (9.29) and in the Mārkaṇḍeya-purāṇa, 16.61 (MP), the two first two *pāda-s* of which are identical with the Mānava-dharmaśāstra text.

The Mānava-dharmaśāstra text contains some variants. In α the commentary of Govindarāja has *dharmo* instead of *yajño* (the same variant occurs also in the Gadādhara-paddhati); in β the commentaries of Medhātithi, the anonymous Kaśmīrian and the *vulgata* have *upoṣitam* instead of *uposaṇam* (the same variant occurs in the Cāṇakya's compendium, the Viṣṇu-smṛti, the Mārkaṇḍeya-purāṇa and the Varṣa Kriyā Kaumudī). Cāṇakya's compendium has also other, but not important, variants in α and γ from the Manu text. The numerous variants in the *nibandha-s* are of no particular importance.

Cāṇakya's text was borrowed undoubtedly from the Mānava-dharmaśāstra but it is difficult to establish its exact source with more precision.

[1]In some other editions, e.g. Jhā's edition, 5.133. [2]*pṛthak CNPh*, *japo* BBh, GaP. [3]*dharmo* Govindarāja's commentary, GaP; *yājo* VyK. [4]*śrāddhaṁ* MP. [5]*upoṣitam* Medhātithi's, anonymous Kaśmīrian commentaries, *vulgata*, *CNPh*, Vi, MP,VRK. [6]*śuśrūṣuyati bhartaraṁ* SRM. [7]*patiḥ* MaP, SC. [8]*saṁsevate CNPh*, VP; *saṁsevyate* MaP. [9]*tena* SRM; *yā tu CNPh*, VP; *yat tu* Vi.

No. 18. *Mn* 6.46.

dṛṣṭi-pūtaṁ[1] *nyaset*[2] *pādaṁ* [3]*vastra-pūtaṁ* [4]*jalaṁ pibet*[5],
satya-pūtāṁ[6] *vaded vācaṁ*[7] [8]*manaḥ-pūtaṁ samācaret.*

"Let him place his foot purified by looking down, let him drink water purified by cloth, let him utter words purified by truth, let him act with pure mind."

The maxim occurs in all edition of the Cāṇakya-nīti-darpaṇa, 10.2 (*CVND*), including the Vṛddha-Cāṇakhyanuṁ (Nirṇaya Sāgara Press, Bombay, 1874) edition, 10.2 (*CVM*); the following seven editions; *Über* 100 *Sprüche des Cāṇakya* by A. Weber (Berlin, 1865), 102 (*CNW*); Rājanitau Cāṇikya-mūni-viracitam (no place, no date), 136 (*CNM*); Cāṇikya-muni-kṛtam (Allahabad, saṁvat 1880), 102 (*CNMN*); Cāṇakya-śloka-saṁgrahaḥ (Calcutta, 1918), 38 (*CNŚl*); Cāṇakya-śloka-saṁgraha (Calcutta, 1915), 38 (*CNŚC*); Cāṇakya-ślokaḥ (Calcutta, 1319), 37 (*CNŚ*); Cāṇakya-nīti-māla (Calcutta, 1324), 77 (*CNNM*); the following three MSs. No. 5119 from Tanjore, 138 (*CNT IV*); No. 5122 from Tanjore, 10 (*CnT VII*); No. 1518a (Eggeling 3990) in the India Office Library in London, 24 (*CNI*); and in the Vṛdha-cāṇakyaḥ, Cāṇakya-praṇītaḥ (Calcutta, 1332) edition, 278.18 (*CPS*).

It also occurs in the Mārkaṇḍeya-purāṇa, 41.4 (MP); and the Śukasaptati, *textus simplicior*, 17 (16.12-3) (ŚS).

It is also quoted in the Parāśara-dharma-saṁhitā, 1.2; 194.2 (PS); in Śūlapāṇi's Dipakalikā, 49.17 (ŚD); and in Aparārka's commentary on the Yājñavalkya-smṛti, 953.24-5 (Apar).

The Mānava-dharmaśāstra text is found in the Vṛddha Cāṇakya, *textus ornatior*, and the Cāṇakya-nīti-śāstra versions; of the latter one, the MS. 1518a in the India Office Library in London has the two verses transposed, viz., $\gamma\delta/\alpha\beta$. The text was incorporated in the Vṛddha-cāṇakyaḥ, Cāṇakya praṇītaḥ edition from the Cāṇakya-nīti-darpaṇa editions.

The maxim deals with the procedure for an ascetic, but at the time when it was incorporated into Cāṇakya's compendia it probably lost its original meaning.

The maxim is well-known. It occurs in the Mārkaṇḍeya-purāṇa, the *textus simplicior* of the Śukasaptati, several *nibandha-s* and commentaries and various Subhāṣita-saṁgraha-s, such as Kavitāmṛtakūpa, 4; Subhāṣitārṇava, 193; and M. W. Carr's *Collection of Telugu Proverbs* (Madras, 1868), 416. Also Böhtlingk quotes it in his *Indische Sprüche*, 2934 (IS).

No variants occur in the Mānava-dharmaśāstra text. The Mārkaṇḍeya-purāṇa has some changes in α and δ; the latter is important. The Cāṇakya text has some variants from the Manu text, of which only one, in γ, is important. The *nibandha-s* follow the Manu text; Aparārka's text has one variant in γ which also occurs in the Mārkaṇḍeya-purāṇa.

The text of Cāṇakya was undoubtedly borrowed directly from the Mānava-dharmaśāstra and not from Mārkaṇḍeya-purāṇa.

[1]*cakṣuḥ-pūtaṁ* MP, LOM$_1$H in ŚS omitted. [2]*kṣipet CNMN*; *nāset CNŚC*; *nyasyet* IS; *sadāt CNM.* [3]*vastraṁ CNM.* [4]*pibej jalaṁ CVND, CPS.* [5]*pivej jalaṁ* A in ŚS. [6](or °*pūtaṁ*); *śāstra-pūtaṁ CVND, CPS, CNŚ, CNŚC.* [7]*vākyaṁ CVND, CNW, CPS, CNŚ, CNŚC,* ŚS; *vāṇīṁ* MP, Apar. [8]*buddhi-pūtaṁ ca cintayet* MP.

No. 19. *Mn* 7.8.

bālo'pi nā'vamantavyo manuṣya iti bhūmipaḥ,[1]
mahatī devatā hy eṣā[2] *nara-rūpeṇa*[3] *tiṣṭhati.*

"Even though a child, the king should not be despised, as if he were a mere mortal; for he is a great divinity in human form."

This maxim occurs in the Vṛddha-cāṇakya-nīti-samuccaya edition, Allahabad, 1913, 16.21.

It also occurs in the Mahābhārata (Bhāṇḍarkar edition), 12.68, 40; the Nītiprakāśika, 8.5; and in the Hitopadeśa (Johnson's edition, 2.81; Schlegel's and Lassen's edition, 2.80; Müller's edition, 2.82; Peterson's edition, 2.74; H. Blatt's Nepālī edition, 2.73, Kale's edition, 2.82; Hamilton's edition, 52.8-9; Colebrooke's edition 68.15-6).

It is also quoted in the Parāśara-dharmasaṁhitā, 1.1; 448.7-8 and 3.1; 4.1-2 (PS); Vīramitrodaya, Rājanīti-prakāśa,

17.21-2; Rājanīti-ratnākara, 68.16-7 (RRK); and the Subhāṣita-ratna-bhāṇḍāgāra, 142.8.

The Mānava-dharmaśāstra text is found in only one Cāṇakya-compendium belonging to the Vṛddha Cāṇakya, *textus ornatior* version, viz., the Vṛddhacāṇakya-nīti-samuccaya edition.

The maxim deals with the obligation to honour a king, even if he is a child. It is a well-known maxim found also in the Mahābhārata, the Hitopadeśa, the Nītiprakāśika and several *nibandha-s* and commentaries. It is also quoted in some Subhāṣita-saṁgraha-s. Also Böhtlingk quotes it in his *Indische Sprüche*, 4446.

No variants occur in the Mānava-dharmaśāstra text. The Cāṇakya's text follows closely the Manu text. In the Mahābhārata the verse is different. Otherwise the variants are unimportant.

The text of Cāṇakya was undoubtedly borrowed directly from the Mānava-dharmaśāstra and not from the Mahābhārata.

[1]*bhūpatiḥ* in Peterson's edition of the Hitopadeśa; *na hi jātvavamantavyo manuṣyair iti bhūmipaḥ* Mahābhārata. [2]*hy etā* gh in RRK; *pūjyā* P in Schlegel's and Lassen's edition of the Hitopadeśa. [3] *'nanta-rūpeṇa* B in PS 3.1.

No. 20. *Mn* 7.22.

sarvo daṇḍajito loko[1] *durlabho hi śucir naraḥ,*[2]
daṇḍasya hi [3]*bhayāt sarvaṁ jagad bhogāya kulpate.*[4]

"It is by the threat of punishment that the whole world is kept under control, for a guiltless man is hard to find; through fear of punishment this universe enjoys its blessings."

This maxim occurs in the Vṛddhacāṇakya-nīti-samuccaya edition, Allahabad, 1913, 16.22.

It also occurs in the Mahābhārata (Roy's edition), 12.15, 34 (MBh) and the Brāhmadharma, 2.11, 4.

It is also quoted in Vīramitrodaya, Rājanīti-prakāśa, 286.2-3, and 292.22-3 (VRR); Rāja-nīti-ratnākara, 63.13-4 (RRK); and Vivādacintāmaṇi, 168.10-1 (VC).

The Mānava-dharmaśāstra text is found only in one Cāṇakya-compendium belonging to the Vṛddha Cāṇakya, *textus ornatior* version, viz., the Vṛddhacāṇakya-nīti-samuccaya edition.

The maxim deals with punishment and forms the basis for the *daṇḍanīti*. It states that only through the threat of punishment men are kept on the right path, because very seldom people are pure by their own nature (VRR 286).

The maxim is well-known. It also occurs in the Brāhma-dharma and the Mahābhārata; the latter text is however different in γδ. It is also quoted in some *nibandha-s* and commentaries. Also Böhtlingk quotes this maxim in his *Indische Sprüche*, 6958.

No variants occur in the Manu text. The text of the Mahābhārata differs in γδ and has two unimportant variants in αβ. The Cāṇakya text follows closely the Manu text but contains one, probably, printing error in β. The texts of the *nibandha-s* and commentaries follow the Manu text; they contain only two unimportant variants in α and δ.

The text of Cāṇakya was undoubtedly borrowed directly from the Mānava-dharmaśāstra and not from the Mahābhārata.

[1]*loke* MBh. [2]*śuci-naraḥ CV*; *naraḥ śucir* CV; *janaḥ* MBh. [3]*bhayād bhīto bhogāyaiva pravartate* MBh. [4]*kalpyate* RRK.

No. 21. *Mn* 7.45.

daśa kāmasamutthāni[1] *tathā'ṣṭau*[2] *krodhajāni ca,*[3]
[4]*vyasanāni durantāni prayatnena vivarjayet.*

"Let him carefully shun the ten vices proceeding from love of pleasure[5] and eight proceeding from wrath[6]; they all end in misery."

This maxim occurs in the Vṛddhacāṇakya-nīti-samuccaya edition, Allahabad, 1913, 16.23.

It is also quoted in the Parāśara-dharmasaṁhitā 1.1; 473.1 (PS); Rājanīti-ratnākara, 6.12-3 (RRK); Kṛtyakalpataru of Bhaṭṭa Laksmīdhara, Rājadharma-kāṇḍa (in *Gaekwad Or. Ser.*), 143.11-2 (KK); and in Vīramitrodaya, Rājanīti-prakāśa, 149.8-10 (VRR).

The Mānava-dharmaśāstra text is found only in one Cāṇakya-compendium belonging to the Vṛddha-Cāṇakya, *textus ornatior* version, viz., the Vṛddha-cāṇakya-nīti-samuccaya edition.

The maxim deals with vices. It states that a man should avoid the ten vices proceeding from love of pleasure and eight proceeding from wrath. It does not enumerate however these vices. They are enumerated in the Mānava-dharmaśāstra in the following verses; the inclusion of this particular verse without the following ones does not make great sense.

The maxim is well-known. It is quoted in several *nibandha-s* and commentaries. The Parāśara-dharma-saṁhitā quotes this verse when describing the vices which should be avoided by the king. Similar thoughts are very often expressed in various sources, in particular in the *arthaśāstra-s*. We find them in Kāmandaki's Nītisāra (1.39-68, 11. 12, 14.65); the Śukranīti-sāra (1.215, 238); the Mārkaṇḍeya-purāṇa, quoted in the Parāśara-dharma-saṁhitā; the Matsya-purāṇa quoted in Vīramitrodaya, Rājanītiprakāśa (146-9); the Viṣṇu-smṛti (3.50-2), etc.

The Mānava-dharmaśāstra text contains some variants. The commentary of Medhātithi has in β *tu* instead of *ca*. Otherwise no variants occur in the Manu text. The Rājanītiratnākara has a small variant in α and the Cāṇakya text has a printing mistake in β. Otherwise it follows closely the Manu text. The Parāśara-dharma-saṁhitā is different in γδ.

The text of Cāṇakya was undoubtedly borrowed directly from the Mānava-dharmaśāstra.

[1] °*sammucchrāṇi* RRK. [2]*taithāṣṭā* *CV*. [3]*tu* Medhātithi's commentary. [4]*mṛgayā'kṣā* (*kṣo*) *divā* *svapnaḥ* *parīvādaḥ* *striyo* *madaḥ* (*damaḥ*) PS. [5]They are enumerated in Mn 7.47. [6]They are enumerated in Mn 7.48.

No. 22. *Mn* 7.105.

nāsya[1] (*c*)*chidraṁ*[2] *paro*[3] [4]*vidyād vidyā*[5] (*c*)*chidraṁ*[6] *parasya*[7] *tu*,[8]
gūhet[9] *kūrma*[10] *ivā'ṅgāni* [11]*rakṣed vivaramātmanaḥ*.

"The enemy should not know his (the king's) weaknesses, but should know the weaknesses of his enemy; he should conceal (before the enemy) the organization[12] of his government, similarly as the tortoise does it with its limbs; he should shield his own weaknesses."

This maxim occurs in the Boddhi Cāṇakya edition by Bhoobhun Chaund Dutt, Calcutta, 107 (*CSBD*); MS. or. fol. 598 in the Universitäts-bibliothek in Tübingen (Weber No. 1591), 2.7 (*CSB I*); MS. or. fol. 599 inthe Universitäts-bibliothek in Tübingen (Weber No. 1592), 107 (*CSB II*); MS. belonging to Professor J. W. de Jong in Leiden, 2. 7 (CSJ); MS. Add. 1359 in the University Library in Cambridge, 2.7 (*CSC I*); MS. Add. 1346 in the University Library in Cambridge, 107 (*CSC II*); MS. Cod. or. 8857 Lub/D 122 in the University Library in Leiden, 2.7 (*CSLd*).

It also occurs in the Mahābhārata (Roy's edition), 12.140, 24; 1.142, 8 and 12.83, 48.

It is quoted in the Kṛtyakalpataru of Bhaṭṭa Lakṣmīdhara, Rājadharma-kaṇḍa (*Gaekwad Or. Ser.*), 152.2-3 (KK); and Vīramitrodaya, Rājanīti-prakāśa, 117.8-9.

The Mānavadharmaśāstra text is found in seven texts of the Cāṇakya-sāra-saṁgraha version, of which one, viz., *CSB II*, is corrupt.

The maxim deals with advice to the king as regards his enemies. In connection with this maxim Vīramitrodaya, Rājanīti-prakāśa, states that the king should try his best to keep his weak points from being known by the enemy, and yet he himself should find out the weak points of the enemy, such as disaffection among the people and so forth; just as a tortoise hides within its body its head and other limbs, in the same manner the king should hide before his enemies the organization of his state and win over to his side, by bestowing gifts and honours, his own ministers and other officers; and if, by chance, some dissatisfaction should arise among his people, he should take remedial measures at once. Similar thoughts are often expressed in the *arthaśāstra* literature, in particular in Kauṭilya's Arthaśāstra.

Although this maxim occurs also in three places of the Mahābhārata it is not often quoted in this wording. It is found only in one *nibandha* and one commentary. Böhtlingk quotes it in his *Indische Sprüche*, 3692 (IS).

The Mānava-dharmaśāstra texts contain some variants: the commentaries of Medhātithi and Nandana have in β *ca* instead of *tu*. The same variant occurs also in most of the Cāṇakya's texts. The Mahābhārata has some important variants in β and unimportant ones in *a*. The Cāṇakya text has several unimportant variants from the Manu text. The other sources follow the Manu text with one exception in β.

The text of Cāṇakya was undoubtedly borrowed directly from the Mānava-dharmaśāstra and not from the Mahābhārata.

[1]*nātma CSBD, CSC II, CSB I*; *ātma CSJ, CSC I, CSB II, CSLd*, MBh 12.140. [2]*chidra CSC II*; *kṣidraṁ CSB I.* [3]*pare CSJ, CSB II, CSLd*; *paraḥ* MBh I.142 and 12.83; *ripur* MBh 12.140. [4]*vidyācchindyācchidraṁ* KK. [5]*dadyād vidyā CSC I, CSB I, CSLd*; *vidyāḥ CSC II.* [6]*chidra CSC II*; *kṣidraṁ CSB I*; *paśye cchidreṇa* MBh; *chidreṣu* IS. [7]*pareṇa CSC II.* [8]*ca* Medhātithi's and Nandana's commentaries, *CSBD, CSC I, CSC II, CSB I, CSLd*; *na*

CSB II. [9]*gṛhe CSJ, CSC I*; *gṛhet CSB I*; *gṛha CSB II.* [10]*karma CSJ*; *kurma CSLd.* [11]*parabhāvaṁ ca labhāyet CSBD, CSC II, CSB I*; *parabhāvaṁ ca lakṣaye(t) CSJ, CSC I, CSC II, CSB I, CSLd* [12]the limbs.

No. 23. *Mn* 7.179.

āyatyāṁ[1] *guṇa-doṣa-jñas tad-ātve*[2] *kṣipra-niścayaḥ,*
atīte kārya-śeṣa-jñaḥ [3]*śatrubhir nābhibhūyate.*

"He (the king), who forsees the good and the evil (which result from his own actions), is quick in forming desisions on present (occasions), and understands the consequences of his acts of his past (conduct), will never be overcome by his enemies."

This maxim occurs in the Cāṇakya-rāja-nīti-śāstram edition (*Calc. Or. Ser.* 2), 8.44 (*CRC*); MS. sansk. f. 15 in the Bodleian Library in Oxford, 8.47 (*CRB*); MS. 1559 in the Library of the University of Pennsylvania in Philadelphia, 8.45 (*CRP*); in MS. No. 347 of 1892-95 in the Bhāṇḍārkar O. R. Institute in Poona, 8.45 (*CRBh I*); and in the Vṛddhacāṇakya, Cāṇakya-praṇītaḥ, Calcutta, 1332, edition, 244.65 (*CPS*).

It is also quoted in the Kṛtyakalpataru of Bhaṭṭa Lakṣmīdhara, Rājadharma-kāṇḍa, 113. 12-3 (KK); Rājanīti-ratnākara, 58. 21-2 (RRK); and Vīramitrodaya, Rājanīti-prakāśa, 328. 18-9 (VRR).

The Mānava-dharmaśāstra text is found in some editions and MSs. of the Cāṇakya-rāja-nīti-śāstra version from which it was incorporated in the text of the Vṛddha-cāṇakyaḥ, Cāṇakya-praṇītaḥ edition.

The maxim deals with the description of an ideal king, a subject dealt with often in the *arthaśāstra-s*. The maxim is not well-known, though a similar thought is expressed in the Mahābhārata (5.38, 55). It is quoted in some *nibandha-s* and commentaries. Also Böhtlingk includes it in his *Indisches Sprüche*, 982.

No variants occur in the Mānava-dharmaśāstra text. The *nibandha-s* and commentaries follow closely the Manu text. Only the Rājanīti-ratnākara notes that some MSs. contain some unimportant variants in *α*. The Cāṇakya texts contain two unimportant variants from the Manu text in *α* and β and one important variant in δ.

The text of Cāṇakya was undoubtedly borrowed directly from the Mānava-dharmaśāstra.

[1]*āyatyā* *CRBh I*; *āyantyā* RRK (var.). [2]*tad-āptau* *CRC, CRB, CRP, CRBh I.* [3]*śatrur alpavalopisan* (?) *CRBh I.*

No. 24. *Mn* 7.213.

āpad arthe[1] *dhanaṁ rakṣed*[2] *dārān*[3] *rakṣed*[4] *dhanair*[5] *api,*
[6]*ātmānaṁ satataṁ*[7] *rakṣed*[8] *dārair*[9] *api*[10] *dhanair api.*[11]

"Let him protect his wealth for time of misfortune; let him protect his wife even with his wealth; (but) let him always protect himself even by sacrificing his wife and his wealth."

The maxim occurs in all editions of the Caṇakya-nīti-darpaṇa, 1.6 (*CVND*), including the Vṛddha-Cāṇakhyanuṁ (Nirṇaya Sāgara Press, Bombay, 1874) edition, 1.6 (*CVM*); the Rāja-nīti. Cāṇakya-muni-viracitam edition (Agra, 1920), 1.6 (*CvA*); Śrī-atha-ṣoḍaśa-cāṇakya-prārambhaḥ edition (Bombay, Saṁvat 1932), 1.6 (*CvṢ*); MS. 17072-4 (D) in the Université de Paris. Institut de Civilisation Indienne, 1.6 (*CvP IV*); MS. 17072-5 (E) in the Université de Paris. Institut de Civilisation Indienne, 1.6 (*CvP Y*); MS. cod. ms. sanscr. 64 in the Niedersächsische Staats-und Universitätsbibliothek in Göttingen, 1.6 (*CvGt*); MS. or. fol. 1037 in the Universitätsbibliothek in Tübingen, 1.6 (*CvTb*); MS. H. 250 in the Harvard University Library in Cambridge, Mass., 1.6 (*CvH*); MS. 2411 in the India Office Library in London, 1.6 (*CvI*); MS. 445 in the Karl-Marx Universität Universitätsbibliothek in Leipzig, 1.6 (*CvL I*); MS. 446 in the Karl-Marx Universität, Universitätsbibliothek in Leipzig, 1.6 (*CvL II*); MS. Cod. or. 8859; UB/123 in the University Library in Leiden, 1.6 (*CvLd*); MS. Walker 205c in the Bodleian Library in Oxford, 1.7 (*CvW*); the Cāṇakya-rāja-nīti-śāstram edition (*Calc. Or. Ser.* 2), 2.1 (*CRC*); MS. sansk. f. 15 in the Bodleian Library in Oxford, 2.1 (*CRB*); MS. 1559 in the Library of the University of Pennsylvania in Philadelphia, 2.1, (*CRP*); MS. No. 347 of 1892-95 of the Bhāṇḍārkar O. R. Institute in Poona, 2.1 (*CRBh I*); MS. No. 348 of 1892-95 of the Bhāṇḍārkar O. R. Institute in Poona, 2.1 (*CRBh II*); the Cāṇakya-śatakam edition (Calcutta, 1926) and all other-editions which republish this text, 29 (*CNJV*); the Cāṇakya-nīti-vyavahāra-sāra-saṁgrahaḥ edition (*Poona Or. Ser.* 71), 12 (*CNS*); *Über 100 Sprüche des Cāṇakya* by A. Weber (Berlin, 1865) edition, 8 (*CNW*); the Cāṇakyam. Codice Indiano edito dal Dre

Emilio Bartoli (Napoli, 1911) edition, 45 (*CNF*); the Recension of Cāṇakya used by Galanos......edition in *Studies in Honor of Maurice Bloomfield*, New Haven, 19 (*CNG*) ; the Cāṇakya-ślokaḥ edition (Calcutta, 1319), A 11 (*CNŚ*); the Cāṇakya-nīti-māla edition (Calcutta, 1334), 68 (*CNNM*); the Cāṇakya-śatakam edition (Calcutta, 1319), 25 (*CNŚT*); MS. 1566 in the Library of University of Pennsylvania in Philadelphia, 4 (*CNPh*); MS. Sanscrit 684 (Cabaton 684 in the Bibliothèque Nationale in Paris, 7 (*CNPN*); MS. 1518a (Eggeling 3990) in the India Office Library in London, 95 (*CNI I*) ; MS. Keith 7204 (Tagore 40b) in the India Office Library in London, 21 (*CNI II*); MS. No. 5119 from Tanjore, 195 (*CNT IV*), and in the Vṛddha-cāṇakyaḥ, Cāṇakya-praṇītaḥ (Calcutta, 1332) edition, 19.51 (*CPS*).

The maxim also occurs in the Mahābhārata (Roy's edition), 1.160, 27 and 5.37, 18; the Pañcatantra (Kielhorn's and Bühler's edition, 1. 356 and 3.86); the Hitopadeśa (Johnson's edition, 1.43, Schlegel's and Lassen's edition, 1.36; Müller's edition, 1.41; Peterson's edition, 1.31; Blatt's Nepālī edition, 1.31; Kale's edition, 1.42; Hamilton's edition, 12.15-6; Colebrooke's edition, 17.1-2); the Vikramacarita (Southern recension, 12.1; Jainistic recension, 20.1); the Śukasaptati, *textus ornatior*, 321.12-3, the Vetālapañcaviṁśatikā, 19.16; Halāyuddha's Dharmaviveka, 14; and the Garuḍa-purāṇa 1.109. 1. *a* is also found in the Hitopadeśa (Peterson's edition, 3.122; Kale's edition, 3.126); and in the Bhotjaprabandha, 198. It forms there a part of another maxim.

It is also quoted in Vīramitrodaya, Rājanītiprakāśa, 413. 2-3 (VRR); Rājanīti-ratnākara, 31. 16-7 (RRK); Kṛtyakalpataru of Bhaṭṭa Lakṣmīdhara, Rājadharma-kāṇḍa (*Gaekwad Or. Ser.*), 142.12 sqq. (KK); and Dharmakośa, 3.1978.

The Mānava-dharmaśāstra text is found in the Vṛddha-Cāṇakya, *textus ornatior*, Vṛddha Cāṇakya, *textus simplicior*, Cāṇakya-rāja-nīti-śāstra and Cāṇakya-nīti-śāstra versions. It is found in addition to the numerous editions of the Cāṇakya-nīti-darpaṇa in twenty-nine editions and MSs.

The maxim deals with one's own preservation. It is one of the best known stanzas in Sanskrit literature and as such was probably incorporated into many Cāṇakya's compendia. It occurs in the Mahābhārata, Pañcatantra, Hitopadeśa, Vikramacarita, Śukasaptati, Vetālapañcaviṁśatikā, Halāyuddha's Dharmaviveka, the Bṛhaspati-Saṁhitā of the Garuḍa-purāṇa from which it was probably incorporated in the Cāṇakya-rāja-nīti-śāstra version (or *vice-versa*), in various Subhāṣita-saṁgraha-s (Subhāṣita-ratna-bhāṇḍāgāra, 761.348). It is also quoted in Böhtlingk's *Indische Sprüche*, 958, and in various *nibandha-s* and commentaries.

The Mānava-dharmaśāstra texts contain some variants. One unimportant variant is quoted in Jolly's edition in α; this edition has *arthaṁ* instead of *arthe*. This variant occurs also in many other sources. In addition, in γ some commentaries of Medhātithi have *satataṁ*, while other commentaries of Medhātithi and the anonymous Kaśmīrian commentary has *sarvato* and Govindarāja's commentary *sarvadā*; Nandana's commentary has *tu tathā*. Some MSs of the Vṛddha Cāṇakya, *textus simplicior*, and Cāṇakya-nīti-śāstra versions have also the same variant as some commentaries of Medhātithi and the anonymous Kaśmīrian commentary. The other variants from the Manu text in Cāṇakya's compendia, epics, the *kathā* and *kāvya* sources, though numerous, are not important.

The text of Cāṇakya was undoubtedly borrowed directly from the Mānava-dharmaśāstra or the Mahābhārata.

[1]*arthaṁ* Hitopadeśa (Peterson's, Nepālī, Kale's P in Schlegel's and Lassen's editions), Vikramacarita, (southern recension but VJENd as above, GŚ in the Jainistic recension), Śukasaptati, Bhojaprabandha, Dharmaviveka, *CNJV*, *CNH*, *CNS*, *CNF*, *CNPh*, *CNG*, *CNŚT*, *CNNM*, *CvP IV*, *CvP V*, *CRP*, *CRBh II*, Mn (all editions with the exception of Medhātithi's commentary), VRR, RRK, KK, Subhāṣita-ratna-bhāṇḍāgāra; *artha CRBh I*; *ārthaṁ* A in Hitopadeśa (Peterson's edition, Pp in Schlegel's and Lassen's editions); *ārthe* B in Hitopadeśa Peterson's edition, *āparthe* (?) *CvH*. [2]*rakṣyaṁ* Ś in Vikramacarita, southern recension; *rakṣet* Hitopadeśa, Peterson's edition 3.122, Kale's edition 3.126; Bhojaprabandha, *CNJV*, *CNH*, *CNW*, *CRC*, *CRP*, *CRBh I*, *CRBh* II; *rakṣe CNPh*. [3]*dārām* Hitopadeśa Hamilton's edition; *dārā CRP*, *CRBh I*, *CRBh II*, *CvW*, Ś in Vikramacarita Jainistic recension, MBh 5.37, VRR. [4]*rakṣyā CRP*, *CRBh I*, Ś in Vikramacarita, Jainistic recension, VRR; *rakṣye CRBh II*; *rakṣet* Dharmaviveka, *CRC*, var. in Mn Jhā's edition; *dārair api CNPh*. [5]*yanair CRBh I*; *dharner CvW*. [6]*ātmānaṁ sarvato* Medhātithi's commentary, old Deccan College MS dated Saṁvat 1649 and the anonymous Kaśmīrian commentary; *ātmānaṁ sarvadā* Govindarāja's commentary; *ātmānaṁ tu tathā* Nandana's commentary; *ātmā tu servato rakṣyā* (*rakṣyo CRC*, *CRP*, *CRBh I*, KK; *rakṣed CRBh II*) Ś in Vikramacarita, Jainistic recension, KK, *CRC*, *CRP*, *CRBh I*, *II*; *ātmā tu servathā* MBh 5.37. [7]*sarvato CvH*, *CvLd*, *CvL II*, *CvA*, *CNP IV*, *CNPh*, VRR; *dhanaṁ CvW* (cf. fn. 6). [8]*rakṣet CNW* (wrongly) [9]*dārer CNI I*, *CvA*. [10]*dānair api* KRB in *Śukasaptati*; *rakṣerakṣarer api CvW* (corrupt); *rakṣet putradāra* Hitopadeśa, Nepālī edition; *paśva dārai Indische Sprüche*, 958. [11]*apīti* RRK (contra metrum); *dhanerapa CvW* (corrupt).

No. 25. *Mn* 8.17.

eka eva suhṛd[1] *dharmo nidhane'py anuyāti yaḥ,*
śarīreṇa samaṁ nāśaṁ sarvam[2] *anyad-dhi*[3] *gacchati.*

"*Dharma* is the only friend that follows one after his death; everything else ceases to exist with the body."

This maxim occurs in the Cāṇakya-ślokaḥ, Calcutta, 1319, edition, A 17 (*CNŚ*); and in the Vṛddha-cāṇakyaḥ, Cāṇakya-praṇītaḥ, Calcutta, 1332, edition, 371.56 (*CPS*).

It also occurs in the Pañcatantra (Nepālī text), 3.30 (PN); Recension β, southern, 3.37 (PS); Tantrākhyāyika, 3.47; oldest Tantrākhyāyika, 3.61; Reconstructed, 3.50; the Hitopadeśa (Johnson's edition, 1.67; Schlegel's and Lassen's edition, 1.59; Müller's edition, 1.64; Peterson's edition 1.49; Blatt's Nepālī edition, 1.50; Kale's edition 1.66, (HK); Hamilton's edition, 16.16-7; Colebrooke's edition, 22. 12-3); and the Brāhmadharma 2.14.10.

It is also quoted in Hemādri's Caturvargacintāmaṇi, Vrata 1.14. 14-5; Vyavahāranirṇaya, 17.7-8 (where it is wrongly ascribed to the Kātyāyana-smṛti); Vyavahārakalpataru, Prajñapathasthala, 15; Vyavahāra-prakaśa 12; Vyavahārārthasamuccaya, 8; Vyavahārasaukhya, 11; Nṛsiṁhaprasāda Saṁskāra, 17a, and Kṛtyakalpataru, 11a.

The Mānava-dharmaśāstra text is found only in one Cāṇakya-compendium, viz., the Cāṇakya-ślokaḥ, Calcutta, 1319, and in the Subhāṣitasaṁgraha composed of Cāṇakya's sayings called Vṛddha-cāṇakya, Cāṇakya-praṇītaḥ. In the first of these editions it is added in the annex.

The maxim deals with *dharma*. It is a beautiful, well-known maxim. It also occurs in the Pañcatantra, the Hitopadeśa, the Brāhmadharma and is quoted in several *nibandha-s*. Also Böhtlingk quotes it in his *Indische Sprüche*, 1345.

No variants occur in the Manu text. Otherwise the variants are unimportant.

The text of Cāṇakya was undoubtedly borrowed directly from the Mānava-dharmaśāstra.

[1]*śataṁ* PN. [2]*sarvan* HK, [3]*anyat tu CNŚ*, Vyavahārakalpataru, PS, Hitopadeśa.

No. 26. *Mn* 8.26.

[1]*ākārair iṅgitair*[2] *gatyā ceṣṭayā bhāṣitena*[3] *ca,*[4]
netra-vaktra[5]*-*[6]*vikārais ca gṛhyate-*[7]*'ntargataṁ manaḥ.*[8]

"The inner mind is revealed by gestures, motions, gesticulations, speech and changes in the eye and the face."

This maxim occurs in the Cāṇakya-rāja-nīti-śāstram edition (*Calc. Or. Ser.* 2), 2.55 (*CRC*); MS. sansk. f. 15 in the Bodleian Library in Oxford, 2.62 (*CRB*); MS. 1559 in the Library of the University of Pennsylvania in Philadelphia, 2.59 (*CRP*); MS. No. 347 of 1892-95 in the Bhāṇḍārkar O. R. Institute in Poona, 2.59 (*CRBh I*); MS. No. 348 of 1892-5 in the Bhāṇḍārkar O. R. Institute in Poona, 2.49 (*CRBh II*); MS. Add. 2525 in the Univeristy Library in Cambridge, 2.49 (*CRCa*); The Recension of Cāṇakya used by Galanos......in *Studies in Honor of Maurice Bloomfield*, New Haven, edition, 259 (*CNG*); MS. 5122 from Tanjore; and the Vṛddha-cāṇakyaḥ, Cāṇakya-praṇītaḥ, Calcutta, 1332 edition, 46.56 (*CPS*).

It also occurs in the Garuḍa-purāṇa, 1.109, 52 (GP); the Pañcatantra (Pañcakhyānaka Recension, 1.21 (PP); and Kielhorn's and Bühler's edition, 1.44 (Pts); the Hitopadeśa (Johnson's edition, 2.47 (HJ); Schlegel's and Lassen's edition, Vol. II, *ad* 2.46 (HS); Müller's edition, 2.50 (HM); Kale's edition, 2.50 (HK); Hamilton's edition, 47.15-6 (HH); Colebrookes edition, 63.5-6 and 106.3-4 (HC); and the Vetāla-pañcaviṁśatikā 1.8 (Vet.).

It is also quoted in Goutama-dharmasūtra with Maskaribhāṣya, 186.12-3 (GMBh); Gautama, Mitākṣara, Haradatta (ĀnSS), 11.23 (GMH); the Parāśara-dharma-saṁhitā, 3.1; 55.12 (PS); the Smṛti-candrikā (Ghārpure's edition) 49.17 (SC); Apararārka's commentary on the Yājñavalkya-smṛti, 620.21-2 (Apar); the Sarasvatīvilāsa, 104.8-9 (SV); Vīramitrodaya, Vyavahāraprakāśa, 71.13-4 (VRV); Vyavahāramātṛkā, 313.11-2 (VyMā); Vyavahāranirṇaya, 70.2-4 (VyN) wrongly ascribed to Nārada-smṛti; Vyavahārārthasamuccaya, 24 (VyS); Vyavahāraprakāśa, 21, 31 (VyP); Vyavahārakalpataruḥ, Prajñapathasthala, 32 (VyK); Vyavahārasaukhyam, 31 (VySau); Vivādavyavahāra, 10 (VVy); Govindarājīyā (Mandlik's edition) (GR); Smṛticintāmaṇi 41, 42 (SCM); and Nītivākyāmṛta, 10.27; 117.10.1 (NV).

The Mānava-dharmaśāstra text is found in the Cāṇakya-rāja-nīti-śāstra and Cāṇakya-nīti-śāstra version and in nine different compendia. It was incorporated in the Vṛddhacāṇakyaḥ, Cāṇakya-praṇītaḥ edition from the Cāṇakya-rāja-nīti-śāstra version.

The maxim deals with false witnesses and is well-known It also occurs in the Pañcatantra, the Hitopadeśa, the Vetāla-pañcaviṁśatikā, the Bṛhaspati-saṁhitā of the Garuḍa-purāṇa from which it was probably incorporated into the Cāṇakya-rāja-nīti-śāstra version (or *vice versa*) and the Gautama-dharma-sūtra. It is also quoted in several *nibandha-s* and commentaries, as well as in Subhāṣita-saṁgraha-s, such as the Subhāṣita-ratna-bhāṇḍāgāra, 147.226 (SRBh); and Vallabhadeva's Subhāṣitāvali, 2803 (VS). Also Böhtlingk quotes it in his *Indische Sprüche* 848 (IS). Similar thoughts are expressed in the Yājñavalkya-smṛti (2.13-5); the Nārada-smṛti (1.193-6) and Pariśiṣṭa (10-1); the Bṛhaspati-smṛti, 5.43a; the Kātyāyana-smṛti, 386; the Śaṅkha Likhita in Vīramitrodaya, Vyavahāra-prakāśa, 124.13 and Vyavahāra-cintāmaṇi, 399-400; and even in the Rāmāyaṇa in Vyavahāradatta, 51. However in most of these sources the stanza is not quoted without the preceding one (8.25), since both form a unit. Mn 8.25 states that the king should discover the internal disposition of men by external marks, such as voices, colour, motions, eyes and gestures; in the following stanza Mn states that by gestures, motions, gesticulations, speech and changes in the eye in the face their inner mind is revealed. Medhātithi states in his commentary to Mn 8.26 that this stanza is a supporting stanza of the preceding one and is therefore not repeated in it.

Only one variant occurs in some texts of Manu. Govinda-rāja's commentary (also quoted in Jhā's edition) has in δ *jñāyate* instead of *gṛhyate*. The same variant occurs also in the texts of the Cāṇakya-rāja-nīti-śāstra version, some texts of the Pañcatantra, the Vetālapañcaviṁśatikā and some *nibandha-s* and commentaries. The texts of the Cāṇakya-rāja-nīti-śāstra version have in addition one variant in β (*vikārābhyāṁ* instead of *vikārais ca*) which also occurs in the Garuḍa-purāṇa and the Subhāṣita-ratna-bhāṇḍāgāra. The various editions and MSs of Cāṇakya contain other unimportant variants, some of which occur also in other sources, in particular in the *kathā* literature. Numerous other variants are unimportant.

The text of Cāṇakya was undoubtedly borrowed from the Mānava-dharmaśāstra but it is not possible to conclude through what source it was incorporated in these compendia. It is possible that it was not borrowed directly from the Mānava-dharmaśāstra. This is not only evidenced by the language used, but also by the fact that this stanza was quoted out of the context. It must be however noted that this is not an isolated case. The Pañcatantra, the Hitopadeśa and the Vetālapañcaviṁśatikā also quoted this stanza without the preceding or the following one.

[1]*ākaraṇe'(ṅ)gitair* *CRP*, *CRBh II*, Apar, SV, VyK; *ākāronauṁgi°* (*sic* !) *CRBh I*. [2]*aṅgitair* Nñψ PL_1PrMBh in PP. [3]*bhāṣaṇena* *CRC*, *CRP*, Hitopadeśa, *Pañcatantra*, C in Vet, VyN, NV, SRBh, SV; *harṣitena* GMBh. [4]*tu* GP. [5]*va°* omitted *CRBh II*. [6]*vikārābhyaṁ* *CRC*, *CRP*, *CRBh I*, *CRBh II*, *CRCa*, *CPS*, GP, SRBh, VS; *vikāreṇa* PP, Hitopadeśa, NV, BDce in Vet, VRV, VyK. [7]*jñāyate* Govindarāja's commentary (also quoted in Jhā's edition), *CRC*, *CRP*, *CRBh I*, *CRBh II*, *CRCa*, A in PP, Vet, VRV, SRBh, VS; *lakṣyate* GP, Pts, d in Vet, VyK; *śaya°* GR. [8]*nṛṇām* *CRC*, *CPS*; *pranaḥ* VRV.

No. 27. *Mn* 8.351.

[1]*nā'tatāyi-vadhe*[2] *doṣo hantur*[3] *bhavati kaścana*[4],
[5]*prakāśaṁ vā'prakāśaṁ vā manyus taṁ manyum ṛcchati.*

"By killing an assasin, either openly or secretly, the slayer incurs no punishment; fury recoils upon fury."

This maxim occurs in the Cāṇakya-rāja-nīti-śāstra edition (*Calc. Or. Ser.* 2), 8.49 (*CRC*); MS. sansk. f. 15 in the Bodleian Library in Oxford, 8.52 (*CRB*); MS. 1559 in the Library of the University of Pennsylvania in Philadelphia, 8.49 (*CRP*); MS. No. 347 of 1892-95 in the Bhāṇḍārkar R. O. Institute in Poona, 8.49 (*CRBh I*); the Vṛddha-cāṇakyaḥ, Cāṇakya-praṇītaḥ, Calcutta, 1332, edition, 233.37 (*CPS*).

It also occurs in the Garuḍa-purāṇa, 1.115, 47 γδ/αβ; the Matsya-purāṇa (in Dharmakośa, 1655); and the Viṣṇu-smṛti, 5.190.

It is also quoted in the Parāśara-dharmasaṁhitā, 3.2; 467.5-6 (PS); Smṛti-candrikā (Ghārpure's edition), 314.22-3 (SC); Mandanaratnapradīpa (*Gaṅga Or. Ser.* 6), 300.24-5; Daṇḍaviveka (*Gaekwad Or. Ser.* 52), 9.19 (αβ only) (DV); Nṛsiṁhaprasāda, Vyavahāra-sāra (Sarasvatī Bhāvana Texts,

53), 208.12-3 (NṛP); Sarasvatīvilāsa, 152.14-5 (cf. 154-5 for αβ) (SV); Mitākṣarā *ad* Yājñavalkya-smṛti, 2.21 (Mit); Viśvarūpa *ad* Yājñavalkya-smṛti, 2.21; Nītimayukha, 62.12 (αβ only); (NM); Vyavahāraprakāśa, 14; Vyavahārodyota, 9; Vyavaharārthasamuccaya, 147; Vivādārṇavasetu, 100; Vivādātaṇḍava, 491 and 757; and Prāyaścittaviveka 60.

The Mānava-dharmaśāstra text is found in the Cāṇakya-rāja-nīti-śāstra version from which it was incorporated in the Vṛddha-cāṇakya, Cāṇakya-praṇītaḥ edition.

The maxim deals with self-defense and is one of the best known maxims and legal rules which states that a killer who acts in self-defence cannot be made responsible for his action. The maxim also occurs in the Viṣṇu-smṛti, the Matsya-purāṇa and the Garuḍapurāṇa. It is also quoted either in whole, or in part in numerous *nibandha-s* and commentaries. The first part of the maxim contains the main thought, i.e. that by killing a killer, the slayer incurs no punishment. The same thought is expressed in the Vāsiṣṭha-dharmaśāstra (3.15-8), the Baudhāyanadharmasūtra (1.10, 18, 11-3); the Kātyāyana-smṛti (800 sqq.); the Bṛhaspati-smṛti in Aparārka (1042); Vyāsa in Aparārka (1043); and the Garuḍa-purāṇa (1.115, 47).

No variants occur in the Manu text. The *nibandha-s* and commentaries follow, with a few exceptions, the Manu text; however the text as found in the Cāṇakya's compendia follows almost without variants the Manu text in αβ only; γδ of the Cāṇakya's compendia is different and follows the text of the Bṛhaspati-saṁhitā of the Garuḍa-purāṇa with which it is usually very closely connected. The same Garuḍa-purāṇa stanza can be also found in the Pañcatantra and in the Vṛddha Cāṇakya, *textus ornatior*, and the Cāṇakya-nīti-śāstra versions.

It is impossible to conclude from where the Cāṇakya text was borrowed. It was neither directly borrowed from the Garuḍa-purāṇa nor from the Mānava-dharmaśāstra. It is a combination, probably an original combination, of these two sources. It may be added that αβ of the Cāṇakya text (which is identical with αβ of the Manu text), similarly as γδ of the Cāṇakya text (which is identical with αβ of the Garuḍa-purāṇa text) include two separate thoughts of which each can stand by itself.

[1]*na tatrāri°* NṛP; *ātatāyi°* SV [2] *°badhe* DV. [3]*karttur CRBh I.* [4]*kaścanaḥ*

CPS; *kaścanā CRBh I*; *kaścaneti* NM. [5]*kṛtaṁ* (*kṛte CRB, CRP, CRBh I*, GP) *pratikṛtaṃ* (°*tiṁ CRB*; °*te CRP*) *kuryād*(*t*) *hiṁsitaṁ* (°*te CRB, CRP, CRBh I*, GP) *pratihiṁsitam* (°*sinam CRP*) *CRC, CRB, CRP, CRBh I, CPS*, GP; *prachannaṁ* Mit, SV.

No. 28. *Mn* 9.3.

pitā rakṣati[1] *kaumāre*[2] *bhartā rākṣati*[3] *yauvane*,[4]
[5]*rakṣanti*[6] *sthavire*[7] *putrā na strī* [8]*svātantryam arhati*[9].

"The father protects them (i. e., women) in maidenhood; the husband protects them in youth; the sons protect them in old age; a woman is never equipped to be free from control."

This maxim occurs in MS. sansk. f. 15 in the Bodleian Library in Oxford, 8.68 (*CRB*); MS. 1559 in the Library of the University of Pennsylvania in Philadelphia, 8.65 (*CRP*); MS. No. 347 of 1892-95 in the Bhāṇḍārkar O. R. Institute in Poona, 8.66 (*CRBh I*); MS. No. 348 of 1892-95 in the Bhāṇḍārkar O. R. Institute in Poona, 8.55 (*CRBh II*); the Cāṇakya, Codice Indiano edito dal Dre E. Bartoli, Napoli, 1911, edition, 58 (*CNF*); MS. 1566 in the Library of the University of Pennsylvania in Philadelphia, 92 (*CNPh*); MS. 1518a (Eggeling 3990) in the India Office Library in London, 155 (*CNI*); The Recension of Cāṇakya used by Gallanos...in *Studies in Honor of Maurice Bloomfield*, New Haven edition, 180 (*CNG*); MS. A 447 in the Universitätsbibliothek of the Karl-Marx Universität in Leipzig, 46 (*CNL*).

It also occurs in the Baudhāyana-dharmasūtra, 2.2, 3, 45; Gautama, Mitākṣarā, Haradatta (ĀnSS), 28.1 (G); Vāṣiṣṭha-dharmaśāstra, 5.3 (Vās); Nārada-smṛti, 13.31 (N); Nāradīya-ṁanu-saṁhitā, 13.31 (NMS); as well as in the Mahābhārata (Roy's edition), 13.20, 21, and 13. 46, 14 (MBh); the Rāmāyaṇa, 2.39. 33 (2.29, 18) (R); the Garuḍa-purāṇa, 1.115, 63 (GP); the Padma-purāṇa, Sṛṣṭikhaṇḍa, 54.23 (Pp); and the Hitopadeśa (Johnson's edition, 1.128 (HJ); Schlegel's and Lassen's edition, 1.113 (HS); Müller's edition, 1.119 (HM); Peterson's edition, 1.91 (HP); Blatt's Nepālī edition, 1.92 (HN); Kale's edition, 1.122 (HK); Hamilton's edition 24.26-7 (HH); Colebrooke's edition, 33.17-8 (HC).

It is also quoted in the Parāśara-dharma-saṁhitā, 2.1; 38.2 and 355.6 (PS); Smṛticandrikā (Ghārpure's edition), 2.240, 16 (SC), Ujjvalā *ad* Āpastambīya-dharmasūtra, 2.14, 2

(U); Vīramitrodaya, Vyavahāra-prakāśa, 406.6-7 (VRV); Dharmattvanirṇaya-pariśiṣṭa, 2.50, 2-3 (DhN); Bālambhaṭṭi, Vyavahāra (Ghārpure's edition), 195. 33 αβγ and 342.24-5 and 3.211, 17 (BBh); Vivāda-ratnākara, 410. 1191 (VRK); Vyavahārakalpataruḥ, Prajñapatahsthala, 128, Vyavahāra-prakāśa, 406, (VyP); Smṛticintāmaṇi in Dharmakośa, 27 (SCM); Vivādārṇavasetu, 281, Vivādabhaṅgarṇava, 2.53 (VBh); Vyavahārārthasamuccaya, 120 (VyS); Vivādātaṇḍava, 821; Nṛsiṁhaprasāda, Saṁskāra, 66b; Saṁskāra-ratnamālā 674. 19-20 (SR); and Smṛtimuktāphalam 154.33 (SMPh).

The Mānava-dharmaśāstra text is found in the Cāṇakya-rāja-nīti-śāstra and the Cāṇakya-nīti-śāstra versions in ten different compendia of which one, viz., *CNI*, is corrupt. The Manu text was incorporated in the Vṛddha-cāṇakyaḥ, Cāṇakya-praṇītaḥ text from the Cāṇakya-rāja-nīti-śāstra version.

The maxim deals with the protection of women in their maidenhood, youth and old age. It is a very well-known maxim. It also occurs in the Mahābhārata, the Rāmāyaṇa, the Hitopadeśa, the Bṛhaspati-saṁhitā of the Garuḍa-purāṇa from which it was probably incorporated in the Cāṇakya-rāja-nīti-śāstra version (or *vice-versa*), in the Padmapurāṇa and in many Smṛti-s, viz., Gautama, Baudhāyana, Vāsiṣṭha and Nārada. Similar thoughts are also expressed in the Viṣṇu-smṛti (25.13), the Yājñavalkya-smṛti (1.85-6), the Smṛtyantara in Aparārka (109) and in another place of the Mānava-dharma-śāstra (5.148) and in the Mahānirvāṇatantra (8.106). Most important *nibandha-s* and commentaries also quote this stanza. It is also quoted in some Subhāṣita-saṁgraha-s, such as the Subhāṣita-ratna-bhāṇḍāgāra, 166.575; and M. W. Carr's *Collection of Telugu Proverbs*, 77. Also Böhtlingk quotes it in his *Indische Sprüche*, 4067 (IS).

Only one variant occurs in some texts of the Mānava-dharmaśāstra. The commentaries of Rāghavānanda and Nandana have in γ *putrās tu sthavire bhāve* instead of *rakṣanti sthavire putrā*. The same variant occurs also in several other sources. In γ several other variants are also noted, some of which are of lesser importance (in the Cāṇakya-compendia). The other variants from the Manu text inthe Cāṇakya's compendia are unimportant and are rather misspellings than variants.

The text of Cāṇakya was undoubtedly borrowed directly from the Mānava-dharmaśāstra, but not in its purest form.

[1]*rakṣata CRBh I*; *rekṣati* (?) *CNI*. [2]*komārye CNI*; *kaumarī CNL*. [3]*rokṣiti* (?) *CNPh*. [4]*yāvane* IS. [5]*putrās* (°*as*) *tu sthavire* (°*rī* B, GMH, U, PS 2.1; 355) *bhāve* Rāghavānanda's and Nandana's commentaries, PS, VRR, B, GMH, VRV, DhNP, VRK, VV, P in HS, HN, BN in HP, SMPh, *CNL*, *CNPh*, SRBh; *putraś ca sthavire bhāve* Vās. MBh 13.46, Pp; *putrāś ca sthāvire kāle* HJ, HS, HM, HP, Pp in HS, MBh 13.20, GP, *CNF*; *putrāḥ sthavira bhāve tu* PS 2.1; 38; *putrāś ca sthavire prāpte CNI*; *putro rakṣati vardhahye* SR. [6]*putrāh* BBh 195. [7]*vārdhake CRP*, *CRBh I*, *CRBh II*, NMS; *sthāvire CNF*, *CNPh*, *CNG*, HM, HC, U, MBh 13.20, SRBh; *sthavira* PS 2.1; 38; *sthāvirī* GMH, B (cd in B as above). [8]*svātantryacam* (?) *CRBh I*; *svātantryaṁ kvacit striyāḥ* SR; *svataṁcam* (?) *CNI*. [9]*arhīti* B.

No. 29. *Mn* 11.9.

śaktaḥ para-jane dātā sva-jane duḥkha-jivini,[1]
madhvā'pāto[2] *viṣāsvādaḥ sa* [3]*dharma-pratirūpakaḥ.*

"He who in order to get reward after death bestows gifts upon strangers to the detriment of persons he is obliged to maintain, fails miserably during his lifetime and after his death."

This maxim occurs in the Vṛddhacāṇākya-niti-samuccaya, Ahmedabad 1913 edition, 14.17.

It also occurs in the Brāhmadharma, 2.9, 10 and is quoted in Aparārka's commentary on the Yājñavalkya-smṛti, 283. 2-3.

The Mānava-dharmaśāstra text is found only in one Cāṇakya-compendium belonging to the Vṛddha Cāṇakya, *textus ornatior* version, viz, the Vṛddha-cāṇakya-nīti-samuccaya edition.

The maxim deals with the bestowing of gifts for purposes of reward to the detriment of persons who, according to law, have to be maintained. This maxim should be read together with the following one where persons who, according to law, have to be maintained, are enumerated. This stanza is taken out of context.

The maxim is not a well-known one. It is quoted only in the Brāhmadharma and in one commentary, viz., Aparārka's.[4] Böhtlingk quotes it in his *Indische Sprüche*, 6343 (IS).

Three unimportant variants are noted in various MSs of the Māṇava-dharmaśāstra. In β the commentary of Govindarāja has *duḥkha-pīḍite* instead of *duḥkha-jīvini* (the same variant is also noted in the Jhā's edition). In γ Jhā in his Mānava-dharma-śāstra with Medhātithi's commentary notes as a variant °*pāno* instead of °*pāto* and in δ three MSs of the Medhātithi's commentary, the Wilkin's MS and the Rāghavānanda's commentary have *dharmaḥ* instead of *dharma*.

The Cāṇakya text follows closely and without any variants the generally accepted Manu text.

The text of Cāṇakya was undoubtedly borrowed directly from the Mānava-dharmaśāstra.

[1]*duḥkha-pīḍite* Govindarāja's commentary (also noted in Jhā's edition). [2] °*pātaḥ* IS; °*pāno* Jhā's edition (variant). [3]*dharmaḥ* MS No. V used by Haughton, MS of the Deccan College in Poona and the old Deccan College MS of Medhātithi's commentary, Wilkins's MS, Rāghavānanda's commentary. [4]According to G. Jhā's edition of the Mānava-dharmaśāstra, part II, p. 794 the maxim is also quoted in Hemādri, Dāna p. 40; however it could not be traced in this place.

It should be noted that we find in all the editions and MSs. of the Vṛddha Cāṇakya, *textus ornatior* version one maxim viz., 6.3[1] which is in thought, but not in language, almost identical with stanza 5.108 of the Mānava-dharmaśāstra.

The CV stanza reads :

bhasmanā śudhyate kāṁsyaṁ tāmram amlena śudhyati,
rajasā śudhyate nārī nadī vegena śudhyati.

The Mānava-dharmaśāstra stanza reads :

mṛttoyaiḥ śudhyate śodhyaṁ nadī vegena śudhyati,
rajasā strī manoduṣṭā saṁnyāsena dvijottamaḥ.

[1]This stanza occurs also in the Bodhi Cāṇakyam edition by Bhoobhun Chaund Dutt, Calcutta, 1888, 281; MS. or. fol. 598 in the Universitätsbibliothek Tübingen (Weber No. 1591), 3.80; MS. belonging to Prof. J. W. de Jong in Leiden, 3.88; MS. Add. 1539 in the University Library in Cambridge, 3.80; MS. Add. 1346 in the University Library in Cambridge, 281; MS. or. fol. 599 in the Universitätsbibliothek Tübingen (Weber No. 1592), 281; MS. Cod. or. 8857, Lub-D 122 in the University Library in Leiden, 81, the Cāṇakyam. Codice Indiano edito dal Dre Emilio Bartoli (Napoli 1911), edition 82; MS. 17072-3 (A) in the Université de Paris. Institut de Civilisation Indienne, 48; MS. 17072-1 in the

Université de Paris. Institut de Civilisation Indienne, 72; MS. Sankrit 684 in the Bibliothèque Nationale in Paris (Cabaton 684), 26; MS. 1518a in the India Office Library in London (Eggeling 3990), 164; MS. No. 5119 from Tanjore, 47; Rājanitau Cāṇikya-mūni-viracitaṁ (no place, no date) edition, 47; Cāṇakya-muni-kṛtaṁ- nīti-sāra (Allahabad, saṁvat 1880) edition, 45; Vṛddha Cāṇakyaḥ, Cāṇakya-praṇītaḥ (Calcutta, 1332) edition, 165.87. It is also quoted in the Subhāṣita-ratna-bhāṇḍāgara, 389.503 and in Böhtlingk's *Indische Sprüche* 4567.

XXVII

MAHĀBHĀRATA VERSES IN CĀṆAKYA'S COMPENDIA[1]

1. *INTRODUCTORY NOTE*

1. This author in his previous study on "Mānava-dharmaśāstra Verses in Cāṇakya's Compendia"[2] emphasized that the origin of the very numerous aphorisms attributed to Cāṇakya (2433) was, in most cases unknown; that they were passed down orally from person to person, just as today wise sayings float among peoples of different nations; and that in India this floating mass of oral tradition and wisdom was very often *in majorem gloriam* attributed to one man—Cāṇakya. The author has endeavoured to show which of the maxims attributed to Cāṇakya originated in the Mānava-dharmaśāstra. In this study he will endeavour to show which of the maxims attributed to Cāṇakya originated in the Mahābhārata.

2. It is a well-known fact that it is impossible to determine the age of the Mahābhārata in its present form and that the age of each part of the Mahābhārata, in reality, of each of its verses, must be determined separately.[3] However, it seems safe to say that the Mahābhārata was the source for maxims attributed to Cāṇakya, rather than *vice-versa*, though some of the maxims might have belonged to the floating mass of oral tradition and wisdom which could have been incorporated independently either in the Mahābhārata or in the collections of maxims attributed to Cāṇakya.

3. It is also a well-known fact that the Mahābhārata is not so much a poem with a single subject, as a vast cyclopaedia or thesaurus of Hindū mythology, legendary history, philosophy and ethics. The main narative of the Mahābhārata acts only as a slender thread to connect a vast mass of independent legends and religious, moral and political precepts; these precepts are scattered throughout the whole epic but some didactic discourses full of setentious maxims are in particular found in the Vanaparva (Āraṇeya-parvan) in which Yuddhiṣṭhira and Yakṣa

1. Previously appeared as JSAIL 30. in JAOS 83.1, pp. 30-67.
2. JAOS 79.4, p. 234-54. Study XXVI.
3. M. Winternitz, *Geschichte der indische Litteratur*, I 396-9,

in their dialogue search for the Brāhmaṇ's fire-stick and discuss the precepts of knowledge and religion; Udyoga-parvan (Prajāgara-parvan) in which in order to beguile a sleepless night, Dhṛtarāṣṭra got Vidura discourse to him; there Vidura gave lengthy ethical teaching and quoted many maxims, frequently advising to concede to just claims of Yudhiṣṭhira; and Śānti-parvan (Āpad-dharma-parvan) which could be considered as an *arthaśāstra* composed of moral and ethical sentences dealing with *artha*. These in particular, but also several other parvan-s of the Mahābhārata, could be considered as Subhāṣitasaṃgraha-s from which many authors drew and then incorporated the sententious maxims included therein in their own works.

4. The aim of this study is to show which of the maxims attributed to Cāṇakya originated in the Mahābhārata.[4] In order to be able to conclude whether the compilor of the Cāṇakya's compendia borrowed directly from MBh or not, it was necessary to analyse each stanza occurring in any of the Cāṇakya's compendia as well as in the MBh separately and to give all variants of this stanza. This has been done in the second part of this study. In particular it was found necessary, first, to give the text of the Mahābhārata, an English translation of each stanza; appropriate places in which the stanza is found in various Cāṇakya's compendia; and other sources; a detailed analysis of each stanza; and in the footnotes different readings which occur in each stanza.

The MBh text used was, in principle, the critical edition, as published by the Bhandarkar Oriental Research Institute. Since at the time this study was written, the Anuśāsana-parvan did not appear yet[4a], this text could not be used for Nos. 113 to 130. Also the Bombay (Roy's edition) and the Calcutta editions were used. The author has given his own new English translation of each stanza.[5] As far as Cāṇakya's compendia are concerned, he used the critical text, as reconstructed by him in the six versions of *C*,[6] and as being published by the Vishvesh-

4. Compare para. 2 above.

4a. In the meantime the Anuśāsanaparvan was published.

5. The translation used in his JSAIL 24 was Johnson's translation in HJ and therefore the translation given here is not always identical with that given in JSAIL 24.

6. As described in detail in para. 2 of JSAIL 27 (*JAOS* 79, 234). See Abbreviations: Cr.

varanand Vedic Research Institute in Hoshiarpur; where the maxims did not occur in the reconstructed versions of Cāṇakya's sayings, but in individual Cāṇakya's texts, he used these texts; they are described in the Abbreviations;[7] the other sources are the Dharmaśāstra-s (including the *nib andha-s*), the *kāvya* and the *kathā* literature.[8]

The maxims are arranged in the order in which they appear in the Mahābhārata. Very often the same maxim appears in two or more places of the MBh; in such a case the stanza is not repeated but figures only once and a reference is made to the places where the maxim is analyzed.

5. This study contains 141 Mahābhārata stanzas which are also found in one or more texts of Cāṇakya's compendia. In reality there are only 98 Mahābhārata stanzas, since in 43 cases the same stanza is repeated in the MBh text more than once.[9]

The Cāṇakya's compendia usually borrowed from those parts of the MBh which could be considered as Subhāṣita-saṃgraha-s.[10] These Subhāṣita-saṃgraha-s which formed part of the MBh deal perhaps more consistently than other well-known Subhāṣita-saṃgraha-s with separate topics; therefore, in one place we find several maxims dealing with king's policy (MBh (Bh) 12.138); fear (MBh (R) 12.83); wife (MBh (Bh) 1.74); previous existence (MBh (Bh) 12.174), etc. From these sources of wise sayings dealing with the same subjectmatter, the editors of Cāṇakya's compendia could borrow, according to their whim. They did so, often not very ably, since they chose only one maxim, omitting the preceding or subsequent maxims which were closely connected with the quoted one. And so, for instance, the maxim quoted in No. 100 is incomplete;

7. The *CnT* texts which have an appearance of note-books of students (*Cf.* L. Sternbach, *Various Versions of Cāṇakya Compendia* in *Akten des XXIV internationalen Orientalistenkongresses, München* 1957; *p.* 546) and do not merit special attention, were in principle not enumerated in this study.

8. However, the Subhāṣita-saṃgraha-s in which the appropriate stanzas also occur were not enumerated in this study; they appear in the critical reconstructed texts of the six versions of Cāṇakya's aphorisms. See Abbreviations : *Cr.*

9. In addition there are several MBh stanzas which are similar to *C* stanzas; sometimes their thoughts have influenced the *C* maxims, but their wording is so different from the *C* text that it was decided not to include them in this study; these MBh stanzas will be the object of a separate study.

10. See para. 3 above.

the next maxim gives additional faults of covetousness; the maxim quoted in No. 91 is incomplete since the next maxim develops the theme contained in the preceding stanza; the maxim quoted in No. 126 is also incomplete, since it forms a part of a longer extract dealing with the same subject-matter; the maxim quoted in No. 44 is also partly incomplete, since the next maxim in MBh gives additional examples of preservation; the maxim quoted in No. 46 is the second part of the same thought which was expressed in the preceding maxim in MBh.

Sometimes the various editors of Cāṇakya's compendia quoted the consecutive stanzas from MBh but included them in different Cāṇakya's compendia. And so, for instance, two maxims dealing with forbearance (Nos. 34 and 35 are included in two completely different texts of the *CR* version: the first in the *CRCa* II text, and the second in the *CRC* text; or five maxims from the Udyoga-parvan (Nos. 61 to 65; MBh (Bh) 5.39, 60 to 66 although consecutive in the MBh have been included in various Cāṇakya's compendia, such as *CVNS* (No. 61), *Cvr*, *CRr* and two texts of the *CN* version (No.62), *CNr* (No. 63); *CRr* and one text of the *CN* version (No. 64);and two texts of the *CN* version (No. 65); or two maxims also from the Udyoga-parvan (Nos. 66 and 67) although consecutive in the MBh have been included in various Cāṇakya's compendia: (No. 66 in the *Cvr* and *CLr* versions and No. 67 inthe *CRr* and *Cvr* versions and in six texts of the *CN* version); or two maxims from the Śanti-parvan (No. 139 and 111) although consecutive in the MBh have been included in various Cāṇakya's compendia; No. 137 in *CRCa II* 3.5 and No. 111 in *CVr* 13.14, *CRr* 6.47 and three individual texts of the *CN* version.

On the other hand, consecutive stanzas in the same Cāṇakya's compendia quote maxims from the same chapter of the MBh omitting one or more maxims quoted in the MBh. And so, for instance, in the *CRr* version 8.40 and 8.41 quote MBh (Bh) 5.35, 34 and 5.35, 44 omitting 5.35, 36 to 43 (Nos. 48 and 49); or the *CRCa II* text quoted in 28 and 29; MBh (Bh) 12.174, 10 and 14 omitting 12.174, 11 to 13 (Nos. 108 and 110).

The Cāṇakya's compendia very often selected indiscriminately from a group of maxims dealing with the same subject-matter (and included in the same chapter in the MBh) some maxims only, although many more maxims in the same chapter dealt with the same subject. And so, various Cāṇakya's compendia selected from the Ādi-parvan (68th chapter) only some stanzas dealing with wives (Nos. 1-3); or selected also from the Ādi-parvan (68th chapter) only one stanza dealing with sons (No. 4); or selected from the Udyoga-parvan (70th chapter) only one maxim dealing with wealth (No. 68); or selected from the Udyoga-parvan (114th chapter) only one maxim dealing with wives (No. 98); or selected from the Śānti-parvan (111th chapter) one of many maxims dealing with fear (No. 87); or selected from the Anuśāsana-parvan (38th chapter) one of many maxims dealing with women (No. 124). The same refers also to the Udyoga-parvan (33rd chapter) Nos. 38 and 39; (34th chapter) Nos. 40-6; Śānti-parvan (27th chapter) Nos. 83 and 84; and particularly Śānti-parvan (332nd chapter of MBh (R) (Nos. 114 to 118) which is a repetition of MBh (R) 181st chapter.[11] Other example could be additionally quoted.

This indiscriminate selection of stanzas from the MBh by different editors of Cāṇakya's compendia proves that they were ignorant of the Mahābhārata text as it is known in its present form. Had they known this text, they would certainly have included all or at least some of the beautiful maxims dealing with the same subject with which they dealt. It is very likely that they did not even known that these maxims originated in the MBh but knew them by heart as part of the floating mass of oral tradition and wisdom, and included them in their compendia and attributed them to Cāṇakya.

Some of these stanzas were very well known (sometimes they were included in the Bhagavadgītā; No. 93), the thought of which was even often repeated in different words in several places, e.g., maxims Nos. 5, 7, 8, 42, 50, 102, 104, 127, 130 etc. Some of these maxims were also adapted in the Tibetan, Mongolian, Burmese (Pāli and Burmese) and Old Javanese Literature[12] (maxims Nos. 1, 5, 8, 18, 23, 36, 41, 42, 44,46, 48, 50, 52, 53, 56, 57, 58, 61, 62, 67, 80, 93, 94, 95, 96, 97, 104, 107, 111, 124, 132, 134, 136, 141, 143, 144, 148 and 149). However, some are less known and it seems rather strange that

11. In MBh(Bh) 174th chapter. MBh(Bh) omits MBh(R)'s 322nd chapter.

12. *Cf.* L. Sternbach, *The Spreading of Cāṇakaya's Aphorisms over "Greater India"* in *Journal of the Greater India Society*, Vol. XVIII.

they were selected from the MBh and included in Cāṇakya's compendia, e.g. No. 24.

6. The detailed analysis of each stanza made it possible to conclude: *A.* whether the maxim, as included in a Caṇakya's compendium, was borrowed directly from the MBh or from other sources of Sanskrit literature; *B.* from what text of the MBh i.e. from what *parvan* it was borrowed; *C.* whether it was borrowed from the classical text of the MBh (as critically edited in the Bhandarkar Oriental Research Institute), or from a Vulgata text of the MBh; and *D.* whether the MBh text, experiencing an evolution, was changed and in *C* or only influenced by the Mahābhārata text.

A. Very often the same maxim is found in the MBh, some other sources and one or more Cāṇakya's compendia. Usually the preliminary source of this maxim was the MBh, but not always.

We find seven maxims which are found in the MBh, the Mn and *C.* Of these one has no different readings (No. 8) and therefore could have been borrowed by *C* either from MBh or from Mn; however, the other six maxims (Nos. 26, 56, 61, 81, 126 and 127) have various readings. Analysing the various readings of these maxims we come to the conclusion that all of them were borrowed directly from the Mn and not from the MBh.[13]

The texts of MBh. R and *C* are usually the same, but in one case (viz. No. 85), analysing the various readings, we can come to the conclusion that *C* borrowed from MBh and not from R.

In two cases different readings are found in MBh, GP and *C.* Analysing these different readings we come to the conclusion that in one case (No. 87) *C* borrowed from MBh, while in the other (No. 108) the *C* text is nearer to GP than to MBh.[14]

B. As stated above the variants between the MBh text and the *C* text are usually unimportant. It must, however, be noted that often the same maxim occurs in the MBh in more

13. Of these six, four viz. Nos. 26, 61, 81 and 126 are found in the *CVNS* text which is a *CV* text with a number of additions from Mn or MBh.

14. The *C* text is the *CRCa II* text which usually follows very closely the GP and may be even considered as a fragment or shortened text of GP. *Cf. CRr* para. 5.8 and L. Sternbach *A new Abridged Version of the Bṛhaspati-Saṃhitā of the Garuḍa-purāṇa.* Ramnagar—Varanasi, 1966.

than one place in various readings; these readings are usually not far apart. The analysis of the various readings permits sometimes to come to the conclusion from what place (*parvan*) *C* borrowed his text. This shows which text of the same maxim of MBh was more popular in India. And so, in the case of maxim No. 10 we see that the text of the Ādi-parvan (and not Sabhā- or Udyoga-parvan) was borrowed by *C*, as well as Pañc. H, Śts, VCjr, etc; in the case of maxim No. 18 we see that the text of the Udyoga-parvan (and not Sabhā-parvan) was borrowed by *C*, as well as Pañc and GP.

C. The analysis of the various variants occurring in the MBh and *C* texts[15] can also throw additional light on the MBh, as critically edited in the Bhandarkar Oriental Research Institute. This analysis shows in what form the MBh maxim was better known in India at the time when *C's* compendia were compiled. When the MBh text of the Vulgata, which appears in the MBh (R) or MBh (C) editions, is identical with the *C* text, it seems to show that that text was better known in India than the "classical" text of MBh and that that text was accepted by the Hindū-s as the "authentic" text of MBh. On the contrary, if the classical text occurs also in the *C* text that seems to show that that text was generally accepted as the text of the MBh.

The critical analysis of the texts given below shows that maxims Nos. 12, 20 and 47 followed the classical text of MBh as critically edited in the Bhandarkar Oriental Research Institute in Poona, while maxims Nos. 37, 41, 46, 69, 91, 97, 99 (*CNP II*), and 106 followed the MBh (R) and MBh (C) texts, it is the Vulgata text of the MBh.

D. If we find a maxim in the MBh, the *kathā* (or *kāvya*) literature and *C*, usually the texts are different,[16] although the main thought is identical; these texts were certainly influenced by the primary source. This proves that the maxim underwent a change, sometimes a radical change; then it is very often impossible to conclude from what particular source *C* borrowed.

15. Sometimes also other texts.
16. But not always. E.g. maxim No. 40 is identical in MBh, H and *C*. Therefore, it is impossible to conclude from where the *C* text borrowed this maxim. The *C* text in case of maxim No. 40 is *CNB*; this text adds to 108 stanza (classical *aṣṭottaraśata*) 37 maxims borrowed from MBh, H and other versions of *C*. *Cf*. *CNr* para. 9.40.

The analysis of the various readings teaches us sometimes, however, from what source the *C* stanza could not have been borrowed. And so, the MBh maxim (No. 74) underwent a change in H only; therefore, we can conclude that the *C* stanza was not borrowed from H. In the case of maxims Nos. 88 and 98, we can conclude that *C* could not have been borrowed directly from MBh.

Sometimes the changes between the various texts are so obvious that we can see what part of the stanza (*pāda*) was influenced by other texts. And so, as far as maxim No. 93 is concerned, its first *pāda* in *C* was influenced by Pañc, or H and in maxim No. 95 the first *pāda* in *C* was influenced by Pañc., or H (Vet.). However, as stated above, in most of the cases when the texts are quite different, it is impossible to conclude from what text the *C* text was borrowed directly, e.g., in the case of maxims Nos. 29, 95, 96.

The same can also be said of maxims Nos. 52 and 92 where λδ are different (both these maxims could therefore be considered as new maxims). In other cases, it seems that the *C* stanzas which contain different readings from the MBh text, were only influenced directly by the MBh text, although the thought included in the MBh was borrowed by the *C* text. That occurs in maxims Nos. 49, 54, 57, 59, 62 and 107,[17] while Nos. 109 and 130 were borrowed from MBh not in its purest form.

E. Sometimes we can also observe in the maxims quoted in this study the development of the thought included therein. In the MBh maxim (No. 99) it was said that a woman does not receive many gifts from her father, mother and son, but only from her husband; therefore she should treat him with respect. The Vulgata text of the MBh, the R, the Pañc, the VC and the Vet substituted the brother for mother. The *C* text went further; probably knowing the different variants of this stanza changed somewhat the reading of the first two *pādas* and included all the four, i.e., the father, mother, brother and son as those from whom a woman did not receive many gifts;[18] the poetical beauty of the verse was partly lost, but its sense was improved.

17. Some Subhāṣita-saṃgraha-s repeat maxim No. 49 in the form as it appears in MBh and not in the form as it appears in *C*.

18. *mitaṃ dadāti hi pitā, mitaṃ mātā* (or *bhrātā*), *mitaṃ sutaḥ* (MBh) was changed to *mitaṃ dadyāt pitā, mātā, mitaṃ bhrātā, mitaṃ sutaḥ* (*CNP II*).

F. Finally, the analysis of the different readings of the stanzas quoted below can show if a MBh stanza was quoted in more than one text of *C*, which of the *C* texts is nearer to the original. E.g., far as maxim No. 50 is concerned, the MBh text was reproduced in the *CNG* text in its original form, while the *CRr* had some variants which occurred also in H or BhŚ. It seems therefore, that the *CNG* text borrowed directly from MBh, while the *CRr* text borrowed through H or BhŚ.

II *DETAILED ANALYSIS OF STANZAS*

1. *MBh*(*Bh*) 1.68, 39; *MBh*(*R*) 1.74, 39; *MBh*(*C*) 1. 3027.
Cf. Nos. 91-2.

sā bhāryā ya gṛhe[1] *dakṣā*[2] *sā bhāryā yā prajāvatī,*[3]
sā bhāryā yā patiprāṇā[4] *sā bhāryā yā pati-vratā.*[3]

She is a (true) wife who is clever; she is a (true) wife who bears offsprings; she is a (true) wife whose life is her husband; she is a (true) wife who is faithful to her husband.

This maxim occurs in the *CR* version and in one text of the *CN* version, viz. in *CRr* 1.27 *ad/cb* and *CNPN* 23. This maxim also influenced *CV* 4.13 *ad/cb*, *Cvr* 7.5 *ad/cb*, *CNP I* 23, *CNT IV* 22 and *CNŚ* 87.

Also found in H (HJ 1.211) and GP 1.108, 18 *ad/cb*. The *śloka* as found in *CVr* is also found in Pañc. (PS 2.32, PN 1.29, PT 2.59, PP 2.80, PRE 2.34), VCsr 21.1, Vet 6.2 and Skanda-purāṇa, Āvanthyakhaṇḍa, Revākhaṇḍa 103.128

The Mahābhārata *śloka* was also adapted in the Old Javanese literature: TK 17.

The *CR* text was undoubtedly borrowed directly from MBh, similarly as the text of H, but *C* transfers *b* and *d*, a change of no consequence.

FOOTNOTES TO NO. 1

[1]*śucir CVr, Cvr.* [2]*priyaṃ vrayāt CNPN.* [3]*satyavādini CVr, Cvr; priyaṃvādinī CNPN; pratiprāṇā* GP. [4]*patiprītā CVr, Cvr.*

For other variants see *CRr* 1.27, *CVr* 4.13, *Cvr* 7.5, MBh(Bh)1.69, 39 and *JSAIL* 24 (*JAOS* 77.114; No. 81).

2. *MBh*(*Bh*) 1.68, 40; *MBh*(*R*) 1.74, 40; *MBh*(*C*) 1.3028.

ardhaṃ bhāryā manuṣyasya[1] *bhāryā śreṣṭhatamaḥ sakhā,*[2]
bhāryā mūlaṃ trivargasya bhāryā [3]*mitraṃ mariṣyataḥ.*

The wife is the husband's half; the wife is the very best of friends; the wife is the root of *trivarga* (i.e. *dharma, artha* and *kāma*); the wife is a friend to anyone who intends to travel happily through life.[4]

This maxim occurs in the *CR* version, viz. in *CRr* 1.31.

The MBh(R) and MBh(C) texts are not completely

identical in *d* with the MBh(Bh) text. Also the *CR* text contains some variants from the MBh text in *d*, as well as some minor variants in *a* and *b*.

The *CR* text seems to be borrowed from or influenced by the MBh text.

FOOTNOTES TO NO. 2:
[1]*śarīrasya CRr.* [2]*'bhiṣṭatamaṃ sukham CRr.* [3]*mūlaṁ tariṣyataḥ* MBh(R), MBh(*C*); *'maitriṇa naśyati CRr.* [4]*tariṣyataḥ.*
For other variants see *CRr* 1.31 and MBh(Bh) 1.68, 40.

3. *MBh*(*Bh*) 1.68, 41; *MBh*(*R*) 1.74, 41; *MBh*(*C*) 1.3029.
bhāryā-vantaḥ kriyā-vantaḥ sa-bhāryā[1] *gṛhamedhinaḥ,*
[2]*bhāryā-vantaḥ pramodante* [3]*bhāryā-vantaḥ śriyānvitāḥ.*

Those who have a wife can perform sacred rites; those who have a wife can lead (happy) domestic lives; those who have a wife can enjoy life; those who have a wife can achieve prosperity.

This maxim occurs in the *CR* version, viz. in *CR* 1.34.

The *CR* text is different in *c* and *d*, but was certainly influenced by MBh or another common aphorism, though not quoted in any of the main Subhāṣita-saṃgraha-s.

FOOTNOTES TO NO. 3:
[1]*satataṁ CRr.* [2]*bhāryā mūlaṁ kulaṁ sarvaṁ CRr.*[3] *tasmād bhāryā parā gatiḥ CRr.*
For other variants see *CRr* 1.34 and MBh(Bh) 1.68, 41.

4. *MBh*(*Bh*) 1.68, 55; *MBh*(*R*) 1.74, 55; *MBh*(*C*) 1.3043.
na vāsasāṃ na rāmāṇāṃ nā'pāṃ sparśas tathā sukhaḥ,[1]
śiśor āliṅgyamānasya sparśaḥ [2]*sūnor yathā sukhaḥ.*

The touch of a robe, the touch of a charming young woman, the touch of (cool) water is not so pleasing as the touch of a child (infant-son) hugged in one's embrace.

This maxims occurs in one text of the *CN* version, viz. in *CNP II* 221.

The MBh(R) and the MBh(C) contain minor variants from the MBh(Bh) text in *b* and the MBh(C) contains one minor variant from the MBh(Bh) text in *d*.

The only *C* text belonging to the *CN* version was borrowed from MBh.

FOOTNOTES TO NO. 4:
[1]*vidhaḥ* MBh(*R*), MBh(C). [2]*sunor*° MBh(C).
For other variants see MBh(Bh) 1.68, 55.

5. *MBh*(*Bh*) 1.69, 1; *MBh*(*R*) 1.74, 81; *MBh*(*C*) 1.3069;

rājan[1] *sarṣapa-mātrāṇi parac-chidrāṇi paśyasi,*[2]
ātmano bilva-mātrāṇi paśyann api na paśyasi.[3]

The faults of others, though they are as small as a mustard seed, one will notice...but one's own faults though they are as large as the *bilva*-fruit one will not notice though one sees them.[4]

This maxim occurs in the *CR*, *CS* and *CL* versions and in three texts of the *CN* version viz., in *CRr* 6.48, *CSr* 3.29 *CLr* 5.8, and *CNN* 51, *CNG* 86, *CNŚK* 70.

Also found in GP 1.113, 56.

The Mahābhārata *śloka* was also adapted in the Old Javanese literature and the Pāli and Burmese literatures of Burma: SS 347, LN 75, DhN 348 and NKy 106.

The variants are unimportant.

The *C* text was undoubtedly borrowed directly from MBh.

FOOTNOTES TO NO. 5:

[1]*khalaḥ CSr* (but some *CS* texts have *rājan* or *kharaḥ*) *CRr*, *CLr*, *CNN*, *CNG*, *CNŚK*; *nīcaḥ* GP. [2]*paśyati CSr* (*CSJ* as above), *CRr*,*CLr*, *CNN*, *CNG*, *CNŚK*, GP. [3]*paśyati CSr* (*CSJ* as above), *CRr*, *CLr*, *CNN*, *CNG*, *CNŚK*, GP. [4]Compare St. Mathew, ch. 7, v. 3; "And why beholdest thou the mote that is in thy brother's eye, but considerest not the beam that is in thine own eye?

For other variants see *CRr* 6.48, *CSr* 3.29, *CLr* 5.8 and MBh (Bh) 1.69, 1.

6. *MBh*(*Bh*) 1. 69, 10; *MBh*(*R*) 1.74, 90; *MBh*(*C*) 1.3078.

prājñas tu jalpatāṃ puṃsāṃ śrutvā vācaḥ śubhā'śubhāḥ,
guṇavad vākyam ādatte haṃsaḥ kṣīram ivā'mbhasaḥ.

(However) intelligent men who in conversation hear good and bad speeches, accept only good speeches, like a *haṃsa* that always separates milk from water (and takes the milk).

This maxim occurs in one text of the *CN* version, viz. in *CNG* 255.

The *C* text was undoubtedly borrowed directly from MBh, but the compiler of MBh unintelligently quoted only the MBh (Bh) 1.69, 10 stanza while omitting the previous stanza which is closely connected with that stanza; that can be clearly seen from the word *tu*. The preceding stanza reads :

mūrkho hi jalpatāṃ puṃsāṃ śrutvā vācaḥ śubhā'śubhāḥ,
aśubhaṃ vākyam ādatte puriṣam iva sūkaraḥ

For other variants see MBh (Bh) 1.69, 10.

7. *MBh*(*Bh*) 1.69, 22; *MBh* (*R*) 1.74, 102; *MBh*(*C*), 1.3095. (*Also MBh*(*Bh*) 12. 156, 26 and 13.23, 14; *MBh*(*R*) 12.162 26 and 13, 75, 31; *MBh*(*C*) 12, 6002 and 13.3651-2).

aśvamedha-sahasraṃ ca satyaṃ ca tulayā dhṛtam,
[1]*aśvamedha-sahasrāddhi satyam eva viśiṣyate.*[2]

If a hundred horse-sacrifices were weighed against Truth, then Truth would outweigh a hundred horse-sacrifices.

This maxim occurs in one text of the *CN* version, viz. in *CNNM* 65.

Also found in MP 8.42, H (HJ 4.135), Pañc (PT, Annex 4.20), Viṣṇu-smṛti 8.36, Nārada-smṛti 4.211 (Nāradīyamanusaṃhitā 1.189) and *nibandha-s* (Smṛticandrikā 47, Smṛtisāraḥ 121, Vivādacandraḥ 147, Vivādārṇavasetuḥ 122, Vyavahāracintāmaṇi 48 and 56, Vyavahārakalpataruḥ 52, Vyavahāramātṛkā 331, Vyavahārattattvam 215, Vyavahārasaukhyam 50, Asahāyabhāṣya 71. Also cf. Ūrdhvāmanāya 1.19 in IS 730), RG 2.61, 10.

This is a well known aphorism which in *cd* is different from the RG and Ūrdhvāmanāya texts. In *d* MBh (R) 12.156, 26; RG and HJ contain an unimportant variant which is characteristic for the Vulgata of MBh.

The *C* text borrowed directly from MBh but from the Vulgata.

FOOTNOTES TO NO. 7:

[1]*tulayitvā tu paśyāmi* RG, *atyaricyata satyaṁ ca iti vedavido viduḥ* Ūrdh. [2]*evā'tiricyate* MBh (Bh) 12.156, 26, RG, *CNNM*, HJ.

For other variants see MBh(Bh) 1.69, 22; 12.156, 26 and *JSAIL* 26, par. 22.

8. *MBh*(*Bh*) *ad* 1.70, 44 (693*. 6-7); *MBh*(*R*) 1.75, 49; *MBh*(*C*) 1.3174. (Also *MBh*(*Bh*) *ad* 1.80, 9 (840* 1-2); *MBh*(*R*) 1.85, 12; *MBh*(*C*) 1.3511).

na jātu kāmaḥ kāmānām upabhogena śāmyati,
haviṣā kṛṣṇavartmeva bhūya evābhivardhate.

Desire is never suppressed by the enjoyment of the object desired; it only becomes stronger as fire is strengthened by clarified butter.

This maxim occurs in a Subhāṣita-saṃgraha composed of aphorisms ascribed to Cāṇakya, viz. in *CPS* 377.16.

Also found in Har 1639; Manu-smṛti 2.94; Viṣṇu-purāṇa 4.10, 9; Vayu-purāṇa 93.95, Bhāgavata-purāṇa 9.19, 14; BrDh 2.13, 3 (No. 103). Cf. Pañcarātra 1.14, 97.

The Mahābhārata *śloka* was also adapted in the Old Javanese literature: SS 429.

This maxim is a well known one and does not contain any variants in any of the sources in which it occurs (Cf. *JSAIL* 27, *JAOS* 79.237; No. 2). It was borrowed either directly from MBh or from Mn.

9. *MBh*(*Bh*) *ad* 1.80, 9; (840*. 1-2); *MBh*(*R*) 1.85, 12; *MBh*(*C*) 1.3511.

See No. 8.

10. *MBh*(*Bh*) 1.107, 32; *MBh*(*R*) 1.115, 36; *MBh*(*C*) 1.4517-8. (*Also MBh* (*Bh*) 2.55, 10; 5.37, 16 and 5.126, 48; *MBh*(*R*) 2.61, 11; 5.36, 17 and 5.127, 47; *MBh*(*C*) 2.2104; 5. 1350 and 5.4307. Cf. No. 56.

tyajed ekaṃ[1] *kulasyā'rthe*[2] *grāmasyā'rthe kulaṃ tyajet,*
grāmaṃ jana-padasyā'rthe[3] *ātmā'rthe*[4] *pṛthivīṃ tyajet.*

Let him forsake one for the family; the family for the village; the village for the country; the whole world for the *ātmān*.

This maxim occurs in the *CV*, *Cv*, *CR* and *CN* versions, viz. in *CVr* 3.10, *Cvr* 1.7, *CRr* 2.3 and *CNr* 29.

Also found in the Pañc (PRE 1.117, PT 1.118, PTem 1.107, Pts 1.355 and 3.84), H (HJ 1.159), VCjr 28.3, Śts 21.4-5, GP 1.109, 2, Kathārṇava (ZDMG 14.574).

The Mahābhārata *śloka* was also adapted in the Pāli and Burmese literature of Burma: LN 156, DhN 205, NKy 180 (cf. 200).

MBh in the Ādi-parvan has another text in *a* than in the Sabhā- and Udyoga-parvan-s; the variant is unimportant. The text of the Ādi-parvan is identical with the Cāṇakya text, as well as with the texts of H. Pañc, Śts, VCjr, etc.

This well-known stanzas was undoubtedly incorporated in several Cāṇakya compendia directly from MBh, as it appears in the Ādi-parvan.

FOOTNOTES TO NO. 10:

[1]*deśaṃ* (°ṣaṃ) CN (var.) (*CRr* as above). [2]*tyajet kulā'rthe puruṣaṃ* MBh (Bh), (R) and (C) in Sabhā- and Udyoga-parvan. °*rtha* Kathārṇava (*sic* !). [4]*svā'tmārthe CRr* (*CRT* as above), Pañc. H, VC.

For other variants see *CVr* 3.10, *Cvr* 1.7, *CRr* 2.3, *CNr* 29, MBh (*Bh*) I.107, 32; 2.55, 10; 5.37, 16; 5.126, 48 and *JSAIL* 24 (*JAOS* 77.173; No. 119).

11. *MBh*(*Bh*) *ad* 1.113, 7 (1189*. 1-2) *MBh*(*R*)—; *MBh* (*C*)—.

See No. 67.

12. *MBh*(*Bh*) 1.122, 8; *MBh*(*R*) 1.132, 10; *MBh*(*C*) 1. 5143.

yayor eva samaṃ vittaṃ yayor eva samaṃ kulam,[1]
[2]*tayoḥ sakhyaṃ vivāhaś ca na tu puṣṭa-vipuṣṭayoḥ.*

Only between two persons who have equal wealth and are of equal family can marriage be concluded and friendship exist, but not between two, one of whom is rich and the other poor.

This maxim occurs in the *CR* version, viz. in *CRr* 3.6.

Also found in the Pañc (PRE 3.75, PP 1.288 and 3.190, Pts 1.281 and 2.27, PtsK 1.313 and 3.220, PT 3.87, PTem 3.76, PS 3.53, PN 3.43).

Variants which occur in the various MBh texts are unimportant; MBh(R) and MBh(C) has in *b śrutam* (learning) instead of *kulam* (family) and in *c* has a different sequence of words, while some texts of Pañc have there *maitrī* instead of *sakhyaṃ*.

The *CR* text was undoubtedly borrowed directly from the classical text of MBh as included in the critical Bhandarkar edition.

FOOTNOTES TO NO. 12:

[1]*śrutam* MBh(R), MBh(*C*). [2]*tayor vivāhaḥ sakhyaṁ ca* MBh(R), MBh (C), PP. PtsK 3.220, PS, PRE; *tayor maitrī vi°* Pts. PtsK 1.313.

For other variants see *CRr* 3.6 and MBh(Bh) 1.128, 8.

13. *MBh*(*Bh*) *Appendix I to I. No.* 81.16-7; *MBh*(*R*) 1.142, 8, *MBh*(*C*) 1.5550.

See No. 94.

14. *MBh*(*Bh*)—; *MBh*(*R*) 1.142, 21; *MBh*(*C*) 1.5563.

See No. 93.

15. *MBh*(*Bh*) *Appendix I to I. No.* 81. 125-6; *MBh*(*R*)1.142, 60-1; *MBh*(*C*) 1.5603.

See No. 58.

15A. *MBh(Bh) Appendix I to I. No*. 81, 151-2; *MBh(R)* 1. 142, 73-4; *MBh(C)* 1.5615.
See No. 138.

16. *MBh(Bh) Appendix I to I. No*. 81, 165-6; *MBh(R)* 1.142, 80-1; *MBh(C)* 1.5622.
See No. 95.

17. *MBh(Bh) ad* 1.148, 26 (1614*. 1-2); *MBh(R)* 1.160, 27; *MBh(C)* 1.6169.
See No. 56.

18. *MBh(Bh)* 2. 5, 101; *MBh(R)* 2. 5, 112; *MBh(C)* 2. 247. *Also MBh(Bh)* 5. 39, 51 *ad/cb*; *MBh(R)* 5.38, 66-7 *ad/cb*; *MBh(C)* 5. 1511-2 *ad/cb*).

agnihotra-phalā vedā[1] [2]*datta-bhukta-phalaṃ dhanam,*
[3]*rati-putra-phalā dārāḥ*[4] [5]*śīla-vṛtta*[6]*-phalaṃ śrutam.*[7]

The result of (having studied) the Veda is the fire sacrifice; the result of (having) wealth is (the possibility of) giving and enjoying (wealth); the result of (having) a wife is (the possibility of) sexual enjoyment and (of getting) sons; the result of learning is (one's own) morality and virtuous conduct.

The maxim occurs in the *CR*, *Cv*, *CS* versions, in four texts of the *CN* version and in one text of the *CL* version, viz. in *CRr* 3.4 *ad/cb*, *Cvr* 8.4 *ad/cb*, *CSr* 3.88 *ad/cb* and *CNP II* 9 *ad/cb*, *CNG* 54 (as above), *CNF* 106 *ad/cb*, *CNPh* 19 *ad/cb*, *CNI II* 78 *ad/cb*, *CLṢ* 3.2 *ad/cb*.

Also found in Pañc (PP 2.150 *ad/cb*, Pts 2.147 *ad/cb*, PtsK 2.154 *ad/cb*), GP 1.110, 4 *ad/cb*.

The Mahābhārata or Pañcatantra *śloka* was also adapted in the Old Javanese literature: TK 17, NŚ 1.14, SS 183.

The Mahābhārata text of the Udyoga-parvan transfers the *pāda-s*, viz. *ad/cb*; in this form this stanza is better known (Pañc, GP, *C*). Otherwise, the MBh contains only unimportant variants. The variants which occur in different texts of *C* are minor.

The *C* text was borrowed directly from the Mahābhārata, as it appears in the Udyoga-parvan.[8]

FOOTNOTES TO NO. 18:

[1]*vedāḥ* MBh(R), MBh(C); °*phalāḥ vedāṁ CNPh*. [2]*dāncabhogya*° *CNPh*;

dāna-bhukti° *CLṢ*; *dāna-bhoga°* *CRr*. [3]*saputra suphalā nārī* *CNF*. [4]*dārā* *CLṢ*, GP, PP; *nārī* *CSr*, *CNI II*, *CNPh*, MBh(R), (C) Udyogaparvan. [5]*dāna-bhoga-phalaṃ* *CRr* (but *dhana-śakti-phalaṃ* *CRC*; *datta-bhukta-phalaṃ* *CRT*, GP); *nīti-śāstra-phalā nṛpāḥ* *CNP II*. [6] *°vṛtt°* *CNPh*, *CNI II*, GP. [7]*smṛtiḥ* *CNF*; *dhanam* *CNI II*. [8]With one exception, viz. *CNG*.

For other variants see *CRr* 3.4, *Cvr* 8.4, *CSr* 3.8, MBh (Bh) 2.5, 101 and 5.39, 51.

19. *MBh*(*Bh*) 2.55, 10; *MBh*(*R*) 2.61, 11; *MBh*(*C*) 2.2104. See No. 10.

19A. *MBh* (*Bh*) 2 *ad* 67.5 (853*); *MBh* (*R*) 2.75,5 See No. 133.

20. *MBh*(*Bh*) 3.2, 15; *MBh*(*R*) 3.2, 15; MBh (*C*) 3.62. (*Also MBh*(*Bh*) 11. 2, 13; 12. 26, 20[1]; 12. 168, 31; 12.307, 2 *and* 18. 5, 48; *MBh*(*R*) 11.2, 13; 12. 25, 20; 12.174, 42; 12. 330, 20 *and* 18.5, 61; *MBh*(*C*) 11.67; 12.751; 12. 6497-8; 12.12483; 18. 204-5).

śakasthāna-sahasrāṇi bhayasthāna-śatāni[2] *ca,*
divase divase mūḍham āviśanti na paṇḍitam.

Thousands of causes for grief and hundreds of causes for fear, day by day bewilder a fool, but not a wise man.

This maxim occurs in four different texts of the *CN* version, viz. in *CNŚC* 103, *CNŚl* 103, *CNŚ* 101 and *CNŚL* 89.

Also found in H (HJ 1.2).

The Mahābhārata *śloka* was also adapted in the Old Javanese literature: SS 512.

Some texts of MBh (R) and MBh(*C*)[3] have a variant in *b* which, though changing slightly the text, changes its sense considerably and to its disadvantage. The *C* text follows the classical text of MBh (Bhandarkar edition) from which it was borrowed directly.

FOOTNOTES TO NO. 20:
[1]Appeared in MBh(Bh) 12.26, 20. [2]*harṣa-sthāna-śa°* MBh(R) 12.25, 20; 12.168, 31; 18.5, 48; MBh(C) 12.751. [3]See fn. 2 above.

For other variants see MBh(Bh) 3.2, 15; 11.2, 13; 12.26, 20; 12.168, 31 and 18.5, 48.

21. *MBh*(*Bh*) 3.2, 39; *MBh*(*R*) 3.2, 39; *MBh*(*C*) 3.86.

yathā[1] *hy*[2] *āmiṣam*[2] *ākāśe pakṣibhiḥ śvāpadair bhuvi,*
bhakṣyate salile matsyais tathā sarveṇa[3] *vittavān.*

For as prey is eaten by birds in the air, by animals on earth, and by fish in the water, so is a nice man exposed to danger wherever he may be.

This maxim occurs in two manuscripts from Tanjore, the originality of which is uncertain, viz. in *CnT II* 20.3 and *CnT III* 53.1.

Also found in Skanda-purāṇa, Nāgarakhaṇḍa 185, H (HJ 1.194). Also compare Pañc (Pts. 1.401 and 2.116.)

The Mahābhārata *śloka* was also adapted in the Old Javanese literature: SS 470.

The variants which occur in the MBh(R) and MBh (*C*) or HJ are unimportant.

The *C* text was borrowed directly from MBh.

FOOTNOTES TO NO. 21:

[1]*tathā* HJ. [2]*hy* om. *CnT II*, *CnT III*. [3]*sarvatra* MBh(R), MBh(C), HJ.

For other variants see MBh(Bh) 3.2, 39 and *JSAIL* 24 (*JAOS* 76.128; No. 21).

22. *MBh*(*Bh*) 3.29, 30; *MBh* (*R*) 3.28, 31; *MBh*(*C*) 3.1059.

See No. 97.

23. *MBh*(*Bh*) 3.32, 32; *MBh*(*R*) 3.31, 24; *MBh*(*C*) 3. 1183.

dharma eva plavo nā'nyaḥ svargaṃ Draupadi gacchatām,
sai'va nauḥ sāgarasy eva vaṇijaḥ pāramṛcchataḥ.[1]

Draupadī, there is no other boat for those who desire to go to heaven, than *dharma*; it is like a ship for merchants who desire to cross the ocean.

This maxim occurs in one MS of the *CL* version, viz. in *CLP IV* 7.4.

The Mahābhārata *śloka* was also adapted in the Old Javanese literature: SS 20.

Variants are unimportant.

The *C* text was undoubtedly borrowed directly from MBh.

FOOTNOTES TO NO. 23:

[1]*paramicchataḥ* MBh (R), MBh(*C*).

For other variants see MBh(Bh) 3.32, 22.

23A. *MBh*(*Bh*) 3.70, 8; *MBh*(*R*) 3.72, 8; *MBh* (*C*) 3. 2815.

See No. 133.

24. *MBh*(*Bh*) 3.82, 85; *MBh*(*R*) 3.84, 97; *MBh* (*C*) 3. 8075. (*Also MBh*(*Bh*) 3.85, 7 *cd* + *ab of* 456*, *MBh*(*R*) 3.87, 9-10; *MBh*(*C*) 3.8305-6).

eṣṭavyā bahavaḥ putrā [1]*yady eko'pi Gayāṃ*[2] *vrajet*
yajeta vā'śvamedhena nīlaṃ vā vṛṣam utsṛjet.

One should wish for many sons, so that at least one may go to Gayā, or offer the horse-sacrifice, or allow a *nīlā* bull to roam.

This maxim occurs in the *CS* version, viz. in *CSr* 2.87.

Similar thoughts are expressed also in MBr (Bh) 13.88, 14, (or MBh(R) 13.88, 14, MBh(C) 4253) and in R (R 2. 107, 13, RG 2.115, 13); all of them refer to *tīrtha-s*.

Variants which occur in the MBh text are unimportant. In most text of *CS* there is also one unimportant variant in *b*, but the *CSBD* text is identical with the classical text of MBh.

The *C* text was undoubtedly borrowed directly from MBh.

FOOTNOTES TO NO. 24:

[1]*gayām eko yadi vrajet* CSr (*CSBD* as above). [2]*apy eko ga°* MBh (R) 3.87, 9, MBh (C) 3.8075 & 8305.

For other variants see *CSr* 2.87 and MBh (Bh) 3.82, 85 and 3.85, 7.

25. *MBh*(*Bh*) 3.85, 7 *cd* + *ab of* 456*, *MBh* (*R*) 3.87, 9-10; *MBh*(*C*) 3. 8305-6.

See No. 24.

26. *MBh*(*Bh*) 3. 133, 11; *MBh*(*R*) 3. 133, 11; *MBh*(*C*) 3. 10631.

na tena sthaviro[1] *bhavati*[2] *yenā'sya palitaṃ śiraḥ,*
[3]*bālo'pi yaḥ prajānāti taṃ devāḥ*[4] *sthaviraṃ viduḥ.*

One is not old because his head is gray; the gods regard one as old who, though young in years, possesses knowledge.

This maxim occurs in one *CV* text which adds to the classical text of the Cāṇakya-nīti-darpaṇa a number of MBh and Mn stanzas viz. in *CVNS* 12.13.

Also found in Mn 2.156, BrDh 2.4.11 (No. 28) and *nibandha-s* (Smṛtimuktāphalam 104.27).

The MBh text does not contain any important variants but the Mn text contains a variant from MBh in *c*. The same variant is repeated in the *C* text. This shows that the *C* text was borrowed directly from Mn and not from MBh.

FOOTNOTES TO NO. 26:

[1]*vṛddho* Mn. *CVNS*, BrDh (latter; hypermetric). [2]*mavati* MBh (R)

(printing error). [3]*yo vai* (*va* BrDh) *yuvā'py adhīyānas* Mn, *CVNS*, BrDh. [4]*devā* *CVNS*, BrDh.

For other variants see MBh (Bh) 3.133, 11 and *JSAIL* 27 (*JAOS* 79.238; No. 5).

26A. *MBh* (*Bh*) 3.245,13; *MBh*(*R*) 3.258,13-4; *MBh*(*C*) 12. 15382-3.

See No. 135.

27. *MBh*(*Bh*) *App. I to III*. 32, 47-8; *MBh*(*R*) 3.312, 108; *MBh*(*C*) 3.17395.

paṭhakāḥ[1] *pāṭhakāś*[2] *cai'va ye cā'nye śāstra-cintakāḥ*[3]
sarve vyasanino mūrkhā[4] [5]*yaḥ kriyāvān sa paṇḍitaḥ*.

Professors, pupils and others who are versed in *śāstra-s*, if addicted to evil passions, are stupid; only those who perform sacred rites are learned.

This maxim occurs in the *CL* and *CS* versions and in two texts of the *CN* version, viz. in *CLr* 2.8, *CSr* 3.24, *CNI I* 18, *CNG* 109.

All the MBh texts are identical; the *C* texts contain some unimportant variants from the MBh text. The text is somewhat nearer to MBh than the *CS* text.

The *C* texts were undoubtedly borrowed directly from MBh.

FOOTNOTES TO NO. 27:

[1]*paṭhakaḥ CLr. CNG, CNI I*; *lekhakaḥ CSr*. [2]*paṭhakaś CLr, CNG, CNI*. [3] °*paṇḍitāḥ CNI I*. [4]*mūḍhāḥ CSr*; *jñeyā CNI I*. [5]*kriyāvantaś ca pa*° *CSr*; *yāḥ kri*° *CNI I*.

For other variants see *CLr* 2.8 and *CSr* 3.24.

28. *MBh*(*Bh*) *App. I to III*. 32; 65-8; *MBh*(*R*) 3. 312, 115; *MBh*(*C*) 3.17402.

tarko'pratiṣṭaḥ[1] *śrutayo vibhinnā*[2]
[3]*nai'ko ṛṣir yasya mataṃ pramāṇam*,[4]
dharmasya tattvaṃ[5] *nihitaṃ guhāyāṃ*
mahājano yena gataḥ sa panthāḥ.

Speculation lacks foundation; *śrūtis* are contradictory; not even one's *ṛṣi's* opinion can be accepted as correct; the very essence of *dharma* is concealed in the innermost heart; (hence) only the path followed by many is the right one.

This maxim occurs in the *CR* version, viz. in *CRr* 2.58.

Also found in GP 1.109, 51.

The variants which occur are not important.

The *C* text was undoubtedly borrowed directly fromMBh.

FOOTNOTES TO NO. 28:

[1] °*tiṣṭhāḥ* MBh(R), GP. [2]*vibhinnāḥ* GP. [3]*nā'sau munir CRr*; *nāsāvṛṣir* GP. [4]*na bhinnam CRr*, GP. [5]*mūlaṁ CRr* (*CRC*, *CPS*, GP as above); *munir* MBh(*C*).

For other variants see *CRr* 2.58.
Indravajrā and Upendravajrā metre.

29. *MBh*(*Bh*) *ad* 4.46, 12 (853*.3-4); *MBh*(*R*) 4.51, 15; *MBh*(*C*) 4.1597.

śatror api guṇā grāhyā[1] *doṣā vācyā guror api,*
[2]*sarvathā sarvayatnena putre śiṣye hitaṃ vadet,*

Virtues even of an enemy should be recognized and faults of a *guru* reproached; one should tell the son and the pupil by one's all means and to the best of one's ability (everything) that can be of use to them.

This maxim occurs in the *CS* version, viz. in *CSr* 2.97.

The variants in the various MBh texts are unimportant. The CS text is however different in *od* and changes the meaning of this maxim. The maxim, if quoted in Subhāṣita-saṃgraha-s (e. g. SRBh 160. 340, Kk 99, Pras 13.5), follows the MBh text.

It is not certain that the *C* text was borrowed from MBh, although it is probable that it was influenced by MBh.

FOOTNOTES TO NO. 29:

[1]*vācyā* MBh(R), MBh(C), *CSr*. [2]*yuktāyuktavaco grāhyā na vaco guru gauravāt CSr*.

For other variants see *CSr* 2.97 and MBh(Bh) *ad* 4.46, 12.

30. *MBh*(*Bh*)—, *MBh*(*R*) 5.32, 25; *MBh*(*C*) 5.990.

yasya saṃsāriṇī prajñā dharmā'rthāvanuvartate,
kāmād arthaṃ vṛṇīte yaḥ sa vai paṇḍita ucyate.

He whose broad judgement follows *dharma* and *artha* and who gives preference to *artha* and not to *kāma*, is considered a wise man.

This maxim occurs in one *CV* text which adds to the classical text of the Cāṇakya-nīti-darpaṇa a number of MBh and Mn stanzas, viz. in *CVNS* 17.18.

No variants occur in this maxim.

The *C* text was undoubtedly borrowed directly from MBh.

31. *MBh*(*Bh*) 5.33, 23; *MBh*(*R*) 5. 32, 28; *MBh* (*C*) 5.993.

nā'prāpyam abhivāñchanti naṣṭaṃ ne'cchanti śocitum,
āpatsu ca[1] *na muhyanti narāḥ paṇḍita-buddhayaḥ.*

Those who do not strive for objects which are unattainable; those who do not grieve for what is lost and gone; those who are not at a loss what to do in case of misfortune; (all) these men are considered wise.

This maxim occurs in four texts of the *CN* version, viz. in *CNŚ* 98, *CNŚL* 98, *CNŚC* 99 and *CNŚl* 99.

Also found in H (HJ 1.181).

Variants from the *MBh* text which occur in the *C* text and in H are unimportant.

The *C* maxim was undoubtedly borrowed directly from MBh.

FOOTNOTES TO NO. 31:
[1]*āpatsv api CNŚ, CNŚL, CNŚC, CNŚl,* HJ.
For other variants see MBh (Bh) 5.33, 23.

31A. *MBh*(*Bh*) 5.33, 26; *MBh*(*R*) 5.32, 31; *MBh*(*C*) 5.996.
See No. 134.

32. *MBh*(*Bh*) 5.33. 31; *MBh*(*R*) 5.32, 36; *MBh*(*C*) 5.1001.

svam arthaṃ yaḥ parityajya parā'rtham anutiṣṭhati,
mithyā carati mitrā'rthe yaś ca mūḍhaḥ sa ucyate.

He who abandons his own affairs (while) concerns himself with the affairs of others; he who deceitfully carries on the affairs of his friends, is considered a fool.

This maxim occurs in one *CV* text which adds to the classical text of the Cāṇakya-nīti-darpaṇa a number of MBh and Mn stanzas, viz. in *CVNS* 17.19.

No variants occur in this maxim.

The *C* text was undoubtedly borrowed directly from MBh.

For other variants see MBh (Bh) 5.33, 31.

33. *MBh*(*Bh*) 5. 33, 42; *MBh*(*R*) 5.32, 47; *MBh*(*C*) 5.1013.

ekaṃ hanyān na vā [1]*hanyād iṣur mukto*[2] *dhanuṣmatā,*
[3]*buddhir buddhimato'tsṛṣṭā hanyād*[4] *rāṣṭraṃ*[5] *sarājakam.*[6]

An arrow shot by a bowman may or may not kill even a single person; but when an intelligent man applies his intellgence (in a vicious manner) he may destroy the entire kingdom together with the king.

This maxim occurs in three texts of the *CR* version and in one text of the *CN* version, viz. in *CRC* 4.53, *CRB* 4.43, *CRBh II* 4.37 and *CNI I* 200.

Also found in the Pañc (PRE 3.105, PT 3.123, Pts 1.206, PtsK 1.219, PS 3.73, PN 3.63), K(Kangle) 10.6,51 and the Śukasaptati (Śts 31.3—101.8).

All texts with the exception of the Śukasaptati and PT contain minor variants; Śts and PT are different in *cd*.[7]

The *C* text was undoubtedly borrowed directly from MBh.

FOOTNOTES TO NO. 33:

[1]*hanyādhanur CNI I.* [2]*iṣuḥ kṣipto(°āḥ)K* [3]*sarāṣṭraṁ saprajaṁ hanti rājānaṁ mantriniścayaḥ* Śts; *prājñena tu matiḥ kṣiptā hanyād parbhagatām api* PT, K.[4]*mṛṣṭā hanti* PtsK, PS. [5]*rāṣṭaṁ CRC, CNI I*: *rājyaṁ* PS. [6]*sanājakaṁ* PtsK. [7]*Cf.* above fn. 2.

For other variants see MBh(Bh) 5.33, 42.

34. *MBh*(*Bh*) 5.33, 47; *MBh*(*R*) 5.32, 52; *MBh* (*C*) 5.1018. (*Also MBh*(*Bh*) 12.154, 34; *MBh* (*R*) 12.160. 34; *MBh*(*C*) 12. 5959). *Cf. No.* 35.

[1]ekaḥ kṣamāvatāṃ,[2] doṣo dvitīyo no'palabhyate,[3]
yad enaṃ[4] kṣamayā yuktam aśaktaṃ manyate janaḥ.

There is one and only one fault with indulgent persons, namely that people consider an indulgent person weak.

This maxim occurs in one MS of the *CR* version which usually follows closely the GP and could be considered as an expurgated text of the Bṛhaspati-samhitā of the GP., viz. in *CRCa II* 53.

Variants which occur in the MBh, *C* and GP texts are not important.

The *C* text was undoubtedly borrowed directly from MBh.

FOOTNOTES TO NO. 34:

[1]*eka eva damedo°* MBh Śānti-parvan; *eka* MBh(R) 5.32, 52. [2]*kṣamāvato CRCa II.* [3]*no'papadyate* MBh(R), MBh(C) Udyoga- and Śānti-parvan. [4]*eva CRCa II.*

For other variants see (MBh(Bh) 5.33, 47 and 12.154, 34.

35. *MBh*(*Bh*) *ad* 5.33, 47 (175.* 1-2); *MBh*(*R*) 5.32, 53-4; *MBh*(*C*) 5.1019-20. *Cf. No.* 34.

kṣamā[1] guṇo hy[2] aśaktānāṃ śaktānāṃ bhūṣaṇaṃ kṣamā,
kṣamā vaśīkṛtir loke[3] kṣamayā kiṃ na sādhyate.

Forbearance is the virtue of the weak; forbearance is the ornament of the strong; forbearance subdues (everything) in this world; what is there that forbearance could not achieve. ?

This maxim is in MBh the continuation of the previous one; in some texts *ab* is added between No. 34 and No. 35 reading: *sosya doṣo na mantavyaḥ kṣamā hi paramaṃ dhanam* (this should, however, not be considered as a fault of him, for forbearance is a greatest treasure).

This maxim occurs only in one text of the *CR* version, viz. in *CRC* 7.57.

Variants which occur in the MBh and in the *C* text are unimportant.

The *C* text was undoubtedly borrowed directly from MBh.

FOOTNOTES TO NO. 35:

[1]*jñamā* MBh(R) (printing error). [2]*balam CRC.* [3]*vasikṛto lokaḥ CRC*; *vasikṛte loke* Subh 238.

36. *MBh*(*Bh*) 5.33, 50; *MBh*(*R*) 5. 32, 58; *MBh* (*C*) 5.1024.
dve karmaṇī[1] *naraḥ kurvann asmil loke*[2] *virocate,*[3]
abruvan[4] *paruṣaṃ kiṃcid asato nā'rthayaṃs*[5] *tathā.*

A man may shine in this world by doing two things; by refraining from the use of abusive language and by ignoring wicked persons.

This maxim occurs in one *CV* text which adds to the classical text of the Cāṇakya-nīti-darpaṇa a number of MBh and Mn stanzas, viz. in *CVNS* 17.20.

The *CVNS* text contains some printing errors and two minor variants of which one occurs also in *d* of the MBh(R) and MBh(*C*) texts.

The Mahābhārata *śloka* was also adapted in the Old Javanese literature: SS 123.

The *C* text was undoubtedly borrowed directly from the MBh (*Vulgata*).

FOOTNOTES TO NO. 36:

[1]*karmaṇi CVNS.* [2]*asmiṃloke CVNS*; *asmilloke* MBh(R), MBh(C). [3]*virājate CVNS.* [4]*abuvan CVNS* (printing error). [5]*'narcayaṁs* MBh (R), MBh (C), *CVNS.*

For other variants see MBh(Bh) 5.33, 50.

36A. *MBh*(*Bh*) 5. 33, 56; *MBh*(*R*) 5.32, 67; *MBh*(*C*) 5.1033.
See No. 135.

37. *MBh*(*Bh*) 5.33, 66; *MBh*(*R*) 5.32, 82; *MBh*(*C*) 5.1048.

ṣaḍ doṣāḥ puruṣeṇe'ha hātavyā bhūtim icchatā,
nidrā tantrī[1] *bhayaṃ krodha*[2] *ālasyaṃ dīrghasūtratā.*

Six faults should be avoided by a man who desires well-being: sleep, laziness, anxiety, anger, idleness and procrastination.

This maxim occurs in two texts belonging to the *CN* version, viz. in *CNŚC* 109 and *CNŚl* 109.

Also found in H (HJ 1.34).

Variants which occur in the MBh, *C* and H texts are unimportant.

The *C* text was undoubtedly borrowed directly from MBh.

FOOTNOTES TO NO. 37:

[1]*tandrā CNŚC, CNŚl*, HJ; *tandrīr* MBh(C). [2]*krodham CNŚC, CNŚl.* For other variants see MBh(Bh) 5.33, 66.

38. *MBh*(*Bh*) 5.33, 69; *MBh*(*R*) 5.32, 85; *MBh*(*C*) 5.1051 *Cf.* No. 39.

ṣaḍ eva tu guṇāḥ puṃsā na hātavyāḥ kadācana,
satyaṃ dānam anālasyam anasūyā kṣamā dhṛtiḥ.

Six qualities should never be given up by a man; veracity, generosity, assiduity, benevolence, forbearance and contentment.

This and the next maxim occur one after the other in one *CV* text which adds to the classical text of the Cāṇakya-nīti-darpaṇa a number of MBh and Mn stanzas, viz. in *CVNS* 17.21 and 17.22.

No variants occur in this maxim.

The *C* text was undoubtedly borrowed directly from MBh.

FOOTNOTES TO NO. 38:

For variants of this maxim see MBh(Bh) 5.33, 69.

39. *MBh*(*Bh*) *ad* 5. 33, 69; (183*. 11-2) *MBh* (*R*) 5.32, 90; *MBh* (*C*) 5.1056. *Cf. No.* 38.

īrṣur[1] *ghṛṇī na saṃtuṣṭaḥ*[2] *krodhano nityaśaṅkitaḥ,*[3]
parabhāgyo'pajīvī ca ṣaḍ ete nitya-duḥkhitāḥ.[4]

The envious, the impetuous, the discontented, the passionate, the ever suspicious and he who lives on another's fortune—these six are always distressed.

As stated above (*cf.* No. 38) this maxim occurs in *CVNS* 17.22. It also occurs in one text of the *CS* version, viz. *CSC I* 3.73.

Also found in H (HJ 1.24) and Vānar 1.

Variants which occur in the MBh, H and Vānar texts (the Vānar text follows the H text) are unimportant.

The *C* text follows closely the classical (reconstructed) text of MBh from which it was undoubtedly borrowed directly.

FOOTNOTES TO NO. 39:

[1]*irṣī* HJ, *Vānar.* [2]*tv asaṃ°* MBh (R), MBh (C), HJ. *CSC I*, Vānar. [3] °*saṅkitā CSC I.* [4]*duḥkhabhāginaḥ* HJ, Vānar.

For other variants see MBh (Bh) *ad* 5.33, 69.

40. *MBh* (*Bh*) 5.34, 12; *MBh* (*R*) 5. 33, 11 *bis*; *MBh* (*C*) 5.1105.

na rājyaṃ prāptam ity eva vartitavyam asāṃpratam,
śriyaṃ hy avinayo hanti jarā rūpam ivo'ttamam.

(The fact) that the kingdom has been secured does not empower (the king) to act improperly, for as unseemly behaviour destroys the king's prosperity, so old age destroys beauty.

This maxim occurs in one text of the *CN* version, viz in *CNB* 128. This text follows closely up to stanza 108 the basic text of *CN* and then adds 37 stanzas which were borrowed from the Mahābhārata, Hitopadeśa and other versions of *C*.

Also found in H (HJ 3.116).

No variants occur in this maxim.

The *C* text was borrowed directly either from MBh or H ?

FOOTNOTES TO NO. 40:

For variants of this maxim see MBh (Bh) 5.34, 12.

41. *MBh* (*Bh*) 5.34, 13; *MBh* (*R*) 5.33, 12; *MBh* (*C*) 5.1106.

bhakṣyo'ttamapraticchannaṃ matsyo baḍiśam āyasam,
rūpā''bhipātī[1] *grasate nā'nubandham avekṣate.*[2]

A fish filled with greed, while swimming, devours an iron hook concealed in dainty food without considering the nature of his behaviour and the consequences (of his act)[3].

This maxim occurs in the Tibetan text of the *CR* version, viz. in *CRT* 3.29 which in the third *adhyāya* adds maxims from other sources.

In *c* and *d* the MBh (R), MBh (C) and *CRT* have the same variants from the Bhandarkar MBh text.

The *C* text was undoubtedly borrowed directly from the Vulgata text of the MBh.

FOOTNOTES TO NO. 41:

[1]*lobhābhipāti* MBh(R), MBh(C) *CRT*. [2]*apekṣatr* MBh(C), MBh(R), *CRT*. [3]MBh(R), MBh(C) and *CRT*.

42. *MBh*(*Bh*) 5.34, 18; *MBh*(*R*) 5.33, 17; *MBh* (*C*) 5.1111.
puṣpaṃ puṣpaṃ vicinvīta[1] *mūlac-chedaṃ na kārayet,*
mālākāra ivā'rāme[2] *na yathā'ṅgāra-kārakaḥ.*[3]

One should pluck one flower after the other without up-uprooting the plants, like a gardener in a garden and not like a producer of charcoal.

This maxim occurs in the *CR* and *CS* versions, viz. in *CRr* 4.3, *CSr* 2.17. It deals with the collection of king's treasury. Similar thoughts are also expressed in *CRr* 4.4 (GP 1.111, 4), *CRr* 4.5 (GP 1.111, 5), *CRr* 5.37, (GP 1.113, 6), *CRT* 4.6, *CRr* 5.38, *Cvr* 6.13, *CNG* 85. (Also known in Tibetan literature: ShD 29, SRN 323; and Pāli literature of Burma: DhN 182, SN 60).

Also found in GP 1.111, 3.

This Mahābhārata or Cāṇakya *śloka* was also adopted in Tibetan literature: ShD 8 and in the Pāli literature of Burma: RN 93.

There are no variants in the MBh text; however the *CSr* text has one important variant in *d* and two unimportant variants in *a* and *c*.

The *CRr* text was undoubtedly borrowed directly from MBh and the *CSr* text was closely influenced by MBh.

FOOTNOTES TO NO. 42:

[1]*vicinvanti CSr* (*CRr*, GP. SRBh 388, 449, SRHt 181.2 as above). [2]*ivā'ṅgāni CSr* (*CRr*, SRBh as above). [3]*yathā jñāti sa ratām CSr* (*CRr*, GP, SRBh, SRHt as above).

For other variants see *CRr* 4.3, *CSr* 2.17 and MBh (Bh) 5.34, 18.

43. *MBh*(*Bh*) 5.34, 32; *MBh*(*R*) 5.33, 33; *MBh* (*C*) 5.1127.
[1]*gandhena gāvaḥ paśyanti vedaiḥ*[2] *paśyanti brāhmaṇāḥ,*[3]
cāraiḥ[4] *paśyanti* [5]*rājānaś cakṣurbhyām itare janāḥ.*

Cows see through smell; Brāhmaṇs see through the Vedas; kings see through (their) spies; ordinary people see through their own eyes.

This maxim occurs in one text belonging to the *CN* version, viz. in *CNP II* 117.

Also found in Pañc (PP 3.58, Pts 3.67, PtsK 3.64), VC (VCsr 8.1, VCjr 8.2), e in Vet after 12.6 and D in Vet after 23.60, 24 (p. 202).

Several variants occur in the various texts but none is of any importance. The *CN* text is somewhat corrupt in *cd*.

The *C* text was undoubtedly borrowed directly from MBh.

FOOTNOTES TO NO. 43:

[1]*gāvo gandhena* (*ghrāṇena* VCjr) PtsK, VCsr, VCjr. [2]*śāstraiḥ* VCjr. [3]*vedenai'va dvijātayaḥ* VCsr; *vai dvijāḥ* MBh(C), Pts. PtsK; *brāhmaṇaiḥ CNP II*; *paṇḍitāḥ* VCjr. [4]*caraiḥ* PP, PtsK. [5]*rājanyo cakṣurātibhyāṁm itare janā CNPII.*

For other variants see MBh(Bh) 5.34, 32.

44. *MBh*(*Bh*) 5. 34, 37; *MBh*(*R*) 5. 33, 38; *MBh* (*C*) 5. 1132.

satyena rakṣyate [1]*dharmo vidyā yogena rakṣyate,*[2]
mṛjayā rakṣyate[2] *rūpaṃ*[3] *kulaṃ vṛttena*[4] *rakṣyate.*[5]

Dharma is preserved through truthfulness; knowledge is preserved through diligence; beauty is preserved through cleanliness; good family is preserved through good behaviour.

This maxim occurs in two texts belonging to the *CR* version, one of which was translated into Tibetan, viz. in *CRCa II* 26 and *CRT* 6.6.

Also found in GP 1.113, 10.

The Mahābhārata *śloka* was also adapted in the Old Javanese literature: SS 168.

The next sentence in MBh is the continuation of the previous one, but erroneously it was not included in any of the sources mentioned above.

The *C* texts contain some very minor variants.

The *C* text was undoubtedly borrowed directly from MBh.

FOOTNOTES TO NO. 44:

[1]*rakṣate dharmaṃ CRCa II.* [2]*rakṣate CRCa II.* [3]*pātraṃ CRT*, GP. [4]*śilena CRT*, *CRCa II*, GP.

For other variants see MBh(Bh) 5.34, 37.

45. *MBh*(*Bh*) 5. 34, 50; *MBh*(*R*) 5. 33, 51; *MBh*(*C*) 5. 1146.

avṛttir bhayam antyānāṃ madhyānāṃ maraṇād bhayam,
uttamānāṃ tu martyānām[1] *avamānāt paraṃ bhayam.*

Men of lowest class dread lack of sustenance; those of the

middle class dread death; those of the highest class, however, dread in particular disrespect on this earth.

This maxim occurs in the *CR* version, viz. in *CRr* 8.11.

Only one variant occurs in *b*; it is unimportant.

The *C* text was undoubtedly borrowed directly fromMBh.

FOOTNOTES TO NO. 45:

[1]*satvānām CRr.*

For other variants see *CRr* 8.11 and MBh(Bh) 5.34, 50.

46. *MBh*(*Bh*) 5. 34, 75; *MBh*(*R*) 5.33, 77; *MBh*(*C*) 5. 1172. (*Also* *MBh*(*Bh*) 13. 107, 58; *MBh*(*R*) 13. 104, 33; *MBh*(*C*) 13. 4987).

[1]*saṃrohati śarair viddhaṃ vanaṃ paraśunā hatam,*[2]
vācā[3] [4]*duruktaṃ bībhatsaṃ na saṃrohati*[5] *vāk-kṣatam.*[6]

The forest pierced by arrows or injured by the use of an axe will grow up (recover) again; a harsh speech is revolving; an injurious speech will never be recovered.

This maxim occurs in one text of the *CN* version, vix. in *CNT IV* 216.

Also found in Pañc (PP 3.99, Pts 3.111, PtsK 3.112).

The Mahābhārata *śloka* was also adapted in the Old Javanese literature: SS 128.

The preceding stanza in the MBh is closely connected with this stanza and it would have been better for *C* to use both texts.

Some variants occur in *b*, *c* and *d*. They are not very important. The *C* text is nearer to the MBh (R) and MBh(*C*) texts than to the classical text of MBh, as reconstructed in the Bhandarkar edition.

The *C* text was undoubtedly borrowed directly from the Vulgata text of MBh.

FOOTNOTES TO NO. 46:

[1]*rohate* (°*ti* PtsK) *śāyakair* (sā°)MBh (Bh), MBh(R), MBh(C), Udyoga- and Anuśāsana-parvan, *CNT IV*, Pts, PtsK; *rohati sāyakaviddhaṁ* PPl [2]*chinnaṁ rohati cāsinā* PtsK. [3]*vaco* PtsK. [4]*duruktayā viddhṃ* MBh(R), MBh(C) Anuśāsana-parvan, *CNT IV*. [5]*prarohati* PP. PtsK. [6]*vākkṛtam* PP.

For other variants see MBh(Bh) 5.34, 75.

47. *MBh*(*Bh*) 5. 35, 33; *MBh*(*R*) 5. 34, 41; *MBh*(*C*)5. 1222.

na devā[1] *yaṣṭim*[2] *ādāya rakṣanti paśu-pālavat,*
yaṃ tu rakṣitum[3] *icchanti buddhyā saṃvibhajanti*[4] *tam.*

The gods do not protect men in the way the herdsmen do, (that is) by using their sticks; but if they wish to protect them they do it with intelligence.

This maxim occurs in the *CR* version, viz. in *CRr* 6.25.

Also found in Pañc (Pts. 3.182).

MBh(R) and MBh(C) have one minor variant in *a*. Otherwise the variants are unimportant.

The *C* text was undoubtedly borrowed directly from the classical text of MBh as reconstructed in the Bhandarkar edition.

FOOTNOTES TO NO. 47:

[1]*devo* MBh(R). [2]*daṇḍam* MBh(C), MBh(R). [3]*vardhitum* Pts. [4]*saṃyojayanti* Pts.

For other variants see *CRr* 6.25 and MBh(Bh) 5.35, 33.

48. *MBh(Bh)* 5. 35, 34; *MBh(R)* 5. 34, 42; *MBh (C)* 5. 1223.

yathā yathā hi puruṣaḥ kalyāṇe kurute manaḥ,[1]
tathā [2]*tathā'sya sarvā'rthāḥ sidhyanta nā'tra saṃśayaḥ.*

In the same way as a man directs his mind towards the excellent, in the same way, there is no doubt, he will succeed in everything he touches.

This maxim occurs in the *CR* version, viz. in *CRr* 8.40.

Also found in GP 1.115, 43.

The Mahābhārata *śloka* was also adapted in the Old Javanese literature: SS 23.

The *CR* and GP texts contain one minor variant in *b* and GP has one quite important variant in *cd* which however does not change the meaning of the text.

The *C* text was undoubtedly borrowed directly from MBh.

FOOTNOTES TO NO. 48:

[1]*matim CRr.* GP. [2]*tathā hi sarvatro* l *śliṣyate lokasupriyaḥ* GP.

For other variants see *CRr* 8.40 and MBh(Bh) 5.35, 34.

49. *MBh(Bh)* 5. 35, 44; *MBh(R)* 5. 34, 52; *MBh(C)* 5. 1232.

śrir maṅgalāt prabhavati prāgalbhyāt saṃpravardhate,[1]
dakṣyāt tu kurute[2] *mūlaṃ saṃyamāt pratitiṣṭhati.*[3]

Prosperity originates in good fortune; grows owing to self-confidence; takes its roots owing to skill; acquires stability owing to self-control.

This maxim occurs in the *CR* version, viz. in *CRr* 8.41.

The *C* text contains some important variants from the

MBh text; some Subhāṣita-saṃgraha-s which repeat this stanza (SRBh 386.349, SRHt 204.1) follow the MBh text.

The *C* text was undoubtedly borrowed from, or was influenced by, MBh.

FOOTNOTES TO NO. 49:

[1]*prakaṭi bhavet CRr.* [2]*prakurute CRr.* [3]*saṃyamāt sthairyam aśnute CRr.* For other variants see *CRr* 8.41 and MBh(Bh) 5.35, 44.

50. *MBh*(*Bh*) 5.35, 49; *MBh*(*R*) 5.34, 59; *MBh*(*C*) 5.1239

na sā sabhā yatra na santi vṛddhā
na te vṛddhā[1] *ye na vadanti dharmam,*
nā'sau dharmo[2] *yatra na satyam asti*[3]
na tat[4] *satyaṃ*[5] *yac chalenā'nuviddham.*[6]

That is not an assembly where there are no elders; those are not elders who do not proclaim *dharma*; there is no *dharma* where there is no truth; there is no truth where deceit exists.

This maxim occurs in the *CR* version and in one text of the *CN* version, viz. in *CRr* 8.53 and *CNG* 330.

Also found in R 7.59(3) 33 GP 1.115, 52, BhŚ 568, H (HJ 3.64), some *nibandha-s* (Maskari Bhāṣya on Gautama-dharmasūtra 220.1-2; Pārāśara-dharmasaṃhitā 3.1; 35.13; Smṛti-candrikā 23.14-5; Aparārka), Prabandhacintāmaṇi (SJS 1) 2.129, Alaṅkāra-kaustubha (VA in KM 66) 385.67; cf. KSS 14.106, 168.

The Mahābhārata *śloka* was also adapted in the Tibetan literature : NM 3.12.

The text contains several variants; all of them are unimportant.

The *C* text was undoubtedly borrowed from MBh; the *CNG* text does not contain any variants from MBh and was borrowed directly from MBh; the *CRr* text may have been borrowed from MBh through BhŚ or H.

FOOTNOTES TO NO. 50:

[1]*vṛ° na te* tr. *CRr* (*CRBh II*, *CNG* as above), HJ, GP, R. BhŚ, PrC, VA. [2]*dharmaḥ sa no CRr* (*CNG* as above), GP, HJ, BhŚ, PrC. [3]*sa° na* tr. *CRr* (*CRC*, *CNG* as above), HJ; *cā'sti satyaṃ* BhŚ, PrC; *nā'ste sa dharmo na hi yatra satyaṃ sa°* V.A. [4]*naitat* GP. [5]*sa° na tad* tr. CRr, BhŚ, PrC. [6]*chalodosayuktam CRr; chalenā'bhyupetam* MBh (R), MBh(C); *yad bhayam abhyupaiti* HJ; *yat kapaṭānu°* (*kṛtakānu°* PrC; *kapaṭena* VA) *°viddham* BhŚ, PrC, VA.

For other variants see *CRr* 8.53, MBh 5.35, 49 and *JSAIL* 24 (*JAOS* 76.125; No. 10). Also see W. Hopkins in *AJPh* 20.29.

Indravajrā and Upendravajrā metre.

51. *MBh(Bh)* 5.35, 51; *MBh(R)* 5.34, 61; *MBh((C)* 5.1241-2.

pāpaṃ kurvan pāpa-kīrtiḥ pāpam evā'śnute phalam,
puṇyaṃ kurvan[1] *puṇya*[2]*-kīrtiḥ puṇyam evā'śnute phalam.*

A wicked man performing evil deeds reaps evil; a virtuous man acting righteously reaps auspicious rewards.

This maxim occurs in one *CV* text which adds to the classical text of the Cāṇakya-nīti-darpaṇa a number of MBh and Mn stanzas, viz. in *CVNS* 12.18.

Also found in BrDh 2.14, 13 (No. 120).

The MBh (*C*) text omits *cd* and adds instead the next half *śloka* reading : *tasmāt pāpaṃ na kurvita puruṣaḥ saṃśita vrataḥ.* The MBh(R) and MBh (*C*) texts have also in *d* another variant which is repeated in BrDh; *CVNS* follows this variant with the transposition of two words; it also contains a minor variant in *c*.

The *C* text was undoubtedly borrowed directly from MBh.

FOOTNOTES TO NO. 51:

[1]*puṇyakur°* *CVNS*. *°kīrtir* 1 *atyantaṁ puṇyaṃ aśnute* *CVNS*; *puṇyaṃ atyantam aśnute* MBh(R), MBh(C), BrDh.

For other variants see MBh(Bh) 5.35, 51.

52. *MBh(Bh)* 5.35, 59; *MBh(R)* 5. 34, 70; *MBh* (*C*)5. 1250-1.

jīrṇam annaṃ praśaṃsanti[1] *bhāryāṃ ca gata-yauvanām,*
[2]*śūraṃ* [3]*vigata-saṃgrāmaṃ gatapāraṃ tapasvinam.*

(These four) are praised; food when it is digested; a wife whose youth has vanished; a hero who has returned from battle; an ascetic who has attained his objective.

This maxim occurs in the *CS* and *CN* versions, viz. in *CSr* 2.79 and *CNr* 77.

The Cāṇakya *śloka* (and not the MBh *śloka*) was also adapted in the Pāli literature of Burma: LN 99, DhN 360 (DhN has a somewhat different version).

The MBh texts have one very minor variant in *c*; however the *C* texts are quite different in *cd* and therefore, can be considered as a different maxim. The *CNr* text also has an unimportant variant in *a*.

The *C* text was undoubtedly influenced by MBh but was not borrowed directly from MBh.

FOOTNOTES TO NO. 52:

[1]*praśaṃsīyād* *CNr*. [2]*raṇāt pratyāgatāṃ śūraṁ* 1 *sasyaṃ ca gṛhaṃ āgataṃ* *CSr*,

CNr. [3]*vijita°* MBh(R), MBh(C).
For other variants see *CSr* 2.79, *CNr* 77 and MBh(Bh) 5.35, 59.

53. *MBh*(*Bh*) 5.35, 64; *MBh*(*R*) 5.34, 75-6; *MBh*(*C*) 5.1255-6.

[1]*suvarṇa-puṣpāṃ pṛthivīṃ* [2]*cinvanti puruṣās trayaḥ,*
śūraś ca kṛtavidyaś[3] *ca yaś ca jānāti sevitum.*[4]

These three are (able to gather) flowers of this earth (viz.) gold : the valiant ones, the learned ones, and those who know how to serve.

This maxim occurs in the *CR* version, one text of the *Cv* version and three texts of the *CN* version, viz. in *CRr* 8.75, *CvTb* 4.20, *CNP II* 126, *CNI I* 53 and *CNT IV* 97.

Also found in Pañc (PP 1.30, Pts. 1.45, PtsK 1.51) and Dhvanyāloka (Hāridas Skṛt. Ser. 66, p. 68).

The MBh *śloka* was also adapted in the Old Javanese literature viz: in Ślokāntara (38) where four kinds of men were able to gather gold: those who knew ways and means (*apāyajña*); the valiant ones (*śūra*); the learned ones (*kṛtavidya*); and those who spoke sweetly (*prayaṃvada*).

The various texts have several variants, neither of them is, however, of any great importantce.

The *C* texts were undoubtedly borrowed directly from MBh.

FOOTNOTES TO NO. 53:

[1] *°puṣpitāṃ pṛthvīṃ* Pts. PtsK. [2]*viracanti trayo janā CvTb*; *viṃciṃta trayo janāḥ CNI I*; *vicinvanti trayo janāḥ* (*narās trayaḥ* PtsK) Pts, PtsK; *cinvanti puru°* PP. [3]*°vighnaś CNP II*; *°vijñaś CvTb.* [4]*yas tu yānāti* (instead of *jānāti*) *sevanam CNP II.*

For other variants see *CRr* 8.75 and MBh(Bh) 5.35, 64.

53A. *MBh*(*Bh*) 5.36, 26; *MBh*(*R*) 5.35, 26; *MBh*(*C*) 5.1285
See No. 138

54. *MBh*(*Bh*) 5.36, 65; *MBh*(*R*) 5.35, 67; *MBh* (*C*) 5.1326.

na manuṣye guṇaḥ kaścid anyo dhanavatām api,[1]
anāturatvād bhadraṃ te[2] *mṛtakalpā hiroginaḥ.*[3]

A man (thinks that he) does not have any other good quality than (his) wealth; if however you are blessed with good health (you are happy), because a sick person is like a dead one.

This maxim occurs in the *CR* version, viz. in *CRr* 4.11.

This MBh stanza has several variants in *b* and *d*; these variants are unimportant; the variants in the *C* text are however important.

The *C* text was undoubtedly directly influenced by MBh.

FOOTNOTES TO NO. 54:

[1]*rājan sadhanatāmṛte* MBh (R), MBh(C); *āḍhyatvam anuvartate CRr.* [2]*arogabhāvādany atra CRr.* [3]*roginaḥ* MBh(C).

For other variants see *CRr* 4.11 and MBh(Bh) 5.36, 65.

55. *MBh(Bh)* 5.37, 16; *MBh(R)* 5.36, 17; *MBh (C)* 5.1350. See No. 10.

56. *MBh(Bh)* 5.37, 17; *MBh(R)* 5.36, 18; *MBh (C)* 5.1315. (*Also MBh(Bh) ad* 1.146, 26 (1614*. 1-2); *MBh(R)* 1.160, 27; *MBh (C)* 1.6169). *Cf. No.* 10.

āpad arthe[1] *dhanaṃ rakṣed dārān rakṣed dhanair api,*
ātmānaṃ satataṃ rakṣed dārair api dhanair api.

Let him protect his wealth for time of misfortune; let him protect his wife even with his wealth; (but) let him always protect the *ātmān* even by sacrificing his wife and his wealth.

This maxim occurs in the *CV*, *Cv CR* and *CN* versions, viz. in *CVr* 1.6, *Cvr* 1.6, *CRr* 2.1 and *CNr* 27.

This is a well-known stanza. It is also found in Mn 7.213, GP 1.109, 1, Pañc (Pts. 1.356 and 3.86), H (HJ 1.43), VC (VCsr 12.1; VCjr 20.1), Śto 321.12-3, Vet 19.16, Halāyuddha's Dharmaviveka 14, Bhojaprabandha 198 and some *nībandha-s* (Vīramitrodaya, Rājanīti-prakāśa 413.2-3, Rājanīti-ratnākara 31.16-7, Kṛtyakalpataru of Bhaṭṭa Lakṣmīdhara, Rājadharma-kaṇḍa 142, 12 sqq. and Dharmakośa 3.1978).

The Mahābhārata *śloka* was also adapted in the Tibetan literature : NM 3.5.

This verse was described in *JSAIL* 27 (study XXVI; *JAOS* 79.248-50). The *C* text was undoubtedly borrowed directly from Mn or MBh.

FOOTNOTES TO NO. 56:

[1]*arthaṃ* MBh(Bh) 5.37, 17.

For all other different readings see *JSAIL* 27, *op. cit.* and *CVr* 1.6, *Cvr* 1.6, *CRr* 2.1, *CNr* 27, and MBh (Bh) 5.37, 17.

57. *MBh(Bh)* 5.37, 53; *MBh(R)* 5.36, 57; *MBh (C)* 5.1390.

strīṣu rājasu sarpeṣu svādhyāye śatru-seviṣu,[1]
bhoge cā'yuṣi[2] *viśvāsaṃ*[3] *kaḥ prājñaḥ kartum arhati.*

What sensible man is justified in trusting women, kings, serpents, those studying the Veda-s, enemies, enjoyment and longevity ?

This maxim occurs in one text of the *CN* version, viz in *CNG* 151. *Cf CR* (*T*) 7.25.

The Mahābhārata *śloka* was also adapted in the Old Javanese literature: SS 392. Also see the Tibetan NM 4.11 and SRN 167.

The various texts contain several important variants.

The *C* text was undoubtedly borrowed directly from MBh

FOOTNOTES TO NO. 57:

[1] °*ya prabhuśatruṣu* MBh(R), MBh(C); *śatruvigrahe CNG.* [2]*bhogeṣu ā°* MBh(R), MBh(C); *agnau durjane CNG.* [3] °*saḥ* MBh(C).

For other variants see MBh(Bh) 5.37, 53.

58. *MBh*(*Bh*) 5.38, 9; *MBh*(*R*) 5.37, 9; *MBh*(*C*) 5. 1406. (*Also MBh*(*Bh*) *App. I to I, No.* 81, 125-6 and 12.136, 138; *MBh*(*R*) 1.142, 60-1 and 12.138, 142; *MBh*(*C*) 1.5603 and 12. 5055-6).

[1]*na viśvased aviśvaste viśvaste*[2] *nā'tiviśvaset,*[3]
viśvāsād bhayam utpannaṃ [4]*mūlāny api nikṛntati.*[5]

One should not trust a man who does not trust us; one should also not trust too much a man who trusts us; the danger that arises from trusting another cuts off one's own roots.

This maxim occurs in the *CS, CR* versions and in three texts of the *CN* version, viz. in *CSr* 3.47, *CRr* 7.42, *CNPh* 39, *CNI I* 102 and *CNG* 87.

Also found in Harivaṃśa 1164 (Calcutta ed.), GP 1.114, 47, Pañc (PP 4.12, Pts. 2.39 and 4.13, PtsK 2.43 and 4.14) and Śts. 70.11.

The Mahābhārata *śloka* was also adapted in the Tibetan literature : NM 4.8.

Variants occurring in the various texts are unimportant; the variants occurring in *CNI I* are due to the corruption of the text.

The *C* text was undoubtedly borrowed directly from MBh.

FOOTNOTES TO NO. 58:

[1]*natiścasenna aviśvasthe CNI I* (*sic* !). [2]*viśvasthe CNI I.* [3]*mitrasyāpi na vi° CNG*; *viśvaste'pi na viśvaset* MBh(Bh) 12.136, 138; *na vikatyayet CNPh*; *'pi na vi° CNI I*, PP, Pts, PtsK, Śts. [4]*api mūlāṃ kṛ°* MBh(R), MBh(C) Śānti-parvan. [5]*nihantati CNI I.*

For other variants see *CSr* 3.47, *CRr* 7.42, MBh(Bh 5.38, 9 and 12. 136, 138.

58A. *MBh*(*Bh*) 5.38.12; *MBh*(*R*) 5.37.12; *MBh*(*C*) 5.1409
See No. 139

59. *MBh*(*Bh*) 5.39, 2; *MBh*(*R*) 5.38, 2; *MBh*(*C*) 5. 1447.

aprāpta-kālaṃ[1] *vacanaṃ Bṛhaspatir api*[2] *bruvan,*
[3]*labhate*[4] *buddhyav ajñānam avamānaṃ*[5] *ca Bhārata.*[6]

O Bhārata, even if Bṛhaspati were to utter words at improper time, he would incur contempt and would be charged with ignorance.

This maxim occurs in one MS of the *CN* version, viz., in *CNPh* 159.

Also found in Pañc (PP 1.23, Pts 1.63, PRE 1.24, PT 1.19, PTem 1.22, PS 1.28) and H (HJ 2.61).

The various variants which mostly occur in P are of no great importance, with the exception of *cd* of PP. The *C* text has some variants of importance.

The *C* text was undoubtedly borrowed directly from MBh.

FOOTNOTES TO NO. 59:

[1] °*kāle* MBh (C), *CNPh*, PS; °*kāla*° HJ. [2] °*tiri CNPh* (scribe's error). [3]*na kevalam asaṃ mānaṃ vipriyatvaṃ ca gacchati* PP. [4]*prāpnuyād* HJ; *prāpnoti CNPh.* [5]*apamānaṃ CNPh*, HJ. [6]*kevalam CNPh*, PRE, PT; *tat kṣaṇam* PS; *puṣkalam* Pts; *śāśvatam* HJ.
For other variants see MBh (Bh) 5.39, 2.

60. *MBh*(*Bh*) 5.39, 51; *MBh*(*R*) 5.38, 66.7; *MBh*(*C*) 5.1511-2.
See No. 18.

61. *MBh*(*Bh*) 5. 39, 60; *MBh*(*R*) 5. 38, 75-6; *MBh*(*C*) 5.1520-1.

abhivādana-śīlasya nityaṃ vṛddho'pasevinaḥ,
[1]*catvāri saṃpravardhate kīrtir āyur yaśo balam.*

He who usually pays respect and constantly pays homage to elders is rewarded by an increase of four things; renown, longevity, fame and strength.

This maxim occurs in one *CV* text which adds to the classical text of the Cāṇakya-nīti-darpaṇa a number of MBh and Mn stanzas, viz. in *CVNS* 12.11.

Also found in Mn 2.121 and some *nibandha-s* (see *JSAIL* 27; *JAOS* 79.237-8 where this stanza was described in detail)[2].

The Mahābharata *śloka* was also adapted in the Old Javanese literature: SS 256.

The text of *C* has, like the text of Mn, variants in *cd* ; therefore, it seems that it was borrowed directly from Mn and not from MBh.

FOOTNOTES TO NO. 61:

[1]*catvāri tasya vardhanta āyuḥ prajñā (āyur vidyā CVNS) ya°* Mn, *CVNS.* [2]See Study XXVI. For other variants see MBh(Bh) 5.39, 60 and *JSAIL* 27 (*JAOS* 79. 238; No. 3).

62. *MBh*(*Bh*) 5.39, 61; *MBh*(*R*) 5.38, 76-7; *MBh*(*C*) 5.1521-2.

atikleśena [1]ye'rthāḥ[2] syur[3] dharmasyā'tikrameṇa ca,
arer vā[4] praṇipātena [5]mā sma teṣu manaḥ kṛthāḥ.

Do not desire objects which can be acquired only with excessive hardship, or by overstepping *dharma*, or by submitting to the enemy.

This maxim occurs in the *CV* and *CR* versions and in two texts of the *CN* version, viz. in *CVr* 16.11, *CRr* 2.37, *CNG* 181 and *CNT IV* 198.

Also found in GP 1.109, 28 and Śukasaptati (Śts 82.6-7, Śto 360.8-9).

The Mahābhārata *śloka* was also adapted in the Old Javanese literature : SS 272.

Variants which occur in *abc* are unimportant; however variants which occur in *C* in *d* are of some importance.

The *C* text was undoubtedly borrowed from MBh with a variant in *d*.

FOOTNOTES TO NO. 62:

[1]*ye hy* (*'py* GP) *arthā CVr*, GP. [2](*dehasya CRr*) 1 *dharmasyā'tikrameṇa tu* (*ca CRr*, Śto, GP) *CVr, CRr, CNG*, GP, Śts, Śto. [3]*syar* MBh(R) (printing error). [4]*śatrūṇāṃ CVr, CNG*, Śts, Śto. [5]*te arthā mā bhavantu me CVr, CNG; mā bhūt so'rthaḥ kadā ca na CRr; mā bhuvaṃ ste kadā ca na* GP; *māmate'rthā bhavantu na* Śto.

For other variants see *CVr* 16.11, *CRr* 2.37 and MBh(Bh) 5.39, 61.

63. *MBh*(*Bh*) 5.39, 62; *MBh*(*R*) 5.38, 77-8; *MBh*(*C*) 5.1522-3.

avidyaḥ puruṣaḥ śocyaḥ śocyaṃ mithunam[1] aprajam,
nirāhārāḥ prajāḥ śocyāḥ śocyaṃ rāṣṭram[2] arājakam.

An ignorant man is to be deplored; sexual intercourse which does not bring children is to be deplored; subjects who do not have enough food are to be deplored; a king less kingdom is to be deplored.

This maxim occurs in the *CN* version, viz. in *CNr* 55.

Also found in Vet 11.12 and MS A 21.12.

The variants which occur in this stanza are of no importance at all.

The *C* text was undoubtedly borrowed directly from MBh.

FOOTNOTES TO NO. 63:

[1]*maithunaṁ* MBh(R), MBh(C). [2]*rājyam CNr.*

For other variants see *CNr* 55 and MBh(Bh) 5.39, 62.

64. *MBh*(*Bh*) 5.39,63; *MBh*(*R*) 5.38,78-9; *MBh*(*C*) 5.1523-4.

adhvā jarā dehavatāṃ [1]*parvatānāṃ*[2] *jalaṃ jarā,*
asaṃbhogo jarā strīṇāṃ[2] [3]*vākśalyaṃ manaso*[5] *jarā.*

Travel wears out people; rain wears out mountains; absence of sexual enjoyment wears out women; abusive speech wears out one's mind.

This maxim occurs in the *CR* version and in one text of the *CN* version, viz. in *CRr* 8.8 and *CNP I* 27. Similarly *CVr* 4.17, *CNr* 39, *CSr* 2, 36.

Also found in GP 1.115,10 and Dharmaviveka 15.

The variants which occur in the different texts are of no great importance.

The *C* text was undoubtedly borrowed directly from MBh.

FOOTNOTES TO NO. 64:

[1]*avadhvā vājināṃ CNP I.* [2]*parvanānām* MBh(R). [3] *°bhogaś ca nāriṇāṁ CRr.* [4]*saṁbhogaḥ kariṇāṃ ja° CNP I.* [5]*vastrasyā'kṣalanaṃ CRr.*

For other variants see *CRr* 8.8 and MBh(Bh) 5.39, 63.

65. *MBh*(*Bh*) 5.39, 66; *MBh*(*R*) 5.38, 82; *MBh*(*C*) 5.1527.

na svapnena jayen[1] *nidrāṃ na kāmena striyaṃ jayet,*[2]
[3]*nendhanena jayed agniṃ*[4] *na pānena*[5] [6]*surāṃ*[7] *jayet.*

One cannot conquer sleep by dreams; one cannot conquer a woman by sexual enjoyment; one cannot conquer fire by fuel; one cannot conquer thirst by drinking spirituous liquor.

This maxim occurs in the *CR* version and in two texts of the *CN* version, viz. in *CRr* 2.42, *CNG* 50 and *CNP II* 237; the latter text is corrupt.

Also found in GP 1.109, 34.

The variants in MBh, the *C* texts and GP are of no great importance.

The *C* text was undoubtedly borrowed directly from MBh.

FOOTNOTES TO NO. 65:

[1]*jayet* GP. [2]*jayet striyaḥ* MBh(R), MBh(C), *CNG.* [3]*na cendhanair yajed vahniṃ* GP. [4]*asiṃ* MBh(R); *vahniṃ CRr.* [5]*mādyena CRr,* GP; *cārthena CNG.* [6]*jayed dhanam CNG.* [7]*tṛṣāṃ CRr,* GP.

For other variants see *CRr* 2.42 and MBh(Bh) 5.39, 66.

66. *MBh*(*Bh*) 5.40, 5; *MBh*(*R*) 5.39, 6-7; *MBh* (*C*) 5.1537-8.

sukhā'rthinaḥ kuto vidyā nā'sti[1] *vidyā'rthinaḥ sukham,*
sukhā'rthi vā[2] *tyajed vidyāṃ vidyā'rthī vā*[2] *sukhaṃ tyajet.*[3]

How can one who is striving for pleasure have knowledge? But there is no pleasure for one who is striving for knowledge. Either one strives for pleasure and gives up knowledge, or one strives for knowledge and gives up pleasure.

This maxim occurs in the *CV* and *CL* versions, viz. in *CVr* 10.3 *cd*/*ab* and *CLr* 7.8. Similarly *CRv* 3.25.

The variants which occur in the various texts are unimportant.

The *C* text undoubtedly borrowed directly from MBh.

FOOTNOTES TO NO. 66:

[1]*kuto CVr, CLr.* [2]*cet CVr.* [3]*su° tya°* tr. MBh(C), *CVr. CLr.*
For other variants see *CVr* 10.3, *CLr* 7.8 and MBh (Bh) 5.40, 5.

67. *MBh*(*Bh*) 5.40, 6; *MBh*(*R*) 5.39, 7; *MBh*(*C*) 5.1538, (*Also MBh*(*Bh*) *ad* 1.113, 7 (1189*. 1-2) *and* 13 38. 25; *MBh*(*R*) 13.38, 25; *MBh*(*C*) 13. 2226).

nā'gnis tṛpyati kāṣṭhānāṃ[1] *nā'papānāṃ*[2]*mahodadhiḥ,*[3]
nā'ntakaḥ sarvabhūtānāṃ[4] [5]*ṃa puṃsāṃ*[6] *vāma-locana.*[7]

Fire is not satiated with fuel; nor the ocean with rivers; nor death with all creatures; nor bright-eyed women with men.

This maxim occurs in the *CR* and *Cv* versions and in six, texts of the *CN* version, viz. in *CRr* 2.48, *Cvr* 7.8, *CNF* 41 *CNI I* 172, *CNP I* 13, *CNT IV* 12, *CNM* 12 and *CNMN* 12.

Also found in GP 1.109.40, Pañc (PP 1.106, Pts 1.137, PtsK 1.153), H (HJ 2.114), VC (VCsr VI 10), BhŚ 571, NPR 1.14, 99. *Cf.* R 5.54, 28-9.

The Mahābhārata *śloka* was also adapted in the Old Javanese literature : SS 437.

The variants which occur in all the texts, with the exception of the texts belonging to the *CN* version and NPR, are unimportant. Some variants occurring in the *CNI I*, *CNM*, *CNMN* and particularly NPR texts are important.

The *C* text, were undoubtedly borrowed directly from MBh.

FOOTNOTES TO NO. 67:

[1]*Kaṣṭena CNI I, CNM, CNMN,* [2]*'pagābhir CNI I; 'pigābhir CNM,*

CNMN. [3] *°dhi CNM.* [4]*bhutebhyo CNM, CNMN.* [5]*nāśa nṛpyati saṁpadām* NPR. [6]*puṁbhir CNM. CNMN.* [7]*nāmalocanā CNI I*; *°nāḥ* MBh(Bh) *ad* 1.113, 17; 1189*, MBh(R), MBh(C) Anuśāsanaparvan.

For other variants see *CRr* 2.48, *Cvr* 7.8, MBh(Bh) 5.40, 6 and *JSAIL* 24 (*JAOS* 77.113; No. 78).

68. *MBh*(*Bh*) 5.70, 23; *MBh*(*R*) 5.71, 23; *MBh*(*C*) 5.2603.
dhanam āhuḥ paraṃ dharmaṃ dhane sarvaṃ pratiṣṭhitam,
jīvanti dhanino loke mṛtā[1] *ye tv adhanā narāḥ.*

It is said that wealth is the highest *dharma*; that everything depends on wealth; that those who have wealth (really) live in this world; however those people who do not have wealth are (like) dead.

This maxim occurs in the *CS* version, viz. in *CSr* 2.43.

Only one variant occurs in the MBh(C) text (*hata* instead o *mṛta*); this variant seems to improve the text; it is not repeated in any *C* texts.

The *C* text was undoubtedly borrowed directly from MBh.

FOOTNOTES TO NO. 68:

[1]*hatā* MBh(C).

For other variants see *CSr* 2.43 and MBh(Bh) 5.70, 23.

69. *MBh*(*Bh*) 5.111, 15; *MBh*(*R*) 5.112, 15; *MBh*(*C*) 5.3887.
(*d identical also in MBh*(*Bh*) 5.39, 32 *etc. and Mn* 4.156 *d*).
[1]*ācārāl labhate dharmam ācārāl labhate dhanam,*
[2]*ācārāc chriyam āpnoti ācāro hanty alakṣaṇam.*

Through good conduct one attains *dharma*; through good conduct one attains wealth; through good conduct one obtains a high position; good conduct scares bad luck away.

This maxim occurs in the *CS* version, viz. in *CSr* 1.93.

The MBh texts and the *CSr* text have variants of some importance. The *C* text follows the variants in MBh(R) and is nearer to this text as well as the MBh(*C*) text, than to the MBh(Bh) text.

The *C* text was undoubtedly borrowed directly from the Vulgata text of the MBh.

FOOTNOTES TO NO. 69:

[1]*ācara* (*°raḥ* MBh(R)); *phalate dharmam ācāraḥ phalate dha° CSr*, MBh (R); *ācāraḥ phalate dharmā'cāraḥ phalate dha°* MBh(C). [2]*ācārāt phalam a° CSr*; *ācārā śriyam* a° MBh(R), MBh(C).

For other variants see *CSr* 1.93 and MBh(Bh) 5.111, 15.

70. *MBh(Bh)* 5. 126, 48; *MBh(R)* 5.127, 47; *MBh(C)* 5.4307. See No. 10.

71. *MBh (Bh)* 5.131, 8; *MBh(R)* 5.132, 9; *MBh(C)* 5.4502.
supūrā[1] *vai*[2] *kunadikā*[3] *supūro*[4] *mūṣikā'ñjaliḥ.*[5]
susaṃtoṣaḥ[6] *kāpuruṣaḥ svalpakenā'pi*[7] *tuṣyati.*

A little stream is, indeed, easy to fill; the joined paws of a mouse are easy to fill; a contemptible man is easy to satisfy since he is content even with little.

This maxim occurs in the *CR* version, viz. in *CRr* 8.36.

Also found in GP 1.115, 38 and Pañc (PRE 1.13, PP 1.14, Pts 1.25 & 2.138, PtsK 1.31 & 2.145, PT 1.11, PTem 1.8, PS 1.14, P 2.10).

All variants which occur in this maxim are un-important.

The *C* text was undoubtedly borrowed directly from MBh.

FOOTNOTES TO NO. 71:

[1]*svapurā* GP. [2]*syāt* Pts, PtsK (2.145 only). [3]*kāpuruṣāḥ* GP. [4]*svāpuro* GP. [5]*mūṣakā°* *CRr*, PP, PtsK (2.145 only), PT, PTem PS, PRE. [6]*tuṣṭaḥ* *CRr*, GP, Pts, PtsK, PT, PTem, PS, PRE. [7]*svalpaḥ ke*[0] PS; *°kenai'va* MBh (R), MBh(C).

For other variants see *CRr* 8.36 and MBh(Bh) 5.131, 8.

72. *MBh(Bh)* 5.131, 21; *MBh(R)* 5.132, 23-4; *MBh(C)* 5. 4516-7.
[1]*dāne tapasi śaurye*[2] *ca*[3] *yasya na prathitaṃ*[4] *yaśaḥ,*[5]
vidyāyām arthatābhe vā[6] *mātur uccaraeva saḥ.*

He whose fame is not founded on respect for charity, piety and heroism, on knowledge and acquisition of wealth is, verily, but his mother's excrement.

This maxim occurs in the *CR* version and in one text of the *CN* version, viz. in *CRr* 8.33 and *CNG* 105.

Also found in GP 1.115, 32 and H (HJ Intr 16).

Some variants occur in the texts of MBh, H and C, but none of them is of great importance.

The *C* text was undoubtedly borrowed directly from MBh.

FOOTNOTES TO NO. 72:

[1]*śau° ta° dā°* tr. GP. *°satye* MBh(R), MBh(C). [2]*vā* *CRr.* [3]*nocchāritaṃ* (or *noccā*[0]) MBh(R),MBh(C), *CNG.* [5]*manaḥ* HJ. [6]*ca* *CRr.* HJ.

For other variants see *CRr* 8.33, MBh(Bh) 5.131, 21 and *JSAIL* 24 (*JAOS* 77.166; No. 90).

73. *MBh*(*Bh*) 6.24, 28; *MBh*(*R*) *and* *MBh*(*C*)*Bhagavadgītā* 2.28. (*Also MBh* (*Bh*) 11.2; 7* 1.1-2; *MBh*(*R*) 11.2, 6 *and* 11, 9.11; *MBh*(*C*) 11.51 *and* 11.56; *d often repeated*; *see MBh*(*Bh*) 6.24, 28 (*fn.*).

avyaktādīni[1] *bhūtāni vyaktamadhyāni*[2] *Bhārata,*
[3]*avyaktanidhanāny eva tatra kā paridevanā.*

The beginnings of things are unmanifest, manifest their middle, son of Bhārata, unmanifest again their ends; why mourn about this. (Edgerton's translation *HOS* 39).

This maxim occurs in the *CR* version among verses, the Cāṇakya's authenticity of which is doubted, viz. in *CRr* "Q."

There are no variants in the Bhagavadgītā text nor in the *CRr* text. However, small variants occur in MBh text found in the Strī-parvan.

The *C* text was undoubtedly borrowed directly from the Bhagavadgītā.

FOOTNOTES TO NO. 73:

[1]*abhāvādīni* MBh (Bh) MBh(R), MBh(C) Strī-parvan. [2]*bhāvana*° MBh (Bh), MBh(R),MBh (C) Strī-parvan. [3]*abhāvani*° MBh(Bh), MBh(R), MBh(C) Strī-parvan.

For other variants see *CRr* "Q" and MBh(Bh) 6.24, 28.

74. *MBh*(*Bh*) 11.2, 3; *MBh*(*R*) 11. 2, 3; *MBh*(*C*) 11. 48. (*Also MBh*(*Bh*) 12.27, 29, 12.317, 20 *and* 14.44, 18; *MBh*(*R*) 12.27, 29; 12.330, 20 *and* 14.41, 19; *MBh* (*C*) 12.829, 12.12501 *and* 14.1230).

[1]*sarve kṣayā'ntā*[2] *nicayāḥ patanā'ntāḥ*[3] *samucchrayāḥ,*[4]
[5]*saṃyogā*[6] *viprayogā'ntā maraṇā'ntaṃ hi*[7] *jīvitam.*[8]

All provisions come (finally) to an end; everything that goes up in the end falls down; union ends in separation; and life ends in death.

This well known maxim occurs in the *CR* version and in two texts of the *CN* version, viz. in *CRr* 8.59, *CNG* 329 and *CNI I* 186.

Also found in R (2.105, 16 and 7.52, 11; RG 2.114, 3), Pañc (PT 2.165, PTem 2.147), H (*ad* HS 1.180, HH 32.25-6). KSS 9.51, 26-7; Gobhila-smṛti 3.43 (ĀnSS 48), Divyāvadāna II p. 27.

The variants which occur in the maxim are of no great importance, with the exception of variants in H.

The *C* text follows the classical text of MBh and was undoubtedly borrowed from MBh.

FOOTNOTES TO NO. 74:

[1]*sarvatra jantor niyamāt* HS, HH. [2]*'nti CNI I.* [3]*'ntā CNI I*; *patataś ca* HS, HH. [4]*samudyanāḥ CNI I.* [5]*saṃyogāś ca viyopā'nta* (°*gāś ca* HS, HH) MBh (R), MBh (C) Āśvamedhika-parvan, RG, HS, HH. [6]*saṃthopā* MBh (R) 11.2, 3 (printing error); *saṃgoga R* 7.52, 11.7.7 *ca* R, MBh (C) 11.42 & 14.1230, KSS. [8]*jīvati* MBh (C) 11.42, *CNI I*, PT, PTem; *jivanam* HS, HH.

For other variants see *CRr* 8.59, MBh (Bh) 11.2, 3; 12.317, 20 and 14.44, 18. Also see W. Hopkins *AJPh* 20.30. *Cf.* B No. 83 below.

75. *MBh* (*Bh*)—; *MBh* (*R*) 11. 2, 6; *MBh* (*C*) 11. 51.
See No. 73.

76. *MBh* (*Bh*) 11.2, 13; *MBh* (*R*) 11.2, 13; *MBh* (*C*) 11.67.
See No. 20.

77. *MBh* (*Bh*) *ad* 11.2, 14. (9*); *MBh* (*R*) 11.2, 24; *MBh* (*C*) 11. 69. (*Also cf. MBh* (*Bh*) 1.1, 188 *ab*; *MBh* (*Bh*) *ad* 1.1. 189 *cd*; 61*; *MBh* (*R*) 1.1, 245 *ab and* 247 *cd.*

kālaḥ pacati[1] *bhūtāni kālaḥ saṃharate*[2] *prajāḥ,*[3]
kālaḥ supteṣu jāgarti[4] *kālo hi duratikramaḥ.*

Time causes all beings to ripen; time destroys (also) all creatures; time is watchful while others are asleep; no one indeed, escapes from it.

This maxim occurs in the *CV*, *Cv*, *CR*, *CS* versions and in three texts of the *CN* version, viz. in *CVr* 6.6, *Cvr* 8.3, *CRr* 1.11, *CSr* 3.2, *CNP I* 53, *CNP II* 78 and *CNT IV* 56.

Also found in GP 1.108, 7 and Utpala *ad* Varāhamihira's Bṛhat-saṃhitā 1.7.

All variants which occur in this maxim are unimportant.

The *C* text was undoubtedly borrowed directly from MBh, Strī-parvan.

FOOTNOTES TO NO. 77:

[1]*sṛjati Utpala, MBh* (*R*) 1.1, 245. [2]*ab* only in MBh (Bh) 1.1, 188 but in *b saṃharati*; also Utpala. [3]*'pi ca CNP II.* [4]*jāgarttā CNP II.*

For other variants see *CVr* 6.6, *Cvr* 8.3, *CRr* 1.11, *CSr* 3.2, MBh (Bh) 11.2, 14 (9*) and 1.1, 188-9.

78. *MBh* (*Bh*)—; *MBh* (*R*) 11.9, 11; *MBh* (*C*) 11. 256.
See No. 73.

79. *MBh* (*Bh*) 12.8. 18; *MBh* (*R*) 12.8, 18; *MBh* (*C*) 12.218-9.

arthena hi[1] *vihīnasya*[2] *puruṣasyā'lpamedhasaḥ*[3]
[4]*vicchidyante*[5] *kriyāḥ sarvā grīṣme kusarito yathā.*

Acts of a man of small wit and deprived of wealth dry up like small streams in the summer season.

This maxim occurs in the *CR* and *Cv* versions, *viz.* in *CRr* 4.13 and *CVr* 6.10.

Also found in R (6.83, 33; RG 6.62, 30) Pañc (PRE 2.32, PP 2.71. Pts 2.85, PtsK 2.92, PS 2.30, PT 2.53, PN 1.27) and H (HJ 1.133).

The various variants which occur in this maxim are of little importance.

The *C* text was undoubtedly borrowed directly from MBh.

FOOTNOTES TO NO. 79:

[1]*eha* MBh(R); *ca* Pts. PtsK; *eha* MBh(C). [2]*vimuktasya* R 6.83, 33. [3] °*tejasaḥ* R 6.83, 33. [4]*kriyāḥ sarvā vinaśyati* HJ.; *prachidyante* RG; *vyucchi°* MBh(Bh), R. [5]*ucchi°* PP. Pts., PtsK.

For other variants see *CRr* 4.13, *Cvr* 6.10, MBh(Bh)12.8, 18 and *JSAIL* 24 (*JAOS* 76, 129-30; No. 27).

80. *MBh(Bh)* 12.8, 19; *MBh(R)* 12.8, 19; *MBh(C)* 12.219-20.

yasyā'rthās[1] *tasya mitrāṇi yasyā'rthās*[2] *tasya bāndhavāḥ,*
yasyā'rthāḥ[3] *sa pumāṁl loke*[4]*yasyā'rthās*[5] *sa ca*[6] *paṇḍitaḥ.*[7]

He who has riches has friends; he who has riches has kinsmen; he who has riches is regarded in this world as an important man; he who has riches is regarded as a learned man.

This maxim occurs in the *CV*, *Cv* and *CR* versions and in five texts of the *CN* version, viz. in *CVr* 7.15, *Cvr* 6.8, *CRr* 4.12, *CNP I* 51, *CNP II* 76, *CNI I* 67, *CNG* 238 and *CNT IV* 50.

Also found in R (6.83, 35; RG 6.62, 32), GP 1.111, 17, Pañc (PRE 2.31, Pts 1.3, PtsK 1.3, PT 2.52, PS 2.31, PN 1.28), H (HJ 1.134), VC (VCsr 12.5), Śukasaptati (Śts 25. 11-26.1, Śto 325. 34-5); *cf.* KṣB 16.422.

The Mahābhārata *śloka* was also adapted in the Tibetan, Mongolian Pāli and Burmese literatures, viz. NM 6.7, SRN 49, LN 167, NKy 41.

All variants which occur in this maxim are unimportant.

The *C* text was undoubtedly borrowed directly from MBh.

FOOTNOTES TO NO. 80:

[1]*'rthas* VC, Śts. [2]*'rthas* VC, Śts. [3]*'rthas CNP I, CNP II*; *'thā CNI I*; *'rthā* HJ. [4]*loki CNI I.* [5]*'rthas* VC, *CNP I, CNP II*; *'rtho CNI I*, *'rthāḥ* MBh(R), [6]*tu* HJ; *hi CRr*, HM, HC. [7]*jivati CVr, Cvr, CNI I*; *rogiṇaḥ CRr*; *bahuśrutaḥ CNI I.*

For other variants see *CVr* 7.15, *Cvr* 6.8, *CRr* 4.12, MBh(Bh) 12.8, 19 and *JSAIL* 24 (*JAOS* 77.127; No. 16).

81. *MBh*(*Bh*) 12.15, 34; *MBh*(*R*) 12.15, 34; *MBh*(*C*) 12.457.

sarvo daṇḍajito loko[1] *durlabho hi śucir janaḥ,*[2]
daṇḍasya hi bhayād bhīto[3] *bhogāyai'va pravartate.*[4]

It is by the threat of punishment that the whole world is kept under control, for a guiltless man is hard to find; through fear of punishment the universe is ruled.

This maxim occurs in one *CV* text which adds to the classical text of the Cāṇakya-nīti-darpaṇa a number of MBh and Mn stanzas, viz. in *CVNS* 16.22.

Also found in Mn 7.22 (and *nibandha-s* viz. Vīramitrodaya, Rājanīti-prakāśa 286.2-3 and 292. 22-3, Rājanīti-ratnākara 63.13-4 and Vivādacintāmaṇi 168.10-1), BrDh 2.11, 4 (No. 91).

The Mn text contains some variants in *bc* and *d*. The BrDh and *C* texts follow the Mn text and not the MBh text.

The *C* text was undoubtedly borrowed directly from Mn and not from MBh.

FOOTNOTES TO NO. 81:

[1]*loke* MBh(R), MBh(C). [2]*naraḥ* Mn. MBh(Bh), BrDh; *śuci naraḥ CVNS*. [3]*sarvaṃ* Mn, *CVNS*, BrDh. [4]*jagad bhogāya kalpate* Mn, *CVNS*, BrDh; *bhogāyeha prakalpate* MBh(Bh).

For other variants see MBh(Bh) 12.15, 34 and *JSAIL* 27 (*JAOS* 79.246-7; No. 20) where the text was described in detail.

82. *MBh*(*Bh*) 12.26, 20; *MBh*(*R*) 12.25, 20; *MBh*(*C*) 12.751. See No. 20.

83. *MBh*(*Bh*) 12.27, 28; *MBh*(*R*) 12.27, 28; *MBh*(*C*) 12.828. *Cf.* No. 74.

saṃyogā viprayogāś ca[1] *jātānāṃ prāṇināṃ dhruvam,*[2]
budbudā iva toyeṣu bhavanti na bhavanti ca.

Inevitably, all union of living beings ends in separation; they arise and vanish like bubbles in water.

This maxim occurs in one *CV* text which adds to the classical text of the Cāṇakya-nīti-darpaṇa a number of MBh and Mn stanzas, viz. in *CVNS* 11.22.

Variants are unimportant.

The *C* text was undoubtedly borrowed directly from MBh.

FOOTNOTES TO NO. 83:

[1] °*yogānta* MBh(R), MBh(C). [2]*dhruvāḥ* MBh(C); also so Böhtlingk in *Indische Sprüche* 6624 (better) .

For other variants see MBh(Bh) 12.27, 28.

84. *MBh(Bh)* 12.27, 29; *MBh(R)* 12. 27, 29; *MBh(C)* 12.829. See No. 74. Cf. No. 83.

85. *MBh(Bh)* 12.28, 36; *MBh(R)* 12.28, 36; *MBh(C)* 12.868-9. (*Also MBh(Bh)* 12.168, 15; *MBh(R)* 12.174, 16; *MBh(C)* 12.6471-2).

yathā kāṣṭhaṃ ca kāṣṭhaṃ ca sameyātāṃ maho'dadhau,[1]
same'tya ca[2] *vyape'yātāṃ*[3] [4]*tadvad bhūtasa-māgamaḥ.*

As two pieces of wood (As a piece of wood and another piece of wood) floating on the great ocean may come together and may again be separated, so even human beings may come together and may again be separated.

This maxim occurs in the *CR* version among verses, the Cāṇakya's authenticity of which is doubted, viz. in *CR*, "N."

Also found in R (2.105, 26; RG 2.114, 12), H (HJ 4.72).

The Mahābhārata *śloka* was also adapted in the Old Javanese literature: SS 490.

Varients occur only in the R text. The *C* text follows MBh and H.

The *C* text was undoubtedly borrowed directly from MBh and not from R.

FOOTNOTES TO NO. 85:

[1]*mahārṇave* R. [2]*tu* R. [3]*vyatiyātāṃ* MBh(Bh) 12.28, 36. [4]*kālamā sādya kañcana* R; *sthitvā kiṃ cit kṣanāntaram* RG.

For other variants see *CRr* "N," MBh(Bh) 12.28, 36, MBh(Bh) 12. 168, 15 and *JSAIL* 24 (*JAOS* 77.170; No. 106). Also see W. Hopkins *AJPh* 20.29.

85A. *MBh(Bh)* 12.68,40; *MBh(R)* 12.68,40; *MBh (C)* 12.2573. See No. 140.

86. *MBh(Bh)* 12.84, 42; *MBh(R)* 12.83, 48; *MBh(C)* 12.3173-4. See No. 94.

86A. *MBh(Bh)* 12.89, 4; *MBh (R)* 12.88, 4; *MBh (C)* 12.3305. See No. 141.

87. *MBh(Bh)* 12.112, 32; *MBh(R)* 12. 111, 32; *MBh(C)* 12. 4114.

[1]*pānīyaṃ vā nirāyāsaṃ svādv annaṃ vā bhayo'ttaram,*
vicārya khala paśyāmi tat sukhaṃ yatra nirvṛtiḥ.[2]

If I reflect which is better: water (i.e. common food), the (getting of which) does not involve trouble, or pleasant tasting food obtained with fear, I come to the conclusion that happiness lies where there is no fear.

This maxim occurs in the *CR* version, viz. in *CRr* 6.49.

Also found in GP 1.113, 57 and H (HJ 1.160).

There are no variants in this maxim but GP 1.113, 57 is different in *ab*.

The *C* text was undoubtedly borrowed directly from MBh.

FOOTNOTES TO NO. 87:

[1]*rāgadveṣādi yuktānāṃ na sukhaṃ kutracid dvija* GP. [2]*pānīyaṃ nirbhayaṃ sukham CRr*.

For other variants see *CRr* 6.49, MBh (Bh) 12.112, 32, and *JSAIL* 24 (*JAOS* 77, 180; No. 147).

87A. *MBh*(*Bh*) *ad* 12.112, 57 (265*); *MBh*(*R*) 12. 111, 59; *MBh*(*C*) 12. 4142-3.

See No. 136.

87A. *MBh*(*Bh*) 12.124, 15; *MBh*(*R*) 12.124, 15; *MBh*(*C*) 12.4564.

See No. 143.

88. *MBh*(*Bh*) *ad* 12.135, 1 (307*); *MBh*(*R*) 12.137, 1; *MBh* (*C*) 12.4889. (*Also MBh*(*R*) 12.137, 20; *MBh*(*C*) 12. 4908).

[1]*anāgata-vidhātā ca pratyutpanna-matiś ca yaḥ*,[2]
dvāv eva[3] *sukham edhe'te* [4]*dīrghasūtrī*[5] *vinaśyati*.

These two: one that provides for the future and one having presence of mind, are always happy; a procrastinating man perishes.

This maxim occurs in the *CV* version and in four texts of the *CN* version, viz. in *CVr* 13.6, *CNP I* 85, *CNP II* 122, *CNPh* 154, *CNT IV* 86.

Also found in Pañc. (PRE 1.127, PP 1.326, Pts 1.318 and 367; PtsK 1.361, PT 1.128, PTem 1.117, PS 1.118, PN 2.95) and H (HJ 4.5). *Cf.* KSS 10.60, 178; *cf.* KṣB 16.336.

The variants which occur in this maxim are unimportant with the exception of one in *d* where instead of *dīrghasūtrī* (procrastinating man) is *yadbhaviṣyo* (what will be, will be). This variant occurs in Pañc, H and the *C* texts.

The *C* text was borrowed directly from Pañc or H, while these two latter texts were undoubtedly influenced directly by MBh.

FOOTNOTES TO NO. 88:

[1]*anāgati*[0] *CNP II*. [2]°*tis tathā CVr, CNP I, CNP II, CNPh*, HJ, Pts, PtsK. [3]*etau CVr*, HJ, Pañc; *ete CNPh*. [4]*yadbhaviṣyo vi*° *CVr, CNP I*, HJ, Pañc; *yad bhaviṣyati bhāvi ca CNP III* [5]°*sūtro* MBh(R), MBh (C) (in both places).

For other variants see *CVr* 13.6, MBh(Bh) *ad* 12.135, 1 (307*) and *JSAIL* 24 (*JAOS* 77.176; No. 129).

89. *MBh(Bh)*—; *MBh(R)* 12.137, 20; *MBh(C)* 12.4908.
See No. 88.

90. *MBh(Bh)* 12.136, 138; *MBh(R)* 12.138, 142; *MBh(C)* 12.5055-6.
See No. 58.

90A. *MBh(Bh)* 12. 137, 89; *MBh(Bh)* 12. 139, 92; *MBh(C)* 12. 5226.
See No. 137.

91. *MBh(Bh)* 12.137, 90; *MBh(R)* 12.139, 93; *MBh(C)* 12.5227. *Cf. No.* 92.

ku-mitre[1] *nā'sti*[2] *viśvāsaḥ ku-bhāryāyāṃ kuto ratiḥ*,[3]
ku-rājye[4] *nirvṛttir nā'sti*[5] *ku-deśe*[6] *na prajīvyate*.[7]

One should not trust a bad friend;[8] what enjoyment can one have from a bad wife ? There is no happiness in a bad kingdom; there is no hope for livelihood in a bad country.

This maxim occurs in the *CS* version, in three texts of the *CN* version and in one text of the *CR* version which was translated into Tibetan and included in the Tanjur, viz. *CSr* 3.53, *CNP II* 241, *CNG* 158 *cb/ad*, *CNPh* 132 (*d* missing with the exception of the word *jīvitam*) and *CRT* 8.3 *cb/ad*.

Also found in GP 1.115, 4 *cb/ad*.

The various variants are unimportant with the exception of one in *a*; MBh(R), MBh(*C*), as well as *CNP II, CNG, CRT* have *kuputre* (bad son) instead of *kumitre* (bad friend). Another variant in *d* is often repeated in MBh(R), MBh(*C*) and some *C* texts.

The *C* text was undoubtedly borrowed from MBh, but not in its purest form. It is nearer to the Vulgata than to the classical MBh text as included in the Bhandarkar edition. (*Cf.* the previous stanza: No. 137).

FOOTNOTES TO NO. 91:

[1]*kuputre* MBh(R), MBh(C), *CNP II*; *kumitraṃ CSr.*[2] *kāsya CRT.* [3]*kutaḥ sukham CNP I.* [4]*kuputre* (°*pā*° *CNG*) *CRT*, GP, *CNG*; *kurāja CNPh.* [5]*ni*° *nā*° tr. *CSr*; *kasya CRT.* [6]*kurājye* (°*je CRT*), *CNG*, GP. [7]*nā'sti jivikā* MBh(R), MBh(C), *CNP II. nā'sti jivitam CSr, CNG, CNPh, CRT*, GP. [8]or a bad son. *kumitre* seems to be better; that can be seen from next maxim. See No. 92.

For other variants see *CSr* 3.53 and MBh(Bh) 12.137, 90.

92. *MBh*(*Bh*) 12.137, 92; *MBh*(*R*) 12.138, 95; *MBh* (*C*) 12.5229. *Cf. No.* 1 and 91.

sā bhāryā ya priyaṃ brūte sa putro yatra nirvṛtiḥ,
[1]*tan mitraṃ yatra viśvāsaḥ sa deśo yatra jīvyate.*

She, indeed, is a (true) wife who speaks pleasingly; he is a (true) son who makes one happy; he is a (true) friend whom one can trust; that is indeed a (true) country where one can live (where one could earn his livelihood.)

This maxim occurs in the *CR* version, viz. in *CRr* 1.26. and in one text of the *CN* version, viz. in *CN*Śap 70.

No variants occur in this maxium but the *CR* text is different in *cd* and therefore partly forms a different maxim.

It seems that the *CR* text was influenced by the MBh text, while the *CN* text was borrowed directly from MBh.

FOOTNOTES TO NO. 92:

[1]*sa bhṛtyo yas tu cittajñas tadvijaṃ yat prarohati CRr.*

For other variants see *CRr* 1.26 and MBh(Bh) 12.137, 92.

93. *MBh*(*Bh*) 12.138, 18; *MBh*(*R*) 12.140, 18; *MBh*(*C*) 12.5264. (*Also MBh*(*R*) 1.142, 21; *MBh*(*C*) 1.5563).

[1]*vahed amitraṃ skandhena yāvat kāla-viparyayaḥ,*[2]
[3]*athai'nam āgate kāle* [4]*bhindyād ghaṭam ivā'śmani.*

One should carry his foe on (his) shoulders as long as the time is unfavourable; when, however, the right moment occurs one should (knock him down and) smash him on the stone like an earthen jar.

This well-known maxim occurs in the *CR* and *CS* versions and in one text of the *CN* version, viz. in *CRr* 5.28, *CSr* 2.10 and *CNI I* 127 *ab* (only).

Similar thoughts are found in the Kāmandakīya Nītiśāstra 10.36, Pañc (PRE 3. 93, PP 3.213, PtsK 3.247 and 252, PT 3.107, PTem 3.94, PN 3.56, PS 3.66) and H(HJ 4.65)

The Mahābhārata *śloka* was also adapted in the Pāli and Burmese literature of Burma and in the Tibetan and Mongolian literature: LN 86, DhN 212, RN 104, NKy 115, NM 3.1, Subhāṣita-ratnanidhi 186 (117 in JRASB).

The variants which occur in this maxim are numerous and important.

The *C* text does not follow exactly the MBh text; in *a* it follows the Pañc text, but undoubtedly was influenced by MBh.

FOOTNOTES TO NO. 93:

[1]*skandhenā'pi vahec chatrum* *CRr*, *cf.* Pañc, H. [2]*kālasya paryayah* MBh (C), MBh (R) (both places). [3]*tatah pratyāgate* MBh (R). MBh (C) Ādi parvan; *prāptakālantu vijñaya* MBh (R), MBh (C) Śānti-parvan; *tam eva kāle-samprāpte CRr.* [4]*bhindhyādhyata* MBh (R) 12.140, 18.

For other variants see *CRr* 5.28, *CSr* 2.10 and MBh (Bh) 12.138, 18.

94. *MBh*(*Bh*) 12.138, 24; *MBh*(*R*) 12.140, 24; *MBh*(*C*) 12. 5270. (*Also MBh* (*Bh*) *App. I to I No.* 81, 16-7 and 12. 84, 42; *MBh*(*R*) 1.142, 8 *and* 12.83, 48; *MBh*(*C*) 1. 5550 *and* 12. 3173-4.

nā'sya[1] *chidram* [2]*paro*[3] *vidyād vidyāc chidram parasya tu,*
gūhet kūrma ivā'ṅgāni [4]*rakṣed vivaramāt manaḥ.*

The enemy should not know his (the king's) weaknesses but (the king) should know the weaknesses of his enemy; he should conceal (before the enemy) the organization (limbs) of his government, similarly as the tortoise does it with its limibs; he should shield his own weaknesses.

This maxim occurs in the *CS* version, viz in *CSr* 2.7.

Also found in Mn. 7.105 (and *nibandha-s* : Kṛtyakalpataru of Bhaṭṭa Lakṣmīdhara, Rājadharma-kaṇḍa 152.2-3 and Vīramitrodaya, Rājanītiprakāśa 117.8-9).

The Mahābhārata *śloka* was also adapted in the Pāli and Burmese literature of Burma: LN 76, DhN 224 and NKy 106.

The MBh texts contain several important variants in *ab* and the *CSr* text in *d*.

The *C* text was undoubtedly influenced by the classical MBh text as reconstructed in the Bhandarkar edition or the Mn text.

FOOTNOTES TO NO. 94:

[1]*nā'tma* MBh (R) 12.140, 24, MBh (C) 12.5270, *CSr.* [2]*paraḥ paśyec l chidreṇa* (°*dreṣu* MBh (Bh) 12.84, 42, MBh (C) 12.3173)*paramanviyāt* MBh (Bh) App. I, MBh (Bh) 12.84, 42, MBh (C) 1.5550 and 12.3173; *paraḥ paśyet chid-reṣu para*° MBh (R) 12.83, 48; [3]*ripur* MBh (R) 12.140, 24 and MBh (C) 12. 5270. [4]*parabhāvaṃ ca lakṣayet CSr.*

For other variants see *CSr* 2.7, MBh (Bh) 12.138, 24, App.I to I; No. 81; 16-7 and *JSAIL* 27 (*JAOS* 79. 247-8; No. 22).

95. *MBh*(*Bh*) 12.138, 33; *MBh*(*R*) 12.140, 33; *MBh*(*C*) 12. 5279-80. (*Also MBh* (*Bh*) *App. I to I, No.* 81, 165-6; *MBh*(*R*) 1.142, 80-1; *MBh*(*C*) 1.5622).

[1]*bhītavat saṃvidhātavyaṃ yāvad bhayam anā'gatam,*[2]
āgataṃ[3] *tu*[4] [5]*bhayaṃ dṛṣṭvā*[6] [7]*prahartavyam abhītavat.*[8]

As long as the (cause) of fear is not imminent, one (*i.e.* the king) should act as if he were terrified; when however the cause of fear is imminent, he must attack fearlessly.

This maxim occurs is the *CV* and *CR* versions and in four texts of the *CN* version, viz. in *CVr* 5.3, *CRr* 8.42, *CNP II* 185, *CNI I* 189, *CNG* 177, *CNT IV* 250.

Also found in GP 1.115, 45, Pañc (PP 1.170, PD 307. 109-10), H (HJ 1.58 and 4.17), and Vet 11.7 (203).

The Mahābhārata *śloka* was also adapted in the Tibetan literature : NM 2.6.

The maxim contains several important variants, some of them being identical in some *C*, Pañc and H texts.

The *C* text, similarly as the Pañc H and Vet texts, were directly influenced by MBh. but it is impossible to conclude from what text the Cāṇakya maxim was borrowed directly.

FOOTNOTES TO NO. 95:

[1]*tāvad bhayeṣu* (*bhoyadhi CRr*; [0]*yat tu* HJ 4.17, *CNP II*; *bhayasya* PP, HJ, GP, Vet) *bhetavyam CVr, CRr, CNG, CNP II*, PP, HJ, Vet, GP; *tāvad bhayaṃ* (°*bhda*°) *ca setavyaṃ yāvabhda*° *CNI I.* [2]*bhayasam ā*° *CNP II.* [3]*utpanne* GP. [4]*ca* HJ. [5]*bhaye tivre vai hy abhitavat* GP. [6]*vīkṣya* HJ. [7]*naraḥ kuryād yatho'citaṃ* HJ 1.58; *tat kāle ca bhayaṃ tyajet* PD. [8]*abhitavam* HJ 4.17; *aśekitaiḥ CNI I*; *aśaṅkayā CNG*; *aśaṅkitaiḥ* PP. Vet.

For other variants see *CVr* 5.3, *CRr* 8.42, MBh(Bh) 12.138, 33, App. I to I, 165-6 and *JSAIL* 24 (*JAOS* 77. 179-80; Nos. 145-6).

95A. *MBh*(*Bh*) 12.138, 37; *MBh*(*R*) 12.140, 37; *MBh*(*C*) 12.5283-4.

See No. 138.

96. *MBh*(*Bh*) 12.138, 58; *MBh*(*R*) 12.140, 58; *MBh*(*C*) 12.5305.

[1]*ṛṇa-śeṣo'gni-śeṣaś*[2] *ca* [3]*śatru-śeṣas*[4] *tathai'va ca,*
[5]*punaḥ* [6]*punar vivardheta svalpo'py anivāritaḥ.*

The (unpaid) balance of a debt, the (smoldering) remainder of fire and the remnant of (undefeated) foes, if unhindered, grow up a new in a short time.

This maxim occurs in the *CR*, *CN* and *CS* versions, viz. in *CRr* 8.45, *CNr* 38, *CSr* 3.58.

Also found in Pañc (PRE 3.99, PP 3.219, Pts 3.178, PT 3.114, PS 3.69, PN 3.59).

This stanza was also adapted in the Tibetan, Pāli and Burmese literature of Burma: NM 3.3, LN 87, DhN 234, NKy 116.

Variants which occur in this maxim are numerous and important, in particular in *cd*. The *C* text does not follow any particular text but is nearer to the Pañc text (PT and Pts) than to the MBh text.

It is impossible to conclude from what text *C* borrowed this stanza; it is certain that it was influenced by the Pañc or MBh text.

FOOTNOTES TO NO. 96:

[1]*ṛṇaśeṣam agniśeṣaṁ* (*cā'gni°* PS, Pts) MBh (R), Pañc; *vyādhiśeṣo CRr*. [2]*agni-śeṣaṁ CSr*. [3]*śatroḥ śeṣa ṛṇasya ca CRr*; *vyādhiśeṣas* (*°ṣaṃ* PRE PS) *ta° CNr*, *CSr*, PRE, PS. [4]*śesaṃ* MBh (R), MBh (C), PP, PT, Pts. [5]*punaḥ punaḥ pravardhante* (*°rteta CRr*, PT) MBh (R), MBh (C), *CRr*, Pts, PT; *punaś ca vardhate yasnāt CNr*, *CSr*; *vyādhiśeṣaṁ* (*ariśe°* PRE, PS) *ca niḥśeṣaṁ* PP, PRE, PS. [6]*tasmāt śeṣaṁ akārayet* MBh (R); *tasmāc cheṣaṁ na dhārayet* (*ca kārayet CNr*, *CSr*; *na kā°* PT) MBh (C), *CNr*, *CSr*, PT, Pts; *tasmān niḥśeṣam ācaret CRr*; *kṛtvā prājño na sīdati* PP, PRE, PS.

For other variants see *CRr* 8.45, *CNr* 38, *CSr* 3.58 and MBh (Bh) 12.138, 58.

97. *MBh*(*Bh*) 12.138, 65; *MBh*(*R*) 12.140, 66; *MBh*(*C*) 12.5313. (*Also MBh*(*Bh*) 3.29, 30; *MBh*(*R*) 3.28, 31; *MBh*(*C*) 3.1059).

mṛdunā sumṛduṃ[1] *hanti*[2] *mṛdunā hanti*[3] *dāruṇam*,
nāsādhyaṃ mṛdunā kiṃcit tasmāt tīkṣṇataraṃ mṛdu.[4]

Gentleness may destroy a mild person; gentleness may destroy a hard person; there is nothing that gentleness cannot achieve; therefore, a gentle person is the stronger (more forcible) one.

This maxim occurs in the *CS* version and in two texts of the *CR* version, of which one was translated into Tibetan and included in the Tanjur, viz. in *CSr* 3.40, *CRC* 7.56 and *CRT* 7.27.

Also found in a different version in GP 1.114, 49.

The Mahābhārata *śloka* was also adapted, in addition to *CRT*, in the Tibetan and Pāli literature : NM 6.15, DhN 64.

The texts contain several variants of no great importance.

One of such variants occurs in the Vulgata text of the MBh; *CSr* follows that text.

The *C* text was undoubtedly borrowed directly from the Vulgata of MBh.

The maxim is closely connected with the previous and following maxims of the Śānti-parvan, where it also appears.

FOOTNOTES TO NO. 97:

[1]*mārdavaṃ* MBh(Bh) 3.29, 30; *dāruṇaṃ* MBh(R) 3.28, 31, MBh(C) 3.1059; *mṛdurṇe'va* (°*nai'va CSr, CRC,* MBh(C) *mṛduṃ* MBh(R), MBh(C) (both in Śānti-parvan), *CSr, CRT, CRC.* [2]*chindhi* MBh(R), MBh(C) (both in Śānti-parvan). [3]*hantya*° MBh(R) 3.28, 31, MBh(C) 3.1059. [4]°*taro mṛduḥ* MBh(R), MBh(*C*) (both in Śānti-parvan), MBh(Bh) 3.29, 30, *CSr*; °*tibrataraṁ mṛdu* MBh(R) 3.28, 31; °*tīkṣṇāt paro mṛduḥ CRC, CRT.*

For other variants see *CSr* 3.40, MBh(Bh) 12.138, 65 and 3.29, 30.

98. *MBh*(*Bh*) *ad* 12.142, 10; 368*, *MBh*(*R*) 12.144, 17; *MBh*(*C*) 12.5509.

[1]*yasya bhāryā gṛhe nā'sti sādhvī' ca priyasādini,*
araṇyaṃ tena gantavyaṃ yathā'raṇyaṃ tathā gṛham.

He who does not have in his home a wife who is chaste and agreeable in speech should go into the wilderness; (for such a person) there is no difference between a wilderness and a home.

This maxim occurs in the *CN* version, viz. in *CNr* 42. Also found in Pañc (PP 4.44, Pts 4.83, PtsK 4.54).

Two important variants occur in the text in *a* and *b*. The same variants occur in the *C* and Pañc texts.

The *C* text was, therefore, not borrowed directly from MBh, but from Pañc (or Pañc from *C*).

FOOTNOTES TO NO. 98:

[1]*mātā yasya gṛ*° *CNr,* Pañc. [2]*bhāryā CNr,* Pañc.

For other variants see *CNr* 42 and MBh(Bh) *ad* 12.142, 10; 368*.

99. *MBh*(*Bh*) 12.144, 6; *MBh*(*R*) 12.148, 6; *MBh*(*C*) 12.5566-7.

[1]*mitaṃ dadāti hi pitā mitaṃ mātā*[2] *mitaṃ sutaḥ,*
amitasya tu[3] *dātāraṃ*[4] *bhartāraṃ kā na pūjayet.*[5]

Limited are the gifts (to a woman) given by the father, mother and son; what woman, therefore, will not treat with respect the husband who gives without limit ?

This maxim appears in two texts of the *CN* version, viz. in *CNP II* 220 and *CNT IV* 175.

Also found in R (2.39, 30; RG 2.38 25 and 4.20, 4), PtsK 3.156, VCsr 30.9 and Vet 4.19.

The various variants which occur in this text are unimportant with the exception of some important variants in *b*. These variants occur in MBh(R), MBh(C), R, PtsK, VC and Vet. In *b* the word *mātā* is changed to *bhrātā*. The *CNP II* text follows this text but also introduces a change in *a* by which it keeps also *mātā*; therefore, according to this text "limited are the gifts given by the father, mother, brother and son."

The *C* text was undoubtedly borrowed with some changes directly from the Vulgata text of the MBh.

FOOTNOTES TO NO. 99:

[1]*mitaṃ dadyāt pitā mātā CNP II.* [2]*bhrātā MBh* (R), MBh (C), *CNP II*, R, PtsK, Vet, VC. [3]*hi* MBh (C) RG, PtsK; *ca CNP II.* [4]*dātaikaḥ* RG 2.38, 25. [5]*sukhyasyārthe patiḥ striyāḥ* RG 2.38, 25.

For other variants see MBh(Bh) 12.144, 6. Also see W. Hopkins, *AJPh* 20.29 and par. 6 E above.

100. *MBh*(*Bh*) 12.152, 4; *MBh*(*R*) 12. 158, 4; *MBh*(*C*) 12.5880.

lobhāt[1] *krodhaḥ prabhavati lobhāt kāmaḥ pravartate,*
lobhān mohaś ca māyā ca [2]*mānas ṭamtambhaḥ parāsutā.*

Covetousness causes anger; covetousness causes lust; covetousness causes loss of judgment, deception, pride, arrogance and apathy....

This maxim occurs in one text of the *CN* version, viz. in *CNMN* 132. (*Cf.* Bhojaprabandha 2).

Variants are unimportant.

The *C* text was undoubtedly borrowed directly from *MBh*. However, the sentence is not finished because the following stanzas in MBh give additional faults caused by covetousness. Also the preceding stanza deals with covetousness.

FOOTNOTES TO NO. 100:

[1]*lobhā CNMN.* [2]*manaḥ sta°* MBh (C).

For other variants see MBh(Bh) 12.152, 4.

101. *MBh*(*Bh*) 12.154, 34; *MBh*(*R*) 12.160, 34; *MBh*(*C*) 12. 5959.

See No. 34.

102. *MBh*(*Bh*) 12.156, 26; *MBh* (*R*) 12.162, 26; *MBh*(*C*) 12. 6002.

See No. 7.

103. *MBh(Bh)* 12.168, 15; *MBh(R)* 12.174, 16; *MBh(C)* 12.6471-2.

See No. 85.

104. *MBh(Bh)* 12.168, 18 *ef* + 460*; *MBh* (*R*) 12.174, 20; *MBh(C)* 12.6475.

sukhasyā'nantaraṃ duḥkhaṃ duḥkhasyā'nantaraṃ sukham,
[1]*sukha-duḥkhe*[2] *manuṣyāṇāṃ cakravat parivartataḥ.*[3]

Sorrow follows immediately after joy; joy follows immediately after sorrow; joys and sorrows of men undergo perpetual cycles as if on wheels.

This maxim occurs in the *CR* and *CS* versions and in one text of the *CN* version, viz. in *CRr* 6.51, *CSr* 2. 48 and *CNP II* 49.

Also found in GP 1.113, 61. Similarly, preceding and following stanzas in MBh, as well as MBh (Bh) 3.245, 13 & 15; 3.247, 45; 12.168, 20; MBh (R) 12.25, 23 and 24, etc., HJ 1.184, Meghadūta 106 *cd*, Subh 99 (IS 7082), TP 481 (IS 7083), etc.

This stanza contains a very well known thought which was also adapted in the Tibetan and Old Javanese literatures viz. in ShD 64, Ślt 76.

The variants occurring in this stanza are unimportant.

The *C* text was undoubtedly borrowed directly from MBh.

FOOTNOTES TO NO. 104:

[1]*sukhaṃ duḥkhaṃ* GP. [2] °*duḥkhe CNP II.* [3]*parivartate CNP II,* GP.

For other variants see *CRr* 6.51, *CSr* 2.48 and *MBh* (*Bh*) 12.168.18 *ef* and 460*.

105. *MBh(Bh)* 12.168, 31; *MBh(R)* 12.174, 42; *MBh(C)* 12.6497-8.

See No. 20.

106. *MBh(Bh)* 12.169, 33; *MBh(R)* 12.175, 35; *MBh(C)* 12. 6557. *Also* *MBh(Bh)* —; *MBh(R)* 12.276, 35; *MBh(C)* 12.9962).

nā'sti vidyā-samaṃ cakṣur nā'sti [1]*vidyā-samaṃ balam,*[2]
nā'sti rāga-samaṃ duḥkhaṃ nā'sti tyāga-samaṃ sukham.

There is no other eye equal to that of knowledge ; no other force equal to that of knowledge; no other suffering equal to that of desire; no other joy equal to that of renunciation.

This maxim occurs in the *CN* version among verses, the Cāṇakya's authenticity of which is doubted, viz. in *CNr* "U."

Also found in the Varāha-purāṇa (Bombay ed.) 153.

The MBh(R) and MBh(*C*) texts, similarly as the Varāha-purāṇa, have a different text in *b*. The *C* text follows the latter text. Other variants are unimportant.

The *C* text was undoubtedly borrowed directly from the Vulgata text of MBh.

FOOTNOTES TO NO. 106:

[1]*satya-samaṃ tapaḥ* MBh(R) 12.175, 35, MBh(C) 12.6557, *CNr*, Var. [2]*phalam* MBh(C) 12.9962.

For other variants see *CNr* "U" and MBh (Bh) 12.169, 33.

107. *MBh*(*Bh*) 12.174, 7; *MBh*(*R*) 12.181, 7; *MBh*(*C*) 12. 6751. (*Also MBh*(*Bh*) —; *MBh*(*R*) 12. 322, 7; *MBh*(*C*) 12. 12144).

pulākā iva dhānyeṣu puttikā[1] *iva pakṣiṣu,*[2]
[3]*tadvidhās te*[4] *manuṣyeṣu*[5] [6]*yeṣāṃ dharmo na kāraṇam.*

Those whose actions are not prompted by *dharma* should be considered among men in the same way as seedless grain is considered among corn, or as white ants are considered among winged animals.

This maxim occurs in the *CS* version, viz. in *CSr* 1.99.

Also found in Pañc (PP 3.90, Pts 3.98, PtsK 3.99).

The Mahābhārata *śloka* was also adapted in the Old Javanese literature : SS 51.

Several important variants occur in this stanza, particularly in *d*, but none of them changes the meaning of the maxim.

The *C* text was undoubtedly borrowed from MBh but with some variants.

FOOTNOTES TO NO. 107:

[1]*pūtyaṇḍā* MBh(R) 12.322, 7, MBh(*C*) 12.12144; *kūtikā* PP; *pūtikā Pts, PtsK*. [2]*jantuṣu CSr*. [3]*maśakā iva martyeṣu* Pañc. [4]*tādṛśas te CSr*.[5] *manuṣyāṇāṃ* MBh(R) 12.181, 7, MBh(*C*) 12.6751. [6]*ye ca dharmavahis kṛtāḥ CSr*.

For other variants see *CSr* 1.99 and MBh(Bh) 12.174, 7.

108. *MBh*(*Bh*) 12.174, 10; *MBh*(*R*) 12, 181, 10; *MBh*(*C*) 12. 6754. (*Also MBh*(*Bh*)—; *MBh*(*R*) 12.322, 10; *MBh*(*C*) 12.12147).

yena yena yathā yadyat[1] [2]*purā karma samācitam,*[3]
[4]*tat tad eva naro bhuṅkte* [5]*nityaṃ vihitam ātmanā.*

Wherever and by whatever means (and under what circumstances) he has performed acts formerly [in previous existence] in the same manner will be enjoy them as reward (in his next life), since he alone has performed [is responsible for] this act.

This maxim occurs in one text of the *CR* version which usually follows closely the GP text and could be considered as an extract from the Bṛhaspati-saṃhitā of the GP, viz. in *CRCa II* 28.

Also found in GP 1.118, 18.

The various variants which occur in this maxim are important. The *C* and GP texts have a different reading in *d*.

The *C* text is identical with GP, but was certainly influenced by MBh.

FOOTNOTES TO NO. 108:

[1]*yadvat* GP. [2]*karmasu niścitam* MBh(R) 12.322, 10. [3]*samīhitam* MBh (R) 12.181, 10, MBh(C) 12.6754; *suniścitam CRCa II*, GP, MBh(C) 12.12147. [4]*tattadevattaraṃ* (*devāntarā* GP; *vi° CRCa II*) *bhu°* MBh (R) 12.322, 10, MBh(C) 121.47, *CRCa II*, GP. [5]*svayam āhitam ātmanaḥ CRCa II*, GP.

For other variants see MBh(Bh) 12.174, 10.

109. *MBh*(*Bh*) 12.174, 12; *MBh*(*R*) 12.181, 12; *MBh*(*C*) 12.6756. (*Also MBh*(*Bh*) —; 13. 17,23; *MBh*(*R*) 12.322, 12; 13.7, 23-4; *MBh*(*C*) 12.12149; 13.366-7).

acodyamānāni yathā[1] *puṣpāṇi ca phalāni ca,*
[2]*svakālaṃ*[3] *nā'tivartante tathā*[4] *karma purā-kṛtam.*[5]

As flowers and fruits, not urged by anybody, never pass their usual time (i.e. bloom at the proper time—in spring), so also the formerly performed acts (i.e. acts performed in previous existence) appear at the proper time.

This maxim occurs in the *CR* version, viz. in *CRr* 6.44.

Also found in GP 1.113, 50 *cd/ef*.

The Mahābhārata *śloka* was also adapted in the Old Javanese literature: SS 360.

The variants which occur in this stanza are unimportant.

The *C* text was undoubtedly borrowed directly from MBh but not in its purest form.

FOOTNOTES TO NO. 109:

[1]*tathā* GP. [2]*svayaṃ svakāle pacyante CRr*. [3]*svaṃ kālaṃ* MBh (C), MBh(R) in Śānti-parvan (both places). [4]*yathā* GP. [5]*karmāṇi dehinām CRr*.

For other variants see *CRr* 6.44 and MBh(Bh) 12.174, 12.

110. *MBh*(*Bh*) 12. 174, 14; *MBh*(*R*) 12. 181, 14; *MBh*(*C*) 12.6758. (*Also* *MBh*(*Bh*) —; *MBh*(*R*) 12.322, 14; *MBh*(*C*) 12.12151).

ātmanā vihitaṃ[1] *duḥkham ātmanā vihitaṃ sukham,*
garbhaśayyām upādāya bhujyate paurvadehikam.[2]

One alone destines his sorrows; one alone destines his joys; from the moment one lies in his mother's womb, one begins to enjoy the acts performed in one's former life.

This maxim occurs in one text of the *CR* version which usually follows closely the GP text and could be considered as an extract from the Bṛhaspati-saṃhitā of the GP, viz. in *CRCa II* 29. This *CRCa II* text quotes No. 108 immediately before this one ; both deal with former life.

Also found in GP 1.113, 19.

Variants are unimportant.

The *C* text was undoubtedly borrowed directly from MBh.

FOOTNOTES TO NO. 110;

[1] °*nā'pi hitaṃ CRCa II.* [2]*bhajate pūrva*° MBh(R) 12.322, 14, MBh(C) 12.12151; *bhuṃjate pūrva*° *CRCa II*; *bhuṅkte vai paur*° GP.

For other variants see MBh(Bh) 12.174, 14.

110A. *MBh*(*Bh*) 12.174, 15; *MBh*(*R*) 12.181, 15; *MBh*(*C*) 12.6759.

See No. 139.

111. *MBh*(*Bh*) 12.174, 16; *MBh*(*R*) 12, 181, 16; *MBh*(*C*) 12.6760. (*Also* *MBh*(*Bh*) —; 13.17.22; *MBh*(*R*) 12.322, 16; 13.7, 22-3; *MBh*(*C*) 12.12153; 13.365).

yathā dhenu-sahasreṣu vatso vindati[1] *mātaram,*
tathā[2] *pūrvakṛtaṃ*[3] *karma* [4]*kartāram anugacchati.*[5]

As the calf finds his mother from among a thousand milch cows, so an act performed in one's previous life follows the doer in his new life.

This maxim occurs in the *CV* and *CR* versions and three texts of the *CN* version, viz. in *CVr* 13.14, *CRr* 6.47, *CNP II* 247, *CNG* 233 and *CNT IV* 261.

Also found in GP 1.113, 53-4, Padma-purāṇa, Bhūmi-khaṇḍa 81.47 and Pañc (PP 2.135, Pts 2.125, PtsK 2.134, PT 2.106, PTem 2.95).

The Mahābhārata *śloka* was also adapted in the Old Javanese literature: SS 359.

The various variants are of no great importance.

The *C* text was undoubtedly borrowed directly from MBh.

FOOTNOTES TO NO. 111:

[1]*gacchati CVr; dhavati CNP II.*[2]*evaṃ* MBh (R) 13.7, 23, PP. GP; *yathā* PtsK. [3]*yac ca kṛ° CVr; purākṛtaṃ* PtsK; *kartṛsahasreṣu* PT, PTem. °*kartāraṃ karma vindati* PT, PTem. [5]*anuvindati* PtsK; *anutiṣṭhati* GP.

For other variants see *CVr* 13.14, *CRr* 6.47 and MBh (Bh) 12.174, 16.

112. *MBh*(*Bh*) 12. 219, 22; *MBh*(*R*) 12.226, 22; *MBh*(*R*) 12.8209-10.

[1]*labdha-vyāny eva labhate ganta-vyāny eva gacchati,*
prāpta-vyāny eva prāpnoti[2] *duḥkhāni ca sukhāni ca.*

One obtains only what he was destined to obtain; one goes only where he was destined to go; only those sorrows and joys are experienced which were detined to be experienced.

This maxim occurs in the *CR* version, viz. in *CRr* 6.42.

Also found in GP 1.113, 49 Pañc (PT 2.120, PTem 2.109).

Variants are unimportant.

The *C* text was undoubtedly borrowed directly from MBh.

FOOTNOTES TO NO. 112:

[1]*labya-vyāny* MBh (R), MBh (*C*). [2]*cā'pnoti* MBh (R), MBh (*C*).

For other variants see *CRr* 6.42 and MBh (Bh) 12.219, 22.

112A *MBh* (*Bh*) 12.263;11 *aδ* 12.166,25 (446*; 27-8); *aδ* 12. 167, 20 (449*; 32-3).

See No. 147

113. *MBh*(*Bh*) —; *MBh*(*R*) 12. 276, 35; *MBh*(*C*) 12. 9962.

See No. 106.

113A. *MBh*(*Bh*) 12.284, 21; *MBh* (*R*) 12.295, 21; *MBh*(*C*) 12.10842.

See No. 148.

113B. *MBh*(*Bh*) 12.309, 45; *MBh*(*R*) 12.321, 46; *MBh*(*C*) 12. 12089.

See No. 149.

114. *MBh*(*Bh*) —; *MBh*(*R*) 12.322, 7; *MBh*(*C*) 12.12144.

See No. 107.

115. *MBh*(*Bh*) —; *MBh*(*R*) 12.322, 10; *MBh*(*C*) 12.12147.

See No. 108.

116. *MBh*(*Bh*) —; *MBh*(*R*) 12.322, 12; *MBh*(*C*) 12.12149.
See No. 109.

117. *MBh*(*Bh*) —; *MBh*(*R*) 12.322, 14; *MBh*(*C*) 12.12151.
See No. 110.

117A. *MBh*(*Bh*) —; *MBh*(*R*) 12. 322, 15; *MBh*(*C*) 12.12152.
See No. 139.

118. *MBh*(*Bh*) —; *MBh*(*R*) 12. 322, 16; *MBh* (*C*) 12.12153.
See No. 111.

119. *MBh*(*Bh*) —; *MBh*(*R*) 12. 330, 2; *MBh*(*C*) 12.12483.
See No. 20.

120. *MBh*(*Bh*) 12. 317, 20; *MBh*(*R*) 12.330, 20; *MBh*(*C*) 12. 12501.
See No. 74.

121. *MBh*(*Bh*) 13.7, 22; *MBh*(*Bh*)13.7, 22-3; *MBh*(*C*)13.365.
See No. 111.

122. *MBh*(*Bh*) 13. 7, 23; *MBh*(*R*)13.7, 23-4; *MBh*(*C*) 13. 366-7.
See No. 109.

123. *MBh*(*Bh*) 13.21, 19; *MBh*(*R*) 13.20, 21; *MBh*(*C*) 13. 1506.
See No. 127.

123A. *MBh* (*Bh* 13.24, 90; *MBh*(*R*) 13.23,93; *MBh*(*C*) 13.1664
See No. 150

124. *MBh*(*Bh*)13.38, 16; *MBh*(*R*) 13.38, 16; *MBh*(*C*)13. 2217.

anarthitvān manuṣyāṇāṃ bhayāt[1] *parijanasya ca,*
maryādāyām amaryādāḥ[2] *striyas*[3] *tiṣṭhanti bhartṛṣu.*[3]

Women who (in general) do not know the bounds of morality, remain in the bounds of morality and with their husbands (only when) no other men solicit them, or if they fear their attendants.

This maxim occurs in the *CR* version, viz. in *CRr* 8.87.

Also found in GP 1.115, 65 and in Pañc (Pts 1.142, PtsK 1.158).

The Mahābhārata *śloka* was also adapted in the Old Javanese literature: SS 435.

Variants are unimportant.

The *C* text was undoubtedly borrowed directly from MBh.

FOOTNOTES TO NO. 124:

[1]*bhayān* MBh(R); *bhiyā* GP. [2]*arthādapetamaryadā* GP. [3]*strayas* GP. [4]*bharttṛṁṣu* MBh(R); *sarvadā* Pañc.

For other variants see *CRr* 8.87.

125. *MBh*(*Bh*) 13.38, 25; *MBh*(*R*) 13.38, 25; *MBh* (*C*) 13.2226.

See No. 67.

126. *MBh*(*Bh*) 13.46, 307*+13.46, 5 *cd*; *MBh*(*R*) 13.46, 5-6; *MBh* (*C*) 13.2488-9.

[1]*striyo yatra ca pūjyante ramante tatra devatāḥ,*
[2]*apūjitāś ca yatraitāḥ sarvās tatrā'phalāḥ kriyāḥ.*

Where women are honoured, there the gods rejoice, but where they are not honoured, there all religious rites are ineffectual.

This maxim occurs in one *CV* text which adds to the classical text of the Cāṇakya-nīti-darpaṇa a number of MBh and Mn stanzas, viz. in *CVNS* 14.14.

Also found in Mn 3.56 and *nibandha-s* (Parāśara-dharmasaṃhitā 1.12; 111.18-9, Smṛtimuktāphalam 143.24, Bālambhaṭṭi, Vivāha-prakarṇa 212. 22 and 230.23, Vivāda-ratnākara 418.1211, Vyavahārakalpataruḥ, Prajñapasthala 130). This maxim forms a part of a longer extract from Mn.

The text has two minor variants in *a* and *b*. Both these variants occur in Mn and the *C* text.

The *C* text, which was described in detail in *JSAIL* 27 *JAOS* 79.241 sqq.) undoubtedly was borrowed directly from Mn and not from MBh.

FOOTNOTES TO NO. 126:

[1]*yatra nāryas tu pū° CVNS*, Mn. [2]*yatraitās tu na pūjyante CVNS*, Mn.

For other variants see *JSAIL* 27. (JAOS 79.241 sqq.; No. 11.).

127. *MBh*(*Bh*) *MBh*(*R*) 13.46, 14; *MBh*(*C*) 13. 2497. *Also MBh* (*Bh*) 13. 21, 19; *MBh*(*R*) 13.20, 21; *MBh* (*C*) 13.1506).

pitā rakṣati kaumāre bhartā rakṣati yauvane,
[1]*putrāś ca sthāvire bhāve*[2] [3]*na strī svātantryam arhati.*

The father protects (women) in maidenhood; the husband protects them in youth; the sons protect them in old age; a woman is never equipped to be free from control.

This maxim occurs in the *CR* version and in five texts of the *CN* version, viz. in *CRr* 8.64, *CNF* 58, *CNPh* 92, *CNI I* 155, *CNG* 180 and *CNL* 46.

Also found in R 2.39, 33, Mn 9.3, Baudhāyanadharmasūtra 2.2, 3, 45, Gautama-dharmasūtra 28.1, Vāsiṣṭhadharmaśāstra 5.3, Nārada-smṛti 13.31 and *nibandha-s*,[4] GP 1.115, 63, Padma-purāṇa, Sṛṣṭikhaṇḍa 54, 23 and H (HJ 1.128). It is a well known aphorism; similar thoughts were expressed often.[5]

The MBh text has some variants in *c* and *d* in MBh (R) 13.46, 14 and MBh(R) 13.20, 21. The *C* text follows with one minor variant the text of MBh (R) 13.46, 14 as well as the text of Mn. The variant occurring in *CRr* in *b* is nearer to Mn than to MBh.

The *C* text was undoubtedly borrowed directly from Mn but not in its purest form or from MBh(R) 13.46, 14.

FOOTNOTES TO NO. 127:

[1]*rakṣanti vardhake putrā CRr*; *rakṣanti sthāvire putrā* Mn. [2]*sthavirībhāve MBh* (*Bh*); *kāle* MBh(R) 13.20, 21, MBh(R) 13.1506. [3]*nā'sti strīṇāṃ svatantratā* MBh(R) 13.20, 21, MBh(C) 13.1506. [4]The numerous *nibandha-s* are quoted in *JSAIL* 27(*JAOS* 79.253). [5]*Cf. JSAIL* 27, *op. cit.*

For other variants see *CRr* 8.64, *JSAIL* 27 (*JAOS* 79, 252 sqq.; No. 28) and *JSAIL* 24 (*JAOS* 77.110 sqq.; No. 67).

128. *MBh*(*Bh*) 13.23. 14; *MBh*(*R*) 13.75, 31; *MBh*(*C*) 13. 3651-2.

See No. 7.

129. *MBh*(*Bh*) 13.107, 58; *MBh*(*R*) 13.104, 33; *MBh* (*C*) 13.4987.

See No. 46.

130. *MBh*(*Bh*)13.149,9; *MBh*(*R*)13. 163, 11;*MBh*(*C*)13.7607.

[1]*na'prāptakālo mriyate viddhaḥ śara-śatair api,*
[2]*tṛṇā'greṇā'pi*[3] *saṃspṛṣtaḥ prāptakālo na jīvati.*

If one's appropriate time has not come yet, he will not die even if pierced by hundreds of arrows; however, when the appropriate time comes one will not live even though touched by a blade of grass.

This maxim occurs in the *CR* version and in one text of the *CN* version, viz. in *CRr* 6.41 and *CNG* 232.

Also found in GP 1.113, 48, H(HJ 2.15), Nārada-pañcarātra 1.3, 20 and Ghaṭarpara's Nītisāra (GhN) 19. This is a well known thought expressed in many Sanskrit literary works. (*Cf*. *CRr* 6.42, Bhāgavata-purāṇa 7.2, 40, VCr 14.9, *cf*. Hopkins in *AJPh* 20.26).

Variants are unimportant.

The *C* text was undoubtedly borrowed directly from MBh but not in its purest form.

FOOTNOTES TO NO. 130:

[1]*nā'kāle mriyate jantur* HJ, GhN. [2]*kuśā°* *CRr*, HJ; *kuśakaṇtaviddho'pi* GhN. [3]*greṇaiva* HJ, NPR, GhN.

For other variants see *CRr* 6.41 and *JSAIL* 24 (*JAOS* 77.175; No. 127).

131. *MBh*(*Bh*) 14.44, 18; *MBh*(*R*) 14.44, 19; *MBh*(*C*) 14. 1230.

See No. 74.

132. *MBh*(*Bh*) 18.5, 48; *MBh*(*R*) 18.5, 61; *MBh*(*C*) 204-5.

See No. 20.

III *ADDENDUM TO THE DETAILED ANALYSIS OF STANZAS*[1]

133. *MBh(Bh)* 2. *ad* 6.75 (583*); *MBh* (*R*) 2.75.5.
asaṃbhave hemamasya jantos...
occurs also in one text of the *CN* version, viz. *CNG* 240.

Also found in HJ 1.27 and Māhānāṭaka 179.
The *C* text was influenced by MBh

134. *MBh(Bh)* 3. 70, 8; *MBh(R)* 3.72, 8; *MBh* (*C*) 3.2815.
sarvaḥ sarvaṃ[1] *na jānāti*[2] *sarvajño nā'sti kaścana,*[3]
nai'katra pariniṣṭhā'sti[4] *jñānasya puruṣe*[5] *kvacit.*

No one knows everything; no one is omniscient; never is knowledge in its entirety concentrated in one person.

Also found in PT 2. 143.

This maxim occurs in one text of the *CR* version, viz. in *CRBh II* 3.42.

The various variants which in this text are unimportant; they are mostly scribes' errors.

The *C* text was undoubtedly borrowed directly from MBh.

FOOTNOTES TO NO. 134:

[1]*savaṃ* MBh(R) printer's error; *sarva* *CRBh II.* *sarvas* PT; [2]*janāti* MBh (C). [3]*kaśca na* Böhtlingk in IS 6941 (wrongly); *kutracit CRBh II.* [4]*ca vittaṣṭhāsti* PT; *pariśiṣṭā'sti CRBh II.* [5]*puruṣah CRBh II.*

For other variants see MBh(Bh) 3.70, 8.

135. *MBh* (*Bh*) 3.245,13; *MBh* (*R*) 3.258, 13-4; *MBh* (*C*) 12. 15382-3.

sukḥaduḥkhe hi puruṣaḥ...
is ascribed in SRBh 382. 216 to *CV* 4.23 (?). II

Also found in BrDh 2.53.
This is probably a MBh verse wrongly ascribed to *C*

[1]After this study was sent to the Press the following stanzas which are identical in MBh and *C* were found.

136. *MBh(Bh)* 5.33, 26; *MBh(R)* 5. 32, 31; *MBh(C)* 5.996.

na hṛṣyaty tāma-saṃmāne[1] [2]*nā'vamānena*[3] *tapyate,*
hrada gāṅgo ivākṣobhyo yaḥ sa paṇḍita ucyate.

A man who does not rejoice at honours; a man who does not torment himself when treated contemptuously; a man who remains calm as a lake filled with water of the Gāṅga, is considered as a paṇḍita.

This maxim occurs in the *CR* version, viz. in *CRr* 6.32.

The first part of this maxim was also adapted in the Old Javanese literature: SS 312.

The wording of *a* in *C* is somewhat different from the usual wording of MBh, but the Southern recension of MBh (S with the exception of T_2 and G_2 in MBh (Bh)) has an identical text as *C*; the same text was also adapted in SS. Also in *b* of *C* same variants occur from the MBh text, but the north-western group (Kaśmirī) of the Northern Recension of the MBh (K in MBh (Bh) have *kapyati* instead of *tapyate.*

The *C* text was borrowed directly from a text of MBh but not in its purest form.

FOOTNOTES TO NO. 136:

[1]*na prahṛṣyati saṁmāne CRr,* Southern Recension of MBh, SS. [2]*nā'vamānaiḥ prakupyati CRr; nindito nānutapyate* SS. [3] °*māne na* MBh(R), MBh (*C*).

For other variants see *CRr* 6.32 and MBh(Bh) 5.33, 26.

137. *MBh(Bh)* 5. 33, 56; *MBh(R)* 5.32, 67; *MBh(C)* 5.1033

[1]*trividhāḥ puruṣā*[2] *rājann*[3] *uttamā'dhama-madhyamāḥ,*
niyojayed yathā vattāṃs[4] *trividheṣv eva karmasu.*

...men are of three sorts: they are superior, inferior and middling; therefore they should be accordingly employed in works of three kinds.

This maxim occurs in one text of the *CR* version, viz. *CRT* 5.11; this text was translated into Tibetan and included in the Tanjur.

Also found in HJ 2.69. Similar thoughts are found in the *CS* version and some texts of the *CN* version, viz. in *CSr* 1.73, *CNI I* 267 and *CNG* 79, as well as in the Rāmāyaṇa 6.6, 6, GP 1.112, 1 and Śabdakalpadruma *ad nītisāra.* The latter texts were also adapted in the Old Javanese literature, viz. NŚ 15.3.

The *CS* version is different from MBh in *a* and *c*; among other changes *C* uses in *a* the word *bhṛtyā* instead of *puruṣa*; by this change it expresses the thought of this maxim more clearly than the MBh text.

The *C* text was undoubtedly influenced by MBh.

FOOTNOTES TO NO. 137:

[1]*bhṛtyā bahu-vidhā jñeyā CSr* 1.73. [2]different recensions of MBh have instead *puruṣā*. [3]*rājan* MBh(*C*). [4]°*yet tathaivaitaṃs* HJ; °*te niyojyā yathā-yogyaṃ CSr*.

For other variants see MBh(Bh) 5.33, 56.

138. *MBh* (*Bh*) 5.36, 26; *MBh* (*R*) 5.35, 26; *MBh* (*C*) 5.1285

devadravyavināśena...

occurs also in the *CR* version (CRr 7.71). Also found in GP 1.114, 68.

The *C* text was influenced by MBh; GP has directly borrowed from MBh.

139. *MBh* (*Bh*) 5.38, 12 *ab/cd*; *MBh* (*R*) 5.37, 12; *MBh* (*C*) 5.1409.

pitur antaḥ puraṃ dadyān

occurs also in the *CS* version (*CSr* 82) and in two texts of the *CN* version viz. *CNPH* 13 and *CNL* 103.

The *C* text was directly borrowed from MBh.

140. *MBh* (*Bh*) 12.68, 40; *MBh*(*R*) 12.68, 40; *MBh*(*C*) 12.2573.

na hi jātvavaṃ antavyo

occurs also in one text of the *CV* version, viz. *CVNS* 16.12.

Also found in Mn 7.8, HJ 2.81 and *nibandha-s*.[1]

The *C* text was borrowed from Mn and not from MBh.

[1]Cf. above Study XXVI No. 19

141. *MBh* (*Bh*) 12.89, 4; *MBh* (*R*) 12.88, 4; *MBh* (*C*) 12.3305.

nadhudohaṃ duhedraṣṭraṃ

occurs also in one text of the *CR* version translated into Tibetan, viz. *CRT* 4.6. Similarly Rāmāyaṇa 6.16, 17.

The *C* text could have been influenced by MBh.

142. *MBh*(*Bh*) *ad* 12.112, 57 (265*); *MBh*(*R*) 12.111, 59; *MBh*(*C*) 12.4142-3.

munerapi vanasthasya[1] *svāni karmāṇi kurvataḥ,*
utpadyante[2] *trayaḥ pakṣā*[3] *nitro'dāsīna-śatravaḥ.*

Even an ascetic who lives in the woods and who performs his own acts will make [lit. raises three parties] friends, neutrals and enemies.

This maxim occurs in three texts of the *CN* version,viz. *CNP I* 250, *CNI I* 181 and *CNT IV* 239. Similar thoughts are expressed in MBh (Bh) 5.3, 69, MBh(R) 5.32, 80 and MBh (C) 5.1046.

The variants are unimportant.

The *C* text was undoubtedly borrowed directly from MBh.

FOOTNOTES TO NO. 142:
[1]*vanasthes ca CNP I.* [2]*utpādyante* MBh(R). [3]*puṃsāṃ CNP I.*
For other variants see MBh(Bh) *ad* 12.112, 57 (265-).

143. *MBh* (*Bh*) 12.124, 15; *MBh* (*R*) 12.124, 15; *MBh* (*C*) 12.4564.

śilena hi trayo lokāḥ...

occurs also in three texts of the *CN* version, viz. in *CNSC* 93, *CNŚI* 98, *CNS* 91.

Also found in SS 165.

The *C* text was directly borrowed from MBh.

144. *MBh*(*Bh*) 12. 137, 89; *MBh*(*R*) 12. 139, 92; *MBh*(*C*) 12. 5226.

ku-bhāryāṃ[1] *ca ku-putraṃ*[2] *ca ku-rājānaṃ ku-sauhṛdam,*[3]
ku-saṃbandhaṃ[4] *ku-deśaṃ*[5] *ca dūrataḥ parivarjayet.*

From afar one should avoid a bad wife, and a bad son, and a bad king, and a bad friend, and a bad kinsman, and a bad land.

This maxim appears in two texts of the *CN* version and in one text of the *CR* version, viz. in *CNG* 162, *CNI I* 78 and *CRT* 8.1. (The latter text was translated into Tibetan and included in the Tanjur). It also occurs in some *C* notebook MSs, viz. in *CnT II* 1.11, *CnT III* 1.11, *CnT VI* 11 and *CnT V* 9.

Also found in Har 1160 and GP 1.115, 1.

The Mahābhārata *śloka* was also adapted in addition to the Tibetan literature (*CRT* 8.1), to the Pāli and Burmese literature of Burma: LN 91, DhN 230, NKy 120.

The various texts contain several variants but they are not important; they consist mostly in placing *ku-bhāryā, ku-putra, ku-rājan, ku-sauhṛda, ku-saṃbandha* and *ku-deśa* in different places; the *C* texts and Har add *ku-mitra*; *CRT ku-saṅga* and GP *ku-kanyā*.

This stanza is closely connected with the following one (see No. 91).

The *C* text was undoubtedly borrowed directly from MBh with some changes influenced by other sources. The Pāli texts follow more closely the *C* text than the MBh text.

FOOTNOTES TO NO. 144:

[1]*kubhā* ca *CNI I* (scribe's error); *kumitraṃ* Har. [2]*kudeśaṃ CNG*, Har; *kumitraṃ CNI I, CRT, GP.* [3]*kuputrakaṃ* GP. *kubandhuṃ ca CNG*; *asaṃbandhaṃ CNI I*; *kusaṅgaṃ ca CRT*; *kukanyāṃ ca* GP; *kuputraṃ ca* Har. [4]*kumitraṃ CNG*; *kadāśrayaṃ CRT*; *kubhāryaṃ ca* Har.

For other variants see MBh(Bh) 12.137, 89.

145. *MBh(Bh)* 12.138, 37; *MBh(R)* 12.140, 37; *MBh(C)* 12. 5283-4. (*Also MBh(Bh) I to I, No.* 81, 151-2; *MBh(R)* 1.142, 73-4; *MBh(C)* 1.5615).

yo'riṇā saha saṃdhāya [1]*sukhaṃ svapiti viśvasan,*
sa [2]*vṛkṣāgra-prasupto vā patitaḥ pratībudhyate.*

He (i.e. the king), who after having concluded peace with his foe, sleeps confortably in trustfulness, is like a man who fell asleep on the top of a tree and awoke (i.e. from his illusion) on the ground (after having fallen down).

This maxim occurs in one text of the *CN* version, viz., in *CNG* 152.

Similar thoughts are also found in the *CR* and *CS* versions, viz. *CRr* 7.44 and *CSr* 1.8, GP 1.114, 48 and HJ 4.11. The latter texts were also adapted in the Tibetan literature: NM 6.13.

The two MBh texts, in the Śānti-parvan and the Ādi-parvan, are not completely identical in *b* and *c*. The *C* text follows the MBh text of the Śāntiparvan with small variants.

The *C* text was undoubtedly borrowed directly from MBh, Śanti-parvan.

FOOTNOTES TO NO. 145:

[1]*śayīta kṛtakṛtyavat* (*kṛtakṛtatyavat* MBh(R); printing error)MBh(Bh), MBh(*R*), MBh(C) in the Ādi-parvan. [2]*vṛkṣāgre pra°* MBh(R), MBh(C) Śānti-parvan; *vṛkṣāgre yathā suptaḥ* MBh(Bh); MBh(C), MBh(R) Ādi-parvan; *vṛkṣāgre supta iva* VS 2756.

For other variants see MBh(Bh) 12.138, 37.

146. *MBh(Bh)* 12.174, 15; *MBh(R)* 12.181, 15; *MBh(C)* 12. 6759. (*Also MBh(Bh)* —; *MBh(R)* 12.322, 15; *MBh(C)* 12.12152).

bālo yuvā ca[1] *vṛddhaś ca yat*[2] *karoti śubhā'śubham,*
tasyāṃ tasyām avasthāyāṃ [3]*bhuṅkte*[4] *janmani janmani.*

Whatever acts, good or bad, one performs in childhood, or in youth, or in old age, the fruit of them one enjoys or endures at precisely the same period (of his future life).

This maxim occurs in one text of the *CR* version, which usually follows the GP text, viz. in *CRCa II* 3.5.

Also found in GP 1.113, 29.

The MBh *śloka* was adapted without change in the Old Javanese literature: SS 361 and Ślt 35.

The two MBh texts are not completely identical. The Bhandarkar edition omits MBh(R) 12. 322, 15 and MBh(*C*) 12.12152; the latter two texts are better known and the Bhandarkar edition adopted this text to 12.174, 15; this is also identical with the *C* text. Other variants are unimportant.

The *C* text was undoubtedly borrowed directly from MBh (i.e. MBh(Bh) 12.174, 15 which is identical with MBh(R) 12.322, 15 and MBh (*C*) 12. 12152).

FOOTNOTES TO NO. 146:

[1]*vā* MBh(R) 12.322, 15. [2]*yaḥ* GP. [3]*tat phalaṃ pratipadyate* MBh(R) 12.181, 15, MBh(C) 12.6759. [4]*bhukte CRCa II.*

147. *MBh(Bh)* 12.263, 11; *ad.* 12.166, 25 (446*;27-8), *ad* 12.167, 20 (449*; 32-3).

brahmaghne ca surāpe ca...
occurs in the *CR* version (*CRr* 7.72). Also found in R 4.34,12, PP 1.248 and 4.10, Pts 3.157 and 4.10, PtsK 4.11, GP 1.114, 69.

The *C* text was influenced by MBh (or R).

148. *MBh(Bh)* 12. 284, 21; *MBh(R)* 12.295, 21; *MBh* (*C*) 12.10842.

mano 'nukūlāḥ' pramadā...
occurs also in the *CR* version (*CRr* 2.52.)

Also found in GP 1.109, 44 and in Old Javanese, viz. SS 29.

The *C* text was directly borrowed from MBh.

149. *MBh* (*Bh*) 12.309, 45; *MBh* (*R*) 12.321, 46; *MBh* (*C*) 12.12089.

dhanasya yasya rājato...
occurs also in one texts of the *CR* version, viz. (included in the Tibetan Tanjur), viz. in *CRT* 2.21.

Also found in GP 1.109, 21 and SS 55.

The *C* text was directly borrowcd from MBh.

150. *MBh*(*Bh*) 13. 24, 90; *MBh*(*R*) 13.23, 93; *MBh* (*C*) 13.1664.

sarvahiṁsānivṛttāś ca
occurs also in one text of thc *CN* version viz. *CNB* 143.

Also found in HJ 1.66.

The *C* text was directly borrowed from MBh.

SUBJECT INDEX

(Roman numbers denote the number of the study; Arabic numbers denote the paragraphs of the appropriate study; asterisks denote footnotes)

ERRATA

Page:	*line*:		
5	4	*read*:	*prabrūyuḥ*[3]
6	4	*read*:	and the treasure-trove
6	27	*read*:	*svanihitad*
10	35	*read*:	Cf. above: Study V
12	27	*read*:	*sambhrānte*
16	32	*read*:	*viditaṁ*)
24	19	*read*:	*gūḍacihnādinā*
27	3	*read*:	*aśvān ṛte*
27	6	*read*:	*kṣudrapaśvan ṛte*
32	29	*read*:	*paraḥ para iti*
33	2	*read*:	allowed to give away jointly their
33	32	*read*:	*udvahed dvijaḥ*
35	10	*read*:	*Smṛti-s*
46	6	*read*:	*prakāmi syāt*
48	7	*read*:	PN 3.42,
49	6	*read*:	PM 4.47)
55	11	*read*:	Śārṅgadhara-pad-
63	17	*read*:	*WEAVER'S*
70	9	*read*:	B. (1.8, 16, 2-5)
70	37	*read*:	*dharmye*
76	22	*read*:	N. (12.28)
77	4	*read*:	seeing
84	13	*read*:	*svaravarṇe'ṅgitā-*
86	15	*read*:	versions of Pañc.
127	30	*read*:	*sudṛḍhaṁ*
155	7	*read*:	19.16, DhV. 14 and the
166	21	*read*:	CNG. *instead of* CNCr.
196	30 &	*read*:	Post scriptum.
203	last		
197	26	*read*:	was known in the second half
215	33	*read*:	C_1 in Śts;
236	29	*read*:	CSBD 212, *instead of*: CSD 2.12,
236	30	*read*:	CSB II 2.12, instead of GSB II; 2.12,
296	2	*read*:	**CĀṆAKYA'S**
296	36	*read*:	study XXIV.
297	35	*read*:	Cf. above pages 289-91.

306 in column Pts 1.361 & 2.130 *read*: CNŚ 1 110

308 in column PP 2.43 & 5.58 *read*: under "CR": 8.3* (8.5)

310 in column PP 2.135 *read*: under "CV": 13.14 (13.15)